The Letters of
William Cullen Bryant

III

Bryant, *c*1857, photographed by Charles D. Fredricks, New York
(see Letter 833).

The Letters of
WILLIAM CULLEN BRYANT

Volume III
1849–1857

Edited by

WILLIAM CULLEN BRYANT II

and

THOMAS G. VOSS

New York
FORDHAM UNIVERSITY PRESS
1981

Printed in the United States of America

Library
UNIVERSITY OF MIAMI

Contents

Illustrations   between pages 280 and 281

Key to Manuscript Sources Often Cited in Footnotes

BCHS   Bryant Family Association Papers, Bureau County Historical Society, Princeton, Illinois.

DuU   Duke University Library.

HCL   Harvard College Library.

HEHL   Henry E. Huntington Library and Art Gallery.

HSPa   Historical Society of Pennsylvania.

LC   Library of Congress.

MHS   Massachusetts Historical Society.

NYHS   New-York Historical Society.

NYPL–Berg   Henry W. and Albert A. Berg Collection, The New York Public Library, Astor, Lenox and Tilden Foundations.

NYPL–BFP   Bryant Family Papers, Manuscript Division, The New York Public Library, Astor, Lenox and Tilden Foundations.

NYPL–Bryant–Moulton Letters   Letters of William Cullen Bryant to Leonice M. S. Moulton, Manuscript Division, The New York Public Library, Astor, Lenox and Tilden Foundations.

NYPL–GR   Goddard–Roslyn Collection, Manuscript Division, The New York Public Library, Astor, Lenox and Tilden Foundations.

NYSL   New York State Library.

Ridgely Family Collection   Letters of William Cullen Bryant to Leonice M. S. Moulton, Hampton, home of the Ridgelys, Baltimore County, Maryland.

UVa   The Clifton Waller Barrett Library of the University of Virginia Library.

WCL   Williams College Library.

YCAL   Collection of American Literature, Yale University Library.

ACKNOWLEDGMENTS

The Bryant letters contained in earlier volumes of this edition were drawn from fifty-eight institutional and private collections. Many of these holdings are again represented in the present volume. Additionally, letters from seventeen other collections appear herein. These are provided by the libraries of Amherst College, Boston University, Brown University, University of California at Berkeley, Johns Hopkins University, University of Michigan at Ann Arbor, Swarthmore College, and Wellesley College, and by the William L. Clements Library, Illinois State Historical Library, Iowa State Department of History and Archives, National Collection of Fine Arts, Presbyterian Historical Society, and Saint Louis Mercantile Library Association. Permissions granted by these institutions to publish letters in their possession are gratefully acknowledged.

Several other organizations have, through their understanding cooperation, been helpful in the preparation of this volume. The editor wishes to express appreciation for their assistance to the officers and staff members of the Ashmolean Museum, Bodleian Library, Bryant Library of Roslyn, Century Association, Frick Art Reference Library, Grolier Club, Rutherford B. Hayes Library and Museum, Horticultural Society of New York, Metropolitan Museum of Art, National Academy of Design, National Archives and Records Service, National Portrait Gallery, Rhodes House, Rockefeller Archive Center, Sleepy Hollow Restorations, and the United States Department of State.

To the roster of individuals whose assistance has previously been acknowledged should be added the names of others who have more recently provided generous advice and information. These are Frederick Aandahl, Lisa Brower, Herbert T. F. Cahoon, J. Fraser Cocks III, Anthony Cucciara, Aldo R. Cupo, James E. Cyphers, Mrs. Melvin Dant, Johanna De Onis, Mark Davis, Rodney G. Dennis, Davis Erhardt, Kenneth Gill-Smith, John K. Howat, Michael L. Lawson, James Lawton, Russell Lynes, Watt P. Marchman, Alice G. Melrose, Edwin Haviland Miller, Larry G. Pardue, Winifred E. Popp, Robert E. Schnare, Marshall Swan, Roland E. Swerczek, Marilyn Symmes, and Charles D. Webster.

The editor is particularly grateful to Director Joseph G. Astman and his colleagues, who organized and conducted the Hofstra University Centennial Conference on "William Cullen Bryant and His America" in October 1978, and the many participants whose perceptive insights into various aspects of Bryant's life and activities will continue to offer enlightenment to those who pursue Bryant scholarship in the future.

Bryant Chronology
1849–1857

1849. March 21–April 28, visits Cuba by way of Georgia and South Carolina. May 10, Forrest–Macready theater riots. June 13–October 20, visits Great Britain and the Continent. November, lodges at 263 Greene Street; *Evening Post* editions for California, Oregon, and Sandwich Islands.

1850. *Poems* published in London and Liverpool. February, mediates between Edwin and Catherine Forrest. March 31, death of John Calhoun. May, *Letters of a Traveller*. September, Compromise of 1850. November, Isaac Henderson made business manager of *EP*.

1851. March, meets Garibaldi. May, Bryant's proposed site for park approved. September 14, death of James Fenimore Cooper. September–October, visits Illinois. October 5, death of Charity Bryant. November 15, *Reminiscences of the Evening Post*. December?, death of David Christie. December 15, banquet for Kossuth.

1852. January, testifies in Forrest divorce case. February 19, death of William Ware; 25, eulogy of Cooper. June 29, death of Henry Clay. July 28, death of Andrew Jackson Downing. October 24, death of Daniel Webster. November 13, leaves for Europe, Egypt, and the Holy Land. December 18, death of Horatio Greenough.

1853. June 22, returns from Europe. July 16, death of Eliza Robbins.

1854. *Poems*, Dessau, Germany; one- and two-volume editions, New York. May 15, Isaac Henderson made equal partner in *EP*; 22, Kansas–Nebraska Bill. May 29–cJune 30, visits Illinois.

1855. September, leaves Democratic Party. September 26, address, "The Improvement of Native Fruits." December 18, death of Samuel Rogers.

1856. February 7, death of Edward Channing. July, supports Republican candidate, John Charles Frémont, for presidency. August 3, death of Charles Sedgwick. December 29, address, "Music in the Public Schools."

1857. March 6, Dred Scott decision. May 2, leaves for Europe and North Africa. October 17–November 17, visits Madrid. December 31, at Marseilles.

Bryant's Correspondents
1849–1857

OF 489 LETTERS WHICH BRYANT certainly wrote during this period, 340 to 107 addressees appear on the following pages. Most of the remaining 149 have not reappeared, but about thirty which have been recovered seem scarcely worth printing, either because they are partial drafts, or because they are brief replies to requests for autographs, literary advice, occasional verses, or public appearances. No significant letters seem to be missing, except for nine which Bryant wrote his wife during his 1852–1853 travels abroad, presumably lost, and six to the Roslyn schoolteacher George B. Cline, who with his family occupied the Bryants' home during their long absence in 1857–1858, and who was thereafter the estate superintendent at Cedarmere.

During this period Bryant passed nearly one-fifth of his time abroad, and although Frances was with him on the last of four trips, he visited Cuba, Great Britain, Europe, and the Near East without her. And he continued a practice of sending her notes from New York to Roslyn while he was busy in the city, and to Great Barrington and upper New York State when she visited there. Thus, she remained his chief correspondent; of 111 letters to her during the period, ninety appear in this volume.

Because of his frequent travels, Bryant's letters to the *Evening Post* form the next largest group, fifty-four, of which all save one are recovered. The prominence of these communications in the editorial columns of the paper brought them growing attention, which was enhanced as they were reprinted in other American newspapers, and occasionally in those published abroad. Their popularity, and the encouragement of Dana and others, induced Bryant to reprint them in book form in 1850, 1859, and 1869.

There are twenty-eight known letters to Bryant's two daughters during this period, of which twenty-five appear herein, and twenty-four to his brothers Cyrus and John in Illinois, twenty-one of which are printed. There are no known letters to his brothers Arthur or Austin, or to his sister Louisa. Bryant and Richard Dana, Sr., kept up a friendly if sporadic correspondence; there are thirteen known letters to Dana, all recovered. And Bryant wrote occasionally to other old friends: George Bancroft, Orville Dewey, Ferdinand Field, Henry Longfellow, Julia Sands, Catharine Sedgwick, William Gilmore Simms, Samuel Tilden, and Gulian Verplanck.

During these eight years he lost through death a number of close friends: in 1851, David Christie, James Fenimore Cooper, and Charity Bryant; in 1852, Andrew Jackson Downing, Horatio Greenough, and William Ware; in 1853, Eliza Robbins; in 1855, Samuel Rogers; in 1856, Charles Sedgwick. But he began to enjoy a new intimacy with others, among them his young partner John Bigelow, who joined the *Evening Post* late in 1848, and whose guidance of the paper's editorial and business affairs during Bryant's first absence thereafter gave the senior proprietor an assurance that his interests would not suffer during future travels. Writing Bigelow in 1857 after half a year abroad, Bryant

commented, "With regard to good sense, justice, impartiality, the bold defence of the weak against the strong, and the exposure of incompetence and rascality in public office I do not know of any paper like [the *Evening Post*]." Bigelow returned his confidence; later in life he recorded, "For full twenty years after my daily intercourse with Mr. Bryant terminated . . . , I would find myself frequently testing things I had done or proposed to do by asking myself, How would Mr. Bryant act under similar circumstances? . . . The influence which Mr. Bryant exerted over me by his example—he never gave advice—satisfies me that every one undervalues the importance of his own example." Of ten known letters to Bigelow during the present period, seven have been recovered for this volume.

Other acquaintances with whom Bryant's letters suggest a growing intimacy were the London lawyer Edwin Wilkins Field, the American novelist Caroline Kirkland, the Scottish-American schoolteacher Christiana Gibson, and his Roslyn neighbor Leonice Moulton, the last of whom would become his most frequent correspondent after the death of his wife in 1866. Among writers, artists, and statesmen appearing for the first time among these letters were James G. Birney, Henry Kirke Brown, Benjamin F. Butler, Salmon P. Chase, Evert Duyckinck, James T. Fields, Hamilton Fish, Daniel Gilman, Andrew H. Green, William L. Marcy, Edwin D. Morgan, Hiram Powers, Henry Rowe Schoolcraft, Alfred B. Street, William J. Stillman, and Charles Sumner.

Though it will be apparent that in the letters written between 1849 and 1857 Bryant touches only occasionally on the domestic political issues with which he was most vitally concerned in his editorial writing and political action—the Compromise of 1850, the Fugitive Slave Law, the Kansas–Nebraska Bill, the rise of the Republican Party, the Dred Scott decision—his many travel letters show a wide acquaintance with foreign cultures and political events, a fluent command of modern European languages, and a narrative and descriptive prose style scarcely evident anywhere else in his correspondence.

XIV

Cuba, Scotland, and Europe under the Bayonet
1849
(LETTERS 667 TO 712)

IN 1849, at FIFTY-FIVE, Bryant had served for twenty years as principal editor of the *Evening Post*. No longer president of the American Art-Union, he was, nevertheless, more intimate than ever with many of the artists who had given it success, and whom he often saw at meetings of the Sketch Club, the Century Association, and the National Academy. He had become a "fireside poet" whose verses drew parody and satire as well as imitation and adulation. In his *A Fable for Critics* in 1848 young James Russell Lowell had conceded Bryant to be "first bard of your nation," but saw him standing "in supreme ice-olation." A Lowell imitator complained, "I like friend Bryant, / But as a man;—I can't endure a giant." A less jocular critic commented that, on reading "Thanatopsis," "one seems to be on the mount of contemplation, elevated above the manifold influences of a striving world, and breathing a purer air."

The *Evening Post* was in good shape. With John Bigelow as its associate editor, and both circulation and the business of the commercial printing office growing, Bryant felt free to travel, and he and Charles Leupp planned two trips abroad that year. On the eve of their departure that spring for the South and Cuba, Bryant reminded his readers of several public issues on which the *Evening Post* had taken stands over the past twenty years which were later vindicated by public approval: its advocacy of free trade, an independent national treasury, and other reforms, and—in the North, at least—its opposition to slavery in the western territories.

On March 21 Bryant and Leupp sailed for Savannah, landing there on the 25th. After visiting with friends, they took another steamer for Charleston, and on the 28th went by railway to Augusta. Here they were shown an immense plantation, and a cotton mill impressive in its demonstration that poor white girls could find clean and respectable work in an operation previously performed by Negro slaves. After a night with the novelist Simms at Woodlands, they returned to Charleston, and on April 1st sailed for Havana, stopping for an evening at Key West, a community engaged solely in salvaging wrecked vessels and succoring their crews. On April 4 they reached the Cuban capital.

It was Holy Week. Bryant was intrigued by the strange processions and customs of the first Spanish-speaking land he had visited. Noticing the "brilliant languor" of the Cuban ladies who shopped without leaving their carriages, or lolled on sofas in their parlor windows, he felt indolent in this tropical climate. He managed to enter crowded churches on Holy Thursday to watch the worshippers, mostly weeping women, kiss the feet of an image of the Saviour, and on Good Friday saw another image of Christ carried past his window with a military escort and somber music. On Saturday evening, Holy Week over, he

mingled with crowds in the Plaza de Armas. As often before, in Europe, he found his way to the public cemetery, the Campo Santo, to see rudely coffined corpses thrown into hastily dug trenches, amid screeches from a nearby madhouse. On Easter Sunday he followed a procession into the cathedral, and that evening attended a masked ball in the vast Teatro Tacón. On Monday he watched the slaughter of gamecocks in cockpits outside the city walls, a "horrid sight," he admitted in his diary.

Bryant's interest in Cuba had arisen during his residence in 1828 with the Salazars, who had introduced him to visiting and exiled Cubans. More recently he had been made aware that American slaveholders were eager to add this lush land to their holdings, by purchase or, if not, by seizure. In 1848 President Polk tried to buy the island from Spain without success. Now, the refugee Narciso López was in New York planning the first of several attempts to seize Cuba and offer it to the United States. Consequently, Bryant inquired into local conditions of race relations and slavery. Leaving Havana on April 10, he and Leupp visited a coffee plantation at San Antonio de los Baños, and at Matanzas inspected the sugar mills and cane fields of an American planter and the plantation, reputed the finest on the island, of an English company. Returning toward Havana, Bryant was drawn, at Güines, to watch the execution of a Negro slave by garroting. The "horror of the spectacle," he confessed later, made him regret having given in to "idle curiosity." Here at Güines he learned of the thriving foreign slave trade which, nominally outlawed forty years earlier, had nevertheless brought nearly half a million Africans to the Western Hemisphere since 1840. A cargo of slaves had been landed near Güines a few days earlier, more than one hundred of whom had died on the voyage. He was further shocked to hear that slavers were bringing in Indians from Yucatán and natives of eastern Asia.

After three more days at Havana, Bryant and Leupp sailed for Charleston on April 22, returning to New York by way of Wilmington and Richmond, and reaching home on the 28th. Within three weeks of their return, New York suffered two catastrophes. On May 10, as tragedians Edwin Forrest and William Macready gave rival performances of *Macbeth*, a large mob attacked the Astor Place Opera House, determined to drive the Englishman from the stage, and a small militia unit, mustered to help police, fired on the crowd in self-defense, killing and wounding scores. And on May 15 the first of more than a thousand deaths occurred in the city from Asiatic cholera. The fact that this epidemic originated in Europe seems not to have deterred Bryant, however, from taking his planned excursion across the Atlantic, and on June 13 he and Leupp sailed from New York on the steamship *Niagara*. Their itinerary:

June 25–28: Liverpool and Manchester; June 29–July 8: London.
July 9–10: Edinburgh; 11–13: en route Wick via Perth, Dunkeld, Blair Atholl, Inverness; 14–17: excursion to Lerwick in the Shetlands and Kirkwall in the Orkneys; 18–25: en route Edinburgh via Aberdeen, Inverness (excursion to Guisachan Forest), Caledonian Canal, Loch Ness, Fort Augustus, Loch Oich, Loch Lochy, Fort William, Loch Linnhe, Oban (excursion to Iona and Staffa), Rothesay, Dunoon, Gourock, Greenock, Dumbarton, Glasgow; 26–27: Edin-

burgh; 28–31: en route Birmingham, via Melrose, Kelso, Berwick-upon-Tweed, Newcastle upon Tyne, York, Manchester.

August 1–3: Birmingham; 4–7: London; 8–9: en route Paris via Dover, Calais; 10–12: Paris; 13–16: en route Munich via Amiens, Douai, Valenciennes, Brussels, Malines, Liège, Aachen, Cologne, Koblenz, Mainz, Kastel, Frankfurt, Darmstadt, Heidelberg, Heilbronn, Stuttgart, Geislingen, Ulm, Augsburg; 17–22: Munich; August 23–September 4: en route Paris via Augsburg, Kaufbeuren, Lindau, St. Gall, Zurich, Horgen, Zug, Mount Rigi, Lucerne, Escholzmatt, Bern, Fribourg, Vevey, Lausanne, Geneva, Lyons, Châlons, Dijon, Tonnerre.

September 5–20: Paris (excursion to Versailles); 21–27: en route London via Amiens, Brussels (excursion to Antwerp, Rotterdam, Amsterdam, Antwerp), Ostend, Dover; September 28–October 1: London.

October 2–4: Manchester; 5: Liverpool; 6–20: en route New York on steamer *Liverpool*.

Reaching Liverpool on June 25, the travelers stopped briefly with David Christie at Manchester, then went to London. Bryant breakfasted and dined with Samuel Rogers, who had feared in 1845 they might never meet again, and was entertained by publisher John Chapman, whose home in the Strand was a haven for writers. He and Leupp went to music halls and to the theater, where they saw Madame Vestris and Charles Mathews in Charles Dance's *A Wonderful Woman*, and Sheridan Knowles's *The Wife*. They visited art exhibitions and picture collections at the Royal Academy, Hampton Court, Dulwich College, Sir John Soane's Museum, the British Museum, the British Institution, the Water-colour Society, and Greenwich. Bryant was invited by John Sheepshanks to see the collection of British paintings which he later gave the National Gallery, and at Robert Thorburn's studio he saw the miniatures of this artist who was just then a little notorious for having quarreled with Queen Victoria and refusing to see her when sent for.

On this third visit to the Old World, Bryant was most drawn to those areas he had not yet seen, the Scottish Highlands and islands, and Switzerland. At Edinburgh he was again entertained by the Christie family, particularly artist Alexander Christie, who showed him through Chambers' publishing house, and introduced him to the secretary of the Scottish Society of the Arts, David Hill. Leaving Edinburgh on July 11, the travelers would be in new territory for nearly two weeks. Bryant was impressed by the old capital, Perth, where he lingered at the graves of the tragic maidens Bessie Bell and Mary Gray. He rode a mailcoach on a misty night past Birnham Wood, Dunkeld, and Blair Atholl, and across the moors to Inverness, then through seacoast villages, noting them as "roses without and dirt within," to Wick, where a little steamer took the companions to Lerwick in the Shetlands. On these windswept, treeless islands, he was intrigued by the little ponies, sheep, and cattle, and supposed their diminutive size, similar to that of the Picts, the original islanders, due to malnutrition.

Returning to the mainland, after a stop at Kirkwall in the Orkneys, the companions visited Aberdeen, where they found amusement at a concert of "Female American Serenaders in the picturesque costumes of their country, six

English women singing negro songs, with faces painted red, short dull red petticoats, and strings of beads round their necks." Crossing again to Inverness, they traveled up the Strathglass to an immense estate in the Guisachan Forest belonging to a descendant of Simon Fraser, the violent seventeenth-century Baron Lovat. Here they traveled on ponies with the present owner, an acquaintance of Leupp's, to the top of Ben Sassenach, to see a broad panorama of the Highlands. After observing an isolated community of cottagers who spoke only Gaelic, they took a little steamer down the Caledonian Canal and the lochs to Oban, whence they visited the caves on Staffa, and Iona, the shrine of early Christianity in Britain. From Oban they went on to Glasgow, "tired," Bryant noted, "of bare mountains." Here they saw James Lawson's family, and went through the great Napier iron foundry. At Edinburgh Bryant learned of a fire which had destroyed the old mill at Cedarmere, and corresponded regarding the insurance. Before leaving he enjoyed an afternoon with Francis, Lord Jeffrey, famous literary critic and jurist.

On July 28 the travelers started southward, stopping at Melrose Abbey and at Walter Scott's home, Abbotsford, where, Bryant recorded disgustedly, "The fellow at the gate, tipsy and crusty, the woman at the house flushed and peremptory would not allow us to see the inside. . . . The house an ugly piece of architecture." But they saw Scott's tomb at Dryburgh Abbey, and at Sandy-Knowe his boyhood home. Passing through Berwick-upon-Tweed, Newcastle upon Tyne, and York, they reached David Christie's in Manchester on July 30. Here they went with geologist Edward Binney to tea with the radical weaver–poet Samuel Bamford. After three days with Ferdinand Field in Birmingham, while Leupp lingered at Christie's, Bryant went on with his companion to London. Here Bryant saw Edwin Field and Reginald Parker, and breakfasted and dined twice with Rogers. At Parker's he met naturalist William Benjamin Campbell and philanthropist Edward Enfield; at Rogers', artist Charles Eastlake, soon to be president of the Royal Academy and director of the National Gallery, and his bride, Elizabeth, who had lately published a bitter criticism of *Jane Eyre*, and Amelia Murray, maid of honor to the queen and writer on the United States; at Field's, artists Clarkson Stanfield and George Fripp, and Rowland Hill, inventor of the adhesive postage stamp. Leaving Rogers' home after dinner one evening, Bryant was touched when his eighty-six-year-old host overtook him and walked with him through St. James's Park and on to his hotel on Grosvenor Street.

Crossing the Channel on August 9, Bryant and Leupp passed three days in Paris, during which they went with John Gadsby Chapman to the Louvre, and Bryant had his first sight of "Europe under the Bayonet"—soldiers everywhere, as the city still suffered under the "convenient fiction," as Bryant called it, of a state of siege following the crushing of the workers' revolution of 1848. Passing quickly through Belgium and up the Rhine, they reached Heidelberg on the 15th. Here they found the streets full of drunken Prussian soldiers, the city in another state of siege—"an invention," Bryant noted, "for exercising a military despotism." His friend Professor Hagen, lately a member of the short-lived revolutionary Diet, despaired that, in this most democratic of German states, the intellectuals had failed the revolution. Bryant was glad to escape from what he had once thought a delightful old city. But as he made his way

toward Munich he saw soldiers lounging everywhere, while women worked in the fields, and in Bavaria he was disappointed by the omnipresent military. And he was lonely among scenes he had visited in Munich with his wife and children fourteen years earlier, when, he wrote Frances, "we were all so much farther from the grave than now—and perhaps so much more innocent."

With relief, Bryant escaped the "perpetual sight of the military uniform" as he crossed Lake Constance to Switzerland on August 25, and he wrote to the *Evening Post*, "I could almost have kneeled and kissed the shore of the hospitable republic." He visited nearly all its principal towns, from St. Gall and Zurich to Lausanne and Geneva, traveling through its mountains and across its lakes. His respect for the Swiss and their open society was heightened by contrast with the despotisms he had passed through; he praised their freedom from passport and customs barriers, their architecture, their sturdy self-reliance, their generosity toward political refugees.

Pausing overnight at Geneva, the two friends pushed on to Paris, reaching there on September 5; during the ensuing fortnight they shopped and dined often with fellow–Sketch Club members Albinola, Chapman, Seymour, and Wright, and at the Théâtre Français they saw Rachel in Racine's *Phèdre*; Bryant thought her acting "as perfect as ever." The American inventor Richard March Hoe showed Bryant through the plant of the newspaper *La Patrie*, where he had installed one of his high-speed rotary presses. The Count Circourt called on the American poet, whose verses he had rendered into French prose. The picture dealer Adolph Goupil introduced Bryant to the Dutch religious painter Ary Scheffer.

Here at Paris Bryant heard that the cholera was raging in London, and he was reluctant to go there directly, particularly since he had suffered during the early part of his journey from diarrhea, then considered a common symptom of the disease. But now, he wrote Fanny Godwin, his health was very good, though he was "becoming a florid old gentleman." The disease soon subsided in London, and after a week's diversion through Belgium and Holland, seeing pictures and meeting artists Louis Robbe and Jakob Eeckhout at Brussels, Bryant and Leupp crossed from Ostend to Dover on September 28 for a third visit to London. Again, Rogers was attentive. At his home Bryant met the Irish poet and wit Henry Luttrell; Mrs. Fox Lane, "a clever masculine woman"; and a son of Lord Littleton, first Baron Hatherton, "a gambler, with a young and very pretty wife." Leaving the capital on October 2, the travelers visited David Christie in Manchester, and sailed from Liverpool October 6.

Reaching home on the 20th, Bryant found his wife rather disconsolate and sick of Roslyn—a disappointment, since he had anticipated happy autumn days at Cedarmere. But, he wrote Leonice Moulton, he succeeded so far in reconciling Frances to the country "that she passed a whole day with me in planting and transplanting trees shrubs and roses." The newspaper was prospering; he and Bigelow were soon engaging new correspondents and reporters and announcing two new "Extras" for California, Oregon, the Sandwich Islands, and Central America, with a "full chronicle of European and domestic news – – – of peculiar interest to the inhabitants of the Pacific." The Bryants took new rooms in town, where Dana visited them and urged Bryant to put into book form his travel letters of the past fifteen years.

667. *To* Frances F. Bryant

Savannah   March 25, 1849.

My dear Frances.

I arrived here this morning about half past eight o'clock after a very pleasant passage. We did not leave the port of New York on Wednesday evening; our steamer, the Tennessee, a capital vessel, as tight and staunch as oak timbers can make her with a good natured and very careful captain ran down to the Quarantine Ground and remained there anchored all night, with the rain beating on the deck. In the morning the wind had chopped about from the south east to the northwest, and was sweeping with a good deal of strength over the waters, but as it came from the land it raised no swell; the light of the sun was white and cold and the decks slippery with ice. As the day advanced we seemed to have glided into a warmer temperature; Friday was milder yet, and when the sun rose on Saturday morning it rose like a sun in June, with orange coloured beams too warm to stand in with comfort. An awning was stretched over one third of the deck and all the passengers, except one or two who declined leaving their berths, on pretence of not being quite recovered from seasickness came up from below and sat in the shade enjoying as pleasant an air it seemed to me as ever blew Our captain gave a wide berth to all the shallows, —being as I have said extremely careful, and not being as I was told well acquainted with the coast, —which probably prolonged the passage somewhat. Last night about twelve o'clock we made the Tybee or Savannah light house, and if we had had a pilot might have come in immediately. As there was no pilot we were obliged to wait till this morning. I have of course had my share of sea sickness and my head swims yet with the motion of the vessel.

I have seen Mr. and Mrs. Tefft[1] and have been to church with them. They inquired about you with much interest and chid me for not bringing you. I have seen also Dr. Arnold[2] whose wife is still comfortable though not well, and Mr. and Mrs. Padelford,[3] all of whom inquired if I had not brought you. I told them I wished I had.

We shall run out on the rail road tomorrow I think to Macon, and then to Charleston taking Midway and Mr. Simms in our way.[4] On Saturday the Isabel, a fine staunch, tight steamer departs from Charleston for Havana. She touches at Key West where she makes a stop of some ten hours and completes the passage to Cuba in about three days. I expect therefore to be in Cuba as early as the fourth of April.

The grass is green here in the squares, the locust trees are in leaf, and the peach trees and flowering almonds in blossom. I wish you could have seen what a beautiful aspect the groves on some of the slopes presented, as we came up to the city this morning; the willows in full leaf, and other trees in their bright new green. The temperature is very agreeable, and we have no occasion for fires.

I shall write to you again very soon. Pray ask the men to water the asparagus plants with sea-water, and let Hermann[5] read a book on American Agriculture by Fleischmann,[6] which you will find among the books brought from town, an octavo volume in light coloured covers.

Yours affectionately
W. C. BRYANT

MANUSCRIPT: NYPL–GR.

1. Israel Keech Tefft and his wife, whom the Bryants had met in 1843. See Letters 454, 463.
2. Dr. Richard Dennis Arnold; see 462.3.
3. Padelford was a Savannah merchant whom the Bryants had met on their visit to that city in April 1843.
4. At Woodlands, William Gilmore Simms's plantation in the Barnwell District, about 100 miles northwest of Charleston, South Carolina. See 453.1.
5. Bryant's new German gardener. See Frances to Cyrus Bryant, April 17, 1849, BCHS.
6. Probably Carl Ludwig Fleischmann, *Der nordamerikanische Landwirth: Ein Handbuch für Ansiedler in den Vereinigten Staaten* (New York, 1848).

668. *To* Frances F. Bryant

Augusta, Georgia   March 29, 1849.

My dear Frances.

We did not go to Macon by railway, as we intended when I wrote to you last, and a project which we next contemplated of coming to this place by water was also abandoned; the reason in both cases was the want of time. After I wrote you, Mr. Leupp and myself went with Mr. Tefft and Dr. Arnold to Bonaventure, where we had another sight of the grand old avenues of live oaks, with their cloudy drapery of moss. The solitude of the place is at an end, in consequence of a house being built close to it, and the oaks are enclosed to form a cemetery. Still they are a very remarkable object and Leupp said they were worth coming five hundred miles to see.

Mr. Tefft and his wife and Dr. Arnold desired me to present you their very particular regards.

We took passage in the steamer General Clinch, for Charleston on Monday evening, commanded by the same Captain Peck with whom we went from St. Augustine to Savannah when the sand-fleas stung us so at St. Mary's.[1] On Tuesday morning we landed about eleven o'clock. In the evening I called on Mr. and Mrs. Gilman who inquired after you with much interest.[2] The next morning at nine o'clock we took the railway to this [city?][3] which is pleasantly situated on the Savannah river 138 miles from Charleston.

We passed by Midway where Mr. Roach lives,[4] and through Aiken famous as a resort for the planters during the hot months. Midway looks

much as it did, a very small village in the midst of a boundless waste of forest; indeed the whole state, to one who passes on this railway seems little else but woods. Aiken is the largest place before you reach Augusta, and it had a pleasant look, consisting as it does of cottages dispersed among the trees. It stands on high ground and immediately west of it begin the declivities by which the country descends to the valley of the Savannah.

We arrived here between five and six o'clock in the afternoon and started out to look at the place; the evening was uncommonly beautiful, though the morning had been chilly. The air was soft like that of an evening with us in early June, and the sun in the midst of purple clouds and making a glorious set. Augusta consists of broad unpaved streets parallel with the river and planted with trees. Some of these are very pleasant, particularly Green Street and Marbury Street where the shade in summer must be quite dense, and where the houses are surrounded with gardens and shrubbery. We walked out into the country; the fields were green and though the season is later here than at Savannah, many of the trees had on their new leaves. A party were returning homeward over the fields, perhaps from a picnic; a gentleman passed us with a fowling piece on his shoulder followed by a little negro boy who trotted after his master carrying his fishing rod and a string of small fish. Negroes with horse-carts and waggons were driving in from the country, raising prodigious clouds of dust; for the soil here is light, and rises in the air as soon as disturbed.

At this place the banks of the river are dry and firm, on the Georgia side stretching away in broad meadows, and on the Carolina side rising in woody declivities, where the dog wood and the thorn trees are in flower, and the azalea shows its pink blossoms through the budding thickets. As I looked at them I thought of Roslyn, and wished that I had one with me for whom I might gather these flowers I saw.

Tomorrow we return to Charleston, taking the Woodlands in our way where we expect to pass a night with Mr. Simms. I have seen much at this place to interest me—more than I have space or time to speak of. I shall write to you from Charleston.

Yours ever,
W. C. BRYANT

MANUSCRIPT: NYPL–GR ADDRESS: Mrs. Frances F. Bryant / Roslyn / Long Island DOCKETED: Augusta.

1. In April 1843; see Letter 459.
2. Samuel Foster Gilman (1791–1858, Harvard 1811, D.D. 1837) and his wife, Caroline Howard Gilman (1794–1888). Since 1819 he had been pastor of the Second Independent Church of Charleston, the earliest Unitarian congregation in South Carolina. Both he and Mrs. Gilman were popular writers.
3. Word omitted.
4. Nash Roach, father-in-law of William Gilmore Simms. See Letter 395.

669. *To* the EVENING POST

Augusta, Georgia, March 29, 1849.

A quiet passage by sea from New York to Savannah would seem to afford little matter for a letter, yet those who take the trouble to read what I am about to write, will, I hope, admit that there are some things to be observed, even on such a voyage. It was indeed a remarkably quiet one, and worthy of note on that account, if on no other. We had a quiet vessel, quiet weather, a quiet, good-natured captain, a quiet crew, and remarkably quiet passengers.

When we left the wharf at New York last week, in the good steamship Tennessee, we were not conscious, at first, as we sat in the cabin, that she was in motion and proceeding down the harbor. There was no beating or churning of the sea, no struggling to get forward; her paddles played in the water as smoothly as those of a terrapin, without jar or noise. The Tennessee is one of the tightest and strongest boats that navigate our coast; the very flooring of her deck is composed of timbers instead of planks, and helps to keep her massive frame more compactly and solidly together. It was her first voyage; her fifty-one passengers lolled on sofas fresh from the upholsterer's, and slept on mattresses which had never been pressed by the human form before, in staterooms where foul air had never collected. Nor is it possible that the air should become impure in them to any great degree, for the Tennessee is the best-ventilated ship I ever was in; the main cabin and the state-rooms are connected with each other and with the deck, by numerous openings and pipes which keep up a constant circulation of air in every part.

I have spoken of the passengers as remarkably quiet persons. Several of them, I believe, never spoke during the passage, at least so it seemed to me. The silence would have been almost irksome, but for two lively little girls who amused us by their prattle, and two young women, apparently just married, too happy to do any thing but laugh, even when suffering from seasickness, and whom we now and then heard shouting and squealing from their state-rooms. There were two dark-haired, long-limbed gentlemen, who lay the greater part of the first and second day at full length on the sofas in the after-cabin, each with a spittoon before him, chewing tobacco with great rapidity and industry, and apparently absorbed in the endeavor to fill it within a given time. There was another, with that atrabilious complexion peculiar to marshy countries, and circles of a still deeper hue about his eyes, who sat on deck, speechless and motionless, wholly indifferent to the sound of the dinner-bell, his countenance fixed in an expression which seemed to indicate an utter disgust of life.

Yet we had some snatches of good talk on the voyage. A robust old gentleman, a native of Norwalk, in Connecticut, told us that he had been reading a history of that place by the Rev. Mr. Hall.[1]

"I find," said he, "that in his account of the remarkable people of Norwalk, he has omitted to speak of two of the most remarkable, two spinsters, Sarah and Phebe Comstock, relatives of mine and friends of my youth, of whom I retain a vivid recollection. They were in opulent circumstances for the neighborhood in which they lived, possessing a farm of about two hundred acres; they were industrious, frugal, and extremely charitable; but they never relieved a poor family without visiting it, and inquiring carefully into its circumstances. Sarah was the housekeeper, and Phebe the farmer. Phebe knew nothing of kitchen matters, but she knew at what time of the year greensward should be broken up, and corn planted, and potatoes dug. She dropped Indian corn and sowed English grain with her own hands. In the time of planting or of harvest, it was Sarah who visited and relieved the poor.

"I remember that they had various ways of employing the young people who called upon them. If it was late in the autumn, there was a chopping-board and chopping-knife ready, with the feet of neat-cattle, from which the oily parts had been extracted by boiling. 'You do not want to be idle,' they would say, 'chop this meat, and you shall have your share of the mince-pies that we are going to make.' At other times a supply of old woollen stockings were ready for unravelling. 'We know you do not care to be idle,' they would say, 'here are some stockings which you would oblige us by unravelling.' If you asked what use they made of the spools of woollen thread obtained by this process, they would answer: 'We use it as the weft of the linsey-woolsey with which we clothe our negroes.' They had negro slaves in those times, and old Tone, a faithful black servant of theirs, who has seen more than a hundred years, is alive yet.[2]

"They practiced one very peculiar piece of economy. The white hickory you know, yields the purest and sweetest of saccharine juices. They had their hickory fuel cut into short billets, which before placing on the fire they laid on the andirons, a little in front of the blaze, so as to subject it to a pretty strong heat. This caused the syrup in the wood to drop from each end of the billet, where it was caught in a cup, and in this way a gallon or two was collected in the course of a fortnight. With this they flavored their nicest cakes.

"They died about thirty years since, one at the age of eighty-nine, and the other at the age of ninety. On the tomb-stone of one of them, it was recorded that she had been a member of the church for seventy years. Their father was a remarkable man in his way. He was a rich man in his time, and kept a park of deer, one of the last known in Connecticut, for the purpose of supplying his table with venison. He prided himself on the strict and literal fulfillment of his word. On one occasion he had a law-suit with one of his neighbors, before a justice of the peace, in which he was cast and ordered to pay ten shillings damages, and a shilling as the fees of the

court. He paid the ten shillings, and asked the justice whether he would allow him to pay the remaining shilling when he next passed his door. The magistrate readily consented, but from that time old Comstock never went by his house. Whenever he had occasion to go to church, or to any other place, the direct road to which led by the justice's door, he was careful to take a lane which passed behind the dwelling, and at some distance from it. The shilling remained unpaid up to the day of his death, and it was found that in his last will he had directed that his corpse should be carried by that lane to the place of interment."

When we left the quarantine ground on Thursday morning, after lying moored all night with a heavy rain beating on the deck, the sky was beginning to clear with a strong northwest wind and the decks were slippery with ice. When the sun rose it threw a cold white light upon the waters, and the passengers who appeared on deck were muffled to the eyes. As we proceeded southwardly, the temperature grew milder, and the day closed with a calm and pleasant sunset. The next day the weather was still milder, until about noon, when we arrived off Cape Hatteras a strong wind set in from the northeast, clouds gathered with a showery aspect, and every thing seemed to betoken an impending storm. At this moment the captain shifted the direction of the voyage, from south to southwest; we ran before the wind leaving the storm, if there was any, behind us, and the day closed with another quiet and brilliant sunset.

The next day, the third of our voyage, broke upon us like a day in summer, with amber-colored sunshine and the blandest breezes that ever blew. An awning was stretched over the deck to protect us from the beams of the sun, and all the passengers gathered under it; the two dark-complexioned gentlemen left the task of filling the spittoons below, and came up to chew their tobacco on deck; the atrabilious passenger was seen to interest himself in the direction of the compass, and once was thought to smile, and the hale old gentleman repeated the history of his Norwalk relatives. On the fourth morning we landed at Savannah. It was delightful to eyes which had seen only russet fields and leaf-less trees for months, to gaze on the new and delicate green of the trees and the herbage. The weeping willows drooped in full leaf, the later oaks were putting forth their new foliage, the locust-trees had hung out their tender sprays and their clusters of blossoms not yet unfolded, the Chinese wistaria covered the sides of houses with its festoons of blue blossoms, and roses were nodding at us in the wind, from the tops of the brick walls which surround the gardens.

Yet winter had been here, I saw. The orange-trees which, since the great frost seven or eight years ago, had sprung from the ground and grown to the height of fifteen or twenty feet, had a few days before my arrival felt another severe frost, and stood covered with sere dry leaves in the gardens, some of them yet laden with fruit. The trees were not killed, however, as

formerly, though they will produce no fruit this season, and new leaf-buds were beginning to sprout on their boughs. The dwarf-orange, a hardier tree, had escaped entirely, and its blossoms were beginning to open.

I visited Bonaventure, which I formerly described in one of my letters.[3] It has lost the interest of utter solitude and desertion which it then had. A Gothic cottage has been built on the place, and the avenues of live-oaks have been surrounded with an inclosure, for the purpose of making a cemetery on the spot. Yet there they stand, as solemn as ever, lifting and stretching their long irregular branches overhead, hung with masses and festoons of gray moss. It almost seemed, when I looked up to them, as if the clouds had come nearer to the earth than is their wont, and formed themselves into the shadowy ribs of the vault above me. The drive to Bonaventure at this season of the year is very beautiful, though the roads are sandy; it is partly along an avenue of tall trees, and partly through the woods, where the dog-wood and azalea and thorn-trees are in blossom, and the ground is sprinkled with flowers. Here and there are dwellings beside the road. "They are unsafe the greater part of the year," said the gentleman who drove me out, and who spoke from professional knowledge, "a summer residence in them is sure to bring dangerous fevers." Savannah is a healthy city, but it is like Rome, imprisoned by malaria.

The city of Savannah, since I saw it six years ago, has enlarged considerably, and the additions made to it increase its beauty. The streets have been extended on the south side, on the same plan as those of the rest of the city, with small parks at short distances from each other, planted with trees; and the new houses are handsome and well-built. The communications opened with the interior by long lines of railway have, no doubt, been the principal occasion of this prosperity. These and the Savannah river send enormous quantities of cotton to the Savannah market. One should see, with the bodily eye, the multitude of bales of this commodity accumulating in the warehouses and elsewhere, in order to form an idea of the extent to which it is produced in the southern states—long trains of cars heaped with bales, steamer after steamer loaded high with bales coming down the rivers, acres of bales on the wharves, acres of bales at the railway stations—one should see all this, and then carry his thoughts to the millions of the civilized world who are clothed by this great staple of our country.

I came to this place by steamer to Charleston and then by railway. The line of the railway, one hundred and thirty-seven miles in length, passes through the most unproductive district of South Carolina. It is in fact nothing but a waste of forest, with here and there an open field, half a dozen glimpses of plantations, and about as many villages, none of which are considerable, and some of which consist of not more than half a dozen houses. Aiken, however, sixteen miles before you reach the Savannah river, has a pleasant aspect. It is situated on a comparatively high tract of coun-

try, sandy and barren, but healthy, and hither the planters resort in the hot months from their homes in the less salubrious districts. Pretty cottages stand dispersed among the oaks and pines, and immediately west of the place the country descends in pleasant undulations towards the valley of the Savannah.

The appearance of Augusta struck me very agreeably as I reached it, on a most delightful afternoon, which seemed to me more like June than March. I was delighted to see turf again, regular greensward of sweet grasses and clover, such as you see in May in the northern states, and do not meet on the coast in the southern states. The city lies on a broad rich plain on the Savannah river, with woody declivities to the north and west. I have seen several things here since my arrival which interested me much, and if I can command time I will speak of them in another letter.

MANUSCRIPT: Unrecovered TEXT: *LT* I, pp. 336–344; first published in *EP* for April 6, 1849.

1. *The Ancient Historical Records of Norwalk, Conn.; With a Plan of the Ancient Settlement, and of the Town in 1847*, comp. Edwin Hall (Norwalk and New York, 1847).
2. Although a legislative act of 1784 provided for the emancipation of all Negroes at the age of twenty-five, slavery was not abolished in Connecticut until 1848.
3. Letter 456.

670. *To* Frances F. Bryant

Charleston   March 31, 1849.

My dear Frances.

I passed one day at Augusta very pleasantly, walking about the city and driving out to see the environs. I was much interested in going over a cotton mill where the sallow complexioned girls of the pine woods and some of the young men find an employment where they are not obliged to work with the blacks. They are scoured, put into shoes and stockings, and taught to read in the Sunday schools and in a short time their whole appearance and demeanor undergoes a favorable change. There are many of these establishments at the south; they weave coarse cloths cheaper than the mill owners at the north can do, and they are effecting immense good by reclaiming from idleness and ignorance a large and degraded class of the whites in South Carolina and Georgia.

In the course of the day I fell in with Mr. Gould who has a law school here; he is a son of the late Judge Gould of Litchfield;[1] he told me that he remembered me at Judge Howe's,[2] and inquired about my mother. We went to the plantation of Mr. De l'aigle, who received us with great hospitality and insisted on opening a bottle of Heidsick before he would allow us to go upon his grounds.[3] The plantation was in excellent order; the garden, full of flowers and shrubs in bloom well-kept; the negro houses comfortable, the fences in perfect repair, and hedges of the Cherokee rose

well-pleached, surrounding the enclosures near the dwelling. They were in full fresh leaf and their white flowers were just beginning to open. Southward from the house stretched fields of maize, just beginning to peep above the ground, fields which seemed almost boundless, it would have seemed so but for the distant forests beyond them. The plantation consists of ten thousand acres.

We drove thence to the Sand Hill, or Somerville as it is called lying west of Augusta and overlooking the city. Here is a drier atmosphere than on the river side, and cooler evenings in the hot months. The more opulent people of the place have their cottages here, dispersed among the oaks and pines, and hither they retire from the extreme heat; some pass the whole year here. The place is of considerable extent, and very pretty with its neat white houses about which the shade is as dense as possible, and its embowered paths leading from one to the other. There is no danger that the shade will cause dampness, the soil is so sandy and porous. In some places however they have gardens, which in so barren a tract must be done with a good deal of expense.

We called on a Mr. Robinson a native of Exeter in New Hampshire,[4] reported to be very rich, who has for many years passed his winters here. He lives in a low cottage, but it is furnished with such elegance and neatness that I almost thought I had committed a desecration by entering it with my boots on. He asked me my opinion of slavery which I gave frankly. I agree with you, said he, but you shall see my negroes. He passed out at the back door, showing us the bedrooms as he went, and then entered a negro house, where sat a lady like—if I may say so—coloured woman neatly dressed, in an apartment floored with oaken plank as clean as scouring could make it, surrounded with her wooly headed children, engaged in sewing. Her bedroom was hung with engravings, and if I had been asked to say who was most elegantly lodged, she or her master and mistress it would have been hard for me to say.

Yesterday morning at six o'clock we left Augusta by the railway for Midway and the Woodlands. We found Mr. and Mrs. Simms quite well. Augusta, become a housekeeper is greatly improved in health.[5] Mr. Roach does not look a day older than when we saw him six years ago. They all chid me for not having brought you with me. Mary Steele is married to a man named Rivers, concerned in the management of the railway, and living somewhere near it. Washy as they used to call her was on a visit to her sister.[6] Miss Kellogg—Nancy[7]—was there, better in health, and looking very bright. They all desired to be particularly remembered to you. We had a pleasant day with them. We sat under the brick portico till we were refreshed and then had some long walks through the forests now beautiful with various shrubs in blossom, and over the fields.

I arrived here today about half past five. I have been obliged to make some additions to my wardrobe of thin clothes for the hot climate of Ha-

vana. Tomorrow we sail in the Isabel, at ten o'clock. I wish you were my companion for the voyage. Your prayers, I am sure, will go with me.

April 1st. I wish you would write to me at Charleston. The probability is that we shall not go to New Orleans but return to this place. Good bye— God Bless you

W C BRYANT

MANUSCRIPT: NYPL–GR ADDRESS: Mrs. Frances F. Bryant / Roslyn / Long Island DOCKETED: Charleston.

1. James Gould (1770–1838, Yale 1791) conducted the Litchfield (Connecticut) Law School from 1820 to 1833, after the retirement of its founder, Tapping Reeve (1744–1823, College of New Jersey [Princeton] 1763).

2. This was probably James Gould's eldest son, William Tracy Gould, later a justice of the Georgia Supreme Court. Bryant had studied law with Samuel Howe in Worthington, Massachusetts, from 1811 to 1814; see Letters 4–8.

3. De l'aigle has not been further identified.

4. Probably William Robinson, through whose bequest the Robinson Seminary for girls was founded at Exeter, New Hampshire, in 1867.

5. William Gilmore Simms's daughter by his first wife was then about twenty-two years old. See 395.1.

6. For these cousins of Mrs. Simms, see Letter 460.

7. Of Great Barrington, Massachusetts; see 316.15.

671.   To the EVENING POST

Barnwell District, South Carolina,
March 31, 1849.

I promised to say something more of Augusta if I had time before departing for[1] Cuba, and I find that I have a few moments to spare for a hasty letter.

The people of Augusta boast of the beauty of their place, and not without some reason. The streets are broad, and in some parts overshadowed with rows of fine trees. The banks of the river on which it stands are high and firm, and slopes half covered with forest, of a pleasant aspect, overlook it from the west and from the Carolina side. To the south stretches a broad champaign country, on which are some of the finest plantations of Georgia. I visited one of these, consisting of ten thousand acres, kept throughout in as perfect order as a small farm at the north, though large enough for a German principality.

But what interested me most, was a visit to a cotton mill in the neighborhood, —a sample of a class of manufacturing establishments, where the poor white people of this state and of South Carolina find occupation. It is a large manufactory, and the machinery is in as perfect order as in any of the mills at the north. "Here," said a gentleman who accompanied us, as we entered the long apartment in the second story, "you will see a sample of the brunettes of the piny woods."

The girls of various ages, who are employed at the spindles, had, for the most part, a sallow, sickly complexion, and in many of their faces, I remarked that look of mingled distrust and dejection which often accompanies the condition of extreme, hopeless poverty. "These poor girls," said one of our party, "think themselves extremely fortunate to be employed here, and accept work gladly. They come from the most barren parts of Carolina and Georgia, where their families live wretchedly, often upon unwholesome food, and as idly as wretchedly, for hitherto there has been no manual occupation provided for them from which they do not shrink as disgraceful, on account of its being the occupation of slaves. In these factories negroes are not employed as operatives, and this gives the calling of the factory girl a certain dignity. You would be surprised to see the change which a short time effects in these poor people. They come barefooted, dirty, and in rags; they are scoured, put into shoes and stockings, set at work and sent regularly to the Sunday-schools, where they are taught what none of them have been taught before—to read and write. In a short time they become[2] expert at their work; they lose their sullen shyness, and their physiognomy becomes comparatively open and cheerful. Their families are relieved from the temptations to theft and other shameful courses which accompany the condition of poverty without occupation."

"They have a good deal of the poke-easy manner of the piny woods about them yet," said one of our party, a Georgian. It was true; I perceived that they had not yet acquired all that alacrity and quickness in their work which you see in the work-people of the New England mills. In one of the upper stories I saw a girl of a clearer complexion than the rest, with two long curls swinging behind each ear, as she stepped about with the air of a duchess. "That girl is from the north," said our conductor; "at first we placed an expert operative from the north in each story of the building as an instructor and pattern to the rest."

I have since learned that some attempts were made at first to induce the poor white people to work side by side with the blacks in these mills. These utterly failed, and the question then became with the proprietors whether they should employ blacks or whites only; whether they should give these poor people an occupation which, while it tended to elevate their condition, secured a more expert class of work-people than the negroes could be expected to become, or whether they should rely upon the less intelligent and more negligent services of slaves. They decided at length upon banishing the labor of blacks from their mills. At Graniteville, in South Carolina, about ten miles from the Savannah river, a neat little manufacturing village has lately been built up, where the families of the *crackers,* as they are called, reclaimed from their idle lives in the woods, are settled, and white labor only is employed. The enterprise is said to be in a most prosperous condition.

Only coarse cloths are made in these mills—strong, thick fabrics, suitable for negro shirting—and the demand for this kind of goods, I am told, is greater than the supply. Every yard made in this manufactory at Augusta, is taken off as soon as it leaves the loom. I fell in with a northern man in the course of the day, who told me that these mills had driven the northern manufacturer of coarse cottons out of the southern market.

"The buildings are erected here more cheaply," he continued, "there is far less expense in fuel, and the wages of the workpeople are less. At first the boys and girls of the cracker families were engaged for little more than their board; their wages are now better, but they are still low. I am about to go to the north, and I shall do my best to persuade some of my friends, who have been almost ruined by this southern competition, to come to Augusta and set up cotton mills."

There is water-power at Augusta sufficient to turn the machinery of many large establishments. A canal from the Savannah river brings in a large volume of water, which passes from level to level, and might be made to turn the spindles and drive the looms of a populous manufacturing town. Such it will become, if any faith is to be placed in present indications, and a considerable manufacturing population will be settled at this place, drawn from the half-wild inhabitants of the most barren parts of the southern states. I look upon the introduction of manufactures at the south as an event of the most favorable promise for that part of the country, since it both condenses a class of population too thinly scattered to have the benefit of the institutions of civilized life, of education and religion—and restores one branch of labor, at least, to its proper dignity, in a region where manual labor has been the badge of servitude and dependence.

One of the pleasantest spots in the neighborhood of Augusta is Somerville, a sandy eminence, covered with woods, the shade of which is carefully cherished, and in the midst of which are numerous cottages and country seats, closely embowered in trees, with pleasant paths leading to them from the highway. Here the evenings in summer are not so oppressively hot as in the town below, and dense as the shade is, the air is dry and elastic. Hither many families retire during the hot season, and many reside here the year round. We drove through it as the sun was setting, and called at the dwellings of several of the hospitable inhabitants. The next morning the railway train brought us to Barnwell District, in South Carolina, where I write this.

I intended to send you some notes of the agricultural changes which I have observed in this part of South Carolina since I was last here, but I have hardly time to do it. The culture of wheat has been introduced, many planters now raising enough for their own consumption. The sugar cane is also planted, and quantities of sugar and molasses are often made sufficient to supply the plantations on which it is cultivated. Spinning-wheels

and looms have come into use, and a strong and durable cotton cloth is woven by the negro women for the wear of the slaves. All this shows a desire to make the most of the resources of the country, and to protect the planter against the embarrassments which often arise from the fluctuating prices of the great staple of the south—cotton. But I have no time to dwell upon this subject. Tomorrow I sail for Cuba.

MANUSCRIPT: Unrecovered TEXT: *LT* I, 345–350; first printed in *EP* for April 9, 1849.

    1. The printed text mistakenly has "from."
    2. The printed text mistakenly has "became."

672. *To* the EVENING POST

Havana, April 7, 1849.

It was a most agreeable voyage which I made in the steamer Isabel, to this port, the wind in our favor the whole distance, fine bright weather, the temperature passing gradually from what we have it in New York at the end of May, to what it is in the middle of June. The Isabel is a noble sea-boat, of great strength, not so well ventilated as the Tennessee, in which we came to Savannah, with spacious and comfortable cabins, and, I am sorry to say, rather dirty state-rooms.

We stopped off Savannah near the close of the first day of our voyage, to leave some of our passengers and take in others; and on the second, which was also the second of the month, we were running rapidly down the Florida coast, with the trade-wind fresh on our beam, sweeping before it a long swell from the east, in which our vessel rocked too much for the stomachs of most of the passengers. The next day the sea was smoother; we had changed our direction somewhat and were going before the wind, the Florida reefs full in sight, with their long streak of white surf, beyond which, along the line of the shore, lay a belt of water, of bright translucent green, and in front the waves wore an amethystine tint. We sat the greater part of the day under an awning. A long line, with a baited hook at the end, was let down into the water from the stern of our vessel, and after being dragged there an hour or two, it was seized by a king-fish, which was immediately hauled on board. It was an elegantly shaped fish, weighing nearly twenty pounds, with a long head, and scales shining with blue and purple. It was served up for dinner, and its flavor much commended by the amateurs.

The waters around us were full of sails, gleaming in the sunshine. "They belong," said our Charleston pilot, "to the wreckers who live at Key West. Every morning they come out and cruise among the reefs, to discover if there are any vessels wrecked or in distress—the night brings them back to the harbor on their island."

Your readers know, I presume, that at Key West is a town containing

nearly three thousand inhabitants, who subsist solely by the occupation of relieving vessels in distress navigating this dangerous coast, and bringing in such as are wrecked. The population, of course, increases with the commerce of the country, and every vessel that sails from our ports to the Gulf of Mexico, or comes from the Gulf to the North, every addition to the intercourse of the Atlantic ports with Mobile, New Orleans, the West Indies, or Central America, adds to their chances of gain. These people neither plant nor sow; their isle is a low barren spot, surrounded by a beach of white sand, formed of disintegrated porous limestone, and a covering of the same sand, spread thinly over the rock, forms its soil.

"It is a scandal," said the pilot, "that this coast is not better lighted. A few light-houses would make its navigation much safer, and they would be built, if Florida had any man in Congress to represent the matter properly to the government. I have long been familiar with this coast—sixty times, at least, I have made the voyage from Charleston to Havana, and I am sure that there is no such dangerous navigation on the coast of the United States. In going to Havana, or to New Orleans, or to other ports on the gulf, commanders of vessels try to avoid the current of the gulf-stream which would carry them to the north, and they, therefore, shave the Florida coast, and keep near the reefs which you see yonder. They often strike the reefs inadvertently, or are driven against them by storms. In returning northward the navigation is safer; we give a good offing to the reefs and strike out into the gulf-stream, the current of which carries us in the direction of our voyage."

A little before nine o'clock we had entered the little harbor of Key West, and were moored in its still waters. It was a bright moonlight evening, and we rambled two or three hours about the town and the island. The hull of a dismasted vessel lay close by our landing-place; it had no name on bow or stern, and had just been found abandoned at sea, and brought in by the wreckers; its cargo, consisting of logwood, had been taken out and lay in piles on the wharf. This town has principally grown up since the Florida war.[1] The habitations have a comfortable appearance; some of them are quite neat, but the sterility of the place is attested by the want of gardens. In some of the inclosures before the houses, however, there were tropical shrubs in flower, and here the cocoanut-tree was growing, and other trees of the palm kind, which rustled with a sharp dry sound in the fresh wind from the sea. They were the first palms I had seen growing in the open air, and they gave a tropical aspect to the place.

We fell in with a man who had lived thirteen years at Key West. He told us that its three thousand inhabitants had four places of worship—an Episcopal, a Catholic, a Methodist, and a Baptist church; and the drinking-houses which we saw open, with such an elaborate display of bottles and decanters, were not resorted to by the people of the place, but were the haunt of English and American sailors, whom the disasters, or the regular

voyages of their vessels had brought hither. He gave us an account of the hurricane of September, 1846, which overflowed and laid waste the island.

"Here where we stand," said he, "the water was four feet deep at least. I saved my family in a boat, and carried them to a higher part of the island. Two houses which I owned were swept away by the flood, and I was ruined. Most of the dwellings were unroofed by the wind; every vessel belonging to the place was lost; dismasted hulks were floating about, and nobody knew to whom they belonged, and dead bodies of men and women lay scattered along the beach. It was the worst hurricane ever known at Key West; before it came, we used to have a hurricane regularly once in two years, but we have had none since."

A bell was rung about this time, and we asked the reason. "It is to signify that the negroes must be at their homes," answered the man. We inquired if there were many blacks in the place. "Till lately," he replied, "there were about eighty, but since the United States government has begun to build the fort yonder, their number has increased. Several broken-down planters, who have no employment for their slaves, have sent them to Key West to be employed by the government. We do not want them here, and wish that the government would leave them on the hands of their masters."

On the fourth morning when we went on deck, the coast of Cuba, a ridge of dim hills, was in sight, and our vessel was rolling in the unsteady waves of the gulf stream, which here beat against the northern shore of the island. It was a hot morning, as the mornings in this climate always are till the periodical breeze springs up, about ten o'clock, and refreshes all the islands that lie in the embrace of the gulf. In a short time, the cream-colored walls of the Morro, the strong castle which guards the entrance to the harbor of Havana, appeared rising from the waters. We passed close to the cliffs on which it is built, were hailed in English, a gun was fired, our streamer darted through a narrow entrance into the harbor, and anchored in the midst of what appeared a still inland lake.

The city of Havana has a cheerful appearance seen from the harbor. Its massive houses, built for the most part of the porous rock of the island, are covered with stucco, generally of a white or cream color, but often stained sky-blue or bright yellow. Above these rise the dark towers and domes of the churches, apparently built of a more durable material, and looking more venerable for the gay color of the dwellings amidst which they stand. The extensive fortifications of Cabañas crown the heights on that side of the harbor which lies opposite to the town; and south of the city a green, fertile valley, in which stand scattered palm-trees, stretches towards the pleasant village of Cerro.

We lay idly in the stream for two hours, till the authorities of the port could find time to visit us. They arrived at last, and without coming on board, subjected the captain to a long questioning, and searched the news-

papers he brought for intelligence relating to the health of the port from which he sailed. At last they gave us leave to land, without undergoing a quarantine, and withdrew, taking with them our passports. We went on shore, and after three hours further delay got our baggage through the custom-house.

MANUSCRIPT: Unrecovered TEXT: *LT* I, pp. 351–357; first published in *EP* for April 16, 1849.

1. The Seminole War; see Letter 459.

673. *To* Frances F. Bryant

Havana   April 8, 1849.

My dear Frances.

I have been here four days and it seems almost as many weeks. The steamer Isabel in which we came departs today for Charleston, and I send this by one of my fellow passengers who returns in her. In a fortnight the Isabel will leave this port again for the United States when we mean to take passage in her. To New Orleans we shall not go—the cholera is too rife there.

We left Charleston on the first of April on a morning as mild as summer. Several of the passengers who came on in the Tennessee were with us—a Mr. Morris, brother of the postmaster of New York and his wife, a Mr. Warren and his wife and sister of Troy, and one or two others.[1] At six o'clock we went up a little way towards Savannah, where we received some passengers on board and sent on shore others. The next day we were off the Florida coast and about noon saw land; the sea was rough and several of the passengers sick. The third day we kept near the Florida reef, in a smooth sea, with a belt of light green water of a glittering translucent appearance close to the land, and nearer to the vessel a tract of amethystine tint. We sat on deck the great part of the day in an atmosphere of most agreeable temperature. A long line with a baited hook at the end, was thrown out from the stern which after some time was seized by a fine king fish, resembling a mackeral in shape and colour. We had him on deck—he weighed nearly twenty pounds, and was served up for our dinner. All about us we saw white sails glittering in the sunshine; they were the vessels of the wreckers who inhabit Key West and who cruize every day about this dangerous coast, to discover any vessels that may have suffered wreck or damage on the reefs, returning at night to their little island.

A little before nine o'clock we were moored in the harbour of Key West. It was a bright moonlight night and we went on shore, to ramble over the town and island. The town contains two or three thousand inhabitants and is built on a rock of porous limestone, apparently of coral formation, with a beach of white sand formed of the disintegrated rock.

Large cocoa nut-trees—a kind of palm—made a loud and sharp rustling in the fresh trade wind that blew from the east; there were other trees of the palm kind which were pointed out to us in the gardens, and various strange shrubs in flower. Yet the isle is a barren place with very little verdure; its people subsist by the allowances which the admiralty court established here makes them for saving and bringing in wrecked vessels.

At twelve o'clock we resumed our voyage and when I went on deck the next morning—a hot morning—the coast of Cuba was in sight. Our vessel rolled from side to side in the restless waves of the Gulf Stream, which beat against the northern coast of the island. The white houses of Havana at length appeared in sight guarded by the lofty castle of the Morro, from which we were hailed as we passed, and entering into one of the finest bays in the world by a narrow passage we anchored in what seemed the quiet waters of an inland lake.

It was now nine o'clock—the hottest part of the day in Cuba, for the sea-breeze had not yet risen. Boats came about us rowed by dark looking men in Panama hats, but nobody could come on board till we were visited by the Health Authorities. These came about eleven o'clock—every thing proceeds slowly in Cuba— They demanded our newspapers and after long questioning the Captain, and consulting long among themselves, consented to admit us without quarantine, and withdrew taking our passports. We then went on shore, engaged rooms in an hotel kept by Fulton an American[2] near the water, and got our baggage on shore about two o'clock.

The sea wind was now sweeping gratefully through the streets and we dined with great comfort and appetite, in an open gallery of our *posada* [inn]. In the afternoon we drove out to the Paseo or Park, Isabel, just without the walls, the Paseo Tacon, and the Tacon gardens, planted with palms, mamey trees, papayas, and other trees of the tropics. We climbed the hill on which stands the fortress of Principe and overlooked the town of Havana and its fortifications, its harbor, the green valley of the Cerro and the sea. At eight o'clock the sound of music from the Plaza de Armas drew us again from our hotel. The Plaza is planted with the beautiful royal palm and other trees intersected by broad flagged stone walks. Here the Creoles and their families sit or walk on fine evenings, and listen to the airs played by a military band. The men were all in white pantaloons with here and there an exception, and the women without bonnets—dark eyed women, with jetty hair and dusky cheeks, their negro servants often sitting on the benches by their sides, and here and there was a group of negro women, occupying as conspicuous and convenient a position as their white sisters, and almost as well dressed. A row of volantes,—the two wheeled carriage of the country—almost the only carriage used—surrounded the plaza, in which ladies were sitting, enjoying the music, the fresh wind and the moonlight, occasionally greeted by some friend who

passed. At nine the music ceased the volantes turned away from the Plaza and gradually the crowd dispersed.

We came to Havana in the midst of the Holy Week, and have seen enough, not without entertainment, however, of Spanish religious processions and ceremonies. We have visited most places in the neighbourhood worth seeing and are thinking of proceeding to Matanzas soon. I wish you could have seen the crowds thronging to kiss the toe of the figure of our Savior bearing his cross, black and white pell-mell—the women returning from the ceremony with their eyes red with tears. I wish you could have beheld with me the procession, which with wailing music and muffled drums bore the effigy of the dead Christ around the city on Good Friday.[3] I wish you could have visited with me the *Quinta del Obispo* [bishop's country seat], with its rows of palms, and alleys of mangos and thickets of bamboos and beds of roses in bloom. I wish—no I do not wish—that you could have accompanied me yesterday to the Campo Santo, —where I saw the dead lowered in coarse coffins by stout negroes into fresh dug tranches, and the mould, mingled with human bones, human hair and fragments of garments shoveled upon them. I have a thousand things to write if I had time—Goodby—love to the children.

W. C BRYANT.

P. S. The weather is delightful—the temperature warm, but not hot—the sea wind, which blows the greater part of the day, seems health itself and the weather is constantly fine.

W. C. B.

MANUSCRIPT: NYPL–GR.

1. The New York City postmaster was then William V. Brady. Perhaps Bryant had in mind William L. Morris, a lawyer and commissioner, of 6 Broad Street. *Rode's New York City Directory for 1849–1850,* pp. 3, 305. Warren is unidentified.

2. Fulton's Mansion House, Calle Tacon. Bryant, "Diary of a Trip to Havana in 1849," April 4. NYPL–GR.

3. Bryant mistakenly wrote "Holy Thursday." See Letter 674.

674. *To* the EVENING POST

Havana, April 10, 1849.

I find that it requires a greater effort of resolution to sit down to the writing of a long letter in this soft climate, than in the country I have left. I feel a temptation to sit idly, and let the grateful wind from the sea, coming in at the broad windows, flow around me, or read, or talk, as I happen to have a book or a companion. That there is something in a tropical climate which indisposes one to vigorous exertion I can well believe, from what I experience in myself, and what I see around me. The ladies do not seem to take the least exercise, except an occasional drive on the Paseo, or public park; they never walk out, and when they are shopping, which is

no less the vocation of their sex here than in other civilized countries, they never descend from their *volantes*, but the goods are brought out by the obsequious shopkeeper, and the lady makes her choice and discusses the price as she sits in her carriage.

Yet the women of Cuba show no tokens of delicate health. Freshness of color does not belong to a latitude so near the equator, but they have plump figures, placid, unwrinkled countenances, a well-developed bust, and eyes, the brilliant languor of which is not the languor of illness. The girls as well as the young men, have rather narrow shoulders, but as they advance in life, the chest, in the women particularly, seems to expand from year to year, till it attains an amplitude by no means common in our country. I fully believe that this effect, and their general health, in spite of the inaction in which they pass their lives, is owing to the free circulation of air through their apartments.

For in Cuba, the women as well as the men may be said to live in the open air. They know nothing of close rooms, in all the island, and nothing of foul air, and to this, I have no doubt, quite as much as to the mildness of the temperature, the friendly effect of its climate upon invalids from the north is to be ascribed. Their ceilings are extremely lofty, and the wide windows, extending from the top of the room to the floor and guarded by long perpendicular bars of iron, are without glass, and when closed are generally only closed with blinds which, while they break the force of the wind when it is too strong, do not exclude the air. Since I have been on the island, I may be said to have breakfasted and dined and supped and slept in the open air, in an atmosphere which is never in repose except for a short time in the morning after sunrise. At other times a breeze is always stirring, in the day-time bringing in the air from the ocean, and at night drawing it out again to the sea.

In walking through the streets of the towns in Cuba, I have been entertained by the glimpses I had through the ample windows, of what was going on in the parlors. Sometimes a curtain hanging before them allowed me only a sight of the small hands which clasped the bars of the grate, and the dusky faces and dark eyes peeping into the street and scanning the passers by. At other times, the whole room was seen, with its furniture, and its female forms sitting in languid postures, courting the breeze as it entered from without. In the evening, as I passed along the narrow sidewalk of the narrow streets, I have been startled at finding myself almost in the midst of a merry party gathered about the window of a brilliantly lighted room, and chattering the soft Spanish of the island in voices that sounded strangely near to me. I have spoken of their languid postures: they love to recline on sofas; their houses are filled with rocking-chairs imported from the United States; they are fond of sitting in chairs tilted against the wall, as we sometimes do at home. Indeed they go beyond us in this respect; for

in Cuba they have invented a kind of chair which, by lowering the back and raising the knees, places the sitter precisely in the posture he would take if he sat in a chair leaning backward against a wall. It is a luxurious attitude, I must own, and I do not wonder that it is a favorite with lazy people, for it relieves one of all the trouble of keeping the body upright.

It is the women who form the large majority of the worshippers in the churches. I landed here in Passion Week, and the next day was Holy Thursday, when not a vehicle on wheels of any sort is allowed to be seen in the streets; and the ladies, contrary to their custom during the rest of the year, are obliged to resort to the churches on foot. Negro servants of both sexes were seen passing to and fro, carrying mats on which their mistresses were to kneel in the morning service. All the white female population, young and old, were dressed in black, with black lace veils. In the afternoon, three wooden or waxen images of the size of life, representing Christ in the different stages of his passion, were placed in the spacious Church of St. Catharine, which was so thronged that I found it difficult to enter. Near the door was a figure of the Saviour sinking under the weight of his cross, and the worshippers were kneeling to kiss his feet. Aged negro men and women, half-naked negro children, ladies richly attired, little girls in Parisian dresses, with lustrous black eyes and a profusion of ringlets, cast themselves down before the image, and pressed their lips to its feet in a passion of devotion. Mothers led up their little ones, and showed them how to perform this act of adoration. I saw matrons and young women rise from it with their eyes red with tears.

The next day, which was Good Friday, about twilight, a long procession came trailing slowly through the streets under my window, bearing an image of the dead Christ, lying upon a cloth of gold. It was accompanied by a body of soldiery, holding their muskets reversed, and a band playing plaintive tunes; the crowd uncovered their heads as it passed. On Saturday morning, at ten o'clock, the solemnities of holy week were over; the bells rang a merry peal; hundreds of volantes and drays, which had stood ready harnessed, rushed into the streets; the city became suddenly noisy with the rattle of wheels and the tramp of horses; the shops which had been shut for the last two days, were opened; and the ladies, in white or light-colored muslins, were proceeding in their volantes to purchase at the shops their costumes for the Easter festivities.

I passed the evening on the *Plaza de Armas*, a public square in front of the Governor's house, planted with palms and other trees, paved with broad flags, and bordered with a row of benches. It was crowded with people in their best dresses, the ladies mostly in white, and without bonnets, for the bonnet in this country is only worn while travelling. Chairs had been placed for them in a double row around the edge of the square, and a row of volantes surrounded the square, in each of which sat two or more

ladies, the ample folds of their muslin dresses flowing out on each side over the steps of the carriage. The Governor's band played various airs, martial and civic, with great beauty of execution. The music continued for two hours, and the throng, with only occasional intervals of conversation, seemed to give themselves up wholly to the enjoyment of listening to it.

It was a bright moonlight night, so bright that one might almost see to read, and the temperature the finest I can conceive, a gentle breeze rustling among the palms overhead. I was surprised at seeing around me so many fair brows and snowy necks. It is the moonlight, said I to myself, or perhaps it is the effect of the white dresses, for the complexions of these ladies seem to differ several shades from those which I saw yesterday at the churches. A female acquaintance has since given me another solution of the matter.

"The reason," she said, "of the difference you perceived is this, that during the ceremonies of holy week they take off the *cascarilla* from their faces, and appear in their natural complexions."

I asked the meaning of the word *cascarilla*, which I did not remember to have heard before.

"It is the favorite cosmetic of the island, and is made of egg-shells finely pulverized. They often fairly plaster their faces with it. I have seen a dark-skinned lady as white almost as marble at a ball. They will sometimes, at a morning call or an evening party, withdraw to repair the *cascarilla* on their faces."

I do not vouch for this tale, but tell it "as it was told to me." Perhaps, after all, it was the moonlight which had produced this transformation, though I had noticed something of the same improvement of complexion just before sunset, on the Paseo Isabel, a public park without the city walls, planted with rows of trees, where, every afternoon, the gentry of Havana drive backward and forward in their volantes, with each a glittering harness, and a liveried negro bestriding, in large jack-boots, the single horse which draws the vehicle.

I had also the same afternoon visited the receptacle into which the population of the city are swept when the game of life is played out—the Campo Santo, as it is called, or public cemetery of Havana. Going out of the city at the gate nearest the sea, I passed through a street of the wretchedest houses I had seen; the ocean was roaring at my right on the coral rocks which form the coast. The dingy habitations were soon left behind, and I saw the waves, pushed forward by a fresh wind, flinging their spray almost into the road; I next entered a short avenue of trees, and in a few minutes the volante stopped at the gate of the cemetery. In a little inclosure before the entrance, a few starveling flowers of Europe were cultivated, but the wild plants of the country flourished luxuriantly on the rich soil within. A thick wall surrounded the cemetery, in which were rows of openings for coffins, one above the other, where the more opulent of the dead

were entombed. The coffin is thrust in endwise, and the opening closed with a marble slab bearing an inscription.

Most of these niches were already occupied, but in the earth below, by far the greater part of those who die at Havana, are buried without a monument or a grave which they are allowed to hold a longer time than is necessary for their bodies to be consumed in the quicklime which is thrown upon them. Every day fresh trenches are dug into which their bodies are thrown, generally without coffins. Two of these, one near each wall of the cemetery, were waiting for the funerals. I saw where the spade had divided the bones of those who were buried there last, and thrown up the broken fragments, mingled with masses of lime, locks of hair, and bits of clothing. Without the walls was a receptacle in which the skulls and other larger bones, dark with the mould of the grave, were heaped.

Two or three persons were walking about the cemetery when we first entered, but it was now at length the cool of the day, and the funerals began to arrive. They brought in first a rude black coffin, broadest at the extremity which contained the head, and placing it at the end of one of the trenches, hurriedly produced a hammer and nails to fasten the lid before letting it down, when it was found that the box was too shallow at the narrower extremity. The lid was removed for a moment and showed the figure of an old man in a threadbare black coat, white pantaloons, and boots. The negroes who bore it beat out the bottom with the hammer, so as to allow the lid to be fastened over the feet. It was then nailed down firmly with coarse nails, the coffin was swung into the trench, and the earth shovelled upon it. A middle-aged man, who seemed to be some relative of the dead, led up a little boy close to the grave and watched the process of filling it. They spoke to each other and smiled, stood till the pit was filled to the surface, and the bearers had departed, and then retired in their turn. This was one of the more respectable class of funerals. Commonly the dead are piled without coffins, one above the other, in the trenches.

The funerals now multiplied. The corpse of a little child was brought in, uncoffined; and another, a young man who, I was told, had cut his throat for love, was borne towards one of the niches in the wall. I heard loud voices, which seemed to proceed from the eastern side of the cemetery, and which, I thought at first, might be the recitation of a funeral service; but no funeral service is said at these graves; and, after a time, I perceived that they came from the windows of a long building which overlooked one side of the burial ground. It was a mad-house. The inmates, exasperated at the spectacle before them, were gesticulating from the windows—the women screaming and the men shouting, but no attention was paid to their uproar. A lady, however, a stranger to the island, who visited the Campo Santo that afternoon, was so affected by the sights and sounds of the place, that she was borne out weeping and almost in convulsions. As we left the place, we found a crowd of volantes about the gate; a pompous

bier, with rich black hangings, drew up; a little beyond, we met one of another kind—a long box, with glass sides and ends, in which lay the corpse of a woman, dressed in white, with a black veil thrown over the face.

The next day the festivities, which were to indemnify the people for the austerities of Lent and of Passion Week, began. The cock-pits were opened during the day, and masked balls were given in the evening at the theatres. You know, probably, that cock-fighting is the principal diversion of the island, having entirely supplanted the national spectacle of bull-baiting. Cuba, in fact, seemed to me a great poultry-yard. I heard the crowing of cocks in all quarters, for the game-cock is the noisiest and most boastful of birds, and is perpetually uttering his notes of defiance. In the villages I saw the veterans of the pit, a strong-legged race, with their combs cropped smooth to the head, the feathers plucked from every part of the body except their wings, and the tail docked like that of a coach horse, picking up their food in the lanes among the chickens. One old cripple I remember to have seen in the little town of Guines, stiff with wounds received in combat, who had probably got a furlough for life, and who, while limping among his female companions, maintained a sort of strut in his gait, and now and then stopped to crow defiance to the world. The peasants breed game-cocks and bring them to market; amateurs in the town train them for their private amusement. Dealers in game-cocks are as common as horse-jockies with us, and every village has its cock-pit.

I went on Monday to the *Valla de Gallos*, situated in that part of Havana which lies without the walls. Here, in a spacious inclosure, were two amphitheatres of benches, roofed, but without walls, with a circular area in the midst. Each was crowded with people, who were looking at a cock-fight, and half of whom seemed vociferating with all their might. I mounted one of the outer benches, and saw one of the birds laid dead by the other in a few minutes. Then was heard the chink of gold and silver pieces, as the betters stepped into the area and paid their wagers; the slain bird was carried out and thrown on the ground, and the victor, taken into the hands of his owner, crowed loudly in celebration of his victory. Two other birds were brought in, and the cries of those who offered wagers were heard on all sides. They ceased at last, and the cocks were put down to begin the combat. They fought warily at first, but at length began to strike in earnest, the blood flowed, and the bystanders were heard to vociferate, *"ahi están peleando"**—*"mata! mata! mata!"*† gesticulating at the same time with great violence, and new wagers were laid as the interest of the combat increased. In ten minutes one of the birds was dispatched, for the combat never ends till one of them has his death-wound.

[Bryant's notes]
    * "Now they are fighting!"
    † "Kill! kill! kill!"

In the mean time several other combats had begun in smaller pits, which lay within the same inclosure, but were not surrounded with circles of benches. I looked upon the throng engaged in this brutal sport, with eager gestures and loud cries, and could not help thinking how soon this noisy crowd would lie in heaps in the pits of the Campo Santo.

In the evening was a masked ball in the Tacon Theatre, a spacious building, one of the largest of its kind in the world. The pit, floored over, with the whole depth of the stage open to the back wall of the edifice, furnished a ballroom of immense size. People in grotesque masks, in hoods or fancy dresses, were mingled with a throng clad in the ordinary costume, and Spanish dances were performed to the music of a numerous band. A well-dressed crowd filled the first and second tier of boxes. The Creole smokes everywhere, and seemed astonished when the soldier who stood at the door ordered him to throw away his lighted segar before entering. Once upon the floor, however, he lighted another segar in defiance of the prohibition.

The Spanish dances, with their graceful movements, resembling the undulations of the sea in its gentlest moods, are nowhere more gracefully performed than in Cuba, by the young women born on the island. I could not help thinking, however, as I looked on that gay crowd, on the quaint maskers, and the dancers whose flexible limbs seemed swayed to and fro by the breath of the music, that all this was soon to end at the Campo Santo, and I asked myself how many of all this crowd would be huddled uncoffined, when their sports were over, into the foul trenches of the public cemetery.

MANUSCRIPT: Unrecovered TEXT: *LT* I, pp. 358–369; first published in *EP* for May 19, 1849.

675. *To* the EVENING POST

Matanzas, April 16, 1849.

My expectations of the scenery of the island of Cuba and of the magnificence of its vegetation, have not been quite fulfilled. This place is but sixty miles to the east of Havana, but the railway which brings you hither, takes you over a sweep of a hundred and thirty miles, through one of the most fertile districts in the interior of the island. I made an excursion from Havana to San Antonio de los Baños, a pleasant little town at nine leagues distance, in a southeast direction from the capital, in what is called the Vuelta Abajo. I have also just returned from a visit to some fine sugar estates to the southeast of Matanzas, so that I may claim to have seen something of the face of the country of which I speak.

At this season the hills about Havana, and the pastures everywhere, have an arid look, a russet hue, like sandy fields with us, when scorched by a long drought, or like our meadows in winter. This, however, is the dry

season; and when I was told that but two showers of rain had fallen since October, I could only wonder that so much vegetation was left, and that the verbenas and other herbage which clothed the ground, should yet retain, as I perceived they did, when I saw them nearer, an unextinguished life. I have, therefore, the disadvantage of seeing Cuba not only in the dry season, but near the close of an uncommonly dry season. Next month the rainy season commences, when the whole island, I am told, even the barrenest parts, flushes into a deep verdure, creeping plants climb over all the rocks and ascend the trees, and the mighty palms put out their new foliage.

Shade, however, is the great luxury of a warm climate, and why the people of Cuba do not surround their habitations in the country, in the villages, and in the environs of the large towns, with a dense umbrage of trees, I confess I do not exactly understand. In their rich soil, and in their perpetually genial climate, trees grow with great rapidity, and they have many noble ones both for size and foliage. The royal palm, with its tall straight columnar trunk of a whitish hue, only uplifts a Corinthian capital of leaves, and casts but a narrow shadow; but it mingles finely with other trees, and planted in avenues, forms a colonnade nobler than any of the porticoes to the ancient Egyptian temples. There is no thicker foliage or fresher green than that of the mango, which daily drops its abundant fruit for several months in the year, and the mamey and the sapote, fruit-trees also, are in leaf during the whole of the dry season; even the Indian fig, which clasps and kills the largest trees of the forest, and at last takes their place, a stately tree with a stout trunk of its own, has its unfading leaf of vivid green.

It is impossible to avoid an expression of impatience that these trees have not been formed into groups, embowering the dwellings, and into groves, through which the beams of the sun, here so fierce at noonday, could not reach the ground beneath. There is in fact nothing of ornamental cultivation in Cuba, except of the most formal kind. Some private gardens there are, carefully kept, but all of the stiffest pattern; there is nothing which brings out the larger vegetation of the region in that grandeur and magnificence which might belong to it. In the Quinta del Obispo, or Bishop's Garden, which is open to the public, you find shade which you find nowhere else, but the trees are planted in straight alleys, and the water-roses, a species of water-lily of immense size, fragrant and pink-colored, grow in a square tank, fed by a straight canal, with sides of hewn stone.

Let me say, however, that when I asked for trees, I was referred to the hurricanes which have recently ravaged the island. One of these swept over Cuba in 1844, uprooting the palms and the orange groves, and laying prostrate the avenues of trees on the coffee plantations. The Paseo Isabel, a public promenade, between the walls of Havana and the streets of the new

town, was formerly over-canopied with lofty and spreading trees, which this tempest levelled to the ground; it has now been planted with rows of young trees, which yield a meagre shade. In 1846 came another hurricane, still more terrific, destroying much of the beauty which the first had spared.

Of late years, also, such of the orange-trees as were not uprooted, or have recently been planted, have been attacked by the insect which a few years since was so destructive to the same tree in Florida. The effect upon the tree resembles that of a blight, the leaves grow sere, and the branches die. You may imagine, therefore, that I was somewhat disappointed not to find the air, as it is at this season in the south of Italy, fragrant with the odor of orange and lemon blossoms. Oranges are scarce, and not so fine, at this moment, in Havana and Matanzas, as in the fruit-shops of New York. I hear, however, that there are portions of the island which were spared by these hurricanes, and that there are others where the ravages of the insect in the orange groves have nearly ceased, as I have been told is also the case in Florida.

I have mentioned my excursion to San Antonio. I went thither by railway, in a car built at Newark, drawn by an engine made in New York, and worked by an American engineer. For some distance we passed through fields of the sweet-potato, which here never requires a second planting, and propagates itself perpetually in the soil, patches of maize, low groves of bananas with their dark stems, and of plantains with their green ones, and large tracts producing the pine-apple growing in rows like carrots. Then came plantations of the sugar-cane, with its sedge-like blades of pale-green, then extensive tracts of pasturage with scattered shrubs and tall dead weeds, the growth of the last summer, and a thin herbage bitten close to the soil. Here and there was an abandoned coffee-plantation, where cattle were browsing among the half-perished shrubs and broken rows of trees; and the neglected hedges of the wild pine, *piña raton*, as the Cubans call it, were interrupted with broad gaps.

Sometimes we passed the cottages of the *monteros*, or peasants, built mostly of palm-leaves, the walls formed of the broad sheath of the leaf, fastened to posts of bamboo, and the roof thatched with the long plume-like leaf itself. The door was sometimes hung with a kind of curtain to exclude the sun, which the dusky complexioned women and children put aside to gaze at us as we passed. These dwellings were often picturesque in their appearance, with a grove of plantains behind, a thicket of bamboo by the door, waving its willow-like sprays in the wind; a pair of mango-trees near, hung with fruit just ripening and reddish blossoms just opening, and a cocoa-tree or two lifting high above the rest its immense feathery leaves and its clusters of green nuts.

We now and then met the *monteros* themselves scudding along on their little horses, in that pace which we call a rack. Their dress was a

Panama hat, a shirt worn over a pair of pantaloons, a pair of rough cow-skin shoes, one of which was armed with a spur, and a sword lashed to the left side by a belt of cotton cloth. They are men of manly bearing, of thin make, but often of a good figure, with well-spread shoulders, which, however, have a stoop in them, contracted, I suppose, by riding always with a short stirrup.

Forests, too, we passed. You, doubtless, suppose that a forest in a soil and climate like this, must be a dense growth of trees with colossal stems and leafy summits. A forest in Cuba—all that I have seen are such—is a thicket of shrubs and creeping plants, through which, one would suppose that even the wild cats of the country would find it impossible to make their way. Above this impassable jungle rises here and there the palm, or the gigantic ceyba or cotton-tree, but more often trees of far less beauty, thinly scattered and with few branches, disposed without symmetry, and at this season often leafless.

We reached San Antonio at nine o'clock in the morning, and went to the inn of La Punta, where we breakfasted on rice and fresh eggs, and a dish of meat so highly flavored with garlic, that it was impossible to distinguish to what animal it belonged. Adjoining the inn was a cockpit, with cells for the birds surrounding the inclosure, in which they were crowing lustily. Two or three persons seemed to have nothing to do but to tend them; and one, in particular, with a gray beard, a grave aspect, and a solid gait, went about the work with a deliberation and solemnity which to me, who had lately seen the hurried burials at the Campo Santo, in Havana, was highly edifying. A man was training a game-cock in the pit; he was giving it lessons in the virtue of perseverance. He held another cock before it, which he was teaching it to pursue, and striking it occasionally over the head to provoke it, with the wing of the bird in his hand, he made it run after him about the area for half an hour together.

I had heard much of the beauty of the coffee estates of Cuba, and in the neighborhood of San Antonio are some which have been reputed very fine ones. A young man, in a checked blue and white shirt, worn like a frock over checked pantaloons, with a spur on one heel, offered to procure us a *volante*, and we engaged him. He brought us one with two horses, a negro postillion sitting on one, and the shafts of the vehicle borne by the other. We set off, passing through fields guarded by stiff-leaved hedges of the ratoon-pine, over ways so bad that if the motion of the volante were not the easiest in the world, we should have taken an unpleasant jolting. The lands of Cuba fit for cultivation, are divided into red and black; we were in the midst of the red lands, consisting of a fine earth of a deep brick color, resting on a bed of soft, porous, chalky limestone. In the dry season the surface is easily dispersed into dust, and stains your clothes of a dull red.

A drive of four miles, through a country full of palm and cocoanut

trees, brought us to the gate of a coffee plantation, which our friend in the checked shirt, by whom we were accompanied, opened for us. We passed up to the house through what had been an avenue of palms, but was now two rows of trees at very unequal distances, with here and there a sickly orange-tree. On each side grew the coffee shrubs, hung with flowers of snowy white, but unpruned and full of dry and leafless twigs. In every direction were ranks of trees, prized for ornament or for their fruit, and shrubs, among which were magnificent oleanders loaded with flowers, planted in such a manner as to break the force of the wind, and partially to shelter the plants from the too fierce rays of the sun. The coffee estate is, in fact, a kind of forest, with the trees and shrubs arranged in straight lines. The *mayoral*, or steward of the estate, a handsome Cuban, with white teeth, a pleasant smile, and a distinct utterance of his native language, received us with great courtesy, and offered us *cigarillos*, though he never used tobacco; and spirit of cane, though he never drank. He wore a sword, and carried a large flexible whip, doubled for convenience in the hand. He showed us the coffee plants, the broad platforms with smooth surfaces of cement and raised borders, where the berries were dried in the sun, and the mills where the negroes were at work separating the kernel from the pulp in which it is inclosed.

"These coffee estates," said he, "are already ruined, and the planters are abandoning them as fast as they can; in four years more there will not be a single coffee plantation on the island. They can not afford to raise coffee for the price they get in the market."

I inquired the reason. "It is," replied he, "the extreme dryness of the season when the plant is in flower. If we have rain at this time of the year, we are sure of a good crop; if it does not rain, the harvest is small; and the failure of rain is so common a circumstance that we must leave the cultivation of coffee to the people of St. Domingo and Brazil."

I asked if the plantation could not be converted into a sugar estate.

"Not this," he answered; "it has been cultivated too long. The land was originally rich, but it is exhausted"—tired out, was the expression he used—"we may cultivate maize or rice, for the dry culture of rice succeeds well here, or we may abandon it to grazing. At present we keep a few negroes here, just to gather the berries which ripen, without taking any trouble to preserve the plants, or replace those which die."

I could easily believe from what I saw on this estate, that there must be a great deal of beauty of vegetation in a well-kept coffee plantation, but the formal pattern in which it is disposed, the straight alleys and rows of trees, the squares and parallelograms, showed me that there was no beauty of arrangement. We fell in, before we returned to our inn, with the proprietor, a delicate-looking person, with thin white hands, who had been educated at Boston, and spoke English as if he had never lived anywhere else. His manners, compared with those of his steward, were exceedingly

frosty and forbidding, and when we told him of the civility which had been shown us, his looks seemed to say he wished it had been otherwise.

Returning to our inn, we dined, and as the sun grew low, we strolled out to look at the town. It is situated on a clear little stream, over which several bathing-houses are built, their posts standing in the midst of the current. Above the town, it flows between rocky banks, bordered with shrubs, many of them in flower. Below the town, after winding a little way, it enters a cavern yawning in the limestone rock, immediately over which a huge ceyba rises, and stretches its leafy arms in mid-heaven. Down this opening the river throws itself, and is never seen again. This is not a singular instance in Cuba. The island is full of caverns and openings in the rocks, and I am told that many of the streams find subterranean passages to the sea. There is a well at the inn of La Punta, in which a roaring of water is constantly heard. It is the sound of a subterranean stream rushing along a passage in the rocks, and the well is an opening into its roof.

In passing through the town, I was struck with the neat attire of those who inhabited the humblest dwellings. At the door of one of the cottages, I saw a group of children, of different ages, all quite pretty, with oval faces and glittering black eyes, in clean fresh dresses, which, one would think, could scarcely have been kept a moment without being soiled, in that dwelling, with its mud floor. The people of Cuba are sparing in their ablutions; the men do not wash their faces and hands till nearly mid-day, for fear of spasms; and of the women, I am told that many do not wash at all, contenting themselves with rubbing their cheeks and necks with a little aguardiente; but the passion for clean linen, and, among the men, for clean white pantaloons, is universal. The *montero* himself, on a holiday or any public occasion, will sport a shirt of the finest linen, smoothly ironed, and stiffly starched throughout, from the collar downward.

The next day, at half-past eleven, we left our inn, which was also what we call in the United States a country store, where the clerks, who had just performed their ablutions and combed their hair, were making segars behind the counter from the tobacco of the Vuelta Abajo, and returned by the railway to Havana. We procured travelling licenses at the cost of four dollars and a half each, for it is the pleasure of the government to levy this tax on strangers who travel, and early the following morning took the train for Matanzas.

MANUSCRIPT: Unrecovered TEXT: *LT* I, pp. 370–380; first published in *EP* for May 26, 1849.

676.   *To* the EVENING POST

Los Guines, April 18, 1849.

In the long circuit of railway which leads from Havana to Matanzas, I saw nothing remarkably different from what I observed on my excursion

to San Antonio. There was the same smooth country, of great apparent fertility, sometimes varied with gentle undulations, and sometimes rising, in the distance, into hills covered with thickets. We swept by dark-green fields planted with the yuca, an esculent root, of which the cassava bread is made, pale-green fields of the cane, brown tracts of pasturage, partly formed of abandoned coffee estates where the palms and scattered fruit-trees were yet standing, and forests of shrubs and twining plants growing for the most part among rocks. Some of these rocky tracts have a peculiar appearance; they consist of rough projections of rock a foot or two in height, of irregular shape and full of holes; these are called *diente de perro*, or dog's teeth. Here the trees and creepers find openings filled with soil, by which they are nourished. We passed two or three country cemeteries, where that foulest of birds, the turkey-vulture, was seen sitting on the white stuccoed walls, or hovering on his ragged wings in circles above them.

In passing over the neighborhood of the town in which I am now writing, I found myself on the black lands of the island. Here the rich dark earth of the plain lies on a bed of chalk as white as snow, as was apparent where the earth had been excavated to a little depth, on each side of the railway, to form the causey on which it ran. Streams of clear water, diverted from a river to the left, traversed the plain with a swift current, almost even with the surface of the soil, which they keep in perpetual freshness. As we approached Matanzas, we saw more extensive tracts of cane clothing the broad slopes with their dense blades, as if the coarse sedge of a river had been transplanted to the uplands.

At length the bay of Matanzas opened before us; a long tract of water stretching to the northeast, into which several rivers empty themselves. The town lay at the southwestern extremity, sheltered by hills, where the San Juan and the Yumuri pour themselves into the brine. It is a small but prosperous town, with a considerable trade, as was indicated by the vessels at anchor in the harbor.

As we passed along the harbor I remarked an extensive, healthy-looking orchard of plantains growing on one of those tracts which they call *diente de perro*. I could see nothing but the jagged teeth of whitish rock, and the green swelling stems of the plantain, from ten to fifteen feet in height, and as large as a man's leg, or larger. The stalks of the plantain are juicy and herbaceous, and of so yielding a texture, that with a sickle you might entirely sever the largest of them at a single stroke. How such a multitude of succulent plants could find nourishment on what seemed to the eye little else than barren rock, I could not imagine.

The day after arriving at Matanzas we made an excursion on horseback to the summit of the hill, immediately overlooking the town, called the Cumbre. Light hardy horses of the country were brought us, with high pommels to the saddles, which are also raised behind in a manner making it difficult to throw the rider from his seat. A negro fitted a spur

to my right heel, and mounting by the short stirrups, I crossed the river Yumuri with my companions, and began to climb the Cumbre. They boast at Matanzas of the perpetual coolness of temperature enjoyed upon the broad summit of this hill, where many of the opulent merchants of the town have their country houses, to which the mosquitoes and the intermittents that infest the town below, never come, and where, as one of them told me, you may play at billiards in August without any inconvenient perspiration.

From the Cumbre you behold the entire extent of the harbor; the town lies below you with its thicket of masts, and its dusty *paseo*, where rows of the Cuba pine stand rooted in the red soil. On the opposite shore your eye is attracted to a chasm between high rocks, where the river Canimar comes forth through banks of romantic beauty—so they are described to me—and mingles with the sea. But the view to the west was much finer; there lay the valley of the Yumuri, and a sight of it is worth a voyage to the island. In regard to this my expectations suffered no disappointment.

Before me lay a deep valley, surrounded on all sides by hills and mountains, with the little river Yumuri twining at the bottom. Smooth round hillocks rose from the side next to me, covered with clusters of palms, and the steeps of the southeastern corner of the valley were clothed with a wood of intense green, where I could almost see the leaves glisten in the sunshine. The broad fields below were waving with cane and maize, and cottages of the *monteros* were scattered among them, each with its tuft of bamboos and its little grove of plantains. In some parts the cliffs almost seemed to impend over the valley; but to the west, in a soft golden haze, rose summit behind summit, and over them all, loftiest and most remote, towered the mountain called the *Pan de Matanzas*.

We stopped for a few moments at a country seat on the top of the Cumbre, where this beautiful view lay ever before the eye. Round it, in a garden, were cultivated the most showy plants of the tropics, but my attention was attracted to a little plantation of damask roses blooming profusely. They were scentless; the climate which supplies the orange blossom with intense odors exhausts the fragrance of the rose. At nightfall—the night falls suddenly in this latitude—we were again at our hotel.

We passed our Sunday on a sugar estate at the hospitable mansion of a planter from the United States about fifteen miles from Matanzas. The house stands on an eminence, once embowered in trees which the hurricanes have leveled, overlooking a broad valley, where palms were scattered in every direction; for the estate had formerly been a coffee plantation. In the huge buildings containing the machinery and other apparatus for making sugar, which stood at the foot of the eminence, the power of steam, which had been toiling all the week, was now at rest. As the hour of sunset approached, a smoke was seen rising from its chimney, presently

puffs of vapor issued from the engine, its motion began to be heard, and the negroes, men and women, were summoned to begin the work of the week. Some fed the fire under the boiler with coal; others were seen rushing to the mill with their arms full of the stalks of the cane, freshly cut, which they took from a huge pile near the building; others lighted fires under a row of huge cauldrons, with the dry stalks of cane from which the juice had been crushed by the mill. It was a spectacle of activity such as I had not seen in Cuba.

The sound of the engine was heard all night, for the work of grinding the cane, once begun, proceeds day and night, with the exception of Sundays and some other holidays. I was early next morning at the mill. A current of cane juice was flowing from the rollers in a long trunk to a vat in which it was clarified with lime; it was then made to pass successively from one seething cauldron to another, as it obtained a thicker consistence by boiling. The negroes, with huge ladles turning on pivots, swept it from cauldron to cauldron, and finally passed it into a trunk, which conveyed it to shallow tanks in another apartment, where it cooled into sugar. From these another set of workmen scooped it up in moist masses, carried it in buckets up a low flight of stairs, and poured it into rows of hogsheads pierced with holes at the bottom. These are placed over a large tank, into which the moisture dripping from the hogsheads is collected and forms molasses.

This is the method of making the sugar called Muscovado. It is drained a few days, and then the railways take it to Matanzas or to Havana. We visited afterward a plantation in the neighborhood, in which clayed sugar is made. Our host furnished us with horses to make the excursion, and we took a winding road, over hill and valley, by plantations and forests, till we stopped at the gate of an extensive pasture-ground. An old negro, whose hut was at hand, opened it for us, and bowed low as we passed. A ride of half a mile further brought us in sight of the cane-fields of the plantation called Saratoga, belonging to the house of Drake & Company, of Havana, and reputed one of the finest of the island. It had a different aspect from any plantation we had seen. Trees and shrubs there were none, but the canes, except where they had been newly cropped for the mill, clothed the slopes and hollows with their light-green blades, like the herbage of a prairie.

We were kindly received by the administrator of the estate, an intelligent Biscayan, who showed us the whole process of making clayed sugar. It does not differ from that of making the Muscovado, so far as concerns the grinding and boiling. When, however, the sugar is nearly cool, it is poured into iron vessels of conical shape, with the point downward, at which is an opening. The top of the sugar is then covered with a sort of black thick mud, which they call clay, and which is several times renewed.

as it becomes dry. The moisture from the clay passes through the sugar, carrying with it the cruder portions, which form molasses. In a few days the draining is complete.

We saw the work-people of the Saratoga estate preparing for the market the sugar thus cleansed, if we may apply the word to such a process. With a rude iron blade they cleft the large loaf of sugar just taken from the mould into three parts, called first, second, and third quality, according to their whiteness. These are dried in the sun on separate platforms of wood with a raised edge; the women standing and walking over the fragments with their bare dirty feet, and beating them smaller with wooden mallets and clubs. The sugar of the first quality is then scraped up and put into boxes; that of the second and third, being moister, is handled a third time and carried into the drying-room, where it is exposed to the heat of a stove, and when sufficiently dry, is boxed up for market like the other.

The sight of these processes was not of a nature to make one think with much satisfaction of clayed sugar as an ingredient of food, but the inhabitants of the island are superior to such prejudices, and use it with as little scruple as they who do not know in what manner it is made.

In the afternoon we returned to the dwelling of our American host, and taking the train at *Caobas*, or Mahogany Trees—so called from the former growth of that tree on the spot—we were at Matanzas an hour afterward. The next morning the train brought us to this little town, situated half-way between Matanzas and Havana, but a considerable distance to the south of either.

MANUSCRIPT: Unrecovered TEXT: *LT* I, pp. 381–388; first published in *EP* for May 30, 1849.

677.   *To* the EVENING POST

Havana, April 22, 1849.

The other day when we were at Guines, we heard that a negro was to suffer death early the next morning by the *garrote*, an instrument by which the neck of the criminal is broken and life extinguished in an instant. I asked our landlady for what crime the man had been condemned.

"He killed his master," she replied, "an old man, in his bed."

"Had he received any provocation?"

"Not that I have heard; but another slave is to be put to death by the *garrote* in about a fortnight, whose offense had some palliation. His master was a man of harsh temper, and treated his slaves with extreme severity; the negro watched his opportunity, and shot him as he sat at table."

We went to the place of execution a little before eight o'clock, and found the preparations already made. A platform had been erected, on which stood a seat for the prisoner, and back of the seat a post was fixed,

with a sort of iron collar for his neck. A screw, with a long transverse handle on the side of the post opposite to the collar, was so contrived that, when it was turned, it would push forward an iron bolt against the back of the neck and crush the spine at once.

Sentinels in uniform were walking to and fro, keeping the spectators at a distance from the platform. The heat of the sun was intense, for the sea-breeze had not yet sprung up, but the crowd had begun to assemble. As near to the platform as they could come, stood a group of young girls, two of whom were dressed in white and one was pretty, with no other shade for their dusky faces than their black veils, chatting and laughing and stealing occasional glances at the new-comers. In another quarter were six or eight monteros on horseback, in their invariable costume of Panama hats, shirts and pantaloons, with holsters to their saddles, and most of them with swords lashed to their sides.

About half-past eight a numerous crowd made its appearance coming from the town. Among them walked with a firm step, a large black man, dressed in a long white frock, white pantaloons, and a white cap with a long peak which fell backward on his shoulders. He was the murderer; his hands were tied together by the wrists; in one of them he held a crucifix; the rope by which they were fastened was knotted around his waist, and the end of it was held by another athletic negro, dressed in blue cotton with white facings, who walked behind him. On the left of the criminal walked an officer of justice; on his right an ecclesiastic, slender and stooping, in a black gown and a black cap, the top of which was formed into a sort of coronet, exhorting the criminal, in a loud voice and with many gesticulations, to repent and trust in the mercy of God.

When they reached the platform, the negro was made to place himself on his knees before it, the priest continuing his exhortations, and now and then clapping him, in an encouraging manner, on the shoulder. I saw the man shake his head once or twice, and then kiss the crucifix. In the mean time a multitude, of all ages and both sexes, took possession of the places from which the spectacle could be best seen. A stone-fence, such as is common in our country, formed of loose stones taken from the surface of the ground, upheld a long row of spectators. A well-dressed couple, a gentleman in white pantaloons, and a lady elegantly attired, with a black lace veil and a parasol, bringing their two children and two colored servants, took their station by my side—the elder child found a place on the top of the fence, and the younger, about four years of age, was lifted in the arms of one of the servants, that it might have the full benefit of the spectacle.

The criminal was then raised from the ground, and going up the platform took the seat ready for him. The priest here renewed his exhortations, and, at length, turning to the audience, said, in a loud voice, "I believe in God Almighty and in Jesus Christ his only Son, and it grieves me to the heart to have offended them." These words, I suppose, were meant,

as the confession of the criminal, to be repeated after the priest, but I heard no response from his lips. Again and again the priest repeated them, the third time with a louder voice than ever; the signal was then given to the executioner. The iron collar was adjusted to the neck of the victim, and fastened under the chin. The athletic negro in blue, standing behind the post, took the handle of the screw and turned it deliberately. After a few turns, the criminal gave a sudden shrug of the shoulders; another turn of the screw, and a shudder ran over his whole frame, his eyes rolled wildly, his hands, still tied with the rope, were convulsively jerked upward, and then dropped back to their place motionless forever. The priest advanced and turned the peak of the white cap over the face to hide it from the sight of the multitude.

I had never seen, and never intended to see an execution, but the strangeness of this manner of inflicting death, and the desire to witness the behavior of an assembly of the people of Cuba on such an occasion, had overcome my previous determination. The horror of the spectacle now caused me to regret that I made one of a crowd drawn to look at it by an idle curiosity.

The negro in blue now stepped forward and felt the limbs of the dead man one by one, to ascertain whether life were wholly extinct, and then returning to the screw, gave it two or three turns more, as if to make his work sure. In the mean time my attention was attracted by a sound like that of a light buffet and a whimpering voice near me. I looked, and two men were standing by me, with a little white boy at their side, and a black boy of nearly the same age before them, holding his hat in his hand, and crying. They were endeavoring to direct his attention to what they considered the wholesome spectacle before him. "*Mira, mira, no te hará daño,*"* said the men, but the boy steadily refused to look in that direction, though he was evidently terrified by some threat of punishment and his eyes filled with tears. Finding him obstinate, they desisted from their purpose, and I was quite edified to see the little fellow continue to look away from the spectacle which attracted all other eyes but his. The white boy now came forward, touched the hat of the little black, and goodnaturedly saying "*pontelo, pontelo,*"† made him put it on his head.

The crowd now began to disperse, and in twenty minutes the place was nearly solitary, except the sentinels pacing backward and forward. Two hours afterward the sentinels were pacing there yet, and the dead man, in his white dress and iron collar, was still in his seat on the platform.

It is generally the natives of Africa by whom these murders are committed; the negroes born in the country are of a more yielding temper.

[Bryant's notes]
   * "Look, look, it will do you no harm."
   † "Put it on, put it on."

They have better learned the art of avoiding punishment, and submit to it more patiently when inflicted, having understood from their birth that it is one of the conditions of their existence. The whip is always in sight. "Nothing can be done without it," said an Englishman to me, who had lived eleven years on the island, "you can not make the negroes work by the mild methods which are used by slaveholders in the United States; the blacks there are far more intelligent and more easily governed by moral means." Africans, the living witnesses of the present existence of the slave-trade, are seen everywhere; at every step you meet blacks whose cheeks are scarred with parallel slashes, with which they were marked in the African slave-market, and who can not even speak the mutilated Spanish current in the mouths of the Cuba negroes.

One day I stood upon the quay at Matanzas and saw the slaves unloading the large lighters which brought goods from the Spanish ships lying in the harbor—casks of wine, jars of oil, bags of nuts, barrels of flour. The men were naked to the hips; their only garment being a pair of trowsers. I admired their ample chests, their massive shoulders, the full and muscular proportions of their arms, and the ease with which they shifted the heavy articles from place to place, or carried them on their heads. "Some of these are Africans?" I said to a gentleman who resided on the island. "They are all Africans," he answered, "Africans to a man; the negro born in Cuba is of a lighter make."

When I was at Guines, I went out to look at a sugar estate in the neighborhood, where the mill was turned by water, which a long aqueduct, from one of the streams that traverse the plain, conveyed over arches of stone so broad and massive that I could not help thinking of the aqueducts of Rome. A gang of black women were standing in the *secadero* or drying-place, among the lumps of clayed sugar, beating them small with mallets; before them walked to and fro the major-domo, with a cutlass by his side and a whip in his hand. I asked him how a planter could increase his stock of slaves. "There is no difficulty," he replied, "slaves are still brought to the island from Africa. The other day five hundred were landed on the sea-shore to the south of this; for you must know, Señor, that we are but three or four leagues from the coast."

"Was it done openly?" I inquired.

"*Publicamente*, Señor, *publicamente*;* they were landed on the sugar estate of *El Pastor*, and one hundred and seven more died on the passage from Africa."

"Did the government know of it?"

He shrugged his shoulders. "Of course the government knows it," said he; "every body else knows it."

[Bryant's note]
* "Publicly, sir, publicly."

The truth is, that the slave-trade is now fully revived; the government conniving at it, making a profit on the slaves imported from Africa, and screening from the pursuit of the English the pirates who bring them. There could scarcely be any arrangement of coast more favorable for smuggling slaves into a country, than the islands and long peninsulas, and many channels of the southern shore of Cuba. Here the mangrove thickets, sending down roots into the brine from their long branches that stretch over the water, form dense screens on each side of the passages from the main ocean to the inland, and render it easy for the slaver and his boats to lurk undiscovered by the English men-of-war.

During the comparative cessation of the slave-trade a few years since, the negroes, I have been told, were much better treated than before. They rose in value, and when they died, it was found not easy to supply their places; they were therefore made much of, and every thing was done which it was thought would tend to preserve their health, and maintain them in bodily vigor. If the slave-trade should make them cheap again, their lives of course will be of less consequence to their owners, and they will be subject again to be overtasked, as it has been said they were before. There is certainly great temptation to wear them out in the sugar mills, which are kept in motion day and night, during half the year, namely, through the dry season. "If this was not the healthiest employment in the world," said an overseer to me on one of the sugar estates, "it would kill us all who are engaged in it, both black and white."

Perhaps you may not know that more than half of the island of Cuba has never been reduced to tillage. Immense tracts of the rich black or red mould of the island, accumulated on the coral rock, are yet waiting the hand of the planter to be converted into profitable sugar estates. There is a demand, therefore, for laborers on the part of those who wish to become planters, and this demand is supplied not only from the coast of Africa, but from the American continent and southwestern Asia.

In one of the afternoons of Holy Week, I saw amid the crowd on the *Plaza de Armas*, in Havana, several men of low stature, of a deep-olive complexion, beardless, with high cheek-bones and straight black hair, dressed in white pantaloons of cotton, and shirts of the same material worn over them. They were Indians, natives of Yucatan, who had been taken prisoners of war by the whites of the country and sold to white men in Cuba, under a pretended contract to serve for a certain number of years. I afterward learned, that the dealers in this sort of merchandise were also bringing in the natives of Asia, Chinese they call them here, though I doubt whether they belong to that nation, and disposing of their services to the planters. There are six hundred of these people, I have been told, in this city.

Yesterday appeared in the Havana papers an ordinance concerning the "Indians and Asiatics imported into the country under a contract to

labor." It directs how much Indian corn, how many plantains, how much jerked-pork and rice they shall receive daily, and how many lashes the master may inflict for misbehavior. Twelve stripes with the cowskin he may administer for the smaller offenses, and twenty-four for transgressions of more importance; but if any more become necessary, he must apply to a magistrate for permission to lay them on. Such is the manner in which the government of Cuba sanctions the barbarity of making slaves of the freeborn men of Yucatan. The ordinance, however, betrays great concern for the salvation of the souls of those whom it thus delivers over to the lash of the slave-driver. It speaks of the Indians from America, as Christians already, but while it allows the slaves imported from Asia to be flogged, it directs that they shall be carefully instructed in the doctrines of our holy religion.

Yet the policy of the government favors emancipation. The laws of Cuba permit any slave to purchase his freedom on paying a price fixed by three persons, one appointed by his master and two by a magistrate. He may, also, if he pleases, compel his master to sell him a certain portion of his time, which he may employ to earn the means of purchasing his entire freedom.

It is owing to this, I suppose, that the number of free blacks is so large in the island, and it is manifest that if the slave-trade could be checked, and these laws remain unaltered, the negroes would gradually emancipate themselves—all at least who would be worth keeping as servants. The population of Cuba is now about a million and a quarter, rather more than half of whom are colored persons, and one out of every four of the colored population is free. The mulattoes emancipate themselves as a matter of course, and some of them become rich by the occupations they follow. The prejudice of color is by no means so strong here as in the United States. Five or six years since the negroes were shouting and betting in the cockpits with the whites; but since the mulatto insurrection, as it is called, in 1843, the law forbids their presence at such amusements. I am told there is little difficulty in smuggling people of mixed blood, by the help of legal forms, into the white race, and if they are rich, into good society, provided their hair is not frizzled.

You hear something said now and then in the United States concerning the annexation of Cuba to our confederacy; you may be curious, perhaps, to know what they say of it here. A European who had long resided in the island, gave me this account:

"The Creoles, no doubt, would be very glad to see Cuba annexed to the United States, and many of them ardently desire it. It would relieve them from many great burdens they now bear, open their commerce to the world, rid them of a tyrannical government, and allow them to manage their own affairs in their own way. But Spain derives from the possession of Cuba advantages too great to be relinquished. She extracts from Cuba

a revenue of twelve millions of dollars; her government sends its needy nobility, and all for whom it would provide, to fill lucrative offices in Cuba—the priests, the military officers, the civil authorities, every man who fills a judicial post or holds a clerkship is from old Spain. The Spanish government dares not give up Cuba if it were inclined.

"Nor will the people of Cuba make any effort to emancipate themselves by taking up arms. The struggle with the power of Spain would be bloody and uncertain, even if the white population were united, but the mutual distrust with which the planters and the peasantry regard each other, would make the issue of such an enterprise still more doubtful. At present it would not be safe for a Cuba planter to speak publicly of annexation to the United States. He would run the risk of being imprisoned or exiled."

Of course, if Cuba were to be annexed to the United States, the slave trade with Africa would cease to be carried on as now, though its perfect suppression might be found difficult. Negroes would be imported in large numbers from the United States, and planters would emigrate with them. Institutions of education would be introduced, commerce and religion would both be made free, and the character of the islanders would be elevated by the responsibilities which a free government would throw upon them. The planters, however, would doubtless adopt regulations insuring the perpetuity of slavery; they would unquestionably, as soon as they were allowed to frame ordinances for the island, take away the facilities which the present laws give the slave for effecting his own emancipation.

MANUSCRIPT: Unrecovered TEXT: *LT* I, pp. 389–401; first published in *EP* for June 6, 1849.

678.   *To* Israel K. Tefft

Richmond, Virginia, April 27, 1849.

My dear sir

I found time, during the last four days of my stay in the island of Cuba, after the novelties of Havana had been exhausted, and during the voyage homeward, after I had recovered from the first horrors of seasickness, to read the volume of Stevens's History of Georgia[1] which you were so kind as to put into my hands.

And, I assure you, I read it with great interest. I had no idea that the annals of your state could be presented in a form which could so deeply engage my attention. Dr. Stevens it appears to me, has executed his work with a great deal of historical talent. He has arranged the facts in such a manner as not only to make their order and relation to each other perfectly clear to the reader, but, also to keep the curiosity of the reader continually awake. The narrative is pervaded by a liberal philosophy, the reflec-

tions are just, and often profound, and the characters drawn with discrimination. The part which relates to the religious history of the colony I like exceedingly.

The work has some faults, however. Portions of documents or entire documents are sometimes given in the text when their import might better have been briefly stated in the author's own language. In that case if there was any reason for publishing the document it might have been placed in the appendix. The tedious original minutes of the formalities attending the surrender of their charter by the original trustees of the colony of Georgia are an example of what I mean. Sometimes the author allows himself to appear too much as the predetermined eulogist of the founders of the colony and commends in warm language acts for which more measured praise would have sufficed, or acts so obviously meritorious as to need no elaborate encomium. In the chapter respecting the slave-trade he begins by speaking of the African slave trade as criminal and condemning Great Britain for fastening the institution of slavery upon Carolina Massachusetts and other of her colonies, and proceeds in what seems to me an attempt to justify the settlers of Georgia for extorting by importunity the consent of the Trustees to introduce slavery within her limits, and after it was established buying negroes of the African traders. The episode of Bosomworth and his wife Mary is not as neatly related as the other incidents of Georgia history.[2] The style is sometimes a little too oratorical; sometimes it bears strong marks of the writer's profession, and now and then I have met with a tag of commonplace finery which I could wish exchanged for simpler and more direct forms of expression. There is my list of defects; perhaps if I were to read the work over I should reduce it—and they are nothing in comparison with its great and essential merits. I promised you to write what I thought of it, and you have just what you asked.

I am here in four days and a half from Havana—my head yet swims with the motion of the steamer in which I came out. Mr. Leupp and myself have stopped for a days rest. — We were eighteen days in Havana—we had a prosperous voyage both in going and returning, temperate weather while there and the opportunity of seeing much that was interesting and new to us. We often speak of your civility and that of your family while we were at Savannah.

Give my best regards to Mrs. Tefft and remember me kindly to your sons.

Yrs truly

W. C BRYANT

MANUSCRIPT: DuU ADDRESS: I. K. Tefft Esq. PUBLISHED: Jay B. Hubbell, "A New Letter by William Cullen Bryant," *The Georgia Historical Quarterly*, 26 (September–December 1942), 288–290.

1. William Bacon Stevens, *A History of Georgia from Its First Discovery* (New York and Savannah, 1847). See 456.4.

2. In their *A Popular History of the United States* (New York, 1879), III, 166–168, Bryant and his collaborator, Sydney Howard Gay, told the story of a bizarre episode in the early history of Georgia in which the half-breed Indian Mary Musgrove and her white husband, Rev. Thomas Bosomworth, played a central role. Mary had served for a time as interpreter for James Oglethorpe, founder of the colony, and Bosomworth, a Church of England clergyman, as his chaplain. In 1747, several years after Oglethorpe's final return to England, the two conspired to set themselves up as supreme rulers of the Creek Indian nation, leading an abortive rebellion against the colonial government—which, however, managed to disperse it without bloodshed.

679.   *To* Frances F. Bryant

[New York] Monday   May 14, 1849

Dear Frances.

I bought one piece of the paper at Kemp's[1] this morning, and one piece of *border*. He did not like to cut it, and the price of the piece is but six shillings. So I took it. The package is to be directed to the care of Mr. Julian,[2] and I spoke to him about it, as I went out. He will bring it to you I doubt not this evening.

All is quiet here. The mobs are over.—[3]

Yours ever
W. C. B.

MANUSCRIPT: NYPL–GR ADDRESS: Mrs. Frances F. Bryant / Roslyn / Long Island.

1. Probably George Kemp, a housepainter, of 90 Grove Street. *Rode's New York City Directory for 1849–1850*, p. 237.

2. Operator of the Roslyn stage; see Letter 651.

3. The long rivalry between the actors Edwin Forrest and William Charles Macready reached a catastrophic climax on May 10, 1849, when a New York mob, determined to drive the British tragedian from the city, disrupted Macready's performance at the Astor Place Opera House so violently that a militia company, called out to disperse the crowd, fired into it with cannon, killing and wounding nearly sixty people. See *EP*, May 9–16, 1849, *passim*; Odell, *Annals*, V, 481–484; 655.2.

680.   *To* Frances F. Bryant

New York   Thursday   May 17   1849.

Dear Frances

Will you be so kind as to ask Julia to be so kind as to copy for me that part of Griswold's introduction to my verses in the Poets of America which is strictly biographical—omitting the critical remarks,[1] so that I can have it when I come.

You thought it possible that you might come to town this week. Why not come tomorrow morning and go out with me on Saturday? Mr. and Mrs. Dewey are here, I saw them at the meeting of the Association last evening—they want to see you. Mr. Dewey will preach next Sunday, and

on Tuesday they return to Berkshire.[2] Tomorrow I have appointed to be at Levetts at twelve o'clock and should be glad if you were with me.

Del Vecchio will not have his picture frames finished till the beginning of next week, when he will send for the engraving at Mrs. Elwell's.[3]

Since I wrote thus far I have got your letter of yesterday noon.[4] I am glad to know what you are doing and that there is some prospect that you will have things in tolerable order at last, but I fear that you have so much work laid out for yourself that you will not be able to come to town tomorrow. Remember, however, that if you can, it is better to come now than after the cholera is here, which I suppose will be very soon. There are rumours that it is in town already and I fear they are not without foundation.[5]

As to Forrest and his wife, the matter stands just as it did, at least so far as I can hear. No letters have been written to any body, and of course no answers to them have been given. Miss Robbins has advised Mrs. F. to put her case in the hands of Mr. McCoun.[6]

Miss Robbins has just called. She tells me that yesterday Mrs. F. saw her husband and that he promised to call tomorrow, Friday, and talk the matter over and make an arrangement as to the allowance she is to receive.

Yrs ever

W. C. B.

MANUSCRIPT: NYPL–GR ADDRESS: Mrs. F. F. Bryant / Roslyn / Long Island.

1. See Rufus Wilmot Griswold, *The Poets and Poetry of America* (Philadelphia, 1842), pp. 125–126.

2. In 1849 Orville Dewey (307.4, 608.4) resigned his ministry of the Unitarian Church of the Messiah on Broadway and retired from New York City to his family home in Sheffield, Massachusetts. Bryant refers, perhaps, to a meeting of the American Unitarian Association, of which Dewey had previously served as president (1845–1847), and of which Bryant would later be a vice president during the last seven years of his life.

3. Since May 1847 the Bryants had lodged when in town with Mary Elwell at 4 Amity Place; see 615.1. The other references are probably to Morris Levett, a dentist, of 628 Broadway, and James R. Del Vecchio, a picture framer, 495 Broadway. *Rode's New York City Directory for 1849–1850*, pp. 256, 123.

4. Letter unrecovered.

5. The Asiatic cholera, brought to New York in December 1848 by steerage passengers from Europe, claimed its first victims in the city two days before Bryant wrote this letter. During an epidemic over the course of the next three months, more than one thousand deaths were officially attributed to this disease, and probably many hundreds more resulted from undiagnosed cases. Charles E. Rosenberg, *The Cholera Years: The United States in 1832, 1849, and 1866* (Chicago: The University of Chicago Press [1962]), pp. 101–114, *passim*.

6. See Letter 665 for the first intimation of the impending divorce suit between Edwin Forrest and Catherine Sinclair Forrest, into which the Bryants and the Godwins would later be drawn. For Eliza Robbins, see 127.6; for Judge William T. McCoun, 535.6.

681.   *To* Richard G. Parker[1]

New York   May 21, 1849.

Sir.

It seems to me very likely that the change you propose in a line of my little poem, called "The Death of the Flowers," is an improvement. Notwithstanding that I wrote "calls" originally, and notwithstanding a poet's paternal fondness for what he produces, I feel no repugnance to adopting the alteration, which convinces me that the expression you desire to substitute is quite as good, to say the least, as the one I used. The term, moreover, is less general, and therefore more descriptive. I freely consent, therefore, that instead of "calls" you read "caws" in the quotation you do me the honor to make, and I shall seriously consider whether I will not myself make the change in the next edition of my poems, if one should ever be published.[2]

You are kind enough to ask whether I have not some favorite poem which I would indicate, in order that you might copy it in the work you are preparing for the press.[3] The poem called "the Past," seems to me better than most of my verses, and another entitled "the Dream" is rather a favorite with me.[4] But poets do not always agree with the critics in regard to the comparative merits of their own productions, and I may therefore be mistaken in my preferences.

I am sir
very respectfully yours
Wm. C. Bryant

Manuscript: NYHS address: To Richard G. Parker Esq.

1. Richard Green Parker (1798–1869), a Boston teacher, was a prolific author of elementary and secondary school textbooks. His letter to Bryant which drew this reply is unrecovered.

2. Nevertheless, Bryant kept the original verb in the concluding line of the first stanza of this poem: "And from the wood-top calls the crow through all the gloomy day." See *Poems* (1876), p. 132.

3. Probably *National Series of Selections for Reading; Adapted to the Standing of the Pupil* (New York and Cincinnati, 1851).

4. *Poems* (1876), pp. 171–173, 283–285.

682.   *To* Frances F. Bryant

New York, May 24, 1849.

Dear Frances.

Fanny saw the girl of whom I wrote to you yesterday and thinks she may come without her friend. I went to inquire her character. I did not find Mrs. Moran with whom she had lived at home, but a nurse, a respectable looking German girl gave a good account of her and was anxious that

I should see Mrs. Moran, in order that she might confirm it. She had the oversight of every thing in the household, and though a chambermaid could turn her hand to any thing. Fanny will see her again today.

I saw Mrs. Robinson[1] last evening. She will come out on Saturday— She said nothing of Mary, but I will see her again. Nothing whatever has been done for Mrs. Forrest.—

I have written to West[2] as you desire.

Yrs ever

W C BRYANT

MANUSCRIPT: NYPL–GR ADDRESS: Mrs. Bryant / Roslyn / Long Island.

1. Probably Therese A. L. von Jacob Robinson; see 399.2.
2. West is unidentified; Bryant's letter to him is unrecovered.

683. *To* Fanny Bryant Godwin

[New York] Thursday May 24, 1849.

Dear Fanny.

I called yesterday at Mrs. Moran's but did not find her at home. A German girl, a nurse, gave me such an account of Matilde, that I am perfectly satisfied of her good qualities. She did every thing in his family, though she was chambermaid, and was sehr geschickt [very skillful] &c &c.

Yrs affectionately

W C BRYANT.

MANUSCRIPT: NYPL–GR ADDRESS: Mrs. F. Bryant Godwin / Fourth Street.

684. *To* Frances F. Bryant

New York Friday May 25 1849.

Dear Frances.

I wrote you yesterday that Mrs. Robinson would come out with me tomorrow. I called on her last evening and learned that no other of the family will come with her. Her cook leaves her the sixth of June, a good servant, except that she takes offence too easily. Perhaps you might engage her, if you get nobody else. Mrs. Hoyer[1] is making inquiries and expects to hear something the beginning of next week. Her indisposition the other day was occasioned by a fall which bruised her cheek and loosened her teeth.

You are invited to Lizzy Gray's wedding[2]—you and Julia—on Wednesday at twelve o'clock. I shall bring out the letters. If Miss Robbins comes out, as I hear she may, hold her fast till I come. She is not I know in one of her very gentlest moods about this time, but I am not afraid of her. Tell her so. I have hardly had a good talk with her since my return.

I forgot to say to you, yesterday, that Fanny intended to come out on Monday, and that she would be glad if you could engage somebody to begin house cleaning at the cottage on that day.—

Yours affectionately

W. C. B.

MANUSCRIPT: NYPL–GR ADDRESS: Mrs. Frances F. Bryant / Roslyn / Long Island.

1. Mrs. Charles F. Hoyer; see 326.5.
2. Probably a daughter of the Bryants' physician, Dr. John Franklin Gray; see 444.1.

685.   *To* Frances F. Bryant

Steamer Niagara

Friday evening   June[1]   15   1849.

My dear Frances.

I write this just as we are going into Halifax. We have had a pleasant passage thus far—three days of pleasant weather and a smooth sea. I have not been quite so sick as usual, and hope to get across to England with less of that misery than the last time.

The day before I left New York Mr. Leupp told me that Mrs. Fisk had arrived from Cuba with the two fans and was at the Bond Street House.[2] I told him I would call and take them, but forgot it entirely.

I did not think to give John[3] a memorandum to look to the plum trees and cut off all the knots which make their appearance. There is a tree in Mrs. Kirkland's garden which needs very much his attention.[4] Will you tell him of it and ask him to cut off the knots immediately.

I hope you will look well to your health this summer and take things as easy as possible. Look up something in the books for your eye which continued, when I left you to be affected longer than it ought, in the case of an ordinary stye.

Farewell again and may God bless you. I shall write again as soon as I touch land at Liverpool, which I hope will be in eight days at least. Do not forget, however, that you are not to wait till you get a letter from me.

I am writing almost in the dark— Love to Fanny and Julia.

Yrs   affectionately

W. C   BRYANT

MANUSCRIPT: NYPL–GR.

1. Bryant mistakenly wrote "May."
2. Mrs. John J. Fisk, apparently Bryant's and Leupp's fellow-passenger on their recent trip to Cuba. See Letter 686.
3. An Irish gardener Bryant had engaged that spring; see Frances Bryant to Cyrus Bryant, April 17, 1849, BCHS.
4. The novelist Caroline Kirkland (517.2) had rented a cottage on the Bryant property for the summer. *Ibid.*

686.   *To* Frances F. Bryant

Liverpool   Monday   June 25, 1849

My dear Frances.

I promised that I would write you as soon as I landed in England and I keep my word, though the letter cannot go till Saturday when the steamer departs for America.

We arrived at half past three this morning after a very prosperous passage—so much so that I often [prayed?][1] that if you and I should make the voyage hereafter we may have just such a one. The weather was quite favorable, the sea uncommonly smooth, and the wind when there was any, generally with us. When we got into the Channel, where we were for more than a day, there was no more motion than in Long Island Sound. We made the entire passage from New York in an hour and twenty minutes sooner than it was ever made before. I suffered very little from sea-sickness; after the fourth day I might be said to feel no remains of it; though my sensations were still not quite natural. A steamer from the Hudson the captain said, might have made the passage not only with safety but with comfort to the passengers and would have arrived at Liverpool three days sooner, where it would have attracted as much attention as the arrival of the sea serpent.

We had a hundred and twenty eight passengers, not more than five or six of whom were Americans—the rest were English commercial agents or merchants, Frenchmen, Germans, Italians and Spaniards; the latter appeared to be the most numerous. There were few of them in whom we took any interest, but they were all good humoured, like the weather.

Manchester, June 28th, Thursday. I write this from the house of my friend Mr. Christie[2] where I have already passed two nights. While at Liverpool, I went to see the Prince's Park, a public ground which had just been laid out when I was here before, and which I now found wonderfully improved and embellished. In one place an artificial sheet of water had been formed, where swans were sailing, and the banks of which, with rock-work, and groups of shrubs amidst the thick turf, some of which were covered with brilliant flowers white and red, formed the prettiest piece of picturesque gardening within a small compass that I think I ever saw. I called on Mr. Rathbone, who had been very attentive to us when we were at Liverpool before,[3] and went with Mr. Leupp to see some good pictures in the collection of Mr. Clow, a Scotchman to whom he had a letter.[4]

I was seized with a diarrhea, the afternoon of the day I landed, which proved violent and obstinate. I studied Dr. Joslin's book on the cholera,[5] and followed his directions in regard to regimen, but I got no better. While I was waiting to get well before travelling further, Mr. Christie came out and on Tuesday evening took us down to his house in this city, thirty one miles from Liverpool. Here I passed another very bad night,

and the next day, yesterday, in a kind of despair I swallowed a plate of strawberries which cured me instantly. I had a good night, and was never better than I find myself this morning. Tomorrow morning we go to London.

Mr. Tilden did not come out with us but he came to see us off and declared that he was determined to follow us in the next steamer. We have lost so much time that it will not be difficult for him to overtake us if he comes, as we shall pass two or three days in London.[6]

The weather has been very chilly since I came, and the skies cloudy, sometimes coyly sprinkling the streets and sometimes opening to let down a gleam of pale sunshine. It is much like the weather we were complaining of in America when I came away—the English however call it fine. I had on a great coat when Mr. Christie came out on Tuesday, and he said it was what he called "a blazing hot day." Since then I have put on my thickest wrapper, and Mr. Leupp wears two thin ones.

I have not yet seen Mr. Field,[7] and having been detained so long by my indisposition I think I must postpone my visit to him till I have seen the Hebrides. After the middle of August I am told that travelling in the Highlands is not so pleasant. I shall write to him, however, today. I am very anxious to hear from you, and hope to get a letter by the steamer the beginning of next week. Take good care of yourself, I entreat you and do not worry yourself too much.

Yours ever
W. C. BRYANT.

[*To* Julia Bryant]
Dear Julia.

You have your frolic tomorrow when I hope you will get better weather than any thing we have here, where we have made an hospitable friend keep his fire in the grate burning at midday. When the festivity is over, I fancy you returning to your studies,—your drawing and perhaps to your Ollendorf.[8] Write to me and tell me what you are doing; how you amuse yourself and how you occupy yourself. As the world is constituted the most fortunate are those who find amusement in occupation. Love to Fanny. Remember me kindly to Mrs. Kirkland and her family.

Yrs affectionately—
W. C. BRYANT

P. S. I have written to Mrs. Fisk apologizing for not calling [to][9] take the fans, and requesting her, if she paid more for them than what I handed her, to send to the office a memorandum of it for you. You will then send her the amount, addressed to the care of John J. Fisk Esq. American Exchange Bank New York.

MANUSCRIPT: NYPL–GR.

1. Word omitted.

2. David Christie (d. 1851), a Scottish manufacturer who had entertained Bryant and Leupp in 1845. See 538.4.

3. William Rathbone, former mayor of Liverpool. See 537.4.

4. Leupp was an avid art patron and collector. See James T. Callow, "The Art Collection of Charles M. Leupp," *The Antiques Magazine*, 118 (November 1980) 998–1009.

5. Benjamin Franklin Joslin (1796–1861), *Causes and Homoeopathic Treatment of the Cholera; Including Repertories for this Disease and for Vomiting, Diarrhoea, Cholera Infantism and Dysentery* (New York, 1849).

6. In June 1849 Samuel Jones Tilden (389.3), then a busy New York lawyer, "was disposed to accept the invitation of his wise friend and counselor, William Cullen Bryant, to accompany him to Europe," and went so far as to secure a passport and letters of introduction to persons abroad, but the pressure of business forced him to give up the trip. Alexander Clarence Flick and Gustav S. Lobrano, *Samuel Jones Tilden: A Study in Political Sagacity* (New York: Dodd, Mead, 1939), p. 87.

7. Ferdinand Emans Field, of Birmingham. See 347.5; Letter 687.

8. Probably Heinrich Gottfried Ollendorff (1803–1865), *A Key to the Exercises in Ollendorff's New Method of Learning to Read, Write, and Speak the German Language* (New York, 1845).

9. Word omitted. This letter is unrecovered.

---

687. *To* Frances F. Bryant

London   July 6, 1849.

My dear Frances.

I am yet you see in this great capital which seems to me and really is larger than when I was here four years since. The overgrown city grows and spreads like a great cancer and if it goes on at this rate will cover the whole island at last. North of Hyde Park where they were building streets of palaces when I was here last they are building streets of palaces yet— rows of tall and stately houses of stuccoed brick inhabited by families who spend I am told not less than two thousand a year or about ten thousand dollars of our money.

We left [for][1] London the day after I wrote you from Manchester, Mr. Christie accompanying us, and it is because he is with us and knows the city and its environs most thoroughly, that we still remain here. He esteems himself under some obligations to Mr. Leupp, and seems anxious to show that he remembers them. He will leave us, however, in a day or two, and then, on Monday probably, the 9th of this month, we set out for Scotland.

On Saturday, the day after I came up to London my complaint returned, and the next day it was so troublesome and obstinate that I went to employ a physician. I called at Dr. Cu[rie?]'s,[2] he was not at home, at Dr. Epps's[3] with the same success, and finally at Dr. Laurie's,[4] whom I

found in. He is a dapper, dark-complexioned young-looking Scotchman. He prescribed pulsatilla and bryonia—the first had a good effect but I was obliged to perfect the cure by mercurius. I paid him a guinea which was his fee he said for the two visits, but I had no occasion to call on him or send for him again.

Since I have been in London I have seen many things, but an enumeration of the sights of London would not interest you much. The original pictures of Hogarth, at Sir John Soane's Museum[5] are exceedingly interesting; they are solidly painted and well preserved and there seems to be even more meaning in them than in the engravings he made from them. I wish you could have gone with me to Dulwich College, in a pretty village, with a very rich collection of pictures mostly by the Flemish masters.[6] We went to Greenwich Hospital[7] and had our fourth of July dinner there, the principal dish being *white bait*, a very small fish, for which the place is famous.

I have called twice at Mr. Rogers's[8] but he did not happen to be in. I have seen Mr. Bancroft[9] and Mr. Edwin Field,[10] from whose hospitalities —I speak of them both—I had some difficulty to disengage myself. I wrote to Mr. Field of Birmingham[11] our friend and received a letter full of kind reproaches that when I was ill I did not come to his house. I shall answer him that I would have done so, but that Birmingham was so much further off than Manchester.

If I have time I shall write a letter this morning for the Evening Post[12] in which you will find notices of some things which I have not mentioned in this letter.

The weather since we have been in England has been very fine for English weather, though we should call it "very cold for the season." There are no open windows, except for a short time in the morning to air the rooms. Yet it is fine weather for exercise, for walking and excursions into the country.

I got your letter of the 17th of June[13] the other day and was very glad to receive it. I read it half a dozen times over. Love to the children. Remember me kindly to Mrs. Kirkland and her family. Tell Julia not to forget to write—and say to Fanny that I shall be very glad of a letter from her.

Yrs ever
W. C. BRYANT

MANUSCRIPT: NYPL–GR ADDRESS: Mrs. F. F. Bryant.

1. Word omitted.

2. Unidentified.

3. Probably John Epps (1805–1869, M.D. Edinburgh 1826), a homoeopathic physician and writer in defense of the Hahnemann system.

4. Joseph Laurie (d. 1865), whose *Homoeopathic Domestic Medicine* (London, 1842) had been edited in five American editions between 1843 and 1849 by Bryant's

physician and friend Dr. A. Gerald Hull, Jr. (405.4; 944.1). Hull had probably recommended Bryant to Dr. Laurie.

5. Established in 1833 by architect Sir John Soane (1753–1837) at 12–14 Lincoln's Inn Fields, in several buildings designed by him as a unit. The pictures by British artist William Hogarth (1697–1764) were the two satiric series "The Rake's Progress" and "The Election."

6. The Dulwich Picture Gallery, opened in 1817, was also designed by Sir John Soane.

7. Now the Royal Naval College at Greenwich on the Thames, within present-day London.

8. Samuel Rogers. See Letter 689; 540.10.

9. Historian George Bancroft, who had been since 1846 the American minister to Great Britain under Democratic President Polk, was about to relinquish this office to the Massachusetts textile manufacturer Abbott Lawrence, appointed by Polk's successor, Whig President Taylor.

10. A London lawyer who was an elder brother of Ferdinand Field. See 540.7.

11. Ferdinand Field. This letter is unrecovered.

12. Letter 688.

13. Unrecovered.

688. *To* the Evening Post

London, July 7, 1849.

I have just been to visit a gallery of drawings in water-colors, now open for exhibition. The English may be almost said to have created this branch of art. Till within a few years, delineations in water-colors, on drawing paper, have been so feeble and meagre as to be held in little esteem, but the English artists have shown that as much, though in a somewhat different way, may be done on drawing-paper as on canvas; that as high a degree of expression may be reached, as much strength given to the coloring, and as much boldness to the lights and shadows. In the collection of which I speak, are about four hundred drawings not before exhibited. Those which appeared to me the most remarkable, though not in the highest department of art, were still-life pieces by Hunt.[1] It seems to me impossible to carry pictorial illusion to a higher pitch than he has attained. A sprig of hawthorn flowers, freshly plucked, lies before you, and you are half-tempted to take it up and inhale its fragrance; those speckled eggs in the bird's nest, you are sure you might, if you pleased, take into your hand; that tuft of ivy leaves and buds is so complete an optical deception, that you can hardly believe that it has not been attached by some process to the paper on which you see it. A servant girl, in a calico gown, with a broom, by the same artist, and a young woman standing at a window, at which the light is streaming in, are as fine in their way, and as perfect imitations of every-day nature, as you see in the works of the best Flemish painters.

It is to landscape, however, that the artists in water-colors have principally devoted their attention. There are several very fine ones in the col-

lection by Copley Fielding,[2] the foregrounds drawn with much strength, the distant objects softly blending with the atmosphere as in nature, and a surprising depth and transparency given to the sky. Alfred Fripp and George Fripp[3] have also produced some very fine landscapes—mills, waters in foam or sleeping in pellucid pools, and the darkness of the tempest in contrast with gleams of sunshine. Oakley[4] has some spirited groups of gipsies and country people, and there are several of a similar kind by Taylor,[5] who designs and executes with great force. One of the earliest of the new school of artists in water-colors is Prout,[6] whose drawings are principally architectural, and who has shown how admirably suited this new style of art is to the delineation of the rich carvings of Gothic churches. Most of the finer pieces, I observed, were marked 'sold;' they brought prices varying from thirty to fifty guineas.

There is an exhibition now open of the paintings of Etty,[7] who stands high in the world of art as an historical painter. The "Society of the Arts" —I believe that is its name—every year gets up an exhibition of the works of some eminent painter, with the proceeds of which it buys one of his pictures, and places it in the National Gallery. This is a very effectual plan of forming in time a various and valuable collection of the works of British artists.

The greatest work of Etty is the series representing the Death of Holofernes by the hand of Judith. It consists of three paintings, the first of which shows Judith in prayer before the execution of her purpose; in the next, and the finest, she is seen standing by the couch of the heathen warrior, with the sword raised to heaven, to which she turns her eyes, as if imploring supernatural assistance; and in the third, she appears issuing from the tent, bearing the head of the ravager of her country, which she conceals from the armed attendants who stand on guard at the entrance, and exhibits to her astonished handmaid, who has been waiting the result.[8] The subject is an old one, but Etty has treated it in a new way, and given it a moral interest, which the old painters seem not to have thought of. In the delineation of the naked human figure, Etty is allowed to surpass all the English living artists, and his manner of painting flesh is thought to be next to that of Rubens. His reputation for these qualities has influenced his choice of subjects in a remarkable manner. The walls of the exhibition were covered with Venuses and Eves, Cupids and Psyches, and nymphs innocent of drapery, reclining on couches, or admiring their own beauty reflected in clear fountains. I almost thought myself in the midst of a collection made for the Grand Seignior.

The annual exhibition of the Royal Academy is now open. Its general character is mediocrity, unrelieved by any works of extraordinary or striking merit. There are some clever landscapes by the younger Danbys, and one by the father,[9] which is by no means among his happiest—a dark picture, which in half a dozen years will be one mass of black paint. Cooper,[10]

almost equal to Paul Potter[11] as a cattle painter, contributes some good pieces of that kind, and one of them, in which the cattle are from his pencil, and the landscape from that of Lee,[12] appeared to me the finest thing in the collection. There is, however, a picture by Leslie,[13] which his friends insist is the best in the exhibition. It represents the chaplain of the Duke leaving the table in a rage, after an harangue by Don Quixote in praise of knight-errantry. The suppressed mirth of the Duke and Duchess, the sly looks of the servants, the stormy anger of the ecclesiastic, and the serene gravity of the knight, are well expressed; but there is a stiffness in some of the figures which makes them look as if copied from the wooden models in the artist's study, and a raw and crude appearance in the handling, so that you are reminded of the brush every time you look at the painting. To do Leslie justice, however, his paintings ripen wonderfully, and seem to acquire a finish with years.

<Upon the whole, I did not see any thing in the exhibition to make it compare very favorably with that of our own Academy of Design.>[14] If one wishes to form an idea of the vast numbers of indifferent paintings which are annually produced in England, he should visit, as I did, another exhibition, a large gallery lighted from above, in which each artist, most of them of the younger or obscurer class, takes a certain number of feet on the wall and exhibits just what he pleases. Every man is his own hanging committee, and if his pictures are not placed in the most advantageous position, it is his own fault. Here acres of canvas are exhibited, most of which is spoiled of course, though here and there a good picture is to be seen, and others which give promise of future merit.

Enough of pictures. The principal subject of political discussion since I have been in England, has been the expediency of allowing Jews to sit in Parliament. You have seen by what a large majority Baron Rothschild has been again returned from the city of London, after his resignation, in spite of the zealous opposition of the conservatives.[15] It is allowed, I think, on all hands, that the majority of the nation are in favor of allowing Jews to hold seats in Parliament, but the other side urge the inconsistency of maintaining a Christian Church as a state institution, and admitting the enemies of Christianity to a share in its administration. Public opinion, however, is so strongly against political disabilities on account of religious faith, that with the aid of the ministry, it will, no doubt, triumph, and we shall see another class of adversaries of the Establishment making war upon it in the House of Commons. Nor will it be at all surprising if, after a little while, we hear of Jewish barons, earls, and marquises in the House of Peers. Rothschild himself may become the founder of a noble line, opulent beyond the proudest of them all.

The protectionist party here are laboring to persuade the people that the government have committed a great error, in granting such liberal conditions to the trade of other nations, to the prejudice of British indus-

try. They do not, however, seem to make much impression on the public mind. The necessaries of life are obtained at a cheaper rate than formerly, and that satisfies the people. Peel has been making a speech in Parliament on the free-trade question, which I often hear referred to as a very able argument for the free-trade policy.[16] Neither on this question nor on that of the Jewish disabilities, do the opposition seem to have the country with them.

MANUSCRIPT: Unrecovered TEXT: *LT* I, 402–407; first published in *EP* for July 28, 1849.

1. William Henry Hunt (1790–1864), outstanding for his still-life and humorous drawings.
2. Antony Vandyke Copley Fielding (1787–1855), president of the Water-colour Society, 1831–1855.
3. The brothers Alfred Downing Fripp (1822–1895) and George Arthur Fripp (1813–1896), secretary of the Old Water-colour Society, 1848–1854.
4. Octavius Oakley (1800–1867), nicknamed "Gipsy Oakley."
5. Frederick Tayler (1802–1889), who was notable for rural and sporting scenes.
6. Samuel Prout (1783–1852), distinguished for his long series of continental street scenes.
7. William Etty (1787–1849), who received very high prices for such works as "Cleopatra" and "Joan of Arc."
8. Cf. Judith 9, 13.
9. James Francis Danby (1816–1875); Thomas Danby (1817?–1886); Francis Danby (1793–1861).
10. Abraham Cooper (1787–1868).
11. Paul Potter (1625–1654), Dutch animal painter and etcher.
12. Frederick Richard Lee (1799–1879).
13. Charles Robert Leslie (1794–1859), London-born painter of American parentage, who was then a professor at the Royal Academy.
14. This sentence, printed in the *EP* for July 28, 1849, was omitted from the text in *LT* I, p. 406.
15. The London banker Lionel Nathan de Rothschild (1808–1879), who was refused a seat after his election to Parliament in 1847, and was thereafter repeatedly re-elected to the same office, was finally seated in 1858.
16. With the repeal of the Corn Laws in 1846, Conservative Prime Minister Sir Robert Peel (1788–1850) had been largely instrumental in implementing a policy of free trade in Great Britain.

689. *To* Frances F. Bryant

Edinburgh   July 11, 1849.

My dear Frances.

I have a few moments leisure before setting out for the Highlands which I employ in finishing a letter for the Evening Post and writing to you. Today we take the railway for Perth, and thence the coach for Inverness. At Inverness we expect to proceed by coach to a place called Wick on the northeast coast of Scotland, where a steamboat will touch on Saturday morning—it is now Wednesday—to take passengers for the Orkneys

and the Shetland Isles—to Kirkwall in the former and Lerwick in the latter. I think you will be able to trace our course on the map. We shall return to Inverness next Tuesday, and after a short stay there proceed to Glasgow by way of the Caledonia Canal and a chain of lakes in the Highlands.

I have been disappointed at not hearing from home before leaving Edinburgh. We supposed the steamer would arrive on Monday which would have given us our letters and papers yesterday and now we shall be obliged to leave Edinburgh before the arrival of the London mail or we may not secure our passage in the steamer from Wick to Kirkwall. I hear nothing of Tilden yet.

Before I left London, which was on Sunday evening at nine o'clock I had called on Mr. Rogers and had breakfasted with him. He was as formerly extremely kind and tried hard to make me pass a day with him. On our return to London we expect to go down to Hampshire Forest—the neighborhood of the Salisbury Cathedral, and Stonehenge, where Mr. Edwin Field expects to pass some days and where his brother Ferdinand will probably join him. *That* is an excursion which I think would please you, and therefore I wish you were here to make it with me—the one which I am about to make I think might be fatiguing for a lady.

We reached this city on Monday between one and two o'clock after a journey of four hundred miles without changing our seats, in a very cold night and a chilly morning. Edinburgh is as beautiful as ever but how the strawberries which I had at old Mrs. Christie's yesterday at dinner were ripened in such a climate puzzles me. One of the Christies, Alexander is an artist,[1] and is engaged to paint the panels[2] of the robing room of the House of Lords with portraits of the ancient sovereigns of England. He has taken us in charge since we have been here, and showed us some of the few antiquities of the place. My health is now excellent—I hope you will take care of yours. I am sorry to hear such reports of the spread of the cholera in the United States, but I do not perceive that it becomes more general in New York. Farewell— Tell Mrs. Kirkland that I have provided myself according to her advice with Walter Scott's journal of his tour among the northern isles.—[3] Love to all—write often.

Yrs ever

W. C. BRYANT

[*To* Julia Bryant]

Dear Julia. I believe that my postscript addressed to you at the end of the letter I wrote to your mother last week contained nothing but exhortations. I will suppose they are followed and inflict no more of them upon you. I suppose you begin to take to the water for coolness sake, while here in Edinburgh we sit with the windows closed, and try to make ourselves comfortably warm. I am just about to set out on a journey to the

very farthest northern extremity of the British Isles and when I get there I will tell you how the descendants of the Danes who inhabit the Shetlands look and what is the price of a Shetland pony, and how it strikes one to be in a country where the daylight, in summer is never out of the sky. I forgot to say to your mother that she must not expect a letter from me by the steamer after this.

Yrs affectionately,
W. C. BRYANT.

MANUSCRIPT: NYPL–GR.

1. Bryant and Leupp were entertained in Edinburgh by the family of David Christie (686.2), whose brother Alexander Christie (1807–1860) was an historical painter.
2. Bryant wrote "pannels."
3. Although Scott's *Journals* were not published in full until 1890, Bryant was probably reading the long extracts from these published in John G. Lockhart's *Memoirs of the Life of Scott* (1837–1838).

690.   *To* the EVENING POST

Aberdeen, July 19, 1849.

Two days ago I was in the Orkneys; the day before I was in the Shetland Isles, the "farthest Thule" of the Romans,[1] where I climbed the Noup of the Noss, as the famous headland of the island of Noss is called, from which you look out upon the sea that lies between Shetland and Norway.

From Wick, a considerable fishing town in Caithness, on the northern coast of Scotland, a steamer, named the Queen, departs once a week, in the summer months, for Kirkwall, in the Orkneys, and Lerwick, in Shetland. We went on board of her about ten o'clock on the 14th of July. The herring fishery had just begun, and the artificial port of Wick, constructed with massive walls of stone, was crowded with fishing vessels which had returned that morning from the labors of the night; for in the herring fishery it is only in the night that the nets are spread and drawn. Many of the vessels had landed their cargo; in others the fishermen were busily disengaging the herrings from the black nets and throwing them in heaps; and now and then a boat later than the rest, was entering from the sea. The green heights all around the bay were covered with groups of women, sitting or walking, dressed for the most part in caps and white short gowns, waiting for the arrival of the boats manned by their husbands and brothers, or belonging to the families of those who had come to seek occupation as fishermen. I had seen two or three of the principal streets of Wick that morning, swarming with strapping fellows, in blue highland bonnets, with blue jackets and pantaloons, and coarse blue flannel shirts. A shopkeeper, standing at his door, instructed me who they were.

"They are men of the Celtic race," he said—the term Celtic has grown to be quite fashionable, I find, when applied to the Highlanders. "They

came from the Hebrides and other parts of western Scotland, to get employment in the herring fishery. These people have travelled perhaps three hundred miles, most of them on foot, to be employed six or seven weeks, for which they will receive about six pounds wages. Those whom you see are not the best of their class; the more enterprising and industrious have boats of their own, and carry on the fishery on their own account."

We found the Queen a strong steamboat, with a good cabin and convenient state-rooms, but dirty, and smelling of fish from stem to stern. It has seemed to me that the further north I went, the more dirt I found. Our captain was an old Aberdeen seaman, with a stoop in his shoulders, and looked as if he was continually watching for land, an occupation for which the foggy climate of these latitudes gives him full scope. We left Wick between eleven and twelve o'clock in the forenoon, and glided over a calm sea, with a cloudless sky above us, and a thin haze on the surface of the waters. The haze thickened to a fog, which grew more and more dense, and finally closed overhead. After about three hours sail, the captain began to grow uneasy, and was seen walking about on the bridge between the wheel-houses, anxiously peering into the mist, on the lookout for the coast of the Orkneys. At length he gave up the search, and stopped the engine. The passengers amused themselves with fishing. Several coal-fish, a large fish of slender shape, were caught, and one fine cod was hauled up by a gentleman who united in his person, as he gave me to understand, the two capacities of portrait-painter and preacher of the gospel, and who held that the universal church of Christendom had gone sadly astray from the true primitive doctrine, in regard to the time when the millennium is to take place.

The fog cleared away in the evening; our steamer was again in motion; we landed at Kirkwall in the middle of the night, and when I went on deck the next morning, we were smoothly passing the shores of Fair Isle—high and steep rocks impending over the waters, with a covering of green turf. Before they were out of sight we saw the Shetland coast, the dark rock of Sumburgh Head, and behind it, half shrouded in mist, the promontory of Fitfiel Head,—Fitful Head, as it is called by Scott, in his novel of the Pirate.[2] Beyond, to the east, black rocky promontories came in sight, one after the other, beetling over the sea. At ten o'clock, we were passing through a channel between the islands leading to Lerwick, the capital of Shetland, on the principal island bearing the name of Mainland. Fields, yellow with flowers, among which stood here and there a cottage, sloped softly down to the water, and beyond them rose the bare declivities and summits of the hills, dark with heath, with here and there still darker spots, of an almost inky hue, where peat had been cut for fuel. Not a tree, not a shrub was to be seen, and the greater part of the soil appeared never to have been reduced to cultivation.

About one o'clock we cast anchor before Lerwick, a fishing village, built on the shore of Bressay Sound, which here forms one of the finest harbors in the world. It has two passages to the sea, so that when the wind blows a storm on one side of the islands, the Shetlander in his boat passes out in the other direction, and finds himself in comparatively smooth water. It was Sunday, and the man who landed us at the quay and took our baggage to our lodging, said as he left us—

"It's the Sabbath, and I'll no tak' my pay now, but I'll call the morrow. My name is Jim Sinclair, pilot, and if ye'll be wanting to go anywhere, I'll be glad to tak' ye in my boat." In a few minutes we were snugly established at our lodgings. There is no inn throughout all the Shetland Islands, which contain about thirty thousand inhabitants, but if any of my friends should have occasion to visit Lerwick, I can cheerfully recommend to them the comfortable lodging-house of Mrs. Walker, who keeps a little shop in the principal street, not far from Queen's lane. We made haste to get ready for church, and sallied out to find the place of worship frequented by our landlady, which was not a difficult matter.

The little town of Lerwick consists of two-story houses, built mostly of unhewn stone, rough-cast, with steep roofs and a chimney at each end. They are arranged along a winding street parallel with the shore, and along narrow lanes running upward to the top of the hill. The main street is flagged with smooth stones, like the streets in Venice, for no vehicle runs on wheels in the Shetland islands. We went up Queen's lane and soon found the building occupied by the Free Church of Scotland, until a temple of fairer proportions, on which the masons are now at work, on the top of the hill, shall be completed for their reception. It was crowded with attentive worshipers, one of whom obligingly came forward and found a seat for us. The minister, Mr. Frazer, had begun the evening service, and was at prayer. When I entered, he was speaking of "our father the devil;" but the prayer was followed by an earnest, practical discourse, though somewhat crude in the composition, and reminding me of an expression I once heard used by a distinguished Scotchman, who complained that the clergy of his country, in composing their sermons, too often "mak' rough wark of it."

I looked about among these descendants of the Norwegians, but could not see any thing singular in their physiognomy; and but for the harsh accent of the preacher, I might almost have thought myself in the midst of a country congregation in the United States. They are mostly of a light complexion, with an appearance of health and strength, though of a sparer make than the people of the more southern British isles. After the service was over, we returned to our lodgings, by a way which led to the top of the hill, and made the circuit of the little town. The paths leading into the interior of the island, were full of people returning homeward; the women in their best attire, a few in silks, with wind-tanned faces. We saw

them disappearing, one after another, in the hollows, or over the dark bare hilltops. With a population of less than three thousand souls, Lerwick has four places of worship—a church of the Establishment, a Free church, a church for the Seceders, and one for the Methodists. The road we took commanded a fine view of the harbor, surrounded and sheltered by hills. Within it lay a numerous group of idle fishing-vessels, with our great steamer in the midst; and more formidable in appearance, a Dutch man-of-war, sent to protect the Dutch fisheries, with the flag of Holland flying at the mast-head. Above the town, on tall poles, were floating the flags of four or five different nations, to mark the habitation of their consuls.

On the side opposite to the harbor, lay the small fresh-water lake of Cleikimin, with the remains of a Pictish castle in the midst; one of those circular buildings of unhewn, uncemented stone, skillfully laid, forming apartments and galleries of such small dimensions as to lead Sir Walter Scott to infer that the Picts were a people of a stature considerably below the ordinary standard of the human race. A deep Sabbath silence reigned over the scene, except the sound of the wind, which here never ceases to blow from one quarter or another, as it swept the herbage and beat against the stone walls surrounding the fields. The ground under our feet was thick with daisies and the blossoms of the crow-foot and other flowers; for in the brief summer of these islands, nature, which has no groves to embellish, makes amends by pranking the ground, particularly in the uncultivated parts, with a great profusion and variety of flowers.

The next morning we were rowed, by two of Jim Sinclair's boys, to the island of Bressay, and one of them acted as our guide to the remarkable precipice called the Noup of the Noss. We ascended its smooth slopes and pastures, and passed through one or two hamlets, where we observed the construction of the dwellings of the Zetland peasantry. They are built of unhewn stone, with roofs of turf held down by ropes of straw neatly twisted; the floors are of earth; the cow, pony, and pig live under the same roof with the family, and the manure pond, a receptacle for refuse and filth, is close to the door. A little higher up we came upon the uncultivated grounds, abandoned to heath, and only used to supply fuel by the cutting of peat. Here and there women were busy piling the square pieces of peat in stacks, that they might dry in the wind. "We carry home these pits in a basket on our showlders, when they are dry," said one of them to me; but those who can afford to keep a pony, make him do this work for them. In the hollows of this part of the island we saw several fresh-water ponds, which were enlarged with dykes and made to turn grist mills. We peeped into one or two of these mills, little stone buildings, in which we could hardly stand upright, inclosing two small stones turned by a perpendicular shaft, in which are half a dozen cogs; the paddles are fixed below, and there struck by the water, turn the upper stone.

A steep descent brought us to the little strait, bordered with rocks,

which divides Bressay from the island called the Noss. A strong south wind was driving in the billows from the sea with noise and foam, but they were broken and checked by a bar of rocks in the middle of the strait, and we crossed to the north of it in smooth water. The ferryman told us that when the wind was northerly he crossed to the south of the bar. As we climbed the hill of the Noss the mist began to drift thinly around us from the sea, and flocks of sea-birds rose screaming from the ground at our approach. At length we stood upon the brink of a precipice of fearful height, from which we had a full view of the still higher precipices of the neighboring summit. A wall of rock was before us six hundred feet in height, descending almost perpendicularly to the sea, which roared and foamed at its base among huge masses of rock, and plunged into great caverns, hollowed out by the beating of the surges for centuries. Midway on the rock, and above the reach of the spray, were thousands of sea-birds, sitting in ranks on the numerous shelves, or alighting, or taking wing, and screaming as they flew. A cloud of them were constantly in the air in front of the rock and over our heads. Here they make their nests and rear their young, but not entirely safe from the pursuit of the Zetlander, who causes himself to be let down by a rope from the summit and plunders their nests. The face of the rock, above the portion which is the haunt of the birds, was fairly tapestried with herbage and flowers which the perpetual moisture of the atmosphere keeps always fresh—daisies nodding in the wind, and the crimson phlox, seeming to set the cliffs on flame; yellow buttercups, and a variety of other plants in bloom, of which I do not know the name.

Magnificent as this spectacle was, we were not satisfied without climbing to the summit. As we passed upward, we saw where the rabbits had made their burrows in the elastic peat-like soil close to the very edge of the precipice. We now found ourselves involved in the cold streams of mist which the strong sea-wind was drifting over us; they were in fact the lower skirts of the clouds. At times they would clear away and give us a prospect of the green island summits around us, with their bold headlands, the winding straits between, and the black rocks standing out in the sea. When we arrived at the summit we could hardly stand against the wind, but it was almost more difficult to muster courage to look down that dizzy depth over which the Zetlanders suspend themselves with ropes, in quest of the eggs of the sea-fowl. My friend captured a young gull on the summit of the Noup. The bird had risen at his approach, and essayed to fly towards the sea, but the strength of the wind drove him back to the land. He rose again, but could not sustain a long flight, and coming to the ground again, was caught, after a spirited chase, amidst a wild clamor of the sea-fowl over our heads.

Not far from the Noup is the Holm, or, as it is sometimes called, the Cradle or Basket, of the Noss. It is a perpendicular mass of rock, two or

three hundred feet high, with a broad flat summit, richly covered with grass, and is separated from the island by a narrow chasm, through which the sea flows. Two strong ropes are stretched from the main island to the top of the Holm, and on these is slung the cradle or basket, a sort of open box made of deal boards, in which the shepherds pass with their sheep to the top of the Holm. We found the cradle strongly secured by lock and key to the stakes on the side of the Noss, in order, no doubt, to prevent any person from crossing for his own amusement.

As we descended the smooth pastures of the Noss, we fell in with a herd of ponies, of a size somewhat larger than is common on the islands. I asked our guide, a lad of fourteen years of age, what was the average price of a sheltie. His answer deserves to be written in letters of gold—

"It's jist as they're bug an' smal'."

From the ferryman, at the strait below, I got more specific information. They vary in price from three to ten pounds, but the latter sum is only paid for the finest of these animals, in the respects of shape and color. It is not a little remarkable, that the same causes which, in Shetland, have made the horse the smallest of ponies, have almost equally reduced the size of the cow. The sheep, also—a pretty creature, I might call it—from the fine wool of which the Shetland women knot the thin webs known by the name of Shetland shawls, is much smaller than any breed I have ever seen. Whether the cause be the perpetual chilliness of the atmosphere, or the insufficiency of nourishment—for, though the long Zetland winters are temperate, and snow never lies long on the ground, there is scarce any growth of herbage in that season—I will not undertake to say, but the people of the islands ascribe it to the insufficiency of nourishment. It is, at all events, remarkable, that the traditions of the country should ascribe to the Picts, the early inhabitants of Shetland, the same dwarfish stature, and that the numerous remains of their habitations which still exist, should seem to confirm the tradition. The race which at present possesses the Shetlands is, however, of what the French call "an advantageous stature," and well limbed. If it be the want of a proper and genial warmth, which prevents the due growth of the domestic animals, it is a want to which the Zetlanders are not subject. Their hills afford them an apparently inexhaustible supply of peat, which costs the poorest man nothing but the trouble of cutting it and bringing it home; and their cottages, I was told, are always well warmed in winter.

In crossing the narrow strait which separates the Noss from Bressay, I observed on the Bressay side, overlooking the water, a round hillock, of very regular shape, in which the green turf was intermixed with stones. "That," said the ferryman, "is what we call a Pictish castle. I mind when it was opened; it was full of rooms, so that ye could go over every part of it." I climbed the hillock, and found, by inspecting several openings,

which had been made by the peasantry to take away the stones, that below the turf it was a regular work of Pictish masonry, but the spiral galleries, which these openings revealed, had been completely choked up, in taking away the materials of which they were built. Although plenty of stone may be found everywhere in the islands, there seems to be a disposition to plunder these remarkable remains, for the sake of building cottages, or making those inclosures for their cabbages, which the islanders call *crubs*. They have been pulling down the Pictish castle, on the little island in the fresh-water loch called Cleikimin, near Lerwick, described with such minuteness by Scott in his journal, till very few traces of its original construction are left. If the inclosing of lands for pasturage and cultivation proceeds as it has begun, these curious monuments of a race which has long perished, will disappear.

Now that we were out of hearing of the cries of the sea-birds, we were regaled with more agreeable sounds. We had set out, as we climbed the island of Bressay, amid a perfect chorus of larks, answering each other in the sky, and sometimes, apparently, from the clouds; and now we heard them again overhead, pouring out their sweet notes so fast and so ceaselessly, that it seemed as if the little creatures imagined they had more to utter, than they had time to utter it in. In no part of the British Islands have I seen the larks so numerous or so merry, as in the Shetlands.

We waited awhile at the wharf by the minister's house in Bressay, for Jim Sinclair, who at length appeared in his boat to convey us to Lerwick. "He is a noisy fallow," said our good landlady, and truly we found him voluble enough, but quite amusing. As he rowed us to town he gave us a sample of his historical knowledge, talking of Sir Walter Raleigh and the settlement of North America, and told us that his greatest pleasure was to read historical books in the long winter nights. His children, he said, could all read and write. We dined on a leg of Shetland mutton, with a tart made "of the only fruit of the Island" as a Scotchman called it, the stalks of the rhubarb plant, and went on board of our steamer about six o'clock in the afternoon. It was matter of some regret to us that we were obliged to leave Shetland so soon. Two or three days more might have been pleasantly passed among its grand precipices, its winding straits, its remains of a remote and rude antiquity, its little horses, little cows, and little sheep, its sea-fowl, its larks, its flowers, and its hardy and active people. There was an amusing novelty also in going to bed, as we did, by daylight, for at this season of the year, the daylight is never out of the sky, and the flush of early sunset only passes along the horizon from the northwest to the northeast, where it brightens into sunrise.

The Zetlanders, I was told by a Scotch clergyman, who had lived among them forty years, are naturally shrewd and quick of apprehension; "as to their morals," he added, "if ye stay among them any time ye'll be able to judge for yourself." So, on the point of morals, I am in the dark.

More attention, I hear, is paid to the education of their children than for-merly, and all have the opportunity of learning to read and write in the parochial schools. Their agriculture is still very rude, they are very un-willing to adopt the instruments of husbandry used in England, but on the whole they are making some progress. A Shetland gentleman, who, as he remarked to me, had "had the advantage of seeing some other countries" besides his own, complained that the peasantry were spending too much of their earnings for tea, tobacco, and spirits. Last winter a terrible famine came upon the islands; their fisheries had been unproductive, and the po-tato crop had been cut off by the blight. The communication with Scot-land by steamboat had ceased, as it always does in winter, and it was long before the sufferings of the Shetlanders were known in Great Britain, but as soon as the intelligence was received, contributions were made and the poor creatures were relieved.

Their climate, inhospitable as it seems, is healthy, and they live to a good old age. A native of the island, a baronet, who has a great white house on a bare field in sight of Lerwick, and was a passenger on board the steamer in which we made our passage to the island, remarked that if it was not the healthiest climate in the world, the extremely dirty habits of the peasantry would engender disease, which, however, was not the case. "It is, probably, the effect of the saline particles in the air," he added. His opinion seemed to be that the dirt was salted by the sea-winds, and pre-served from further decomposition. I was somewhat amused, in hearing him boast of the climate of Shetland in winter. "Have you never observed" said he, turning to the old Scotch clergyman of whom I have already spoken, "how much larger the proportion of sunny days is in our islands than at the south?" "I have never observed it," was the dry answer of the minister.

The people of Shetland speak a kind of Scottish, but not with the Scottish accent. Four hundred years ago, when the islands were transferred from Norway to the British crown, their language was Norse, but that tongue, although some of its words have been preserved in the present dialect, has become extinct. "I have heard," said an intelligent Shetlander to me, "that there are yet, perhaps, half a dozen persons in one of our re-motest neighborhoods, who are able to speak it, but I never met with one who could."

In returning from Lerwick to the Orkneys, we had a sample of the weather which is often encountered in these latitudes. The wind blew a gale in the night, and our steamer was tossed about on the waves like an egg-shell, much to the discomfort of the passengers. We had on board a cargo of ponies, the smallest of which were from the Shetlands, some of them not much larger than sheep, and nearly as shaggy; the others, of larger size, had been brought from the Faro Isles. In the morning, when the gale had blown itself to rest, I went on deck and saw one of the Faro

Island ponies, which had given out during the night, stretched dead upon the deck. I inquired if the body was to be committed to the deep. "It is to be skinned first," was the answer.

We stopped at Kirkwall in the Orkneys, long enough to allow us to look at the old cathedral of St. Magnus, built early in the twelfth century—a venerable pile, in perfect preservation, and the finest specimen of the architecture once called Saxon, then Norman, and lately Romanesque, that I have ever seen. The round arch is everywhere used, except in two or three windows of later addition. The nave is narrow, and the central groined arches are lofty; so that an idea of vast extent is given, though the cathedral is small, compared with the great minsters in England. The work of completing certain parts of the building which were left unfinished, is now going on at the expense of the government. All the old flooring, and the pews, which made it a parish church, have been taken away, and the original proportions and symmetry of the building are seen as they ought to be. The general effect of the building is wonderfully grand and solemn.

On our return to Scotland, we stopped for a few hours at Wick. It was late in the afternoon, and the fishermen, in their vessels, were going out of the harbor to their nightly toil. Vessel after vessel, each manned with four stout rowers, came out of the port—and after rowing a short distance, raised their sails and steered for the open sea, till all the waters, from the land to the horizon, were full of them. I counted them, hundreds after hundreds, till I grew tired of the task. A sail of ten or twelve hours brought us to Aberdeen, with its old cathedral, encumbered by pews and wooden partitions, and its old college, the tower of which is surmounted by a cluster of flying buttresses, formed into the resemblance of a crown.

This letter, you perceive, is dated at Aberdeen. It was begun there, but I have written portions of it at different times since I left that city, and I beg that you will imagine it to be of the latest date. It is now long enough, I fear, to tire you and I therefore lay down my pen.

MANUSCRIPT: NYPL–GR (draft) TEXT: *LT* I, 408–425; first published in *EP* for August 27, 1849.

    1. Tacitus, *Agricola* 10; Pliny, *Natural History* IV.xvi.104.
    2. Walter Scott, *The Pirate* (1822), a novel set in the Shetland Islands in the seventeenth century.

691.   *To* Julia S. Bryant

Guisachan, Strathglass, North
Highlands of Scotland, July 22, 1849.

Dear Julia.

    I promised I think to write to you after I had visited Shetland. The journey or rather voyage to Shetland has been made and here is the letter.

    But before going to the Shetland Isles Mr. Leupp and myself being

detained a day at the ancient town of Perth, on account of not being able to obtain seats in the mail coach, made a sort of romantic pilgrimage in a drosky to the graves of Bessy Bell and Mary Gray, who in 1666 "biggit a bower on the burn side and theekit it owre wi' rashes,"[1] to which they retired for safety, but were smitten, notwithstanding, by the plague of that year, and were buried not far from their bower close by the stream of the Almond. An iron railing incloses the spot where they are supposed to have been buried, and an old yew tree stands near, planted probably by order of the noble families to which these two young girls belonged. On the banks of a little brook which flows into the Almond, and about half a mile from the graves, the foundations of their woodland habitation are shown, a regular parallelogram, out of one corner of which springs a Norway spruce of considerable size. All around, the banks of the river are closely embowered in shade, and the woods for a considerable distance, above and below are uninterrupted by cultivated grounds or habitations, except the Lynedock cottage, and that of the gardener, a civil Scotchman who acted as our guide. I am thinking that I may write an account of my visit to this place for the Evening Post, so I will reserve the minuter particulars and the sentimentalities proper for the occasion for that letter.[2]

We passed nearly two days in the Shetlands, went to church, the Free church, for the schism in the Presbyterian church has extended even to that remote region, walked over three of the islands, and climbed the headland called the Noup of the Noss, which impends almost perpendicularly six hundred feet over the sea. Near to it is the Holm a rocky islet, with perpendicular sides, separated from the island of Noss by a very narrow chasm, over which two strong ropes are stretched, and on these a kind of wooden chair or rather box slides to and fro, to convey the shepherds with their sheep to the grassy summit of the Holm. The box was made fast by a lock, that it might not be used by visitors. But the Noup or Head of the Noss is really a sublime object. The immense height makes you dread to look down where the breakers are constantly dashing and roaring and flinging up their white foam at the foot of the rock, and rushing into the caverns which they have hollowed out for themselves by beating against it for hundreds of years. Myriads of sea fowl are constantly wheeling and screaming before the precipice and high overhead, we could see them sitting in ranks on the narrow shelves of rock. In places, particularly near the summit the face of the rock was tapestried with green plants and flowers; the crimson phlox, nodding daisies in profusion, and butter cups, and a pink flower the name of which I did not know. From the top of the precipice the ground slopes smoothly, in green pasturage, to the strait which divides the Noss from the island of Bressay. A strong south wind was blowing all the while from the sea and drifted, at times the low clouds against the headland on which we stood; they came by us in cold streams of mist and often hid the sea and the islands from our sight.

The Shetlanders are said to be a civil, hospitable people, kindhearted, of quick apprehension, active, dirty and healthy; their health, I suppose is owing to the perpetual coolness of their climate. Sir Arthur Nicholson, a native and resident of the island who was one of our fellow passengers,[3] attributed it to the saline particles in the air—in other words he thought the dirt was preserved from putrefaction by being salted. The men fish for a living, and the women dig and carry home peat and knit fine woollen stockings and knot the Shetland shawls which sometimes come to our country.

I asked the price of a Shetland pony, or sheltie—a lad of fourteen gave me this intelligent answer—It's jist as they're bug an' smal'. I learned afterwards that they can be had at various prices from two pounds to eight or nine. I saw a drove of them upon the Noss, and when we came away, there was a cargo of them in our steamer, some of them not much larger than a sheep and nearly as shaggy.

I did not sit up to see whether it ever became dark in the course of what we call the night, but when I went to bed at half past ten o'clock I could see very well to read and it seemed to me like going to bed in the day time. Of course the twilight continued till midnight, and then the light again began to increase. In travelling, from Perth to Inverness a few days before, I perceived—for I was on the outside of the coach all night— that a sunset blush remained in the sky all night travelling from the north west to the north, and so on to the north east, where the sun rose.

I find that I have reached the bottom of my page, and I have a letter yet to write to your mother. At Edinburgh I expect to meet a letter from you as well as letters from her. Farewell and be good—

Yrs affectionately
W. C. BRYANT.

MANUSCRIPT: NYPL–GR.

1. Bryant quotes here from the short ballad "Bessy Bell and Mary Gray," to be found in the first volume of Walter Scott's *The Minstrelsy of the Scottish Border* (1802).
2. Apparently this letter was not written.
3. Not further identified.

692.   *To* Frances F. Bryant

Oban, in the Scottish Highlands,
July 24th   1849.

My dear Frances.

After I wrote to you on the 11th of July, I went to Perth, the ancient capital of Scotland, by railway intending to proceed immediately in the mail coach, to Wick where we were to take the steamer for the Shetlands and the Orkneys. There was no room, however, and we were obliged to

wait another day which we did not regret, as the environs of the town are very beautiful and there are several places worth visiting. The next day at five in the afternoon we took our seats on the outside of the coach, that is on the top, and traversed a country of extraordinary [beauty?][1] by Birnam wood, and Dunkeld, and through the forests of the Duke of Athol, the finest I think I ever saw, gigantic beeches, mingled with Scotch firs and other trees, through which we had occasional glimpses of the river Tay and the mountain tops among which the road conducted us. The country was beautiful nearly as long as there was light enough to see it distinctly, and then it became a region of dark moorland without trees and broad mountain summits covered with heath. It was extremely cold, but I had provided myself with a shawl or plaid at Perth, which I wrapped round me. Of course I dozed now and then, but to prevent myself from falling from the top of the coach I lashed myself by my pocket handkerchief to the iron rods which formed the back of my seat, and this answered the purpose very well. Whenever I woke there was the same dreary country around me, and just light enough from the sky to enable me to distinguish its character. The glow in the northwestern horizon shifted gradually to the north, and after midnight to the east, for in this high latitude at midsummer the light of day on the other side of the globe streams up into the atmosphere on this. About two o'clock as we were passing by a high mountain the moon, in her wane, showed herself suddenly through an opening in the summits, looking very broad and shedding a pale glow which contrasted with the blush in the northeastern sky seemed almost frightful. Shortly afterwards a fog rose and grew more and more dense till it changed into a regular Scotch mist, cold and penetrating. In this mist we journeyed the rest of the night, and reached Inverness, an old town, the capital of the North Highlands, where King Duncan was murdered by Macbeth.[2]

Inverness is a town of good appearance, overlooking the meadows of the river Ness. The streets were full of people from the country talking Gaelic, and among them was here and there a kilt and a pair of bare knees. We breakfasted here and went on through a pleasant country on the Firth of Cromarty, and the sea shore, travelled all day and all the next night till one or two in the morning; a very cold and foggy night but we were inside the coach, and at last arrived at Wick a considerable fishing town on the northern coast of Scotland. The steamer which we expected was delayed by the fog, so that we had plenty of time for rest and sleep. At half past twelve we were on our way for the Orkneys but after proceeding for two or three hours the steamer stopped on account of the fog. Late in the evening we were in motion again, and reached Kirkwall in the Orkneys a little after midnight, but I did not get up to look at it. Next morning when I rose we were passing under the dark steep rocks that formed the shore of

an island; it was Fair Isle, between the Orkneys and Zetland or Shetland. We landed at Lerwick in the Shetland Isles about mid day, Sunday the 15th of July. In my letter to Julia I have given some account of my visit.

On our return we stopped for an hour at Kirkwall in the Orkneys and looked at the old cathedral built there by the Norwegians, which the English government is now repairing and completing. It is a most venerable pile, and offers the best specimen of what is called Norman architecture that I ever saw. In coming from Shetland, the sea was terribly rough, and I was seasick. One of the ponies which formed our cargo, a Faro Island pony, gave out in the course of the night and lay dead the next morning on deck. We did not stop at Wick but kept on in the steamer to Aberdeen, and crossed over the country by coach to Inverness. From Inverness we went to Guisachan, where my letter to Julia is dated a valley deep in the Highlands owned by Mr. William Frazer[3] a friend of Mr. Leupp's who has twice visited America, and who has a vast hereditary estate of many square miles of heathery and rocky mountains and narrow glens between them. His sister a very agreeable young lady was with him. We made an excursion of fourteen miles to the west end of his estate, upon ponies, the young lady accompanying us. After leaving the little Highland settlement near his house, we met with but one habitation, where a shepherd lived in the wilderness. We called and looked at the interior. The abodes of the Highlanders are not so comfortable nor so desirable as those of the Indians at Sault St[e]. Marie.[4]

We returned to Inverness—thirty two miles distant and came down the Caledonian Canal to this place, in steamers, through the locks and mountains of the Highlands, visiting in our way the Fall of Foyers, the island of Iona with its ruins, and the island of Staffa with its basaltic caves. Tomorrow we take the steamer for Glasgow and the next day we expect to be in Edinburgh where I hope to meet with letters from you. My health is good, but I am obliged to be careful in my diet. Remember me affectionately to all. I have had a very fatiguing journey to the north, and though I have often wished you with me, yet I could not wish that you should travel in the same manner.

Yrs ever
W   C   Bryant

Manuscript: NYPL–GR.

1. Word omitted.
2. *Macbeth*, II.ii.15.
3. Apparently a great-grandson of Simon Fraser, twelfth Baron Lovat (1667?–1747), a follower of Charles Edward, the "Young Pretender" (1720–1788), and an heir to the vast Fraser property. See Bryant, "Diary, 1849," July 20, 21.
4. See Letter 590.

693. *To* Frances F. Bryant

Edinburgh   July 27, 1849.

Dear Frances.

I reached Edinburgh last evening, where I found two letters from you, one from Julia with a postscript by you, letters from Dr. Neilson and Bigelow and a note from Mrs. Moulton.[1] I thank you for writing so regularly. The burning of the mill I am sorry for;[2] I was attached to the old building, and by making it a house for John and his family it promised to be a great convenience to us. You do not say to what extent the surrounding trees were injured, and whether the boats were burnt up with the mill but I suppose they were.

As to the money coming from the Insurance Company you shall have your own way in the application of it. It would be just the sum to pay on the mortgage in General Wool's hands, as it would extinguish that part of the debt which is properly General Wool's, and make the payment of the interest more convenient.[3] But if it is paid into the bank in my name, my check would be necessary to draw it out. I propose therefore to send Mr. Howe[4] a power of attorney to receive the money, and that you write to Maj. General John E. Wool, to inquire whether at the time he calls for the interest due on the 20th of September, he will also receive seven hundred dollars on the principal which he will readily do, I am sure. In the mean time the use of the money might be a convenience to the office.

I have enclosed a letter to Mr. Neilson[5] in answer to the one from him. Read it and put it in an envelope, but do not make its contents or the subject of them public. It certainly was fortunate for me that the building was insured, and Mr. Neilson very kindly congratulates me on having had the prudence to keep it so.

I saw Mr. Lawson's[6] mother and sisters at Glasgow—the old lady has been unable to leave her bed for twelve years, but seems very cheerful. They expressed great concern for the estrangement of Mr. Forrest from his wife, knowing as they do both parties. I could tell them little in addition to what they already knew.

A kind of presentiment haunted me before I came to Edinburgh that something unpleasant had happened, and I was very uneasy till I got the letters. It was rather a relief to me to find that nothing worse had taken place. I hope that this fire will be the worst that befalls us in the time that shall elapse before I see you again. It was my intention to return in September, but the first of September will make my visit rather short for seeing all that we have planned to see, and after the tenth of September the weather is so variable and stormy that I have been advised to defer my return till October. On this matter, however, I must think further. I am extremely sorry for the trouble that the fire has given you—more sorry

than for the loss of the mill itself—but the inconvenience I hope is quite over before this time, and your men able to go on with their work.

While you were suffering with heat I have been suffering with the cold. This season is unusually cool and unusually late. Cloudy weather prevails for the most part, particularly in the northern parts which I have visited with frequent sprinklings of rain, and drizzling uncomfortable mists. We are here just in the midst of the strawberry season, and the first ripe gooseberries, rather poor yet, have made their appearance. We shall stay here a day or two and then go southward.

Accompanying this is an answer to Mrs. Moulton's letter.[7] Will you be so good as to put it in a cover and address it to her if you know where she is— If you do not, I suppose the best way would be to direct it to the care of Joseph W. Moulton New York.

The time has arrived when I must send off this letter and I therefore can write no more. My love to the children and thank Julia for her letter.

Yours ever
W. C. Bryant

MANUSCRIPT: NYPL–GR ADDRESS: Mrs. F. F. Bryant.

1. Neilson (204.1, 329.6) apparently handled Bryant's insurance. None of the letters referred to has been recovered.
2. A paper and fulling mill, which Bryant soon replaced by the picturesque structure of brick and wood which still stands on the edge of the salt water. Goddard, *Roslyn Harbor*, p. 70.
3. See 563.3.
4. Timothy Howe (503.2), then business manager of the *EP*, as well as a proprietor.
5. Bryant mistakenly wrote "from." This letter is unrecovered.
6. James Lawson; see 154.4; Letter 665.
7. Letter 695.

694. *To* Edwin W. Field

Edinburgh   July 27, 1849.

My dear sir

I promised that I would mention some Saturday, about the end of this month or the beginning of the next, when Mr. Leupp and myself would be in London. We have made our tour to Shetland and through the Highlands, and arrived last evening in Edinburgh. We expect to be in London about the middle of next week and to remain there a day or two beyond Saturday the 4th of August.

Yours faithfully
Wm C. Bryant.

MANUSCRIPT: HCL ADDRESS: E. Field Esq.

695. *To* Leonice M. S. Moulton[1]

Edinburgh July 27, 1849.

My dear Madam.

I thank you for your letter[2] which had but two defects—one that it was too short, the other that it did not mention what office had fallen to the lot of your husband in the new arrangements of the Custom House.[3]

I am sorry that I did not get your letter earlier so that I might have fulfilled your commission to bring you a leaf or flower from the Shetlands. It is not my habit to collect relics of the sort, but I mentioned the matter to Mr. Leupp, who has promised me one of the daisies which he gathered on the main island.

What you say of the sea is true, if you mean the sea beheld from the land; there is no pleasure to me in looking at the sea when you are on its bosom; the sensation of physical discomfort predominates over the idea of sublimity. One should see it as I have lately seen it breaking and roaring and foaming at the foot of the huge precipice of six hundred feet in height called the Noup of the Noss and rushing into the caverns which it has hollowed out in the rock. Or one should stand as I stood three days since in Fingal's cave on the island of Staffa and hear the grand murmur of its green translucent tides, echoed from the roof of the high vault every time the wave comes in and retires. But there is no need to go to Shetland or Staffa to know what a grand thing the ocean is and I am only talking nonsense. It is grand every where.

Of mountains I have almost had a surfeit—[4] In this country they are bare and bleak with woods only on their lower declivities, and sides and summits dark with heather, which makes a spongy boggy soil through which streams are trickling. But if the summits are not shaded with woods, they are often shrouded with fogs, and the traveller among the Highlands is often surprized by mists which wet him to the skin. The Highlanders are yet but a half civilized race, living in miserable cabins with no floor but the earth, and without sheets to their beds. In some districts they speak only Gaelic yet, and the Lowlanders speak of them as wanting in industry, and indisposed to any advance in civilization.

The women of this country are no beauties. I think I have seen more coarse featured women, more women absolutely ugly in Scotland, than elsewhere— If you were here, now, I think you would be stared at as a wonder; in our own country you are only admired. The English women also are far inferior to the American in beauty.

There is a letter as long as yours I think. I send it to my wife who I hope knows your address.

Yrs truly
W C BRYANT

MANUSCRIPT: NYPL–Bryant–Moulton Letters ADDRESS: Mrs. L. M. S. Moulton.

1. See 648.1.
2. Unrecovered.
3. A John W. Moulton, of 82 Charlton Street, is listed as an employee of the New York Custom House in *Rode's New York City Directory for 1851–1852*, p. 389. Mrs. Moulton's husband, Joseph White Moulton, is there listed as a lawyer at 5 State Street.
4. Bryant wrote "surfiet."

696.   *To* Frances F. Bryant

Birmingham   August 3, 1849.

My dear Frances.

I am passing a day or two with our friend [Ferdinand] Field, who often speaks of you and "little Julia" as he calls her, and wishes that you were here. I am sure I wish so too. He is very comfortably established here, in a house on what is called the Bristol road with green fields and cottages and country seats about him, with two servant maids, and a Scotch gardener who works for him half the time and keeps his conservatory in order, where he amuses himself with raising calceolarias from the seed, and other flowers, which take prizes at the horticultural exhibitions. He defended himself for preferring this sort of culture to common horticulture, by saying that it furnished him with occupation in the winter. In his garden is a bath, a huge tub supplied with water from a pipe, under a tent. I came just in time to take the last of his strawberries, enormous things they were, and quite sweet, of the variety called "British Queen," —this and the Keene's seedling, he says, are esteemed here the only varieties worth cultivating—the first is the earliest, and the other is the least acid strawberry I ever tasted. Meantime there is an abundance of raspberries in his garden, so you can imagine that I am doing very well for the present. I have missed the usual summer fruits since I came to this country very much, and sometimes to the prejudice of my health.

Before leaving Edinburgh we called on Lord Jeffrey,[1] to whom we had a letter from Colden, of the Sketch Club, his brother-in-law.[2] He was quite indisposed with an attack of bronchitis, from which he was partially recovering, but he still seemed quite ill. He received me, however, with great distinction and said many kind things. He is a very small man, smaller than our poor friend Dr. Bliss,[3] and thinner, but though pale with illness, bearing a certain look of vivacity and elasticity, and by no means seeming as old as he really is, which is seventy five or seventy six. He had lain down when we arrived, which was about half past eleven in the morning, and his son-in-law Mr. Empson[4] walked us about the grounds till he should be ready to see us. The grounds are beautiful, commanding a distant view of Edinburgh, with its old castle, its hills and monuments, and of the Firth of Forth and the shores of Fife and the Pentland Hills &c.

The house in which Jeffrey lives is an antiquity, belonging once to the abbey of Holyrood, and of an architecture similar to the Holyrood palace. He has greatly enlarged it in the same style, so that the whole of it now appears like a building of the 14th century.

Our companion in these walks was civil and well informed, but when we were admitted into the presence of Lord Jeffrey, the contrast between Mr. Empson's somewhat prosy talk and the pithy, weighty, yet lively conversation of Lord Jeffrey was as great as one can well imagine. I was much gratified with the visit, and glad to have seen so eminent a man, though I certainly should not have gone but for Mr. Leupp.

From Edinburgh we went by railway to Melrose, and after viewing the fine ruins of the old Abbey, and taking a drive to Abbotsford,[5] we hired a conveyance to Kelso pleasantly situated at the junction of the Tweed and the Teviot. From Kelso the mail coach took us along the banks of the Tweed and by the ruins of Norham Castle, to Berwick-on-Tweed, a little place lying among its ancient ramparts of earth and stone now dismantled. We here took the railway for Newcastle, the capital of a great coal district, a large town with several magnificent streets lately built, and many old streets and lanes remarkable for dirt and bad air. It was there that the cholera raged so terribly in the year 1832. At Newcastle we stopped for half a day Mr. Leupp having some business in the neighbouring town of North Shields. In the afternoon we took the train and passing through York and in sight of its grand old minster reached Manchester at midnight.

I passed a day at Manchester, where I attended to the making of the affidavit and letter of attorney necessary to obtain the money on the insurance of the mill, and walked out about four miles from the city, through the village of Blakely, pleasantly seated on the Irk, and inhabited by hand-loom weavers, many of whom are learned botanists, to the cottage of Samuel Bamford, author of "Passages in the life of a Radical," an extraordinary book of which the Manchester literati are rather proud.[6] An intelligent Manchester solicitor, said to be a good geologist, Mr. Binney[7] accompanied us—Mr. Christie was also of our party. We found the old radical an interesting man, of an original turn in conversation, and quite well informed. His occupation is that of a weaver, and he took me into one of the neighbouring cottages to see the process of weaving poplin. It was a clean Lancashire cottage—the Lancashire people are very cleanly; a decent looking young man and his decent looking wife were at the loom, he driving the shuttles and she superintending some other part of the work. Half the warp was blue silk the other half orange, and the shuttles crossed it first with a thread of blue cotton and then a thread of purple silk alternately. The process produced a beautiful tissue. Mr. Bamford gave our party a dish of tea, and a glass of homebrewed, which was brought by his fresh coloured good looking wife, and we returned by moonlight

over hill and dale by pleasant walks among the trees. Day before yesterday I came to this place. Today I expect Mr. Leupp and tomorrow we go up to London. Love to all.

Yrs ever.

W. C. BRYANT

The steamer Canada which arrived last Saturday brought me no letters from America. I hope to get some by the next, at all events.

MANUSCRIPT: NYPL–GR.

1. See 546.22; Letter 697.
2. Francis Lord Jeffrey's wife, the former Charlotte Wilkes of New York, was a sister of the wife of David Cadwallader Colden (1797–1850, Union 1817), a New York lawyer. Cooper, *Letters & Journals*, V, 325.
3. Elam Bliss (1779–1848), Bryant's former publisher. See 241.1; 616.2.
4. William Empson (1791–1852), editor of the *Edinburgh Review* from 1847 to 1852.
5. The home of Sir Walter Scott for the last twenty years of his life.
6. Samuel Bamford (1788–1872), *Passages in the Life of a Radical* (1840–1844).
7. Edward William Binney (1812–1881), a founder of the Manchester Geological Society, and later its president.

697.   *To* Eliza Robbins

Paris   August 11, 1849.

My dear Miss Robbins.

I arrived in this city yesterday from London at an early hour, and have since looked at the Annual Exhibition of Manufactures under the auspices of the government, a magnificent spectacle, & the annual exhibition of recent pictures—a wretched one, and then refreshed myself with a walk through the galleries of the Louvre, which seemed to me richer in masterpieces than ever, closing the day with a visit to the *Champs Elysées* where temporary stages were erected, and singers were performing to crowds of people seated before them in the open air. I find Paris little changed, externally I mean, from what it was four years ago, before the revolution, except that it appears to me that there is less bustle in the streets.

One of the first things we did was to call on Mr. Chapman.[1] He and his wife seemed very glad to hear from you. Mrs. Chapman has quite recovered from her cough, and he from his ill-health and despondency, and now instead of coming to America as they had made arrangements for doing, he has gone industriously to work, and as soon as he has finished one or two copies of pictures which he has on hand, will hasten to Florence.

At London where we passed a few days Mr. & Mrs. Edwin Field inquired concerning you with much interest, and the Chapmans, at whose house I was twice—you know I promised you to call on them—seemed much pleased to hear the report I gave them from my wife's last letter,

that you were in better health than usual. Chapman tells me that your friends, the Walshes were near being carried off by the disease which killed poor Franconi.[2] I hope you will forgive the juxta-position, for Franconi was a much better circus-rider than Walsh is a critic.[3] Mr. and Mrs. Walsh were greatly frightened by the cholera and went to St. Germain where both had it, but fortunately did not die of it.

I suppose my wife may have told you something of my wanderings— how Mr. Leupp and myself have traversed Scotland in various directions, strolled on the banks of the Tay, the Dee and the Don, visited the graves of Bessie Bell and Mary Gray on the Almond, navigated the Ness and the Clyde, and half a dozen lochs, sailed to the distant Orkneys & the more distant Shetlands, made an excursion into the wildest part of the Highlands, where we could only travel on ponies, where we met with but one habitation in a journey of fifteen miles, and where from the top of Ben Sassenach, we looked upon a vast wilderness of heathy mountains and lochs, and scattered hamlets, at a great distance from each other inhabited by a race living in extreme poverty and strongly attached to dirt and the Gaelic speech and the Catholic religion; that we have stood in the Giant's Cave in Staffa, and seen the ruins of Iona, where the Free Church has erected a place of worship, close[4] by the kirk of the establishment, and almost in the shadow of the old cathedral, for the benefit of the few people who inhabit a row of Highland huts by the shore.

At Edinburgh we called on Mr. Jeffrey—I beg his pardon Lord Jeffrey, to whom we had a letter. We left the letter and our cards at his residence in town, and soon after received a note from his son-in-law Mr. Empson who said that his lordship regretted that he could not call at our hotel, but that he was confined by illness at his seat in the country called Craig Crook a little way out of Edinburgh. Mr. Empson invited us to come out to Craig Crook to lunch, at one o'clock, on any day we chose. On our return from the north of Scotland we went. Mr. Empson received us and informed us that Lord Jeffrey had been confined for three weeks with a dangerous attack of bronchitis and was just beginning to find himself somewhat better, that he was then taking a little rest, but would be able to see us shortly. He then took us over the grounds, which are handsomely laid out, most of the trees having been planted by Lord Jeffrey himself. They command fine views of Edinburgh with its hills and crags and old castle, and of the Frith and its shores, and of the Pentland Hills.

When we returned we found the owner of the mansion ready to receive us. In stature he is one of the smallest of men, and quite thin, but his movements show an elastic frame, and his manner is that of one whose conversation has always been listened to with attention and deference. He received me with great consideration, said that he had long known my name and was glad to know me personally, and was complimentary enough to add that he felt honoured and flattered by my visit. I had to say some-

thing, of course in reply to this, so I spoke of the Edinburgh review which I read from its commencement,[5] and of the early deference I was accustomed to pay to its critical decisions. "I believe I never had the pleasure of cutting you up in it," said he. I replied that he had not. "Then, if you were in the habit of reading it, I hope," said he, "that you forgave what you found amiss, as I forgave you your trespasses."

The conversation happening to turn on Puseyism[6] he said, "There are but two great divisions of the religious world—those who are inclined to an intense devotion and who delight in the contemplation of mysteries, and those on the other hand who take a hard and rationalistic view of religious subjects. The tracterians belong to neither of these and therefore can never have the large majority or any considerable number of mankind with them. What is peculiar to them consists in the revival of certain usages of antiquity which had been laid aside; they complain that the Church of England at the reformation abolished certain observances which might advantageously have been retained. It is an affectation, a fashion which like other fashions will be temporary; it has no root in any great principle of human nature."

Mr. Jeffrey is about seventy five years of age, but he does not look so old, though pale and apparently in ill-health. I was struck both with the dignity of his manners and the point and vivacity of his conversation. His house is an antiquity, and the older part of it is said to have once belonged to the Abbey of Holyrood. He showed me his study which is in the ancient part of the building, with thick walls and deep windows, the interior somewhat elaborately fitted up in the Gothic style. The new part of the house is built precisely like the other—it was added by Lord Jeffrey—and it looks quite old. The building has round turrets with pointed roofs.

I thought you might like to see these notices of a man who has left the impression of his mind upon the literature of the first half of this century and therefore I have written this letter. I have since visited a man of humble literary pretensions Samuel Bamford author of "Passages in the Life of a Radical," a remarkable book and some poetry less remarkable. The old hand loom weaver, now subsisting by his literary labours, lives in a hamlet—a "fold" they call it in Lancashire, near the village of Blakely and not far from Manchester. We were accompanied by Mr. Binney a solicitor who has written a work on geology. "Here" said he, as we approached Blakely, by a pleasant path among the trees, "live, among the weavers, a society of learned botanists, who meet once a week, to communicate their researches. One of these weavers has just written a book on the plants of the neighbourhood of Manchester, which has kept him out of the poor house. In another village just beyond the hill, called Chatterton, are, or rather were, for they are dying out now, a set of profound mathematicians, also mechanics." We found Mr. Bamford at home, living in a clean Lancashire cottage like those of his neighbours. He is a hale old

man, of pithy conversation and uses the Lancashire dialect. He seemed glad to see me, and gave our party a glass of homebrewed and a cup of tea. —I am at the end of my paper.

Yrs truly
W C BRYANT.

MANUSCRIPT: UVa.

1. The American artist John Gadsby Chapman (526.1).

2. The bookseller and publisher John Chapman (1822–1894), editor and publisher of the *Westminster Review*, lived with his wife and children over his shop at 142, The Strand. Here he entertained many literary friends, including Emerson—for several weeks in 1848—George Eliot, who helped him with his review, and others. Bryant, "Diary, 1849," July 2; Ralph Leslie Rusk, *The Life of Ralph Waldo Emerson* (New York: Scribner's, 1949), p. 341. For Franconi, see 558.1.

3. Bryant had often written contemptuously of the critical judgments of the Philadelphia journalist Robert Walsh, who was United States consul-general at Paris, 1844–1851. See Letters 80, 159, 194, 195.

4. Bryant mistakenly wrote "closed."

5. As the authoritative *Edinburgh Review* was first published in 1802, this suggests that Bryant began to read it at the age of eight!

6. A schismatic high Anglican movement within the Church of England, now commonly known as the Oxford Movement, was led by Rev. Edward Bouverie Pusey (1800–1882, M.A. Oxford 1825), professor of Hebrew at Oxford University, 1828–1843.

698. *To* Frances F. Bryant

Paris   August 13   1849.

My dear Frances.

We have been delayed in this city two days longer than we wished, for having shortly after our arrival made up our minds to go to Munich, we began to look after our passports, and found that they had not been sent to the police of this city from Calais where they were taken from us. We arrived here on Friday morning early—the 10th of the month—by railway—today, which is Monday we shall set out, at eight in the evening, if we can get our passports, for Brussels and Cologne, on our way to the capital of Bavaria.

After writing to you on the 8th[1] we went by railway from London to Dover on the sea coast, and there passed the night. Here a long line of chalk cliffs, high and white, rise directly from the sea, and in a vale forming a recess between two of them Dover, an old looking town with narrow streets, is situated. A castle built on one of the cliffs in the time of Henry II—a dark looking edifice—overlooks it, and near this are two towers and part of the wall of an old Roman castle, prodigiously massive, the stones intermixed with Roman tiles. We climbed up to it, on a wet morning, and were shown by a soldier the opposite coast of France.

We left Dover for Calais at twelve o'clock on a steamer, and were two hours in making the passage. Calais has nothing of any importance to show

to the stranger, but we could not leave it till half past six in the afternoon when the first train departed for Paris. The train took us eastward through St. Omer, Lille and Douai, a flat and in many places a marshy country reminding me of Holland, with canals and rows of willows and poplars, and often with Dutch or Flemish names to the stations—as Steenwerck, Ebingham &c. From Douai we turned southward towards Amiens Arras and Paris and I went to sleep.

Almost the first thing which arrested my attention when I awoke next morning in the daylight was the remains of a building at one of the stations, not far from Paris, which had been destroyed by fire, and portions of iron rail scattered about on the ground. This was the work of the late revolution when the communication between the capital and the country was cut off. The next station presented a like spectacle. Shortly afterwards we were in Paris and about six o'clock were established in the Hôtel des Étrangers, near the Place de la Bourse.

I do not see much to remind one of the change in the government and of the terrible and bloody days which followed it. The paving stones have been put back to their places, the damaged buildings have been repaired and the mourning for the dead is over. The words, liberty, equality, fraternity are inscribed in staring letters on the churches, but soldiers with fixed bayonets are marching before them, and every where you see armed men, the signs of a government of force. People have as much trouble with their passports as ever, and you cannot go from place to place without the leave of the police. There is you know no liberty of the press, nor liberty of assembling.

There is I think less appearance of activity and bustle than formerly; the number of strangers residing here I am told is far less than formerly, owing unquestionably to a belief that the present state of things is not to last, and that another revolution, sooner or later, must come.

I miss you very much in this city where there are so many interesting objects which we once looked at together. The Louvre, enriched with new monuments of antiquity from Nineveh and elsewhere, is as glorious, and the Boulevards almost as gay as ever. I shall miss you still more at Munich where I expect to see completed the magnificent works of which you and I fourteen years since witnessed the beginning.[2]

Our absence from Paris on this excursion will probably not much exceed a fortnight, or if we return by way of Zurich and the north of Switzerland three weeks. This will bring us back to Paris about the first of next month. It is not probable that I shall write by the next steamer.

My health is just now extremely good; the fresh figs which we get at Paris agree with me surprisingly—and if there were no figs I could make a shift with the pears. I have had several returns of the complaint which gave me so much trouble soon after my landing, but the[y] do not last long, and I find that the best cure and best preventive is fruit.

Enclosed is a letter for Miss Robbins which after you have read I will thank you to put into a cover and send to her.[3]

I have no letter from you since the one dated July 22d, which I answered by the steamer of last week. I hope to get a letter at Munich. In the meantime, I trust you do not let your cares weigh so heavily upon your mind as to make you thin. Do not suppose that I mean to laugh at you—I understand too well the extent to which I am obliged to you, for consenting to be perplexed, during my absence, with affairs properly belonging to me, to think of doing that.

Remember me kindly to Mrs. Kirkland and her family. Love to Fanny and Julia.

Yours ever
W. C. Bryant

MANUSCRIPT: NYPL–GR ADDRESS: Mrs. F. F. Bryant.

1. This letter was lost; see Letter 704.
2. The Bryants had lodged in Munich from June 30 to October 2, 1835. See Letters 303–309.
3. Letter 697.

699. *To* Frances F. Bryant

Munich   August 22d   1849

My dear Frances.

I am sitting in a chamber at the Goldener Hirsch, in the Theatinerstrasse, not far from the Bazaar in which we passed a summer. The cold morning reminds me of the weather we then had in the latter part of August when we were obliged to make a fire in our room. Yesterday I took a long walk alone in the English Garden. I recognized the same winding paths in which we used to walk, there were the same swiftly running streams, as turbid with clay crossed by the same bridges but the woods had grown taller and darker and what then seemed thickets of shrubbery had now become groups of tall trees. It was a sad walk for me; I am not sure but it would have been sad even if you had been with me for I thought every moment of the time when we used to ramble there with our children, when we were all so much farther from the grave than now—and perhaps so much more innocent.

Munich has been greatly enlarged and beautified since we saw it together. The Allerheiligen Capelle, where we saw them putting in the frescos, sumptuous as it is, is not to be compared in beauty with the Ludwigskirche, the Basilica in the neighbourhood of the Glyptothek and the Aukirche in the suburbs on the other side of the Isar. The two first of these are in the Byzantine style with round arches—the last is in the pure Gothic. Ludwigstrasse from the Bazaar northwards is a broad street of magnificent public buildings ending with the university and the Catholic

Theological Seminary, and the grand vista closed with an arch, almost finished, bestriding the street and upbearing groups of colossal statuary. In another quarter of the city side by side with the Pinacothek to which the public collection of pictures is now removed, is another large building destined for the reception of modern paintings. The suburbs have been extended, and the taste for roomy houses of massive architecture is shown every where. Bronze statues of gigantic size representing the great men of the kingdom have been set up in all the public squares. Overlooking the Teresienwiese, the meadow in which the Octoberfest is annually held a building is now rising destined to contain memorials of the great men of Bavaria, and before it is to stand a colossal statue of bronze, an armed female representing Bavaria. They are casting the figure in this city; the upper part is finished. I visited it the other day and crawled into the head which they say will contain fourteen persons.

We have been through the Pinacothek, the Glyptothek, and the new palace with its statues and frescoes, seen an opera at the Hoftheater, and visited the studio of Kaulbach,[1] the most imaginative of the German painters, where a woman showed us among others his grand [painting?][2] of the Destruction of Jerusalem, a work just on the verge of extravagance, representing the entrance of Titus into the conquered city and the terrible scenes which attended it. We have looked into the Kunst Verein [Art Union] and peeped into the churches.

At Eichthal's—our banker's—I have seen the son of our old landlord Grandi.[3] He had forgotten us, and speaks Italian with difficulty. He is a bookkeeper in the banking house. His father he told me went back to the Milanese territory, but having been long accustomed to the climate of Germany, the change disagreed with his constitution, and he died about four years since. Mariana, the daughter is married and lives near the lake of Como. Our other acquaintances, and they were few, I have not seen.

On the evening of the day I wrote you from Paris the 13th of this month, we set off by the railway at eight o'clock, and sweeping round, in the night, through Amiens, Lille, Douai and Valenciennes were in Brussels at sunrise, whence turning eastward we passed the cities of Malines and Louvain, in a level region, and next Liège, a prosperous manufacturing town charmingly situated in a valley of the Meuse. We then threaded a narrow glen full of mineral springs, one of which is a spa, with here and there an old castle on the cliffs and emerging from this, came upon a country resembling England, —green hills and dales divided by hedge rows and shaded by scattered trees. We had entered Germany—the possessions of Prussia on the Rhine. At Aix La Chapelle, which the Germans call Aachen, we stopped to let our passports be examined, and regretted that time did not allow us to stop a day at this ancient watering place and to see the cathedral where nearly two score of emperors had been crowned. At five in the afternoon we were at Cologne where we dined and at half

past nine took a steamer going up the Rhine. When the morning broke we had just entered the picturesque part of the valley of the river. At eleven we stopped at Castel opposite to Mayence, where that part ends. Here I had a feast of yellow plums, the *Mirabellen*, juicy sweet and fragrant. We took the railway to Frankfort, ran to look at Danneker's Ariadne,[4] set off again at three o'clock, and, passing through Darmstadt, and a fertile country got to the Badischer Hof in Heidelberg at half past six; hastened to look at the old castle by daylight and returning sat down to the best dinner I have eaten in Europe. I next went to call on Mrs. Hagen.[5] The streets had a strange air; they were full of Prussian soldiers.

I found your friend sitting with her husband at a table in the twilight; she knew me by the sound of my voice, and expressed great satisfaction at hearing from you and your children. Her husband was a delegate to the diet or parliament of the German Confederation, a government the authority of which was acknowledged but for a few months. The Diet was first obliged to leave Frankfort, whence it went to Stuttgardt and there a few weeks ago was broken up by the military force, after which Professor Hagen removed to Heidelberg. He is quite disheartened at the political prospects of his country. The cause of liberty he said had been injured by the *Gelehrten* or learned class who knowing nothing of practical liberty had first insisted on their own fantastic schemes and then, frightened at their own work had thought it their duty to aid the reaction which was sweeping every thing back to absolutism. Heidelberg was now in a state of seige, in other words, under the worst form of military despotism, and any man, in the least suspected or dreaded was arrested and imprisoned as long as the government pleased; there was in fact no security for any body against the most arbitrary oppressions. Mrs. Hagen told me that her husband had thus far owed his exemption from arrest to the mildness of the policy he had supported in the diet, but she did not appear to think him quite safe, and talked of the possibility of their coming to America. Her health had suffered much by anxiety and the traces of this were too visible on her countenance. She desired to be most kindly remembered to you and your daughters, and said that she wrote to you not long since. Eva[6] she sometimes hears from, and she was well at the last accounts. Of Mr. Barrault[7] I could hear nothing; he was not in town and Mrs. Hagen believed that he had gone with his family to Weinheim.

Next morning at four o'clock we took the eilwagen [mailcoach] for Heilbronn, travelling in lovely weather through the lovely valley of the Neckar, amid fruit trees and nut trees and vineyards, and reeking manure tanks at the doors of the dwellings. Soldiers were pitched on the villages, marching in companies on the roads, quartered at the inns. At Heilbronn after a late breakfast we took the railway which carried us to Stuttgardt, where we snatched a look at the royal palace, and its garden, and proceeded through a winding fertile valley to where the railway ends at the

little town of Geisslingen, looking like a remnant of the middle ages dropped in that gorge of the mountains. An omnibus took us some twenty miles further to Ulm on the Danube, where we were obliged to pass the night, the vehicle in which we expected to proceed having gone on just before our arrival.

Ulm is a picturesque old city, the several stories of the houses overhanging each other so that its streets are almost caverns, but it has little to detain the traveller. On Friday morning at eight o'clock we were again on our way travelling over a monotonous country of broad plains unenclosed, and broad woods, to Augsburg where we had an hour or two to look at the handsome fountains and fine old town houses, and to get dripping wet in a tempest of rain. At three we took the railway and about nine in the evening reached Munich in the rain. We made the journey from Paris in four days and one hour, and from Paris to Heidelberg in less than two days.

Munich August 22. After I wrote thus far I visited the Schloss at Schleissheim a country seat of the royal family three leagues north of the city a mouldy old palace built in 1601 on a dreary plain, where the late King Ludwig[8]—you know he has abdicated in favour of his son—has a private gallery of paintings, many by modern artists, and some very beautiful, Wilkie's[9] Reading of the Will for example, and some landscapes by Achenbach.[10] Returning we took Nymphenburg in our way which you and I once saw together. The buildings have been whitewashed, the walks are neatly tended, though formal, and the weather being beautiful they looked very pleasant to me amidst the thick shades overhanging swift currents of clear water. The two beavers, one from the Danube and the other from the Mississippi, which used to fight whenever they met, are long since dead, but there is a fat beaver from the Danube in their place whom a woman stirred up for us with a pole. In the afternoon we went to the Aukirche, very symmetrically built, but mostly of a mean material brick. The interior, however, realizes my idea of what a Gothic church ought to be; the clustered columns support a nave of great height, seeming to carry the eye up to heaven, and nothing breaks the view between the principal gates of the temple and the altar at the farther end. There is perfect unity and great grandeur of effect and a certain severe and noble simplicity in the details. A priest was chanting vespers and the people responding; the reverberations of sound in the arches of the church reminded me of those of the tides in Fingal's cave.

Lyons September 3d. I am giddy with being whirled through Switzerland. So many sights have passed before my eyes within these last ten days— great mountains green vallies, blue lakes rushing streams, tall woods and picturesque cities that my head swims when I think of them. On the 23d of August we left Munich in the afternoon and ran down through Augsburg to Kaufbeurn, an old Swabian town in the south part of the kingdom

of Bavaria. Next morning we went on with some other travellers in a hired coach, with the Alps in sight for a considerable part of the way. The country in many parts reminded me of my own, by its scattered houses woods and orchards. In a day and a half we reached Lindau still in Bavaria, on the Lake of Constance or Bodensee, skirted by vineyards with the Alps overlooking it from the south and southwest. Crossing the lake in a steamer, we landed at Roorschah in Switzerland, on a beautiful declivity, and climbing the green slopes in a diligence reached St. Gall—St. Gallen the Germans call it—beautifully situated among the hills and groves of spruce trees. A discharge of fire arms was heard from a neighbouring meadow where all the boys of the city schools from twelve to sixteen were engaged in a sham fight, for in Switzerland every man is educated to be a soldier. Next day we had another beautiful drive through the rich and fresh Swiss valleys, with great Swiss houses—the house and barn in one—the snowy summit of Sentis looking down upon us, to the lake of Zurich, the descent to which is prodigiously beautiful. A steamer took us to the town at the west end of the lake. But I must be less minute. I have climbed Mount Righi, passed a night on its summit, looked thence on the Swiss lakes, towns, and white mountain peaks, crossed the lake of Zug in a row boat, the lake of the Four Cantons in a steamer, visited successively the picturesque towns of Luzern Bern and Freiburg, passed into the warmer region of French Switzerland, eaten figs at Vevey contemplated the fine old cathedral of Lausanne, refreshed my recollection of Geneva, and having arrived here this morning too late to take the steamer to Châlons employ a moment in adding this paragraph. I wish you could have seen Switzerland with me. The northern part of it is more beautiful than I could have imagined.

Paris. September 6. I took the steamer up the Saône on the morning of the fourth, and was broiled all day on deck without an awning. You remember how uncomfortable the steamer on that river was fifteen years ago—there has been no improvement since. We reached this city yesterday at one o'clock partly by diligence and partly by railway. I found your letter of the 12th of August with Fannys and Julias of the 3d, and before night got yours of the 20th, with Julia's of that date, and Miss Robbins's, and one from Mrs. Moulton.[11] I am glad to hear that you are all doing so well, for I had become quite uneasy not having heard from you so long. Farewell—God bless you—[See another note enclosed][12]

W. C. Bryant.

MANUSCRIPTS: NYPL–GR (draft and final).

1. Wilhelm von Kaulbach (1805–1874), who was made director of the Munich Academy that year. The opera was by the Italian Alessandro Stradella (1642?–1682). Bryant, "Diary, 1849," August 19.

2. Word omitted.

3. See letter 409.

4. Johann Heinrich von Dannecker (1758–1841), one of whose outstanding sculptures was entitled *Ariadne on a Panther.*

5. See Letter 558.

6. Eva (Hepp) Mercier; see Letter 540.

7. See 305.1; Letter 408.

8. Louis I (1786–1868), king of Bavaria, 1825–1848.

9. Sir David Wilkie (1785–1841), Scottish genre and historical painter.

10. Andreas Achenbach (1815–1910), marine painter, and a founder of the modern German landscape school.

11. None of these letters has been recovered.

12. Letter 700. The brackets are Bryant's.

700.   *To* Frances F. Bryant

Paris   September 6   1849.

My dear Frances.

Please to thank Miss Robbins for her short note.[1] I have already written to her[2] so that debt is paid in advance. Tell Fanny I should answer hers[3] if I were not already fatigued with copying out legibly what I had scribbled down for you—a very long letter you will see it is.[4] I thank you for writing so minutely about matters at home, and for the care you have taken of every thing, this unpleasant summer. You ask what shall be done with the clover field next to Miss Mudge's.[5] Will you be so good as to speak to Mr. Hicks[6] about it. If he agrees with the men that it is best to till it again very well. If he thinks that a top dressing of ashes would do, let it have that— I do not want so much land under tillage if I can help it.

You inquire if I take care of myself. I assure you I think I am in pretty good hands. The complaint of which I spoke in my former letters recurs about as often as once in a fortnight, but passes off in the course of twelve hours.

I am sorry that your own health has been so delicate. The cooler weather I hope will complete your restoration. *You* I hope will be careful— it is an admonition of which you stand more in need than I. What you say of the gratitude we owe to Providence for the safety we have found amidst so many dangers, I feel very strongly.

Give my kind regards to Miss Robbins and to Miss White[7] and my love to the children and remember me to Mrs. Kirkland and her family.

Yrs affectionately
W C BRYANT.

MANUSCRIPT: NYPL–GR.

1. Unrecovered.

2. Letter 697.

3. Unrecovered.

4. Letter 699.

5. The spinster sisters Amy and Elizabeth Mudge occupied an old homestead bordering on Bryant's property. Goddard, *Roslyn Harbor,* pp. 10–11.

6. Postmaster William Hicks owned a lumber yard and several other properties on Hempstead Harbor near Bryant's Cedarmere. *Ibid.*, pp. 13, 24, [104].

7. Unidentified.

701. *To* Fanny Bryant Godwin

Paris   September 11, 1849.

Dear Fanny.

I thank you for your note,[1] short though it was. It was something to have found time to write it amidst your many cares and anxieties. I hope they are happily over by this time. My own health which you so kindly inquire about is very good. I am becoming a florid old gentleman, particularly about the nose.

You have seen I suppose my last letter to your mother which gives a sort of bird's eye view of my journey to Germany and Switzerland. Since my return to Paris I have seen little worth writing about. The most remarkable sight was one which I saw in the Rue de la Paix the other day. A man was sitting in a vehicle about as large as a one horse waggon; it had four wheels and a box of very fair dimensions, but was without any animal to draw it. The vehicle, without any apparent motion of his body or limbs he caused to run backward or forward with great velocity, and to turn with great suddenness. A bystander explained to me that he did it by first pressing on one foot and then on the other, the wheels being moved by a machinery to which the impulse was thus given, and that he had been ten years in bringing this invention to its present state.

Paris is not so gay a place as when you knew it. There is less bustle and movement in the streets; the splendid carriages and gay liveries have disappeared. The[y] still supply the people with amusements, and a fete is now holding at St. Cloud, which began on Sunday the 9th. All Paris trooped out to St. Cloud, some on foot, some in cabs, some in omnibuses and some by the railway. There had been rows of booths erected for the occasion, swinging machines set up, shows and spectacles of all kinds provided, and tents for those who wished to dine, and places where children could gamble for macaroons. The *grandes eaux* were made to play, but though the sculpture and other arrangements of the fountains were quite elaborate, the volume of water to one who had seen our fountains would appear rather scanty. The grounds of St. Cloud are fine, and the old trees make noble avenues. The view of Paris from the higher grounds is prodigiously fine. The place is a kind of Richmond Hill with a clearer atmosphere. On the heights were a crowd of people looking at the city through enormous telescopes and not far off young women in white playing tag among the trees.—

So you see, French gaiety is not quite dead. The political condition of France is bad enough, but the friends of liberty are not discouraged. They see that if they can but keep the *form* of government as it now is the

substance of liberty will be attained at last. At present there is very little of liberty here except the name. The number of strangers in the city is considerably less than usual, and the reason I hear given is, and it is no doubt the true one, that the late revolutions and attempts at revolution, and the dissatisfaction of the people with the present government, make strangers afraid to live here. A year of quiet would bring them all back, and if no attempt is made to alter the constitution so as to make it more monarchical or aristocratic the probability is that there will be no popular disturbance. At present the principal resort of tourists and summer residents is Switzerland. At Munich they complained very much of the absence of strangers this season.

September 13. I have been trying to look up Madame Mercier—Eva Hepp—of whom I thought you and your mother would like to hear. Mrs. Hagen told me to apply to Professor Quinet[2] for her address; Professor Quinet is not in town, and I have written to him at Seineport but have received no answer though sufficient time has elapsed. I heard however from Mrs. Hagen that she was well at the last accounts they had received from her.

I hoped to get letters from home by the steamer which was due at Liverpool the beginning of this week, but though we hear she has arrived we have no mails from her yet. The weather has been exceedingly stormy for a day or two past, and we have nothing from England this morning. We do not choose to pitch ourselves head foremost into the cholera, and therefore we do not go to London at present where the deaths by it are from four to five hundred a day. We make a short excursion to Holland hoping that the cholera in England will have subsided by October.

Farewell. I would send my love to the little ones[3] if they were old enough to know what is meant.

W   C   BRYANT

MANUSCRIPT: NYPL–GR ADDRESS: To Mrs. F. Bryant Godwin.

1. Unrecovered.
2. Edgar Quinet (1803–1875), historian and professor at the Collège de France, and a leading opponent of Napoleon III.
3. Bryant's grandchildren, Minna Godwin (612.3) and her sister Annie (born 1848).

702.   *To* Frances F. Bryant

Paris   September 13, 1849.

Dear Frances.

I suppose you will have seen, before you receive this, accounts of the ravages which the cholera is making in London and other parts of England. Of course we are in no haste to get to that country as we at first intended to do. The distemper rages in the south of England which we had

hoped to visit. We shall therefore direct our way to Holland and pass a few days at Ghent and Amsterdam in hopes that the cholera will subside before the time for our departure arrives.

I send with this a letter for Fanny[1] which I wish [you][2] to put in an envelope for her, after you have read it. By this steamer I have written a long letter for the Evening Post.[3] I have had more matter for such letters than either time or inclination to write them. The worst of it is that I must write them on the spot or the vividness of the impression made by what I have seen or heard is lost and my account of it becomes flat and meagre.

I hoped to get letters from you by the last steamer before writing this, but it has arrived late at Liverpool, and yesterday there was a storm in the channel which prevented the mails from being brought over. I shall expect them tomorrow, and in the mean time I must write or lose the steamer which leaves Liverpool on Saturday.

Mr. Leupp wants to go to America in the steamer which sails on the 20th of October. I am for going on the 6th, and I think that if the cholera in England is not too bad at that time I shall take passage in the Niagara on that day. Love to Julia and regards to all my friends.

Yrs affectionately
W. C. B.

MANUSCRIPT: NYPL–GR ADDRESS: To Mrs. Frances F. Bryant.

1. Letter 701.
2. Word omitted.
3. Letter 703.

703. *To* the EVENING POST

Paris, September 13, 1849.

Whoever should visit the principal countries of Europe at the present moment, might take them for conquered provinces, held in subjection by their victorious masters, at the point of the sword. Such was the aspect which France presented when I came to Paris a few weeks since. The city was then in what is called, by a convenient fiction, a state of siege; soldiers filled the streets, were posted in every public square and at every corner, were seen marching before the churches, the cornices of which bore the inscription of Liberty, Equality, and Fraternity, keeping their brethren quiet by the bayonet. I have since made a journey to Bavaria and Switzerland, and on returning I find the siege raised, and these demonstrations of fraternity less formal, but the show and the menace of military force are scarcely less apparent. Those who maintain that France is not fit for liberty, need not afflict themselves with the idea that there is at present more liberty in France than her people know how to enjoy.

On my journey, I found the cities along the Rhine crowded with sol-

diers; the sound of the drum was heard among the hills covered with vines; women were trundling loaded wheel-barrows, and carrying panniers like asses, to earn the taxes which are extorted to support the men who stalk about in uniform. I entered Heidelberg with anticipations of pleasure; they were dashed in a moment; the city was in a state of siege, occupied by Prussian troops which had been sent to take the part of the Grand Duke of Baden against his people. I could hardly believe that this was the same peaceful and friendly city which I had known in better times. Every other man in the streets was a soldier; the beautiful walks about the old castle were full of soldiers; in the evening they were reeling through the streets. "This invention," said a German who had been a member of the Diet of the Confederation lately broken up,[1] "this invention of declaring a city, which has unconditionally submitted, to be still in a state of siege, is but a device to practice the most unbounded oppression. Any man who is suspected, or feared, or disliked, or supposed not to approve of the proceedings of the victorious party, is arrested and imprisoned at pleasure. He may be guiltless of any offence which could be made a pretext for condemning him, but his trial is arbitrarily postponed, and when at last he is released, he has suffered the penalty of a long confinement, and is taught how dangerous it is to become obnoxious to the government."

From Heidelberg, thus transformed, I was glad to take my departure as soon as possible. Our way from that city to Heilbronn, was through a most charming country along the valley of the Neckar. Here were low hills and valleys rich with harvests, a road embowered in fruit-trees, the branches of which were propped with stakes to prevent them from breaking with their load, and groves lying pleasantly in the morning sunshine, where ravens were croaking. Birds of worse omen than these were abroad, straggling groups, and sometimes entire companies of soldiers, on their way from one part of the duchy to another; while in the fields, women, prematurely old with labor, were wielding the hoe and the mattock, and the younger and stronger of their sex were swinging the scythe. In all the villages through which we passed, in the very smallest, troops were posted, and men in military uniform were standing at the doors, or looking from the windows of every inn and beer-house.

At Heilbronn we took the railway for Stuttgart, the capital of Wurtemberg. There was a considerable proportion of men in military trappings among the passengers, but at one of the stations they came upon us like a cloud, and we entered Stuttgart with a little army. That city, too, looked as if in a state of siege, so numerous were the soldiery, though the vine-covered hills, among which it is situated, could have given them a better occupation. The railway, beyond Stuttgart, wound through a deep valley and ended at Geisslingen, an ancient Swabian town, in a gorge of the mountains, with tall old houses, not one of which, I might safely affirm,

has been built within the last two hundred years. From this place to Ulm, on the Danube, the road was fairly lined with soldiers, walking or resting by the wayside, or closely packed in the peasants' wagons, which they had hired to carry them short distances. At Ulm we were obliged to content ourselves with straitened accommodations, the hotels being occupied by the gentry in epaulettes.

I hoped to see fewer of this class at the capital of Bavaria, but it was not so; they were everywhere placed in sight as if to keep the people in awe. "These fellows," said a German to me, "are always too numerous, but in ordinary times they are kept in the capitals and barracks, and the nuisance is out of sight. Now, however, the occasion is supposed to make their presence necessary in the midst of the people, and they swarm everywhere." Another, it was our host of the Goldener Hirsch, said to my friend, "I think I shall emigrate to America, I am tired of living under the bayonet."

I was in Munich when the news arrived of the surrender of the Hungarian troops under Görgey, and the fall of the Hungarian republic.[2] All along my journey I had observed tokens of the intense interest which the German people took in the result of the struggle between Austria and the Magyars, and of the warmth of their hopes in favor of the latter. The intelligence was received with the deepest sorrow. "So perishes," said a Bavarian, "the last hope of European liberty."

Our journey to Switzerland led us through the southern part of Bavaria, among the old towns which formed a part of ancient Swabia. The country here, in some respects, resembles New England; here are broad woods, large orchards of the apple and pear, and scattered farm-houses—of a different architecture, it is true, from that of the Yankees, and somewhat resembling, with their far-projecting eaves, those of Switzerland. Yet there was a further difference—everywhere, men were seen under arms, and women at the plough.

So weary had I grown of the perpetual sight of the military uniform, that I longed to escape into Switzerland, where I hoped to see less of it, and it was with great delight that I found myself at Lindau, a border town of Bavaria, on the Bodensee, or Lake of Constance, on the shores of which the boundaries of four sovereignties meet. A steamer took us across the lake, from a wharf covered with soldiers, to Rorschach,[3] in Switzerland, where not a soldier was to be seen. Nobody asked for our passports, nobody required us to submit our baggage to search. I could almost have kneeled and kissed the shore of the hospitable republic; and really it was beautiful enough for such a demonstration of affection, for nothing could be lovelier than the declivities of that shore with its woods and orchards, and grassy meadows, and green hollows running upward to the mountain-tops, all fresh with a shower which had just passed and now glittering in the sun-

shine, and interspersed with large Swiss houses, bearing quaintly-carved galleries, and broad overhanging roofs, while to the east rose the glorious summits of the Alps, mingling with the clouds.

In three or four hours we had climbed up to St. Gall—St. Gallen, the Germans call it—situated in a high valley, among steep green hills, which send down spurs of woodland to the meadows below. In walking out to look at the town, we heard a brisk and continued discharge of musketry, and, proceeding in the direction of the sound, came to a large field, evidently set apart as a parade-ground, on which several hundred youths were practicing the art of war in a sham fight, and keeping up a spirited fire at each other with blank cartridges. On inquiry, we were told that these were the boys of the schools of St. Gall, from twelve to sixteen years of age, with whom military exercises were a part of their education. I was still, therefore, among soldiers, but of a different class from those of whom I had seen so much. Here, it was the people who were armed for self-protection; there, it was a body of mercenaries armed to keep the people in subjection.

Another day's journey brought us to the picturesque town of Zurich, and the next morning about four o'clock I was awakened by the roll of drums under my window. Looking out, I saw a regiment of boys of a tender age, in a uniform of brown linen, with little light muskets on their shoulders, and miniature knapsacks on their backs, completely equipped and furnished for war, led on by their little officers in regular military order, marching and wheeling to the sound of martial music with all the precision of veterans. In Switzerland arms are in every man's hands; he is educated to be a soldier, and taught that the liberties of his country depend on his skill and valor. The worst effect, perhaps of this military education is, that the Swiss, when other means of subsistence are not easily found, become military adventurers and sell their services to the first purchaser. Meantime, nobody is regarded as properly fitted for his duties as a member of the state, who is not skilled in the use of arms. Target-shooting, *Freischiessen*, is the national amusement of Switzerland, and has been so ever since the days of Tell;[4] occasions of target-shooting are prescribed and superintended by the public authorities. They were practicing it at the stately city of Berne when we visited it; they were practicing it at various other places as we passed. Every town is provided with a public shooting-ground near its gates.

It was at one of the most remarkable of these towns; it was at Freiburg, Catholic Freiburg,[5] full of Catholic seminaries and convents, in the churches of which you may hear the shrill voices of the nuns chanting matins, themselves unseen; it was at Freiburg, grandly seated on the craggy banks of her rivers, flowing in deep gulfs, spanned by the loftiest and longest chain-bridges in the world, that I saw another evidence of the fact that Switzerland is the only place on the continent where freedom is understood, or allowed to have an existence. A proclamation of the authorities

of the canton was pasted on the walls and gates, ordaining the 16th of September as a day of religious thanksgiving. After recounting the motives of gratitude to Providence; after speaking of the abundance of the harvests, the health enjoyed throughout Switzerland, at the threshold of which the cholera had a second time been stayed; the subsidence of political animosities, and the quiet enjoyment of the benefits of the new constitution upon which the country had entered, the proclamation mentioned, as a special reason of gratitude to Almighty God, that Switzerland, in this day of revolutions, had been enabled to offer, among her mountains, a safe and unmolested asylum to the thousands of fugitives who had suffered defeat in the battles of freedom.

I could not help contrasting this with the cruel treatment shown by France to the political refugees from Baden and other parts of Germany. A few days before, it had been announced that the French government required of these poor fellows that they should either enlist at once in the regiments destined for service in Algiers, or immediately leave the country—offering them the alternative of military slavery, or banishment from the country in which they had hoped to find a shelter.

I have spoken of the practice of Switzerland in regard to passports, an example which it does not suit the purpose of the French politicians to follow. Here, and all over the continent, the passport system is as strictly and vexatiously enforced as ever. It is remarkable that none of the reformers occupied in the late remodelling of European institutions, seem to have thought of abolishing this invention of despotism—this restraint upon the liberty of passing from place to place, which makes Europe one great prison. If the people had been accustomed to perfect freedom in this respect, though but a short time, it might have been found difficult, at least in France, to reimpose the old restraints. The truth is, however, that France is not quite so free at present as she was under Louis Philippe.[6] The only advantage of her present condition is, that the constitution places in the hands of the people the means of peaceably perfecting their liberties, whenever they are enlightend enough to claim them.

On my way from Geneva to Lyons I sat in the *banquette* [outside seat] of the diligence among the plebeians. The conversation happened to turn on politics, and the expressions of hatred against the present government of France, which broke from the conductor, the coachman, and the two passengers by my side, were probably significant of the feeling which prevails among the people. "The only law now," said one, "is the law of the sabre." "The soldiers and the *gens d'armes* have every thing their own way now," said another, "but by and by they will be glad to hide in the sewers." The others were no less emphatic in their expressions of anger and detestation.

The expedition to Rome is unpopular throughout France,[7] more especially so in the southern part of the republic, where the intercourse

with Rome has been more frequent, and the sympathy with her people is stronger. "I have never," said an American friend, who has resided some time in Paris, "heard a single Frenchman defend it." It is unpopular, even among the troops sent on the expedition, as is acknowledged by the government journals themselves. To propitiate public opinion, the government has changed its course, and after making war upon the Romans to establish the pontifical throne, now tells the Pope that he must submit to place the government in the hands of the laity. This change of policy has occasioned a good deal of surprise and an infinite deal of discussion. Whatever may be its consequences, there is one consequence which it can not have, that of recovering to the President and his ministry the popularity they have lost.[8]

MANUSCRIPT: NYPL–GR (draft) TEXT: *LT* I, 426–435; first published in *EP* for September 28, 1849.

1. Professor Hagen; see Letter 699.
2. On August 13, at Világos, Rumania, the young Hungarian revolutionary general Arthur Görgey (1818–1916) had surrendered his Magyar army to Russian officers who had come to the aid of his Austrian opponents. Priscilla Robertson, *Revolutions of 1848: A Social History* (Princeton: Princeton University Press, 1952), p. 301. Two years later, while presiding over a banquet given by the New York press to another Hungarian revolutionary, Louis Kossuth (1802–1894), Bryant characterized Görgey's capitulation as a betrayal of Hungary's cause. "Address at the Banquet Given by the New York Press to Louis Kossuth, December [15], 1851," in *Orations and Addresses*, p. 264.
3. The printed text has "Roorschach."
4. William Tell, legendary Swiss patriot of the thirteenth century, who, under compulsion by Austrian oppressors, successfully shot an apple from his son's head with bow and arrow.
5. More properly, "Fribourg."
6. Louis Philippe (1773–1850), "Citizen King" of France from 1830 until his abdication in the 1848 revolution.
7. On July 3, 1849, after a siege of three months, a French expeditionary force had entered Rome, forcing Giuseppe Garibaldi's revolutionary army to flee to the Adriatic, whence its leader sailed to New York. Here, according to Parke Godwin, he and Bryant first became acquainted, and in 1867 they met again in Florence. See *Life*, II, 258; *EP*, March 10, 1851.
8. Louis Napoleon Bonaparte (1808–1873), elected president of France in 1848. In 1852 he was proclaimed Emperor Napoleon III, reigning until 1870, when he was captured during the Franco-Prussian War and subsequently deposed by a revolution in Paris.

704.   To Frances F. Bryant

Paris   September 17, 1849.

Dear Frances.

Professor Quinet was polite enough to send me the address of Victor Mercier, and at the same time to enclose to Mr. Mercier my note of inquiry.[1] Mr. Mercier called immediately at the Hotel de Paris to see me. I

was not in at the time, but he told Mr. Leupp that his wife thought that you were with me and would be disappointed to find that you were not. He fixed an hour for calling again and at the time appointed was at the door of my room, with Eva herself, who is a lively, bright looking, slender woman, speaking English quite well, for they resided two or three years in England. I should not have known her for any recollection I retained of her looks. She spoke of you in affectionate terms as well as of Fanny and Julia and appealed to her husband to bear witness how often she had spoken of little Julia. She had really supposed, she said, when she saw my name, that I had brought *you* at least with me. You *must* come, she said, to Paris,—there were some nice apartments, in the hotel in which she and Mr. Mercier lived, which would suit you exactly, and where you could be very comfortable. She spoke of her health, as being very good—though neither she nor her husband were of a robust constitution—and of her life as a happy one. He is a literary man of some sort—journalist or book maker—I could not ask which—and seems to be a [rather?] quiet man. Very different he is certainly from the flippant voluble Frenchmen whom you so often meet. I am to call at their lodgings before I leave town.

We have concluded to take passage in the steamer Niagara which leaves Liverpool for New York on the sixth of October. If you do not hear from me otherwise you may expect me by her. Leaving England on the 6th I may be in New York on any day from the 18th to the 21st. You remember you said that you should be in New York to receive me, and I need not tell you how much pleasure it would give me to meet you so much the sooner.

We are still waiting here for letters from America. The cholera is rapidly decreasing in London, and it may be that we shall not take our trip to Amsterdam but proceed directly to England. In the south of France meantime the cholera is increasing and Mr. Chapman, who was preparing to go with his family to Florence told me last evening that in consequence of the spread of the distemper in that direction he had given up the plan.

I went on Saturday—it is now Monday—with Mr. Leupp and Mons. Goupil[2] to the studio of Sheffer[3] the painter, whose Christ the Consoler we have in an engraving. He has just finished a picture of Christ the Rewarder, intended as a companion piece to that. It is very fine, perhaps superior to that in some respects, but, as appeared to me, not equal to it in pathos and therefore not so great a picture. Christ is represented as separating the benevolent and the repentant from the wrong-doers. The aspect of Jesus is certainly nobler than in the other picture. The artist received us politely. He is a broad bottomed man, with white mustachios, and though he seems to be nearly sixty, paints, his friends think, with more vigour of talent than ever. I saw in his studio the original of Christ the Consoler, a picture of the Three Marys, another of Francesca da Rimini, from the story in Dante,[4] and a remarkable painting called St. Augustine

and Monica, representing the saint and his mother in a moment of religious meditation. The devout thoughts of the two personages are so plainly expressed in their countenances that they need no interpretation of language.

Paris   September 18.

Yesterday I called on Madame Mercier at No. 10 Rue St. Hyacinthe St. Honoré a short street parallel with the Rue Rivoli. Mr. Leupp took a fancy to go with me. I found her in a little chamber among papers and manuscripts; her husband soon made his appearance from another room. She made a great many inquiries about you and the children and the Americans she had known at Heidelberg. She said that I would render them a service if I could recommend such Americans as had need for a French master to Mr. Mercier which I promised to do when I found opportunity. In England she gave lessons in German to young ladies and would be willing to do so here. She desired to be affectionately remembered to you all. Mr. Leupp was quite pleased both with her and her husband and so was I.

Last evening Monsieur Circourt—he was a Count under Louis Philippe—called on me. It was he, you may remember, who wrote a review of my poems for a Geneva literary periodical, giving a prose translation of some of them.[5] He had come into town from the country for a day and hearing I was here came immediately to see me. He is a very well informed and accomplished man, speaking English, with great volubility but with so decided a French accent, that I was obliged to listen with almost painful attention to be always sure of what he said. He regretted he said that his wife could not have the opportunity of knowing me and said a good many other kind things.

I have just learned that the steamer Hibernia which was due at Liverpool last week ran aground at Halifax and that the steamer Cambria arrived at Liverpool yesterday bringing the mails and passengers of the Hibernia. We expect letters tomorrow after getting which I shall finish this.

Paris   September 19th. I have just received a letter from you of the 2nd of August— I suppose it means the 2nd of September, and one from Fanny of the same date.[6] I wrote to you last week and the week previous—my letters were dated the 6th of September and the 13th; the last letter written previously to these was dated August 13th on which day I also wrote to Miss Robbins. I am sorry you lost my letter of the 8th[7] as it continued the narrative of my journey and its incidents up to that date, though I believe it was not very long. Tell Fanny I am much obliged to her for her letter. I sent her a letter on the 13th as long as three of hers.[8] Mr. Leupp is now writing a letter to England to take our passage in the steamer which departs on the 6th of October. If the berths are not all

taken and we are alive we shall go then. The cholera at London is greatly abated and now gives no alarm. Love to all.

Yours affectionately
W. C. BRYANT.

MANUSCRIPTS: NYPL–GR (draft and final).

1. Unrecovered.

2. Adolf Goupil (1806–1893?), a partner with Theodore Vibert (1816?–1850) in the Paris firm of art dealers Goupil, Vibert & Co., which had opened a gallery in New York in 1848. This was succeeded by the present firm of M. Knoedler and Company.

3. Ary Scheffer (1795–1858), Dutch painter of religious subjects, who worked chiefly in Paris.

4. *Inferno*, V.73–138.

5. It was apparently this review which was published by Count Adolphe Marie Pierre de Circourt (1801–1879) as *Poésies de William Cullen Bryant* (Geneva: Bibliothèque Universelle de Genève [1847?]).

6. Neither letter has been recovered.

7. Unrecovered.

8. Letter 701.

705. *To* the EVENING POST

Paris, September [17], 1849.

There are many here who affirm that the French expedition against the Roman people was the most fortunate thing that could have happened for the liberties of France, and that it has in fact proved the salvation of the republic. There may be some exa[g]geration in this, but there is no doubt that the expedition has made the men who now administer the government, so unpopular that they have been obliged to give up their favorite scheme, with all the other plans it was intended to introduce—the scheme of re-electing President Bonaparte, and extending his term of office to ten years.

The French constitution you know, forbids a second election of the same person as President, and makes his term of office four years. The members of the present administration began to intrigue for expunging the prohibition, and enlarging the term of office as soon as they stepped into their places. In due time Leon Faucher,[1] one of their instruments, was sent to make the tour of the departments, and harangue the people in favor of the change, and at length the *Consuls Generaux* of the departments, which I shall take leave to translate General Councils, were desired to take the question into consideration and give the nation their advice. Certain members of these Councils are appointed by the ministry, and it was thought that they would have sufficient influence with their colleagues to secure a majority in favor of the scheme, and give it the appearance of being strongly supported by public opinion.

The legitimate party co-operated with great zeal in this movement; it was an attempt to bring the government nearer to monarchical forms, and they favored it, of course. It is said here, very confidently, that the ultimate design of the men in power, was to make Mons. Bonaparte, President for life. In this the legitimists could not have concurred, inasmuch as they are dreaming of Henry V. as king, and the restoration of the Bourbons.[2] They were ready, however, to give their help in diminishing the frequency of elections, and to keep the power for the present in the hands of men who manifestly bear no good will to republican doctrines.

In the meantime the Roman expedition had given great offence to the people, and excited an indignation which they were desirous of an opportunity of expressing. They could not do this by means of public meetings, for they are forbidden; nor by their votes, for there were no elections at hand; and the feeling was perhaps more intense and impatient on account of this suppression. When the question of recommending a revision of the constitution therefore, came before the General Councils of the Departments, it found them pervaded with that distrust of the men in power which pervaded the nation generally. The friends of the ministry in the councils were overruled, and out of eighty-six departments, all but two or three reported against the project. It was a complete defeat of the ministry in the very quarter in which it thought itself strongest. The whole combination of Bonapartists, legitimists, men in office, presses, and emissaries of the ministry, were put down by the mere force of public opinion, operating upon the General Councils. The result is highly creditable to the French nation,—to its good sense, and what is a part of good sense, its sense of justice. The project of changing the constitution is now given up, and if there was any intention of giving to the shallow coxcomb who is now President, a life estate in his office, it is postponed to a more favorable period, if not for ever.

The French politicians do not seem to be aware of what we know very well in the United States, that a popular candidate does not always make a popular officer. A man who is elected to a post of great responsibility by the general good will of his fellow-citizens, must possess extraordinary qualifications for public life, to keep the same measure of popular favor to which he owed his election. Let him do his best, he will offend many, and disappoint more. Particularly is this the case, when he happens to be, like the present Chief Magistrate of France, a man of weak understanding and no principles.

I find that nobody here, except perhaps the American Consul,[3] believes that any conspiracy existed to overthrow the government by force on the 13th of June last. The story of a plot is regarded as one of those. humbugs which the government of Louis Philippe, and the governments which preceeded it, used to get up from time to time to frighten the timid

and credulous and make them believe that to be a republican is the same thing as to be a ruffian and a cut-throat.— The proceeding which led to the flight of Ledru Rollin[4] is looked upon as an act of folly and imprudence, and nothing more. Its object was to present a petition with an imposing display of numbers, and such of the petitioners as belonged to the National Guards, appeared in their uniform with their military equipments. The trial of those who were engaged in this affair is to be opened on the 10th of October, and nobody expects that any thing will be proved against them, but the simple fact of the intended procession.

Meanwhile the public confidence in the stability of the present form of government, though it is now administered by men who are objects of public distrust, seems to be gaining ground. If the constitution is not meddled with, the people, by and by, as they begin to understand their rights, will assert them in a peaceable and proper manner, that is, by legislation, which the constitution gives them power to do, whenever they are disposed. At present there is very little political liberty in France, except the liberty of suffrage. The police can seize the printed sheets of any journal containing expressions which the government happen to dislike, and prevent its circulation. The law punishes with severe penalties the vague offence of printing and publishing any thing which is calculated to bring hatred and contempt on the government, and therefore a trial by jury is allowed in such cases; all that the jury has to do, is to say whether the obnoxious article was published or not; the judges, who are the creatures of the government, decide whether the law is violated or not. There is no chance, therefore, of escape, when the government has marked out its victim. People are arrested and detained, by order of the government, and there is no process like that of our *habeas corpus*, to deliver them, if confined on a frivol[o]us or insufficient pretext. There is no liberty of assembling to express public opinions on political questions, in addresses and resolutions, or we should have seen the entire people moving, on the Roman question. In short, here is a government, with popular forms, conducted in the worst spirit of oligarchy, and allowing ample scope for the exercise of the most capricious tyranny.

The remedy, however, is in the hands of the people, and if the friends of liberty are guilty of no acts of rashness and violence, but confine themselves to the task of enlightening the people in regard to their rights and interests, the remedy will yet be applied.

I have lately been to look at the printing press constructed by our countryman, Hoe,[5] for the administration paper, *La Patrie*. It is a beautiful piece of machinery, tended by four men, and delivering eight thousand impressions an hour. The perfection and simplicity of the arrangements, as well as the celerity of its operation, are greatly admired here; but I have heard that the workmen are jealous of it, as a labor saving

machine, and are not inclined to favor its working. It prints for *La Patrie* forty thousand copies daily, of which thirty thousand are without the advertisements, and are sold for a single sou each; the others, containing the advertising department, are sold for three sous. It is the most perfect printing press in Europe. The London Times has a more complicated and expensive machine, occupying three times the room, and tended by sixteen men, which prints about the same number of impressions hourly.

Among the recent arrangements for the accommodation of Americans in Paris, is the Reading Room of Livingston & Wells, which has almost entirely drawn them away from Galignani's, where they found but one or two American journals.[6] The reading room of Livingston & Wells, on the contrary, is abundantly supplied with American papers, though the assortment, as a merchant would say, is by no means complete. The room is becoming a place of much resort, and in an address-book, lying on its desk, are registered the name and residence of most of the Americans who arrive at Paris.

Our countryman, Chapman, has recovered from his indisposition, and is applying himself to his art, with all his former activity. He has lately been making some admirable copies of Van Ostade and Gerard Douw.[7] His keen eye and extraordinary ingenuity, make him a very perfect copyist, whenever he condescends to a work of that nature. He seems to penetrate, at once, the mechanical methods of the artist whose work is before him, and in his copies there is no trace of Chapman except his fidelity. I believe he is almost the only man in the world who could perfectly reproduce Denner's Old Men and Women,[8] if he thought it worth the trouble.

Scheffer, the French artist, who paints so much in the German manner, and whose "Christ the Consoler" is already known in America by means of an engraving, has lately finished a companion-piece to that beautiful work; he calls it Christ the Rewarder. It represents Jesus separating the good from the bad—those who practice his precepts, from those who reject or neglect them. It does not appear to me that it possesses the pathos and interest which belong to the other picture—the subject, perhaps, does not admit of them—but in some respects it is finer. The countenance of the Savior, for example is nobler and of higher dignity. The group of the good at the right hand, in whose faces the traces of human suffering yet remain, is well conceived, but the group at the left hand, the wicked and the men of violence, make a feebler impression on the beholder than any thing in the other picture. It is intended, I was told, to send the picture to the United States for exhibition.

W. C. B.

MANUSCRIPT: NYPL–GR (partial draft) TEXT: *EP*, October 5, 1849; not published in *LT* I.

1. Léon Léonard Joseph Faucher (1803–1854), representative from the Marne district in the French parliament, was a frequent writer on financial matters.

2. Henri Charles, Comte de Chambord (1820–1883), claimant to the French throne as Henry V, was never crowned.

3. Robert Walsh; see 697.3.

4. Alexandre Auguste Ledru, called Ledru-Rollin (1807–1874), who had been minister of the interior in the provisional government formed after the revolution of February 1848, turned against the government during the unsuccessful workingmen's revolt in June 1849, and was forced into exile in England. Among his many published writings were *Le 13 Juin* (Paris, 1849) and *The Decline of England* (London, 1850).

5. Richard March Hoe (1812–1886), a New York manufacturer whose invention of a rotary press in 1847 revolutionized newspaper printing. In 1850 the *EP* acquired a high-speed Hoe press. Nevins, *Evening Post*, pp. 236–237.

6. Messrs. Jean and Guillaume Galignani, Paris dealers in English books. They also published an English-language newspaper, *Galignani's Messenger*, for which Bryant had earlier expressed contempt. See Letter 310.

7. Probably Adriaen van Ostade (1610–1685), a Dutch genre painter, and Gerard Douw (1613–1675), Dutch genre and portrait painter.

8. Balthazar Denner (1685–1749), French miniaturist and genre painter, whose many realistic studies of elderly men and women were most characteristic of his work.

706. *To* Julia S. Bryant

Paris September 19, 1849.

Dear Daughter.

I think you would have been amused had you heard Madame Mercier talk the other day about the dear little Julia, whom she represented as a most accomplished creature, speaking not only English and German but Italian and French with the greatest facility. She inquired whether you possessed these accomplishments yet. I was obliged to give up your Italian and to confess that your German had fallen off, but I made a stand in favour of your French and, if I had thought of it, I might have told her that you had made some proficiency in English since she knew you. I should almost be ashamed to have her see you, her recollections of you are so favorable. It would be a pity if she should institute any disparaging comparisons between the little child of 1836 and the grown up girl of 1849. If you should ever see her you must be upon your good behavior. I wrote a long letter to your mother on my return from Bavaria and Switzerland—a very long and minute one which I hope will have come safely to her hands before this. I am now about starting for Belgium and Holland whence I shall go to England reaching London in the last week of September, to embark for America on the 6th of October. I have remained in Paris till it seems a little dull to me, and I want to be moving again. Mr. Seymour[1] is here, and has been of much use to Mr. Leupp and myself. Mr. Chapman has also been very kind and hospitable to us. Albinola[2] is here also—I dined with him and Wright[3] & [others?] yesterday. I shall bring home some views of Switzerland which Chapman found for me.

Give my regards to Mrs. Kirkland and her daughters and Willie. Your

house has not been very lonesome this summer I think with such entertaining people as you have had for neighbours and inmates.

Yrs affectionately

W   C   BRYANT

MANUSCRIPT: NYPL–GR ADDRESS: To Julia Bryant.

1. Probably Daniel Seymour (d. 1850), a member of the Sketch Club and an honorary member of the National Academy of Design. NAD Exhibition Record, II, 117; information from James T. Callow.

2. G. Albinola has been identified only as a member of the Century Club from 1851 to 1870, when he resigned.

3. Probably Charles Cushing Wright (1796–1854), an engraver and medalist who was a founder of the National Academy and exhibited his work there and at the American Art-Union. From 1823 to 1827 he had been a member of the engraving firm of (Asher) Durand and Wright in New York, and he was long a member of the Sketch Club. DAA; NAD Exhibition Record, II, 217; information from James T. Callow.

707.   To Frances F. Bryant

London   September 28th   1849.

My dear Frances.

I have just arrived in this city from Belgium which I left this morning at half past twelve—it is now the same hour in the afternoon—travelling with all haste that I might learn whether a berth had been secured for me in the Niagara which leaves Liverpool on Saturday week and that I might answer any letters I might find here, in time to send off the answers by the steamer which departs tomorrow. In one respect my hopes have been fulfilled, in another they have not. A state room has been taken for us in the Niagara and we go out to America on the 6th of October. But I receive no letters from you nor any body else in America. Mr. Leupp has several brought by the last steamer. I hope however, to hear from you by the steamer which arrives the beginning of next week, and if I do, I shall bring the answer in person.

The Evening Post of the latest dates—September 7th and 11th, has come to hand and I perceive, by that, that the cholera has so greatly subsided that no more is thought of it than of any of the common distempers and that people are returning to the city and business is becoming active. I rejoice that this great fear is at length taken off from men's minds, and my thoughts recur again and again to the relief which you and all our friends must feel. Here to[o] the cholera, which has been more fatal than in New York, has abated so far that it no longer causes alarm. There are still deaths by it in Paris, and in many other cities of Europe—in Amsterdam for example where I was two days ago, but in no part of northern Europe, is it, I believe, at all the subject of much apprehension.

My journey to Belgium and Holland was as pleasant as fine weather could make it, but it was not particularly interesting to me. It was very

short, and most of the novelties which these two countries have to offer to one who merely goes to their principal cities and passes a day or two had been exhausted in my first visit. At Antwerp, however, I saw an exhibition of modern paintings like the exhibitions of our Academy of Design; and a very fine one it was, better than any I have ever seen abroad, though I have seen two Academical Exhibitions in London, one in Paris, the present season, two at different times in Florence, one at Vienna and one at Naples. The exhibition was a large one, the proportion of decidedly bad pictures small, and the number of really good ones very considerable. The Flemings I find, keep their ancient skill in the art, if not their ancient reknown. It was the last day of the exhibition, the rooms were crowded, and I had the opportunity of observing the physiognomy and personal appearance of the Flemish race under its best aspect, and the result of my observation was favorable. They are a good looking healthy looking race, and their physiognomy certainly comes nearer to that of our branch of the human family than the German does. There were a good many people in the country garb among the crowd.

At Brussels where we arrived on the same day that we left Paris, we called on Mr. Clemson the American minister.[1] He has been a Professor of chemistry in the University of Paris, but his conversation does not strike one as that of a highly educated or intellectual man. His wife, however who is a daughter of John C. Calhoun appears to have much the most talent of the two—at all events is much the better talker. It was but an hour before we called upon them, entirely unexpected that she had been reading with her children my poem of the Death of the Flowers. In the evening we saw at Mr. Clemson's, two of the present Flemish artists, Robbe[2] whom his friends claim as the best cattle-painter living, and Eckhout,[3] who is a portrait painter and a painter of cabinet pieces—domestic scenes after the manner of the old Flemish masters. Mr. Leupp ordered two pictures of Robbe, and afterwards bought a picture by Eckhout, and a very fine one, of Mr. Vesey the American consul at Antwerp, by whom, let me say by the way, we were very kindly received.[4]

Holland is as poor, as dear and as green as ever. Not a touch seems to have been given to Amsterdam since we were there four years ago. There are the same girls, the neatest cleanest looking creatures in the world, with the whitest caps and the purest complexions, and some of them exceedingly pretty stooping and wiping the pavement with wet cloths, and there is the same long row of strong, clumsy vessels idly moored along the curving edge of the huge basin in which they lie. Of the two hundred and sixty thousand people who make the population of Amsterdam, eighty thousand I was told are supported either wholly or partly by charity. A good deal of this charity is voluntary, and our *valet de place* told us, that in providing for these poor the Catholics of Amsterdam were the least liberal of all the religious denominations.

At Amsterdam we saw what we were not able to see when we visited it before, the Museum, a collection of pictures belonging to the public, quite large and containing some of the very finest things of the old Flemish masters. We obtained also permission to see the collection of Van der Hoop,[5] the banker which [is][6] an exceedingly choice one, and for a private collection quite ample. There is scarce any of the old Flemish painters of any note of whom there are not specimens of his best things.

In returning from Rotterdam to Antwerp I saw what might be called the original material out of which Holland was made. This part of the journey is performed in steamers, which run when the tide serves; often in the night, when you are accommodated, instead of a berth, with a sleeping place on a narrow bench covered with hair cloth, there are no sheets of course. We went on board at Rotterdam late in the evening, and about half past one in the morning the steamer left the wharf. After proceeding a little way the captain stopped her on account of the fog and she remained motionless till morning. With daylight we were again on our way and after winding through various narrow channels between rows of houses willows and windmills, we entered upon a broad expanse of water, with distant shores in sight and channels marked out for the shipping by buoys and poles planted in the sand. Once or twice our steamer touched the ground but was got off again, but finally about twelve o'clock she struck and would go no further. We remained on the spot for several hours; the tide fell till we saw nothing for miles around us but bare dark-looking flats intersected with watercourses looking like large brooks. If on the margins of these water courses banks were to be erected ten or fifteen feet in height, it would do for these flats what the dykes have done for the greater part of Holland and would reclaim them from the dominance of the sea. I suppose that the greater part of that country was at an early period much like the bare oozy waste which I saw about me.

In consequence of the delay occasioned in the manner I have related I did not reach Antwerp till eleven o'clock at night instead of ten o'clock in the morning as I had expected. This occasioned the loss of a day in our journey to London. We took the railway to Brussels the next morning, and in the evening took the railway from Brussels to Ostend. From Ostend a steamer, a little light vessel with no accommodations for sleeping brought us in the night to Dover, and a most uncomfortable night it was. Towards morning the motion made me very sick but the voyage lasted but five hours and a half, and after showing our baggage to the custom house officers, we took the railway to London at eight o'clock. If this letter is a stupid one, as part of it is I am sure, you must ascribe something to the sea sickness with which I am giddy yet.

For the last three weeks I have not wished you to be with me—you will excuse my frankness—but I have wished to be with you on Long Is-

land. A few days I hope will realize the wish. In a week after receiving this letter you will probably see me, very glad to get home again, and to see you all as I pray that I may be permitted to do as well at least as when I sailed for Europe.

I have bought a microscope at Paris, a very good instrument of the kind, which Mr. Seymour who sails today from Havre in a packet ship belonging to one of the lines is kind enough to take charge of. I shall perhaps be in New York before him. Mr. Leupp has remembered you, as you will see when I return. Remember me most kindly to Mrs. Kirkland and her family— Love to Fanny and Julia. Miss Robbins I suppose is gone by this time; if not tell her that I will inquire particularly concerning Mr. Delft[7] and his family before leaving London.

Yours ever

W. C. BRYANT

MANUSCRIPT: NYPL–GR.

1. Thomas Green Clemson (1807–1888), by profession a mining engineer. Through his bequest, Clemson Agricultural College was founded in 1889 on the site of John C. Calhoun's South Carolina plantation.
2. Louis Marie Dominique Romain Robbe (1800–1887).
3. Jakob Joseph Eeckhout (1793–1861).
4. William Henry Vesey of New York was United States consul at Antwerp, 1847–1853. *U. S. Consular Officers, 1789–1939.* See also 974.5.
5. Not further identified.
6. Word omitted.
7. Unidentified.

708. *To* John Bigelow[1]

New York   Friday   Nov. 2   1849

Dear sir

Mr. D[oherty][2] called yesterday according to his appointment. He declined the offer of $12—which I made him—said that Hallock[3] had paid him at the rate of $500 a year, and talked of wanting $900— I did not feel authorized to make any other arrangement without further consultation. We had a long talk as to what was expected of him if he came &c. and he is to call on you on Monday morning. I think well of his capacity, if he would exert it industriously, and would be willing myself to give him what he had at the Journal of Commerce rather than not have him.

He had scarcely gone out, however, before another man presented himself, Geo. W. Peck,[4] who said he knew you, and who is much in want of occupation. He was at one time employed on the Courier[5] where they paid him ten dollars a week and employed him to read proof and to do all kinds of things that were required. His politics are not of our sort, and he is I fear of a temper which imagines slights when they are not intended,

but I am inclined to believe he is diligent, and he is certainly very well educated, and has a good deal of literary expertness. He asked when you would be in town and is to call some time on Monday morning.

I will give you a *carte blanche* to make any arrangement with Doherty you think just and judicious—but I must have a talk about our Montreal correspondent who costs us I believe ten dollars a week.

Yrs truly
W. C. BRYANT

MANUSCRIPT: NYPL–GR.

1. A year earlier three-tenths of the shares in the *EP* had been transferred from William G. Boggs (341.2) to John Bigelow (1817–1911), a New York lawyer who had previously contributed to the newspaper articles and editorials on constitutional matters. Bigelow, *Retrospections*, I, 73–79; 615.1.

2. Not further identified.

3. Gerard Hallock (1800–1866), editor of the *New York Journal of Commerce*, 1828–1861.

4. George Washington Peck; see 647.4.

5. The New York *Courier and Enquirer*, edited by James Watson Webb. See 212.2.

709.   *To* Leonice M. S. Moulton

New York   November 14th. 1849.

My dear Mrs. Moulton.

I did receive your note from Duxbury, for which I was greatly obliged to you. It was considerably longer than your first, and I was glad to hear of your pleasant visit to Roslyn, and your still pleasanter rambles in the region where you were born and which I am sure was glad to see you again. You are one of the few friends who took the trouble to write to me while I was abroad, and to whom, accordingly I cherish a special gratitude. I wrote to you, in my last, that I brought away no memorial of the Shetlands, but I quite forgot a small parcel of little shells which I gathered on the shore of the strait which divides the island of Bressay from that of the Noss, with the waters of the North Sea—clear green waters—dashing at my feet. One of them is yours, and if you are good a sprig of heath, from the summit of the Righi shall be added thereunto.

I am afraid you were not accurately informed concerning the disconsolateness of the *Frau*. I found her in tolerable health, though she has been far from well during the summer; but she seemed quite sick of our place at Roslyn which I was sorry for as I hoped to pass many pleasant days there yet. However, I succeeded in reconciling her so far to the place that she passed a whole day with me in planting and transplanting trees shrubs and roses. In the course of another season the cure, I trust, will be complete.

We have pleasant rooms in New York, at No. 263 Greene Street where

we shall expect to see you often when you come to town. At present we have nothing to plague us but the marriage of Victoria Gibson[1] to a young Scotchman, Mr. Campbell, son of a *millionaire*.[2] Julia is to be one of the bridesmaids, and we are all in a bustle to equip her for the occasion. The ceremony is to be performed tomorrow at twelve o'clock at the Ascension church, after which the couple will set out upon their travels.

We are glad that you find yourself so much the better for your residence in New England. When you return to town we shall expect to see you amplified from a Sylph to a Juno. You *do* mean to come back, I suppose, sometime or other, notwithstanding that you say nothing about it in your letter, and when I see you I will tell you what I think of the *crumb* you speak of.

My wife desires her love. She has been either very busy or else sick all summer, which is her apology for not answering your lively and witty letter—you always write to her in your sprightly vein and keep your gravity for me.

Yours faithfully
WM C. BRYANT.

MANUSCRIPT: NYPL–Bryant-Moulton Letters.

1. See 502.3.
2. During a trip abroad with her father in 1867, Julia Bryant visited her former schoolmate Victoria and her husband at 6 Clarendon Crescent, Edinburgh. Bryant to John Durand, June 23, 1867, NYPL–Berg.

710. *To* Richard H. Dana

New York   November 15, 1849.

Dear Dana.

We took your hint, and drank your health today and wished you many more birth days; all as pleasant as this, which is one of the most beautiful and sunshiny of our autumnal days. The grass in the fields is almost as green as ever and the willows have lost scarce any of their leaves. You are a November birth as well as myself I find, only twelve days later in the season.

We have pleasant rooms in town, and though we have not quite broken up housekeeping in the country we have been passing a few days here and shall be here next week, including Friday and Saturday and the Sunday following. You can come directly to *263 Greene Street, near Eighth Street*, where there is a room in which you can have a fire, and the "lady as keeps the house" will give you your meals at the same table with us—we have a separate table. If by any casualty, which is not at all likely, the room with a fireplace should be occupied when you arrive there is another room without one, in which you could make yourself comfortable for two or three nights, and our own parlour shall be yours while you stay. My wife

has arranged all these matters for you in case you have not another place engaged.

I have several times thought of what you counsel me to do in regard to the publication of my letters. They have, I know been received in rather a friendly manner by readers, and this is what made me think of reprinting them—but when I look them over it does not appear to me that there is much in them. I shall, however, turn the thing over again in my mind now that you advise me to publish them.[1]

They tell me that you have been busy in preparing your works for the press, and I think you have done well. If nothing else comes of it, I shall get back the copy I lent to Park Benjamin,[2] and get it back with interest. It is high time that we had another edition of your writings, for your fame is much wider and more deeply rooted than when the first appeared, and whereas you then belonged to New England you now belong to the United States. I am glad that you are to lecture in Philadelphia. Besides the immediate good it will do to those who hear you, it will increase the demand for your book. As you go to Philadelphia early in the season, you may pass on further south as the weather grows colder, repeat your lectures in Baltimore, and even find yourself in South Carolina, where the rice-birds, and bobo'lincolns pass the winter.[3]

I have had in some respects a pleasant time of it abroad, and have come back a little stouter and a good deal stronger—with a stock of health, I hope to last for some months. But I will talk over these and other matters with you when you come.[4]

Faithfully yours

WM   C. BRYANT.

MANUSCRIPT: NYPL–GR DOCKETED: Wm. C. Bryant / Novr 15/49.

1. These letters, published in the *EP* between 1834 and 1849, were gathered in *Letters of a Traveller; or, Notes of Things Seen in Europe and America* (New York: Putnam, 1850).

2. Park Benjamin (1809–1864, Trinity 1829), a New York newspaper and magazine editor, and a minor poet.

3. Bryant may have tried that fall, through William Gilmore Simms, to arrange a lecture engagement for Dana in Charleston. Simms wrote from Woodlands to the painter Charles Fraser (1782–1860) in that city that "steps ought to be taken immediately to invite Mr. Dana" to lecture on Shakespeare. But Fraser "wrote a very chilling reply, on December 20, 1849, saying that Dana's whole object was to levy a contribution on the South 'in pursuance of a system in which the scholar and mechanic of New England are always alike happy to exert their best efforts.'" William P. Trent, *William Gilmore Simms*, "American Men of Letters" (Boston and New York, 1892), p. 157. Trent attributes this attitude to a "growing feeling of hostility in Carolina to anything hailing from New England," which is the more surprising in Fraser's case, since he had been a close friend of Dana's brother-in-law, the late Washington Allston. And he himself had paid many visits to the North, where his works were exhibited at the Boston Athenaeum, as well as at the National Academy, of which he had long been an honorary member,

and at the American Art-Union. *DAA*; *NAD Exhibition Record*, I, 168; Cowdrey, *AAFA & AAU*, II, 138.

4. Dana apparently visited the Bryants the following week; he and Bryant attended a Sketch Club meeting on November 23 at the home of Dudley B. Fuller. Information from James T. Callow.

711.   *To* Messrs. Carey & Hart

New York   Nov   24   1849.

Gentlemen.

Please send me one copy of the illustrated edition of my poems and three copies of the cheap edition,[1] with a bill which I will discharge by return mail.

About a year since in a letter to me you said you hoped to get out another edition of my poems for the holidays. I have heard of no new edition since that time. I hope the demand for the book has not ceased. If it has not, I should be much [pleased?][2] to know that the previous edition has been cleared off and that there is room for another.

I am gentlemen
Yours respectfully
WM C. BRYANT

MANUSCRIPT: DuU ADDRESS: To Messrs Carey & Hart ENDORSED: 250 fine — 125 / 500 cheap 62.50 / 250 cheap 31.25 / —— / $218.75.

1. See Letters 594, 642.
2. Word omitted.

712.   *To* Abraham Hart

New York   December 3, 1849.

Sir.

I got your letter[1] and the four copies of my poems this morning, and remit you five dollars, the amount of your account, which please return to me receipted.

I shall immediately draw on Carey & Hart for the $218.75 due on the thousand copies of my poems published since the last settlement. Mean time I am much obliged to you for your attention to my letter.

Yrs truly
W   C   BRYANT

MANUSCRIPT: HSPa ADDRESS: A. Hart Esq. / [late Carey & Hart] / Bookseller / Philadelphia POSTMARK: [New York] / 3 / DEC POSTAL ANNOTATION: PAID.

1. Unrecovered.

XV

Retrospections and Projections
1850–1852
(LETTERS 713 TO 809)

ENTERING THE YEAR 1850, Bryant had reason for satisfaction in the condition of his newspaper and the performance of his partner Bigelow. Early that year the firm moved into a larger building nearby and installed a high-speed Hoe press. The third partner, Timothy Howe, was persuaded to relinquish the management of business affairs to Isaac Henderson, a bookkeeper who had developed a profitable job printing office as an annex to the paper. As the year opened Charles Francis Adams of Boston, renewing his annual subscription, called the *Evening Post* "the best daily journal in the United States."

After a visit to the island of Jamaica in January and February, Bigelow wrote a series of letters for the paper on the condition of Negroes in this former slave colony sixteen years after their emancipation, and he soon began to compose weekly interviews with "John Brown, the Jersey Ferryman," whose reports of eavesdropping on his politician passengers carried inside information given Bigelow by his friends Charles Sumner, Samuel Tilden, and other Free Soil leaders. The newspaper also carried articles by Adams, Thomas Hart Benton, Salmon P. Chase, and Gideon Welles. A different sort of contributor in 1850–1851 was the former editor of the *Brooklyn Eagle*, Walt Whitman, who wrote on art and civic improvements in Brooklyn, and several "Letters from Paumanok" describing the summer delights of eastern Long Island.

During much of the year Bryant drew editorial strictures on the compromise, introduced in Congress by Henry Clay and supported by Daniel Webster, which would admit California as a free state provided territories should be organized in New Mexico and Utah without provision against slavery, which would be continued in the District of Columbia. The final bill—anathema to Bryant and other Free Soilers—would replace an ineffective Fugitive Slave Law with a stringent one which empowered federal marshals to recapture runaways in northern states. Bryant cited Webster's flat statement in the Senate only two years earlier, "I shall oppose all slavery extension and all increase of slave representation in all places, at all times, under all circumstances," charging the Massachusetts senator with a "traitorous retreat" from principle.

Though Bryant published no original verse during this period, his poetic reputation grew steadily, at home and abroad. Fenimore Cooper said he "always put him at the head" of American literature. Nathaniel Hawthorne, who might have occupied a summer home near Bryant's in Roslyn in 1850, joined Oliver Wendell Holmes and Herman Melville that summer at a picnic on Monument Mountain in the Berkshires, where they listened to a recitation of Bryant's verse tale of a lovelorn Indian maiden who leaped from its summit, and later they toasted the "dear old poet" in champagne. Edgar Allan Poe's mother-in-

law, Maria Clemm, begged an inscribed copy of Bryant's *Poems*, for, she wrote, "There are so many beautiful things in that book which my dear son has so often recited to me." In the volume which he sent her she underscored two poems to which the late Poe had accorded special praise, "June," and "The Death of the Flowers." Bryant's collected poems were published in 1850 at London and Liverpool; in the second instance he was described as the "most popular of American poets," in England as well as in his own country. At times, however, his politics got in the way of his poetic reputation. Southern editor Thomas Ritchie refused to print in his Washington *Union* a favorable notice of a book dedicated to Bryant. An historian of Long Island sketched the poet's biography in unflattering terms, concluding, "It is to be regretted that he should . . . prostitute his fine talents and improved taste to the humiliating pursuit of party politics, . . . in the advocacy of doctrines and measures worthless in themselves and injurious in their operation and tendency to the best interests of the country."

During this period Bryant lost a number of close friends, most through death, and in one instance as a result of the most sensational divorce in New York's history. The actor Edwin Forrest and his English wife, Catherine, had been intimates of the Bryants' since their marriage in 1837. When the couple separated in 1849 amid charges of infidelity, Mrs. Forrest fled to the home of Fanny and Parke Godwin. Early in 1850 Bryant was asked to arrange amicable terms for divorce, an effort which failed. In 1852, after widely publicized court proceedings at which Bryant and the Godwins testified, the suit started by Forrest ended in his wife's favor. The actor alienated many of his friends by threatening Godwin in Bryant's presence, and by attacking Nathaniel Parker Willis in public. Although Bryant seems to have taken no sides in the case, and was eulogized at the trial's conclusion as "a man [who,] all parties in this case . . . have united to say, is a model of all that is morally worthy in public and in private," it is evident that he saw little or nothing afterward of either party.

Fenimore Cooper died in September 1851, and Bryant was asked by the novelist's friends to offer a public eulogy the following February. Though they had never been very close, the two men had held each other in high respect for nearly thirty years. Bryant's warm but judicious appraisal of his friend's genius was widely applauded; Charles Sumner wrote a day or two later, "it will be a more durable monument to Cooper than any other." A present-day critic remarks that it "has been the source both for the facts of Cooper's life and for a keen analysis of his writing." Later that fall, with the death of his aunt Charity Bryant, Bryant's last link with his parents' generation was broken. He was on a short visit in Illinois when these deaths occurred, and soon after his return he learned of a third, that of his British friend David Christie, who had been extremely attentive during Bryant's visits to England in 1845 and 1849. In February 1852 William Ware, who had become Bryant's pastor when he settled in New York in 1825 and remained a revered friend, died in Cambridge, where the Bryants had visited him. In July a tragic accident took the life of the brilliant young landscape architect and cottage designer Andrew Jackson Downing, who, it has been aptly said, "made over the face of rural America." Only thirty-seven, at the height of his career, Downing drowned during a steamboat fire on the Hudson River as a result of his repeated attempts to save his fellow-passengers. He had, Bryant wrote the next day, "made himself a high reputation in the

peculiar walk of art to which he had devoted his life," and "few will be more generally deplored." The last sad loss of 1852 was in the death of Horatio Greenough soon after Bryant left in November on his journey to the Middle East.

Bryant must have lingered over other memories as he searched the files of the *Evening Post* for the past fifteen years, preparing his collection, *Letters of a Traveller* (1850), and those of half a century for his *Reminiscences of the Evening Post* (1851), his account of the newspaper's history on its fiftieth anniversary. These were his only separate publications during this period.

By mid-century Bryant's poems as well as his person had become frequent subjects for interpretation by artists. In 1849 Asher Durand exhibited, at the National Academy, "A Pastoral Landscape," on the theme of Bryant's "Green River" (1821), and in 1850 two of his most successful paintings, "Landscape, Summer Morning"—later called "Early Morning at Cold Spring"—after "A Scene on the Banks of the Hudson" (1828), and "Landscape, Scene from 'Thanatopsis.'" In 1849 Emma Stebbins worked on an "illumination" of "Thanatopsis," and John James Audubon's son Victor illustrated "The Murdered Traveller" (1825). Notes on these works in exhibition catalogues included quotations from Bryant's verses. Two portraits of 1850 are good of Bryant in middle age: Henry Kirke Brown's marble bust, and Henry Peters Gray's oil painting, one of four portraits of its presidents commissioned by the American Art-Union. Others were done during this period by Charles G. Crehen, Peter Paul Duggan, and Daniel Huntington—the last a group portrait of Bryant, Irving, and Webster at the Cooper memorial in 1852.

Bryant's kinship with the arts was generously recognized by their practitioners. Thanking him for presiding over the annual meeting of the International Art Union, its French director, Theodore Vibert, remarked on the "general esteem which your admirable talent and your honourable character inspire." Thomas Cole's first biographer, Louis Noble, dedicated his book to Bryant. Sculptor Hiram Powers wrote from Florence of his wish to "stand well in the opinion of a man who has won overlasting fame for himself, and added so much glory to our common country." During the last two years of his life Horatio Greenough confided to Bryant some of the aesthetic theories later set forth in *The Travels, Observations, and Experience of a Yankee Stonecutter* (1852), and his elaborate dreams of monuments to Washington, Jackson, Cooper, and other great Americans.

In articles for his influential magazine, *The Horticulturalist*, in 1848, Downing had joined Bryant in urging the development of a large central park in New York City. The writings of these proponents proved effective when, in 1850, both candidates for mayor supported their proposals. In May 1851 the state legislature approved the site first suggested by Bryant in 1844, Jones's Woods, on the east side of Manhattan Island. Bryant stoutly advocated the plan, and refuted claims that it would be too costly. Although seven years would pass before work on Central Park was actively underway, its realization was assured.

In December 1851 Bryant presided at a banquet given by New York journalists to the Hungarian revolutionary Louis Kossuth. In his own toast to Kossuth, he pledged the American press to a prominent role in "this great attempt of man" against the "mightiest despotisms of the world" to "repossess himself of

the rights which God gave him." A few weeks before, discussing in the *Evening Post* the riots caused at Syracuse by marshals trying to enforce the Fugitive Slave Law, he declared, "It is the curse of this law that the people of the free states can never get reconciled to it. . . . The impulse toward freedom is one which no legislature can extinguish or control." On the paper's fiftieth anniversary he promised that it would "continue to battle for human rights in preference to human sovereignties." And, writing Senator Salmon P. Chase of Ohio of party struggles in New York, he concluded, "We must fight this battle, but we shall not neglect higher and more permanent questions. The controversy concerning slavery will be kept open, and nothing of the zeal of an opposition to the fugitive slave law and the kindred enormities will be abated." In August 1852, telling his brother John of his impatience with the sluggishness of Free Soil politicians and his consequent purpose to support the Democratic presidential candidate Franklin Pierce, Bryant commented, "I see not the least chance of a repeal or change of the fugitive slave law. Its fate is to fall into disuse. . . . We must make it odious, and prevent it from being enforced. That the *Evening Post* can do . . . just as effectively by supporting Pierce as Hale [the Free Soil candidate]." Bryant's return to the Democratic Party was no more than a reluctant expedient; in 1856 he would throw his growing influence behind the incipient Republican Party. But his course was the warrant of his political strength as well as his integrity. On the newspaper's fiftieth anniversary the Whig politician Hamilton Fish, now a United States senator from New York, had written that, "Although it has been my lot to differ in my views of many of the important questions which it has discussed from those which the Post has advanced, I have always admired the force, the ability & the fearlessness with which it has maintained its own views. I have appreciated the honesty with which it adopted those views however differing from my own."

713. *To* John G. Chapman

New York. January 10   1850.

My dear Sir.

I send you an appletree by [Asher] Durand which he copied from one of his studies, a little modified for the occasion. If you should see that it wants any further change, you of course are *padrone* [boss] as the Italians say and can adapt it to your purpose. It is a fine tree, and an old one.[1]

Along with this I send a daguerreotype likeness of myself in profile. It was not practicable to get a daguerreotype of the bust without a great deal of trouble, and the transportation of the bust to some distance. The daguerreotype takers would not carry their instruments to it for the reason that it was liable to put them out of order.[2]

The face on this profile is a little inclined towards the spectator, but of course you can make allowance for that.

I am glad to learn that you are domiciliated at last in the pleasant city of Florence among the remains of ancient art, and under that brilliant sky and in the midst of that picturesque scenery. My regards to Mrs. Chapman and love to the little ones.

Yours truly
W. C. BRYANT.

MANUSCRIPT: Unrecovered TEXT: *Century Magazine*, 50 (July 1895), 321.

1. Chapman was apparently then projecting a series of illustrations to accompany Bryant's poem "The Planting of the Apple Tree," composed in 1849 but unpublished until it appeared in the *Atlantic Monthly* in January 1864. At Paris Bryant had noted on September 12 that he had finished the poem and planned to show it to Chapman. "Diary, 1849"; *Poems* (1876), pp. 320–323. But by the time Bryant saw Chapman in Rome three years later, the artist had abandoned his project, explaining to the poet that he had "collected materials by different studies and planned several designs but finished none, on account of his engagements and his health." Bryant, "Diary, 1852–1853," May 15, 1853.

2. It is uncertain to which bust Bryant refers. That done by Henry Kirke Brown in 1849 (now in NYHS) seems the most likely possibility. The daguerreotype was apparently that which appeared with a facsimile of this letter in the *Century Magazine*, 50 (July 1895) [322].

714. *To* James Fenimore Cooper

[New York] January 31, 1850.

Dear Sir:

I am sorry not to find you in this morning, as I went to ask you to go to Mr. Leupp's tomorrow evening, No. 66 Amity Street, where the Sketch Club meet, and where you will probably find some of the members of the old Lunch, Mr. [Gulian] Verplanck, Mr. [Asher] Durand, and myself certainly, with several others of your acquaintance.[1]

Each member has the right to take any stranger who may be in town,

and Mr. Leupp I know would be offended with me if he knew I had seen or written to you, and did not ask you. I hope you will do us all the favour to come.

Yrs truly
W. C. BRYANT

MANUSCRIPT: Unrecovered TEXT: *Correspondence of James Fenimore Cooper*, ed. James Fenimore Cooper (New Haven: Yale University Press, 1922), II, 655–656.

1. Cooper was then staying at the Globe Hotel at 66 Broadway, as he did often when in New York City. Cooper, *Letters & Journals*, VI, 85, 121. Although no reply to Bryant's invitation has been found, the minutes of the Sketch Club for February 1 indicate that Cooper did not attend the meeting at Charles Leupp's home that evening. Information from James T. Callow.

715. *To* Oliver C. Gardiner[1]

New York   March 27   1850

Dear Sir.

You desired me to inquire whether there were any places at Roslyn to let for the summer or the year.

A gentleman, Mr. A. W. Leggett[2] has a little cottage which he would partly furnish and let for $80.—It has a garden.

There is another house, intended for two families—having two kitchens, a very large house and finely situated, which without any furniture might be had for from 75 to 100 dollars, with garden &c.

Yrs truly
W. C BRYANT[3]

MANUSCRIPT: HEHL.

1. Oliver Cromwell Gardiner (642.1) had written a study of the Free Soil movement which was published in 1848 under the imprint of W. C. Bryant and Company, entitled *The Great Issue; or, The Three Presidential Candidates; Being a Brief Historical Sketch of the Free Soil Question in the United States from the Congresses of 1774 and '87 to the Present Time.*
2. Augustus W. Leggett; see 648.2.
3. No reply to this letter has been found, but it is evident in a letter from Nathaniel Hawthorne to Gardiner dated at Salem on April 3, 1850, that Gardiner had undertaken to find a summer home for the novelist, who had just published *The Scarlet Letter.* Hawthorne wrote him, "Sometime before your letter reached me, I had engaged a house at Lenox [Massachusetts]; otherwise, I think I should have been tempted by the cheapness of the rents, and other desirabilities, at Roslyn." MS in St. Lawrence University Library.

716. *To* Frances F. Bryant

New York   Thursday   March 28, 1850.

My dear Frances.

After I left you on Wednesday morning I recollected, to my great

vexation, that I did not make you promise to write. You will write, however, I am sure. I am anxious to know whether you made your journey comfortably in this storm[1]—for though it did not snow much the day you left us, the snow began to fall some time last night and has fallen all the morning till now—about two o'clock.

I bought an umbrella yesterday as a protection, and when I got home Julia informed me that one of the missing ones had been discovered at Mrs. Gibson's. It was brought to me in the afternoon, and proved to be the brown gingham one; the other I fear is too valuable to be found.

It was precisely seven o'clock and no more, when the coachman set me down yesterday at my door in Greene Street. I breakfasted and went to the Doctor's. He did nothing, but gave me another dose of medicine and bid me call in the evening when he would puncture the gum. In the evening I called again—another dose of medicine and a direction to call this morning. The pain left me last evening—and I had a comfortable night, and a long sleep. When I called on Gray this morning he told me that the tooth would now take care of itself and declined making any incision.

Fanny was not quite so well yesterday as usual, but today she is better again.

This morning the whole testimony in the Forrest case is published in the Herald. There is a bill before the Pennsylvania Senate for giving the Circuit Court of the state, authority to hear and decide the suit for a divorce. On the question of passing this bill, the votes stood 16 to 16; so the bill was lost. But Mr. Parker one of the members moved a reconsideration of the vote, and the question will come up again. Before taking the vote the affidavits and other documents were read in open Senate. Probably some of the other papers here, the Sunday papers certainly, will publish the testimony. I must get a copy and send you.[2]

Now, you will not neglect to write. If you do, I must see what I can do by stopping supplies, that is, newspapers &c.

This morning a letter from Dr. Tobey of Rochester came for you.

Remember me kindly to all our friends in Bloomfield, Rochester and elsewhere.

Yours affectionately
WM C. BRYANT.

MANUSCRIPT: NYPL–GR.

1. Frances was then on a brief visit to her relatives in western New York State, returning within the week. See Letter 718.

2. A "Proposed Agreement," drafted in Bryant's handwriting, indicates that he tried, about this time, to arrange an amicable separation between Edwin Forrest and Catherine Sinclair Forrest, an effort which he later wrote William Gilmore Simms was broken off. See 665.3; Letter 760.

717. *To* Orville Dewey

Roslyn, March 29, 1850.

. . . Your letter was read by me to the Sketch Club, at Mr. William Kemble's,[1] a fortnight ago last evening, and received with clapping of hands. All expressed their satisfaction at the invitation, and all are coming.[2] How many will come you will probably know on the day appointed. The secretary made a note of it in due form. I offered to add something to the letter by way of commentary or explanation, but not a word was I allowed to say; the members were so well pleased with the letter they would suffer nothing to take the taste of it out of their mouths. With Mr. Durand I have especially conferred, and Mr. Durand has specially promised to be one of the party.

Now, I really hope that you will see that the country is in its best trim on the occasion; that there be no late frosts to spoil the freshness of early summer, that just at the time the roads be in good order, the weather fair and not too hot or too cold, and the atmosphere reasonably clear. It will not be amiss if there should have been a pretty copious shower the night before, just to lay the dust. I mention these things because you who live in the country are very apt to fall into the habit of taking them as they come, and neglect them very much. . . .

MANUSCRIPT: Unrecovered TEXT (*partial*): *Life*, II, 52.

1. William Kemble (1795?–1881), a Sketch Club member then living at 24 Beach Street, was a founder of the Century Association and an amateur member of the National Academy. He was the secretary of the West Point Foundry, with offices at 79 West Street. Kemble was a generous patron of American artists. *NAD Exhibition Record*, I, 274; II, 296. Further information from James T. Callow.

2. Dewey had written Bryant on February 25 asking him to relay an invitation to Sketch Club members to meet at the Dewey home in Sheffield, Massachusetts, on June 19, and proposing that they pass the following day "among the mountains,—seeing Bash-Pish [Falls] and, if possible, the Salisbury." Quoted in *Autobiography and Letters of Orville Dewey, D.D.*, ed. Mary E. Dewey (Boston, 1884), pp. 215–216. However, the surviving minutes of the Sketch Club do not record a meeting that summer at Dewey's. Information from James T. Callow.

718. *To* Orville Dewey

New York   April 8, 1850.

My dear Sir.

Lest you should rashly enter into some other engagement, I write this to tell you that the Academy of Design will have its private exhibition on Friday or Saturday evening next, when the members all hope to see you.[1] They have found the trouble of getting into the new gallery and making all the necessary arrangements so great that they have been obliged to post

pone the *probable* day of opening from one time to another, but beyond the times I have mentioned they are resolved it shall not be deferred.[2]

If I learn any thing more precise in season, I will write you again. If you do not hear from me, however, I hope you will come down on Friday which will allow you to be present either on Friday or Saturday evening.

Yrs truly
W C BRYANT.

P.S. Your sister was here yesterday[3] very well and in good spirits—My wife came back safe and sound at twelve o'clock the other night. Regards to all.

W. C. B.

MANUSCRIPT: NYPL–GR (draft?) ADDRESS: Rev. O. Dewey.

1. A feature of this exhibition was Asher Durand's large canvas "Landscape—Scene from 'Thanatopsis,'" introduced in the catalogue by nine lines from Bryant's poem beginning "The hills / Rock-ribbed and ancient as the sun. . . ." This painting is now in the Metropolitan Museum of Art. *NAD Exhibition Record*, I, 139; Albert Ten Eyck Gardner and Stuart P. Feld, *American Paintings: A Catalogue of the Collection of the Metropolitan Museum of Art. I. Painters Born by 1815* (New York: The Metropolitan Museum of Art [1965]), p. 211.

2. In 1849 the National Academy occupied a new building on the west side of Broadway south of Amity Street, the cost of which was largely underwritten by Charles M. Leupp and Jonathan Sturges. *Morse Exhibition of Arts and Science Presented by National Academy of Design . . . January 18 to February 28, 1950* ([New York: National Academy of Design, 1950]), p. 23.

3. Dr. Dewey's unmarried sister Jerusha, long a friend of the Bryants', later occupied a cottage on their Roslyn property. Goddard, *Roslyn Harbor*, pp. 70–72.

719.   *To* Edward A. Stansbury[1]

New York April 10th. 1850.
Office of the Evening Post

My dear sir.

Sometime since a prospectus was issued by the proprietors of this paper at the close of which they offered that if any weekly journal would give it three insertions, the daily edition of the Evening Post should be sent to it for one year as a compensation. We have since given our prospectus another form and made it considerably longer. With a slight change at the commencement we have made it into a circular, which you will find on the outer leaf of this sheet.[2] We have not offered to make the same terms in regard to it as with regard to the other prospectus, but if you will publish it in the Burlington Courier as many times as you think our paper is worth for one year, we will send you the daily.

I have made a slight change in the first sentence of the paper, to adapt it to the purpose of an advertisement and have ordered the Daily Evng Post to be sent to the address of the Burlington Courier.

Yrs truly
WM C. BRYANT

MANUSCRIPT: DuU ADDRESS: E. A. Stansbury Esq.

1. Edward A. Stansbury (1817?–1873), a journalist who for some time practiced law in New York, was then apparently editing the Burlington, Vermont, *Courier*, a Free Soil weekly. Franklin B. Hough, *American Biographical Notes . . .* (Albany, 1875), p. 375.

2. Unrecovered.

720. *To* John Ellis Wool[1]

New York   April 15, 1850.

My dear sir.

I am sorry that I have missed your communications on account of my supposed absence from the paper. The article from the Kentucky paper you will see I have inserted in the Evening Post.[2] In looking it over this afternoon I find that some typographical errors have crept into it which are to be amended in the edition for the country. It does you what I believe will be acknowledged to be no more than bare justice.

As to the proper time for the appearance of the history of the Battle of Buena Vista, I am rather inclined to think with such of your friends as advise a postponement of it. It is very likely that the period will by and by arrive when there will be less objection on the part of many to see a full and impartial discussion of the degree of credit due to the different commanders on that occasion than there now is, and there certainly is less bigotry now in regard to General Taylor than there was a year or two since.[3]

Yrs truly
WM C. BRYANT

MANUSCRIPT: UVa ADDRESS: Genl Jno E. Wool.

1. See 563.3.

2. "General Wool in Mexico," *EP*, April 15, 1850.

3. General Wool, whose "celerity and efficiency were largely responsible for the victory of Buena Vista," fought between Americans and Mexicans on February 22–23, 1847, was later given a sword and the thanks of the United States Congress for his "skill, enterprise and courage" in that battle (*Dictionary of American Biography*). In the article cited by Bryant, a former officer under Wool's command wrote, "[Zachary] Taylor and [Winfield] Scott and Wool are the leading heroes of this war. The first two we have seen, as party dictated, raised or depressed, while the latter, because separate from party factions, has failed to receive that just meed which is his due." In 1848 Scott had failed to win the Whig presidential nomination from Taylor, who had gone on to win the presidency.

721. *To* Cyrus Bryant

New York   April 22   1850.

Dear Brother.

When I went the other day to see to the stopping of Merry's Museum[1] they told me that it had been paid for in advance for some time to come, and would be stopped, according to the usage of the proprietors, as soon

as the term was out. They only forward the periodical to those who pay in advance. As to Holden's Magazine,[2] it is not exactly the thing, but I do not know of any dollar magazine which is. Chambers's Edinburg[h] Magazine[3] is much better but it is dearer.

You have seen, I suppose that the Weekly Evening Post is enlarged. This makes its publication more expensive, of course, so much so as to leave a very slender profit, and if the circulation be not considerably increased by it, the change will prove to be a great mistake. We are in hopes, however, that the number of subscribers will be greatly increased.[4] We are getting additions by every mail. If the cheapest newspaper has the largest sale as is reasonable to expect, there should be no doubt of our success, for the Evening Post, if the quantity of its reading matter be considered is the cheapest paper in the United States, and, of course, the cheapest in the world.

I am publishing a book, as I suppose you know. It will contain such letters as I wrote last summer,—there were four of them in all—for the Evening Post. I am mistaken—one of them, a merely political letter is omitted.[5]—It will contain besides, those from Cuba, those from Florida and the other parts of the South; a dozen or thereabouts from the west, and those written and published during my other two visits to Europe, together with a few which have not before been printed. I expect it will be out in a day or two.

You mention my voyage to Europe. I was absent four months and one week. I saw some parts of Scotland which I had not visited before, besides the Shetlands; made a second visit to Holland and to Munich in Bavaria, saw the northern cities of Switzerland for the first time, climbed the Righi and returned by the way of Geneva and Lyons to Paris. With the exception of two or three of the first weeks in England, when I had the prevailing complaint, the diarrhoea, and was obliged to consult a physician—a homoeopathic one of course, Dr. Laurie[6]—my health was exceedingly good, and towards the end of my absence, I became almost, as it seemed to me, incapable of fatigue.

Our family are all well. I write this at Roslyn though I have dated it, from habit, at New York, where I expect to be tomorrow, and where this will be mailed. The weather just begins to be spring like; it has been extremely cold for the whole month hitherto, —a harsh temperature, with strong north-west winds. The peach trees are generally in bloom before this time, and my apricots have put out their flowers in some seasons nearly a month earlier, but not a blossom has yet shown itself.

Please hand the accompanying letter to John.[7] My regards to your wife and to the young gentlemen. Frances desires to be kindly remembered by you all.

Yrs affectionately
W C BRYANT.

MANUSCRIPT: BCHS ADDRESS: To Cyrus Bryant Esq.

1. See 413.5.
2. *Holden's Dollar Magazine,* a monthly published in New York, 1848–1851.
3. *Chambers's Edinburgh Journal,* 1832–1853.
4. The *EP* offices had recently been moved from 18 Nassau Street to larger quarters on the corner of Nassau and Liberty streets, with a new steam-driven Hoe press which facilitated the printing of larger sheets and greater daily runs. From this time on the paper's circulation steadily increased. Nevins, *Evening Post,* pp. 236–237; *EP,* March 22, 1847.
5. Letters 688, 690, 703, 705. The last of these was not reprinted in *LT* I.
6. See 687.4.
7. Letter 722.

722. *To* John Howard Bryant

New York   April 22, 1850.

Dear Brother,

Before this time I suppose you have my wife's letter, which I hope has convinced you that we had not quite forgotten you in this quarter. It was written I believe about the same time with yours to me.

With regard to my land, I am in no hurry to sell it. Say to those who call upon you, if you please, that I do not care to part with it at present.

I should like, however, by and by, when you and Mr. Olds are ready, to build another house upon the lot in the village which is now vacant. The payments from Galer,[1] who seems to be of the class of slow [coaches?], might be applied to that purpose, if he is ever to pay any thing more, and if any additional cash is necessary I might advance it.

I should have answered your letter[2] earlier, but that I was in town when it arrived and my notes of hand and other papers were in the country, so that I could not give you the information you desired. Your note is dated June 1, 1848, and is for five hundred dollars with seven per cent interest. There is an endorsement of which the following is a copy.

"Rec^d. on this note Dec. 1, 1848, two hundred and forty one dollars and one cent in building a stable and addition to a house. $241.01."—
From this I suppose you will be able to ascertain what you did with the wheat received from Galer in the year 1848. I shall be glad to receive the statement you speak of as soon as may suit your convenience to send it, and shall be obliged to you if you will consult with Mr. Olds and see if you can do any thing about building me another house. I suppose it ought to be a better one than the one built upon the other lot, inasmuch as the lot is in a more conspicuous situation, but on this point I desire your advice.

We are all quite well, my wife in better health than usual, and Julia too I believe. A few weeks ago I was nearly killed by a gumbile. Our poor aunt Mrs. Fish[3] died of a similar complaint in November, and I did not hear of it till the other day when I received a letter containing the history of her last moments from Elisha. The younger Mrs. Rankin[4] is now at

Brooklyn for medical advice. She visited aunt Charity last summer and found her and Miss Drake in comfortable health;—much more so than formerly. They had given up their habit of tea drinking, in which they once indulged immoderately, and were greatly better for the reformation. Edwin Bryant has lately returned from California, where he has made money by the rise in real estate, which he owned at the time of his first visit to the country.

We have just broken up our winter quarters in town and transplanted ourselves to the country—later than usual—but the season is late. We have had a very mild and pleasant winter; February as mild as April usually is, and more calm; but March has been colder, and April has been until now worse than March.

I am getting out a book, made up of my letters written during my travels, for the Evening Post, together with a few from the manuscript. It should have been out before this but for the delay of the printer.—

Remember me to your wife and boys. Frances desires her kind regards to you all. Yrs affectionately

W. C. BRYANT

MANUSCRIPT: NYPL–BFP ADDRESS: John H. Bryant Esq. / Princeton / Bureau County / Illinois.

1. See 597.7. For Justin H. Olds, see 520.1.
2. Unrecovered.
3. See 723.2.
4. See 772.2.

723.   *To* Elisha S. Fish[1]

Roslyn   Long Island   April 22   1850.

Dear Cousin.

I thank you for the interesting account you gave me of the last moments of my excellent aunt.[2] The news of her death I had not received before. It must have been a great consolation to you all that her departure was so calm and happy, and that she went to her rest in Christian hope. To me she always appeared to be one of those who "possess their souls in patience,"[3] a person "of a meek and quiet spirit"[4] and it seems fitting that so serene a death should crown a life which had always been so submissive to Providence. She had reached a patriarchal age, the age at which or about which the ancient prophets and leaders of Israel were allowed to depart. The period of probation and discipline which belongs to the natural term of human life was fully completed—more than completed—in her case, she had passed through all the stages of education for another state of being, and so far as that may assist in giving maturity to the powers of the soul, was fitted for the employments of the future life by all the preparation which this life could afford her.—

I am glad to hear in other respects of your continued welfare, and of the health of your family. You ought certainly to be healthy if a rational mode of living, conformed to the laws which God has established for the maintenance of the bodily powers in their vigour can make you so. I hope also that your affairs are prosperous.

My wife and I often speak of our visit to your place, and remember it with pleasure. Whether we ever repeat it or not, it is something to have made it, and for my part I remember the two or three days I passed there with a peculiar vividness. We shall all be glad to see yourself and Mrs. Fish and your daughters here, and will show you Long Island and make you as comfortable as it is in our power to do.

I write this at Roslyn on Long Island to which I have just come with my wife and where I am passing four or five days, getting our garden in order, and looking to our little place. But if you write to me, my proper address is always New York, to which you know all letters come more directly and speedily than to such a little place as this. Julia is still at New York engaged in her studies. It was a great pleasure to hear from you through your daughters, in their joint letter to Julia. She has often talked of answering it, and I shall have to scold her seriously if she defers it much longer.

With regard to David Nelson Harris I do not know that I can get the information you desire without going to Staten Island,[5] which is something of an expedition, but if I can learn any thing about him by any shorter process I will write to you again.

Remember me kindly to your wife and daughters, and to your sisters and to your brother if he is with you. My wife desires love to you all.

Yours
W C BRYANT

MANUSCRIPT: NYPL–GR (draft) ADDRESS: To my Cousin Elisha S. Fish.

1. See Letters 472, 465.
2. This was apparently Sarah Snell Bryant's elder sister, Abigail Snell Fish (b. 1764), the mother of Elisha S. Fish. See Sarah Snell Bryant to Cullen Bryant, June 12, 1833, NYPL–GR.
3. Luke 21:19.
4. I Peter 3:4.
5. Harris is unidentified.

724.   *To* Leonice M. S. Moulton

New York   May 21. 1850

. . . I send you along with this a copy of my letters[1] which I am glad to learn that you are disposed to receive so graciously.

The report which you mention as affecting my good name, does not disturb me. It is true enough that when I am at work in the garden I like to have Mrs. Bryant at my side, not on account of my ignorance of the

proper method of putting seeds into the ground, but for two other reasons. In the first place, I do not like to work in the garden alone. In the second place—and I am partly indebted to you for the discovery of the fact—I must do as my wife says, and how could that be if I had not her at hand to direct me.

In this chilly weather I suppose you do not regret your return to the city. Yet the cool days and nights have given a long blooming-time to the fruit trees, and with your keen enjoyment of the beautiful in nature, you could endure some inclemency of the weather for its sake. . . .[2]

MANUSCRIPT: Ridgely Family Collection TEXT: Hoyt, "Bryant Correspondence (I)," 64.

1. *LT* I.
2. The salutation, complimentary close, and signature have been deleted from the printed text.

725.   *To* Frances F. Bryant

New York   Wednesday   June 12th   1850.

Dear Frances.

I found this morning a letter from Mrs. Hinckley[1] for you, informing you that her daughter was now *really* recovering. Ellen she did not engage, having already made arrangements with another servant. The letter enquires anxiously about your health. In the course of the morning Mr. [Jonathan] Sturges called and confirmed the account of Miss Hinckley's improved health.

I had a call from another visitor, your cousin Elvira Fairchild, now Mrs. Hallett and a widow. She and her husband lived for some time among the Shakers, where he died, and with whom she remained till she got tired of them, and came away. She was in pursuit of her brother Edward who owes her fifty dollars, but he has removed from Brooklyn into the State of New Jersey, nobody knows to what particular place, and so she can neither find him nor the money. He has a son Edward somewhere in town a clerk with somebody but she does not know with whom. I recommended that she should write a note to him through the post-office. She is, as formerly, anxious for a *situation*, and would for the present assist in the care of any respectable family for her board, until a situation can be had. She inquired whether there was any vacancy in our family. Possibly she may come out to Roslyn yet.

Yours ever
W. C. B.

MANUSCRIPT: NYPL–GR.

1. Possibly Eliza H. Hinckley, who kept a boardinghouse at 2 Clinton Place. *Rode's New York City Directory for 1850–1851*, p. 244.

726. *To* Richard H. Dana

Roslyn, July 4th, 1850.

Dear Dana.

It is long since I have heard from you. I hope you are so comfortable somewhere, in this hot weather, that you have no occasion to go far either for occupation or entertainment, and therefore need not trouble yourself about your friends at a distance. I have been passing a few days at my place on Long Island, and tomorrow must go back, to the town—the foul, hot, noisy town. How it will smell of the tons of gunpowder that have been burnt in it today! I hear the thunder of its guns even here, but it does not disturb the birds. The fire-bird and the song-sparrow have been singing all day among my locusts and horse-chestnuts in spite of it.

We have quite given the world the go-by today. We have been no further than the garden, from the foot of which we saw in the morning, a sloop go down the bay, with a fiddle on board, and a score of young women in sunbonnets. Nobody has been to see us but a little boy of two years old, whom at his particular desire I took to the barn to see the pigs and chickens, and whom I was obliged to refresh with a liberal handful of cherries which I climbed the tree to gather. Between eleven and twelve o'clock I had rather a sweltering time in the garden gathering the first of the raspberries and the last of the strawberries. If we had a quiet friend or two like yourself, the day, I know, would pass more agreeably, but we get a good deal of contentment from it, as it is. And it is not wishing you any great ill-luck to wish you here, for the temperature all day has been delightful, and since two o'clock—it is now four—a fresh breeze has sprung up, full of spirit—which is now bringing in at the windows the scent of the flowers of early summer and some faint odour of the hayfields. If you care for sea-bathing, the tide is swelling up, and when it meets the grass, I think I shall take a plunge myself.

A copy of my Letters of a Traveller was sent to you some time since, from Putnam's who is my bookseller, and who seems to be a very well behaved man in his vocation. I hope you got it. You are the instigator of its publication, and if it be a bad book must bear your share of the blame.[1] I know very well that it is light matter, and that the world would be no wiser if it were to get it by heart, but I hope it will do no harm. It is a tolerably good book in the bookseller's sense of the phrase, for it sells pretty well. The periodical press has been civil to it, and Raymond of the Courier had the magnanimity to set the example of commending the style.[2]

Does it not make one egotistical to write letters? I am sure you must suspect this to be the case when you read mine.

It was well done of your son to give the world Mr. Allston's Lectures and Poems.[3] We wanted another edition of his poems which have been

long out of print, and the lectures were needed by our artists and our judges of art, to teach them how to think on such subjects, how to look at nature and how to compare nature with the representations of her on canvass.

This place is very beautiful just now. I think I never saw its vegetation so rich. Shall we never see you here again? My wife wants another chance to try to make you comfortable. She desires to be very kindly remembered. Our regards to your daughter and sisters. Mrs. Ripley[4] is passing the 4th in this neighbourhood and is to take tea at Fanny's this afternoon.

Yours faithfully
WM C. BRYANT.

MANUSCRIPT: NYPL–GR (draft and final) ENDORSED: Wm C. Bryant, July 4/50 / Ans. July 31st. PUBLISHED (*in part*): *Life*, II, 52–53.

1. See Letter 710.

2. Henry Jarvis Raymond (1820–1869, Vermont 1840), once Horace Greeley's chief assistant on the New York *Tribune*, and since 1843 editor of another Whig paper, the *Morning Courier*, would become in 1851 a joint founder with George Jones (1811–1891) of *The New York Times*.

3. Washington Allston, *Lectures on Art, and Poems* . . . , ed. R. H. Dana, Jr. (New York, 1850).

4. Probably the wife of Rev. George Ripley (1802–1880, Harvard 1823), first president of Brook Farm, a communal colony at West Roxbury, Massachusetts, and since 1849 literary critic of the New York *Tribune*. In 1847 Parke Godwin had succeeded Ripley as editor of *The Harbinger*, socialistic organ of the colony.

727.   *To* Frances F. Bryant

New York   July 30, 1850

Dear Frances.

Yesterday and today were so hot that I am fairly parboiled in my own perspiration. I went over to Dr. Gray's last evening as soon as the sun was fairly down and conveyed your message. At present it is Dr. Gray's plan to come out on Friday in his carriage, in which case he will not bring a nurse, but all the children.

I shall send to Mrs. Forrest's the parcel you left. There is an old umbrella in my room, very much "dilapidated" as Miss Robbins would say. Did you leave it there? If so what shall I do with it—whither is it to be sent? If I have a failing in the world, it is a desire to return umbrellas. I cannot bear to see a strange umbrella on my premises—particularly an old one.

Miss Sands[1] will get the pine apples for Friday when I shall come down, but they have grown scarce she says. It would have been better if I had got them last week.

Yrs ever
W. C. B.

MANUSCRIPT: NYPL–GR ADDRESS: Mrs. Frances F. Bryant / Roslyn / Long Island.

1. Julia M. Sands. See 203.10.

728. *To* Frances F. Bryant

[*c*August 1, 1850]

Dear F.

I got some tools at Newbould's[1] this morning which will come in the sloop. As most of the ones I wanted were in a tool chest which he had, I thought I would get the chest. I shall bring the key. I met Mr. Lawson today in the street; we shook hands very cordially.[2]

Sherwood[3] called this morning. He has just returned from Barrington. All our friends there, he says, are well.

Mr. Bigelow is here today;[4] so that I can come out tomorrow if I think fit.

Yrs ever
W C B

P.S. Do not forget to take care of the plums and peaches if there are any.

W. C. B.

MANUSCRIPT: NYPL–GR ADDRESS: Mrs. F. F. Bryant / Roslyn / Long Island.

1. Probably John A. Newbould, of Newbould & Russell, hardware, 13 Gold Street. *Rode's New York City Directory for 1850–1851*, p. 380.
2. No reason is apparent for the estrangement between Bryant and James Lawson which is suggested here.
3. William Sherwood. See 100.9.
4. See Letter 730.

729. *To* Frances F. Bryant

New York   Tuesday   August 6, 1850.

Dear F.

I copy Mrs. Ver Bryck's[1] letter.

"My dear Mrs. Bryant. I was very sorry to miss both the visits of your kind husband, particularly as he could have no definite answer to his errand. Most happy will I be to accompany you to Catskill. As you leave the naming of the day to me, I will mention Thursday. I should like to hear how you go. If you have any time to spare mother will be glad to have you come directly to Pierrepont Street from Roslyn. Had you not better inform Mrs. Cole[2] of our intention, as her family is sometimes large.

"For several days we have all been occupied with the last sickness of Mr. Huntington's father.[3] He was released on Saturday last and buried yesterday. The family are well but weary. As soon as possible they will now leave town. I trust you have all kept well. Remember me very kindly to Mr. Bryant and your daughters. If any other day would be more agreeable to you, just name it to your attached friend.

S. E. Ver Bryck

Monday noon   August 5th.["]

[over][4]

I have written to Mrs. Ver Bryck that it was doubtful if you could go any day this week and gave her the reason.

Yesterday I had a letter from Dr. Dickson.[5] He has shipped he says a barrel of rice for us. They are quite well but suffering from the heat.

Godwin went away yesterday morning, to be absent the whole week.

Yours ever

W. C. B.

MANUSCRIPT: NYPL–GR ADDRESS: Mrs. F. F. Bryant / Roslyn / Long Island.

1. Widow of the artist Cornelius Ver Bryck. See 486.1.
2. Maria Bartow Cole, widow of the artist Thomas Cole. See 647.3.
3. Father of the painter Daniel Huntington. See 499.3.
4. Bryant's note.
5. Samuel Henry Dickson. See 646.3.

730.   To Leonice M. S. Moulton

New York   August 7   1850

My dear Mrs. M.

You recollect perhaps the story of him who in a letter apologizes to a lady for writing to her in his shirt sleeves. The weather is now so warm that I am committing an indecorum of a like kind—I write without a cravat and a shirt or shoes. It is hot—hot hot continually—the thermometer in my room in New York always as high as eighty for the last ten days and often higher. Hanging against the wall for several days past, at five o'clock this morning was at 84, and now at six in the afternoon in a current of air in the window it stands at 85.

You ask for news from my wife. She is quite well, much cumbered with seeing of company, and bathing every day in the harbour. She had been to pay a visit to some friends in Berkshire where Julia now is, and she is soon to go with Mrs. Ver Bryck and myself to Catskill. Fanny is well and her children are healthy bonny and good tempered. I have been pent up in the town all summer—Mr. Bigelow got married in the beginning of June and took a honeymoon of two months, the [experience?] of the great-er part of which was passed at Rye Beach somewhere on the New England coast where the weather was so cool—so cold they called it, as to allow of their very soon being quite social.[1]

The order for . . .[2] came to hand and the Damascus peas also. I planted them duly—and duly they came up, and blossomed and bore fruit. The plants are about three inches in height, with small narrow pinnacle leaves, and of the pods some contain a single pea and some none at all. I fancy they should have been planted earlier—but really they are the most in-significant crop I ever saw and appear little worth bringing all the way

from Damascus. However I shall try to preserve the seed that when you again become a farmer you may have wherewith to sow your fields.

I am glad to hear that you are become such a Jehu—or to give it a feminine termination such a Jehua—such a driver of steeds in harness[3]—so expert a charioteer—that the most timid female may trust herself to your charge. You should be in Roslyn now to astonish your old acquaintances with your dexterity as a whip—Roslyn which is as green and fresh as if it decked itself out in [decent?] expectation of your presence. I think I have never known so [luxuriant?] a summer on the island or a more well proportioned alternation of showers and sunshine. Just now a thunder storm is rising and the mighty wind is on hand to the right and left, and the tree tops on the streets are tossing in the wind and a romantic youth in long hair and a linen sack coat is standing on the top of a chimney on the house opposite looking into the wind's eye.

It is a dull summer here in New York. The heat has driven every body out of town, and I have been at Roslyn less than usual. You I doubt not have had a delightful time at Meadow Side. Your plan of life is perfectly captivating—all but washing at the pump—I must have pails, tubs floods of water in my chamber—but then I would cheerfully draw the water and empty what is called the "slops." Do not however I pray you become so independent that it will cost you a great effort to return to civilized life.

Have you read Rural Hours by Miss Cooper a daughter of Fenimore Cooper[?] It is the most charming book I have read for a long time.[4] It would suit your taste exactly all the objects of country life as they present themselves daily throughout the year are made the subject of pleasant notices full of knowledge and good sense and good taste and kindly feeling. You must read it—if you do not see it earlier, it will be a treat for you when you come to Roslyn—

My letter is ended. I have given you ten times the quantity of phrase which your note to me contained—yours had the advantage in quality I confess, but that you could not help, so you must claim no merit on that account. I should like to get a chronicle of your adventures at Meadow Side. My wife I doubt not would send her love if she were here.

Yours faithfully
W   C   B.

MANUSCRIPT: NYPL–GR (draft) ENDORSED (by Bryant): My Letter.

1. On June 11, 1850, John Bigelow married, in Baltimore, Jane Poultney (1829–1889), formerly of that city and lately of New York. After a honeymoon spent at Niagara Falls and traveling through Canada, the couple occupied rooms on Fourth Street, New York City. Margaret Clapp, *Forgotten First Citizen: John Bigelow* (Boston: Little, Brown, 1947), pp. 85–86, 334.

2. Several words illegible.

3. Cf. II Kings 9:20.

4. Susan Fenimore Cooper (1813–1894), *Rural Hours* (New York, 1850). Several months later Cooper exulted to his wife, "I wish you could have heard Bryant last night, on R[ural] H[ours]. 'Yes' said I 'it is a nice book' 'Pooh!' he answered—'it is a *great* book—the greatest of the season, and a credit to the country!' Was not my heart glad!" Cooper, *Letters & Journals*, VI, 237.

731. *To* George Bancroft

Wednesday   August 14   1850.

Dear Bancroft.

You could hardly take a pleasanter excursion than the one you propose. The best way to reach the [Delaware] Water Gap is by the New Jersey Central Railroad which leaves New York at 9 in the morning from the foot of Cortlandt Street. At a place called White House not far from Easton are stage coaches to take passengers to Easton to Wilkesbarre to Bethlehem and the Water Gap.

Bethlehem is an interesting place, a Moravian settlement you know founded by Loskiel,[1] *Episcopus Fratrum* a little more than a hundred years since, on the pleasant banks of the Lehigh, with vineyards on the declivities. Here they speak the best German in America. Nazareth in the neighbourhood is another Moravian village of a characteristic appearance. Of Wilkesbarre I can tell you nothing—but you should see Bethlehem. You might go by the way of Easton and return by the way of Schooley's Mountain and Morristown.[2]

Yrs truly

W   C   BRYANT.

MANUSCRIPT: MHS.

1. George Henry Loskiel (1740–1814), Russian-born bishop of the Moravian Church, who came to Bethlehem, Pennsylvania, in 1802, in the year of his consecration. Bethlehem was first settled in 1740–1741.

2. Bryant's visits to this area in 1840 and 1846 are recounted in Letters 384 and 604–605.

732. *To* John Howard Bryant

New York   August 30, 1850

Dear Brother.

I thank you for the statement you have given me of my account with you. I wish I had mentioned to you that I should be glad to know how many bushels of wheat you had received from Galer at different times and what price the wheat brought in market, in order that I might judge what sort of bargain I made in selling him the land. I should also like to know how much is yet coming to me on his notes. Will you be so kind as to inform me when you receive this?

With regard to the building of a house, your advice I doubt not is judicious. I do not see, however, that I can send out any money for the purpose this fall—money is not so plentiful with me as that. I have been in hopes that Galer would pay enough on his interest to buy the timber for the building. [If this] cannot be done I think the building of the house must go over to another year at least. I had thought of offering you, if you would build the house, the first year's rent, which I suppose would be about ten per cent of the value. I did not offer any thing for the trouble taken in building the first house because I made an abatement from the interest stipulated in the notes.

The terms on which you wish to exchange lands with me I am not sure that I perfectly understand. I have no objection to any arrangement of that kind however, on fair business principles. If you will give me for my lands near the village lands the same value in lands elsewhere within reasonable distance, I am content, and I am willing that Mr. Olds shall say what amount of land I shall take for what I transfer to you.

The monument for our mother's grave certainly ought to be attended to, and I take shame to myself that it has been so long neglected. I must see for what a simple monument of good marble can be had and order it to be made. I have not at hand the memorandum of the day of her death,[1] though I have I believe that of her birth. Will you send it to me?

I had entertained some thoughts before you wrote of coming out to Illinois in the last half of September. If I do, I shall bring out my wife with me, but it is very uncertain yet. I thank you however, and so does my wife for your hospitable invitation.

The plum trees you sent me succeeded very well and make flourishing little trees. Of the gooseberry cuttings some appeared to take root: they put forth leaves, but last winter the frost threw them nearly out of the ground, and the spring rains, while I was absent in town, washing away the earth completed the mischief. One only yet maintains a starving existence with two or three little leaves but it must inevitably die. I should like more of the gooseberry cuttings this fall.

You do not say whether you have tried any [Em?] or [Eledie's?] for the hurt on your shoulder. If you have not you should try [Elius?]. Perhaps there are some other remedies.[2]

We are all well—my wife is at [our] place in Roslyn and Julia on Staten Island and Fanny with her children at her cottage by the water where they have the benefit of a dip now and then in the salt water which keeps them strong and hearty. Part of the summer has been uncommonly hot, but it is now rather cooler than usual. Last week I took my wife and Julia to Easthampton and Montauk Point, the eastern extremity of Long Island. Easthampton consists of large ancient houses and green level ground, with a ridge of sand hills on the sea shore and a belt of sandy woods on the other three sides. Montauk Point is a peninsula of grassy

hills bare of trees, pastured by cattle, and separated from the rest of the island by an isthmus of sand. It is very cool in the summer time and the sea views are very fine.

Remember me kindly to your wife and boys and to all our friends in your neighborhood.

Yrs affectionately,
W. C. BRYANT

MANUSCRIPT: Mrs. Mildred Bryant Kussmaul, Brockton, Massachusetts ADDRESS: J. H. Bryant Esq.

1. Sarah Snell Bryant had died in Illinois on May 6, 1847. See Letter 617.
2. As Bryant wrote them, the names of these homoeopathic medicines are virtually illegible.

733. *To* Eliza Robbins

[New York? cAugust 1850]

My dear Miss Robbins—

My wife is perpetually asking me why I do not write to you—"so here goes" as the cant phrase is.

I have two things, however, on my mind which would be sufficient reason for writing if I were not the laziest man in the world.

One is to ask how you find yourself—how you are getting on—whether you are getting well as fast as you ought, and in the meantime whether you are passing the days of your convalescence as pleasantly and happily as one could wish. We can hear little of you from any one that we see. Your friends here with whom you are intimate can tell us nothing about you, and I suppose you write to nobody except by special request. We have just heard from Mrs. Moulton who made several attempts to see you but always called when you were out.—

The next matter on which I have to speak to you is to tell you that I sent to Boston to your address a copy of my Letters of a Traveller.[1] Have you got it? I find it is at some of the Boston Booksellers for you.

That is all. News I have little to give you. And at this present writing— my wife and Fanny and Julia and little Minna are all in Berkshire—all well when they went of course. Everybody that I know is out of town except Miss Sands and her mother—driven forth by the hot weather, and confounded hot it has been at times I assure you—sweltry exceedingly—and the city almost an oven sometimes at night, and by day fuller of all things abominable to sight and smell than I ever saw it before. Mr. Bigelow is married—married about the beginning of June and has gone off taking two whole months to his honeymoon, so much more extravagant has the world gone in these days than formerly, for who is a greater squanderer than he that spends his time?

The season in the country has been rather finer than usual—the herb-age always fresh and the shades thicker than usual—the trees were [loaded absolutely down?] with foliage till the terrible southeast wind came last [month?] with the rain on its [wings?] and [strained?] them and broke the [heavy?] and brittle branches, and [strewed the earth with their spoil?]—

Would it had been contented with [blowing down trees?]; it has covered our shores with wrecks. You have heard of the sad fate of Margaret Fuller & young son[2]—but perhaps . . .[3]

MANUSCRIPT: NYPL–GR (draft) ENDORSED (by Bryant): My Letter— / 1850?.

1. See 710.1.
2. Sarah Margaret Fuller, with her husband, Angelo Ossoli, and infant son, drowned on July 14, 1850, when the ship on which they were returning from Italy was wrecked off Fire Island, New York. See 583.2; Goddard, *Roslyn Harbor*, pp. 62–63.
3. The rest of the manuscript is unrecovered.

734.   *To* Frances F. Bryant

Thursday   Sept   12, 1850
Dear F.

Mrs. Goddard[1] died on Tuesday morning at Mamaroneck of the Typhus fever. Her son has just called to give me the intelligence. She had been ill eight or ten days and seemed to be getting better until very shortly before she died. Dr. Wilsey and Dr. Curtis[2] were out to see her a few days before her death and found her in so good a way that they thought it unnecessary to visit her again. The fever seemed to be entirely subdued. On Monday she began to sink and rapidly grew worse. The young man said that it was supposed the debility occasioned by her previous low state of health left her no strength to bear up against the disease, and when the fever left her there did not remain suf[f]icient energy in her constitution to carry on the functions of life. I told him I should inform you immediately of the event.

Mrs. Goddard will be buried on Saturday from the lower church—Mr. Bellows's.[3] The funeral is postponed that every chance for resuscitation may be allowed.

Your rage at the article in the paper[4] made me laugh heartily.

Yrs ever
W. C. B.

MANUSCRIPT: NYPL–GR ADDRESS: Mrs. F. F. Bryant / Roslyn / Long Island ENDORSED: Informing me of the death of Elizabeth Goddard.

1. Elizabeth Goddard (Mrs. Joseph Goddard). See 317.6.
2. Ferdinand L. Wilsey, a physician, of 588 Houston Street, was apparently a founder of the Hahnemann Academy of Medicine. Curtis may have been either A. M. Curtis, of 59 Grand Street, or Alva Curtis, 43 Bowery. See *Rode's New York City*

Directory for 1850–1851, pp. 588, 125; Leonard Paul Wershub, *One Hundred Years of Medical Progress: A History of the New York Medical College Flower and Fifth Avenue Hospitals* (Springfield, Illinois: Charles C. Thomas [1967]), p. 16.

3. Henry Whitney Bellows (1814–1882, Harvard 1832, Harvard Divinity School 1837) was minister of the Unitarian Church of All Souls, then at Broadway and Crosby Street, from 1839 to 1882. He was the founder and president of the United States Sanitary Commission during the Civil War, and from 1866 to 1877 edited the *Christian Examiner*.

4. Unidentified.

735.   *To* [Christiana?] Gibson[1]

New York, September 26, 1850.

Dear Miss Gibson.

Do not let the dull weather, if dull it should be, prevent you from going out to Roslyn tomorrow. When you make a visit to the country it is better to choose the end of a storm than the end of an interval of fine weather. If you had gone to Roslyn yesterday, for example, it would have been a mistake, for you would have arrived just in time to see the beginning of the rain; if you go tomorrow, provided the weather does not clear up in the mean time you will probably arrive just in time to see the end of it, and to enter upon a new lease of fine weather with the earth refreshed, the dust laid, and the roads firm.

Yrs truly
W. C. BRYANT.

MANUSCRIPT: DuU.

1. See 502.3.

736.   *To* Hiram Powers[1]

New York   October 14th. 1850.

Dear Sir.

The bearer of this, Theodore Sedgwick Esq.[2] who has a high appreciation of your genius, has desired of me an introduction to you, which I am proud to be able to give him. He goes abroad for his health, with his mother and sister, and with the intention to pass some time in the country [Italy] which your residence and that of a few other great men continues to make the principal seat of the fine arts. I need say no more in favour of Mr. Sedgwick than that he belongs to the family of that name, distinguished for worth and talent, with the reputation of which you are well acquainted.

I am sir
very truly and respectfully yours
WILLIAM C   BRYANT

MANUSCRIPT: National Collection of Fine Arts, Washington, D. C. ADDRESS: To H. G. Powers Esq. ENDORSED: Wm C. Bryant / 14 Oct 1850.

1. See 542.3.
2. See 209.8; 475.1.

737. *To* Mrs. Richards[1]

New York, Monday October 14th 1850.

My dear Mrs. Richards,

I send you in the enclosure with this a note from my wife and two
letters for your daughter which reached Roslyn after her departure.

My wife's note has something about your going out with me to Roslyn
on Saturday next. I have been obliged to make arrangements for going out
on Friday. I hope that day will be convenient for you and Mrs. Verbryck.
If it should not there is nothing to make your journey to Roslyn on Saturday inconvenient without my attendance. You stop at the *Branch* and
Julian's Stage is always there to bring you to our door.

Yrs truly

W. C. BRYANT.

MANUSCRIPT: HEHL.

1. Apparently the sister of Mrs. Cornelius Ver Bryck. See 729.1.

738. *To* Parke Godwin

Roslyn   October 18, 1850.

Dear Sir.

Yesterday my niece Mrs. Mitchell[1] of Cummington was to come out
to this place with me. Her husband was to bring her to the South Ferry
at a quarter past three P.M. where I was to take charge of her. I waited till
half-past 3 and then crossed over thinking she might be on the other side,
but she was not there and I came on without her.

They were staying at the American Hotel, and he was to set out for
Boston at 5 the same afternoon. Will you do me the favor to call at the
Hotel as early as you can spare time, and inquire the reason why Mrs.
Mitchell did not come, and let her come out with you.

Yrs respectfully

W C BRYANT

MANUSCRIPT: NYPL–GR ADDRESS: Parke Godwin Esq.

1. Ellen Theresa Shaw Mitchell (1822–1891), Mrs. Clark Ward Mitchell, was the
only child of Bryant's sister Sally (Mrs. Samuel Shaw), who died in 1824. See 106.2.

739. *To* John Howard Bryant

New York   October 25, 1850.

Dear Brother.

I suppose you have before this given up looking for me this autumn.
I thought at first of coming out with my wife, and then, as she did not

much like the journey I thought of coming out alone, but I found on reflection, that there was no business to call me very imperatively to Illinois, and that the money which I should spend would be very convenient
to make some necessary payments with, so I concluded to stay at home.

With regard to the land which you wish to exchange, I am willing
that you and Mr. Olds should arrange the matter just as you please; only
let me know what you have determined on, and what I am to do in regard
to it.

I should very much like if you can get the items to have that statement of what money I have had of Galer and what is yet coming to me. It
would satisfy what I am sure you will consider as a rational curiosity to
know how the sale of the land to Galer has turned out, whether I have
gained or lost by the transaction. There has been a good deal of delay on
Galer's part and a good deal of inconvenience occasioned by the delay,
and if the wheat has not brought good prices, the bargain is nothing to
brag of.

We have passed rather a pleasant and quite a healthy summer. Part
of the time the weather was quite hot, but always showery, and the earth
green, and the woods thick with foliage. We had frequent thunderstorms,
and several violent gales of wind, one of which did considerable mischief
to me by shaking off my apples, which are not very abundant on Long
Island this year. We had large crops of hay good crops of wheat and corn,
and excellent potatoes, but little injured by the disease, which in some
parts, on the mainland has done considerable damage. The cherries this
year were particularly abundant the strawberries very fine and lasted long,
the raspberries almost equally good, the summer pears abundant and
[watery?], the later pears good for nothing; the peaches on Long Island
poor and ripening early; but in New Jersey and elsewhere plentiful to a
degree I never knew before though not of so good a flavor I think, as usual.

The autumn thus far has been uncommonly fine, a warm sunshiny
September, a still more sunny October, and great brilliancy of color in
the woods, owing I suppose to the strong summer heats, which brought on
the old age of the leaf before the frosts. We have had no severe frosts yet.

In September, the latter part of the month, we made an excursion to
the east end of the Island visiting Easthampton, a level country, of fields
of heavy loam in the midst of sandy woods, inhabited by a primitive race
of people much like the New Englanders. From this place we went to
Montauk Point the extreme eastern end of the island, a hilly region of
hard loam, with cliffs of gravel forming its shore. There are scarce any
trees on the point which is nine or ten miles long, and is almost all pasturage, with eight or ten Indian houses on it, and three inhabited by white
people, the keepers of the herds, besides the house of the keeper of the
light-house. It is a great place for fishing.

We have all been quite well during the greater part of the time. My

family are yet on Long Island and will probably remain there till December.

Ellen Shaw or Mitchell has been with us a few days. Her husband brought her down to my house on Long Island on Saturday last and she came away yesterday, Thursday. She is in quite delicate health, but her lungs are apparently sound. If she should sink under ill-health it will not be consumption that kills her but frequent child births. She has had [four?] children, the last died in infancy. The short visit she made us improved her looks. She told me that Deacon Briggs[1] had been two years an inhabitant of Lanesborough.

Remember me kindly to your wife and the boys and to all my friends in Princeton.

Yours affectionately

W. C. BRYANT.

P. S.—Please give the letter which comes with this to Cyrus[2]

W. C. B.

MANUSCRIPT: NYPL–BFP ADDRESS: John H. Bryant Esq. PUBLISHED (*in part*): *Life*, II, 54.

1. Probably James L. Briggs, formerly of Cummington. See 224.1.
2. Letter unrecovered.

740.   *To* Frances F. Bryant

New York   Wednesday, October 30, 1850.

Dear F.

Dorothea Lisner[1] called this morning, and will go down on Saturday to Roslyn.

Miss Robbins called also and will go down the same day she thinks.

There was a very severe frost last night I perceived as I went to the Branch. The grass was white with the hoar frost, and after I got up the hill near Haviland's I saw ice in the puddles beside the road.

Twenty people have called to see me this morning, and I believe I should have something more to tell you if I could remember who they were and what they said. The room has been a perfect theatre of Chinese shadows.—

Yrs ever

W. C. B.

MANUSCRIPT: NYPL–GR ADDRESS: Mrs. F. F. Bryant / Roslyn / Long Island.

1. Apparently a prospective housemaid.

741.   *To* Frances F. Bryant

New York, Wednesday, November 13th, 1850.

Dear F.

I hope you got the letters sent you yesterday[1] informing you that I

had seen Mr. Spring[2] and that there was no special inducement for you to leave home.

Mr. Dewey has been here for several days. He came down last week, I think on Friday, on purpose to hear Jenny Lind,[3] and staied at Mr. Lane's.[4] On Friday evening he was at Leupp's, and as I heard in fine spirits. He was to return to Berkshire yesterday morning and I suppose did so; for I have not seen him.

I have a note from Mrs. Verbryck desiring that I will put her in the way "of procuring a good German servant." I wish I could with all my heart.

Yours ever

W. C. B.

MANUSCRIPT: NYPL–GR.

1. Unrecovered.
2. Marcus Spring (1810–1874). See 583.2.
3. The Swedish soprano Jenny Lind (1820–1887) had made her spectacular American debut at Castle Garden, New York City, on September 11, under the management of Phineas T. Barnum, later the great circus impresario. Odell, *Annals*, VI, 83–85.
4. Probably David Lane (1801–1885), a New York merchant, and a trustee of the Unitarian Church of All Souls. See Walter Donald Kring, *Liberals Among the Orthodox: Unitarian Beginnings in New York City, 1819–1839* (Boston: Beacon [1974]), pp. 259–260.

742.   *To* Frances F. Bryant

New York   November 14, 1850. [Thursday.][1]

Dear F.

I wrote the enclosed yesterday, but the newspaper was sent off before I got down stairs.

Mr. Dewey preached here on Sunday morning. On Tuesday when he got to Bridgeport he was called back by a telegraphic dispatch to attend the funeral of Ferris Pell.[3] You will see by the paper that Mrs. Edmonds the wife of the Judge[4] is also dead.

Mr. Dewey made a good many apologies to Fanny for not coming out to Roslyn.

We had a pleasant dinner at Mr. Springs yesterday. The furnace and a fire in the grate—the new grate—of their parlour made the temperature quite comfortable. By the bye, read the extract from the *Horticulturist* in today's paper concerning heated rooms. Mrs. Kirkland was there and Mr. Brown;[5] his wife was not well enough to come. He appeared to be wholly unconscious of the engagement made for him by Mr. Marquand;[6] he had never heard any thing about it. Great regret was expressed that you and Julia were not there. It was a fine moonlight evening when we returned. We all walked to the Ferry and after crossing, the ladies took the omnibus, but I walked home.[7]

Miss Cooper has sent in her bill for four weeks and in her moderation has concluded not to take the additional dollar weekly.

Yrs ever

W. C. B.

P.S. I think I shall come to Roslyn tomorrow.

MANUSCRIPT: NYPL–GR ADDRESS: Mrs. F. F. Bryant / Roslyn / Long Island.

1. The brackets are Bryant's.
2. Probably Letter 741.
3. Ferris Pell, a New York lawyer and political writer who had been a close associate of Governor De Witt Clinton (1769–1828).
4. John Worth Edmonds. See 492.4.
5. Probably the sculptor Henry Kirke Brown, a member of the Sketch Club and the National Academy of Design, whose marble bust of Bryant had been shown at the Academy earlier that year. NAD Exhibition Record, I, 54. See Letter 561.
6. Henry Gurdon Marquand (1819–1902), a New York banker and art collector, who owned a number of Brown's sculptures, including four which had been exhibited at the National Academy the preceding spring. NAD Exhibition Record, I, 54.
7. Marcus and Rebecca Spring then lived on State Street in Brooklyn.

743. *To* Frances F. Bryant

New York, Wednesday   November 27, 1850.

Dear F.

I went to the wedding party last evening at half past nine and was at home again at twenty minutes past ten. The bride behaved as composedly and seemed as much at her ease as if she had been married every day of her life. She is hardly handsome enough to "look sweetly," as they say of all brides. Poor Ellery certainly looked as if he had never been married before—a spot of bright red on each cheek bone close to the eyes, and the rest of the face quite pale.[1] I spoke with Mrs. Robert Sedgwick and Miss [Catharine] Sedgwick and several of the young ladies. Mrs. Kirkland was there and Mr. Bellows, and Dr. Anderson and Mr. Beckwith and Mr. McCracken and Alfred Pell's oldest son, now a tall young man, and young men whom I did not know in scores. I saw Mr. Hackley yesterday. He is afraid he shall figure again in Forrest's affidavit, though he pretends not to care for it. He is evidently tender-skinned yet.[2]

They are making a Bishop today. Seabury,[3] high church, and White-house,[4] low church, are the candidates. I saw Mr. [Fenimore] Cooper last evening at Leupp's; he is full of the subject and wanted he said to persuade the low church party to support Dr. Wainwright who is somewhere, in doctrine between Seabury and Whitehouse.[5]

Yrs ever

W. C. B.

MANUSCRIPT: NYPL–GR ADDRESS: Mrs. F. F. Bryant / Roslyn / Long Island.

1. The bridal couple were William Ellery Sedgwick (1825–1873), son of Bryant's late friend Robert Sedgwick, and Constance Irving Brevoort, daughter of the late Henry Brevoort (1782–1848), longtime friend of Washington Irving. Cooper, *Letters & Journals*, VI, 240; *EP*, November 30, 1850.

2. For Henry James Anderson, see 126.1; for Alfred Pell, 329.7. J. L. N. McCracken was an amateur playwright (Cooper, *Letters & Journals*, VI, 118). Hackley, apparently named in Edwin Forrest's divorce, has not been further identified. N. M. Beckwith (d. 1887) was a fellow-member of the Century Club.

3. Samuel Seabury (1801–1872), rector of the Episcopal Church of the Annunciation, New York, 1838–1868.

4. Henry John Whitehouse (1803–1874, Columbia 1821) was then rector of Saint Thomas' Church in New York. In 1852 he became bishop of Illinois. *Ibid.*, III, 340.

5. This conclave was adjourned without agreeing on a choice, but the following year Jonathan Mayhew Wainwright (1792–1854), rector of Trinity Parish, was consecrated bishop of New York. *Ibid.*, VI, 234–241, *passim*.

744.   *To* Frances F. Bryant

New York   December 4th   1850.—

Dear F.

I wrote to you yesterday[1] desiring that a bottle of hock in your bedroom closet might be transferred to the cellar. Lest you should not have received the note I write again. I sent a letter for Julia in the paper with your note.[2]

Do not forget the thermometer—nor the lens—nor the letters to be answered. If you do not come tomorrow, see that the white raspberry bushes are covered.

Yours ever
W. C. B.

MANUSCRIPT: NYPL–GR ADDRESS: Mrs. F. F. Bryant / Roslyn / Long Island.

1. Letter unrecovered.
2. Unrecovered.

745.   *To* John Ellis Wool

New York   February 25th, 1851.

My dear sir.

I have your letter concerning the payment of my mortgage.[1] By Friday's mail I will forward you a check for the amount of principal and interest,—dated Saturday, March 1st.

I am sir
yours faithfully
W. C. BRYANT

MANUSCRIPT: NYSL ADDRESS: Gen Jnº E. Wool.

1. See 563.3; Letter 747.

746. *To* John Ellis Wool

New York February 26, 1851.

My dear sir.

I did not I believe say in my note of yesterday that it was a *certified* check that I intended to send you on Friday. This, however, is what I meant, which will make it the same thing as cash in hand the moment it is received.

Yours faithfully
Wm C. Bryant

MANUSCRIPT: NYSL ADDRESS: Genl Jno. E. Wool.

747. *To* John Ellis Wool

New York February 28th 1851.

My dear sir.

I enclose you my check on the Mechanics Bank for $3093.78, which is the principal and interest on my mortgage up to March 1st, if I have computed the interest right. The check as you will see by a scrawl on the face is certified at the Bank. Will you do me the favour to send me the mortgage discharged by mail.

I cannot allow this opportunity to pass without thanking you for the courtesy and the disposition to oblige, which you have always shown in the business relations I have had with you.

I agree with you that there seems to be little chance at present for any of the "Richmonds" in the field. Benton you have seen positively declines becoming a candidate in any event—his refusal I understand will not be reconsidered. He means to fight his own battle over in Missouri.[1] The remarks made by you at the Troy dinner, as you give them, were quite pertinent and proper. I know very well how much the newspaper reporters, if they have a purpose to serve, are disposed to <put a false> give an unfair turn to words spoken by a public man.

I am dear sir
yrs truly
W C Bryant

MANUSCRIPTS: NYSL (final): NYPL–GR (draft) ADDRESS: Genl Jnº E. Wool ENDORSED: New York Feb. 28, 1851. / W. C. Bryant / To / Major Genl. Wool / Enclosing his check / $3093.78.

1. Thomas Hart Benton (1782–1858) had been United States senator from Missouri from 1820 until 1850, when he was defeated for re-election. In 1852 he was elected to the House of Representatives.

748. *To* Cyrus Bryant

New York   March 26, 1851.

Dear Brother,

I have just opened again your letter of February 10th,[1] the business part of which was attended to as soon as I received it, but there is a question at the end which I have not yet answered. You ask what you shall do with Cullen[2]—keep him at school or set him to work? I would be governed very much by his turn of mind and inclination. We must have somebody in the professions and it is rather a pleasant thing to have one or two of this sort of people among one's relatives. If he takes to learning and has a decided bent to become a scholar I would indulge him. In this respect the Bryants are not apt to be deficient, and I should not wonder if he inherited a fondness for books from the Everett side.[3] If he does not like to work better than you and I, there is perhaps some ground for fear that he will not distinguish himself in that line.

We are all well here— My own health is very good, and that of my wife is better than usual this winter. I am making arrangements to go out to my place, for the summer next week. I am obliged to part with the man who has been with me for several years and I have just engaged an Irishman in his place, concerning whom I am not wholly free from misgivings, for it is next to impossible to know whether an Irishman is good for any thing or not until you have tried him. I am now looking for another man to work with him—but I think that one Irishman is enough and I am trying for a German or a Scotchman. Americans are out of the question. I am glad you have undertaken the chemical lectures;[4] it will give your people something better to think of and talk about than village scandal, but I suppose they are concluded before this time. If you gave your auditors exhilerating gas, I think you must have drawn better houses than Lovejoy.[5]

My wife desires to be kindly remembered to you and your wife and children, and says that as soon as she gets time she will answer your letter. My regards to all.

Yrs affectionately

W   C   BRYANT

MANUSCRIPT: BCHS ADDRESS: Cyrus Bryant Esq. / Princeton / Illinois.

1. Unrecovered.
2. Cyrus' third son, Cullen (1839–1909, United States Military Academy 1864).
3. Mrs. Cyrus Bryant had been Julia Everett of Worthington, Massachusetts.
4. Cyrus, who had lectured on the sciences at George Bancroft's Round Hill School in Northampton, Massachusetts, before moving west in 1831, had recently given a course of similar lectures in Princeton, Illinois. *The Bryant Record for 1895–96–97–98: Being the Proceedings of the Bryant Association, at its First Four Annual Reunions, Held at Princeton, Illinois* (Princeton, Illinois, 1898), p. 75.
5. Owen Lovejoy (1811–1864), an Illinois legislator and radical Abolitionist, was later a close friend and supporter of Abraham Lincoln. A United States congressman

from 1857 to 1864, he was a younger brother of the anti-slavery editor Elijah Parish Lovejoy, whose murder by a pro-slavery mob at Alton, Illinois, in 1837 had prompted Bryant to a vigorous defense of freedom of the press. See Letter 363; *EP*, November 18, 1837.

749. *To* Richard H. Dana

New York   April 8th   1851.

Dear Dana.

I should have written to you before, but that I could not till now answer one of the material points in your letter.[1] I have just installed my wife in her home for the summer at Roslyn, and made inquiries about the boarding houses. There is a family near us where I supposed that comfortable lodgings might be had for a reasonable compensation, and which is situated close to the water, where Charlotte[2] might have taken a plunge twice a day if she pleased. But I learn that they mean not to take boarders this summer—one of the daughters intending to be married in June. There is no other good place here within a convenient distance of the salt water. Along the shores of the Sound, at Glen Cove and other places are boarding houses, but their terms are five or six dollars a week, most often the latter. Dr. Bryant thinks highly of sea-bathing, and his opinion is confirmed by the experience which your daughter had of its beneficial effect last summer. If you have any doubt of it, come down with her in June and let her try the experiment in the little cove at the foot of my dyke. A fortnight's trial, I am sure, would determine the question, and then we might see whether there were not a comfortable and quiet place to be found somewhere in the neighbourhood.

I read your son's argument, which certainly was an able one and does him great credit.[3] Equally great, still greater in my opinion, is the credit due to him for the boldness with which he came forward to do his duty to the uttermost in a matter in which it seemed that there was much to lose and nothing to gain. I am not certain, however, that it will not hereafter appear that what seems only courage, would deserve to be called by those [who] could see the end along with the beginning, the highest policy. Let people be convinced that what has been done was not from a love of contention or an itch for notoriety, but from a disinterested determination to decline no duty which his profession might cast upon him, —and he will stand far far higher in men's estimation for his courage. Nor will they fail to be convinced of this in time.

I suppose you saw the little article I made up concerning Channing[4] for the Evening Post from your letter, making use of your own expressions, for which I hope you bear me no grudge. Since you wrote I have heard some of his pupils speak of what they owed to him in much the same terms as those you mentioned having heard from a clergyman.

Cooper is now in town—in ill health,—a disease of the liver. When I

saw him last he was in high health apparently and in excellent spirits. He has grown thin and has an ashy instead of a florid complexion.[5] The other night there was an annual supper at the Academy of Design just before the opening of the exhibition. They toasted [Asher] Durand the shyest of men, unexpectedly to him, and he answered in a brief speech entirely unpremeditated and simple in manner and phrase, but most happily turned and as they said really affecting. It was allowed to be the best made in the evening.[6]

Remember me very kindly to your sisters and daughter.

Yrs sincerely

Wm C. Bryant

MANUSCRIPT: NYPL–GR ADDRESS: R. H. Dana Esq. ENDORSED: Wm C. Bryant, Apr / 8/51—Answered June 26/51. PUBLISHED (in part): Life, II, 61.

1. Unrecovered.

2. Dana's daughter, a semi-invalid, was long a friend and frequent guest of the Bryants.

3. On February 15 a runaway slave, Shadrach, had been seized in Boston under the Fugitive Slave Law and taken before United States Commissioner B. F. Hallet; the same day he was rescued in court by a crowd headed by two Negroes, and hastened away. One of his lawyers, a black named Davies, was charged with aiding in his escape. Davies was represented at his trial on February 20–24 by Richard H. Dana, Jr., whose "Argument in Behalf of Charles G. Davies" on February 25 effected his acquittal the next day. Dana's argument was printed in several newspapers at the time, and later in Richard Henry Dana, Speeches in Stirring Times . . . , ed. Richard Henry Dana, 3d. (Boston and New York: Houghton, Mifflin, 1910), pp. 178–209. See also EP, February 25, 26, 1851; Nevins, Ordeal, I, 388.

4. Edward Tyrell Channing (54.1), who, as editor of the North American Review in 1817–1818 had published Bryant's early verses, retired in 1851 from an outstanding teaching career at Harvard. Bryant's article on Channing has not been found.

5. James Fenimore Cooper, ill since the preceding November with a liver ailment, died on September 14, 1851. Cooper, Letters & Journals, VI, 256.

6. With characteristic reticence, Bryant does not mention the final toast of the evening, offered by Rufus Griswold, and reported in the Bulletin of the American Art-Union (May 1851), p. 32: "Dr. Griswold was here called upon. He said he would not make a speech, but he would supply an omission. The greatest of all American artists was absent—a man of whom Fenimore Cooper had said that day in his (Dr. Griswold's) presence, 'However we may be praised, he is the author of America.' "

750.   To Amasa Walker[1]

New York   April 20, 1851.

My dear sir.

I was absent in the country when your letter[2] arrived or I should have written you earlier. I was about to say that I could send nothing for the Bazaar, when on opening my desk for a sheet of paper my eye fell upon the lines which I subjoin. I hope this will not reach you too late.

Yours faithfully,

W. C. Bryant.

From the French.

Sere leaf, severed from the bough!
Tell me, whither goest thou?

Ask me not, the leaf replies;
Lately was my parent oak
Smitten by the tempest's stroke.
Since that hour, with every gale,
Soft or strong, that sweeps the skies,
I am borne from grove to plain,
From the mountain to the vale,
Wandering wide where'er they blow.
Yet I fear not nor complain;
I but go where all things go,
Where the rose's leaf, at last,
And the laurel-leaf are cast.[3]

MANUSCRIPT: YCAL, bequest of Norman Holmes Pearson ADDRESS: Hon Amasa Walker ENDORSED: Boston Apl 23 / 50—[sic] / Miss Henshaw, / Agreeably to your / request I wrote my friend / W. C. Bryant for a few / lines for the London Ba- /zaar, and have received / in reply the subjoined, / which I trust you will / transmit to our friends / in England in season / for the Fair, or, what / would suit me better, / I hope you will go / & be the bearer of / it yourself— / Yours for Human / Brother-hood / Amasa Walker.

1. Amasa Walker (1799–1875) was a Boston shoe merchant, as well as a state legislator and congressman. After his retirement from business he taught political economy at Oberlin College, and published several books on economics. Bryant had first known him while studying Latin, as a boy of fourteen, with his Uncle Thomas Snell in North Brookfield, Massachusetts. Bryant, "Autobiography," *Life*, I, 31.
2. Unrecovered.
3. The original verses in French are unidentified.

751. *To* Charles Sumner[1]

New York, April 24, 1851.

My dear Sir.

Allow me to add my congratulations to those of Mr. Bigelow on your success. I am glad that my native state is once more worthily represented in the United States Senate.

Yrs truly
W. C. BRYANT.

MANUSCRIPT: HCL.

1. Charles Sumner (1811–1874, Harvard 1830, Harvard Law School 1833) entered the United States Senate as a Free Soiler from Massachusetts in December 1851. See illustration. John Bigelow had written him on April 2, "I will bear your request

about Mr. Bryant's autograph in mind," and again on the 23rd, "I have not forgotten your request for the autograph." Both letters in HCL.

752.   *To* Leonice M. S. Moulton

New York   April 30, 1851.

. . . I looked among the Bridgewater Howards and found Abigails in abundance—it seems to have been a favorite name—but none who married a Moulton. It may be among the Haywards, which name was formerly pronounced Howard. I shall look.

On Sunday, little Minna [Godwin] was taken with the bilious colic. Her nurse being obliged to come to town, I staid to look to the child till yesterday morning. The case was a bad one but I hear, this morning that she is better.

I think you must have had a guilty consciousness of running away too soon from Roslyn, or you would not have been put to such hard service as you say you were in your dreams, to improve the walks about my place. . . .[1]

MANUSCRIPT: Ridgely Family Collection TEXT: Hoyt, "Bryant Correspondence (I)," 65 ADDRESS: Mrs. L. M. S. Moulton, 1 Broadway.

1. Salutation, complimentary close, and signature omitted from published text.

753.   *To* Salmon P. Chase[1]

New York   May 12th, 1851.

My dear sir.

I am sorry not to be able to direct you to any person who would be likely to conduct the paper you propose to establish, in such a manner as would satisfy you.[2] It is the most difficult thing in the world to find a man of whom you could say beforehand that he would conduct a political paper with ability, and in conformity with a high standard of morals. Sometimes the talent is wanting, sometimes the principles, and sometimes both. Some faculties require to be thoroughly drilled in journalism before they have any aptness dexterity or discretion in the work.

You free soil democrats in Ohio are taking the right course, and will reap, I doubt not, the reward of your firmness directness of purpose and fidelity to principle. Here in the state of New York, we are in some confusion. Seward, by forcing upon us the question of the nine million loan for enlarging the canal, has created a new issue of a local nature, which, for the present, predominates over every other.[3] It will have the effect of uniting the whigs, which was probably intended; it will in a considerable degree, bring together the democrats also. The only friends of the nine million bill among the democrats in this city, are the rankest of the pro-slavery faction. The free-soilers of this state are strictly the economical

party and nothing could be more distasteful to them, or bring them out in direct warfare with Seward's friends more effectually than such a project as this loan. Here in the city, a good many of the hunker whigs are against the nine million loan, but at Albany the *Register* Fillmore's organ for the state[4] is vehemently in its favor; the whig party of the city are on the same side, without an exception.

We must fight this battle, but we shall not neglect higher and more permanent questions. The controversy concerning slavery will be kept open, and nothing of the zeal of an opposition to the fugitive slave law and the kindred enormities will be abated.[5]

The enclosure of your letter,—one dollar for Mr. [Skiner?] was safely received and the paper sent to him.

I am sir
yours faithfully
W   C   BRYANT

MANUSCRIPT: HSPa ADDRESS: Hon S. P. Chase.

1. Salmon Portland Chase (1808–1873, Dartmouth 1826), a former Whig, had been elected United States senator from Ohio in 1849 by Democrats and Free Soilers.

2. Chase's request has not been located; consequently, the newspaper referred to is unidentified. But one of his biographers wrote that Chase "valued and cultivated . . . the anti-slavery press," and "subscribed for many of these papers, and raised, lent or gave outright money to keep some of the more important of them afloat." Albert Bushnell Hart, *Salmon Portland Chase*, "American Statesmen" (Boston and New York, 1899), pp. 61–62.

3. William Henry Seward (1801–1872, Union 1820), governor of New York from 1839 to 1843, entered the United States Senate in 1849. On May 2, 1851, the *EP* published a pamphlet entitled *Pay as You Go; or, The Unconstitutionality of the Nine Million Debt Demonstrated*, which included letters from prominent Democrats Samuel J. Tilden and John A. Dix, as well as an address from twelve Democratic state senators who had resigned in April in protest against the senate's plan to float a large loan to enlarge the Erie Canal. In editorials on May 1 and 2, under captions reading "The Plan to Ruin the Erie Canal," and "Another Feature of the Nine Million Loan Fraud," Bryant charged that such an expenditure, without a public referendum, would be unconstitutional. However, in 1854 this proposal was put to the voters and carried by an overwhelming margin. Nevins, *Ordeal*, II, 231.

4. Millard Fillmore (1800–1874) of Buffalo, New York, a Whig congressman who was elected to the vice presidency in 1848, had succeeded to the presidency in July 1850 upon the death of Zachary Taylor. The Albany *Register* was established in 1849, in opposition to the *Evening Journal*, long the champion of the Seward–Thurlow Weed faction of the state's Whig party. Glyndon G. Van Deusen, *William Henry Seward* (New York: Oxford University Press, 1967), pp. 132–133.

5. Bryant was unremitting in his opposition to the Fugitive Slave Law of 1850. Commenting in the *EP* (October 4, 1851) on riots in Syracuse, New York, touched off by "slave-catchers," he called the law "offensive, . . . revolting. The people feel it to be an impeachment of their manhood" to be asked to help manacle "one who has lived among them the life of an industrious and honest citizen. . . . The impulse toward freedom is one which no legislature can extinguish or control."

754. *To* Charles Sedgwick[1]

New York   May 30   1851.

My Dear Sir.

I expect to leave this place on Monday after noon with my wife and perhaps my daughter—I cant tell yet—and pass a day at Great Barrington on my way to Lenox. This will bring me to your house—unless female influence should disturb my arrangements on Tuesday evng.

In great haste
yrs sincerely
W   C   BRYANT

MANUSCRIPT: YCAL ADDRESS: C. Sedgwick Esq.

1. See Vol. I, 14–15.

755. *To* Charles Sedgwick

Roslyn, Long Island, June 16, 1851

. . . I wish you were here just now to enjoy our season of roses and strawberries; you might have your own afterward. I would ask your advice, who are a practical landscape gardener, as to some walks which I am laying out in my woods, and you should decide for me at which point we could have the finest peeps at the water. Our neighborhood is now very beautiful; the later summer heats parch and wither the verdure of [our?][1] island. But now one might almost fancy that the clouds had dropped leaves with the rains, and buried us in a flood of foliage. We have nothing here, I acknowledge, like your mountains, with their infinite variety of aspects, the lakes they embosom, and their broad woods—a wood, to have its true majesty, must be seen on a mountainside—nor have we your swift streams. But what we have you should be welcome to. Meantime I entertain myself with comparing the images of beauty presented by the two regions. I am indebted to you and your "amiable family," as the Spanish say, for some of the finest landscapes in the picture-gallery of my memory, collected during our late pleasant visit to Berkshire. Claude Lorraine's[2] are a trifle *warmer* in the atmosphere, but in all other respects they leave him far behind. Ruskin, you know, says that Claude was a clumsy artist,[3] so that this would be no compliment in his estimation to the pictures of which I speak. . . .

MANUSCRIPT: Unrecovered TEXT *(partial)*: *Life*, II, 54–55.

1. The printed text has "an."
2. Claude Lorrain, born Claude Gelée (1600–1682), French landscape painter.
3. "Claude had, if it had been cultivated, a fine feeling for beauty of form, and is seldom ungraceful in his foliage; but his picture, when examined with reference to essential truth, is one mass of error from beginning to end." John Ruskin, *Modern Painters, by a Graduate of Oxford* (New York, 1848), I, 75.

756. *To* Frances F. Bryant

New York June 26, 1851. Thursday.

Dear F.

I forgot yesterday to say that Miss Robbins called the night previous. Some business relating to her books brought her to town, and she had completed it to her satisfaction. She complained that she was not so well for the sea-air and must hasten back to Newburgh. She desired her love to you and Julia.

Last night Mr. Rand and his wife[1] called. It is possible that he may come out on Saturday.

Minna gets on slowly, very slowly indeed. Fanny thinks the best way to get her to Roslyn will be to put her into the Glen Cove steamer, and let our rockaway come for her. Dr. Warner was at the house yesterday and said that the sooner she was sent into the country the better.

Do not let every thing dry up—trees &c. It is very hot here and must be very dry with you.

Yrs ever

W. C. B.

MANUSCRIPT: NYPL–GR ADDRESS: Mrs. F. F. Bryant / Roslyn / Long Island.

1. Portrait painter John Goffe Rand and his wife, Lavinia Brainerd Rand. See 287.1, 289.1.

757. *To* Richard H. Dana

New York, July 1, 1851.

Dear Dana.

I got your letter today and this goes tomorrow.[1] It is bad news both for myself and my wife that you and your daughter could not find it con-venient to try the sea-bath at our place on Long Island where it is now very pleasant—that is the sea-bathing. I am sorry that you give so bad an account of Charlotte's health. It is a double misfortune—as great a one to you, to whom she is so necessary as to herself. Before the summer is over I hope she will have found health somewhere; in the waters of some sea coast or some healing fountain, or some friendly atmosphere. It is one of the melancholy things of our existence, one of the sorrowful exceptions to what seems the natural and proper order of things when the young become infirm before or as soon as their parents.

Hillard[2] has written a letter for the Evening Post which I have printed today, as well as the article from the Daily Advertiser which he desires should follow it; but I took occasion to reprimand him a little for helping on the attempt to persecute your son, under the semblance of arguing the question. I believe you are right when you say that these people begin to be dissatisfied with what has been done.

How came you to suppose that the article concerning the "Son of a Merchant" was not mine[?] I sat down and threw it off immediately on receiving Richard's letter[3] enclosing the article cut from the Daily Advertiser. On looking it over again, I see marks of haste in it, and some blunders in the composition.[4]

You are too despairing concerning your works. I wish they were more profitable, but that you get little from them is no proof that they are not esteemed. How much more money Byron made by his works than Wordsworth, and yet which of them is now most spoken of and quoted? Byron is no longer read with pleasure, and the impression made by his works on the public mind is nearly worn out. Wordsworth never seems to have been a successful author, so far as gain is concerned. Your writings may have a slow sale, but they will last.[5]

I came to town today and am almost dissolved with the heat. I pine for the hour of release from this daily toil at the mill, but will my condition be any better then? I fear I should become lazy or fancy myself too old or too unwell to do any thing but scratch the ground a little in the garden.

My regards to your daughter and son. I am sorry that I did not see Richard when he was here on Saturday.

Yours ever

W   C   BRYANT

MANUSCRIPT: NYPL–GR ENDORSED: Wm C. Bryant / July 1/51 / Ans. Decr 9th.

1. Dana's letter is unrecovered.
2. George Stillman Hillard. See 341.4.
3. Unrecovered.
4. Sometime early in June Richard H. Dana, Jr., had spoken at Worcester, Massachusetts, in support of Congressman Charles Allen, a Free Soiler who had recently charged Secretary of State Daniel Webster with taking bribes from a syndicate of bankers. Several of Webster's Boston admirers, among them Hillard, had attacked Dana in letters to the Whig Boston *Daily Advertiser*, charging him with "treasonable language," and suggesting that merchants withdraw their business from him; that he be "silenced or starved." Discussing this correspondence in the *EP* for June 11 under the caption "Boston Political Morality," and supposing Hillard to have written a letter signed "A Son of a Merchant," Bryant commented, "Perhaps there is no place in the United States where intolerance takes a more odious shape than in Boston." Hillard's letter of June 25 appeared in the *EP* on the 30th; in it he denied writing the "A Son of a Merchant" letter, while reiterating some of its charges against Dana. In an editorial in the same issue Bryant admonished Hillard for contributing indirectly to the persecution of Dana. *EP*, June 11, 21, 31, 1851; Irving H. Bartlett, *Daniel Webster* (New York: Norton [1978]), p. 287.
5. Dana, Sr.'s *Poems and Prose Writings*, first published in 1833, were brought out in a new edition in 1850 by Baker & Scribner of New York, and reprinted by them in 1857 and 1859. In 1857 his poems appeared, under his name, in *The Poetical Works of Edgar Allan Poe*, published in London by George Routledge.

758. *To* Leonice M. S. Moulton

New York   July 8th   1851.

. . . I have just got your letter of the 7th.[1] which must be yesterday, if there is any trust to vulgar arithmetic. I answer it immediately because it asks for medical advice, which, I think, the doctors say ought to be given early.

Nux vomica, I have found, is not likely to produce a good effect after sea-sickness. Of late I have been obliged to abandon its use, though at one time it was of the greatest service to me. Sulphur, perhaps, might suit your case; or you might choose among Bryonia,[2] Hepar Sulphuris and Mercurius according to the symptoms. The other day my wife and I effected an extraordinary cure. A young girl the sister of our cook came to see her. She had been a patient in a hospital, and had taken a great deal of medicine, and was now subject to great weakness of the stomach and frequent nausea, which in the morning was constant. One dose of Hepar put the nausea in the morning to flight, and she declared that she felt stronger and better than for months before.

Minna, Fanny's eldest has been ill for weeks with an abdominal abcess succeeding an attack of dysentery. At one time it was feared that she would not live, and her situation now is very critical. Fanny has had her in town, till within ten days, for medical advice and she has now just moved into her cottage at Roslyn.

Roslyn meantime is as beautiful as ever. It began to fade a little with the drought but the rains of the third and fourth of July revived it. I have lengthened the walk in the woods, so that one can now pass over the greater part of them. All that now remains to do is to put up seats and open views by thinning or pruning the trees here and there. You should be there with your quick observation and accurate taste to tell where and how it should be done.

I come to this dirty town, as usual every week, to be poisoned by the bad air. In a year or two, if I live I hope to be relieved from the necessity of being here in the hot weather. In your Paradise at Plympton, I doubt not you think with a sort of compassion on those who at this season swelter and pant in the cities. I shall write to you again, by and by, with a genealogical commission for your friend and the deacon. . . .[3]

MANUSCRIPT: Ridgely Family Collection TEXT: Hoyt, "Bryant Correspondence (I)," 65–67 ADDRESS: Mrs. L. M. S. Moulton, Meadow Side, Plympton, Massachusetts.

1. Unrecovered.
2. The printed text has "Bryonic."
3. Salutation, complimentary close, and signature omitted from printed text.

759. *To* John T. S. Smith[1]

Roslyn   Long Island   July 27th, 1851.

Dear Sir.

Please send me the following named medicines in two shilling vials—

low dilutions—either tincture or powder as the case may be. The *Express* which runs between this place and New York will call for them on Wednesday and I write that you may have them ready

Aconite	Nux Vomica
Arsenic	Mercurius
Bryonia	Tartar Emetic
Chamomelle	Sulphur
China	Pulsatilla.—
Belladonna	
Ipecac	

Yrs truly

W   C   BRYANT

MANUSCRIPT: YCAL.

1. The recipient of this letter was almost certainly John T. S. Smith, proprietor of Smith's Homoeopathic Pharmacy, at 488 Broadway, New York. A former patient of Dr. A. Gerard Hull's, Smith had begun in 1843 to prepare "tinctures and titurations" for Hull and his partner, Dr. John Franklin Gray, and by 1846 had established his pharmacy. *Homoeopathic Bibliography of the United States from the Year 1825 to the Year 1891* . . . , comp. Thomas L. Bradford (Philadelphia, 1892), p. 550.

760.   *To* William Gilmore Simms

[Roslyn? *c*July 1851]

Dear Simms.

As soon as I can get sight of one of the gentlemen who have the active management of the testimonial to Mrs. Cowden Clarke[1] I shall acquit myself of the commission you ask me to execute.

The Forrest affair is really a most unhappy one. I believe it has had somewhat the effect you mention.[2] I have not seen Lawson for many months— It is more than a year and a half since I have seen Mrs. Forrest. —The last I saw of her was when a well meant attempt on my part to effect an arrangement between the parties was broken off.[3] What the end of the litigation between them will be I can not guess or whether there will be any end. It is kept along in the courts for a long time.

You speak of coming to New York in August—I shall claim a visit from you at my place in the country. It is very beautiful now—but the summer which is already almost a little too dry for Long Island will take off some of its freshness. I hope your wife and Augusta will accompany you. My best regards to both of them. My wife who has read your letter joins me in the invitation and in the desire to welcome you at our place. . . .

MANUSCRIPT: NYPL–GR (draft).

1. The British writer Mary Victoria Cowden-Clarke (1809–1898) had compiled *A Complete Concordance to Shakespeare* in 1844–1845. At a Shakespeare birthday din-

ner in New York on April 23, 1851, Bryant had been appointed to a committee charged with soliciting funds from American writers to buy her a testimonial chair, which was delivered to Mrs. Clarke in London the following January. Richard D. Altick, *The Cowden-Clarkes* (London and New York: Oxford University Press, 1948), pp. 173–175.

2. Since the letter to which Bryant is apparently responding is unrecovered, Simms's comment on the Forrests is undetermined.

3. See 716.2.

761. *To* L. P. Frod[1]

New York   August 6th, 1851.

Sir

When I wrote the little poem called "The Waterfowl" I certainly intended to refer the adjective weary to the wings of the bird.[2] If a different construction should seem to any one to be an improvement, I have no objection that he should make it. That there should be any question as to the meaning makes me fear that the composition of the stanza is defective.

I am sir
yours respectfully
W. C. BRYANT.

MANUSCRIPT: HCL ADDRESS: L. P. Frod Esq.

1. The addressee, who had apparently questioned Bryant on the point discussed below, has not been identified.

2. In the fifth stanza of "To a Waterfowl" (1815) Bryant had written
"All day thy wings have fanned,
At that far height, the cold, thin atmosphere,
Yet stoop not, weary, to the welcome land,
Though the dark night is near."
See *Poems* (1876), p. 31.

762. *To* Frances F. Bryant

[New York] Wednesday   Aug. 27, 1851.

Dear F.

I got a note yesterday morning from Mrs. Kirkland asking me to her house on Tuesday evening to meet "two or three conversible people" as she called them. I went and found Mr. Duyckinck[1] and Mr. Whipple[2] the Review writer and his wife.

Mrs. Kirkland is coming out to Roslyn on Saturday. I wish you would send word to Saunders[3] that I expect to be at Roslyn on Monday and hope he will be ready for me.

I received the manuscript for which I wrote, at a very seasonable hour this morning and am much obliged.[4]

Yrs ever
W. C. B.

MANUSCRIPT: NYPL–GR ADDRESS: Mrs. F. F. Bryant / Roslyn / Long Island.

1. Evert Augustus Duyckinck. See 471.2.

2. Edwin Percy Whipple (1819–1886) was a Boston broker and a highly respected lecturer and literary critic, whose articles in the *North American Review* and other periodicals were widely read and later collected into several volumes. A few years after this meeting he published a judicious but sympathetic notice of Bryant's poetry in *Graham's Magazine*, 46 (January 1855), 90–94, which was reprinted in Whipple's *Literature and Life* (Boston, 1871), pp. 303–321.

3. Probably a Roslyn carpenter.

4. The letter requesting this unidentified manuscript is unrecovered.

763.   *To* James G. Birney[1]

New York   Sept. 8th 1851.

Dear Sir.

As I am wholly unable to answer any of the questions put in your letter, my sole agency in regard to the Tract on Colonization[2] being to receive any manuscripts sent to the office of the Evening Post and hand them over to the writer of the communication alluded to in your letter,[3] I have sent your letter to him that he may satisfy you on those points concerning which you request information.

Yrs truly

W. C. BRYANT.

MANUSCRIPT: William L. Clements Library, University of Michigan ADDRESS: To James G. Birney Esq. DOCKETED: William C. Bryant / R. Sep. 17.

1. James Gillespie Birney (1792–1857, Princeton 1810), a southerner who had freed his slaves and become an early anti-slavery leader, had run unsuccessfully for the presidency in 1840 and 1844 as the candidate of the Liberty Party. An early advocate of colonization in Africa as a means of gradual emancipation, he had soon abandoned that method as ineffectual. By 1851, however, he was again urging colonization because of what he saw as a growing discrimination in the northern states against free Negroes. Nevins, *Ordeal*, I, 140–142. Russell B. Nye, *Fettered Freedom: Civil Liberties and the Slavery Controversy, 1830–1860* ([East Lansing?] Michigan State University Press [1963]), pp. 128–134; Vol. II, 5.

2. Probably Birney's "Address to the Free Colored People," in James Gillespie Birney, *Examination of the Decision of the Supreme Court of the United States, in the Case of Strader, Gorman and Armstrong vs. Christopher Graham Delivered at its December Term, 1850 . . .* (Cincinnati, 1852), pp. 33–46.

3. Unrecovered.

764.   *To* Leonice M. S. Moulton

New York   September 9th, 1851.

. . . I did not answer, in my last, one of the most important parts of your letter, that, I mean, which relates to the young invalid.[1] I think you may without hesitation undertake to prescribe for him, provided you do it like a sensible woman as you are, and with due caution as to the repetition of

the doses and the length of time allowed to elapse between them. Do not let him go on with the same medicine more than three days and let a week or more intervene between the administration of the different remedies, and I think you will do no mischief, and may possibly do good.

It is very hot and close here in this noisy and dusty city, and every body is languishing for cooler weather. We are devoured too by mosquitoes which come up, they say, from the mouths of the sewers, as soon as the sun sets and make merciless war upon all human kind. You have chosen the better part, among the sandy pastures and whortleberry fields of Plympton, and I only wish that I was as free a denizen of the country. Since my German John[2] left me I have been much at a loss for a faithful and intelligent man in his place. In July I dismissed one whom I engaged in the Spring; and now I am going to dismiss another. On Thursday—it is now Tuesday—I go down with my new man who gives all manner of good accounts of himself—but so did his predecesser. Do you not find it more comfortable, on the whole, to let other people own the farms, and the pleasant places on the seashore and elsewhere, and go yourself occasionally to enjoy them while others have the trouble of them? Let me have a frank answer to this question when you have turned it over—revolved it Johnson would say—in your mind.[3] You have no laborers to hire and pay, and discharge, and look up others in their places; you have no anxiety lest thieves should take your choice fruit; you perplex yourself with no question whether a field be ill or well ploughed, or whether the weather be too wet or too dry. But yours are the fresh air and the sunshine, and the grateful shade of trees, and the verdure of the fields, and the hues and fragrance of the flowers and the sparkle and murmur of the waters, just as much as if you had forty acres to worry you. Your husband goes down on Saturday to see his old place and I dare say will take more pleasure in it than when he owned it.

I believe I gave you all the gossip of Roslyn with which I was acquainted, in my last. The most remarkable thing, in my private opinion, which happened in the neighbourhood this season, is that I had a young plum-tree in the garden, loaded with fruit, loaded to breaking, which ripened perfectly. It was of the sort called Prince's Yellow Gage. It seems to resist the curculio perfectly. I must have another of the sort. My Bartlett pears, some on quince stocks and some on the pear stock, also begin to yield fruit. The peaches fail this year. —But we will talk over the horticulture of the place,—a subject in regard to which you are most kindly patient with me—when you come out this autumn. . . .[4]

MANUSCRIPT: Ridgely Family Collection TEXT: Hoyt, "Bryant Correspondence (I)," 67–68 ADDRESS: Mrs. L. M. S. Moulton, Meadow Side, Plympton, Massachusetts.

1. Mrs. Moulton's marginal note: "Charles Sherman."
2. Bryant's Roslyn steward, 1844–1849. See Letter 502.

3. Samuel Johnson; see Letter 451.
4. Salutation, complimentary close, and signature omitted from text.

765. *To* Frances F. Bryant

New York   Sept. 10, 1851. Wednesday—

Dear F.

Julia has just called and says she will come with me tomorrow. Last night she passed at Mr. Morton's[1] in Hoboken.

Fanny was well when I saw her last evening between seven and eight o'clock.

A copy of verses in a female hand from Roslyn ["]On Following a Path in the woods traced by the hand of William C. Bryant," has been sent to the office, but there is too much about me in it to admit of its publication in the E.P.

Yrs ever

W. C. B.

P.S.—One o'clock. On coming down stairs to leave this letter for you I find your note to me. Caroline[2] has called and got her ten dollars—so you may charge them to her as soon as you get this.

W. C. B.

MANUSCRIPT: NYPL–GR ADDRESS: Mrs. F. F. Bryant / Roslyn / Long Island.

1. Probably George W. Morton; see 505.1.
2. Presumably a household servant.

766. *To* Frances F. Bryant

Rochester   Friday   Sept. 19   1851.

Dear Frances

I write this from Dr. Tobey's.[1] We got to Geneva at ten o'clock on Tuesday night and staid till Thursday morning. Mrs. Lee[2] says she will be very glad to see you and Julia, if you come out this fall and that if we let her know when we are to arrive she will send the carriage to the village for us—which is about two miles distant from her house.

Yesterday morning we came into Rochester, and went immediately to the Fair Ground. The town is crammed and at the hotels people sleep four in a small bed room. I came to the Doctor's and demanded hospitality. On my way I found Barnum Fairchild and his wife in the train. At this house are Tobey of Bloomfield and his wife and Mary White and John Fairchild Edwin's oldest son.[3] Their families are all well.

I shall proceed to Buffalo today, and expect to be in Detroit tomorrow morning, when I shall take the railway across Michigan, making the best of my way to Chicago.

When you write to me, which I expect you will do frequently, I wish

you would address your letters, postpaid of course, to the care of W. B. Ogden of Chicago.[4] If I do not hear that you are coming to this place, I shall not return by the way of Rochester, but shall take the Erie Railroad at Dunkirk which is the most expeditious way to New York.

Will you say to George[5] that I wish him when he and the men can spare time, to remove the earth from the peach trees in the garden and in the two yards that of the house and the Titus cottage[6] and supply its place with earth from the woods. I would also have manure put round the fruit trees on the hill and elsewhere.

I am sorry that you are not with me—you and Julia—to make the journey to Illinois. Here at Rochester just now it is not very pleasant. The air is constantly full of dust and the streets full of foot passengers and waggons. I hope, however, to find you somewhere before my return.

Yrs ever
W. C. B.

MANUSCRIPT: NYPL–GR ADDRESS: Mrs. F. F. Bryant / Roslyn / Long Island.

1. Frances Bryant's brother-in-law.
2. Not further identified.
3. Barnum Fairchild was evidently Frances' nephew; John Fairchild was a son of her brother Edwin; Dr. P. G. Tobey of Bloomfield was the husband of her sister Mary. See 38.1. Mary White is unidentified.
4. William Butler Ogden; see 581.2, Letter 597.
5. Evidently the new steward Bryant had engaged a week earlier; see Letter 764.
6. On April 7, 1845 Bryant had bought, for $1,100, an adjoining house and lot from Jacob Titus, who had farmed Bryant's land during the first year of his ownership of the property acquired from Joseph W. Moulton in 1842. MS agreement between Bryant and Titus dated February 23, 1843, Bryant Library, Roslyn; MS account with Titus, April 4, 1845, in The William Cullen Bryant Homestead Collection of the Trustees of Reservations, Cummington, Massachusetts.

767. *To* the EVENING POST

Rochester, Sept. 19, 1851.

This city lies under a dense cloud of dust which only subsides by night. Foot passengers throng the ways as in Chatham street[1] at seven o'clock in the morning, and the middle of the streets is occupied by long processions of vehicles of all sorts, forming knots where the streets cross each other, which are tediously slow in unravelling. Owners of horses and carriages at a distance send them up to Rochester and make their hundred dollars a day, by conveying people through the dust to the Fair Ground, as it is called, at the rate of twenty-five cents a passenger. The population of Rochester was, in 1850, thirty-six thousand—at present nearer forty—yesterday it was computed that there could not be fewer than ninety thousand in the place. At the hotels there is a perpetual banquet from morning to night; as fast as one set rises from the long tables another

is ready to take its place; and incredible quantities of tough beef, potatoes snatched in haste from huge cauldrons, and tomatoes stewed in vats, are served up to hungry guests on the same table cloth. The people of the city contributed about seven thousand dollars, as I hear, to the expenses of the fair, the greater part of which was subscribed by the keepers of hotels and boarding houses.

The field occupied by the fair lies about a mile and a half from the town, in the possessions of Mr. Wadsworth[2]—a grassy pasture, full of hillocks, with the Genesee flowing on the south side. Beyond the river is the woody ridge of Mount Hope, and a foot-bridge has been thrown across the stream that the visitors to the fair may pass over to that beautiful cemetery. The most remarkable part of the exhibition consists in the show of animals and agricultural implements. In both respects, the present fair is said to be altogether superior to any other ever held in the state. I should mention also the fruits, of which there was a very fine display. The apple which Atalanta ran for, could not have been fairer than hundreds of those ranged on the tables in the building appropriated to fruits and flowers. In this region the apple is larger and more uniformly handsome in shape than in the country near the sea-coast. It is scarce ever stung by insects. Plums and pears also are in the greatest abundance, and of the largest size and most inviting appearance.

The short-horn cattle of Mr. Wadsworth, fed in the rich pastures of Genesee, made a fine appearance, but as there was some obscurity in their pedigree, they were not entered for the prizes. Mr. Morris, of Westchester county, has some very fine short-horns at the fair, and some remarkably beautiful samples of the Devonshire breed, with their long slender horns, their deer-like heads, and shapely, active limbs. From these are bred the best working oxen of the country. In one part of the field I saw three spayed heifers of this breed, as large as oxen, and said to be superior to the ox, as working animals, in activity and docility. The short-horns of Mr. Sherwood of Auburn, a very early introduction of this breed, are among the very finest samples seen at the fair. Two animals of the Hungary breed are also there, sent by Mr. Colt, of Paterson; [they] are gray in color, not however equal to our own breeds. There was a considerable display of Herefords, ungainly looking animals, and some fine samples of Ayrshire cattle, with their clean looking sharp horns and mottled hides, sent by that judicious breeder, Mr. Prentiss, of Albany.[3]

It is curious to see the evidence which the short-horn breed, both the pure specimens and those of the mixed breed, give of their aptitude for fattening. In the rich pastures of this region they soon swell into prodigious obesity. The broad frame of the back is filled out so that they look almost like stuffed animals, and masses of fat are deposited wherever the skin is loose enough to allow them room, rising in lumps about the rump and other parts of the body.

A good deal of attention is drawn to the reaping machines, which are drawn on the ground by teams of horses; the drills of several different constructions, the advantages of which are elaborately explained to the spectators; the winnowing machines, and so forth. Of ploughs there is an assortment almost large enough to till the fields of the whole country. Two book stores on the ground contain all the American publications on agriculture, gardening and husbandry, and among them are several of which I had not before heard. I look on their appearance at the fair as an indication that the habit of reading books on agriculture is becoming more general.

I find that there is some complaint among the farmers of the unwieldiness of a state agricultural fair. It draws, they say, too large crowds; nobody can thoroughly examine the objects exhibited in such a press of visitors. They complain, too, that the judges who award the prizes are not always taken from the class who understand the matter in hand, but too often from men of note, whose presence and whose name, it is thought may give a sort of eclat to the occasion. I have heard some grumble, that politicians are allowed to make the fair an occasion to add to their own notoriety. I should not wonder if there were not some ground for these complaints.

Today the fair will close, after the prizes are awarded and the addresses are made.

W. C. B.

MANUSCRIPT: Unrecovered TEXT: *EP*, September 22, 1851.

1. Then a business thoroughfare in lower Manhattan.
2. James Samuel Wadsworth (1807–1864), a lawyer and large landowner in Geneseo, New York.
3. These other exhibitors have not been further identified.

768. *To* Rufus W. Griswold

Rochester, Friday, Sept. 19, 1851.

My Dear Sir:

I am sorry that the arrangements for my journey to the West are such that I cannot be present at the meeting which is about to be held to do honor to the memory of Mr. Cooper,[1] on losing whom not only the country, but the civilized world and the age in which we live, have lost one of their most illustrious ornaments. It is melancholy to think that it is only [when][2] such men are in their graves that full justice is done to their merit. I shall be most happy to concur in any step which may be taken to express, in a public manner, our respect for the character of one to whom we were too sparing of public distinctions in his life-time, and beg that I may be included in the proceedings of the occasion as if I were present.[3]

I am, very respectfully yours,
WM. C. BRYANT.

MANUSCRIPT: Unrecovered TEXT: *EP*, September 25, 1851 ADDRESS: Dr. R. W. Griswold.

1. James Fenimore Cooper died at Cooperstown, New York, on September 14, 1851. On the 24th, at a meeting in the New York City Hall, a committee which included Bryant was appointed to plan a suitable tribute to the late novelist. *EP*, September 25, 1851.
2. The printed text has "until."
3. On February 25, 1852, a memorial meeting was held in Metropolitan Hall, New York, at which Bryant delivered the principal eulogy of Cooper. See "James Fenimore Cooper, A Discourse on His Life, Genius and Writings, Delivered at Metropolitan Hall, New York, February 25, 1852," in *Orations and Addresses*, pp. 45–91.

769. *To* Frances F. Bryant

Princeton   September 24th   1851. Wednesday.

Dear Frances.

I wrote you from Rochester just as I was about to set out for Chicago. On the same day Friday last I took the accommodation train for Buffalo where I arrived in the evening. The cars were fairly crammed with persons returning from the fair, and many among whom was myself had to stand up for a considerable part of the distance. We arrived in the evening, and I took passage for Detroit in the *May Flower*, a large and magnificent steamer, which was also crowded. I had a rather uncomfortable night in the "gentlemen's cabin," as it is called, but the next day was pleasant and the temperature delightful. We reached Detroit about four o'clock on Saturday afternoon, and about five were on our way across the peninsula of Michigan by the railway. The aspect of Michigan from the railway is not very attractive—a new country, not apparently the most fertile; flat, in many places marshy, in some sandy. The sun set in thick clouds, the darkness came on early, and ere long we ran into a violent rain. I slept well and the next morning showed us the earth drenched and the woods dripping. About seven o'clock we reached the end of the railway at New Buffalo, and after breakfasting, at the pier took a wretched steamer the Samuel Ward, for Chicago where we arrived between eleven and twelve o'clock. I got my dinner and then went to Mr. Ogden's who was not at home, not yet having returned from the east. I did not look for any body else, but at five o'clock took passage in the mail packet boat on the canal for Peru—or rather La Salle, about one mile north of Peru. The day was fine and I continued on the deck till dark. At night the passengers were hung up, as usual, on the sides of the boat, in three tiers on a side. I was up as soon as it was daylight, and passed the rest of the day—a mild cloudy day, on deck delighted with the scenery about me, till four o'clock when we arrived at the termination of the canal.

A gentleman from La Moille [Greenfield][1] engaged to see if any person from Princeton was in Peru who would take me to that place. He could find nobody, but put me on the track, and I fell in with a man, who

was going the next morning, and promised to take me. I passed a sleepless night with the fleas and mosquitoes at Peru, and the next morning at eight o'clock started in a lumber waggon—the stage coach goes only every other day—for Princeton, in a shower of rain. We had two big iron kettles turned upside down a barrel of molasses and two passengers besides myself in the waggon. I secured my travelling bag from the rain by pulling it under one of the kettles. We reached Princeton at two o'clock in the afternoon. This was yesterday.

I find every body well here. My brothers appear to be doing well, and are living more comfortably than before. I shall stop and see our friends at Chicago in my return and [at]² that place I hope to hear from you. I shall be very glad to learn that you are coming out as far as Rochester— but if you are not, I shall on my return make all haste to New York by way of Dunkirk. They all inquire with interest, here, about you and your children, and seem disappointed that I did not bring you and Julia with me. I have had on the whole a pleasant journey till yesterday, and think you would have been pleased with it. Probably I shall leave this place to return on Monday.—

Yours affectionately

W C BRYANT

MANUSCRIPT: NYPL–GR.

    1. The brackets are Bryant's.
    2. Word omitted.

770. *To* Frances F. Bryant

New York   Wednesday   Oct. 15, 1851.

Dear F.

I wrote to you yesterday in haste to tell you that Mr. Field's¹ waggon would be at the landing on Staten Island to meet Julia when the one o'clock boat arrived from New York on Thursday. She will not get to Brooklyn much before eleven and probably could not be in New York in time to take the eleven o'clock boat for Staten Island. There is no boat at twelve.

I was run down yesterday. Bigelow is ill and was not at the office. I arrived at 20 minutes past eleven and had to write a leader. First Judge Phillips, Willard Phillips,² came. Then after a while came Dr. Simmons of St. Augustine.³ Then came Mr. Sedgwick, Theodore. Next came Mr. [Alfred] Pell. Finally came Miss Cooper. There were several other calls of less importance.

I find that Miss Coopers furniture is mortgaged to her landlord, Dr. Smith, for $300. This, when she told me of it had the effect of making me the less willing to engage her rooms.⁴

It may be that Bigelow will not be well enough on Saturday to come to the office, in which case I may perhaps be unable to come out on Friday—but I shall try very hard to do so.

What I feared is true—they want me to give a eulogy on Cooper[5]—Tripler Hall and a dollar a ticket.— The committee waited for this— They say I may be as short as I please and other persons will speak after me. A bronze monument in New York is talked of.

Yrs ever
W. C. B.

P.S. Since I wrote what goes before, Miss Cooper has called again. Dr. Smith is going to sell her furniture unless she gets the $300. I could do nothing of course.

W. C. B.

MANUSCRIPT: NYPL–GR ADDRESS: Mrs. F. F. Bryant / Roslyn / Long Island.

1. Alfred Field; see 406.5; Letter 643.
2. See Vol. I, 13–14; 479.2.
3. See 460.1.
4. It seems probable that Miss Cooper was the Bryants' landlady in their winter lodgings at 263 Greene Street, into which they had moved in November 1849. See Letters 709, 710, 742.
5. See 768.3.

771. [*To* George Bancroft

New York, October 22, 1851.

My dear Bancroft,

I send you the interrogations you placed in my hands with such answers to them as I am able to give. . . .]

QUESTIONS RESPECTING THE COMMON SCHOOLS OF NEW ENGLAND[1]

1. Have you reason to believe that the system of Instruction, adopted in the Common Schools of New England, interferes with the special religious tenets of any particular denomination of Christians?

I have no reason to believe that as at present conducted the system interferes with the tenets of any religious persuasion.

2. Is it within your knowledge, that, apart from the Common Schools, the children educated in them do practically receive Instruction in the tenets of the religious denomination to which they respectively belong?

I know that the different religious denominations in New England have their sabbath schools in which their peculiar doctrines are taught, and that religious instruction is also given by parents in families and by the distribution of tracts designed for young persons, and likewise in visits by clergymen to the families under their care.

3. If they do receive such Instruction, what are the agencies by which it is communicated to them?

This is answered in the reply to the second question.

4. In your opinion, is the system of Instruction pursued in the Common Schools of New England indirectly favorable to the cultivation of the religious sentiments and to the promotion of morality?

I think it is decidedly so.

5. Generally, do you approve or do you disapprove of that system; and what are the main grounds on which your approbation or disapprobation of it is founded?

I should be very sorry to see the public school system of New England where it has been so long established, and where it has worked so well, and where, as it seems to me it is more wisely administered than elsewhere, abrogated. An answer to the general question here put would lead to the consideration of points in regard to which I am still an inquirer and I must therefore decline attempting to make it.

New York   October 20th   1851,

WILLIAM C. BRYANT.

MANUSCRIPTS (letter) Unrecovered; (questionnaire) Chicago Historical Society LETTER TEXT: N. K. Black, Montclair, New Jersey, Catalogue No. 126, Item No. 70, March 1971.

1. The origin of this questionnaire is unknown, as is George Bancroft's connection with the matter. Bryant's replies to the questions are printed in italics.

772.   *To* Cyrus Bryant

New York   November 6th   1851.

Dear Brother.

You have doubtless heard before this of Aunt Charity's death.[1] I had a telegraphic despatch acquainting me with the event—it came to New York during my absence.

Since that time, I have seen Mrs. Rankin [Caroline][2] and her husband. A very short time before our aunt's death, Caroline had paid her a visit. She found her somewhat relieved from the unpleasant and painful symptoms which she formerly complained of, but she was in quite delicate health. Her faculti[e]s, however, seemed uncommonly bright, and she took great interest in every thing that was going on.

Not long before her death—a very few days—Mrs. Rankin had a letter from her. Her case had been mentioned by Mrs. Rankin to some physician in Boston who called it, I think, spasmodic neuralgia, and another said it was *angina pectoris.*

She died in her chair, of one of those attacks which she so frequently had the year before, and which were so distressing—a sort of constriction about the region of the heart, as I understood, accompanied with pain, and I think a sense of suffocation—agreeing with the symptoms of what is called *Angina* pectoris, or stricture of the chest. My former partner Mr.

Burnham[3] in the latter part of his life, had attacks of this sort, which compelled him sometimes to stop in the street and sit down. He died of what the physicians called a disease of the heart.

Will you be kind enough to let the other members of our family see this letter. It may give them some particulars of which they have not heard. I have been thinking of writing to Miss Drake[4] on the subject, but I have not yet done it.—

We are all very well. Fanny has another child, a little girl,[5] and is doing well. Her eldest is recovering. The autumnal rains have filled the springs, which before were very low, and have made the earth green again. I have been planting some apple trees, making a little orchard of a dozen trees or so—in which I include the Northern Spy. In Ontario County where it originated they call it the finest apple in the country; if this be true, it is the finest in the world.

Will you hand the accompanying letter to John.[6]

Remember me to your wife and children, and to all our friends in Princeton.

Yours affectionately
W   C   BRYANT.

MANUSCRIPT: BCHS ADDRESS: C. Bryant Esq.

1. Dr. Peter Bryant's unmarried sister Charity (58.1) died at Weybridge, Vermont, on October 5, 1851, at the age of seventy-four.

2. Caroline A. (Bryant) Rankin was the daughter of Peter Bryant's sister Silence (b. 1774) and her cousin Ichabod Bryant. Caroline's brother Edwin N. Bryant (1805–1869) wrote one of the first popular books on the Far West, *What I Saw in California* (1847). The brackets are Bryant's.

3. Michael Burnham; see 146.5; 339.1.

4. Bryant's aunt Charity and her devoted companion, Sylvia Drake (58.1), were buried under the same headstone in the Weybridge Hill Cemetery.

5. Nora Godwin (1851–1914).

6. Unrecovered.

773.   *To* Charles Gould[1]

Nov   12th   1851.

My dear sir.

I am sorry to forego the pleasure of a dinner with you and Mr. Leutze,[2] and the agreeable people whom you know how to assemble about you, but my engagements for this week are so many and so pressing that I am obliged to decline your kind invitation.

Truly yours
W. C. BRYANT

P.S. I have received your note of this morning[3] informing me that the

dinner is postponed to Friday. I am sorry to be obliged to say that even this change will not put it in my power to come.

W. C. B.

MANUSCRIPT: HCL ADDRESS: Ch. Gould Esqre.

1. Charles Gould was a New York broker and art patron who owned paintings, exhibited in 1851–1853, by Asher Durand, Regis Gignoux, John Kensett, and other members of the National Academy. *NAD Exhibition Record*, I, 139, 184, 276, and *passim*. Gould was Bryant's occasional guest at Sketch Club meetings. Information from James T. Callow.
2. The painter Emanuel Leutze; see 531.1.
3. Unrecovered.

774.   *To* Hamilton Fish[1]

Office of the Evening Post,
New York, November 16, 1851.

Sir:

Accompanying this you will receive a History of the EVENING POST for the Last Half Century.[2] We shall be happy to commence the next, with the addition of your name to the list of our subscribers.[3]

Yours respectfully,
WM. C. BRYANT & Co.
18 Nassau St.

MANUSCRIPT: (printed circular): LC.

1. Hamilton Fish (1808–1893, Columbia 1827), Whig governor of New York, 1849–1851, was thereafter United States senator, 1851–1857, and Secretary of State, 1869–1877.
2. Bryant's account of his newspaper's history, since its founding in 1801 by Alexander Hamilton and William Coleman, was printed in the *EP* for November 15, 1851, and simultaneously in a pamphlet, *Reminiscences of the Evening Post: Extracted from the Evening Post of November 15, 1851. With Additions and Corrections by the Writer* (New York: Wm. C. Bryant & Co., Printers, 18 Nassau Street, N.Y., 1851). It was reprinted in Bigelow, *Bryant*, pp. 312–342. Bigelow's account of its composition (p. 109) is illuminating in its revelation of Bryant's work habits:

> When the semi-centennial anniversary of the "Evening Post" was approaching, it was proposed to him to prepare for its columns a sketch of its career. He cheerfully accepted the task, and in order that he might be free from interruption he was advised to go down to his country-home at Roslyn and remain there until it was finished, and have such of the files of the paper as he might have occasion to consult sent to him there. He rejected the proposal as abruptly as if he had been asked to offer sacrifices to Apollo. He would allow no such work to follow him there. Not even the shadow of his business must fall upon the consecrated haunts of his muse. He rarely brought or sent anything from the country for the "Evening Post"; but if he did, it was easy to detect in the character of the fish that they had been caught in strange waters. This separation of his professional from his poetic life must be taken into account in any effort to explain the uniform esteem in

which he was always held as a poet by his country people, while occasionally one of the least popular of journalists.

3. See Letter 776.

775.   *To* Edward W. Leggett

Roslyn   November 27, 1851.

Dear sir.

If my people have at any time obstructed your passage through my land east of the house, I am sorry for it. It was contrary to my directions and I hope you will find neither vehicle nor any other implement of mine in your way hereafter.[1]

With regard to the wood of which you speak I have been to look at it this morning and find that it is piled close to the fence and not in the way at all. If I were in your place I should never think of making it the subject of complaint.

You inquire whether it is to remain there. As you have merely the right to pass and repass, while the land is mine, I certainly expect to put the land to any use which does not interfere with your right—whether it be to lay wood or any thing else upon it, leaving always ample space for your passage. At the same time, whatever be my rights it is my desire to [do][2] nothing to which a reasonable man would object.

I understand that the wood was piled by the fence that it might be measured, after which it was to be removed to the wood piles at the convenience of my people. It will probably remain where it is for a few days.

I am sir

very respectfully yours

W. C. Bryant

MANUSCRIPT: NYPL–GR (two drafts) ADDRESS: Edward W. Leggett Esq.

1. Leggett, whose property adjoined Bryant's, apparently enjoyed an easement through his neighbor's land in order to reach the highway. On the previous day he had written a curt note complaining that Bryant's "people" had so littered the drive with wood and a wheelbarrow that on the evening before he was "compelled to drive over the latter," and that he had hoped, after their earlier discussion, that "such nuisances would have been discontinued." Leggett to Bryant, November 26, 1851, NYPL–GR.

2. Word omitted.

776.   *To* Hamilton Fish

Office of the Evening Post

New York, December 9, 1851.

Dear Sir,

We cannot refrain from expressing the satisfaction we have experienced in reading your letter, the kind expressions in which concerning the *Evening Post* prove your superiority to party prejudice.[1] Nothing, we

hope, will occur to lower it in your esteem, since it would be a source of real pain to us to lose the good opinion of one whom we hold in such high respect.

Yours respectfully
WM. C. BRYANT & CO.

MANUSCRIPT (in Bryant's handwriting): Fish Letter Books, LC.

1. On November 29 Fish had replied to Letter 774 that he was already a subscriber to the *EP*, of which his father, Nicholas Fish (1758–1833), had been an initial backer, and that "I remember it from my earliest boyhood, & rarely have I allowed a day to pass without seeking information from it—& yet more rarely have I sought in vain." He continued,

Although it has been my lot to differ in my views of many of the important questions which it has discussed from those which the Post has advanced, I have always admired the force, the ability & the fearlessness with which it has maintained its own views. I have appreciated the honesty with which it adopted those views however differing from my own. Since I became the father of a family of children I have been made conscious of the security with which the Evening Post may be placed in their hands—its high toned morality, its general teachings (barring some "political heresies"!) its literary ability & the character of its selected matter have pointed to it as one of the papers which a parent may safely & with advantage place in the hands of his child. . . . I most sincerely hope that your Paper may continue to prosper [LC].

On the day this tribute to his paper's integrity was written, Bryant published a prospectus of the *EP* for its second half century, renewing what many of Fish's Whig friends would have considered a "political heresy." "We think its past history," he wrote, "no unimportant guarantee that the *Evening Post* will continue to battle for human rights in preference to human sovereignties; for the welfare and improvement of the multitude, rather than for exclusive privileges to classes and tribes; for freedom of industry and thought, regardless of the frowns and the blandishments of power or wealth." *EP*, November 29, 1851.

777. *To* John W. Francis[1]

New York   Dec. 11, 1851.

My dear sir.

I cannot find the account of the dinner given to Mr. [Fenimore] Cooper before his departure for Europe. I have written to Mr. King,[2] who cannot give me the date of it, but is sure that it was before 1830 and after 1827. Can you give me any thing more precise—if so you will oblige me by communicating it.[3]

Yours faithfully
W. C. BRYANT.

MANUSCRIPT: MHS.

1. See Letter 148.
2. Charles King; see 196.3. Bryant's letter to King is unrecovered.
3. This tribute to Cooper was paid him by fellow-members of the **Bread and Cheese**

Lunch Club, among them Bryant, at the City Hotel, New York, on May 29, 1826, where Charles King, then editor of the New York *American*, was one of those who offered toasts. Cooper, *Letters & Journals*, I, 139–140.

778. *To* Horatio Greenough

New York   December 30, 1851.

My dear sir.

I like the idea of your letter very much,[1] and though I have no definite idea of the method in which you propose to apply to architecture in general the principles on which the style which distinguishes our shipbuilding is founded, I shall be glad to see it done. It will give me great pleasure to hear your paper read, at almost any time you may appoint after your return to New York.[2] Mr. Godwin is about to set out for Europe so that he cannot be present.

Yrs faithfully

W. C BRYANT

MANUSCRIPT: Century Association ADDRESS: H Greenough Esq.

1. Horatio Greenough (195.1, Letter 299, 451.1, 472.1) had returned to America in October 1851 after long residence in Florence, having finally completed the heroic statuary group *The Rescue*, commissioned in 1837 for the east front of the Capitol in Washington. From Boston, on November 4, he wrote Bryant (YCAL), "I thank God from the bottom of my heart that I have once more put my foot on my own, my native soil and I hope though new arrived to the 'mezzo del camin de nostra vita' ["the middle of our life's journey"—Dante, *Divine Comedy*, *Inferno*, I.1] to be of some use here both in illustrative art and structure for here I mean to stay." His mind was feverish with projects he proposed to tackle: a monument coupling the treason of Benedict Arnold and the executions of the spies, British John André and American Nathan Hale; a memorial of James Fenimore Cooper; statues of Washington and Jackson. And on December 27 he sent Bryant from Washington a summary of the creed which he would soon after develop in his influential book, *The Travels, Observations, and Experience of a Yankee Stonecutter* (New York, 1852):

I have since my arrival in this city prepared a paper on Structure and Ornament, in which I seek to show—1st that we have many dialects in our buildings, but no language—2nd that we have developed in our ships, our carriages and engines a new style. 3d that this style, which I call the Yankee Doric, is strictly in harmony with the great primal laws of Gods own structures, and is in these partial exhibitions of it, as near perfection, as our knowledge is to pure science—4th that it is high time to rouse the country to introduce in structures of a civil character, the sound logical doctrine embodied in the engine; and thus by demonstrating practically its beauty as well as utility, to check the influx of foreign and *hostile* aesthetics— Can you and Mr Godwin spare time to hear me read this paper and give me your suggestions? [NYPL–GR].

2. From January through May 1852 Greenough spent much of his time in New York and Brooklyn, discussing his plans and theories with Bryant and others; soliciting funds to support an heroic equestrian statue of George Washington, which he and the sculptor Henry Kirke Brown were to execute jointly (this was completed in 1856 by Brown and John Quincy Adams Ward); and writing letters to the *EP* about this project. In February he described to Bryant his elaborately conceived symbolic monu-

ment to Cooper which he hoped to erect in Washington Square, New York, and he was several times a guest at Sketch Club meetings. "Some of the leading men of letters in New York," he reported to his brother Henry on May 20, "have whispered to me of a professorship of Art in a university on a grand scale." But before the year ended Greenough had died of brain fever. Greenough to Bryant, February 5, 1852, NYPL–BG; *Letters of Horatio Greenough, American Sculptor*, ed. Nathalia Wright (Madison: University of Wisconsin Press [1972]), pp. 389–420, *passim; Letters of Horatio Greenough to his Brother, Henry Greenough, with Biographical Sketches and Some Contemporary Correspondence*, ed. Frances Boott Greenough (Boston, 1887), p. 240.

779. *To* Abraham Hart

New York   January 6, 1852

Dear sir.

I am sorry to hear of the loss which you sustained by the late fire.[1] With regard to the publication of an enlarged edition of my poems I am now so much engaged in various matters that I could not possibly attend to the preparation of any additional poems for the press. At present, therefore, for aught I can see, the cheap edition must remain as it is, and the consideration of an enlarged edition be postponed till I have more leisure.

I am sir
Yours truly
W. C. BRYANT.

MANUSCRIPT: HSPa.

1. On December 26, 1851, a fire in "Harts' Buildings" at the corner of Sixth and Chestnut streets, Philadelphia, caused the destruction of about twenty-five stores, the loss of two lives, and a financial loss of about $300,000. *EP*, December 27, 1851.

780. *To* Horatio Greenough

February 8th. 1852.

My dear sir.

I have just got your letter and answered it immediately, because there is one inquiry in it which might better be answered now than hereafter.[1]

The house which Cooper owned in the village is to be sold. I have this in a letter from the Revd Mr. Battin, the pastor of the church to which Cooper belonged.[2] The family cannot afford to keep it. They ask ten or twelve thousand dollars for it, and it is said to be a most desirable residence. Do you know of any man worthy to live in Cooper's house who will buy it[?] There are five or six acres of land with it, and the dwelling is beautifully embowered with trees planted by his own hands. It would be a great comfort to the worthy Mr. Battin if the purchaser should be a good Episcopalian.

I learn from the same authority that there will be but about $20,000 to be divided among the five children.

Yours cordially
W. C. BRYANT

P.S. I hope to be able to command a few hours leisure at some time not far off, to talk over the subjects of your letter.[3]

W. C. B.

MANUSCRIPT: Brown University Library ADDRESS: H. Greenough Esq.

1. In his letter of February 5 (NYPL–BG), Greenough had written Bryant, "I am very anxious to know how Mr. Cooper's family is now situated as regards their means—and whether the possession of the paternal estate is secured to them."

2. Stephen Henry Battin (1814?–1893, Trinity 1839, General Theological Seminary 1842) of Cooperstown, New York. See Cooper, *Letters & Journals*, V, 388–390. Battin's letter to Bryant is unrecovered.

3. See 778.2.

781.   *To* Henry R. Schoolcraft[1]

New York   February 14, 1852

My dear Sir.

I should have written to you earlier, on the subject of your letter of the 15th of December, but I mislaid it and was not sure of your address.

I like the sample of Mr. Hetherwold's poetry which you have sent me.[2] The sentiments are generous, the imagery poetical and the versification sonorous. Yet I doubt its success with the public, if it appear as Mr. Hetherwold's. A poetical reputation at the present time is made very gradually and slowly; nobody jumps into it at once. I fully believe that the best verses in the world, published in a volume, by an author not yet known to fame, would be inevitably neglected. There is another obstacle to Mr. Hetherwold's success. Poetry you know has its fashions, which change with the time. Poetry of the form you sent me was the mode some twenty or thirty years since—perhaps I should put the era still further back. At present poetry bears a somewhat different shape, and the reader, or rather the mass of readers who feel the influence of the reigning mode, will be repelled by the sight of what does not conform to it.

I have thus written to you frankly what I think on the subject of your letter. It is a delicate matter to advise a poet, but you are also a man who knows the world, and are more easily dealt with. My opinions in such matters are not of much value, but such as they are you have them.

I am Sir
Yours faithfully
WM. C. BRYANT

MANUSCRIPT: LC? TEXT: Frank Smith, "Schoolcraft, Bryant, and Poetic Fame," *American Literature*, 5 (May 1933), 170.

1. See 589.3. Schoolcraft was then engaged in his major work, *Historical and Statistical Information Respecting the History, Condition and Prospects of the Indian Tribes of the United States*, 1851–1857.

2. Schoolcraft had asked Bryant's opinion of some verses written by his "protégé"

"William Hetherwold" (apparently of Schoolcraft's own composition). The final paragraph of Bryant's letter suggests that he was aware of their true authorship. See Smith, "Schoolcraft, Bryant, and Poetic Fame," 170–72. The verses were later published in "William Hetherwold," *The Man of Bronz; A Poem on the Indian Character. In Six Books* (Philadelphia, 1852).

782. *To* Cyrus Bryant

New York   March 12, 1852.

Dear Brother.

I have your letter concerning Mr. Moseley[1] as a subscriber. With respect to Harper's Magazine,[2] I think it is not quite so good as it ought to be. There is one special objection to it—namely that the periodicals from which its articles are taken are not mentioned, which is done I suppose to make people fancy that they are original. To one who desires to know something of the character of the English periodicals this is very unsatisfactory.

The International Magazine[3] edited by Dr. [Rufus] Griswold, is free from this objection. It has besides a greater variety of matter, particularly in relation to what authors are doing or expecting to do, and what learned and scientific societies are occupying themselves with. The editor is particularly well fitted for collecting this sort of information. I should take the *International Magazine,* if I were to give up Littell.[4] Stringer & Townsend of this city are the publishers.

Remember me kindly to your wife and children.

Yrs affectionately

W. C. BRYANT.

MANUSCRIPT: BCHS.

1. Possibly Fred Mosely, who married Austin Bryant's daughter Frances Elizabeth (1828–1882). Austin to Cullen Bryant, April 22, 1859, NYPL–GR.

2. *Harper's New Monthly Magazine* had been established by Harper & Brothers in June 1850.

3. *The International Monthly Magazine of Literature, Art, and Science*, founded in July 1850. It is ironic that the following month this was merged with *Harper's New Monthly Magazine.*

4. *Littell's Living Age*; see 638.3.

783. *To* Richard Dana

New York   March 15th. 1852.

Dear Dana.

I perceive that I have dated this letter at New York, according to my usual habit; but in truth I write it at Roslyn, where I am now with my wife for two or three days, for the first time since the middle of January. I wish you were here too. There is a glorious genial sunshine on the light green water in the little lake and on the darker water of the harbor; the frost is entirely out of the ground, and the roads are becoming settled as

fast as they can. The robins are whistling[1] here and there and the song sparrows are twittering everywhere. Since you were here, I have added about two acres and a half to my woodland, and have made walks in that part of it which I owned before, which are to be extended still further, so that if you *should* ever come to Roslyn you will find solitary and shady walks beginning almost at our door. I have had the trees cut away in several places, and the view opened to the water, and a bench or two put up. for you, if you are inclined to sit.

But I did not mean to speak of this, when I began my letter. I meant principally to set you right concerning [Charles] Sumner's letter, which you suppose was hissed at the meeting when I delivered my discourse.[2] I doubt whether the audience heard Sumner's name at all. Dr. Griswold was not very audible and they had become tired of hearing or trying to hear the letters. He mentioned half a dozen different names of the writers and all had the same reception. I do not mean that it was his manner of reading them that caused the dissatisfaction, but it was getting late, and some of the audience, disrespectfully enough it is true to the Committee, took the arrangements into their own hands.[3]

Webster spoke in a very low voice, and was heard only by a small circle immediately about him. The applause which he received was of a different kind from that given to any of the other speakers, it was more noisy and consisted more of drumming and stamping; it seemed, too, that the noise was made by a different set of people, a great number of whom could not have heard a syllable he said. My daughters sat about two thirds of the way between the platform and the door, and were quite unable to make any thing of what he said; but they observed a set of rather queer looking fellows near them who were very loud in their demonstrations of applause, and who tried to get away after he had finished his introductory speech, but were obliged to remain, being wedged in by the crowd. That speech was deplorably common place, —poor in thought, and clumsy in expression. The man seemed in a sort of collapse and actually moved my compassion. The discourse which he gave before the [New-York] Historical Society[4] was not heard by half the people present, and it was very disrespectfully said by the reporters for the whig papers, whispering to each other at the commencement of his discourse, that he was drunk. I do not vouch for the truth of what they said, but the scandal had a very wide circulation. On the whole I think his visit to New York did a good deal of mischief to his reputation. The meeting called to nominate him for the presidency was thinly attended, and is much laughed at here.[5]

I had the good fortune to be heard by all who were present, though the hall is a large one, and I have no reason to be dissatisfied with the reception of my discourse, either when it was delivered or since it has been published.[6] But enough of this matter.

When Brackett's group arrives in New York I will do what I can for it. I read to Mr. Bigelow that part of your letter which relates to it.[7] Godwin has taken a trip to Europe.

What a funny book that is about your old friend Margaret Fuller.[8] The authors of it seem to think very highly of her, but they say things of her which do not justify, or rather which contradict their conclusions. She seems to have been extraordinary as a scholar, and to have had the gift of talking plausibly and without being at a loss for convenient modes of expression—but beyond this she does not seem to have been endowed with any uncommon talent. Her conceit appears, as they describe it to have been almost maniacal, and she seems to have been without either practical good sense or good manners.

Do you never mean to come down to my place, and see how the spring opens in this somewhat milder latitude? You shall have the run of the new walks which my wife and I have made in our woods, and I think there is sherry enough in the cellar to give you a glass daily with your dinner. Remember me kindly to your sisters and your daughter. My wife asks to be remembered—to you and them.

Yrs sincerely

W. C. Bryant

P.S. Cooper's house in Cooperstown is to be sold. The Rector of the Church, of which Cooper was a member Mr. Battin, has written to me to ask if I knew of anybody who would buy it—anybody worthy to be Cooper's successor, and like him a good Episcopalian. A very nice house with five or six acres of land, made a solitude in summer by the trees which Cooper planted, and which shut it out from sight of the village—price ten or twelve thousand dollars. Do you know a purchaser? Cooper left about $20,000 to his five children.

W. C. B.

MANUSCRIPT: NYPL–GR ADDRESS: R. H. Dana, Esq. DOCKETED: Wm C. Bryant. / Mar. 15/52. Ans / Ap. 14th.

1. Bryant wrote "whislling."
2. See 768.3.
3. At the memorial meeting for James Fenimore Cooper on February 25 Daniel Webster gave the opening address, at the end of which he turned toward Bryant with a bow and said, "Mr. Bryant will now pronounce a discourse upon the life, character, and genius of Fenimore Cooper." But, continues the *EP* report of the next day, Rufus Griswold intervened and read letters from sixteen writers and politicians, of which Sumner's letter was the fourteenth. "Mr. Bryant commenced his address at half-past eight, and concluded about a quarter before ten. He was frequently interrupted by the most flattering applause." Webster closed the meeting "with a short address, which was delivered in a low tone of voice, so much so as to be inaudible except to those who sat very near him."
4. On February 23 Webster addressed an audience of five thousand at Niblo's

Garden and Theatre, on the forty-eighth anniversary of the New-York Historical Society. *EP*, February 24, 1852.

5. During 1851 and the early months of 1852 Webster made what Allan Nevins characterized as "pathetic efforts" to secure the Whig nomination for the presidency the following June. *Ordeal*, II, 23. The meeting Bryant refers to was held on March 5. *EP*, March 6, 1852.

6. Bryant's "Discourse on the Life and Genius of Cooper" was printed in the *EP* for February 27, and later in *Memorial of James Fenimore Cooper* (New York: Putnam, 1852), pp. 39–73. Charles Sumner thought Bryant's address a "truthful, simple & delicate composition; and much as I value sculpture and [Horatio] Greenough, I cannot but add that it will be a more durable monument to Cooper than any other. Webster's historical article," he added, "was crude & trite enough." Letter to John Bigelow, March 2, 1852, quoted in Bigelow, *Retrospections*, I, 125–126.

7. Dana's letter is unrecovered. No comment on the sculpture of Edward A. Brackett (401.1) appears in the *EP* for the two weeks following the date of this letter.

8. *Memoirs of Margaret Fuller Ossoli*, 2 vols. (Boston, 1852), edited by Ralph Waldo Emerson, William H. Channing, and James Freeman Clarke.

---

784.   *To* Lydia L. Brown[1]

New York, April 2d, 1852.

My dear Mrs. Brown:

My wife handed me a letter for you this morning which I was to bring to the office and send over to you. I inadvertently left it on the mantel piece and thus you have escaped, for one day the reproaches due to your misconduct of yesterday in leaving the house without seeing her. Tomorrow you shall have the letter and I write this that you may prepare yourself for the result.

Yours truly,
W. C. BRYANT

MANUSCRIPT: Unrecovered TEXT: "Henry Kirke Brown, the Father of American Sculpture," ed. E. Bush-Brown, typescript in Yale University Library, p. 620.

1. Wife of the sculptor Henry Kirke Brown. See 561.7; Letter 742.

---

785.   *To* George Bancroft

New York   April 8th   1852.

Dear Bancroft.

The Sketch Club will meet at 53 Lexington Avenue on Friday evening. I shall be very happy and so will the members if you will favour us with your company.[1]

Yrs faithfully
W   C   BRYANT

MANUSCRIPT: MHS ADDRESS: Mr. Bancroft.

1. On April 9 Bancroft was a guest at the Sketch Club meeting in Bryant's home, as was Horatio Greenough. Information from James T. Callow.

786. *To* [John?] Dempster[1]

New York   April 16, 1852

My dear sir,

I left a note[2] at your lodgings this morning. The bearer will bring me your answer—verbal or written, as you please.

Yrs truly

W. C. BRYANT

P.S. You will remember that I am at 53 Lexington Avenue—and that Lexington Avenue is the street lying immediately east[3] of Fourth Avenue and parallel with it. I am just above the Twenty Fifth Street.

W. C. B.

MANUSCRIPT: University of California Library, Berkeley.

1. Possibly John Dempster (1794–1863), a Methodist minister and a founder of Wesley Theological Institute, later the Theological School of Boston University.
2. Unrecovered.
3. Bryant mistakenly wrote "west."

787. *To* Gulian C. Verplanck

New York   May 3, 1852.

My dear sir.

The bearer of this note is Mr. William Sampson,[1] who desires to obtain the post of Assistant Superintendent of the New York Hospital which I understand is now vacant. I have no personal acquaintance with Mr. Sampson, but the representations of those in whom I have confidence lead me to believe that he is well qualified for the place by his probity industry, capacity and good character in every respect. He has been employed as an assistant in the House of Refuge in which capacity I hear that he has given great satisfaction. I take leave to commend his application to your favorable consideration.[2]

I am sir

very truly yours,

W   C   BRYANT.

MANUSCRIPT: NYHS ADDRESS: Hon. G. C. Verplanck.

1. Not further identified.
2. Verplanck was then a governor of the New York Hospital. Robert W. July, *The Essential New Yorker: Gulian Crommelin Verplanck* (Durham, North Carolina: Duke University Press, 1951), p. 215.

788. *To* Frances F. Bryant

New York   Wednesday   May 26, 1852.

Dear Frances.

I saw Mr. Bancroft on Monday evening; his wife was ill with a cold,

and did not come down. She was trying hard, he said to get well in order to go next week to Newport.[1]

He told me that he could not bring her out to our place, but afterwards went up to see her and returned with a different plan. They are coming out in their carriage on Sunday morning, and will reach our place about eleven o'clock, or there about. The horses he insists shall be accommodated at Pinckneys.[2] On Monday morning they will return to town.

Yours ever

W. C. BRYANT

MANUSCRIPT: NYPL–GR.

1. Soon after they settled in New York in 1849, the George Bancrofts had bought a summer home, "Roseclyffe," at Newport, Rhode Island. Russell B. Nye, *George Bancroft: Brahmin Rebel* (New York: Knopf, 1945), pp. 185, 282. The Bryants visited them there several times.

2. Probably a Roslyn livery stable.

789.   *To* Frances F. Bryant

New York   June 7th   1852   Monday morning.

Dear Frances.

The Colocynth performed its office perfectly, and removed the difficulty of which I complained in the morning. The hurt of my eye has somewhat affected my sight today. I went down to the paper store in Pearl Street but was too late; the man had already gone out with the paper by the morning train. I have a letter for you from Mrs. Dewey but there is nothing particular in it.

Yrs ever

W. C. BRYANT

MANUSCRIPT: NYPL–GR.

790.   *To* Frances F. Bryant

New York   July 14   1852   Wednesday

Dear F.

I have a letter from Mrs. Eliza Leggett[1] for you, which I shall bring out on Saturday. I do not recollect any thing particular in it.

On going out to the [Hempstead] Branch I saw a rainbow—and the sign of rain has since been fulfilled here. It is now raining gently. Yesterday morning there was a drenching shower in Brooklyn and part of this city.

Godwin has got his ticket for the White Mountains.

Yrs ever

W. C. B.

MANUSCRIPT: NYPL–GR ADDRESS: Mrs. F. F. Bryant / Roslyn / Long Island.

1. Eliza Seaman Leggett (Mrs. Augustus W. Leggett), a Roslyn neighbor. Goddard, *Roslyn Harbor*, p. 19.

791.   *To* Frances F. Bryant

New York   Friday   July 25   1852.

Dear F.

I got your letter this morning by Mr. Willis.[1] I cannot very well come out today, but tomorrow you shall see me without fail. I am in no hurry to make the acquaintance you mention, and am very well here in spite of the weather. I sleep well in a cool house.

I wish you had mentioned whether you got yesterdays paper or not. I wrote to you[2] that Fanny had gone directly to the White Mountains; that Mrs. Kirkland and Cordelia would come out to Roslyn on Saturday with Mr. Stansbury,[3] and that I wished you to say to George that I could get no cabbage, and cauliflower plants in New York and that he might get them at Haviland's if he could.

I heard yesterday that Mrs. Hoyt[4] died on Tuesday night, or perhaps early Wednesday morning. She passed away at last without pain; they thought her asleep.

Bishop Henshaw[5] who died this week was the brother of our friend Mrs. Richards.

yrs ever

W. C. B.

MANUSCRIPT: NYPL–GR.

1. Richard Storrs Willis (1819–1900), a Roslyn neighbor, was editor of the New York *Musical World*, as well as a composer, whose most important publication was *Our Church Music* (New York, 1856). He was a brother of the popular poet and essayist Nathaniel Parker Willis; see 309.3. Frances Bryant's letter is unrecovered.
2. Letter unrecovered.
3. Probably Edward Stansbury, Caroline Kirkland's brother.
4. Probably Mrs. Jesse Hoyt. See 230.6; Letter 341.
5. John Prentiss Kewley Henshaw (1792–1852), Episcopal bishop of Rhode Island since 1843.

792.   *To* Frances F. Bryant

New York   Monday   August 17th   1852.

Dear F.

Will you tell George that I wish he would put the half a dozen leaders for the water in the garden under cover in the barn? I forgot to speak to him this morning.

I have a letter from Simms, in which he says that he has been applied to for some information about himself and his residence and has referred

Mr Putnam to me. I did not mean to write any thing for the book, "Homes of American Literary Men." I shall see if I can get off with a paragraph or two.[1]

The monthly statement which was handed me this morning looks well.

Yrs ever

W. C. B.

MANUSCRIPT: NYPL–GR.

1. See "William Gilmore Simms," *Homes of American Authors* (New York: Putnam, 1853), pp. 257–262; reprinted in *Little Journeys to the Homes of American Authors* (New York, 1896), pp. 157–166.

793.   *To* Eliza Robbins

[Roslyn?] August 24, 1852

Dear Miss Robbins,

My wife and I have been talking a great deal about you lately and wondering what has become of you. We had almost made up our minds to go to Newburgh to see whether you were alive when, making a visit yesterday to Mill Hill we learned from Mrs. [Mackey?] that you were on a visit to Boston. The other day a Mrs. Earle of Philadelphia[1] who I was glad to see, for the first time, and whose appearance and manners are very attractive called at the office to inquire concerning you. I was almost ashamed to be so little able to answer her inquiries. Since you have made the journey to Boston I infer that you are rather better than when I saw you—though I fear that the air of Boston will not agree with you quite so well as that of the interior. I hope you will answer this and tell me precisely how you are and when we may hope to see you again in these latitudes.

Mr. McCoun is on a visit to Massachusetts—the first journey for pleasure he has made since his youth if not the first in his life. He passed some days with Charles Sedgwick at Lenox, and was expected to be absent several days yet. Joseph was with him, and Mary, being relieved for a while from the task of looking to him was on a visit to Mill Hill.[2] Mrs. Holland had been ill and seemed still in bad health.

If the Boston atmosphere should agree with you my wife and I will hope to see you at Roslyn before the fine weather is over. Here the autumn lingers later than either at Newburgh or at Boston, the nights are much warmer at that season and roses bloom in the beginning of December. We have missed you very much; it has not often happened that so long a time has elapsed without our seeing you or hearing from you.

Our own health has been very good in general—but two or three days since Fanny returned from a little visit to one of her cousins at Cummington and has kept her bed ever since, and today my wife is in bed also with

something like a cold or a fever. Both patients now seem on the mend here. Julia is on a visit to her uncles family at Ogdensburgh—

There—I have written what you will I know call an empty letter—but you may say with Justice Shallow—"his meaning is good["].[3] My wife desires her love.—

W. C. B.

MANUSCRIPT: NYPL–GR (draft).

1. Possibly the widow of the Pennsylvania journalist and reformer Thomas Earle (1796–1849).
2. A country estate near Stony Brook, Long Island.
3. *The Merry Wives of Windsor*, I.i.263–264. Bryant mistakenly attributes to Shallow words spoken by the Welsh parson, Sir Hugh Evans.

794.   *To* John Howard Bryant

[New York? cAugust, 1852]

. . . The Free-Soil Party is now doing nothing. Its representatives in Congress have wasted their time till all chance of repealing or modifying the fugitive slave law is gone by, if there ever was any. They have left everything to be done by the journals. Now, at the end of the session, when it is too late for serious debate, Sumner gets up and wants to make a speech. They refuse to consider his resolution, as might have been expected. He might have stated the subject a score of times in the early part of the session. The whole conduct of the public men of the party has been much of a piece with this. What is the use of preserving a separate organization if such be its fruits? But, as I intimated, I see not the least chance of a repeal or change of the fugitive slave law. Its fate is to fall into disuse. All political organizations to procure its repeal are attempts at an impracticability. We must make it odious, and prevent it from being enforced. That the *Evening Post* can do, in a certain measure, just as effectively by supporting Pierce as Hale.[1] Nay, it can do it far more effectually. A journal belonging to a large party has infinitely more influence than when it is the organ of a small conclave. In speaking against slavery, the *Evening Post* expresses the opinions of a large number of people; in exhorting them to vote for Mr. Hale it expresses the opinions of few. The Free-Soil members of Congress—Hale and Sumner,[2] and many others—are not more than half right on various important questions. Freedom of trade is not by any means a firmly established policy in this country. I do not know where these men are on that question. They vote away the public money into the pockets of the Hunkers—Collins, for example.[3] The only certainty we have of safety in regard to these matters is in a Democratic administration.

These are some of my reasons for supporting Pierce. I think the slavery question an important one, but I do not see what is to be done for the cause of freedom by declining to vote for the Democratic candidate. . . .

MANUSCRIPT: Unrecovered TEXT (partial): Bigelow, Bryant, p. 105.

1. In mid-August 1852 a Free Soil Party convention at Pittsburgh nominated John Parker Hale (1806–1873, Bowdoin 1827), United States senator from New Hampshire, for the presidency, and George Washington Julian (1817–1899), a former Indiana congressman, as his running-mate. Franklin Pierce (1804–1869, Bowdoin 1824), a lawyer and former congressman and senator from New Hampshire, was already the Democratic presidential candidate, and General Winfield Scott had been chosen by the Whigs over the incumbent president Millard Fillmore. Nevins, Ordeal, II, 20, 28–29, 33.

2. The ex-Whig Charles Sumner, who had entered the Senate in 1851 as the choice of a coalition of Massachusetts Democrats and Free Soilers, refused to support Pierce. Ibid., p. 33.

3. Edward Knight Collins (1802–1878), a New York shipowner who received large government subsidies to build ships which would carry transatlantic mail. See EP, March 3, 1851.

795.   To Frances F. Bryant

New York   Wednesday   Sept. 8, 1852

Dear Frances

I am sorry to hear such ill news of your health—Mrs. C.[1] called this morning and seemed confident that a change of air would do you good. It is a fact that air often does more good than medicine.

If you would make George bring you tomorrow to the Glen Cove steamboat, I think the object would be attained. The weather is now comfortably cool, and I would go back with you the next day or Saturday, as you pleased.

The Scotch girl Catherine Horne[2] cannot come. I called yesterday at 81 West Twenty Sixth Street and found her with a sickly looking child on her arm a little skeleton with a countenance prematurely old and an expression of anxiety on its little face. In the cradle lay another—they were twins. Her sister she said had not yet risen from her bed; though the children were five weeks old; and she could not tell when she would be able to come to you. She was very sorry &c. and had called once at the office of the Evening Post, and once at Mr. Godwin's in 29th Street, but finding neither of us had not the sense to leave a message for us.—

If you stay tomorrow would it not be well to have the Seckel pears gathered. The white plums in the garden should be watched a little. There are a great many of them—Coe's Golden drop—on the fruit stalls here.

yrs ever

W. C. B.

P.S. I believe I left my knife—the new one which I had from Mr. Pell lying about somewhere. Will you keep it safe for me?

MANUSCRIPT: NYPL–GR.

1. Probably Ann Eliza Cairns (1800–1866), Roslyn neighbor, and wife of William Cairns (1786–1860). See 565.2.

2. Presumably a prospective household servant.

796. *To* Frances F. Bryant

New York   Sept. 14th   1852   Tuesday

Dear F.

Julia is here without any of her cousins or other friends, and stays in town tonight for Alboni's concert.[1] I send a note from her with this.

I left my carpet-bag and Field's basket on the stoop at the Branch,—the first trick of the kind I ever played, and I am quite ashamed of it. I discovered my blunder before I proceeded far and the conductor Mr. Searing promised to get the things for me and bring them to Brooklyn by the noon train. At the Branch Eastman[2] told me that Edward Leggett wanted the rest of the purchase money on the first of May;[3] and Richard Albertson[4] came running up to tell me that he had not received the weekly *Evening Post* since he handed me a dollar for it three weeks since, and these things I suppose put my baggage out of my head.

Yrs ever

W. C. B.

MANUSCRIPT: NYPL–GR.

1. The Italian contralto Marietta Alboni had made her American debut on June 23, 1852, at Metropolitan Hall, New York. Odell, *Annals*, VI, 186–187.

2. Unidentified.

3. This suggests that Bryant may have bought out his cantankerous neighbor at about this time. See Letter 775.

4. Unidentified.

797. *To* Frances F. Bryant

New York, Wednesday, September 15, 1852.

Dear F.

I wish you would tell Fanny that she has some fine looking peaches on two little trees back of the house, and in sight of the nursery window. It would be well to take care of them before any body else does. Will you speak to Julia about the white plums in the garden?

This morning I got my bag and Mr. Field's basket—all safe—

Yrs ever

W. C. B.

P.S. It is now raining rather hard. What Julia will do I cannot tell. We are about despatching a boy to tell her to take a hack. She was to be at the ferry at a quarter past three and a porter was to go for her trunk; but the porters will not go in the rain. It may be that the boy will not find her in.

Half past one p.m.

W. C. B.

MANUSCRIPT: NYPL–GR ADDRESS: Mrs. F. F. Bryant / Roslyn / Long Island.

798.   *To* Frances F. Bryant

New York, Wednesday, September 22   1852.

Dear F.

I thought of coming out tomorrow, but I have changed my mind for this reason.

Yesterday Dr. Gilman of South Carolina called on me. He said his wife and daughters were in town, and his wife would be very glad to see me. I promised to come, and intended to make the call today.

This morning Mr. Pell writes me a note reminding me that I am engaged to dine with Mr. Dawson, at Staten Island. Mr. Dawson is the partner of Mr. Wood[1] Pells brother-in-law. I must therefore put off calling on Mrs. Gilman till tomorrow, and if I do I cannot come that day. The promise to dine at Staten Island had wholly escaped my recollection.

Mrs. Sands was pleased with the flowers you sent her and bade me thank you. I called last evening on Miss Robbins. She has had the complaint which you have just recovered from, and is very weak. I called also at Mrs. Gibson's and saw her only. She is again nervous and cannot sleep. Miss Leclerc[2] has had the neuralgia, which, it is thought, proceeded from an ulcerated tooth that has now been drawn, and they hope she will be better. I have not seen Mr. Simms.

—I shall come on Friday.

Yrs ever

W. C. B.

MANUSCRIPT: NYPL–GR.

1. Benjamin F. Dawson and William Wood were bankers with offices at 58 Wall Street. *Rode's New York City Directory for 1850–1851*, p. 563.

2. Miss Leclerc, not listed in New York City directories for this period, was apparently a teacher of French at the Gibsons' school on Union Square (502.3).

799.   *To* Frances F. Bryant

New York   Sept 28, 1852   Tuesday.—

Dear F.

On arriving at the office this morning I found Margaret's mother waiting with a five dollar bill which she said she had of Margaret[1] and which was counterfeit. I gave her another.

Eastman was in the stage waggon this morning. He said that one of the schoolmasters at Roslyn is going away, because his wages are too small. He gets $350.— yearly and wants more. If Mr. Brown[2] wants the place he should apply now. Will you communicate this to him?

Yrs ever

W. C. B.

[Theodore?] Sedgwick writes[3] that his youngest child is at deaths door—or rather has been—but is now beginning to get better.

MANUSCRIPT: NYPL–GR.

1. Probably a servant.
2. Unidentified.
3. Letter unrecovered.

800. *To* Frances F. Bryant

Thursday, October 14, 1852.

Dear F.

I send out two letters for Julia. Arthur has written to me that he cannot come east this season. His little daughter has been extremely ill, and has not yet recovered.[1] He wants a peck of appleseeds.

Bigelow has not been at the office this week, though he returned on Saturday from the country. He is broken down with hard work, they say. However, I must try to come out tomorrow. I may invite somebody to come on Saturday.—

If I could have come today, I should have brought a parcel for Minna with a letter, from "George Bancroft." But they will not be unseasonable, I hope, tomorrow.

Yrs ever
W. C. B.

MANUSCRIPT: NYPL–GR ADDRESS: Mrs. F. F. Bryant / Roslyn / Long Island.

1. Arthur Bryant's younger daughter, Henrietta Raymond Bryant, died on October 10 at the age of fourteen months. Undated memorandum in his handwriting, in NYPL–GR. His letter is unrecovered.

801. *To* Frances F. Bryant

New York   Oct. 27, 1852   Wednesday.

Dear F.

I went in search of your Scotch girl[1] yesterday, but the door was locked, though there was a twittering of birds within. I shall try again.

Miss Sands has a seamstress and waiter on hand, an Irish Catholic girl.

Mr. Leupp called today to say that the *Arctic*, a very fine steamer, goes out on the 13th. of November, with Gourlie's[2] brother on board as mate. It goes to Liverpool.[3]

Yrs ever
W. C. B.

MANUSCRIPT: NYPL–GR ADDRESS: Mrs. F. F. Bryant / Roslyn / Long Island.

1. See Letter 795.
2. John Hamilton Gourlie; see Letter 653. His brother was apparently Robert Gourlie, sometimes a guest at Sketch Club meetings.
3. Bryant and Charles M. Leupp were then planning the trip to Europe and the Near East described in Bryant's letters between November 1852 and June 1853.

802. *To* Frances F. Bryant

New York Oct. 28¹   1852   Thursday.

Dear F.

I am glad you mentioned the harness in your note. I should inevitably have forgotten it.

Yesterday on going up I called at the Carlton House. Mrs. [Ives?] and her daughter were at dinner, and I did not see them, nor could I wait as I had an engagement with the dentist. This morning at 9 o'clock I went again, and the man at the office told me they had "gone to Jersey."

I made a second journey to Twenty Sixth Street and found Catherine in. She did not seem very desirous of a place, and said that she thought she would take a month to herself before going out to service. I wonder if she is not going to be married. The child is alive, and put with a nurse.

It is true that I do not expect to come to Roslyn till Saturday. I shall stay till Wednesday morning, for the election will take place on Tuesday. I shall be glad when it is off our hands.

Probably it will be well for me to bring out the money for the man who won't get up till seven. I hear nothing yet of John.² Perhaps he may not come this week.

Yours ever

W. C. B.

MANUSCRIPT: NYPL–GR ADDRESS: Mrs. F. F. Bryant / Roslyn / Long Island.

1. Bryant mistakenly wrote "29."
2. Probably John Howard Bryant; see Letters 803, 804.

803. *To* Frances F. Bryant

New York   Oct   29, 1852.

Dear F.

I neglected to tell you, in writing to you yesterday, how I found Miss¹ Robbins on Wednesday evening. A letter for her came addressed to my care and I went to 15 Stuyvesant Street to deliver it. They told me that she had gone to pass a little time at Mrs. Wrights on Eighth Street. There I found her, much worse than when I saw her last, very weak, breathing with labor, coughing frequently and violently, and with a hectic flush on her cheek. Mrs. Wright had gone in a carriage to the boarding house in Stuyvesant Street where there was no suitable room for her, and had brought her away, to remain until better accommodations can be provided. Her voice, however, does not seem to be affected; it is still clear and sometimes even strong. I do not believe she can live long unless she goes into the interior.²

I hear nothing from John yet.

Yesterday I bought a single harness in the Third Avenue for $25—

which I ordered to be sent on board the Sarah Elizabeth.³ Will you tell George to bring it to the house as soon as the sloop arrives, and see immediately whether the collar is large enough. If not the maker will give me another.

Yrs ever
W. C. B.

MANUSCRIPT: NYPL–GR ADDRESS: Mrs. Bryant / Roslyn.

1. Bryant mistakenly wrote "Mrs."
2. Eliza Robbins died at Cambridge, Massachusetts, on July 16, 1853. See 842.1.
3. A sloop carrying freight between New York City and Roslyn. Goddard, *Roslyn Harbor*, p. 24.

804. *To* Frances F. Bryant

New York   Thursday   November 4th   1852.

Dear F.

I was quite well all day yesterday and almost without any symptoms of a cold, but today I cough somewhat.

Mr. Charles Butler¹ has just called with an invitation for you and me to meet Professor Robinson² at his house tomorrow evening. Mr. Ogden is in town and will be there. If you could come in, now,—Perhaps you will be able, and I will go back with you on Saturday.

Warden has promised me a better harness. Of John I hear nothing yet.—³

Yours ever
W. C. B.

MANUSCRIPT: NYPL–GR ADDRESS: Mrs. F. F. Bryant / Roslyn / Long Island.

1. Charles Butler (1802–1897), a brother of Benjamin Franklin Butler (374.1), was a New York lawyer and philanthropist. He, like William Butler Ogden (581.2), was active in the early development of Chicago, and of midwestern railroads. He was also a founder in 1836 of Union Theological Seminary, New York City.
2. Edward Robinson; see 399.2.
3. No other evidence has been found that John Howard Bryant visited the East that year.

805. *To* the Editor of the NEW-YORK DAILY TIMES¹

[New York, November 4, 1852]

Sir—

As you have used my name in a paragraph which appears in your sheet of this morning, giving the purport of an alleged conversation between a person whom you call "Mr. BENSON, the well-known shipping-merchant," and myself, I trust you will do me the justice to publish this reply.²

I never had a moment's conversation with Mr. BENSON on the subject of Mr. WEBSTER and the Lobos Islands, nor, to my knowledge, on any other subject whatever. Mr. BENSON is personally unknown to me, and certainly, if the statement in your paper is a sample of his veracity, I desire never to know more of him than I do now. What Mr. WEBSTER may have said I do not know, but if the account of it be derived from the same source with the account of the conversation between BENSON and myself, it is probably equally authentic.

I am, Sir, yours respectfully.

W. C. BRYANT.

MANUSCRIPT: Unrecovered TEXT: *New-York Daily Times*, November 5, 1852, p. 4.

1. The *New-York Daily Times*, first published on September 18, 1851, was edited by Henry Jarvis Raymond (1820–1869), a Whig politician who was chosen that year as speaker of the New York State Assembly.

2. During the last months of his life Whig Secretary of State Daniel Webster, who died on October 24, 1852, had been attacked in the Democratic press for first supporting and later opposing a practice of American shipowners of taking rich cargoes of the fertilizer guano from the Pacific Lobos Islands, claimed by Peru. On September 24 the *EP* had charged that Webster had been speculating in guano with one A. G. Benson. In the *Times* article of November 4 Webster was quoted as saying, shortly before his death, that his conscience was clear before Heaven, adding, "I can only hope that when Mr. Bryant stands on the brink of the grave, as I now do, his conscience will be as clear of having performed the duty of justice towards my name." The *Times* editor continued, "We understand that Mr. Benson, the well-known shipping merchant of this City, called upon the principal editor of the *Post*, and made such explanations of the whole affair, as silenced his arguments to prove the corruption, if it did not force from him a positive admission of the injustice done Mr. Webster." For a further discussion of Daniel Webster and the Lobos Islands affair, see Irving H. Bartlett, *Daniel Webster* (New York: Norton [1978]), p. 280; Nevins, *Ordeal*, II, 180–182.

806.   *To* Frances F. Bryant

                                New York   Nov   5   1852   Friday—
Dear F.

I brought out a draft as you know, of a certain document of which I intended to make a clean copy and execute it, but I cannot find it any where. Is it possible that I left it behind at Roslyn? Will you look a little— not much for I can make another when I come out.

Things are going on well here. Fanny has been delayed about her house-cleaning, but expects somebody today to begin. We shall have a thumping dividend this half year.[1]

                                                        Yrs ever
                                                        W. C. B.

P.S. Susan[2] says you have another hand. We must not forget the seeds for Arthur.[3]

MANUSCRIPT: NYPL–GR ADDRESS: Mrs. F. F. Bryant / Roslyn / Long Island.

1. Since bookkeeper Isaac Henderson had replaced Timothy Howe as business manager of the *EP* in 1850, its income had risen sharply. Nevins, *Evening Post*, pp. 237–238.

2. A Bryant servant.

3. Arthur Bryant had written Frances on August 1 asking for eastern apple seeds. NYPL–GR.

807.   *To* John Bigelow

New York   Nov. 6   1852

Dear Bigelow

You have seen the *Times* I suppose. I have spoken of the story of Benson as a misstatement and have promised in the *Evening Post* that it shall be exposed on Monday. Col. Thomas was here today and was quite indignant at Benson. He heard nothing said about not liking to take the back track. Barney has sent word that he was present and that Benson's story is a lie.[1]

Yours truly,
W. C. B.

MANUSCRIPT: NYPL–GR DOCKETED: Nov 6 1852.

1. On November 6 the *Daily Times* carried a statement from A. G. Benson which quoted his earlier charge, in a letter of September 27 to "Messrs. W. C. Bryant & Co.," that when he had called on the editor of the *EP*, in company with a Colonel John Addison Thomas, to demand a retraction of the suggestion that he and Daniel Webster had speculated in guano, "You still declined, on the ground, that having made the statement you would not appear well before the public to take the back track." On Monday, the 8th, the *Times* printed a letter from Colonel Thomas stating that he had been present when Benson called on John Bigelow (*not* Bryant), that Bigelow was wholly fair and proper, and that Benson was "entirely incorrect" in his published version of their conversation. On the same day the *EP* printed "A Card" over Bigelow's signature charging Benson with gross misrepresentation, and quoting in full letters to the *EP* from Thomas and Hiram Barney, a lawyer and Democratic leader who happened to be in the office at the time, to support his charge. On November 9 the *Times* disclaimed any further dealings with Benson, and, by implication, offered a grudging apology to the editors of the *EP*. See *New-York Daily Times*, November 4–6, 8–9, 1852, *passim*; *EP*, September 9–10, 24, and November 4–6, 8–9, *passim*.

808.   *To* Mrs. M[yron?] H[olley?] Clark[1]

New York   Nov 6, 1852.

Dear Madam,

I have looked in vain for the letter of yours which relates to the Jenny Lind affair.[2] It was laid by in a moment of haste to be looked at and thought of again, and is now not to be found. Please write, if it is not too much trouble and state the substance of what you wrote at first. But do not write to me for in a week from this time I shall be on my way to Europe—write to the Editors of the Evening Post. When you want the

money for the letters we have published of yours please send on a statement of them &c. I hope you have got duplicates of them all as you desired.

Yours respectfully
W   C   BRYANT

MANUSCRIPT: University of Michigan Library, Ann Arbor ADDRESS: Mrs. M. H. Clark.

1. Mrs. Clark was apparently the wife of Myron Holley Clark (1806–1892), governor of New York, 1854–1858.

2. The extraordinarily popular Swedish soprano Jenny Lind (1820–1887) had been married at Boston on February 5, 1852, to pianist Otto Goldschmidt, and after giving a farewell concert in Castle Garden, New York, on May 24, she returned with her husband to Europe. Bryant's reference to the "Jenny Lind affair" is obscure.

809. [To John Bigelow?]

[New York? cNovember 10   1852]

Mr. George Catlin author of a book on the Aborigines of this country and the collector of a very rich cabinet or gallery of Indian curiosities portraits and pictures representing their customs has returned in his old age to his country bringing with him a great part if not all of his collections.[1] This, or a considerable proportion of it is to be sold.

Mr. George Harvey[2] has promised to write a notice of them for the Evening Post. I wish that something friendly may be said about it, for I hear that Mr. Catlin whom I formerly knew very well is now in need of the money which he hopes from the sale.[3]

W. C. BRYANT.

MANUSCRIPT: WCL (draft?).

1. George Catlin (1796–1872). Pennsylvania-born artist whose drawings and paintings of American Indians, and published accounts of their lives and customs, made him pre-eminent in this field in the 1830s and 1840s, had spent the years 1839–1852 in Europe exhibiting his work. In 1852 he became impoverished through speculation and returned to the United States. He had been an early member of the National Academy in 1826–1827, and in 1847 had exhibited at the American Art-Union. *NAD Exhibition Record*, I, 73; Cowdrey, *AAFA & AAU*, II, 61.

2. An English landscape artist who spent much of his life in the United States. See 553.2.

3. No article on Catlin or his collections has been located in the *EP* for this period.

XVI

Voyage to the East
1852–1853
(LETTERS 810 TO 837)

ON NOVEMBER 13, 1852, Bryant and Charles Leupp left New York on the steamship *Arctic* for Europe and the Near East, expecting first to visit Spain and Portugal. Their itinerary was as follows:

November 25: arrival Liverpool; 26–29: London; 30: Boulogne.

December 1–7: Paris; 8–12: en route Marseilles via Châlons, Lyons, Avignon, Nîmes; 13: Marseilles; 14–18: en route Naples via Genoa, Leghorn, Pisa, Civitavecchia; 19–22: Naples (excursion to Herculaneum, Pompeii, Nocera, Salerno, Amalfi, Paestum); 23–24: en route Malta via Messina; 25–29: Valetta; December 30–January 4, 1853: en route Cairo via Alexandria.

January 5–11: Cairo; 12–27: voyage up the Nile to Aswân, stopping at Tell el 'Amarna, Jirja, Thebes, Luxor, Isna, Philae, Biggeh, Karnak, Dandarah, Asyût, Bani Hasan; 28–29: Cairo; January 30–February 15: en route Jerusalem via El 'Arîsh, Rafah, Khan Yunis, Gaza, Askelon, Isdud, Ramla.

February 16–22: Jerusalem (excursion to Jericho, Bethlehem); 23–25: en route Nazareth via Ramah, Bireh, Bethel, Nablus, Jenin; February 26–March 1: Nazareth (excursion to Cana, Tiberias).

March 2–4: en route Beirut via Haifa, Tyre, Sidon; 5–17: Beirut (excursion to Baalbek, Damascus); 18–25: en route Smyrna via Latakia, Aleppo, Tarsus; 26–30: Smyrna; March 31–April 2: en route Constantinople.

April 3–10: Constantinople and Scutari; 11–14: en route Athens via Smyrna, Syros, Piraeus; 15–18: Athens; 19–26: en route Venice via Corinth, Corfu, Trieste; 27–30: Venice.

May 1–3: en route Florence via Padua, Ferrara, Bologna; 4–5: Florence; 6: en route Rome via Siena, Radicófani; 7–17: Rome; 18–23: en route Paris via Civitavecchia, Marseilles, Avignon, Lyons, Châlons; May 24–June 4: Paris.

June 5–6: en route London via Le Havre, Southampton; 7: London; 8–22: en route Cowes–New York.

On the way to Liverpool Bryant talked with the American naval officer William Francis Lynch, whose report on his exploration of the Dead Sea and the River Jordan had just been published. The travelers read Edward William Lane's *Account of the Manners and Customs of the Modern Egyptians* (1836), and Bryant was already acquainted with the *Biblical Researches in Palestine* (1841) of his friend Edward Robinson. Leaving Liverpool, he and Leupp stopped briefly in London, where they visited picture galleries and saw a poor performance by veteran actor William Farren—"His utterances paralytic and unintelligible," Bryant noted. Samuel Rogers was at Brighton; but at tea with publisher

John Chapman, Bryant met Mary Ann Evans ("George Eliot"), then an editor of Chapman's *Westminster Review*.

While in Paris Bryant and Leupp were joined on their journey by John Durand, son of the artist, and engaged a Maltese courier, John Muscat, to conduct the party through the East. Here, on a rainy December day, Bryant stood in the Tuileries Gardens to see Napoleon III proclaimed Emperor, and heard Paris acquaintances call prospects for the Second Empire as poor as that day's weather. Bryant shopped, dined with artists and other friends, saw pictures in the Louvre, and enjoyed the *opéra comique*. He bought a new guide book to Spain, only to be dissuaded by Muscat from visiting the Iberian Peninsula until spring should bring better weather. So the travelers went southward, stopping at Avignon and Nîmes, and at Marseilles boarded a ship for Naples. It docked at Genoa for a day, and at Leghorn long enough for Bryant to visit Pisa, where he was chagrined to find that old Professor Rosini did not remember his American friend of seventeen years past.

From Naples the party visited Salerno, Amalfi, Paestum, and other places on the Sorrento Peninsula which Bryant and Leupp had missed seven years earlier, then took passage for Malta. Stopping at Messina, and bribing an officer to take them ashore, they found the cathedral closed and Mount Etna hidden by a shower. On Christmas they reached Valetta. Bryant admired the immaculate little city built of creamy stone, and was interested to hear of British efforts to ensure freedom of worship among a people wholly Catholic in tradition. During a voyage to Alexandria he held long conversations with the English botanist Robert Fortune, who was taking Chinese plants to India, and whose suggestions for the domestication of Oriental teas, grapes, and fruits in the United States Bryant discussed before the New York Horticultural Society in 1855.

At Alexandria and Cairo the Americans toured monuments and ruins, and were fascinated by their first glimpses of Oriental life. Before deciding on short notice to join a cruise up the Nile, they engaged a dragoman, Emanuel Balthas—an Athenian who spoke ancient and modern Greek, French and Italian, Arabic, and Turkish—to provide transportation and catering for their two-week crossing of the Sinai Desert. Bryant enjoyed greatly the trip of seven hundred miles up the ancient river on a modern steamer with fifteen passengers, doubting whether "chance ever threw together a better-natured and more obliging set of men." They saw "old temples and tombs to our hearts' content," he wrote Frances, and, sitting in the great temple ruins at Karnak, he thought that "after such a sight no building reared by human hands could affect me with a sense of sublimity." There were lighter diversions; at a native dinner the party watched dancing girls whose "agitations and writhings of the body" left Bryant "feverish."

A fellow-passenger named Keith, from New Orleans, asked to join the party in its eastward journey, and on January 30 the four Americans set out from Cairo for Jerusalem. Their caravan must have been a striking sight. Thirteen camels, tethered by their Arab drivers in single file, were accompanied by two donkeys, on one of which sat a chattering, half-wild Nubian monkey. Dragoman Balthas, a choleric little man "with the manners of a nobleman," was perched on the first camel, carrying a saber, a rifle, and two horse pistols, and snapping a long whip which he used impartially on drivers and passers-by. Next came the

four Americans, followed by the self-proclaimed "father of couriers," Muscat, short and thick like the Persian sword he proudly wore, and, Bryant maintained, "the most honest of his tribe." Then Balthas' cousin Gianneco, a Smyrniote Greek with a "brow like that of the bust of Hippocrates," and, in the rear, the Roman cook Vincenzo, "whose whole soul was in his art," and who rode his camel plucking chickens as he went. The tourists were provisioned with carpeted tents and beds with mattresses and pillows, a dining table with campstools, linen, tin plates, and cutlery; pack camels carried three charcoal stoves and a hencoop. At their first night's stop Bryant recorded, "Vincenzo gave us the very best dinner we had eaten in Egypt."

Finding his first camel inclined to bite, Bryant shifted the next day to one more docile—except when he threatened to unseat his mounting rider by rising suddenly from his knees. The Americans were surprised by the great variety of aspects shown by the desert, which was littered with potsherds, graves, and other relics of the past, and teemed with animal and vegetable life. They encountered sand-fleas and flies, mosquitoes, black beetles, snails and rats, lice, poisonous snakes, and venomous centipedes in their beds. One night their tents were blown down and their belongings scattered by a violent sandstorm.

The travelers saw flocks of small birds, ravens, and herons, heard jackals cry, and surprised herds of gazelles, animals so swift and lovely that when they fled from Balthas' futile gunshot Bryant wondered to see "fear . . . manifest itself so gracefully." He walked often beside the caravan, or strayed aside, remarking on shrubs and flowers—purple and white broom, lilies, pink phlox, scarlet poppies—and his companions were fascinated, John Durand recalled later, by the range of his botanical knowledge and the poetic associations suggested to him by what he saw. Sometimes, as their camels plodded along, the Americans read to each other descriptions of their surroundings, or at evening camps various Biblical accounts of Hebrew journeys to and from Egypt. They were amused by passing parties of agile cavalrymen, charged with protecting travelers, but, in Muscat's words, the "greatest robbers of all." They passed caravans carrying silks from Damascus to Cairo, and dervishes returning from Mecca. At Bedouin villages Bryant marveled at the beauty and grace of these desert nomads, and was touched by pathetic evidences of their family devotion in burial grounds.

At the Syrian border the travelers were quarantined at Khan Yunis and Gaza, and at Ramla, where they bid goodbye to the camel drivers and shifted to horses, passed a night in a hospitable Franciscan convent. From here they were escorted through Judea by a janizary sent from the American consulate in Jerusalem, which they reached in mid-February.

Bryant's surviving letters give only a brief account of his stay in the Holy City, and none of his visits to Jericho and Bethlehem; perhaps he described these in the lost letters to his wife. From his diary we learn that he heard from the Anglican bishop of Jerusalem about Christian efforts to convert the Jews; rode on horseback to the Mount of Olives, where he was shown the tomb of Lazarus; swam in the Jordan and bathed in the Dead Sea; spent a night at the Convent of San Saba, into which no females—even cats or hens—were admitted; and at Bethlehem drank the best wine in the Holy Land.

Leaving Jerusalem, the travelers were stoned at Nablus by children and

threatened by angry women, whose frowns became smiles when Bryant blew kisses at them. They stopped at Arab homes, and in Nazareth spent several nights in a Franciscan convent. At Cana they saw the jars in which water had been converted to wine, and on the shore of the Sea of Galilee the place where the miracle of the loaves and fishes was performed. In Tiberius they stayed with a German Jew, and on Mount Carmel, at the Convent of Lebanon, ate an "excellent" dinner with wine. They galloped their horses along the beach near Tyre, where they bathed in the Mediterranean and lodged with a French-speaking Greek Christian. Still following the sea, they reached Beirut on March 5.

Here Bryant learned of disrespect shown American consuls by Arabian pashas, and, through his letters to the *Evening Post*, he lectured his government for not making a show of naval might in eastern Mediterranean ports. While at Beirut the travelers digressed to Damascus, where Bryant bought the Arab costume in which he would later amuse his grandchildren and puzzle his friends. Back at Beirut he saw much of the American missionary colony, visiting schools and hearing with gratification of a growing Moslem tolerance of other faiths. Boarding a little steamer for Smyrna, the Americans found it crowded by the retinue of a Turkish governor, the chattering members of whose large harem covered the deck with their bedding and "tottered about" in their seasickness, making it impossible for others to exercise and difficult for them to sleep. At Smyrna Bryant was disturbed to learn that American law made our consuls in Turkey the sole judges in crimes charged against United States citizens, even to the point of capital punishment, and he warned his newspaper readers of the grave dangers in such a law.

The travelers reached Constantinople only a few months before the outbreak of the Crimean War, and on the eve of the British ambassador's return with intimations of his country's support in Turkey's threatened struggle against Russia. They saw the sultan ride to his mosque, and watched the worship of howling dervishes and heard them howl. Before sailing for Athens and Trieste they listened to a performance of Verdi's *Nabucco*. At the Greek island of Syros Bryant was glad to see Christos Evangelides, the subject twenty-five years earlier of his poem "The Greek Boy," and now the American consul there. Bryant questioned him, as he did later the teachers at an American school in Athens, on the progress of public education. In Athens he pursued his inquiries into freedom of worship. He was "not disappointed" in the Acropolis, which he climbed easily, but found the ascent of the almost vertical Lycabettus "a tiring walk for me." Near the Pnyx, where Athenians had once gathered in assembly, he was amused by the rock which "Greek women used to slide down to insure their fecundity."

After four days at Athens, the party sailed by way of Corinth to Corfu, where Bryant began his long account of their desert crossing. On Palm Sunday they took another steamer for Trieste, where they parted from Keith, and crossed to Venice. Bryant found the city "much less interesting" than on his earlier visits, and was impatient to get on. He seems to have been impressed only by the new monument to the artist Titian in the Church of Santa Maria dei Frari. In Venice he ran across Marcus Spring, who knew him only with difficulty under a long white beard he had grown on the Sinai. From Venice the travelers retraced the route Bryant and Leupp had taken in 1845, passing through Padua,

Ferrara, Bologna, Florence, and Siena, and reaching Rome on May 8. In Florence Bryant saw Hiram Powers in his studio, and at Rome many of the American artists resident there, enjoying their social gatherings. At the Chapmans' one evening the travelers took part in *tableaux vivants* in their Damascus gowns and turbans. Chapman, Bryant recorded, "explained to me why he has not gone on with the work of making illustrations from my poem of the Appletree." And the artist asked Bryant to "put into good English" a chapter from one of his drawing books. While at Rome Bryant had his "magnificent white beard" daguerreotyped, he wrote Frances, lest he should shave it off before getting home. Perhaps the "palmer's beard," as well as his sack coat, was a reason he was at first refused admission to a mass celebrated in the Sistine Chapel by Pope Pius IX, but he slipped in later with a group of nondescript visitors to be impressed by the pontiff's "dignified" form and attitude. He was displeased, however, by the current newspaper censorship and military occupation of Rome by French troops sent by Napoleon III to sustain the papal dominion, and thought it likely that "a sudden exasperation on the part of the people, may, at almost any time, be exchanged for a state of open and bloody revolt."

Bryant was disappointed that his friends' wish to linger in Italy had made it inadvisable to visit Spain as hot weather drew on. Instead, they sailed to Marseilles and went on to Paris, losing their baggage on the way and having to go to court in Lyons to retrieve it. During ten days in Paris they shopped for clothes and visited friends, including Beckwith and John Gourlie, with whom they dined sumptuously one evening before Durand left their party to visit Italy with Gourlie. Bryant heard from Lieutenant Washington Bartlett of the navy's plan to install new French navigation lights in American coastal waters. He watched another performance at the *opéra comique*, attended an art show largely composed of "simpering, leering, and sprawling" Venuses and nymphs, and on the Champs Elysées saw women "of an equivocal cast, at least," dancing the polka. The new tomb of Bonaparte in the Hôtel des Invalides prompted gloomy reflections on that "terror of the world." A colossal winged figure with a trumpet near the sarcophagus suggested to Bryant the angel of the resurrection, awaiting the day when Napoleon would be "confronted by the multitudes slain in his wars," and he left the tomb with a "strong impression of the yet imperfect civilization of mankind."

Crossing from Le Havre and spending only a day in London, Bryant left Leupp behind and went down to Cowes on June 8 to board the steamer *Humboldt* for New York. He was attentive during the voyage to his wife's goddaughter, later Mrs. Frederick Law Olmsted, whom he found traveling alone with a small baby and very seasick. Another passenger was the young landscape painter, William J. Stillman, later to be co-editor with John Durand of the art journal *The Crayon*, as well as art editor of the *Evening Post*. The voyage was festive; on its last evening Bryant and Stillman toasted the ship's competent commander in champagne. On June 22 they docked at New York.

810. *To* Messrs. William C. Bryant & Co.

Liverpool   Nov. 25   1852.

Gentlemen.

I arrived at Liverpool this morning, safe and sound.[1] I send you two notes one addressed to my wife and the other to Mr. King of the House of Representatives,[2] which I wish you would put into envelopes addressed to them. For the Evening Post I do not think of writing till I get upon less familiar ground.—

Please send to Professor Henry Reed of Philadelphia ten dollars, to be applied to the monument they are erecting in England to the poet Wordsworth.[3] I promised to send something for the purpose, but I neglected it in the haste of my departure. If Mr. Henderson in the note sending on the money will say as much, I shall be obliged to him.

Charge the postage of this letter to me as it concerns my affairs.

respectfully &c

W. C. BRYANT

MANUSCRIPT: Humanities Research Center Library, The University of Texas at Austin ADDRESS: Mr. Henderson, / Office of the Evening Post / New York PUBLISHED: *William Cullen Bryant and Isaac Henderson: New Evidence on a Strange Partnership* . . . , ed. Theodore Hornberger (Austin: The University of Texas Library, 1950), p. 1.

1. Bryant and Charles Leupp had sailed from New York on November 13 on the steamer *Arctic*.

2. Neither note has been recovered. Preston King (1806–1865), then a Free Soil representative in Congress from New York, was later (1857–1863) a Republican United States senator.

3. Henry Hope Reed (546.15), then gathering American contributions toward a memorial window to William Wordsworth (d. 1850) in the church at Ambleside, England, listed Bryant's name the following year as a donor. *William Cullen Bryant and Isaac Henderson*, p. 1.

811. *To* the EVENING POST

London, November 29th, 1852.

I did not think of writing to you from England, but there are one or two things which occur to me as worthy of mention.

One of the vexations which a traveller meets on his arrival in this country is the search for contraband books. The booksellers in England have furnished the Custom-houses with a list of American works of which they claim the copyright. When a book is found among the baggage of the traveller, which is carefully overhauled for the purpose, the examining officer looks to see if it is printed in America; and if it be, he consults his manuscript list, to see whether it be also published in England by a person claiming the copyright. If its title appears on the list, the book is seized.

Considerable delay is occasioned by the strictness with which the examination is made.

Among my fellow-passengers who left New York in the steamer Arctic, was Captain Lynch, the enterprising and successful explorer of the Dead Sea. He made, as you know, an official report of his expedition to the government, which has been printed by order of Congress.[1] Besides this, he prepared a personal narrative of his expedition, a very interesting work, which was published at Philadelphia by Lea & Blanchard.[2] Bentley, the London publisher, imported into England a number of copies of the work in sheets, procuring them to be bound; and to secure himself from competition, took out a copyright for the work, and sent the title to the Liverpool Custom-house, that any other copies introduced from America might be seized and stopped.

When Captain Lynch's baggage was undergoing examination, he asked the officer what disposition would be made of a copy of his narrative printed in America, if it was found among its effects. "Most certainly," answered the officer, "it would be my duty to retain it. Not a single work patented in this country can be introduced from abroad, and I should be obliged to seize it, even in the hands of its author."

One of our passengers[3] had, in his portmanteau, three works published in the United States, of two of which he was the author, and to the third of which he was a contributor. One of them, a volume of poetry, required no long examination; poetry is a drug in both countries, and the publishers do not find it worth their while to maintain a very fierce rivalry for so unsalable a commodity. The volume which next engaged the officer's attention was a prose work, and this led to a long and close examination. The officer went over the list, apparently more than once, looking at the title of the book again and again, and once or twice appeared to hesitate, while the assistant inspectors stood unemployed, waiting his decision. At length he handed back the book. The third volume, a recent publication of Putnam's, was also subjected to a close scrutiny, which was, however, soon brought to a close.

On my way to this city, it seemed to me that I had never seen a country drenched like England. Seven weeks of almost constant rain have saturated the ground with water, swollen the springs, turned the ditches into streams, and raised the rivers till they have in many places swept away their bridges, and everywhere drowned the low grounds. Such numbers of wet women and children I never saw before; wet wagoners walking by the side of their dripping teams; wet laborers, male and female, digging turnips in the muddy fields; wet beggars in the towns, their rags streaming with water; wet sheep staggering under their drenched fleeces, nibbling the grass in the yellowish-green fields—for the pastures wear, at this season, a sallow verdure—or biting the turnips scattered for them by the farmers in long rows. I saw, frequently, mills standing, with their motionless

wheels deep in turbid currents of water; fields prepared for grain, which cannot be sown, and others ready for the plough which cannot be ploughed. In some places, houses and even hamlets have been carried away and the inhabitants drowned; and drowned cattle, I am told, are seen floating in the currents. It is said that the country has not seen such floods since the year 1795.[4]

Almost everybody in England speaks of the present condition of the country as extremely prosperous. The partisans of free trade insist that there has been a gradual diminution of pauperism, and an improvement in the condition of the working-classes ever since the repeal of the corn-laws. At present it is admitted that this effect has been greatly heightened by the emigration to Australia and the United States. "We have sent out," said an intelligent gentleman to me, "great numbers of laborers to Australia, the very men by whom our soil was tilled last year; the paupers, having succeeded to those places, receive the same and even better wages, and are paupers no longer. Besides these, we have sent out from other classes, particularly from the class of merchants, numbers of intelligent, enterprising men, some of the best men of England; and next year we shall give Australia a still larger host of colonists. They have gone out for a purpose of which they themselves are scarcely aware; they have gone out to found the structure of that new community on solid and liberal foundations. Within thirty years you will see a populous, prosperous, powerful, and enlightened community in Australia; and long before that time it will be independent of the mother country, for the men who have migrated to that country will not endure that it should remain in a state of dependence on a distant government a moment beyond the time when dependence is a necessity, or at least a convenience."

In the mean time I hear a good deal said of the difficulty of procuring workmen for the ordinary tasks of agriculture. During the season which has just closed, the ordinary dependence upon laborers from Ireland failed; and when the grain was to be cut, the soldiery, in order to save the crops from destruction, were sent into the fields with sickles in their hands, instead of muskets and swords. Many kinds of work, which were formerly cheaply executed, are now neglected; the more necessary employments are filled, and the others are postponed. I hear a great deal said of the depopulation of Ireland.[5] "Ireland," said a gentleman to me, "is already half Protestant"; but this is, doubtless, an exaggeration. It is true, however, I believe, that English proprietors and farmers are going over in some numbers, and I heard of one case of an emigrant to America, who returned because he could buy land in Ireland of the same quality and nearness to the market, cheaper than in the United States.

MANUSCRIPT: Unrecovered TEXT: *LFE*, pp. [9]–15; first published in *EP* for December 15, 1852.

1. William Francis Lynch (1801–1865), a United States naval officer, explored the Holy Land in 1848 and later wrote an *Official Report of the U. S. Expedition to Explore the Dead Sea and the River Jordan* (1852).

2. *Narrative of the United States Expedition to the River Jordan and the Dead Sea, by W. F. Lynch, U.S.N., Commander of the Expedition* (Philadelphia, 1849).

3. Probably Bryant himself.

4. On January 28, 1853, the *EP* reprinted portions of an article in the *London Weekly News* which remarked on the scant notice given by the British press to notable American visitors, and quoted the foregoing paragraph from Bryant's letter with the comment, "There is not in the whole of his exquisite pieces of pastoral poetry a sketch more faithful to fact than this."

5. As a result of the potato famine and consequent malnutrition and disease, and, above all, of emigration. "In Ireland . . . the potato blight of 1846–7 initiated a rapid reduction of the population from over eight millions to under five millions by stimulating emigration to America." George Macaulay Trevelyan, *History of England* (London: Longmans, Green, 1926), p. 603.

812. *To* Frances F. Bryant

Paris   December 7, 1852

Dear Frances.

I have been waiting here for two or three days for letters from America, for when we are once on our way there is no knowing how long it may be before I hear from you again. We have engaged a *Courier*, John Muscat a Maltese, who brings from various quarters recommendations which make him to be that prodigy among couriers, a strictly honest man. He advises us strongly to go first to the East, on account of the warm weather which is experienced there in the latter part of winter, and to see Spain and Portugal when the severity of the season begins to be mitigated. It is likely we shall take his advice. John Durand is here and will go on with us.[1]

We left London on the 30th of November and were two days in getting to Paris. We came by railway to Folkstone on the coast, and crossed the channel to Boulogne, a very uneasy passage of more than two hours, and I was sick of course, for the steamer was a little uncomfortable thing and was tossed about like an egg shell. We could not get our baggage through the custom house, on time to proceed to Paris before eight o'clock, and we determined to remain, where we were, at the Hotel de l'Europe, a very good inn. The next morning it was quite cold, but we had a brilliant sun the first and only one I have seen since I came to Europe, and we took our places in the railway carriage between nine and ten o'clock. The fields were swimming with rain and the ice stood on the pools. At six o'clock we were in Paris, and one of the omnibuses provided for the purpose took us and our baggage to the Hotel du Prince Regent where Madame Mercier lives. We saw her the next day with her husband. She is looking well and comfortable, but her husband has nothing to do, and I have had long conversations with her about his coming to the United

States, which I infer he has neither the means nor the enterprize to do. Mrs. Maxwell and Agnes are here.[2] I called on them, day before yesterday. Agnes was a little indisposed, and the mother did not look by any means well, though she says she is better. They think of going to Italy this winter—but Mrs. Maxwell seemed a little undecided. Cronkite[3] has been here for some time, but is now on a short visit to London. He too is going to Italy. Mr. Beckwith[4] and his wife are here also. Huntington is settled here for the winter and is painting a picture of the Good Samaritan taking the wounded man to the inn.[5]

The day after I arrived, a rainy day, the empire was proclaimed, and standing amidst a crowd in the garden of the Tuileries I saw the new Emperor,[6] escorted by the military to the Palace of that name. There were some cries of *Vive Napoleon vive l'Empereur*, but mostly from the soldiery. In the crowd about me not one opened his mouth. The absence of enthusiasm was really extraordinary.

The weather is continually foggy and dark. I have looked in at the Luxembourg and the Louvre; seen Notre Dame again; been to church at the Oratoire, a Protestant place of worship and heard an exhortation to peace and quietness; visited Huntington's studio, and passed an evening in his apartments; been twice to the dentist's; shopped with Madame Mercier, &c &c, and think of setting out for the south of France early tomorrow morning.

The letters by the Humboldt have arrived but there are none for me, I am greatly disappointed—but I shall go in the morning nevertheless— Leupp has letters from home. When I shall hear from you I cannot even guess. My love to Fanny and Julia and all.

Yours, notwithstanding as ever
W   C   Bryant.

Manuscript: NYPL–GR address: Mrs. Frances F. Bryant / Roslyn docketed: 3rd / Received Dec 27th / Paris Dec 7th.

1. John Durand (1822–1908), eldest son of the artist Asher Brown Durand, and himself an amateur member of the National Academy, was the joint founder and editor, with William James Stillman (1828–1901), of *The Crayon*, 1855–1861, the first real American art magazine. Later in life he wrote a history of the Sketch and Century Clubs, and a biography of his father, *The Life and Times of A. B. Durand* (New York, 1894). *NAD Exhibition Record*, I, 140; James T. Callow, *Kindred Spirits: Knickerbocker Writers and American Artists, 1805–1855* (Chapel Hill: University of North Carolina Press, 1967), pp. 115–116.

2. Probably the wife and daughter of Hugh Maxwell (1787–1873, Columbia 1808), Collector of the Port of New York, 1849–1853. Cooper, *Letters & Journals*, VI, 33, 89.

3. Probably James P. Cronkhite (d. 1860), a fellow-member of the Sketch Club.

4. N. M. Beckwith; see 743.2.

5. In 1854 Daniel Huntington exhibited a picture entitled "The Good Samaritan" at the National Academy. *NAD Exhibition Record*, I, 248.

6. Napoleon III.

813. *To* the EVENING POST

Paris, December 7th, 1852.

Three years ago, when I was in Paris, the country was suffering under that breaking up of regular employments which necessarily attends a revolution. Nobody seemed sure that another revolution, or at least an attempt at a revolution, was not close at hand; the greater part of those foreigners who make Paris their residence had flown the place. I missed the usual bustle of the streets, and saw here and there long rows of shops untenanted, with the shutters closed. At present these shops are again open, glittering with showy wares, and thronged with customers; the city is full of foreigners,—they count two thousand Americans, birds of every feather,—and the concourse of English visitors and residents seems more numerous than ever; solid English carriages rumble along the streets, and the English signs over the shop-doors seem to me nearly twice as frequent as I ever saw them before. The gayeties of the place, never extinct, are pursued with new spirit; the theatres, the public ball-rooms, and other places of entertainment, are crowded. A vehement desire of magnificence has seized upon the government; the public buildings are beautified and enlarged; workmen are busy in places, scraping from them the mould which, in this damp climate, darkens the cream-colored stone of which they are built; and all the ancient churches are undergoing extensive repairs and restorations. Old frescoes discovered on their walls under the whitewash of centuries, have been cleaned, retouched, and brightened; and eminent artists have been employed on new designs. Couture, for example, who is placed by his disciples at the head of modern French painters,[1] is engaged on new frescoes for the church of St. Eustache. The *rue de Rivoli*, which faces the gardens of the Tuileries, is to be extended so as to traverse the entire city; a track of ruins has been opened to the west for its passage, where houses have been levelled. The magnificent parallelogram of the Louvre is to be completed, and workmen are pulling down a part of the structure not consistent with the grander plan now contemplated. Everybody is employed, and Paris, and as I am told, the whole of France, now presents an appearance of great material prosperity.

To stimulate the activity of trade the Emperor has projected a great financial scheme, a bank with an enormous capital, to be enlarged according to circumstances and the demands of borrowers, which is to lend money on mortgages of property in the country. In this way, to use an expression which I once heard from the lips of an eminent speculator in the United States, real estate is to be made fluid,—a process as much for the welfare of the body politic as it would be healthful for the human body if its solid parts were converted into a liquid state. This plan, which is to be immediately carried into effect, will stimulate speculation to a degree of which France has had no experience since the time of John Law and the South Sea bubble.[2]

In the midst of the general activity and consequent contentment of the laboring-classes, France ceases to be a republic and becomes an empire. "I prefer the empire," said an intelligent lady to me the day after it was proclaimed, "because it is just what it pretends to be; when liberty is at end it is time that the forms of liberty should be abandoned." It was the evening before the proclamation of the empire that I arrived in Paris. The next morning the town was waked by the firing of cannon, and as the day wore on, the shops were shut, and notwithstanding the rain, for it was one of the gloomiest and saddest days of a Parisian winter, the population flocked to the Boulevards and the broader streets where detachments of the army and of the national guards were marching to the sound of music. I was present as the newly proclaimed emperor was conducted to the palace of the Tuileries by a military escort. The ceremony was rather imposing. A party of cavalry, in plumed and glittering casques, first dashed briskly forward through the space opened for them in the immense multitude which thronged the Champs Elysées and the garden of the Tuileries, like the gust which sweeps the streets before a tempest. Then came the Emperor, on horseback, amidst his generals and marshals. A few cries of *Vive l'Empereur* rose, which he answered by taking off his hat and bowing to the people. He appeared of shorter stature than most of the officers of his suite, but he sat his horse well, a spirited creature, which pranced and curvetted, and seemed proud of bearing the sovereign of the French Empire. The party entered the palace gates, and not long afterward the emperor showed himself at the balcony. The troops in front of the palace greeted his appearance with acclamations, but from the crowd which stood around me, not a single cry was heard. They were persons of all conditions and ages; well-dressed men and ladies, men in blouses and women in caps, all looking on in silence, as on a spectacle in which they had no part. There was an utter absence not only of enthusiasm but even of the least affectation of enthusiasm.

The city was illuminated in the evening—meagerly illuminated, except in a few instances. The illumination was a part of the prescribed ceremonies of the occasion, and was commanded by the government. Twice in the course of the day a message from the police was brought to the hotel where I lodge, intimating that it was expected that the house would be illuminated in the evening. The order was obeyed, of course.

It is admitted, however, I believe on all hands, that a large, at least a considerable majority of the people of France is in favor of the present order of things. At the hotel where I passed the night in Boulogne, I asked one of the attendants, a man of mature age and not unintelligent, what he thought of the empire. "What the people now want," he replied, "is the opportunity of earning their livelihood by their labor in peace. That they now have, and they are not ambitious of anything beyond it. I gave

my voice for Louis Napoleon and his plans, because I believe he can and will maintain things in their present state." Another man, of nearly the same class in France, answered the same question thus: "As long as Louis Napoleon remains at peace with other nations, we shall have good times, and the people will be with him. If he should get us into a war, he will disappoint the people, and we may have another change of government."

I was in conversation the other day with an intelligent and reflecting Frenchman, no friend of the present order of things, who said: "The character of the French race is unstable; they are swayed to and fro by the impulse of the day. A little while since they shouted *Vive la République*; now the same voices raise the cry of *Vive l'Empereur*; what may be the next cry I cannot tell; but, if we are to judge by the past, the empire of Napoleon the Third cannot last long. I do not see any elements of duration in it which did not belong to the government of Charles X. or Louis Philippe.[3] Each of the governments which has risen and fallen since the time of Louis XVI.[4] has promised itself eternal duration. I am waiting to see what will come next."

I give these conversations because they are more instructive than any speculations of mine would be. On Sunday I attended worship in the *Oratoire*, a French Protestant church, where I listened to an exhortation from the preacher of the day, M. Vermeuil, who dwelt on the duty of a quiet and peaceable demeanor, and admonished his hearers with much earnestness to "possess their souls in patience,"—evidently, as it seemed to me, alluding to the political circumstances of the time. Enough of French politics.

Huntington, the artist, is here, settled for the winter. He is painting a picture of the Good Samaritan, bringing to the view the man who had fallen among thieves. He has made the studies for it with great care, and it promises to be one of his best and most interesting works.

MANUSCRIPT: Unrecovered TEXT: *LFE*, pp. 16–23; first published in *EP* for December 27, 1852.

1. Thomas Couture (1815–1879).

2. Between 1716 and 1720 the Scotsman John Law (1671–1729) gained control of French finances through his government-chartered Banque Générale, which precipitated ruinous speculation in a so-called "Mississippi Scheme" of investment in Louisiana properties. At almost the same time the English chancellor of the exchequer, Robert Harley, first Earl of Oxford (1661–1724), initiated a scheme for funding the British national debt through his South Sea Company (1711). This "South Sea bubble" burst disastrously in 1720.

3. Charles X (1757–1836), king of France, 1824–1830; Louis Philippe (1773–1850), "King of the French," 1830–1848.

4. Louis XVI (1754–1793), king of France from 1774 until his execution by the revolutionary Convention.

814.   *To* the EVENING POST

Marseilles, December 14th, 1852.

To those who find themselves in France and have not the time to make a journey to Rome, I would recommend a visit to Nismes. In that city and its neighborhood they will be able to obtain almost as good an idea of the remains of ancient Roman architecture as they could at Rome itself. The amphitheatre would entirely represent the Colosseum, if we were to suppose it somewhat more extensive, and somewhat more magnificent in its external architecture. The *Maison Carrée*, or Square House, a building of the Corinthian architecture, is one of the finest remains of antiquity in the world, and gives as perfect an idea as one can well have of the public edifices of the Romans. Besides these, there are the ruins of the Temple of Diana; the Gate of Augustus, a sample of their city gates; the Grand Tower, a fragment of what was probably an immense mausoleum, and the Pont du Gard, a magnificent portion of an aqueduct which once conveyed water to the city. Not far from Nismes is the city of Arles, where is another amphitheatre and other interesting remains; and at nearly the same distance, in another direction, is Orange, with its triumphal arch in almost as good preservation as either of the triumphal arches at Rome. The monuments of antiquity at Nismes have been cleared of all encumbering rubbish, and of all the buildings erected within or against them in the course of centuries, and are thus seen to the very best advantage.

Modern Nismes is a very beautiful city. By the side of its *boulevards*, at the foot of the Temple of Diana, a vast spring, ninety feet in depth, pours forth a river of transparent water. Near it we find some remains of Roman baths, and these have been restored according to what was supposed to be their original plan, with recesses and columns, and a broad stone floor, over which the water hurries toward the town. They are overlooked by groups of statues, and protected by a massive stone balustrade. Beyond this the water is received into broad canals, bordered by walls and parapets of hewn stone, which convey it in different directions through an extensive promenade planted with trees. At the extremity of one of these, it is received into a broad circular basin of stone, the sides of which slope by an easy descent, and here the washerwomen of Nismes ply their vocation, slapping and rubbing the wet linen, and make the slow current froth with soap. On the rocky hill which rises above the fountain a public garden has been laid out. The bare cliffs, about the middle of the last century, were covered with soil brought up from the plain, intersected with winding walks and planted thickly with pines and cypresses, among which are thickets of laurels, myrtle, the tree-box, the lauratinus, with its clusters of white flowers, now beginning to open, and a variety of other shrubs and trees which never drop their leaves in the season of winter. You might walk here in one of the sunny winter days of this soft climate

and fancy it to be May. Above the garden on its foundation of rock rises the lofty Roman ruin, the Grand Tower.

Those parts of the town which lie near these public grounds have an uncommonly agreeable aspect. The streets are very broad and the houses are in a pleasing style of architecture, built of the cream-colored stone of the country, which is easily wrought, and which in the dry climate of this place long retains its original rich light tint in the open air. It appears to me that the aridity of the climate has much to do with the preservation of the ancient buildings. At Lyons and Avignon, on the Rhone, the exhalations from the river darken the churches and houses almost to a sooty hue, and here at Marseilles on the Mediterranean, I perceive the same effect. The Frescoes of Devéria,[1] in the Cathedral at Avignon, painted twelve years since, and well worthy of a longer date, are already peeling in flakes from the walls and the ceiling, so damp is the atmosphere there. Nismes is situated on a plain elevated considerably above the meadows of the Rhone, and beyond the reach of its mists. I was told that rain is sometimes known not to fall in this region for ten months together. I inquired what, in that case, became of the crops. "They are gathered early," was the answer, "except our principal harvests, grapes and olives, and these are best in a dry climate. We have our last showers in April, and then we expect no more rain till October." In such an atmosphere moss and mould are slow in gathering upon walls and sculptures in the open air, and the oldest remains of those at Nismes, such, for example, as the rich Corinthian columns of the *Maison Carrée*, only acquire a warm brown tint after the lapse of centuries.

One of the modern ornaments of Nismes is the Fountain of the Esplanade, adorning the principal public square, a work of the French sculptor Pradier,[2] who died about six months since by a stroke of apoplexy. It is a group representing Nismes with a crown of towers and palaces, copied from the Roman remains, and the streams which water the neighboring lands sitting at her feet, among which is the little river gushing from the ground in the public garden, a beautiful female figure just emerging from girlhood, her fair brows shaded with a chaplet of the leaves of the water-lily. It is a work of considerable merit, but there is a finer one of the same artist in the cathedral at Avignon, a Virgin of great beauty of form and an ethereal sweetness of expression. The *Maison Carrée* is turned into a Museum, that is to say, into a public gallery of pictures. It has some fine portraits by Vanloo,[3] several good cabinet pictures of the Flemish school, and a few larger ones by French painters; but the most striking of them all, as it seemed to me, was Delaroche's[4] painting of Cromwell contemplating the dead body of Charles the First in its coffin. Delaroche is among painters what Crabbe[5] is among poets; he confines himself to rugged, unidealized nature. One would hardly suppose it possible for a French artist to renounce so completely, not only all that is theatrical in

the French school, but all attempt at grace of any sort, as he has done in this work. As I looked at the rough old Roundhead uncovering, with that sad expression which speaks so much of the feelings within, the lifeless face of his king, I could not help fancying myself with him in the chamber of death.

It is impossible for me here in the south of France, to help imagining myself in Italy. The mild climate, the vast tracts covered with olive-trees and intermingled vineyards, the Italian character of the architecture, the women drawing water from the fountains in jars of antique form, the people showing in their features and physiognomy a certain kindred to the Italian race, and speaking an accented language bequeathed to them by the troubadours, almost as different from the language of the northern provinces as that of Spain or Portugal, make it hard for me to convince myself that I am still within the boundaries of France. Around me are the descendants of Roman and Greek colonists, who have founded prosperous and flourishing communities; of those who came hither when the family of Constantine fixed the seat of the Roman empire at Arles,[6] and of those of a later age, when the Italian church migrated, for a time, to Avignon, and made it an Italian city.[7]

To judge by appearances, this part of the population of France, as well as that of the north, is as perfectly satisfied with the present government as if they had lived under an empire from the days of Constantine. No external indication, certainly, bespeaks discontent; there is nothing of gravity or of gloom—no silence, sulkiness, or sadness. It is characteristic of the French race, that it conforms itself easily to any change of circumstances, provided you do not interfere with its amusements. "What a people!" said a German lady to me at Paris. "Three or four thousand unoffending and unresisting people—men, women, and children—were shot in the streets, at their doors, at their windows, or sitting in their apartments, a year ago, when Louis Napoleon abolished the French constitution. In a few weeks all recollection of the dreadful event seemed to have passed away. What a people, that such things should have been done, and that, after a few days, nothing should be said of them; that they should have been forgotten and pardoned!"

Yet there are some who speculate on political events in this country, and who occupy themselves in working out the problem by what sort of process the present government will by and by follow its predecessors to the place where they are all to sleep together. One of them lately said to me: "The Emperor is surrounded by able men, very able and wholly unprincipled, whose advice and assistance he has had in the well-managed intrigue which has made him the absolute sovereign of France. Hitherto, while the project was yet unconsummated, they all acted harmoniously together, for they had but one object. Now the time has arrived for rewarding their services with honors and emoluments, and from this time

each will have a particular aim of his own; each will claim the highest reward for himself. It will be impossible for the Emperor to satisfy them. It is not that they will be discontented with what they receive, but that they will be indignant to see others placed over them. Then will be the time of feuds and factions, which as yet under the new order of things have been unknown; then will secret intrigues be set on foot to excite discontent against the government, which, after being adroitly kindled and inflamed for a few years, may unseat Louis Napoleon as easily as it unseated Charles the Tenth or Louis Philippe!"

There may be much truth in this view, but it seems to me that one of the greatest dangers which the new Emperor has to dread will arise from another cause. In the circumstances in which he has hitherto been placed, audacity has been the highest policy. He is now about to apply the same policy to measures of finance, in which it is madness. Everything indicates that the reign of speculation has begun in France, under the auspices of the new bank, established to increase the number of borrowers to an extent hitherto unknown in the country. The unhealthy prosperity of a period of speculation will be followed most certainly by a period of embarrassment, bankruptcy, and the want of employment among the working-classes. Man, like all beasts of prey, is fierce when famished. A hungry Frenchman has something in him of the nature of the wolves which in a severe winter descend from the mountains of his own country and attack the peasants at their doors. It was the want of employment, it was idleness and famine, which gave rise to the several attempts to change the government by violence that so soon followed the revolution of 1848.

MANUSCRIPT: Unrecovered TEXT: *LFE*, pp. 24–33; first published in *EP* for January 12, 1853.

1. Eugène Devéria (1805–1865), French historical painter.
2. James (Jean Jacques) Pradier (1792–1852).
3. Probably Jean Baptiste Vanloo (1684–1745).
4. Hippolyte ("Paul") Delaroche (1797–1856).
5. George Crabbe (1754–1832), an English poet best remembered for his *The Village* (1783) and *Tales in Verse* (1812).
6. *c*A.D. 314.
7. 1309–1378.

815. *To* the EVENING POST

Valletta, Island of Malta, Dec. 29, 1852.

At Marseilles they told me that though there are more than fifty steamers now on the Mediterranean, not a shipwreck or disastrous accident of any kind has happened to any of them since steamers were first introduced on these waters, with the exception of a single instance, and that happened some twenty years since. They all have low-pressure engines, are carefully navigated, and the greater number of them merely make coasting voyages, stopping at one port after another, and never put-

ting to sea when the weather is tempestuous.[1] It was in one of these steamers that on the 14th of this month I took passage for Naples—a little Neapolitan boat, short and broad, tumbling about with every impulse of the
waves and wind, and working her way as well as might be with a weak
engine. The motion, as we proceeded out of the harbor, soon drove all
the passengers to their berths, except those who were proof against the
causes of sea-sickness. In passing between a rocky island and the coast, our
poor boat had her wheels entangled among the ropes of a net, and was an
hour or more getting clear of them.

I had, some years before, travelled the road along what is called the
Maritime Alps, from Marseilles to Nice,[2] and thought the scenery extremely grand, but I am not quite sure that it is not finer when viewed
from the water. You take broader views of it, at least, and see how its several parts add to each other's effect. As the mountain summits, one by one,
rise before you—the loftiest, at this season, glistening with snow—as the
gulfs, and bays, and valleys, and ravines, one by one, open upon you; as
town after town shows itself, spread out upon the shelving shore, or nest-
ling in the lap of hills, or seated on the craggy heights, the attention is
kept ever awake with ever-new images of sublimity and beauty. A sea-
voyage is a comfortless thing always, at least I have found it so—but a sea-
voyage which shows such sights as these, brings some compensation for its
discomfort.

In about thirty hours our steamer brought us to Genoa, where the
passengers were counted like sheep, to see that their number was neither
too large nor too small; and then, after an hour's delay or more, we were
permitted, by the police of the place, to land, in a dark, rainy evening, and
proceeded to an hotel—for these boats, while in port at any of their stopping-
places, do not concern themselves with providing for their passengers. We
had a day—a bright, sunny, cheerful, winter-day of Italy—to look at the
palaces and churches of Genoa, and all the glorious views seen from its
heights; and, leaving the place in the evening, were early the next morning at Leghorn, where the examination of the passports of those who
wished to land occasioned still longer delays. We received, however, at
last, permission to go on shore, and having breakfasted went by railway to
Pisa, to get a hasty look at its antiquities. Another night on the water
brought us to the port of Civita Vecchia, where we thought we should be
starved before the police would allow us to land. At last an officer made
his appearance on board with written permissions for all of us, between
fifty and sixty in number; our names were called, and as we answered to
them we were permitted to step down to the boats, waiting to convey us
to the shore. We had just time to breakfast, see the greater number of our
fellow-passengers depart on their way to Rome, and make a rapid circuit
of the little town, to be convinced that it contained nothing worth seeing,
when the time arrived for returning to our steamer. It had been lightened

of the greater part of its cargo, and now in going out of port bobbed and danced like a cork upon the waves. After a most unpleasant passage, the early light of the fifth morning from our embarking saw us rounding the coast of Baiae, and making our way slowly against a north wind. At half-past nine we dropped anchor, but nobody was permitted to go on shore till an hour and a half afterward, when we stepped into boats, were taken before the police authorities, and received written permission to remain in the capital of the kingdom for twenty-four hours, at the end of which we were to make application either for leave to remain still longer, or leave to depart. We got to our hotel, and breakfasted about twelve o'clock. I have been the more particular in this recital because it illustrates the beauty of the passport system, and shows what a pleasant thing it is for the traveller. In France, since the late revolution, this system has been somewhat modified, and made more tolerable, but in the other countries of Europe it prevails at the present moment in its worst rigor. The other day a party of dragoons came on board one of the steamers touching at Messina, and took the English passengers before the police, where they underwent an examination.

During our stay at Naples we made an excursion to Paestum, of which, however, I should not have said much, were it not for the episode of a visit to Amalfi on our way—a place remarkable for the exceeding beauty of its scenery.

We left Naples by the earliest railway train for Nocera, a little town ten miles, perhaps, beyond Pompeii. It had been a cold night for Naples; the tramontane winds had been blowing for two days, a calm still night had succeeded, and the hoar-frost was now glistening by the side of the way. As we dismounted to take a look at Pompeii in passing, I found by touching the earth with the end of my umbrella that the frost had hardened to thin crust on the surface of the soil, though the fields of lupines and broad-beans around us, already half grown, seemed uninjured by it. This was a Neapolitan winter in its greatest severity. Our cicerone, after a few minutes' flourish with his hands, would stop to rub them vehemently, and complain of the cold. As the sun mounted the day became warm and genial. We returned to the railway, reached Nocera in a few minutes, and made a bargain with the most respectable looking of the carriage-drivers who crowded shouting around us, to convey us to Salerno.

We passed up among the mountains, through a beautiful and fertile valley, among vineyards and plantations of the fig-tree and rows of olive-trees, and crops of every green thing the season could produce, except grass—but let no one look for grass in Southern Italy. Every spot of earth which will bear tillage is furrowed with the plough and turned with the spade, and the only places where grass is allowed to spring up are the borders of the road and the narrow edges of the fields. Of course you never see any broad expanse of greensward, such as with us is so fresh and grate-

ful to the eye, and forms so pleasant a carpet for the feet, unless in those tracts from which the cultivator is driven by the malaria.

After a drive of four or five miles, we began to descend toward the sea-shore. We had left on our right the grand mountain promontory on which stand the towns of Sorrento and Castellamare, and now the broad gulf of Salerno lay before us, embraced by a semicircle of lofty mountains. Far to the southeast, on a level between the base and the sea, our driver pointed out to us the site of Paestum. About midday we were at Salerno, a city of twenty thousand inhabitants, dirty and noisy, and full of beggars, with olive groves on the rocky slopes back of it, and the finest orange orchards along the shore which I have seen in Italy, loaded and bending with their yellow but not fully ripened fruit. It was now too late, they told us, to think of going to Paestum and returning the same day; we therefore engaged a boat to take us to Amalfi.

It was a clumsy thing, manned with four rowers, each of whom, standing upright, pushed instead of pulling a huge oar, held to a pin in the edge of the boat by a thong, or piece of rope. The principal among them was a merry fellow from Amalfi, about five feet in height, wearing a Phrygian cap, and a dress composed of a canvas shirt and drawers. He and one of his companions took us on their shoulders, and carried us through the shallow water to the boat. As the oarsmen struck out into the bay, he pulled off his cap, threw it on the seat, and encouraged them by calling out, "*Allez*, pull away, pull away, ugh." The boatmen in this part of the Mediterranean appear to have adopted the words "pull away" from the English sailors, for I heard them using it again at Messina. At every repetition of "*Allez*, pull away, pull away, ugh," the boatmen would lean to their oars and redouble the strokes.

As we passed along beside the rocks which rise out of the transparent water of the Mediterranean, we were struck with the wonderful beauty of the region.

"Earth has not anything to show more fair." [3]

In the recesses of the mountains, close to the sea, nestled the white villages of the fishermen; the dwellings of those who tend the olive-tree and the vine were clustered on the heights; the midway declivities were clothed with the gray-green of olive groves, with thickets of the prickly pear hanging from the cliffs in masses of uncouth vegetation; higher up grew trees of deeper verdure, the corob, which bears a sort of bean, imbedded in a sweet pulp, the food of horses; and above them all, bare pinnacles of rock rose into the clear blue sky. Here and there we descried a convent, perched far up in a spot that seemed inaccessible; and on the precipices by the sea rose old towers, built to protect the country from the invasions of the Saracens, and long since abandoned. The whole scene was bathed in a mild golden sunshine, and the smooth waves rippled softly on the beaches, or rolled with gentle dashes into the caverns of the rocks.

Our boatmen sang as they rowed, keeping time to the stroke of their oars. Their songs were sometimes plaintive and sometimes comic, but as they were in the Neapolitan dialect, I could not make out their meaning. Our courier, however, who was four years and a half dragoman to the Grand Turk at Constantinople, and who, besides Turkish, Arabic, and modern Greek, understands all the dialects of Italy, explained them to us, and made, what I dare say was sprightly enough in the original, very tedious in the interpretation. Besides other peculiarities, which are numerous enough, the people of the Neapolitan dominions have an odd way of pronouncing Italian, which may be exemplified in English thus:

> "Faindly as dolls the evening gime
> Our voices geep dune and our oars geep dime."

And again,

> "The rabids are near and the daylighd's bast."[4]

Just before arriving at Amalfi, we passed the village of Atrani, seated in a steep and narrow gorge, where a little stream comes down from the mountains, and high up among the precipices a small white house was pointed out, by our merry friend the boatman, as the house of Masaniello, the fisherman who became a politician and a revolutionist. "And who was Masaniello?" I asked.

"He was a great king of the country," answered the boatman.[5]

This is all that the large majority of Masaniello's countrymen know about him. The patriot and republican is confounded by the people with the common rabble of dead kings.

As we approached Amalfi, our little boatman raising his cry of "*Allez,* pull away, pull away, ugh," looked over his shoulder at us, nodded and smiled, and our boat was soon upon the beach, where a crowd of swarthy fellows, in woollen caps and tattered pantaloons, were waiting to carry us to the shore on their shoulders; and as soon as our boat touched the sand, they gathered round it, up to their knees in the water, thrusting each other aside, and all shouting at once. We tried to select the best only for our bearers, and when at length we landed, the whole crowd ran after us, every man of them, as it seemed to me, demanding to be paid. Our train was further re-enforced by the beggars, blind and lame, who always haunt the places where strangers are expected to pass. We obtained a guide, looked at the old cathedral, which contains little of interest, and then proceeded to what is called the Valley of the Mills, a deep ravine between precipices of immense height at the mouth of which this little town of seven thousand inhabitants is built. A stream—a brook rather—rushes along at the bottom, and turns seventeen paper-mills. Orange-trees, loaded with fruit, overhang the path from the walls of narrow gardens, and other fruit-trees of various kinds, not now in leaf, and trailing plants in full verdure, nourished by the perpetual moisture, mantle the rocks with their

luxuriant growth. High above rise the crags, crowned with old dwellings, castles, and convents; and, seaward, through the chasm, you have a glimpse of Salerno, and the mountains of the opposite coast. It is a spot for the pencil, and not for description.

We climbed to the Franciscan convent overlooking the shore, and from a natural grotto extending deep into the rock, had a magnificent view of the shore, the sea, and the distant mountains. Part of the nearer crags were lying in shadow, yet distinct, a sort of clear-obscure, and part were crimson with the descending sun. We returned to Salerno by moonlight, our boatmen singing the popular ballads of the country, as they passed under the rocks of the shore.

We set out the next morning for Paestum at half-past four. For miles beyond Salerno, we found the road, at that hour, full of men and women trooping to the town, with donkeys bearing loads of vegetables and roots, and wagons and carts drawn by white oxen, loaded with wine, grain, and pulse, the productions of the country. Herds of swine were driven by us, squealing as they went, and several flocks of sheep. If early rising be a sign of industry, the people of this part of Italy well deserve to be called industrious. We could perceive that we were passing through a highly cultivated region, though with but few inhabitants; but when at length the daylight came we found ourselves travelling alone in a solitary level tract of pasturage, spotted with luxuriant tufts of thistles, in which herds of white cows and black buffaloes were grazing. To our left were the mountains with villages and towns on their sides, and the sea was moaning on our right. Further on, tracts of springing wheat made their appearance, fields of turnips and lupines luxuriantly green, with here and there a building apparently intended as a storehouse for the crops.

"There is Paestum," said one of our party. Looking before us, we saw at a little distance the majestic columns of the temple of Ceres, and in a few minutes passed through the opening made by the road in the ruined walls of the ancient town, and stopped at the door of a house which answered, in some respects, the purpose of a hostelry. We found a *cicerone*, who carried a bunch of keys and opened for us the iron gate of the enclosure in which the Temple of Ceres stands. I will not repeat for you what is said in the guide-books of these fine remains of Greek architecture. The Temple of Neptune, as it is the most ancient, is the noblest and most imposing in aspect. It is wonderful how this atmosphere, in which man sickens and dies, spares the work of his hands. In many parts, the architectural ornaments of the Temple of Neptune are as perfect and as sharp in outline as if they were cut yesterday, and nowhere is the stone incrusted with moss, or darkened with mould; time has only given it a warmer tint. The ground, within their grand colonnades, was spotted with December daisies, in bloom, and the morning air was scented with the sweet alyssum, which grows here in profusion, its white flowers, at

that time, looking at a little distance like hoar-frost. I was surprised to see so much cultivation; the fields were enclosed with stone walls and rude hedges; there was a vineyard near, and plantations of fig-trees; and wheat had been sown and was just springing up, close to the foundation-stones of the Temple of Ceres. Nor was the place so solitary as I expected to find it. Travellers were passing to and fro on the highway by which we came; a diligence full of passengers went by; a party of sportsmen, with their fowling-pieces, stopped at the inn; we saw several soldiers in uniform in the road, and when we were not within the enclosures containing the temples, we had a train of followers, some of whom wanted to sell us old coins, which they pretended to have found, and others importuned us for alms.

I asked our guide if the soil of the place was productive. "By no means," he replied; "the earth is full of salt, and there are no springs; in summer these fields are scorched by a severe drought. Those who cultivate them live at Carpaccio, yonder, where there is good air and good water." Here he pointed to a village in sight, half-way up the mountain-side. "In summer," he continued, "this place is so unhealthy that nobody dares to sleep here; those who look to the crops come down in the daytime, and return before night-fall. It swarms with snakes, too, which in summer crawl out of the old walls, and are very dangerous. There are some of the people who remain here during the summer."

As he said this, he pointed to a group of half a dozen people, none of whom seemed to have reached the middle term of life, emaciated, pale, and ragged, most of them wearing a look of helpless debility. We were then about entering our carriage, to take the luncheon which we had brought with us. One of our party threw on the ground the thigh-bone of a chicken, which had been well picked. A boy stepped from the sickly group, took it up, examined it narrowly, and finding it perfectly bare, threw it back again. It was evident that the poor creatures were hungry. We made a pretty liberal distribution of bread and cheese, and bits of meat, among the ghastly women and pallid children, and drove off for Salerno, from which we proceeded to Nocera, and reached Naples by the last train for the day.

To the island of Malta we came by a French steamer—the Hellespont, plying between Marseilles and Alexandria, a more powerful and commodious boat than the Maria Antoinetta. We shot over smooth water by the now harmless rock of Scylla, with a little town behind it on the Calabrian coast, and ran close by the inoffensive eddy of Charybdis, near a village of fishermen on the Sicilian side. "They make a great deal of Scylla and Charybdis in romances," said the second captain of our steamer, "but they are nothing." Of Messina, where we touched, and remained for two or three hours, I have only one remark to make—that the people, though slight and short of stature, have incredibly powerful voices; they are noisier than even the Neapolitans. We passed through the market-place, where

they were screaming their wares at the highest pitch of their voices, and I think I was never in so deafening an uproar. In about forty-two hours from the time of leaving Naples we were in the port of Valletta, the principal city of Malta.

To a New Yorker it is worth a voyage across the Atlantic to see so clean a city as Valletta. It is admirably well built, of a cream-colored calcareous rock, which they hew with axes, and shape with ease into any form that suits the architect. The streets are paved with the same material, which is almost as little soiled under the feet of passengers, as the walls of the houses themselves. Seaward and landward the town is protected by fortification beyond fortification, rampart beyond rampart, and several of its gates are cut through the living rock. From the ramparts, or from the flat housetops of the town, you have a view of the interior of the island, which presents a very uninviting aspect. High walls of stone divide it into little enclosures, where the rock is covered with soil, brought, for the most part, it is said, from Sicily. At first sight one would say that there are no trees on the island, but on looking more closely, you perceive rows of sprawling fig-trees planted by the walls, their boughs given off close to the ground, and here and there a corob-tree, an evergreen, larger but equally sprawling. All the trees on this island, except those which grow in the lower and moister situations, have this tendency to put out their branches close to the earth, and to creep rather than to rise. Whether it be the effect of the sea-winds which sweep over the island from every point of the compass, or of the want of depth of soil, I do not profess to decide.

Just now a question of local politics has arisen in the island, which is not without general interest. When the English took possession of the Island of Malta, they engaged to maintain the Roman Catholic church in all its existing rights. This does not seem to have been understood to imply that other modes of worship were not to be tolerated, and, accordingly, other denominations of Christians have established their worship here. When, however, some years since, the Methodists built a church in Valletta, they were prohibited from giving it any of the external indications of a place for public devotions. Since that time, and within a few years, a very fine building, in which the service of the Anglican church is performed, has been erected: the most conspicuous in appearance of all the churches in Valletta. This seems to have given some displeasure to the Catholic priesthood, and to the original Maltese population, who, to a man, are devout Catholics.

A new criminal code has lately been drawn up for the island; a code very judiciously framed, in general, as I am told, and to which it is very desirable that validity should be given as early as possible. It has, however, been the subject of long debate and consideration in the Council of the island. Malta you know is ruled by a governor and a council the members of which are partly appointed by the home government, and partly

elected by the people. In one of the articles providing punishment for the disturbance of public worship, the Roman Catholic church is styled the dominant church of the country. This expression, after a vehement struggle on the part of the Catholics to retain it, has just been struck out of the code. Those who desired to retain it argued with some plausibility that the British government found the Roman Catholic church dominant in Malta, and by promising to maintain it in the exercise of its rights, had engaged to keep it so. Those who insisted on striking out the expression, took the higher ground of liberty of conscience, and argued that under a just government all forms of religion should be placed on a footing of equality in the eye of the law.

The archbishop of Malta has written a letter to the governor of the island, protesting against the omission of the epithet "dominant," as applied to the church of which he is a dignitary, and declaring that if the word is not restored, he and his clergy will petition the home government for its restoration. The governor has answered that there is no probability that the home government will grant the petition. The petition has probably by this time been forwarded.

To-morrow we shall probably leave this place in an English steamer for Egypt.

MANUSCRIPT: Unrecovered TEXT: *LFE*, pp. 34–54; first published in *EP* for January 28, 1853.

1. The frequency of accidents on American inland waters among steamboats carrying high-pressure boilers was probably much in Bryant's mind just then, for only a few months earlier, on July 28, 1852, his young friend the landscape architect Andrew Jackson Downing (628.1) had died in an explosion and fire aboard the Hudson River steamboat *Henry Clay*, ending a spectacularly successful career in his thirty-seventh year.

2. In September 1834; see Letter 292.

3. Wordsworth, "Composed Upon Westminster Bridge" (1803).

4. Cf. Thomas Moore, "A Canadian Boat Song," from *Poems Relating to America* (1806):

"Faintly as tolls the evening chime
Our voices keep tune and our oars keep time. . . .
Row, brothers, row, the stream runs fast,
The rapids are near and the daylight's past."

5. Masaniello (Tommaso Aniello, 1620?–1647) was a Neapolitan fisherman who led a brief revolt against high taxation in 1647.

816. *Memorandum of an Agreement Made at the City of Cairo in Egypt, between Emanuel Balthas, Dragoman, and Charles M. Leupp of the United States of America, This Eighth Day of January 1853—*

The said Balthas engages to convey the said Leupp and his two friends William C. Bryant and John Durand with their travelling baggage, from Cairo to Jerusalem by way of El Arcesh in eighteen days, including the quarantine at Gaza; and from Jerusalem to Jaffa in twelve days, of which

twelve, ten are to be employed in seeing Jerusalem within and without, including Jordan, the Dead Sea, Jericho, Bethlehem, San Saba &c. The said Balthas engages to furnish the camels, mules and horses necessary for the journey and for visiting the above named places, and to bear the expenses of the journey generally, including the tributes to the Arab Sheiks. He is to supply the necessary furniture namely tents, beds, straw mattresses, bed linen, table linen, towels &c and cooking utensils. He is to give the said Leupp and his two friends, each day, for breakfast, four dishes, two hot and two cold, and for dinner, six hot dishes together with soup, and in the course of the thirty days twelve bottles of Marsala or Bordeaux wine and six of Cognac Brandy. He is to pay for their board and room at their hotel in Jerusalem.

For all this the said Leupp agrees to pay for each of the three persons above mentioned one Napoleon[1] a day. If they shall desire it, their stay at Jerusalem may be shortened, and they may proceed to Beyrout or go by way of Damascus to the sea-coast, paying always at the rate of one Napoleon a day for each person while the journey shall last.

The said Balthus agrees to furnish conveyance and lodging during the journey, to John Muscat, Courier of the persons named above for five francs a day. It is understood that the journey shall begin on the twelfth, thirteenth or fourteenth of this month, as the travellers above named may choose.

signed Emanuel Balthas, DRAGOMAN
signed Chas. M. Leupp

Witness.
[signed] Wm. C. Bryant.[2]
[Endorsed on reverse] Received twenty Napoleons on this contract, making with twenty other Napoleons paid me by the American Consul and for which he has my receipt, forty Napoleons in all, in advance on the within contract, and I hereby agree that the time for beginning the journey herein specified shall be the thirtieth day of the present month.
Cairo, Egypt,
January 29th 1853—

[signed] Emanuel Balthas
dragoman

Received of C. M. Leupp twenty four Napoleons on the within contract. Jerusalem, February 18th, 1853.

signed Emanuel Balthas
dragoman

Received of C. M. Leupp fifteen Napoleons on the within contract. Jerusalem, February 22, 1853—

signed Emanuel Balthas
dragoman

Received of C. M. Leupp this 6th day of March 1853, twenty one Napoleons on the within contract.

signed MANUEL BALTHAS

Received of C. M. Leupp this 15th day of March 1853 nine and twenty
five francs in full of the within contract.

signed MANUEL BALTHAS
dragoman

MANUSCRIPT: NYPL–GR DOCKETED: Emanuel Balthas / Contract Jan. 8, 1853. / In Cairo
Egypt—.

1. Twenty French francs.
2. Only Bryant's signature and the docketing entry are in his handwriting.

817. *To* the EVENING POST

Cairo, Egypt, January 12th, 1853.

I left Malta on the 30th December in the British steamer Ripon, proceeding to Alexandria in one of her monthly voyages from Southampton.
Her commander was Captain Moresby, a veteran in the British naval service, known to geographers by his chart of the Red Sea and the Maldive
Islands.[1] We found a crowd of English on board on their way to India,
army-officers, civilians, medical men, a score of ladies, a lord or two, the
Governor of Hong Kong, a Chief Justice of the India bench, and a large
number of cadets, some of them scarcely full grown, sent out to fill the
civil and military employments, which are kept for young men who must
be provided for.

"These youths," said a Major in the British service, who had been my
fellow-passenger on board of the Arctic, and whom I was very glad to meet
again, "will find, in the climate of India, a severe trial for their constitutions; and yet it is necessary that they should go out thus early, in order
to qualify them properly for the posts they are to hold. A great many of
them will die, and leave their places vacant for other adventurers." I
looked at their fresh and healthy countenances, as he said this, and wished
them well through the trial; but a fate was hanging over one of them more
sudden and disastrous than any of us could possibly anticipate.

The cabins in the Ripon, called with us staterooms, contain each
generally four berths, and when occupied by more than two persons, are
particularly inconvenient. As we found no one of them vacant, our party
was billeted in different chambers, among persons who doubtless wished
us back to America with all their hearts. The proportion of ill-bred people on board was greater than I expected to find. Passengers, late at night,
would come singing to their berths, or whistle perseveringly as they turned
over and arranged the contents of their portmanteaus, or bore you with
their elbows, and commit various other acts of petty rudeness. One day—
it was the first of January—the captain gave champagne at dinner. and

immediately a strife arose among about a third part of the passengers, as it seemed to me, to see who should get possession of the bottles, and swallow the most of their contents. The supply was liberal, and we had a noisy night.

Among the passengers was Mr. Fortune, the botanist and traveller, who had already made two visits to China,[2] with a view of ascertaining which of the vegetable productions of that country might be advantageously introduced into the British dominions, and was now proceeding on a third voyage to Shanghae, by way of India. I sought an acquaintance with him, which he did not decline, and I was much interested by his conversation. "You are attempting the introduction of the tea-plant into America," he said, "but I doubt whether you will succeed. Your climate, with its warm summer, is well adapted to its cultivation, and you will probably have no difficulty in finding soils suitable for its growth; but labor is so dear in the United States, and so cheap in China, that the Chinese will send it to your doors at far less cost than you can produce it at home. I am at present engaged in the experiment of introducing the tea-plant into India. On the slopes of the Himalaya mountains are a soil and climate perfectly adapted to its cultivation; a country where land can be had for almost nothing, and labor costs very little. Here we are now forming gardens of the tea-plant, and I have, for my part, no doubt of the success of the undertaking."

We talked of the culture of the grape in America. "If, as you say," said Mr. Fortune, "the European grape does not succeed well with you, I should advise you to import stocks from those varieties of it which are cultivated in China, where the climate so much resembles your own in its changes and extremes. In the northern parts of China which I visited, I found a table grape very common, though they make no wine. You might easily have the plants brought over, as you are now beginning to have a pretty extensive commerce with the ports north of Canton. We have better fruit of the kind in Europe than I saw there, but you might perhaps improve it.

"There is one kind of fruit," he continued, "which I am introducing into Northern India, and which, I am sure, would succeed in some parts of your country. It is called in China the *yang-mae*—a fruit of the size of a plum, resembling that of the arbutus, but larger—a crimson berry, covered all over with small projecting points, very agreeable to the palate, and with just acidity enough in its flavor to make it refreshing. You have in America some plants of the genus to which it belongs, the *myrica*."

I instanced the *myrica cerifera*, or candleberry myrtle, bearing large quantities of berries.

"The *yang-mae* also," proceeds Mr. Fortune, "is an abundant bearer. It will not answer for England, as our summers are not warm enough, but in those parts of the United States, where the mercury in Fahrenheit's

thermometer does not fall in winter below twenty, or, at the utmost, twelve degrees, and where you have a nice warm summer"—such was his phrase—"to ripen it, the fruit would be produced in perfection. It would be well worth the while of some of your horticulturists to take measures for introducing it from the northern parts of China."   ,

In a subsequent conversation, Mr. Fortune mentioned a hardy kind of palm, the only one which will grow in cold climates, and very common in some parts of China. "It requires," he observed, "a warm summer, and will bear a severe winter, and is the very tree for the United States. It is a *chamoerops*, a genus of the palm family, of which there are several species, all of them tropical plants but this. It looks strange, in the depth of winter, to see this tree, apparently a production of the tropics, with its large evergreen leaves loaded with snow. The Chinese obtain from the upper part of it a kind of network, the sheathing of the young leaves, knotted with the most perfect regularity, which they apply to many useful purposes."

On his way to China, Mr. Fortune was taking out with him to Calcutta several cases containing cinchona plants—the tree which produces the Peruvian bark—brought from South America, with the design of introducing it into India.

As we approached Egypt, the weather grew rainy, and at length the pharos of Alexandria appeared above a low, flat shore. A pilot of slender figure, a little stooping, with a dirty white turban on his head, and a loose blue bag covering his legs from the waist to a little below the knee, came on board. Our steamer made a sudden turn, swept into the harbor, and dropped anchor in a violent shower, under fortifications bristling with guns placed in full sight. On landing we were at once surrounded by a mob of fellows in white turbans or fez caps, and blue cotton shirts tied round the waist by a string, offering us their donkeys with loud shouts, thrusting each other aside to get at us, and blocking our way so that we could not get forward a single step. As there was apparently no alternative, I took the one who stood immediately before me by the throat, shoved him out of my way, and then attacked the next in like manner, till I made my escape out of the crowd. The good-natured Mussulmans smiled at finding themselves thus unceremoniously handled by an infidel, and I jumped upon one of the best-looking of their animals, and trotted off through streets swimming with white mud to the hotel, followed by a shouting donkey-driver, who brandished a long stick, which he occasionally brought down on the quadruped's flanks to encourage his speed.

Brief space was allowed us to look from our hotel windows at the strange spectacle of people in oriental costumes, men and women, walking the streets, or trotting gently by on asses, or urging forward laden camels. We had a gallop on donkeys, attended by a dragoman richly dressed for the occasion, to attract custom, and three or four donkey-drivers running on foot, to Cleopatra's Needle and Pompey's Pillar, which

I will not tire you with describing. I have scarcely time to notice a spacious garden by which we passed, full of lofty date-palms and large-leaved bananas, or to observe the beauty of an avenue through which we went, planted with cassia-trees in full verdure. In a short time we were on board the boat destined to take us to the Nile, through the broad canal opened by the late pacha, Mehemet Ali.[3] Here forty or fifty passengers, who had come by the steamer Ripon to Alexandria, passed the night, as well as they might, on benches, tables, and camp-stools. I grew tired of my hard couch, and went on deck before the day dawned. The moon, in her wane, was in the firmament, which seemed enlarged to an immense depth; and the deck, in the transparent atmosphere, was drenched with dew. A small steamer was dragging us along the canal, and at the helm of our boat stood an Egyptian, in a shaggy brown capote, motionless as a statue, with one or two in the same garb squatted on the deck near him. To the right and left nothing was to be seen but the heaps of mould formed in digging the canal.

When the day broke we found ourselves gliding on between rows of large trees in luxuriant leaf: the cassia, the thorny acacia, called by the ancients the acanthus, and the sycamore, a tree producing a kind of fig, which forms a considerable part of the food of the Egyptians. From time to time we passed villages on the bank, built of unburnt brick, with low, flat roofs, looking like the habitations of mud-wasps magnified. Each had its mosque, with a minaret of hewn stone, from which the hour of prayer is proclaimed. Their inmates, in turbans and long blue or white cotton shirts, were creeping out of them in the early sunshine, and walking carefully on the wet and slippery declivity. Among them were women in blue cotton gowns, barefooted, with infants perched on their shoulders. This is the way in which the Arab mothers, of the laboring class in Egypt, carry their children; as soon as the little creatures get the primary use of their limbs, they are transferred from the arms to the shoulders. I have seen instances of this custom which would supply striking subjects for the pencil. At Old Cairo, the other day, a Coptic woman, in the loose blue dress of the country, barefooted, her face unveiled, with dark symmetrical features, silent and sad-looking, opened to us the door of the old worm-eaten church in which is the little grotto where the Holy Virgin, with her child, is said to have eluded the pursuit of Herod. On the woman's shoulder sat an infant of seven or eight months, as silent as the mother, with well-formed brown cheeks and long dark eyelashes, its head bowed upon hers, and one little hand pressed against her forehead while the other arm was passed around the back of the neck. The Egyptian mothers treat their children with great tenderness, and though I see infants everywhere, I do not know that I have yet heard one of them cry. The expression of quiet resignation in their faces is often quite touching. The Egyptian, born to a lot of dirt, poverty, and oppression, may well learn patience early.

At eight o'clock in the morning we reached the Nile, and were transferred to a steamer. About half the passengers of the Ripon had been sent on a little before us by another. We passed a day on the Nile, and had ample opportunity to observe the character of the great river and its banks. It is a turbid stream, like the Mississippi, flowing rapidly toward the ocean, between banks of fine mould, which are easily undermined, and crumble into the current. The broad, level tracts by which it is bordered have the same dark rich soil as that which lies about our rivers of the West. Along the bank where the current has worn it away, you see distinctly the layers of mould, which, year after year, have been deposited by the successive inundations, and which attest that the land of Egypt has been gradually rising for ages. The bed of the river appears to have been raised also in an equal degree, and I have been told by those who have made the examination for themselves, that, although in some places the sands of the desert, blown by the winds, have encroached upon the fertile grounds, in others the area of fertility has been extended. Broad tracts of sand, which the waters never reached before, have been overlaid by the slime of the river, and, after one or two inundations, covered with harvests.

The country on each side of the Nile was green with tracts of clover, lentiles, barley, and other grains and pulse. Groves of the date-palm appeared by the river-side, and showed their lofty tops at a distance; here and there were seen clumps of the cassia and acanthus, or a huge branching sycamore, overshadowing the tomb of a Mahommedan saint. As the day wore on, we saw men beginning their daily toil of raising water from the river by means of a wheel turned by a donkey, and furnished with buckets, to irrigate the surrounding fields. Women, some of them carefully concealing their faces, and others leaving them exposed, came down to the stream, and filled large earthen jars with the water, which they bore off on their heads. People in turbans, carrying long pipes, were seen walking, or riding donkeys, sometimes with an attendant, or running on foot, along the causeys built to form a passage from place to place during the floods.

Our captain and his crew were Egyptians, though the engineer was an Englishman. They set us an edifying example of Mahommedan devotion. As the Mussulman prays four times a day, and not more than one of the hands could be spared from his employment at any one time, there was scarcely an hour of the day in which some one of them was not in the act of prayer. Each of them, as his turn came, mounted the right wheel-house, and made his prostrations, and murmured his devotions with closed eyes and moving lips in the presence of all the passengers.

At length, after a second uncomfortable night passed on benches and stools, we reached the landing-place of the steamer Bulak, a mile or thereabouts below Cairo. We were conveyed by omnibuses through a fine avenue of trees with dense foliage to our hotels, in the Frank[4] quarter of the

city. Here we heard of the fate of one of our fellow-passengers in the Ripon. He was a fair-haired youth, scarcely grown to his full stature, of the name of Frazer, who, with another of the same age, was going out to his father in India, leaving a mother in England. I had observed him always with his young friend, and had been interested not a little by his ingenuous physiognomy. In coming on from Alexandria to Cairo the passengers by the Ripon had been separated into two divisions, and sent on by different steamers; the one which had the young Frazer on board, preceded by three or four hours the one in which I was. In climbing some part of the rigging, the evening before our arrival, he missed his hold and fell into the river. The steamer was immediately stopped, and everything done to save him, but to no purpose. He strove to swim toward the steamer against the strong current; he breasted it gallantly for a while, but it carried him down, and he appeared no more. He sleeps with the Pharaohs and the shepherd-kings. His father and mother will hear of his death almost at the same moment; the one by the caravan of adventurers who came on with us on their way to India, and the other by the return of the Ripon to England.

MANUSCRIPT: Unrecovered TEXT: *LFE*, pp. 55–68; first published in *EP* for March 2, 1853.

  1. Probably Admiral Sir Fairfax Moresby, R.N. (1786–1877), *Report on the Northern Atolls of the Maldivas* ([London] 1835).
  2. Robert Fortune (1813–1880), who visited China for the Horticultural Society in 1842, and the East India Company in 1848, and sent botanical specimens home to England.
  3. Mohammed Ali (1769–1849), governor of Egypt, 1805–1849.
  4. A common term in eastern Mediterranean countries for a western European.

818.   *To* Frances F. Bryant

Cairo, Egypt, January 29, 1853

... I have just returned from a voyage on the Nile to Upper Egypt, about seven hundred miles, if we include the windings of the river, and somewhat over four hundred in a direct line. We stopped at the most interesting places long enough to see them as thoroughly as we wished, besides making short stoppages at several towns to take in coal. The steamer in which we went was Number 14 of those belonging to Abbas Pa[s]ha, the sovereign of the country, or, as he is called, the Viceroy.[1] Parties of twelve or more are made up from time to time for visiting Upper Egypt on these steamers, and they pay the government twenty-eight pounds sterling each, which includes the expense of the table. Several Americans were waiting at Cairo for the arrival of travellers to make up the requisite number, when they heard of us and immediately came to propose the voyage to us. Our party consisted of fifteen—nine Americans, namely, Mr. Balch, a

Universalist minister, with three young men under his care, one of whom was a son of Mr. Havemeyer, another a son of Moses Taylor, and the third a Mr. Barley, of Philadelphia; the other Americans were Mr. Keith of New Orleans, a Mr. Reding, of California, and ourselves. We had, besides, Dr. Barclay, a Scotch clergyman, a very well-informed man; Mr. Neel, a Methodist teacher of an academy in the island of Jersey; Mr. Budget, a young English Methodist; Mr. Skirving, a Scotch writer for the press; Mr. Clements, an Oxford student, and M. Guillaume, a Frenchman. Our captain was a Turk, the purser was an Englishman, the crew Egyptians, and the waiters Smyrniotes and Greeks. Mr. Skirving was on a bridal tour with his wife, and had just come from Palestine. It was his intention to take her up the Nile, but she was indisposed; so we had no ladies on board.[2]

Nevertheless, we had a pleasant time of it, although I was glad when we got back to Cairo again, after an absence of sixteen days. The weather was monotonously fine, and I believe we had all seen old temples and tombs to our hearts' content. We were very well pleased with one another, and agreed perfectly in regard to all the arrangements of the voyage, except on the point of being out of bed in the morning, some of us being remarkably early, and others very late, risers. It is not often that a company of passengers in any vessel, so casually thrown together as we were, contains so many intelligent, rational, and amiable persons.

Besides the ruins and tombs of Thebes, the first of which are very grand, and the others the most striking of their kind, we saw the ruins of Philae above the first cataract, the ruins of Denderah, of Edfoo, of Esné, and Kom Ombo, the grottos of Tel el Amarna and Beni Hassan, and one or two places less interesting. We paid a visit to the Coptic priests at Negadeh, who seemed well pleased with the compliment, and brought down almost the entire population of the town, except the women, to see us depart. It is remarkable that the reserve and exclusion of the women should be as strict among the Copts of this country, although Christians, as among the Mussulmans. Our journey took us almost to the twenty-fourth degree of north latitude, and we have come back considerably browner for the constant and strong sunshine to which we have been exposed. The nights have been very cold, almost frosty, and the days warm, once or twice hot. The country through which we passed south of Cairo has a very uniform aspect—palm-trees, mud towns, a strip of green level land on the shore of the river, and always of the same height—four or five hundred feet—forming the background on either side. From these cliffs the desert stretches away to a vast extent; the valley of the Nile is a green stripe dividing the wilderness of rock and sand.

The people seem to be a good-natured race, easily amused, with wants which are easily satisfied. They are lively, noisy, ignorant, abject, but are capable of regular industry when tolerably well paid, at least so I am told

by foreign residents in the country. Their habits seem to me dirty, though Lane in his book on Egypt[3] calls them cleanly; a people who never wash their clothing, and whom you see at every turn picking the lice from their garments, cannot deserve the epithet cleanly. They squat in the dust and sand whenever they are not standing at their work, and, with their mud-floors and mud-walls, they are, of course, begrimed more or less with the dry mould with which they are almost always in contact.

I should have mentioned that just above Assouan, or Essouan, where our steamer stopped, there is a region where the face of the country is quite picturesque. Here the Nile breaks its way through rocks, forming rocky islands, of which Philae, the sacred island of the Egyptians, is one. The granite cliffs are piled upon each other in pinnacles, and the river rushes rapidly between them. Here is the frontier of Egypt proper, and farther south lies Nubia, the inhabitants of which are negroes. Elephantiné, the most southern of these islands, has a negro settlement; and at Essouan we saw forty or fifty half-naked black men and women, brought from the interior—mostly women—to be sold as slaves to the Egyptians.

Yesterday our steamer landed us near Cairo, and we are now just ready for beginning our journey on camels from this place to Gaza, whence we shall proceed on horses to Jerusalem. The journey to Gaza is principally across a desert—the Little Desert it is called. We travel with tents and beds, and a stock of provisions, furnished by a dragoman, who is paid twenty francs a day by each of the party. At Gaza we submit to a quarantine of three days, and then enter the territory of Syria.

I expect to hear from you at Smyrna, to which place we have ordered our letters to be sent from Malta. It is doubtful whether we shall go back by way of Malta, as we first thought of doing. I pine to hear from home—from you and my dear friends around you—and am sometimes tempted to end my journeyings in this region and go to some country where I can, at least, have news from you. Here all journeys are slow and subject to a thousand impediments, and the mails are brought at intervals of a fortnight or more. My health is good, and no fatigue that I meet with affects me; indeed, I have met with nothing which I can call fatigue, except when I write letters for the "Evening Post." Love to all. . . .

MANUSCRIPT: Unrecovered TEXT (partial): Life, II, 69–72.

1. Abbas I (1813–1854), pasha and viceroy of Egypt, succeeded his grandfather Mohammed Ali (817.3) in 1849. A tyrant, he was strangled in 1854.

2. Of these passengers, two were sons of William Frederick Havemeyer (1804–1874, Columbia 1823), a sugar refiner who was twice mayor of New York (1845, 1848), and Moses Taylor (666.3). Barclay was probably Thomas Barclay (1792–1873, M.A. Kings College, Aberdeen, 1812, D.D. 1849), principal of Glasgow University, 1858–1873. Mr. Keith of New Orleans, not otherwise identified, joined Bryant's party for their trip through the Holy Land, leaving them afterward at Trieste. Bryant, "Diary, 1852–1853,"

January 30, April 21, 1853. The other passengers Bryant names have not been further identified.

3. Edward William Lane (1801–1876), *Account of the Manners and Customs of the Modern Egyptians* (1836).

819. *To* the EVENING POST

Cairo, Egypt, January 29th, 1853.

My last letter closed with my arrival at Cairo. As I left my hotel that morning, forcing my way with some violence through the crowd of Moslems offering their donkeys, I found myself walking in crooked, unpaved streets, on the ancient mould of the Nile, trodden by human feet since Cairo was first founded, and still almost as soft and elastic as a Turkey carpet. About me were flat-roofed houses, with projecting, covered balconies, a palm-tree here and there rising over them, or a minaret with its encircling balconies. It seemed as if I had been introduced at once into a dirty masquerade. I was among swarthy-bearded men, with glittering white teeth, passing to and fro on foot or on asses—men in turbans or close caps of every color, their feet in red or yellow slippers, or bare; their legs in loose blue or white bags, or concealed by a robe of striped silk, reaching to their feet, or by a long white shirt, over which was worn a black, brown, or green robe, with wide, flowing sleeves. Sometimes a Greek passed in his white petticoat, sometimes a priest of the Greek church, or an Armenian ecclesiastic in his ample black robe. Barefooted women in loose blue cotton gowns came in the crowd, bearing water-jars on their heads, or bundles of green clover freshly cut, and holding with one hand their coarse blue mantles closely over the lower part of the face. These were of the laboring class; but here and there was seen one of their more opulent sisters, moving along the street, in wide slippers, with a waddling gait—a pile of glistening silks or of white muslin, with a pair of eyes visible at the top, and on each side the tips of her fingers, where they held the mantle drawn closely over her forehead. Sometimes the lady was mounted astride on a donkey, with a domestic to hold her in her seat, and keep her from being jolted; her mantle, gathering the wind as she went, made her look like an enormous sack, placed upright on the saddle.

Water-carriers, with their legs bare from the middle of the thigh downward, were driving asses laden with the water of the Nile in goat-skins. Sometimes a large procession of asses, carrying panniers filled with fresh masses of plaster of Paris, would block the way. At other times, in the narrower passages, we had to wait till half a score of camels had gone by, bearing on each side a block of stone just cut from the quarries, or an enormous beam of wood. Now and then the street was occupied with a train of carts—almost the only vehicle seen with wheels in Cairo. The wheels were singularly loose on the axles, and as they staggered along and

wavered from side to side, threatened to knock down the unwary passenger. We passed through the bazars—as the streets occupied by the traders are called—over-canopied for the most part by mats stretched across from the uppermost stories, or by roofs of thin boards with openings for ventilation. Here sat the merchants of Cairo, cross-legged, in the dark little recesses which serve them as shops, some smoking, some chaffering volubly with their customers, some occupied in marking the articles they sold, a few lying asleep on their mats. In the open squares the barbers had brought out their mats and begun their work. Taking the head of a Mussulman between his knees and pulling off the turban, the squatting operator would ply his razor with surprising quickness of motion, and in a few minutes turn out the skull of his patient as smooth as a turnip. Here women were sitting in the dust, bare-legged, with bosoms more than half exposed under their loose garments, but with their faces concealed under a dirty rag, selling oranges and dates from broad, shallow baskets. Here squalid men, the filthiest of their race, were sitting with their backs against the walls, smoking, or sunning themselves, and in the angles of the buildings were young puppies huddling together where they were littered, while the prick-eared mother had left them to prowl for food or bark at the Frank stranger. Our arrival in one of these squares was sometimes the signal for a general chorus from all the dogs of the neighborhood.

As we went on, we peeped into the doors and windows of several of the mosques, of a venerable appearance without, but ill-built, ruinous, and ill-patched within, the carved wooden portions going to decay and dropping to the floor. In them squatted groups of the faithful on their mats, with rosaries in their hands, chanting their morning prayers. Near the mosques we often heard a clamorous chorus of shrill voices; it was from the schools, where the boys were committing their lessons to memory, by repeating them aloud.

From all the multitude engaged in these employments arose a perpetual noise, not of the clanking and humming of machinery, and the rattling of carriages, and the striking of iron hoofs on the pavement, as in our cities; but of human voices, greeting, arguing, jesting, laughing, shouting, scolding, cursing, praying, and begging, mingled with the bleating of camels, the braying of asses, and the barking of innumerable dogs. It is a mistake to speak of the Oriental as grave, solemn, and quiet; the Egyptian, at least, is the liveliest and noisiest of slaves. Everything in this country is done with noise. Two rowers never pull their oars, even for five minutes, without alternate chants and responses; not a stone is moved to its place in a building without the same accompaniment; the quarries east of Cairo resound with a shrill and ceaseless clamor of tongues. The most trivial affairs of life are the subject of discussions that seem to have no end. Every new object or new incident is a signal for a volley of words from old and young. The camel-driver sings all day to the animals he leads; and when

he watches them by night in the desert, keeps himself awake by the exercise of his voice.

I was much struck with this chorus of sounds, when the other day I visited the citadel, and from the site of the magnificent mosque of Mohammed Ali, beheld the city below me with its swarming streets, and the fields and gardens of vivid green surrounding it, intersected with thronged roads. All around this scene of life and noise lay the silence and desolation of the desert—the vast Lybian desert to the west, with the everlasting pyramids at its edge, around which millions of human beings of the elder world sleep in their pits and caves;—and to the east, a desert as broad and still, on the skirts of which stand the tombs of the later sovereigns of Egypt among the graves of their subjects.

The mosque of which I have spoken is one of the very finest works of Oriental architecture; but it is built under the superintendence of European architects, though with Egyptian materials, by the munificence of an Egyptian sovereign. A vast colonnade of Egyptian alabaster, in the Moorish style, surrounds the building and its court. You are struck at first with the lightness and airiness of its appearance, but you are somewhat disappointed when you perceive that the columns of this beautiful mosque are held in their place by a horizontal bar of iron, passing from capital to capital, and that each capital has also a transverse iron bar connecting it with the wall opposite. This expedient is a common one in Egyptian architecture, but the older mosques have bars of wood. No such disappointment awaits you when you enter the mosque itself. It is spacious and lofty, and the simplicity of its design gives to its amplitude and height their full effect. Four lofty half-domes rich with gildings, and resting on pilasters of polished alabaster, carry up the eye to a loftier and ampler dome in the midst, where rays of gold stream from a central point, and golden stars glitter on a blue ground. You have above you what reminds you of the glory and breadth of the firmament in a starlight night. The light from without comes through windows the glass of which is stained with the richest colors. In one of the corners is the tomb of Mohammed Ali, separated from the rest of the church by an enclosure, within which a group of Moslems were seen in prayer. The tomb itself was covered with a pile of Cashmere shawls. The mosque is not yet quite finished, and artisans are still at work within it.

It is almost the first business of travellers in Egypt to visit the pyramids of Ghizeh, and we made it ours; but do not suppose that I am going to weary you with a description of them. We set out on one of the glorious winter-days of Egypt, with a one-eyed dragoman at the head of our little train, brandishing a long stick, and attired in a costume which, though considerably the worse for wear, was very showy at a little distance. Three brown Arab boys in blue shirts, and close-fitting dirty white caps, came trotting and screaming after us to urge on the donkeys we rode. For two

or three miles we kept along the Nile, among trees and gardens, and then crossed to the west bank in a boat manned by three men, one of whom, a fine-looking Arab, in a single garment of coarse white linen, handled the sail, and his two companions the oars. As they rowed, one sang, "God is great"; to which the other responded, "God give me strength." Arriving on the other side, we rode through a village, where the dogs barked at us fiercely from the tops of the mud-cottages, and the dirty inhabitants, squatting by the way, clamored for *bakhshish*, as we appeared, the children running after us. We passed through a palm-grove where turtle-doves were flying about, and the hoopoe, a bird of beautifully-speckled plumage, descended in search of its food close to our path. Then we struck out upon the fields where the peasant women and children were watching their camels and buffaloes, tethered and grazing among the clover and crisp helva-grass. We came at length to where an ancient canal, now a broad hollow with a little water in it, wound along not far from the western edge of the fertile country. A score of Arabs, Bedouins from a neighboring village, came about us, prepared to carry us over on their shoulders. I could not but admire the fine figures of these men, with their muscular, shapely limbs, uniting strength with agility, and their striking countenances. A sculptor could not find a better model, as it seemed to me, for the perfection of the human form. Throwing off their upper garments, and fastening their lower ones considerably above the waist, two of these strapping fellows lifted me up by the legs, while I supported myself by the hands on their shoulders, and in this way waded with me through the mud and water. The others were carried over in the same manner, as well as a French gentleman and lady who had come up with us just as we were about to cross.

We were soon on the bare sands, ascending gradually to the range of rocks skirting the desert, on the brow of which the pyramids are placed. Of course we climbed to the top of the great pyramid. "If you no go up, what for you come to pyramid?" asked one of the Arabs, who spoke a little English, and the question seeming to me a very pertinent one. From the summit of this vast pile of hewn stones, which would cover all Washington Square with its base,[1] we looked over the green Delta, stretching north, with dark groves spotting it like broad shadows of clouds. To the west of us was the Lybian desert, a waste of rocky hill-tops and sandy hollows; to the north rose the summits of pyramid after pyramid, and eastward lay Cairo, below the pinnacles of the mosque of Mohammed Ali, beyond which gleamed the white edge of another desert.

As I stood amidst the pyramids, where, all around, the skirts of the desert are one vast cemetery, full of tombs and mummy-pits, and remains of pyramids of smaller size, I could not but wonder that there should ever have arisen any doubt as to the design of these immense structures. They were meant as monuments of the dead, and, in my opinion, nothing more.

They are the same in shape as some of the smaller monuments, and no more exceed them in size than the kings to whose memory they were erected, excelled in power and riches the most distinguished of their subjects.

A day or two afterward we visited the pyramids of Sakkara, lying to the north of those of Ghizeh. We had a letter to M. Mariette,[2] who is here, employed by the French government in making excavations among the tombs and other remains of the ancient cemetery of Memphis. He received us very politely, and ordered the tomb of Apis to be lighted up for us. We descended into the rock by an inclined passage leading from a portal graven with numerous hieroglyphics. A gallery of about four hundred feet in length lay before us, regularly arched overhead, with chambers, at intervals on each side, the floor of which was about five feet below that of the gallery. Each of these chambers contained its sarcophagus of black or gray granite, exquisitely polished, about twelve feet in length, ten in height, and seven in width. They were covered with hieroglyphic characters. On each lay a massive lid of the same material, weighing tons, which, centuries since, had been shoved a little aside by iron levers, the marks of which are yet visible, giving us an opportunity of looking into the interior. It was empty. "This," said M. Mariette, "was done by the Persians, by order of their king, Cambyses, to show his contempt for the worship of the Egyptians."

One of the sarcophagi was found which had escaped the general desecration. M. Mariette had ordered it to be opened, and its contents were lying on the lid when I saw it. They were the bones of the sacred bull of the ancient Egyptians, the Apis, for which this tomb was destined. Every one of these enormous chests of stone had formerly contained similar remains, which, thousands of years since, had been dragged forth and scattered, and trampled upon, by a foreign soldiery from the north.

We slept that night in a chamber of M. Mariette's house, a building which he said had cost him eleven francs. Its walls were made of the unburnt brick, part of the structures of earlier ages, which his workmen had dug from the sands, and it was roofed over with logs of the palm-tree. In the morning we looked at the excavations made by M. Mariette in front of the tomb of Apis, revealing the remains of an extensive temple of white marble, which he has identified as the Egyptian temple of Serapis. Here are pedestals of columns, the lower part of walls, and other remains of a sumptuous edifice long covered up in sand. Strabo[3] speaks of the sand as drifting into the courts of this temple in his time. "It must have been the same from the first," said M. Mariette; "the temple itself rests on a base of sand."

The excavations had been suspended for a day or two when I visited Sakkara, but they were soon to be resumed. Three or four hundred workmen are generally employed; and objects of ancient workmanship are fre-

quently found, of an interesting character, which are immediately packed up and sent to the museums of Paris. "These men," said M. Mariette, "whom I have with me, are the fellahs, the peasantry of the neighborhood, not the Bedouins, for it is not easy to make the Bedouin engage in any regular employment. These fellahs work hard, receive small wages, live on little, and are faithful, good-tempered, and cheerful. They are the same patient race which built the pyramids."

Not far from the tomb of Apis is a village inhabited by Bedouins. "I am obliged," said M. Mariette, "to keep watch against the men of that tribe. These fellahs, whom you heard singing all last night to keep themselves awake, are my watchmen. About eighteen months since the Bedouins attacked the place in the night, armed with their matchlocks, a clumsy weapon, with which they did not succeed in doing any harm. We disarmed them, took them prisoners, and brought them before the authorities; but they were released on the ground that I had no right to be here, and that they committed no crime in attempting to drive me off. Since that time an understanding has been had with the Egyptian government, and this enterprise is now under its protection."

"These Bedouins," pursued M. Mariette, "as well as those fine-looking fellows whom you saw at Ghizeh, were settled in these villages by Mehemet Ali. It was his policy to allure them to settle in regular communities, and to quit their roving life. He assigned them these lands which they now cultivate, and exempted them from many of the burdens borne by the fellahs, but which a Bedouin would not endure. Formerly these men would commit robberies and assassinations, and then hide themselves in the desert, where it was vain to pursue them. Now, if any of them are guilty of crimes, the government has them in its power. They intermarry with the fellahs, and their character is undergoing a gradual change."

We visited at Sakkara one of the repositories of the mummies of the sacred bird Ibis. It was a long passage cut in the rock of the desert, with branches in various directions, full of earthen jars, about a foot and a half in length, in which these mummies are contained. Every traveller, as a matter of course, brings out and breaks one of these jars, and we followed the general practice. In some of them we found only a handful of brown dust and two or three lumps of bitumen, wrapped in folds of linen cloth, which looked as if scorched by fire, and fell to pieces on being touched; in others the wrappings were tolerably white, and on being unrolled showed the figure of the bird tolerably perfect, with all its bones, its beak, and even its feathers in tolerable preservation. The ground around the spot was strewn, to a considerable distance, with fragments of these jars and pieces of mummy-cloths, and among them were here and there portions of human mummies, a skull, a thigh-bone, blackened with bitumen, or a torn part of the cloth in which the corpse had been swathed. Hollows nearly filled with sand, showed where recent excavations in search of

tombs and mummy-pits had been made; but the government, I hear, has prohibited all such undertakings for the future.

After examining a tomb in the precipice overhanging the plain of the Nile, the chambers of which, cut in the living rock, are graven with colored hieroglyphics, we returned to Cairo by way of Memphis. Descending the height, we followed a high causey, built of the fine dark mould of the region, through fields green with crops, to the village of Mitrahenny. It stands in the midst of an extensive circle of mounds, from three to thirty feet in height, which are all that remain of the renowned metropolis of Egypt in the time of its early splendor. These mounds appear at first to be of the dark earth which forms the soil of the plain, but on looking more nearly you perceive that they are heaps of unburnt brick, among which a few burnt bricks are scattered. A vast grove of palms, with trenches leading to their roots for the purpose of irrigation, overshadows them, and extends to a considerable distance on every side. In the midst is a shallow pool of water, over which I saw the kingfisher hovering and striking his prey, and beside it the women of the village were filling their water-jars. The branches of the palms were rustling pleasantly in the morning breeze, and birds of various kinds were flitting about with little fear of man, for the people of this country are not allowed to carry arms. Among them was the beautiful hoopoe, seeking its food at the roots of trees, sometimes erecting its brilliant crest into a semicircle, and then laying it backward in a long slender pencil, so as to seem almost another bird.

Beside the little lake, the ancient reservoir doubtless of the city of Memphis, stood a tent, the tent of Hakakyin Bey—I hope I have the right orthography of his name—an Armenian, formerly interpreter to Mohammed Ali, who possesses a taste for antiquarian researches.[4] He has made several excavations in this spot, uncovering a colossal statue of granite lying on its face, and several smaller figures, one or two of them the most pleasing samples of ancient Egyptian statuary to be seen here, and that is not saying much in their praise. They stand ranged on each side of the entrance to the tent, into which we were permitted to enter and take our lunch, the proprietor being absent.

Such is Memphis now, the once great city to which Martial attributes the building of the pyramids, those miracles of barbaric art, *barbara miracula*,[5] as he calls them. Seen from its site, they appear to stand around it in a semicircle, from those of Dashour on the south to those of Ghizeh on the north. Its builders wrought for the present age in a way they little dreamed of. I could not imagine at first to what cause it was owing that these mounds, apparently of the same rich mould which composed the soil of the plain, were wholly barren of herbage, even in those parts which were irrigated by the trenches conveying water to the palms. On examining their surface, I found it covered in many parts with a nitrous effervescence, looking at a little distance like hoar-frost. The soil is everywhere

highly impregnated with nitre—so highly as to prevent the growth of plants, except where it is washed by the annual overflow of the Nile. How they contrive to make the palm grow in places where no other vegetable will take root, I am sure I cannot tell. In emerging from the forest of these trees, in the midst of which lie the mounds of Memphis, we come to a small circle of mounds almost as high, through which our road lay. It was a manufactory of saltpetre, conducted by the government. The earth which forms the mounds of Memphis is brought hither in panniers slung on the backs of asses, and steeped in the waters of the Nile; the water in which it is infused is evaporated in broad, shallow vats, and the residue is crude saltpetre. In one sense, therefore, the ancient inhabitants of Memphis may be said to have built for posterity.

MANUSCRIPT: Unrecovered TEXT: *LFE*, pp. 69–88; first published in *EP* for April 18, 1853.

1. Eighteen acres.
2. Auguste Edouard Mariette (1821–1881), a French Egyptologist then collecting Coptic manuscripts for the Louvre.
3. *Geography* 17.1.32.
4. This "antiquarian" has not been further identified; perhaps Bryant, as he suggests, misspelled the name.
5. *Epigrams* 1.1.1.

820.   *To* the EVENING POST

Cairo, Egypt, January 30th, 1853.

When we were just ready to set out for Sakkara, we learned that a party was making up to visit Thebes and Philæ in a government steamer, which was to go and return in seventeen days. The price for each passenger was two thousand eight hundred piastres, or about one hundred and fifty dollars of our money; and as soon as twelve passengers could be found, the steamer immediately was to proceed up the Nile. We had already concluded a bargain with a dragoman, as the men who engage in these undertakings are called, to convey us over the smaller Arabian desert to Jerusalem, and thence to one of the seaports of Syria. He was to provide us with the means of seeing all the most interesting places and objects on the journey, which was to begin on the 13th of January. But the temptation of seeing Upper Egypt, with its magnificent monuments of a remote antiquity, in less than three weeks, was too strong to be resisted. We therefore added our names to those of the passengers already engaged. The requisite number was soon completed. We found means to induce our dragoman to wait for our return, and on the very day when we should have started with him for Jerusalem, we left Cairo in the steamer for Essuan, just below the first cataract of the Nile, and within a short distance of the island of Philæ.

Hitherto the voyage up the Nile has generally been performed in

boats driven by sails. These are well fitted up for the purpose with comfortable cabins, but with calms or contrary winds the voyage becomes extremely tedious, and its duration is always uncertain. We passed these boats frequently on the river, overtaking or meeting them, and sometimes found them moored to the shore where we stopped. There were four or five on the Nile bearing the American flag, and as in our party of fifteen there were nine Americans to four Englishmen and one Frenchman, we ran up, by common consent, the American flag also. Our party was probably the first which had made the voyage to Upper Egypt with a satisfactory degree of comfort. The steamer had just been fitted up expressly for these voyages, with a separate chamber for each passenger, which had never been the case in any of the Nile steamers before; the furniture was new and perfectly clean; our larder was abundantly stored, though the cookery was not the most skilful; and the waiters, Greeks and Smyrniotes, were attentive and obliging. We had an ill-looking Bulgarian for a captain, who seemed, however, to understand his duty pretty well; a Scotch Highlander for an engineer, and a crew of good-natured Arabs, of whom it generally took four to manage the helm.

We left Cairo on a beautiful evening, performed our voyage to the lower cataract of the Nile in sixteen instead of seventeen days—for the steamer outstripped the estimates which had been made of her passage from place to place, and here we are again at Cairo. We could not have wished for finer weather, with the exception of one sultry day, in which, however, the steamer kept on her passage. The temperature was that of an English summer; the sky always clear, the evenings like those of Italy at the finest season, a blaze of orange-colored light brightening every object and illuminating every recess; the nights refreshing and without mosquitoes, which torment us so much at Cairo; and the mornings cool—sometimes, I confess, quite unpleasantly so for those who had, as was my case, their cabins on deck. We took our meals on deck, under an awning, and before breakfast was ready the temperature had become quite genial, so quickly did the rays of the sun warm that transparent atmosphere. The temper of our party was as pleasant and genial as the weather; I doubt whether mere chance ever threw together a better-natured and more obliging set of men.

Upper Egypt is easily described. It is a narrow belt of verdure, stretching from the Delta far south into the desert. A river of turbid water rushes swiftly through its whole length, on the sand-banks of which stalk flocks of cormorants and pelicans, with here and there a crocodile basking in the sun—a timid monster which slides into the water at the first notice he has of the approach of man. On each shore, within a short distance of each other, wheels moved by buffaloes and donkeys, or buckets suspended to a pole which turns on a pivot, and lifted by peasants naked to the waist, shaded from the sun by a screen of palm-leaves, distribute over the fields,

at all seasons except that of the annual flood, the waters to which the country owes its three crops a year. From time to time, a town or village, built of unburnt bricks, formed from the mould of the fields, mixed with chopped straw, rises on the banks of the river, resounding with the shrill cries of children. The poorer and lazier portion of the population are seen basking and smoking by the walls of the dwellings, and overhead are aviaries full of flocks of pigeons, for the convenience of which, an additional story is built on many of the housetops. The villages are always near, and sometimes within, a lofty grove of date-palms, which supplies the inhabitants with food, and the tending of which, in conducting the water to their roots, forms part of their occupation. Of other trees there are few; here and there, perhaps, a broad sycamore, or a thick-leaved cassia, or a tamarind; but in Upper Egypt trees seem never to be planted for shade; even fruit-trees, with the exception of the palm, are rare, and a little distance south of Cairo, the country most congenial to their growth, the orange-gardens disappear, and the banana is never seen.

On each side a range of rocky hills without a shrub or plant, sometimes approaching close to the river, and sometimes retreating to form a plain of considerable extent on its border, overlooks this fertile tract. At their base is generally a hard, gravelly level, or a sheet of loose sand, a little elevated above the meadows, and always bare of herbage, but at times they flank the river, with a long wall of sandstone or granite. Old sepulchres yawn in their sides, and kites and eagles sail above them. One morning on my excursion to Upper Egypt, I crossed the gravelly waste near Beni Hassan, and climbed what seemed to be the highest peak in the range to the east of the river. All before me, as far as the sight could extend to the eastward, the region was broken into rough pinnacles of rock, with narrow valleys and passes filled with loose sand.

I will not tire you with describing what has been so often described—the ancient tombs and temples of Upper Egypt. The grandest of them all are the remains of Thebes, consisting of the temples at Karnac and Luxor, and the tombs and colossal statues on the other side of the river. As I sat among the forest of gigantic columns in the great court of the temple at Karnac, it appeared to me that after such a sight no building reared by human hands could affect me with a sense of sublimity. Seen through the vista of columns to the east was a small grove of palms close to the ruins, and another to the west; their tall and massive trunks looked slender and low, compared to the enormous shafts of stone around me. I looked up to where the clouds, floating slowly over, seemed almost to touch them with their skirts, and perceived that two or three of them, shaken perhaps by an earthquake from their upright position, stood leaning against their fellows, still bearing upon their capitals portions of the enormous architrave which belonged to them. Thus they have stood, and thus they doubtless will stand for ages; scarce anything, but another earthquake, can bring

them to the ground. The spoilers of this vast temple, extending over miles of surface, the annihilators of its rows of sphinxes, and the destroyers of its magnificent colonnades, seem to have confined their work of mischief to those parts of it less massively built, and to have shrunk from attempting to overthrow the columns of the great court.

At Thebes we found M. Mounier, a French artist,[1] who is employed by the Pacha to clear away the rubbish from the temples of Upper Egypt. I was walking along the shore, near to his boat, with two gentlemen of our party, when he perceived us from the cabin, and coming out upon the deck, politely invited us to enter. Of course we did not refuse. Many of the finest of the ancient temples of Egypt, that for example at Esneh, are half buried in heaps of earth, accumulated from age to age by the mud cottages built within them by successive generations of the peasantry. The larger portion of the magnificent temple at Esneh is actually filled by them to the roof, and the fellahs are now building on the roof itself.

"My business," said M. Mounier, "is to cause these people to leave the temples, and then to clear them entirely of rubbish, both within and without. The temple at Edfoo and that at Denderah were partly cleared, by order of Mohammed Ali, a few years since, but all that was removed from the interior was heaped about the walls, so that no idea could be formed of the effect of their exterior."

M. Mounier had already uncovered and excavated a very fine portion of the temple of Luxor, to which he conducted us. He informed us that he generally had about three hundred workmen employed. "I have," he continued, "the authority of the government to make requisitions on each of the villages in turn for a certain number of laborers, who are bound to work a certain number of days. Such objects of curiosity, works of art, domestic utensils, etc., as I find in these excavations, I send immediately to Cairo, where the Pasha is forming a museum. As fast as the different temples are completely uncovered, I make drawings of them, which are hereafter to be engraved and published in a volume."

In the cabin of M. Mounier's boat we found Madame Mounier, an elegant French lady, who assists her husband by taking photographic views of the temples, and copying them on drawing paper, a pursuit by which she said she beguiled the years of exile from her native country.

I inquired of M. Mounier if the workmen employed by him on the ruins were paid. He replied that they were not. "I have made up my mind, however," he added, "to advise the Pasha to give them wages. The expense would not be great, as the wages of a laborer are but thirty paras a day, and they would work much more cheerfully and diligently if they were paid."

Thirty paras, you must understand, are about four cents of our money. I shall be glad to learn hereafter that M. Mounier has succeeded in persuading the Egyptian government to treat its subjects a little less like

slaves. Its manner of proceeding is extremely summary. As I have mentioned, the steamer in which we went up the Nile belonged to the government. A little before arriving at Siout, our captain had occasion for a pilot. He pounced upon a boat and took out three persons, whom he compelled to serve in that capacity till he arrived at Siout, where he procured from the local authorities an order compelling the most expert of them to act as pilot so long as he was wanted. At Ghizeh, some miles further south, we stopped to take in coal. Two men in red slippers, with long staves, came driving on, like cattle, the barefooted peasants who were to weigh the coal lying in woollen sacks on the shore, and carry it on their shoulders to our steamer. Our captain himself performed the functions of his office under fear of the bastinado. It happened that Abbas Pasha, the Viceroy of Egypt, was himself on a voyage up the Nile in a steamer, for the purpose of collecting tribute at the time of an excursion to Essuan. On his way up the river, he found a government steamer aground, an accident which often happens on the Nile, and which had happened two or three times to our own steamer. The Pasha ordered the captain to be taken out of his boat and soundly bastinadoed.

One of the most interesting incidents of our voyages was a visit we paid to the Coptic community of Negadeh, on the west bank of the Nile, about four hundred miles above Cairo. We landed at their little town before breakfast, and proceeded to the Latin convent, the superior of which, in a red turban and Arab dress, received us with great civility. He was a Neapolitan, who had resided in the country seventeen years. He showed us the church of his convent, one of those crazy edifices, with rude Moorish columns, which are so common in Egypt, and the several parts of which seem with difficulty to hang together. He then passed us over to several respectable looking men in white turbans and black gowns, who, we understood, were Coptic priests. When they were told that we were Christians, from the distant land of America, who had called to pay them our respects, they expressed their satisfaction at this mark of regard, and seemed desirous to pay us every possible attention. They took us to their place of worship, through an open court, used as a school, in which the boys, squatting on the dusty pavement, were learning to read and write from a lesson written with ink in Coptic and Arabic, on a leaden tablet. The Copts are the clerks and scribes of Egypt. The church was of the same class of edifices with the Latin one. As we entered, the morning service was near its close, and the priest, in reciting its last words, took the hands of several of the worshippers between his own. Both in this and the Latin church were screens of lattice-work, behind which the female worshippers concealed themselves; for the custom of seclusion among the women is national, and is almost as strong among the Copts as among the Mussulmans. From behind these lattices we could observe female figures silently departing. The priests showed us their books in the Coptic language, and attended us to

our steamer. I believe the boys had been let out of the schools on our account, for of a sudden the beach was thronged with a great, but most quiet and well-behaved multitude, as if the whole male population of the place, young and old, had been suddenly assembled to do us honor. At our express desire, three of the priests were allowed to come on board and look at the steamer, after which they took their leave; we moved from the shore, and left the crowd gazing upon us in silence. During the whole of our visit, not a single person of our party was asked for money; it was the only instance of this sort of reserve which we met with in all Egypt.

We are now on the point of crossing what they call here the Little Arabian Desert, on our way to Palestine.

MANUSCRIPT: Unrecovered TEXT: *LFE*, pp. 89–101; first published in *EP* for April 19, 1853.

1. Not further identified.

821. *To* the EVENING POST

Jerusalem, Palestine, Feb. 22d, 1853.

Our arrangements being completed for the journey from Cairo to Jerusalem, by way of what is here called the Little Desert or the Shorter Desert, our dragoman sent forward his camels with the baggage in the morning, and in the afternoon we set out on donkeys. On leaving the town, we passed among gardens fenced by rows of the prickly pear, which here grows to an enormous size. You know its peculiar mode of growth—one broad oval leaf, bristling with spines, proceeding from another; but as the plant becomes old the lower leaves take a rounded form, run into each other, and form large crooked trunks of a dark-brown color. They make a hedge which neither man nor beast can penetrate. Beyond the gardens we entered a country of green fields, where the road was planted on each side with the sycamore, or Egyptian fig, the acacia, and the tamarisk, all in full foliage. Sometimes our way led us among the lofty stems of a palm-grove, with its numerous trenches, dry at that season, for conducting water to the roots of the trees. The road was full of people—men leading loaded camels, women with water-jars on their heads, or fagots of dry branches, and people of both sexes on donkeys. One of these, kicking his donkey's sides to make him keep pace with us, would occasionally join our party and hold a conversation with our dragoman and his companions.

It was only on this road that I saw the olive-tree growing in Egypt. On a large estate belonging to some distinguished Egyptian, who wears the title of Pasha, and whose name I beg his pardon for having forgotten, the culture of the olive has been introduced or perhaps revived. I have never seen finer orchards of the tree than those which, at the distance of twelve or fifteen miles from Cairo, shaded the soil to a great extent, on

both sides of the way; they were young, but not too young for an abundant fruitage, and were growing luxuriantly. It was evident that they were well watered, for in two or three places, where irrigation had apparently been neglected, I saw some plantations of the olive which had not a very thriving appearance.

Our conductor turned aside from the main road, and led us to a garden on the same estate, full of orange, citron, and pomegranate trees, with a few roses and other flowering plants. "In this garden," said he, "is the sycamore tree under which the Virgin rested with her child, in her flight to Egypt.[1] It is much visited by pilgrims, and a jar of sweet water is kept standing by it for their sake." We were admitted to the garden by the Arabs who tended it, and saw the tree, a fine sample of the old sycamores of the country, with an enormous leaning stem, and a scanty circumference of boughs, looking as if it had survived several centuries. By its side was a large earthen jar, with water for the pilgrims. It is one of the principal works of Mussulman piety and charity to supply the traveller with water. Jars of water are kept in little niches at the tombs of the Santons, and charitable people when they die, instead of endowing an hospital, leave a legacy to set up a fountain.

In another garden we stopped to see the obelisk of Heliopolis, a beautiful shaft of polished red granite, standing upright where it has stood for thousands of years,[2] while the temples by which it was surrounded have long ago disappeared. Only a few fragments of their cornices and columns remain to attest that they once existed.

Toward sunset we overtook our camels, and pitched our tent just beyond the village of Khankia, among some scattered palms. The spot was full of wells, and the work of drawing water for the thirsty fields was carried on with great activity; the *sakkia* or wheel, turned by buffaloes, was creaking, and the *shadoof*, or pole and bucket, was going up and down. Near us was an old mosque, apparently just ready to fall into ruins, as is the case with all the mosques in Egypt. A few curious villagers gathered around us to see our people set up their tents, and our cook make his preparations for dinner. We strolled to a little lake near the village, named *Birket el Hoj*, or Lake of the Pilgrims. It is on the way from Cairo to Mecca, and is probably so called because the pilgrims here lay in their provision of water before crossing the desert. We found it a shallow sheet of water, with a gravelly shore, where camels were drinking, and women washing their feet and filling their water-jars. The day had been beautiful—a genial summer temperature, the sunshine tempered by clouds—and the sun now went down in a glow of orange-colored light. A short twilight succeeded—the twilight is always short in Egypt—the women hastened away from the lake, the *sakkia* ceased to creak, the *shadoof* was still, and darkness was upon us before we returned to our tent.

Next morning we sent back our donkeys to Cairo, and prepared for a

journey on the backs of camels. The villagers were again on the ground to
see us strike our tents, and several hoopoes came down from the palms,
and ran about gleaning the scattered grains left where the camels had been
fed. This beautiful bird, unfortunately for itself, is a game-bird, and our
dragoman shot two of them. The camels were kneeling on the ground,
the more impatient of them having their fore-legs tied under them, to
prevent their rising, and were uttering a harsh, angry bleat, as the loads
were put on their backs. At length we were ready; I placed myself on the
back of the camel destined for me, and was nearly thrown over his back,
and then over his head, as he lifted me by three different jerks to the
height of nine feet in the air. We left the village, passing by the Lake of
the Pilgrims, and entered the desert, which here was a vast plain of hard
ground, strewn with pebbles.

Our caravan consisted of thirteen camels, tethered to each other, and
walking in a row. By the side of one of them trotted a young donkey, and
on the back of another, among some baggage, sat a monkey from Nubia,
not yet quite tamed, and making a fearful grimace every time he was approached. Four Arabs from El Areesh, a little town in the desert, on the
sea-shore, walked with the camels; they were the owners of the animals,
and one of them guided the first of the troop by a halter.

At our head, armed with a long sabre and carrying a rifle, rode Emanuel Balthas, our dragoman, an Athenian by birth, speaking the ancient
Greek as well as the Romaic, fluent in Italian, Turkish and Arabic, intelligible in French, and in a fair way to learn English, which he was picking up
very fast from those with whom he travelled. If any of my countrymen
should have occasion for a dragoman in Syria or Egypt, I can with a safe
conscience refer them to Emanuel Balthas, a little man, with the manners
of a nobleman, active, prompt, anxious to satisfy his employers, as choleric
and as generous as a prince, a little too much given to flogging his Arabs,
but always attaching them to him by the liberality with which he treats
them. He engaged, for a Napoleon a day from each of us, to provide us
with conveyance, shelter, beds, and food, in our journey across the desert
and through Syria, paying our expenses at Jerusalem, Damascus, and the
other places we might have occasion to visit, till we should reach Jaffa or
some other seaport on the Mediterranean.

The rest of our party consisted of four American travellers, myself
included; John Muscat, our courier, the father of couriers, as he called
himself, and the most honest of his tribe, a native of the little island of
Malta, fertile in men, which has its representatives in every port of the
Mediterranean, from Gibraltar to Scanderoon; Gianneco, the cousin of
our dragoman, a Smyrniote Greek, with a brow like that of the bust of
Hippocrates;[3] and lastly, Vincenzo, our cook, a Roman, whose whole soul
was in his art, who plucked his chickens as he sat on his camel, and had no
worldly ambition higher than that of hearing his dinners praised. I doubt

whether such capital dinners as he gave us are often eaten in the desert. Our camels carried two tents, one for the travellers, the other for our dragoman and his companions; four camp bedsteads, with mattresses, pillows, and bedclothes; a table; four camp-stools; mats and carpets for the floor of our tent; a water-cask; a provision-chest, with table-linen, tin plates, and knives and forks; three small furnaces, with a supply of charcoal and kitchen utensils; a hen-coop, crowded with chickens, and a small crate filled with oranges. Our Arabs had their blankets on their camels, and passed the night with them in the open air. I have mentioned the rifle and sabre carried by our dragoman, but these were not his only weapons; there was, besides, a pair of horse-pistols, ready loaded, and the father of the couriers, on the morning of our departure, had astonished us by making his appearance equipped with a sword of Persian manufacture, short and thick, like himself, which he now wore, and was ready to employ, as he assured us, against the brigands with which the road to Syria was beset. With such ample arrangements for our comfort and security, we entered with stout hearts upon our journey over the desert.

We dismounted from our camels at half-past twelve, to take our lunch. Mats were spread for us on the ground, and we shaded ourselves from the sun by umbrellas, while we took a short repast, sitting as well as we could in the oriental manner, or reclining on the ground. My camel was a vicious animal, bleating horribly whenever he was made to kneel or to rise, and occasionally offering to bite. I declined remounting him again for the day, but went on foot till we halted for the night. It was an easy matter to keep pace with the camels; they walk at the rate of about three miles an hour, and eight hours, or twenty-four miles, is the ordinary day's journey of a caravan like ours. Our way was on the skirt of the desert, with the palm-trees of the cultivated land in sight on one hand, and the hills of the desert on the other. All day, on looking back, the rocky heights immediately east of Cairo were in full view, with the mosque of Mohammed Ali and its tall minarets gleaming on their western edge.

At every step we set our feet among small fragments of pottery thickly strewn among the gravel—the only vestiges of the millions of human beings by whom this barren waste had been trodden since Egypt was first peopled.

In the course of the day we saw the glimmer of water to the northwest of us. It was a part of the ancient canal of Arsinöe, which reached from the Nile to the Red Sea. Toward sunset, a village of dark-colored mud houses, with white minarets of stone rising over them, appeared in sight, surrounded by palms, and I found myself in the midst of an Arab burial-ground; for the old practice of burying the dead in the desert is still common throughout Egypt. They were vaults of brick, underground, some of them fallen in; those which were entire were each surrounded by a narrow piece of masonry, about six feet in height, composed of bricks or stones

laid in a crumbling kind of cement, and none of them bore inscriptions. Another hour's walk through loose sand brought me to a circle of mounds of dark mould, wholly bare of herbage, among which stands the little village of Belbays, on the site of an ancient town. Within this circle, under some palm-trees, we set up our tents. A caravan of Egyptians was already on the ground; they had unloaded their camels, spread their mats, and disposing their bales of goods around them, were preparing to pass the night in the open air. I find it recorded in my notes that this evening, in this wretched place, Vincenzo gave us the very best dinner we had eaten in Egypt.

MANUSCRIPT: Unrecovered TEXT: *LFE*, 102–112; first published in *EP* for May 16, 1853.

1. Matt. 2.13–14.
2. Dating from the Twelfth Dynasty, 2000–1786 B.C.
3. Greek physician (*c*460–*c*370 B.C.), generally called the "father of medicine."

822. *To* the EVENING POST

Jerusalem, Palestine, Feb. 22d, 1853.

Our tents were struck at sunrise, and we breakfasted in the open air, the wonder of several spectators from the village, who came to see the monkey and the Franks. As they approached a little too near the provision chest and other goods of the caravan, our dragoman drove them off with a fierce shout, and a flourish of his long cowskin. An old woman and a young one came to gather the camels' dung, which is used here for fuel, and the remains of barley and chopped straw with which the camels had been fed. The old woman asked alms; her young companion amused us by an exhibition of innocent coquetry. On her tawny but plump right arm she wore a bracelet of some cheap metal, and on her right hand three rings of the same material. In the intervals of her occupation, she covered the lower part of her face, which was not an unpleasing one, with her blue cotton mantle; but was careful to keep that brown handsome arm with its ornaments in full sight, resting it on her basket.

In the mean time, a muster of cavalry was going on at the gate of a large enclosure opposite our camping-ground. Now and then a horseman would strike his spurs into the side of the animal he rode, dash forward swiftly for a few rods, stop suddenly, wheel and dash forward again as swiftly, brandishing his carbine, while the horse's mane and tail streamed in the air. "Those soldiers," said the dragoman, "are going to El Areesh; their business is to keep the road of the desert clear of robbers. Three hundred of them are to be sent forward in the course of the day." Several small parties of those horsemen left the village before us, and when we at length mounted our camels and entered the desert, we found the road full of them. They soon, however, left us behind.

I had a better camel to-day; an exemplary animal in all respects save one—he was not satisfied to remain long in a kneeling position, and was apt to rise before he was bid. The motion of the camel, tossing its rider backward and forward, is at first extremely fatiguing; and it is customary to wear a belt, by which the muscles of the back are supported, while making these journeys. Our party had all provided themselves with these belts; but as I found that I could avoid the fatigue by varying my position on the back of the animal, sitting sometimes astride, sometimes with both legs on one side and sometimes on the other, and occasionally dismounting to walk, I laid my belt aside after the second day.

It was with no little delight that, toward the end of a day's journey over the herbless plain, we found ourselves again entering among green fields. A narrow tract of cultivation stretched far into the desert, a long cape of verdure putting out from the Delta, and we were crossing it at a place called Rassel Wady. Here were trenches of transparent brackish water, rippled by the wind; marshy spots producing a luxuriant crop of weeds; cotton-fields with bolls ready to be gathered, and a few trees. The reeds and trees were bending with the weight of hundreds of small birds perched upon them, keeping up a chorus of twitterings; and larger game-birds were hovering about in great numbers. There are two reasons why birds abound in Egypt: in the first place, the people are not allowed to own arms; and secondly, the Mussulman is tender of the lives of animals, never taking them wantonly. Balthas could not resist the temptation of adding to the stores of his larder, and getting down from his camel, began a war upon the birds. He shot several hoopoes and plovers, a pigeon, and a beautiful black and white bird—jetty black, and glistening white—which he called the *kinkinazo*.

Beside our way stood a tower of stone, one of a line of telegraphic stations established by Mohammed Ali, between Syria and Egypt, but now disused. Near it were the ruins of a village, roofless walls of unburnt brick, among which our road wound for awhile, and then emerging, passed by orange-gardens richly loaded with fruit. We were soon in the desert again, or rather passing between barren ground on one side, and luxuriant barley-fields on the other. These fields were kept fresh by little rills of water raised by a wheel from a neighboring well, one of which had overflowed its channel, and softened the earth for a little way in our path. One of our loaded camels was incautiously allowed to step into the moistened place; as soon as he touched it with his feet, he slipped and fell heavily to the ground. The Arabs took off his load, and after some floundering he was made to rise.

We pitched our tents on the clean gravel, and filled our cask with sweet but turbid water from a canal which was said to come from the Nile. Our Arabs sang, as they called it, all night, making a monotonous quavering sound, both guttural and nasal. They sang, I was told the next morn-

ing, to keep themselves awake while they watched the camels and the tents. Small parties of cavalry occasionally passed us in the night, on their way to El Areesh. "They keep the road clear of robbers," said our courier, "and are themselves the greatest robbers of all."

Next morning our road proceeded for several miles along the northern border of the green tract I have mentioned, which is a little lower than the adjacent desert on both sides. One of our camels dropped a part of his load, which had bee[n] badly adjusted by the Arabs. Two of them immediately ran to replace it; and Balthas, jumping to the ground, flew at them with his cowskin, with which he dealt them several vigorous blows. Meantime the camel shook the rest of his load to the ground, and breaking into a gallop, scoured away over the desert, and was soon out of sight. The Arab who accompanied him, a well-limbed man, and a good runner, took after him, and was soon out of sight also. The chests and bags which had fallen were distributed among the other camels, and we went on, turning away from the green fields, of which we now took our last look. The day was somewhat sultry; a chain of arid hills rose to the southeast, and before us, from time to time, appeared the illusion so common in the desert, of lakes or pools of water, with trees on their borders reflected in the seeming fluid, where there was only a waste of gravel and stunted shrubs. After travelling for some miles, we overtook our runaway camel, with his Arab, and compelled him, notwithstanding his loud cries of remonstrance, to take his proper load. We encamped that night in the desert, at some distance from any human habitation, but a fire which we saw in the evening, at the distance of a mile or two, showed that there was another encampment in our neighborhood.

An hour's journey the following day brought us to a little hollow, in which were some remains of dwellings, a well, a few stumps of palms, and several young trees of the same kind. After we had filled our water-vessels, I walked on, over a tract of fine sand, among numerous little hillocks tufted with shrubs. I amused myself with observing the tracks of large and small birds, of lizards and jackals, on the smooth surface. We lunched in a place where we were attacked by a swarm of sand-flies, indicating that the sands had been steeped by a recent rain. The shrubs grew more numerous as we went on, and finally we halted for the night at a place called Barook by the Arabs, who have a name for every place in the desert, where there is water, or a palm-tree, or an eminence, or a hollow. At Barook there is a well of brackish water, and we saw the signs of many previous encampments—heaps of ashes from fires made with shrubs growing around, and innumerable foot-prints of camels and horses. In my walk this day, I observed several small plants in flower, feebly rooted in the sand, and I gathered a peculiar species of sorrel, with thick, juicy, brittle leaves.

The next day, as we were about to set out on our journey, two men, a mulatto and a young Arab, made their appearance and lighted a fire

near us. They were pilgrims, they said, returning from Mecca, and had yet two days to walk before reaching their homes. They had eaten nothing, they told us, for the last twenty-four hours. Our provisions were all packed up and on the backs of camels, but we found half a chicken for them and an orange, which they seemed to accept gladly. One of our Arabs became offended at the manner in which his camel was loaded, took off its burden and rode forward upon the animal by himself. We set out in the midst of a strong wind, which had begun to blow before sunrise, and shifted toward the south as the day wore on, till it became a sirocco. Our way was still over a region of fine sand, spotted with shrubs, but all the traces of living things which had been so numerous the day before were effaced by the wind. We lunched at a place which seemed to promise a shelter, but even here the gale blew the sand in showers over our plates. A little beyond we passed a group of palms in a hollow, on which the sand-hills were gaining; the trees on its western side were buried half way to their summits. Here were a few habitations of Bedouin Arabs, made of the long, stiff leaves of the palm stuck into the ground; and here was a well from which we made an addition to our supply of water. Further on, some enormous drifts of sand, loose, almost white, and bare of vegetation, approached the way. A camel lay dead in our path, and ravens were devouring it; they rose croaking as we came on, and flew aside. A mile further on was another camel, the bones of which were almost picked clean by the jackals and birds of prey. The wind became hotter and drier as we proceeded, keeping the sand in motion like snow, though it did not often raise it as high as our faces while we sat on our camels. About half-past four we came to a kind of shallow valley, where the shrubs and other plants of the desert seemed most numerous, and here, as the camels were fatigued with their day's march, it was judged best to pass the night. The little donkey, too, seemed weary with walking so long in the deep sand, and the monkey, as soon as he was taken down from his perch, began to dig up the juicy sorrel, which he ate greedily.

As the sun was going down, the wind abated somewhat in violence, but our dragoman and his assistants took the precaution of heaping the sand about the canvas of our tents at its lower edge, by way of confining the sheets in their places and keeping out the air. As the darkness came on the gale rose again, and at ten o'clock blew with more strength than ever. We were all in bed, but I could not sleep, and lay listening to the perpetual flapping of our canvas, and the sand striking against it in showers. At one o'clock in the morning came a furious gust, and wrenched up the stakes of our tent from the sand, dragging its poles and sheets over us, breaking down the bedstead on which I lay, overturning one or two of the others, and carrying away with the tent our clothes, watches, and books. I felt the current of sand sweeping over me, and was on my feet in an instant, shouting to Balthas and his assistants, who immediately came with

lanterns. While they were struggling to raise our tent, their own was struck by a second gust, and laid even with the ground. After much effort the two tents were raised again and firmly secured with stakes and ropes. We groped in the sand for our stray watches, pen-knives, and other articles of value, which we recovered with little difficulty. My bed was made up again, on the carpet which floored our tent, and I had a nap of about three hours in sheets powdered with sand. The accident I have related happened on the morning of the fifth of February, the windiest and the warmest morning I had known in Egypt.

As we were taking down our tents the next morning, a centipede was found under ours—a frightful insect, with a multitude of legs and feelers, which has the reputation of being venomous. With considerable difficulty, our dragoman got it into a bottle of spirits, for it curled itself back from the mouth of the bottle again and again, and made a thousand efforts to escape the fate destined for it. A smaller one was found the evening before, running on the bedstead of one of our party.

The Arab who had taken away his camel on the morning of the day before, had returned in the evening, and assisted in raising our tents when they were blown down. At our request he was spared the flogging intended for him; his camel was loaded with the rest, and we set forward, intending to stop at Gatieh, a kind of oasis in the desert, once the seat of a considerable town, but now abandoned to the Bedouins. After a ride of two hours and a half, we saw its palms, towering at a distance, and passing to it over a plain thickly covered with shrubs, as it doubtless had once been with harvests, we set up our tents, at a little past mid-day, in a hollow shaded by a fine little grove of palms. The wind, though it was veering to a northerly direction, and had become cooler, still blew with considerable strength, and we made our tent-ropes fast to the trunks of the trees. The Arabs of the place came about us from a larger grove hard by, bringing fresh eggs and baskets for sale—children attracted by our monkey, which, tethered to a stake, was dancing backward and forward, and occasionally springing with his fiercest look toward the strangers who approached too near; and men, some of whom made a formidable appearance, with muskets slung on their shoulders. They complained, however, of the want of ammunition, and one of them offered to shoot a wild pig for us, if we would furnish him with powder. The offer was declined, but to let the Arabs know that we had powder enough for our own purposes, a gun was let off at a thievish-looking dog which came skulking about our encampment.

I could not but admire the grand looks of these brown people of the desert, the perfection of their forms, combining activity and strength, their well-formed features, eyes full of life, and white, even, undecayed teeth. The women wore on their foreheads and cheeks, a row of little circular plates of brass and coins, depending from a kind of cap, and the corners of their blue cotton mantles were sometimes neatly fastened to-

gether with a shell of the size of a pigeon's egg. I bought of them a little basket, handsomely wrought of a kind of rush, but before putting it into my travelling bag, I bethought me of a passage in Lane's account of the modern Egyptians. "Lice," says that minute and candid describer, "with the most scrupulous cleanliness, are not always to be avoided." I struck the basket lightly on a table, to see what might fall out of it, when one of the crawling nuisances made its appearance. I gave a smarter blow; two or three more followed, and I tossed the basket from me into a thicket of young palms.

MANUSCRIPT: Unrecovered TEXT: *LFE*, 113–126; first published in *EP* for May 17, 1853.

823.   *To* the Evening Post
Jerusalem, Palestine, February 22d, 1853.

We went to look at the habitations of the Bedouins in a larger grove near us; they were huts made of the leaves of the date-palm, within little enclosures, formed by setting these leaves upright in the ground. We looked into one or two of these enclosures, where hand-mills were humming, and saw the women grinding millet. The quern they used was composed of two circular stones, with an iron handle on one side of the upper stone, and a raised border of dry mud and chopped straw on the lower, to prevent the escape of the meal. There were none but women and children about the dwellings. An old woman, tall, gaunt, and shrivelled, came up to us scowling, and accosted us in harsh, sharp tones, pointing in the direction of our encampment, and evidently ordering us away. A short old woman enforced the command in a milder voice, with the same gesture; so we bowed to the two ladies, and retired.

Close to this grove I saw the first instance of what travellers in the desert call a salt-plain. It was perfectly level, with a smooth, hard surface, bare of shrubs, except in a few hillocks, and wherever it was fully dry, white with a thin crust of salt. At the end next to the grove was a shallow pool of crystalline water, intensely salt, and near it several salt-wells, evidently deepened by human hands, full to the surface. We crossed the grove to the east side, where are the remains of the town destroyed by the French in their invasion of Egypt, under Bonaparte.[1] They consist of mounds of earth, fragments of brick walls, and the tombs of two Santons—little Moslem chapels, with whitewashed domes. Not far from one of them grew an enormous tamarisk, with a thick head of boughs and foliage. Some of the richer portions of the ground were formed into little enclosures, with palm-branches set in the centre, where the Bedouins had cultivated their millet last year, and the rank weeds had just been plucked up to make room for another crop. Another grove of palms stood to the east of the ruins, and here in a little green hollow, where asses were feeding, were the remains of a higher antiquity—portions of a marble column or two, which

had belonged to some temple of ancient Egyptian or Greek architecture.

In the afternoon our people repaired such of our furniture as had been broken by the accident of the night, and filled our water-cask from a broad, deep well lying in a hollow, to which we saw the young Bedouin women going along a well-beaten path, with jars on their heads. It was dug and lined with stone, by Mohammed Ali, while he was master of Syria, and provided with a spacious watering-trough of brick, covered with cement, for the camels of his military caravans. The water was brackish and unpalatable, but it was the best that could be had. We mounted our camels the next morning, amidst a throng of male and female Arabs, old and young, some diverting themselves with the monkey, and others clamoring for *bakhshish*. They pressed so near while the camels were loading, that our dragoman thought proper to flourish his cowskin over their heads. They scampered away to a little distance, laughing, and came back almost immediately. The clamors for *bakhshish* became louder as we began to move off, men and women lifted up their ragged children, and boys and girls held out their hands to us till we were fairly on our march.

We passed a shepherd of Gatieh driving a flock of about fifty sheep and goats toward a small palm-grove standing by itself, around which the shrubs grew more luxuriantly than elsewhere. The sheep were black, with coarse long wool, from which the Bedouins weave their cloaks and the sheets for their tents. Farther on we entered a hollow formed by heaps of sand, where were many shrubs and sometimes a little water. A swarm of flies came buzzing about us, insisting most perseveringly upon establishing themselves at the corners of our eyes. Diseased eyes are common among people of the poorer class in Egypt, and I never saw any effort made to drive away the flies that settle upon them. Children with a circle of flies around each eye are among the first things of which the traveller takes notice, and the grown-up Egyptian, accustomed to them by long habit, never thinks of brushing them off. It seems to me possible that the contagion of the ophthalmia, so prevalent in that country, may be propagated in this way.

Several camels appeared in sight. "It is a caravan," said one of our party, and so it proved. To meet a caravan in the desert, is an occasion of as much interest as to speak a vessel in a voyage from America to Europe. A train of ten camels was coming toward us in our path, loaded with large bales wrapped in coarse dark-brown woollen cloth, and bound with strong cords. On one of the camels sat the principal of the caravan, in his turban and gown, with a long gray beard and a long pipe, and a brace of pistols in his girdle. With him were seven other persons, some of whom were armed, three on the camels and four walking. Our dragoman stopped and conferred with the principal for a moment. "It is a merchants' caravan," said he, when we resumed our journey. "They are from Gaza, and are conveying silks and other merchandise of Syria to Cairo."

We did not think of being exposed to the persecutions of the mosquitoes in this arid region, but this day, as we were taking our lunch near a hollow where the sand had a moist appearance, they came about us, hungry and sharp-bitten, and with them a cloud of midges, or sand-flies, extremely troublesome. There were other living things of the desert with which we had now become familiar—sand-colored lizards, one kind slender and swift, which often shot across our path; another, clumsily shaped and slow, scarcely able to get out of the way of our camels; moths fluttering about the flowers of the desert, and here and there a butterfly; snails clinging to every shrub, and the surface for several feet around strewn with their white shells, now empty; land-tortoises creeping beside the way; sluggish chameleons, of which we took several; black-beetles, rolling along fresh balls of camel's dung; and snakes, of which we killed a small, spotted one, said by our Arabs to be venomous. Now and then a heron would rise from a pool of brackish water, where he sought his food, and ravens, on their glistening black wings, were always hovering near us.

Close to our path were the burrows of the jackal in the hillocks, and the marks of their feet in the sand, as well as those of the jerboa, or leaping rat, which has numerous holes all over the desert. Less frequently seen was the track of the gazelle, a delicate triangular foot-print. The skeletons of camels were scattered all along the way, where they had fallen and perished, for when the camel gives out under his load, his owner knows that his end is come, and leaves him to die. In a night or two, nothing is left of him but the bones.

It was a fine, cool day, with a bracing northwesterly wind. The sky, which during the sirocco that overturned our tent had been filled with a thick, white haze, from the fine particles of sand, blown up and suspended by the force of the wind, had become perfectly transparent, and the currents of air passing through it came to us directly from the Mediterranean. In ascending a bank, we had the sea before us—the solitary sea—murmuring along a vast extent of uninhabited shore. That night we pitched our tent in a wide plain, with a steep, low bank on the south, beside which the rain-water gathers in the winter, and forms a kind of marsh. The mosquitoes came swarming into our tent, and unlike any of their tribe we had seen before, plunged into the flame of our candles. We made the tent-door fast, and in a short time the greater part of them had singed their wings, and were heaped about the foot of the candles, so that we were little disturbed by them during the night.

The morning of the 7th of February was chilly with the air from the sea, and we were later than usual in leaving our encampment. A journey of an hour and a half over heavy sand brought us to another of the salt-plains I have mentioned, perfectly level, hard under foot, with large patches of a bare smooth surface. In other places it was covered with a growth of bushes. Beyond, we entered upon a winding hollow, looking al-

most like a regular highway, with many shrubs on the left hand, from which rose myriads of mosquitoes and midges, bred by the recent rains. Of the shrubs of the desert nearly all are evergreens; some are thorny, but the greater number are of a jointed growth, somewhat like the rush, in the younger or greener stems of which the moisture imbibed from the soil during winter is secreted and preserved in store for the dry season, supplying a juicy pasturage for the camels. Among these shrubs the *retem*, or broom of the desert, is one of the most conspicuous as well as the most beautiful, bearing a profusion of white flowers veined with purple. The shrubs send their roots far into the loose soil in search of moisture, and the sand being heaped about them by the winds, they form hillocks, held in shape by a net-work of roots, in which the jackal and jerboa have their habitations. The ground in many places at this season was starred with a multitude of little flowers—a small pink phlox, a plant of the geranium family, with a purple bloom; another of the mustard family, of a delicate white; and several compound flowers, both white and yellow, some of them fragrant, all dwarfed by the meagre soil, but making the banks gay under the shrubs. The scarlet poppy showed itself to-day, in little groups on a declivity beside our path.

In our journey this morning several camels appeared in sight, which at first we thought to be a caravan. As we came nearer, camel after camel was seen, a numerous troop, scattered over a considerable space, browsing among the bushes and herbage. They were the property of the Bedouins, feeding in the broad pasture of their owners, the desert. Further on we descended into an oval salt-plain lying among drifts of sand, with a surface as even as a mirror, and wholly bare of vegetation except at the edges to the right and left of our way. A winding path among sand-hills led us from this to another, and in this manner we traversed, in the course of the day, four salt-plains, one of which in the direction we were travelling, we computed to be at least a mile and a half across, and in two of which were shallow pools of water, intensely salt, clear and colorless, and sparkling as they were rippled by the wind. On coming to these plains we immediately dismounted and walked; it was a luxury, after riding through drifts of sand, to tread a surface so firm and even. We followed a path made by the broad and heavy foot-prints of the camel, but this was crossed by the tracks of the gazelle and the jackal in all directions.

On climbing out of these plains we had glimpses of the Mediterranean to the north of us, and salt-pools in the hollows between us and the sea. To the southeast rose the varied peaks of a range of mountains lying along the shore of the Red Sea. When I was in Upper Egypt, I fell in with an Italian who was employed to obtain sulphur from a mine among these mountains. "They are incredibly rich," said he, "in beds of ore of various metals and other mineral productions; but these cannot be worked for want of fuel. Egypt has no mines of coal; all that is used in her steamers

and her manufactures, is brought from England. She has springs of mineral oil, the indication of beds of coal, and wherever they are to be found, the government has made excavations to a great depth, and at great cost, but without success. An Arab in wandering among the mountains near the Red Sea, not long since, found a little pool of quicksilver, where it had flowed from the rocks. He attempted to scoop it up with his hands, but it slid through his fingers; he then drew it up into his mouth, filled with it the leathern bottle in which he carried water, and brought it home. He was taken ill immediately afterward and died, probably from the effect of the quicksilver he had swallowed, so that the spot where he found it is still unknown, though diligent search has been made for it."

We stopped for the night as usual, in a hollow, where we might be sheltered from the wind, and toward morning I heard the cry of the jackals for the first time, though for several nights they had been our neighbors. They were answered by our donkey with a gallant bray, after which I heard them no more. This was succeeded, as the day dawned, by a more welcome song, the cheerful twittering of birds about our tent. The morning was clear and cold; the weak herbs of the desert were flattened to the earth beneath a load of dew; and as we were taking our breakfast in the open air at sunrise, a troop of small birds, apparently of the sparrow family, were busy about us, gathering their early meal on our camping-ground.

This day, the 8th of February, was to bring us to the lonely little town of El Areesh, on the shore of the sea. As we approached it, we observed that our path became more like a beaten highway, and the region better suited to pasturage. We passed a large herd of young camels belonging to the people of El Areesh, feeding under a steep bank, at the foot of which the shrubs were more numerous and the herbage greener than elsewhere. We lunched in a little salt-plain, in the neighborhood of which the declivities seemed on flame with scarlet poppies, and a liliaceous flower on a long stalk made its appearance among the shrubs. Within about three miles of El Areesh, we heard a chorus of shrill cries, and saw grazing in a deep circular basin of a few rods over, covered at the bottom and sides with luxuriant herbage of the liveliest green, a dozen or more camels, wearing the rude wooden frames which serve as saddles, and tended by boys. We now overtook women driving home donkeys loaded with brushwood gathered in the desert, and camels almost hidden under enormous piles of coarse hay, made of a grass which grows in large solitary tufts. Here and there stood a cluster of palms in a hollow, and in some places little plantations of the young tree were formed, with circular depressions about the stem, to receive the water necessary to keep them from perishing.

To the left of our path, on the side next to the sea, were banks of freshly drifted sand, with towering crests, and among these we at length entered by a deep hollow path, within which the rays of the sun beat upon us with sickening force. Climbing out of it by a steep ascent, we came upon

a dreary waste utterly without vegetation, where the arid wind sifted the sand and piled it in broad hills all around us. In all my journey I had seen no aspect of nature so melancholy as that on which I now looked. With every wind from the west or the northwest, these enormous drifts, elevated above the surrounding region, must continue to extend themselves, burying all vegetable growth far below their surface, and carrying with them the desolation which everywhere met my eyes. We followed a broad track, like one made over fresh-fallen snow, and which the next wind must efface, for nearly two miles, amidst a crowd of people returning from the desert. At length the walls of the fortress of El Areesh, built by the French in the time of the Directory,[2] were before us. The drifts had reached the foot of its western wall, covering the site of former habitations, traces of which were yet visible, and half burying one or two structures of stone which had been abandoned. The town is a little collection of huts, within the walls of the fortress, and on its eastern side. The inhabitants subsist by rearing camels, which find a broad range and abundant pasturage in the neighboring desert.

The Arabs of our party were all inhabitants of El Areesh; their friends came about us to help them unload their camels, and our tents were soon pitched on the edge of the loose sands, to the south of the fortress. Meantime we strolled into the town, which presented the usual aspect of the Arab villages we had seen—rows of low flat-roofed houses built of mud, put into the shape of brick—narrow streets, filth, and people asking alms. In that part of the town which lay east of the fortress was a well, with a large wheel for raising its brackish water, which the people of the place, who had probably never tasted any better, assured us was excellent. A little eastward of the village stood a small building of stone, with four open arches on the sides. It covered a broad, deep well, regularly lined with hewn stone, from which the neighboring fields might have been irrigated a hundred years ago, but it was now dry. At a little distance to the southwest of our encampment was an enclosure of fruit-trees, the fig and apricot, protected by a wall; the hills of sand were already peeping over it, and had invaded one corner, threatening to overwhelm the whole in a short time.

MANUSCRIPT: Unrecovered TEXT: *LFE*, pp. 127–142; first published in *EP* for June 3, 1853.

1. In 1798–1799.
2. I.e., 1795–1799.

824.   *To* the EVENING POST

Jerusalem, Palestine, February 22d, 1853.

Next morning, as we were striking our tents and loading our camels, we were surrounded by a large circle of admiring spectators, men, women,

and children, who came to see the Franks and the monkey. "Thieves, all," said the father of couriers—I believe he slandered them—"every one of them thieves," and drawing his short sword, the first time he had employed it in our defence, he rushed among them with a terrific shout and dispersed them. In the mean time, a little party of cavalry belonging to the detachment which we had seen leaving Belbays, rode up to the fortress, from their camp in a palm-grove, north of the town, on the sea-shore. We could not but admire their picturesque costume, so gracefully worn; that of each individual differing in some respect of color or arrangement from those of all the rest. Some had muskets slung on their backs, one or two carried theirs on their shoulders, with the butt behind them, and one bore the black ensign of the Egyptian cavalry. They rode spirited and well-trained horses, which they managed with perfect ease, galloping swiftly to and fro, and stopping or wheeling them in mid-speed. I have seen nothing more showy and striking in all the East, and scarce anywhere else, than the spectacle of one of these horsemen, armed and arrayed in the Oriental fashion, and managing his horse in the Oriental manner. The government here is beginning to put its soldiers into a clumsy uniform of jacket and pantaloons, in which they make an insignificant appearance.

El Areesh is the frontier town of the dominions of the Egyptian Viceroy. Two men came early in the morning for our passports, telling us that they would be examined, and returned in a few minutes. We were ready to depart, and they had not arrived; we sent our dragoman to demand them. In the mean time we had leisure to observe the people who gathered about us. The peculiarities of the Egyptian physiognomy, which give it a resemblance to the faces sculptured in the old hieroglyphics, had entirely disappeared. Some of the men had fine persons and majestic beards, and a few light hair and gray or blue eyes.

Our dragoman returned with the passports in about an hour. Ten minutes would have sufficed to examine and countersign them, but the governor of the place, a lazy Turk, declared that he would not look at them till he had his coffee. When he had got his coffee, he declared that he would not attend to any business till he had finished his pipe. After smoking till he had brought himself to a more complying humor, he wrote two or three words in Arabic on each of the passports, and handed them to our messenger.

We set forward about half-past nine o'clock, amidst flocks of sheep and goats, with a few camels and asses which the herdsmen of El Areesh were driving afield. The region immediately east of the town had the appearance of being susceptible of cultivation, and here and there we saw patches of barley which showed that the soil was not naturally unfruitful. Crossing a dry water-course, about a mile and a half from the town, we entered a tract of pasturage and bushes where women were cutting up with mattocks an evergreen shrub, apparently a sort of heath, which they

used to heat their ovens. In an Arab household, it is the goodwife whose business it is to provide the fuel. A troop of women, barefoot, in the usual loose dress of blue cotton, passed us, bearing bundles of this brushwood on their heads, and looking at us shyly from under the mantles which they drew over the lower part of their faces. The country here was full of flocks, each tended separately by its keepers, men or women; and in the more fertile places were little fields of springing barley.

At a distance of three or four miles from El Areesh, we entered upon a territory possessed by the race of Arabs who dwell in tents. Here the traveller pays a fixed tribute, which has the sanction of the government, to the sheikhs, in consideration of which they engage to protect him against robberies within their respective districts; in other words, they accept the tribute as a compensation for the robberies they would otherwise commit. Our dragoman was to pay these tributes, among the other expenses of our journey.

Two men, one on foot and the other on horseback, were seen coming over an eminence to the east of our path; our dragoman stopped, held a spirited parley in Arabic with the one on foot, and ended by giving him money. I was much struck with the showy costume of this chief, and quite as much with a certain grim beauty in his aspect. He wore a snowy white turban, a long white shirt with a red tunic over it, a sabre by his side, and thrown over one shoulder an Arab cloak, with broad stripes of white and black. His person was thin and sinewy, his features regular, with a jetty beard, a keen restless eye, and two rows of even, glittering teeth, that were visible to the very corners of his mouth at the least motion of his lips. His companion, who was scarcely less showily arrayed, was an elder and graver man; he wore a sabre and carried a long pipe, which he smoked during the conference. I asked our dragoman what was the subject of the dispute.

"The tribute allowed by the government," he replied, "is three piastres for each traveller; the servants pay nothing. That sheikh insisted on having three piastres from each of us, with the exception of our four Arabs. I paid him twelve piastres for our four travellers, and three more for *bakhshish*. He knew he was not entitled to any more, for he thanked me and wished us a good journey."

The country now wore a pastoral look; on each side of our way were flocks tended by groups of men and women, whose voices are often heard before they are in sight. The herbage became more abundant as we went on, and the flowers larger, but everywhere the verdure was overlooked by a range of smooth hills of sand on our left, threatening to overwhelm us. We took our lunch in a salt-plain, from which we entered on a long, narrow, green vale, fragrant with a yellow flower of a plant called by our dragoman the wild camomile. I was walking on with two of my companions, when we saw before us, sitting on a bank by the path, four men, two of them armed with muskets, who were soon joined by a fifth. They were

the collectors of the revenue for the sheikh of a new district. We saluted them and passed on, but they stopped our caravan as it came up; another parley was held, and another tribute of twelve piastres paid.

We walked on through a flock of sheep and goats feeding on both sides of our way, tended by women, who ran away at our approach; all but one slender brown maiden, who kept watch of her charge and us from a neighboring bank. We stopped to observe the beauty of the animals, which had a well-fed appearance. The goats were black, with long, wavy hair, which glistened like silk in the sunshine. The sheep, many of which were young, and had not yet parted with their first fleece, were beautifully marked; they had black feet, coal-black heads for the most part, and fleeces of clean white, with broad spots of raven black. As we stood looking at them, the maiden stretched her little brown neck above the shrubs, as if she were not perfectly sure whether we were not making our choice of the best of her flock.

After we had again mounted our camels, we came to a sandy ridge crossing our path, close by which stood a young Arab, of placid features, who seemed to be waiting for us. We stopped, and after a moment's conversation the young fellow was joined by a tall, thin black man, a Nubian, as they call them here, wearing a white turban, a long white shirt, and a sabre, who took up the discourse and spoke with much energy and gesticulation. Here was another demand for tribute. Twelve piastres were put into the palm of the negro, who handed them over to the Arab, the sheikh of the district, or the sheikh's son.

As we went on, Arabs and their animals were seen everywhere around us, but nowhere a trace of human habitation. Larger tracts of land under tillage appeared than we had before seen in the desert, some green with barley, others just ploughed, others lying fallow. At length our road ran for a short distance along the banks of a clear little lake. I dismounted and tasted its waters; they were as salt as the ocean. To the north of this lake was a smooth round hill of sand, evidently advancing into it, and there, half buried by the drifts, stood a little grove of palms. To the east of the lake was a salt-plain, into which we passed, ending in smooth slopes, clothed with short herbage, where cows, sheep, and camels, tended by Arabs, were grazing. Here were the walls of a few ruined cottages, a cemetery beyond them, in which stood a *wely*, or tomb of a Mohammedan saint, with a whitewashed dome, and near the cemetery a few palm-trees.

"This place," said our dragoman, "is called Safzayda, and here we stop for the night. A few years ago there was a village on this spot, and in former times, I am told, a considerable town." Our people immediately began to unload the camels and to pitch our tents in the midst of the flocks, while I strolled toward the cemetery.

Within the tomb of the saint was a rude sarcophagus of stone, plastered over with mortar, and covered with a faded green cloth. Above it

was stretched a cord, on which were strung bits of cloth, shells, and little frames of wood and paper stained with various colors, which I afterward learned were suspended there by persons afflicted with diseases, in the belief that there was a virtue in the tomb of a holy man which would work a cure. A marble slab, at the door of the tomb, bore a long Arabic inscription, the only one in all that place. The tombs around were numerous, formed of small stones covered with coarse mortar, but the more recent graves merely had loose stones piled over them, or were heaped with earth. The Bedouins had made this their burial-place.

The sun was now setting; women, in blue gowns, and shrill-voiced boys, were running about, hastily gathering their herds and flocks, and driving them over the hill to the south of us till the last of them had disappeared; thousands of small birds, keeping up an incessant twittering, were settling on the palms about us, their perch for the night, till the rigid branches bent with their weight. I returned to our tent, where our Arabs had collected brushwood and had kindled a fire, by which they were to keep watch during the night against the Bedouins and the jackals. At El Areesh we had left behind our donkey, which had grown thin with wading through the sand, and had re-enforced our caravan with two more Arabs, one of whom, a young fellow, rode one of the camels, and the other, a stout-legged man, armed with a brace of pistols, which he carried in his gay-colored sash, walked with the rest. The young man had made a luxurious bed on the ground with mats and quilts, but the other was preparing to pass the night with the camel-drivers.

One of the entertainments of our journey through the desert was reading books of travels relating to the country through which we were passing. Sometimes as we sat on our camels one would read aloud for the benefit of the rest, and in the evening, before we became drowsy, which was early enough, a little time was generally employed in this way. For these evening readings we frequently took parts of the Scriptures, to which the scenes around us gave a new interest—narratives of the journeys of the early Hebrews to the land of Egypt. Their abode in the country, their passage out of it, and wanderings in the desert, which once brought them to the very region in which we were travelling. This evening, while we were thus engaged, we were startled by loud cries, close to our tent, and almost in our ears. The sounds had in them something frightfully human. "It is a jackal," said one of the attendants. The animal had come prowling about our tent, but must have been scared away immediately, for we afterward heard the same cries from a distance.

Next morning, soon after sunrise, I went to the top of the hill which lay south of us, but nowhere could I descry the habitations of the Arabs, though we had heard their dogs answering the jackals all night. I returned to our encampment, where, as we were at breakfast, we observed a troop of ten men on foot approaching by the road we had travelled the day be-

fore. About half their number wore high, shaggy woollen caps, of a brown color, the costume of the dervishes, and two of them carried on their backs loads of dry brushwood. They halted at a little distance from us, sat down in a circle on the ground, and sent one of the wearers of the shaggy caps to borrow a live coal or two from our cook's fire. We learned from him that this was a troop of holy men, pilgrims from Persia and Bokhara, who had been to Mecca, and were now on their way to the holy places in Syria. The dervish was a good-natured looking fellow, with a pair of blinking eyes, ragged, barefooted, and fat. He returned to his companions, and probably made a report to them of what he saw on our breakfast-table, for immediately another deputation was sent, asking for something to eat. Our dragoman, thrifty in his charity, gave them two loaves of bread, brought from Cairo, which had begun to be a little mouldy.

While our camels were loading, I walked again to the Arab burial-place. Even in this desert is felt the instinct which prompts us to beautify the resting-places of the dead. The region produces a liliaceous plant, with a large bulb and large thick leaves of a deep-green color. Bunches of these were planted at the head and foot of many of the graves. A singular custom, I perceived, prevails here, of laying the garments of the dead on the ground above them. At the head of one of the graves lay a woman's blue cotton dress, as fresh, almost, in appearance, as if it had just come from the loom. I remarked several articles of male attire, some of them much decayed by the length of time they had remained on the ground. On one poor fellow's grave lay only his thrum-cap, probably the sole part of his raiment which was thought in a fit condition to serve as his monument. The grave of a child fixed my attention, at each end of which a tuft of the plant I have already mentioned was growing freshly, and between them lay a little garment of blue cotton, and another of white, with a crimson stripe running through it. Near by, and probably dragged away by the jackals, was the skin of a lamb, with a soft silky fleece, which had formed the child's outer garment in winter. I replaced it on the grave, and could not help thinking how tenderly, to judge by these tokens, that child must have been cherished, and that, when it was carried out dead from the humble abode of its parents, their low brown tent pitched on the green-sward, the heart of its mother must have been pierced by a sorrow as sharp as is felt at such a loss in the most civilized country.

MANUSCRIPT: Unrecovered TEXT: *LFE*, pp. 143–156; first published in *EP* for June 4, 1853.

825. *To* the EVENING POST

Jerusalem, Palestine, February 22d, 1853.

It was a cool morning, and on leaving Safzayda, I walked on before the caravan, with two of my companions, in a long valley, between culti-

vated fields on each side of the way for a considerable distance, in the midst of which a broad irregular stripe of greensward and shrubs was left for travellers. Arab men and women appeared from time to time on the heights with their sheep and camels, and groups of women were chattering in the road before us, who took good care to be out of our way as we approached. The long line of bare sand-hills which border the sea continued in sight to the northwest, and once we had a view of the Mediterranean over it. Not long afterward we came to a region of pasturage, where the ground was covered with short herbage, consisting principally of a kind of trefoil, with very minute leaves, and here, in a shallow vale, sheltered on the east and north, and opening to the southwest, lay the dark brown tents of the Bedouins, made of a coarse cloth, woven from the fleeces of their sheep. Cows, sheep, goats, and camels were grazing about us, and from the tents the whooping of children was heard.

On the right of our path, at a little distance before us, appeared a mound, on which stood two columns, their pedestals buried in the earth, which was full of bits of marble and fragments of pottery. Here was the site of Rhaphia, once a populous city. "These columns," said the dragoman, "belonged to a Greek church, built where the Virgin rested in her flight to Egypt, and you will see more of them a little further on, in a place where we shall take our lunch. There is a fountain of sweet water there, which came out of the ground by a miracle, to quench the Virgin's thirst." We descended from the mound into a hollow, where this miraculous fountain was. It was a deep well, with a very little water in it, around which lay scattered several marble columns, and broken pedestals of columns. The herbage was here luxuriant, and our camels cropped it eagerly.

At a little past two o'clock on that day, the 10th of February, we found ourselves among the gardens of Khan Yoonas, the frontier town of Syria. They were hedged with rows of the prickly pear, and full of almond, peach, and apricot trees, in full bloom, with here and there a tamarisk and sycamore next to the way. Just at the entrance of the town, which is a wretched one, we were conducted into an enclosure serving as a lazarette, surrounded by a fence formed by the branches of a thorny tree, called the *nebek*, set upright in the ground—and were informed that we were in quarantine. Part of a Turkish cemetery had been taken into the lazaretto, and we pitched our tents and spread our carpets on the old neglected graves. In that part of the cemetery which lay without were more than fifty women, nearly all in white, with long white mantles covering the head and reaching nearly down to the feet, sitting around the graves or moving silently among them like ghosts. "They are mourning for the dead," said Vincenzo.

Our new acquaintances, the pilgrims, two or three of them bearing a load of brushwood, entered the enclosure along with us and squatted down in one corner. In another part a company of Arabs, men, women,

and children, had established themselves; the men, after taking their midday meal, rolled themselves in their cloaks, covering their heads from sight, and lay asleep on the ground. The keepers of the quarantine had a hut of dry reeds and boughs within the lazaretto, before which they were posted with clubs and boughs of trees, to keep the travellers from going out, and from coming too near the people of the place when they entered the lazaretto. One of our caravan bought some oranges of one of the keepers. He threw a piastre toward the keeper, who poured a pitcher of water over it as it lay on the ground, to purify it from the contagion we were supposed to bring from Egypt, and then taking it up, tossed back four oranges.

Next morning, before sunrise, the pilgrims were heard chanting their prayers. While we were breakfasting and loading our camels, three men, of a remarkably striking appearance, entered the lazaretto, and after standing awhile to observe us, sat down on a mat before the hut, and watched our proceedings at their leisure. One of them, in a snowy-white turban, had a beard as white, and was wrapped in an ample black gown; another, of tall stature and lofty air, in a costume of intermingled white, red, and yellow, wore red morocco boots and a sabre with a glittering handle and scabbard; the third, younger than either, had on the amplest and whitest of oriental petticoats. About eight o'clock, a man on a spirited horse, and wearing a sabre, presented himself at the entrance of the lazaretto; it was our guardian who was to accompany us to Gaza. The term of quarantine performed by travellers arriving in Syria from Egypt is five days. The day on which they arrive at Khan Yoonas, if they enter the lazaretto before sunset, is counted as the first; the day passed in traveling from Khan Yoonas to Gaza is the second; two days and three nights are then passed in the lazaretto at Gaza, and the day on the morning of which they leave the lazaretto completes the five.

At half-past eight we left the lazaretto under the conduct of our guardian—a long train of Franks, pilgrims, Arab men, women, and children, camels, and asses. Of the children, eight or nine in number, some were put on the donkeys, others were carried by their parents, and our good-natured Arabs gave a woman and her baby a seat on one of their camels. One of the donkeys trotted along under a cluster of three children, clinging to each other, the eldest of whom, not more than eight years old, guided the animal. We had left the desert, and now entered on a grassy plain with a range of sand-hills on its western boundary, and verdant eminences to the east. It was gaudy with yellow flowers, and in some places red with the scarlet anemone, and over it were scattered, at considerable distances from each other, sycamores centuries old, with enormous gnarled and twisted trunks. Our pilgrims, as they marched before us, sang in chorus one of their hymns, the sound of which came to us on the wind.

Two or three miles north of Khan Yoonas appeared, far to the east, a cluster of the dark tents of the Bedouins, with smoke rising from them. They were probably inhabited by the keepers of the flocks which were feeding near our path, and which our guardian, with drawn sabre, chased out of our way, lest peradventure we should give them the plague. As the people of the country met us, the cry of *carantina, carantina!* was raised, and they turned to the right or the left, allowing us a broad passage over the plain.

As we approached Gaza, the number of trees diminished, and the tilled fields became more numerous. We saw people ploughing with camels; the ploughs were of wood, light, and with a slender upright handle; the wooden share merely scratched the surface of the ground. At length we came in sight of the minarets of Gaza, situated amidst gardens and trees and gentle eminences. The guardian made our whole train enter the lazaretto, an enclosure with high walls, just at the entrance of the town, having a large well in the midst, and a long low building near the side, opposite to the entrance. At each end of this building was a second story, consisting of two small chambers, one set of which was assigned to us, while our drago-man and his people occupied a room below.

It was now one o'clock in the afternoon, and we had the rest of the day and two more days more to pass in the lazaretto. We did not find our imprisonment so tedious as we expected. We read, we wrote, we paced the wall at our end of the lazaretto; we looked at the surrounding country from our windows; a green, treeless plain to the south; and to the north a region rising into pleasant slopes, covered with trees, mostly the olive, among which stood the flat-roofed buildings of the town and its towering minarets. Over this scene were sweeping the shadows of clouds brought by a cool wind from the sea. We observed the women of the place washing clothes at a little sheet of water at the east of us, almost under the walls of the lazaretto, or sitting on the grass in their long white mantles, with their children playing beside them. We watched our friends, the dervishes and pilgrims, at their devotions, prostrating themselves on their faces from time to time, in their prayers, which they uttered inaudibly, with moving lips. These holy men had their time fully occupied with prayers, sleeping in the sun, and picking the vermin—the lice, if you must have the word—from the inside of their garments, which they took off and carefully examined once a day at least, during their stay at the lazaretto. Five of the party, we now learned, were regular dervishes; the others, ordinary pilgrims. The dervishes were particularly ragged, with patched garments of many colors; but they looked well-fed, and had a foolish expression of face. The only man among them who was not ragged was one of the ordinary pilgrims, a lean fellow, with an anxious look, who wore a sabre by his side. The der-vishes manifested a great desire to amuse themselves with our monkey,

after an example which we had set them; but the creature, though tolerably well-behaved toward our party, would endure no familiarities from strangers. He was fastened by a long cord to the iron grate of our dragoman's window, but whenever the dervishes approached him, he sprung at them into the air, with his fiercest grin, and tore their rags and their sacred skins without mercy. We saw the blood trickling down the plump, swarthy leg of the principal dervish of the party, after a brief interview with the monkey.

Among those who entered the lazaretto with us was an Arab family with several children, the mother of which was endowed with a shrill voice and a most voluble tongue. She was in constant dispute with one of the keepers, who brought us bread from the town, and who insisted upon having his profit on every loaf. For this the woman attacked him whenever he appeared, with reproaches, uttered in the most rapid Arabic. To do him justice, he stood his ground bravely, and answered like one who was practised in such quarrels, but after they had shouted and gesticulated at each other for a quarter of an hour, he generally gave in and retreated, the woman screaming after him as he went. One of our party hearing the cause of her complaint, gave her a few Turkish coins to buy bread for her children. This brought upon him a torrent of thanks and blessings, and it was observed that the disputes of the woman with the keeper were carried on with less animation.

On the third day after we entered the lazaretto, a little before sunset, a message was brought us from the physician, desiring that we would do him the favor to come down stairs. We descended to the court of the lazaretto, and stood in a row before Dr. Eperon,[1] a slender Frenchman of, perhaps, thirty years of age, who planted himself at a safe distance from us, and politely asked us in his native language if we were quite well.

"Perfectly so," was our answer.

"I am glad of it," said the doctor; "but you must excuse me if I go through with certain formalities. Will you be so kind as to let me see your tongues?"

We all put out our tongues together.

"That will do," said he; "to-morrow morning, after sunrise, you are at liberty to leave the lazaretto." We bowed and returned to our rooms, whither we were followed by one of the keepers, who brought a brazier full of live coals, and throwing into it a small quantity of sulphur, fumigated our persons and our clothes.

MANUSCRIPT: Unrecovered TEXT: *LFE*, pp. 157–167; first published in *EP* for June 10, 1853.

1. Not further identified.

826. *To* the Evening Post

Jerusalem, Palestine, February 22d, 1853.

On leaving the lazaretto next morning, our dragoman took us through a part of the dirty town, to show us some things which, he said, were always visited by travellers. He stopped us at a remnant of an old wall, on the side of which was seen the beginning of an arch that had once, apparently, extended over the way. "This," said he, "is the gate of Gaza, the doors of which were carried away by Samson. There," pointing to some granite columns lying on the ground, "are part of the temple which Samson pulled down upon the heads of the Philistines."[1] We did not linger long to look at these apocryphal antiquities, but went on through the vast olive-grove lying north of the town, a monument of past ages, concerning which there could be no doubt. It fills the whole breadth of the valley, from east to west, and extends northward to the distance of about four miles. The trees are old and venerable, with enormous stems of an irregular growth, and on that morning the sunshine came down pleasantly among them upon the verdure, which was sprinkled with flowers. We met many of the people of the neighborhood in their picturesque oriental costume, coming into town; some of them driving asses loaded with green crops, freshly gathered. On one of these animals a cradle, made for carrying an infant, was swinging, supported by two upright posts, fastened to the sides of the saddle, in which the little traveller might ride as much at his ease as in the arms of his mother.

Our dragoman had promised to show us the ruins of Askelon.[2] He took us across a spur of the sand-hills, that border the sea, a waste in which, to judge from the huge sycamores still scattered over it, harvests had once been gathered, and descending into a little green vale planted with olive-trees, led us again up the banks of sand, and finally brought us to the remains of a massive wall, with a broad arched door, about a quarter of a mile from the sea-shore. "These," said he, "are the remains of a Christian church of the City of Askelon. The columns belonging to this church were dragged to the sea and thrown into it, when the city was destroyed, and its port filled up." The loose sands had drifted about the spot where we stood. Between us and the shore were other remains—portions of ancient walls and fortifications, against which the sand was heaped, and the waves of the sea were breaking on fragments of old quays, now wholly deserted. Only in a little valley to the northeast, green with herbage, and planted with fruit-trees, stood a cluster of mud cottages; all that is left of that great commercial city for which the east and the west contended so fiercely for so many centuries.

From this scene of desolation we turned away, and descending the sand-hills where the wind has piled them about the olive-trees almost to

their upper branches, we came to green meadows, with pools of rain-water lying among them, overlooked by the little town of El Medjal. It is pleasantly situated on a bank, with tall minarets rising above its trees. Fortunately, our road did not pass through it, so there was nothing to mar the agreeable impression made by the beauty of its aspect at a little distance. Beyond, the peasants were ploughing their fields with light ploughs, drawn by little oxen, of a size, which in our country, would make them pass for steers of two years old. One hand held the upright handle of the plough, and the other guided the oxen. The shares, as they traced a shallow furrow, uprooted tufts of narcissus in bloom.

When at length we overtook our loaded camels, they had stopped for the night on a tract of pasturage, where herds and flocks were feeding, and a pool of fresh water lay beside the ridge of sand-hills. At a little distance was the town of Esdud, the Ashdod of the Philistines[3] and the Azotus of later times, seated on a little eminence, not far from which lay the ruins of a spacious khan or caravanserai. As the sun was going down, the women and boys of the village came about us, collecting the sheep and cattle, and driving them to their folds for the night, and laborers, one after another, passed us, returning from the fields, with donkeys, bearing their ploughs, harrows, and mattocks—for no vehicle on wheels, even of the humblest kind, is ever seen in any part of Syria.

It was a luxury to dine again in our tent, unmolested by flies, which swarmed in the lazaretto we had left; and, at a later hour, to stretch our limbs on our beds, sure that our slumbers would not be disturbed by fleas, with which the lazaretto was alive in every part. There was a hoarse chorus of frogs from the pool, but this mingling with the roar of the Mediterranean as it broke on the sand-hills to the west of our encampment, was really sleep-inspiring. In the morning, while our camels were getting ready, we visited the ruins of the khan. Massive piers of hewn stone, six feet in diameter, uphold a row of pointed Saracenic arches, surrounding a quadrangle of a hundred and fifty feet square, the pavement of which yet remains. Here are the vaults, some of them yet entire, in which travellers and merchants once stabled camels, or had their merchandise locked up for the night; and traces of the hinges are yet seen upon which the huge gates of the place were turned. The khan in these parts seems once to have served not only as a place of shelter, but as a stronghold, in which the caravans were safe against surprises by night.

We walked up to the town, from which we had a view of the surrounding country. A broad, shallow basin lay before us, green, treeless, fenceless, uninhabited, like the prairies of the West. Along the bottom of this vale we followed a path leading almost due north, among extensive fields of grain and wastes of pasturage. About noon, one of our train pointed to the declivities on the eastern side, and said: "There are gazelles feeding." We looked, and saw twelve of these beautiful creatures, quietly

grazing on the green slope, seven in one troop and five in another. Immediately Balthas was on the ground, with his rifle, in pursuit of them. They took the alarm, and began to move off slowly; he fired while yet at too great a distance for any certain aim, and the instant the smoke broke from the muzzle, they were in full flight, bounding airily away to the southeast, till they were out of sight. I should have hardly thought it possible for fear to manifest itself so gracefully.

Our caravan made its halt at noon, on a green near the village of Zebna, where, as we sat on the grass, we had before us a fine broad valley; the village, with a square tower in the midst, seated on a little hill, and beyond it the dark range of the mountains of Judea. Going up to the village, we found the tower to belong to what was once a Christian church, now used for a school, built, as was manifest from its architecture, in the time of the Crusaders, who have left the tokens of their occupation scattered through the country. Part of the walls had fallen, leaving the building open on one side, but the rest, with its pointed arches, was in perfect preservation. There was nobody in or about the building, but the space within had been carefully and neatly swept; perhaps it had served as a school that morning.

Both beyond Zebna, and before arriving at it, we crossed several Saracenic bridges over small streams, vestiges of the dominion of a race as energetic as the Crusaders, and in their day, perhaps, considerably more civilized. Many people passed us, who greeted us kindly with the Arabic word for "welcome," which sometimes broke from their lips with an energy that startled me; but the good impression made by this civility was counteracted by the manner in which they behaved to their women. It is women who carry the burdens, when there is no donkey to carry them; and it is a frequent sight in Syria to see a lazy Arab travelling along on a donkey, with two or three women trotting on foot beside him.

Our journey brought us to the top of an eminence, on the slope of which, eastward of where we stood, the town of Ramleh lay before us, the centre of a vast circle of huge old olive-trees, amidst which grew fields of luxuriant barley. A little without the terrace, in the midst of a quadrangle of ruined walls, arches, and vaults, two hundred feet square, stands a lofty tower of white marble with Saracenic arches. We entered the enclosure at its principal gate; a row of massive piers and vaults, partly entire and in part fallen, stood on each side of a spacious court, covered with fresh herbage. The ground beneath was hollow with pits, the vaults of which, in places, had fallen in. We descended by one of these openings, and found ourselves in a sort of crypt, spacious, and with lofty pillars supporting pointed arches. The sides of this subterraneous apartment are lined with a smooth stucco, and I have no doubt that it was once a reservoir into which the winter rains were gathered. There were two of them, one on the south and another on the north side of the quadrangle.

A man with a sabre by his side was sitting in the shade of the wall, as we entered the court, engaged in the usual oriental manner of passing time, that is to say, smoking a long pipe. He rose and followed us when we went into the vaults below; and when we came out, he kept near us: he was probably the keeper of the place. We ascended to the top of the tower by its narrow staircase; we heard his steps behind us, and while we looked at the glorious view from the summit, he seated himself near us and smoked his pipe tranquilly till we were ready to go down again. The atmosphere was beautifully transparent; the sea was in sight to the west; the mighty range of rocks which forms the greater part of the territory of Judea, bounded the view on the east; between these was the plain of Sharon—green and fresh, but no longer famed for its roses;[4] still nearer lay the town of Ramleh, with its multitude of little domes forming the house-tops, and just under our feet was an Arab cemetery, crowded with tombs of a rude masonry, plastered over with mortar and whitewashed.

Our dragoman, in the mean time, had proceeded with the camels and the baggage to the Latin convent in Ramleh, which, on descending from the tower, we had some difficulty in finding. We wandered about in the outer streets of the town looking for it, until our appearance began to attract some attention. The boys shouted after us, and two of our party, lingering behind the others, were complimented with a volley of small stones, for which, however, the young rogues were rebuked by an elderly Arab. At length, we discovered our camels in a little enclosure, hedged with the prickly pear. Close at hand was the convent, to which we were admitted, and in which we found our rooms already assigned us. "I hope you like them," said the Superior, a Spaniard of prepossessing physiognomy and agreeable, courteous manners—"I hope you like them; they are the best we have."

In fact we had no reason to be dissatisfied; the day had been hot, and the coolness of our chambers on the ground-floor, vaulted with masonry, was very agreeable. Our cook had his convenient kitchen near us, with a small dining-room next it, and our attendants were provided with a spacious dormitory. The Franciscan convent at Ramleh, like most of the Latin convents in the castle, had but few inmates—there was but one friar besides the Superior, a Spaniard also, and with them was associated an Arab lay-brother, who had lived with them so long that he spoke Spanish fluently. The convent is a spacious building, erected round three or four different courts, all of them clean and silent. They told me that the convent was poor, which I thought not unlikely. While the bell was ringing for vespers, I happened to be in the main court, and looking round the corner, saw the gentlemanly Superior pulling the rope with great activity.

Our chambers swarmed with mosquitos, bred in the numerous cisterns of the convent, containing rain-water, some of which were yet full to the

brim, and open to the air. We had not been an hour in our beds before we wished ourselves again in our tents.

MANUSCRIPT: Unrecovered TEXT: *LFE*, pp. 168–178; first published in *EP* for June 11, 1853.

1. Judg. 16:3, 29–30; Acts 8:26.
2. Jer. 47:5–7; Zeph. 2:4–7.
3. Josh. 13:3.
4. Cf. Song of Solomon 2:1.

827. *To* the EVENING POST
Jerusalem, Palestine, February 22d, 1853.

In the morning when we left our rooms, we found the Arab camel-drivers preparing to return with their animals to their little town on the desert. Their journey ended here, and for each camel which they had led in their caravan from Cairo to Ramleh, the compensation to the drivers was about four dollars, to say nothing of a flogging or two thrown in, to sweeten the bargain, by our free-handed dragoman. We had been so long together in the solitude through which our journey lay, that we had conceived a sort of friendship for these people. We had found them respectful, laborious, and always ready with their services; and we now took leave of Mohammed and Mohammed Ali and Achmed, and the two others whose names I forget, with something like regret. The poor fellows seemed half-sorry to part with us, and Mohammed, the oldest and most responsible man among them, kissed the hands that were offered him to shake.

Meantime, a gigantic Syrian had brought to the convent-gate a troop of fifteen horses and mules, with which to perform the journey from Ramleh to Jerusalem. The horses were equipped with patched bridles, compounded of leather, worsted, ribbon, and rope, ragged saddles, and stirrups of various patterns, but principally of the Turkish, with a broad plate for the foot to rest upon. A janizary of the American Vice-Consul at Jerusalem, on his way home from Jaffa, had heard that there was a party of American travellers at the convent, and had come to offer us his company and protection during the rest of our journey. He wore a sabre, with a pair of pistols clumsily stuck in his sash, after the fashion of the country, and carried in his hand a long staff with a large silver head, the symbol of his office. We put into the hand of the Arab lay-brother, who spoke Spanish, the expected gratuity, and mounting our horses, proceeded through the streets of the town. Before us rode the janizary, resting his long staff on his Turkish stirrup, and occasionally wielding it to poke the people aside when they obstructed the way.

Crossing a rich plain, we entered upon a hilly country with frequent villages on the heights, and finally followed a road into a deep ravine, running far up into the mountain-country of Judea. At its bottom was a

narrow bridle-path, choked with loose stones, and its steep sides were tufted with evergreen shrubs; on the right hand were olive-trees planted on terraces among the rocks, and on the left were flocks of goats, under the care of keepers, browsing among the cliffs. We made our mid-day halt at a spot where the ravine, widening, left a little valley, and a clump of evergreen oaks made a pleasant shade. Close at hand were the ruins of an old building—our dragoman called it a mosque, but I had little doubt it was once a khan, and that the spacious subterranean chambers, which were the only remarkable part of its remains, had once been reservoirs of rain-water.

Out of this ravine, after following it for a great distance, we climbed into an extensive plantation of olive-trees, by a path among the rocks, so steep, slippery, and obstructed with blocks of stone, that the attempt to travel it on horseback seemed to me scarcely less than an act of madness. I soon, however, perceived that there was no cause of fear. The horses of this country, though not otherwise a fine race, are wonderfully sure-footed, and pick their way in safety up and down precipices over which one of our own would infallibly break his neck.

We had a tedious journey up and down the bare hills, and across the stony valleys. The soil of Judea is everywhere full of loose stones, yet it seemed to me, from such examination as I was able to give, that the rocks of the country in disintegrating, resolve themselves into a rich mould, which, as soon as it is touched with moisture, starts into fertility. The barrenness that prevails is owing to the want of water; wherever that flows, the herbage is luxuriant, rich grasses spring up, and abundant harvests are reared.

At length, after crossing a bleak table-land, where the soil seemed to have been washed away by rains from the spaces between projecting rocks, we came in sight of the walls, the towers, and the domes of the Holy City. The ancient metropolis of Palestine, the once imperial Salem,[1] had not lost all its majesty, but still sat like a queen in her place among the mountains of Judea. To the north stretched a broad grove of olive-trees, and under the western wall the green vale of Hinnom wound, deepening as it extended to the south, till it turned eastward to join the deeper glen of the Kedron; and eastward of the city were the steeps of Mount Olivet. I will not attempt the description of a place described so often, nor dwell upon the reflections which arose in my mind at the first sight of that spot from which the light of that religion now professed by all the civilized world, dawned upon mankind, and to which the hearts of millions in every zone of the globe yet turn with a certain reverence.[2]

We approached the city by the road leading to the Yafa Gate, which at that hour—it was now nearly five o'clock—was pouring out its men and women to enjoy the rays of a most pleasant sunshine. Among those who were walking into the country were small parties of young men in the

academical garb of the Colleges, Armenian and Greek priests in their flowing black robes, and Latin priests in their brown gowns. I thought I had never seen so fine an assortment of beards of different tinges of color, as those which hung from those reverend chins. We entered the gates without being asked for our passports, and winding through narrow, dirty streets, and vaulted passages under houses which were built directly over the ways, we stopped at the door of the Melita Hotel, close to the Church of the Holy Sepulchre, kept by Antonio Zanieni, one of that race which is found everywhere dispersed through the East—the Maltese. We were shown into clean, comfortable rooms, after taking possession of which, we went to the church, where Greek mass was performing and the devout of the Greek communion were pressing to the place of the sepulchre, kneeling before it, and kissing the sacred stone in which it is enclosed. That evening, as the day was closing with great splendor of light and color, we heard the muezzin, from a minaret rising close to the church, shouting and quavering his proclamation of the hour of prayer, with extraordinary energy, as if he protested against the Jewish and Christian unbelief surrounding him on every side. Jerusalem is the resort of enthusiasts of every creed and clime;—Jews, who are here to lament the destruction of their temple[3] and wait for the coming of the Messiah; pilgrims and devotees of the Greek Church, the Latin and the Armenian, and religious adventurers from America, of the Protestant faith, who have crossed the Atlantic to assist in preparing for the return of the Jews.

Since we have been here we have visited most of the places within and without Jerusalem, associated by history or tradition with important events. We have just now returned from an excursion to the valley of Jordan and the Dead Sea, the narrative of which I thought to have given you. This letter, however, is already so long, that I have relinquished the design of writing out, at present, my notes of that journey. I have executed my principal purpose, which was to give an account of our passage through the desert and the southern part of Syria to Jerusalem.

MANUSCRIPT: Unrecovered TEXT: *LFE*, pp. 179–185; first published in *EP* for June 14, 1853.

1. Gen. 14:17–18.
2. Mark 16:8; Acts 1:11–12.
3. In A.D. 70 by Titus (39–81), later emperor of Rome.

828. *To* the EVENING POST

Smyrna, Asia Minor, March 29th, 1853.

This letter is written from the lazaretto of Smyrna, the great commercial city of the Turkish empire, seated on the borders of one of the finest harbors in the Levant. Before the long, yellow building in which I have my chamber, spreads a broad sheet of transparent water, remote from

the agitations of the Mediterranean, and apparently surrounded by land like a lake. It is sheltered and overlooked in part by lofty mountains, with masses of forest on their sides, and summits of bare rock, and in part by green hills, up one of which the city has been climbing, of late years, from the low plain on the southern shore. Here whole navies might ride in safety, and never feel the storms that vex the open sea.

It is sometimes asked by Americans, why it is that our squadron in the Mediterranean never makes its appearance in the waters of this excellent harbor. The design of maintaining vessels of war in this quarter of the world is, of course, to inspire respect, by creating an impression of our power to assert our rights against encroachment. A whole fleet of frigates anchored at Port Mahon or at Spezzia, would not have this effect in a much greater degree than if they were stationed at Brooklyn or Norfolk. Nobody makes a voyage to Port Mahon to admire the strength of our men-of-war, their capacity for speed, the excellence of their discipline, or the terrible beauty and perfection of their arrangements for dealing death upon our enemies. At Naples they are already so familiar a sight that their appearance does nothing to strengthen the impression already made. Our naval officers, at these places, interchange civilities with the people of the country, give balls on board their vessels, which are the admiration of the ladies, and do their best to make their time pass agreeably. But if the Navy Department would give a little attention to this matter, they might be employed to somewhat better purpose.

In a conversation on this subject, which I had with the American consul at Beyroot, he said, "In the event of any controversy arising between me and the Pasha here, it would be far more easily settled if there were an American vessel of war in the harbor." These words fully express the true use of the American squadron in the Mediterranean. The authorities of a barbarous country and an arbitrary government naturally pay as little attention to the rights of foreigners as to the rights of their own subjects, unless they find themselves forced to do otherwise. Let a nation bring the evidence of its strength and greatness to their doors, and their sense of justice is surprisingly quickened. A few years since, the English poured a storm of rockets and bombs upon Acre—Akka, as they now generally call it—and battered the fortifications and the town to fragments. Since that time the slightest complaint of the representatives of the English government has received immediate attention.

There is not a port of any consequence in the Levant which the American squadron ought not to visit in its turn. Here, at the principal centre of Turkish commerce, it might find a shelter in the most inclement season, and at Beyroot, the great port of Syria, with which our commercial relations are acquiring more and more importance, though the north winds in winter sometimes render the anchorage insecure, they would find the water as calm as a lake from the first of April to the first of November.

The Turks will never be convinced of our power to exact satisfaction for injuries by what they read, for they never read; they must be convinced by what they see; and it is the proper business of our navy to instruct them on this point. The sight of our superb vessels, riding in their pride and strength upon the Turkish waters, would make the matter clear to their minds.

When our present consul first arrived at Beyroot,[1] the Pasha was disposed to treat him as he treated the consuls of the minor powers, that of Tuscany, for example: he neglected to return his official call, a point of etiquette the strict observance of which is reserved for powers of the first and second rank. Our consul was not of a temper to submit to this, and wrote to the Pasha that if his call was not returned without delay, he should report the matter to the government of the Sultan at Constantinople. This had its due effect,—the call was returned. A short time afterward, the English consul at Beyroot gave an official dinner, at which the Pasha and the consuls of the foreign governments were guests, and at which the American consul was placed next to himself. A new light seemed to break on the Pasha's mind, and he afterward treated our consul with great consideration. But it is not fitting that the respect with which our country is regarded, should be left to depend on circumstances like these.

In the behavior of the people of this country towards the Franks, a great change has taken place within a few years. The ancient bigotry of the Moslems is fast relaxing. Not only do the Turks get drunk like Christians, of which I was sorry to see some examples on board the Austrian steamer that brought me hither from Beyroot, but they submit to contact with the Christians, and do not think themselves, as once they did, contaminated by it; and they suffer our presence in their most holy places. We had on board of our steamer a distinguished officer of the Turkish empire, Mohammed Pasha, the military governor of Damascus, a seraskier.[2] There are but five seraskiers in the empire, and the office is equivalent to that of marshal in France. He dined with us occasionally, and his son always.

In Cairo, you may enter any of their mosques with a janizary, when the faithful are not at their devotions; at Beyroot you may enter them, if you will only take off your shoes. At Damascus, the idea that a mosque is profaned by the entrance of a Christian is still entertained, but even there the old fanaticism is giving way. "Ibrahim Pasha did a great deal of good when he was master of this country,"[3] said an old Jew waiter at the Palmyra Hotel in Damascus. "Before he came, no Frank, no Christian, no Jew, could ride on horseback through the streets; the Moslems would have pulled him down, and perhaps torn him in pieces. He was obliged to dismount at the city gate, and lead his horse through the streets. Ibrahim Pasha decreed that men of all religions should have equal privileges in the community. After Ibrahim Pasha was driven out, the English used

their influence to keep for the Franks and Christians the rights he had granted them, and we are allowed to ride on horseback still."

This thaw of prejudices so strong and so long cherished, this disregard of the precepts of the Koran, encouraged as it is in high places, is very likely to become far more general in the next generation than it now is. There are some who think they see in it a sign of the approaching day, when the followers of Mohammed will have become gradually weaned from their false revelation, and be prepared to embrace a purer religion. There are others who imagine that this day has been postponed by the interference of the English in the controversy between Ibrahim Pasha and the Sultan. I was, not long since, at the Latin Convent on Mount Carmel, the procurator of which, Father Charles, an intelligent and agreeable man, is well known to travellers in Syria. "It was a great mistake of the English government," said he, "that it took the part of the Sultan against Ibrahim Pasha. The English fear that Russia may obtain possession of Constantinople. It was, without doubt, the ultimate design of Ibrahim, to seize upon the seat of the Turkish empire, and if it had once fallen into the hands of so able a prince, would have given England the barrier against the further advances of Russia, which she so much desires. But beyond all this, it was the policy of Ibrahim Pasha, as it was that of Mohammed Ali, his father, to break down the religious prejudices of the Mohammedans, to put all religions on a footing of perfect equality, to adopt European institutions, and to cause the Franks to be treated with courtesy and deference wherever they went. In this way, the gates of the East would have been opened to civilization and Christianity."

Meantime, I would not have you suppose that the old Mussulman hatred of the Franks, though so much diminished, is extinct. A sense of decency, or the fear of the bastinado, often restrains its expression in grown persons—for the foreign consuls, when an insult is offered to an individual of their nation, have the means of subjecting the offender to exemplary punishment—but it breaks out in the behavior of children, who feel no such restraints. I cannot say that I observed anything of this in Egypt, but it was apparent enough the moment we entered Syria. As we passed through Khan Yoonas, the frontier town—a train of eight persons in the Frank costume, on camels—we were saluted by the boys and young girls from the open doors, the windows, and the house-tops, with shouts and gestures of derision. At Ramleh, a village one day's journey from Jerusalem, as our party were walking through the streets, two of them, lingering behind the rest, were followed by boys who threw stones at them, until they were stopped by an Arab coming out of his house, accosting them in an angry manner, and apparently commanding them to desist. I was one day walking near the Mohammedan cemetery, just without the walls of Jerusalem. It was Thursday, the day before the Mohammedan Sabbath; the women were praying at the graves of their friends. Two chil-

dren—beautiful creatures they were—a boy and girl, with brilliant eyes, and gayly dressed, came forward from one of the graves, where two women were sitting, and sang, with great glee and spirit, a song current in the country, composed in ridicule of the Franks. At the entrance of the town of Nablous, in Samaria, where the women and children were assembled in hundreds, in their holiday dresses, in a beautiful olive-grove, the little stones thrown by juvenile hands rattled about us like hail, and we were pursued for a quarter of a mile by a chorus of shouts and songs, till we were fairly within the city gates. There are Protestant missionaries from America at Smyrna, at Beyroot, at Damascus, and other places, but they depend very much on the American consuls for protection. "We could not remain in Damascus," said one of them to me, "we could scarcely maintain ourselves here for a day, but for the support which is given to our rights by the vice-consul."

It is remarkable, as it is a proof of the almost ineradicable nature of Mohammedan prejudices against the Christians, in Syria, that the missionaries never attempt to make proselytes from among the professors of Islamism; they only seek to persuade to their faith those that belong to the Greek Church, or those who acknowledge the supremacy of the Pope. It is well understood that if a Mohammedan were to abjure his creed, and embrace Christianity, his life would be forfeited. "If the criminal tribunals did not meddle in the matter," said our vice-consul at Damascus, "the people would, and we should have a tumult at once. There was, not long since, in this city, a Mohammedan who professed to believe the doctrines of Christianity, and who went to India, promising the missionaries to make a public profession of his faith in that country, but I know not whether he did so." The missionaries, it seems, do not insist upon the Moslems becoming candidates for the crown of martyrdom.

The foreign consuls in the Turkish empire have great power, under the laws of the country, and great weight with the government of the Sultan. If a Pasha or Governor of a province misbehaves himself, and gives them just cause of complaint, an application from them addressed to the Sultan is sure to procure his removal. "I can commit any man to prison, within the district for which I am consul," said our consul at Beyroot to me, "for any cause whatever; and it is only after he has been a prisoner for three days, that the Pasha has a right to send to me inquiring the reason of his detention."

But this is not all. A law passed by the Congress of the United States, in August, 1848, makes the American consuls appointed for the Turkish empire judges in all causes of a criminal nature, in which a citizen of the United States is the accused party. I pray you to look at the statute, and see if it is not an extraordinary one. The consul is both the judge and the jury, and from his sentence there is no appeal. The usages of the Turkish empire, and, if I am not mistaken, a special treaty with the Porte,[4] sanc-

tion the exercise of this power on the part of the consul. Mr. Offley is the American consul at the port of Smyrna.[5] He may not only throw me and the American friends who are with me, and the two Smyrniotes who came on with us from Cairo, and are now in this lazaretto, into prison and keep us there for three days, on no accusation at all, but he may hang all the Americans of our party to-morrow morning, without allowing us a moment's delay, or any opportunity of procuring the revision of a hasty or capricious sentence. If you should find the law to be as I have stated, I hope you will inquire whether it ought not to be immediately amended.[6]

Powers like those which I have mentioned, ought not to be intrusted to any but the most able and upright men. An American consul in a port of the Turkish empire is the sultan of all the American citizens who are within his district; he holds their lives and liberties in his hands. As much caution ought to be used in selecting competent persons for the post, as for that of the most important judicial office—the highest conscientiousness and the soundest judgment are not qualities too exalted for it. Yet it is sometimes strangely misbestowed.

Not long since, a Prussian subject, who was obliged to leave Constantinople for some misbehavior, and who could not return to it in a private capacity, went to the United States, and after an interview with Mr. Webster, obtained from Mr. Fillmore the appointment of American consul at the port of Constantinople. He arrived at Syra, in Greece, with the commission in his pocket, and was waiting for an American vessel of war to convey him to his place of destination, where he expected to make a sort of triumphal entry, when Mr. Marsh, our minister at Constantinople,[7] hearing of his appointment, wrote instantly to Mr. Fillmore, assuring him of the man's utter unworthiness, and advising that his commission should be immediately revoked. This was done, and the Prussian received notice of his dismissal as soon as it could be forwarded to him. I do not give you his name, because I am not quite sure that I remember it, and being in the lazaretto, have no means of informing myself by inquiry, but you may perhaps find it in the list of recent appointments; at all events you shall have it in my next, after I am let out of this prison. The case ought to be put on record as a warning against hasty appointments to office. I can hardly suppose that the office was bestowed, in this case, with any distinct recollection of its powers and responsibilities.

I have spoken on the American missionaries at Beyroot. They are learned and laborious men. One of them, Dr. Eli Smith, distinguished as an orientalist, is preparing, with the help of a well-educated native, a new Arabic translation of the Scriptures from the original languages, the one now used being from the Vulgate.[8] Mr. Calhoun[9] has a school for young men, at Abeih, on the western declivity of Lebanon, in which a regular course of four years' instruction is given, ending with some of the higher branches of mathematics and chemistry. All the pupils learn English, and

some of them Greek. They are twenty-two in number, and one of them is a Druse Emir. Dr. Deforest has at Beyroot a girls' school of sixteen pupils, in which he is assisted by Mrs. Deforest.[10] I was present at a part of the annual examination of this school. The girls acquitted themselves well in English composition—and the specimens of their drawing exhibited, did them great credit. They are clever geographers, I hear. They are from families of different denominations of Christians, and their parents, brothers, and sisters were present, their faces shining with the delight they felt at seeing their little friends becoming such accomplished scholars. The girls were neatly dressed; a spencer, or bodice, of printed calico, a skirt of the same material, but of lighter color, and a tarboosh or red cap, with a blue tassel, round the lower part of which was wound a gay-colored handkerchief, were the principal articles of their costume. They had mostly a healthy look, fine large black eyes, and large full lips. Some of them had a decidedly Jewish cast of countenance, though there were no Jewesses among them.

Both these schools are successful, and on them depend, I should suppose, the only hopes of the mission in Syria. The school for girls is so much in favor, that more persons apply for admission than can be received. As soon as the education of one of these girls is completed, her hand is immediately sought in marriage by some wealthy suitor. An impulse has been given to female education which is likely to spread over the whole country, and as mothers have, far more than fathers, the forming of the minds and dispositions of their children, may entirely change the character of the population, almost before the world is aware of the means by which the change is effected. The demand for female education has induced the Sisters of Charity, a Catholic order, to found a rival school, which I hear is largely attended.

MANUSCRIPT: Unrecovered TEXT: *LFE*, pp. 186–201; first published in *EP* for April 30, 1853.

1. J. Hosford Smith of New York was the United States consul at Beirut, 1850–1854. *U. S. Consular Officers, 1789–1939*.

2. War minister.

3. Ibrahim Pasha (1789–1848), son of Mohammed Ali (817.3), conquered Syria in 1832–1833, ruling until 1838, when he was compelled by British and Austrian intervention to withdraw to Egypt.

4. The Turkish government.

5. E. S. Offley, United States consul at Smyrna, 1848–1862, was probably a son of David W. Offley (d. 1846), a Philadelphia merchant who established the first American commercial house at Smyrna in 1811, and who served there as American consul from 1838 to 1846. A. L. Tibawi, *American Interests in Syria, 1800–1901: A Study of Educational, Literary and Religious Work* (Oxford: Clarendon, 1966), pp. 2–3; *U. S. Consular Officers, 1789–1939*.

6. This law was apparently amended in June 1860 to require equitable "regulations, decrees, and orders for the government of the United States consular courts in

Turkey." See United States Senate Document No. 25, Thirty-Seventh Congress, Third Session.

7. George Perkins Marsh (1801–1882, Dartmouth 1820), United States minister to Turkey, 1849–1854.

8. Eli Smith (1801–1857), a Congregational missionary, and a founder of the first American mission at Urumiah, *post* 1826.

9. Simeon Howard Calhoun (1804–1875, Williams 1829) went to the Near East, in the year of his ordination under Mark Hopkins in 1836, as an agent of the American Bible Society. Joining the Syrian mission in 1844, he took charge of the Mission Seminary at Abeih, where he spent the rest of his life. *The Encyclopaedia of Missions . . .* , ed. Edwin Munsell Bliss (New York and London, 1891), I, 229.

10. Dr. Henry De Forest, a medical missionary of the American Board of Commissioners for Foreign Missions, went to Beirut in 1842, at a time when the American Female Seminary there had been crippled by the death of its headmistress. He and his wife established a school for girls in their home, conducting it until a year after Bryant's visit, when Dr. De Forest retired, and his school was closed by the American Board after complaints that, since classes had been conducted in English, they were unsuitable for girls who were expected to marry native Christian missionaries and preachers! Tibawi, *American Interests in Syria*, pp. 103, 125, 133, 329.

829.   *To* the EVENING POST

Constantinople, April 11th, 1853.

The echoes of the Bosphorus and the Golden Horn—and they are very fine echoes—were awakened on the morning after my arrival at Constantinople, by a salute fired in honor of the arrival of Lord Stratford, the British Ambassador.[1] It was quite time for him to be at his post, for the Russian government seemed on the point of bringing over the Sultan to its projects. What they were, I have learned from good authority, but perhaps before this letter reaches your hands you may have the information from some other quarter. Meantime, I give it to you, as nearly as I can, in the words in which I received it.

"The Russian government has pretended to interest itself very much in the dispute between the Greek and the Latin Church respecting the possession of the Holy Sepulchre and other sanctuaries in Palestine. It has also professed a strong desire to be recognized by the Sultan as a kind of protector of the Greek Christians within his dominions. These, however, were the public pretexts of a deeper design. Russia was in reality laboring to engage the Turkish government in a triple alliance, offensive and defensive, in favor of the principle of absolutism, with Austria for the third power. By means of this, it was hoped to mould the policy of the Porte to a perfect conformity with that of Russia, and to make it in effect a Russian province. You know that Turkey has been a place of refuge to the liberals of Europe from the persecution of the absolute governments; you know, too, that in Turkey perfect freedom of opinion concerning questions of European politics is allowed. This was to be so no longer, if the scheme of Russia could be carried into effect.

"The Sultan was not much inclined to the proposed alliance; the

Grand Vizier was decidedly against it; but the Minister of Foreign Affairs, who had resided in western Europe, was as strongly in its favor. Pressed by his minister on one side, and the Russian embassy on the other, to make common cause with the two great absolute powers of Europe against the enemies of monarchy in its purity, there was danger that the Sultan would give way.

"Since the arrival of Lord Stratford, affairs wear a new face. The project of a triple alliance is now given up, and the negotiations on the part of Russia have fallen back upon minor questions. In resisting this project, the French government has been quite as decided and active as that of Great Britain, inasmuch as France has, or imagines she has, the same interest in preventing Russia from aggrandizing herself in the East."

In this account of the matter we have an explanation of the ordering of the French fleet to the waters of Turkey, the haste with which the British government despatched Lord Stratford to Constantinople, and the reported sailing—I do not yet know whether the report be true, but suppose it must be—of the British squadron at Malta for the Levant. The history of the affair illustrates in a remarkable manner both the weakness of the Turkish empire and the skill of Russian diplomacy. The foreign policy of the Porte does not depend upon its own views or inclinations, but on the accidental influence which any of the great powers of Europe obtain over it. The Russian negotiators are the ablest and wiliest of Europe. Now, when they are just on the point of becoming by superior dexterity winners in the Turkish question, England tosses a sword upon the chess-board, and breaks up the game.[2]

The Turkish government is as feeble in its administration at home, as it is in its dealings with other powers—feeble to enforce its own authority, feeble to preserve order, feeble to execute any work of public importance.

"The people who surround the Pasha," said an American, long a resident at Constantinople, "are the most rapacious and shameless of plunderers. No project on which money is to be spent can be set on foot, which they will not contrive the means of making an occasion of unbounded pillage. Not long since a road was laid out from this city to Adrianople and a large sum of money was raised for the purpose, enough, as was estimated, to complete it. Ten miles of the road was made, and the money was gone. It was computed that if the rest of the road were to be constructed at the same rate, it would bring the empire to bankruptcy, and the project was accordingly abandoned. Every public work is as wastefully managed."

While at Smyrna, the other day, I heard many accounts of robberies committed by banditti who have their haunts in the neighboring mountains. The city is fairly invested by them; and no man whose life is worth the ransom of a thousand piastres, ventures to trust himself at any considerable distance from the city, or to inhabit any of the neighboring villages,

except that of Boornabat, on the plain of Smyrna. Yet in these villages many merchants still possess country-houses and gardens, grateful and pleasant retreats, where they once lived with their families a part of the year, when the heat made Smyrna, a closely-built city with very narrow and very dirty streets and not a single open square or public promenade, disagreeable and unwholesome. At present, they never visit them. Smyrna is now a sort of prison watched by a guard of robbers. About two years ago they seized Mr. Van Lennep, a respectable merchant of Smyrna, who was walking out with two of his children.[3] They demanded a hundred thousand piastres for his ransom; which was negotiated down to fifty thousand— about twenty thousand dollars—on the payment of which, he was allowed to return home. One of the most remarkable of their recent captures was that of a Frenchman, the proprietor of a silk factory, who a short time since was by some means decoyed to a village not far from the city, seized, and released on the payment of thirty thousand piasters—about twelve thousand dollars. "He deserved his fate," said a Smyrniote, who acted as our guide through the city. "He had seduced several young women employed in his factory, and the people of Smyrna all say that the robbers served him right."

A lady, a native of the East, who had lived many years in Smyrna, related to me an incident which shows how little regard this community of robbers have for human life. "A young man of Smyrna, a Christian, had fallen in love with a Turkish girl, and eloping with her, sought refuge with the banditti, among the mountains. They gave him shelter, and urged him to become one of them, but he declined, hoping yet to escape to Greece or some of its islands, where to have run away with a Moslem would not be punishable as a crime. One day the chief of the troop renewed his instances, which were again firmly rejected. The chief drew one of his pistols, aimed it at the young woman, shot her dead on the spot, and turning again to her lover, said to him, 'Now you are ours.' Since that time the young man has been a robber. He knew that if he returned to society, the blood of the Turkish girl would be required at his hands."

The present chief of the banditti is one who, amidst the atrocities he is committing, has shown himself capable of generous actions. On one occasion, hearing that a member of a family in which he had been a servant was in some pecuniary embarrassment, he made his appearance and offered him the means of extricating his affairs, which, however, were not accepted. He resolutely withheld his companions from committing any robbery or act of wrong on Franks or Christians. "The Turks," he said, "are our tyrants and oppressors, and in plundering the Turks we perform an act of justice; but let us spare the Christians, who have never done us harm."

Some time since this man was taken and carried to Constantinople, where he was long detained a prisoner. During his confinement, the troop

Marble bust of Bryant, 1849, by Henry Kirke Brown (see Letter 713).

Bryant as president of the American Art-Union, in an oil portrait by
Henry Peters Gray, 1850 (see p. 118).

"Early Morning at Cold Spring," by Asher Durand, 1850 (see p. 118).

"Thanatopsis," by Asher Durand, 1850 (see Letter 718 and p. 118).

Bryant in 1854, in an oil portrait by Asher Durand (see
Letters 867, 869, 878).

Horatio Greenough, c1851–1852, in a photograph from a portrait by an unidentified artist (see Letters 778, 780).

Andrew Jackson Downing, watercolor by Calvert Vaux, 1864, "from the only existing Daguerreotype" (see Letters 815, 922).

Daniel Huntington's group portrait of Bryant, Daniel Webster, and Washington Irving at the memorial for James Fenimore Cooper, held February 25, 1852, at Metropolitan Hall, New York (see Letters 768 and 783).

William Cullen Bryant II

William Cullen Bryant II

Charles Sumner's carte de visite; photograph by Matthew Brady (see Letters 751, 976).

Christos Evangelides, "The Greek Boy," and his son; photograph by G. Damianos, Hermopolis (see Letters 830, 832).

William Cullen Bryant II

Bryant in Turkish costume bought in Damascus, 1853; photographs by Charles D. Fredricks, New York (see Letters 833, 838, and 842).

William Cullen Bryant II

William Cullen Bryant II

Carte de visite of Julia Bryant, *c*1857; photograph by Charles D. Fredricks, New York.

Carte de visite of Carolina Coronado de Perry; photograph by J. Laurent, Madrid (see Letter 993).

broke through the rules he had laid down, and robbed Franks, Christians, and Turks indiscriminately. "He is now at large," said the person who gave me this account, "and I hear that in returning to his companions he manifested great indignation at their conduct during his absence."

I expressed my astonishment that the Turkish government, having had him once in their hands, should have allowed him to be again at liberty.

"He bribed high," was the reply; "that is the way we explain such things in this country."

When I was waiting at Beyroot, about four weeks since, for the Austrian steamer to bring me to Smyrna, I heard that a Druse chief, a prisoner of the government, had been exposed at the barracks, without the city, chained to a post, with his hands tied behind him. On inquiry, I learned it was a Mohammed Daoud, a noted robber, who, for some time past, with a band of followers, has infested the road over Mount Lebanon, between Beyroot and Damascus, and committed many robberies and murders. They relate of him, that a man having a wife whom he coveted, he entered his house by night, slew the husband, and carried off the woman to his retreat in the mountains.

Mohammed Daoud was one of the boldest villains of his class. He wrote to the Turkish authorities enumerating the robberies and assassinations of which he had been guilty, and added: "You do not know by whom these things were done. I am the man—Mohammed Daoud; they were done by my hand or by my order. Take me if you can." The government had made various attempts to seize his person, but without success, until at length a Druse family named Joubelat, possessing high rank and great influence among their people, engaged to apprehend him and deliver him up. They watched his movements, and finding him at a convent, entered the room where he was dining. He asked them if they came in peace, and being told that they did, allowed them to approach him, and found himself their prisoner. He now complains that he was taken by treachery. He is to be taken to Constantinople, and if he has the means of paying a heavy bribe, I shall not be surprised to hear that he, like the robber-chief from Smyrna, is again at liberty, hovering about the road from Beyroot to Damascus.

While I am speaking of the Druses, I will add a word concerning those who inhabit the country to the south of Damascus, and their quarrel with the Turkish government.

These people possess a region, the passes to which among the mountains are easily defended by a few men. It is the rule of the Turkish empire to allow none to become soldiers in its armies who are not Mussulmen. The Mohammedans are subject to a conscription; the Christians, instead of this, pay a tax. The Turkish government says to the Druses, "We consider you as Mohammedans, and require of you a certain number

of soldiers proportioned to your population." The Druses of Lebanon and Anti-Lebanon submit to the demand, but the Druses to the south of Damascus say, "We will pay a tax, but we will give you no soldiers."

For the present—for this year at least—the quarrel has been compromised. In February the Druses said to the Turkish government: "We want time to attend to our crops: receive the value of a thousand yoke of oxen, and withdraw your troops the present year." The government, thinking it better to take the tribute than to get neither tribute nor conscripts, agreed to the postponement of the quarrel, accepted the conditions, and recalled their troops. The dispute meantime stands good for another season; it will be duly renewed, and the roads in that quarter will again become unsafe. It is possible that if the controversy is ever settled the Druses will make their own terms.

Last Friday—three days since—I saw the man who is the nominal head of that ill-compacted and scarcely cohering empire, once held in rigorous obedience by fierce and mighty monarchs, whose names were the dread of Christendom. From a wooden palace immediately on the Bosphorus—a finer is building for him, of marble, and a florid Palladian architecture— he rode forth, on a handsome black horse, a pale, slender man, dressed in a blue frock and pantaloons, wearing the tarboosh or red cap, which here, with the French, has taken the place both of the hat and the turban. Before him rode his Pashas, his high officers of state and war, the men who dispose of the money that comes into his treasury—stout men, for the most part, with tolerably florid complexions. They were dressed in the same garb with himself. The enormous turbans and barbaric robes which officers of this class wore twenty-five or thirty years ago, are now only to be found in the Museum of Ancient Costumes, established by this Sultan's father in the Atmeidan or Hippodrome. As Sultan Abdool Medjid[4] rode leisurely along, women who were standing in groups beside the way reached forth petitions wrapped in green silk, which were taken by some person belonging to the Sultan's train, and handed to an officer on horseback, carrying a box, in which they were deposited. It is said that the Sultan is always careful to read them. He is represented as a man of mild, amiable disposition, who would be glad to govern his empire better than he does, if he only knew how, or if those who surround him would only let him.

The different parts of the Turkish empire are now held together by the pressure applied to them from without. There are many who think it better that this should be so, than that its different provinces should be distributed among the powers of Christendom. For the interests of religious liberty it is most certainly better. The Mussulman government interferes less with liberty of public worship than most of the governments of Christian empires. To what degree civil and political liberty may yet

be developed from amidst the elements now in effervescence in the Turkish empire, I will not undertake to conjecture, but I would as soon take
my chance of freedom in Turkey as in most of the countries east of the
British Channel.

MANUSCRIPT: Unrecovered TEXT: *LFE*, 202–214; first published in *EP* for May 14, 1853.

    1. Stratford Canning, first Viscount Stratford de Redcliffe (1786–1880, Cambridge 1805), British ambassador to Turkey, 1825–1827, 1842–1846, 1848–1858.

    2. The Crimean War, precipitated by the events which Bryant recounts, began in October 1853, when Turkey declared war on Russia, to be joined by England and France in March 1854.

    3. Henry John Van Lennep (1815–1889, Amherst 1837), born in Smyrna, and the son of the merchant to whom Bryant refers, was a Congregational missionary whom Bryant met at Constantinople at the home of the American chargé d'affaires, John Porter Brown (1814–1872). Bryant, "Diary, 1852–1853," April 9, 1853.

    4. Abdul-Mejid (1823–1861), sultan of Turkey, 1839–1861.

830.   *To* Christos Evangelides[1]

Syra [Syros]   April 14, 1853
On board the Steamer Egette.

My dear sir.

    I was in hopes to have seen you on shore, but the steamer leaves port this evening before completing her quarantine. As I cannot come to you I am constrained to ask you if you have nothing more important to do this evening to come a moment to the side of the steamer in the boat which brings this letter. I have nothing important to communicate but my friends and myself would be glad to see our consul and make some inquiries.

I am sir
yours truly
W C BRYANT
of New York

MANUSCRIPT: NYPL–Thomas F. Madigan Collection.

    1. See 832.4.

831.   *To* Frances F. Bryant

Corfu   April 24   1853

Dear Frances

    In going from Athens to Trieste we took passage in a little steamer which brought us to this island. From Corfu it proceeds to Trieste by a circuitous route stopping at several places and making a long voyage. We have therefore left it on arriving at this place, the seat of government for the little republic of the Ionian Islands under the protection of Great Britain. After a stay of two days here we shall depart this afternoon in an-

other Austrian steamer, the Imperatore, larger and more commodious, less subject to motion, and proceeding directly to Trieste.

After I had written my last letter,[1] I went with my companions to call on Dr. Jonas King, who is the acting American consul at Athens. He seemed very glad to see me and told me anecdotes of my boyhood till I was glad to change the conversation.[2] He is you know a most learned Orientalist and is employed here as a missionary by the Presbyterians. For some time past he has been engaged in a controversy with the Greek church principally in the question of the worship of the Virgin. All denominations of religion are allowed by the constitution of Greece the most perfect liberty but by the Greek law none of them is permitted to revile any other. Dr. King has been sentenced to imprisonment as a reviler of the Greek religion—a most unjust sentence, as I understand the case, for he simply declared his opinion that the virgin was not a proper subject of worship and quoted the fathers of the Greek church to prove that even its own recognized teachers held the same opinion. He was shut up in a most foul dungeon, among common malefactors—a place so crowded damp, destitute of necessary accommodations, and with such a polluted atmosphere that he declared to me that if he had not been allowed to pass the greater part of the term of his imprisonment in the house of the jailer he must have died. After his imprisonment he was sentenced to exile.[3] He remains in Athens, however, preaches in Greek every Sunday, to a congregation of thirty or forty persons, acts as Consul, and was invited, though he did not go, to the last ball given by the Queen at the palace. He intends he says to remain, till he is taken and carried out of the country which I suppose will never be done.

Meantime I like his spirit and courage. He is doing for Greece, what no other man ventures to do, at least to the same extent, teaching it the great lesson of religious liberty, and he seems in a way to do it pretty thoroughly. He has been excommunicated by the Greek church—nobody was to enter his house, eat bread at the same table, engage in conversation with him or have any communication with him. This prohibition was obeyed for a while, but the Greeks, a mercurial race, have now forgotten it. He was once or twice in danger of being torn in pieces by the mob. One Sunday they filled his house and garden, and after his discourse which was on the duty of toleration, were becoming furiously turbulent when he bethought himself of displaying the flag of the United States which he had just received. In five minutes the house and garden were clear of the disturbers.

We called on Mr. Hill, formerly of Hoboken, an Episcopalian clergyman, who has a large school here—or rather Mrs. Hill has.[4] It numbers about three hundred pupils, of whom one hundred and thirty belong to poor families; these girls form what is called the ragged school. There is

also a pretty large infant school. Another department is a Young Ladies School—the pupils in which are boarders, and are taught the higher branches of education including English and ancient Greek. The assistant teachers with the exception of one American lady Miss Baldwin, were all formed at this school, and one of them, who conducted us through the several classes, spoke English with great elegance. In one room the little girls with their Greek teacher sang for us an English hymn. The Greeks I think would realize Miss Robbins's ideal of a scholar—please tell her so. Their thirst for knowledge, is, I should think, beyond that of any other people, and is represented to me as universal in all classes. "These little creatures," said the Greek teacher whom I have already mentioned, Miss Elizabeth, in showing us the infant school, "sometimes forget their lunch but never their lesson." "Offer a child" said Dr. Hill, "the choice of a book or sweetmeats or a toy, and he invariably chooses the book. Offer him a book or a coin, no matter what the value of the coin, he takes the book." Their aptitude in acquiring knowledge, and their quickness of apprehension are said to be as remarkable as their propensity to study. Dr. Hill's school is undoubtedly doing great good. He keeps on good terms with the government and the Greek church, and would be quite unfit for the work which Dr. King is doing.

In the afternoon of the same day we drove out to Eleusis, about nine miles from Athens. Here is a Greek village on the site of the ancient town and some few remains of a temple of Ceres, but the thing to be seen is that part of the Gulf of Salamis where the small fleet of Athens overcame the numerous one of Xerxes,[5] and freed Greece from further fear of the invader. It is a beautiful sheet of clear blue water surrounded by lofty mountains of most picturesque form. In the evening we went to Dr. King's. Here was Mrs. King a Greek lady, Miss King their daughter born in Greece who had lived fifteen years in New York, Mr. Arnold and Mr. Buel, Baptist missionaries,[6] at the Piraeus, with their wives, who were quite agreeable ladies— No, Mr. Buel was not there but his wife was. The gentleman was Professor Kendrick of Rochester[7] a traveller. Besides those there were two officers from the French fleet in the Gulf of Salamis and a young lady of Athens who spoke French. We had a pleasant evening, though I was a little unwell. The water of Athens is highly impregnated with lime and disagreed with me.

Next morning we took a little Austrian steamer at the Piraeus, and went to Calamaki on the Isthmus of Corinth. We ascended the Acropolis of Corinth and were delighted with the magnificent view of land and sea it presented us. Immediately before us was Mount Helicon and more distant Parnassus covered with snow. In the afternoon we took at Lechaeum on the western side of the isthmus another small Austrian steamer bound for Trieste. We had a most pleasant passage through the Gulf of Lepanto

and the next morning stopped at Patras an Italian looking town, nobly situated in a fertile but not healthy country at the foot of the Achaian mountains. We landed and walked over it. While here my complaint left me.

Another day of uneasy navigation, in our little tub of a steamer, brought us to this place, passing among the Ionian islands which are mountanous rising with rocky sides out of the sea. Corfu is a green fertile island, covered, except its rocky mountain peaks, with olive groves. In February it was visited with a terrible tornado which made frightful havoc among the trees breaking off their branches and uprooting them. The roads are fine, and the views very beautiful. The city is now full of country people in their peculiar costume; it is Palm Sunday. I must go on board; it is eleven o'clock.

Trieste April 26—I have just arrived at this place. From hence we go to Rome, where we all expect letters; after receiving which we shall decide whether we shall make all haste for America or not. I am quite impatient of the slow progress of my companions, who are not for putting on to Rome as rapidly as I should.

Yours ever
W. C. B.

Love to Fanny and Julia and all. It seems to me a year or two since I have seen either you or them. W. C. B.

MANUSCRIPT: NYPL–GR.

1. This letter, written at Athens on April 16, according to Bryant's "Diary, 1852–1853," and others to Frances from Cairo on February 12, Beirut on March 6 and 17, and Smyrna on March 29, are unrecovered.

2. Jonas King (1792–1869, Williams 1816, Andover Theological Seminary 1819), of Hawley, Massachusetts, had prepared for college under Moses Hallock at Plainfield while Bryant was studying there in 1809–1810. See Vol. I, 18; George Tremaine McDowell, "The Youth of Bryant: An Account of the Life and Poetry of William Cullen Bryant from 1794 to 1821," Unpublished Ph.D. Diss., Yale University, 1928, p. 85. After studying Arabic in Paris with the Orientalist Antoine Isaac, Baron Silvestre de Sacy (1758–1838), he had gone as a missionary to Greece, where he translated English works into modern Greek. In 1851 he was appointed United States consular agent at Athens, and served until 1858.

3. This sentence was revoked through the intervention of United States minister to Constantinople George P. Marsh (828.7).

4. John Henry Hill (1791–1882, Columbia 1807?, Protestant Episcopal Seminary, Norfolk, Virginia 1830) went to Greece in 1831, and, with his wife, the former Frances Mulligan, opened the first school in Athens after the expulsion of the Turks in 1829.

5. Xerxes I, king of Persia, 485–465 B.C., in 480 B.C.

6. Arnold and Buel have not been further identified.

7. Asbel Clark Kendrick (1809–1895, Hamilton 1831), professor of Greek at Colgate, 1831–1850, and Rochester, 1850–1888, who developed a new method for the study of Greek.

832. *To* the EVENING POST
Austrian steamer Imperatore,[1] on the Adriatic
between Corfu and Trieste, April 26, 1853.

Though my visit to Greece has been a short one, I ought not to pass through so interesting a country without giving you a few notes of what I have seen and heard.

Within a few days past I have seen three of the most beautiful views in the world, all of them of different character. Just before leaving Constantinople, I made, with my companions, an excursion up the Bosphorus, the shores of which were noisy with the beginning of the mackerel fishery—people dragging full nets to land, with eager shouts, and men, women, and children, from the interior, hastening to the shore that they might secure their share.

In returning we stopped at Scutari, took horses and galloped to the hill of Bulgoulu. As we ascended, the prospect opened upon us with new beauty at every step, until at last we stood on the summit in the midst of a scene of inconceivable magnificence and splendor. All Constantinople was at our feet, with its domes and sky-piercing minarets, dark masses of cypress, bright green fields, and blooming gardens, its shining waters sprinkled with sails, the winding Bosphorus, the Golden Horn, and the Sea of Marmora and its lofty islands; to the eastward, a country of cultivated fields and villages, and scattered dwellings; and to the south, rising above ranges of distant mountains, the summits of the Asiatic Olympus, white with snow. It was a scene, half the effect of which was owing to the extraordinary brilliancy and variety of the coloring.

In a few days afterward I was at Athens. I could not but acknowledge the beauty of the scenery which surrounds the city, but I missed something at first, which seemed necessary to its proper effect. The country, as some traveller says, is of the color of withered herbage. The soil, which is far from fertile, is almost white, and everywhere shows itself through the meager vegetation. The more, however, I looked, the more I admired—so varied and so harmonious were the outlines of the surrounding mountains. "The beauty of the place grows upon you," said one who had long lived at Athens, and I felt the truth of the remark every time I went out. In the aspect of nature here, there is that grand and severe repose, which, whether observed in the works of art or those of nature, makes the deepest and most durable impression on the mind.

We left Athens, crossed the Isthmus of Corinth, and took a steamer for the island of Corfu, the ancient Corcyra, a fertile and beautiful spot, its valleys and declivities shaded with old olive-trees, and gay, at this season, with innumerable flowers. "You should see the view from Goruno," said an English gentleman whom we met at our hotel. "Stanfield, the

landscape-painter,[2] declared it was the finest he had ever seen in any part of the world." We drove to Goruno and saw what might almost deserve the praise he gave it. Here was every element of the picturesque, both in color and form—mountain peaks, precipices, transparent bays, woods, valleys of the deepest verdure, and pinnacles of rock rising near the shore from the pellucid blue of the sea.

The remains of ancient art, which are to be seen at Athens, have the character of the surrounding scenery—repose and harmony. Of all that antiquity has left us in the way of architecture, they are the only ones which fill and satisfy the mind. Here is nothing too large or too little, no subordination of the whole to the parts—all is noble, symmetrical, simple; there is not a grace that does not seem to arise naturally out of the general design. It is wonderful how time has spared them. They are mutilated, defaced, and in great part overthrown, yet the marble, in many places, is as white as when it was hewn from the quarries of the Pentelicum Mount, and the outlines as sharp and clear as when the chisel had just finished its task.

All this destruction is the work of man, and but for human wickedness and folly the temples of the Acropolis would now be in almost as perfect a state as when Paul, in passing by, beheld the altar erected to the Unknown God.[3]

In looking at these remains, one can hardly help asking himself whether the Greeks of that early age, which produced works of art wearing such a stamp of calm greatness and employing such a fine harmony of the intellectual faculties, were not of a different character from the Greeks of the present day. The modern Greeks are not wanting in capacity; on the contrary, they are exceedingly clever and ingenious, but they are restless and mercurial beyond almost any other family of mankind.

The schools of Greece are now flourishing, and crowded with pupils, whose parents deny themselves the necessaries of life that their children may be educated. We shall see in the next generation what are the influences of a general diffusion of knowledge upon a national character so volatile.

On our voyage from Constantinople to Athens, the steamer stopped for some time in the port of Syra, where we began a quarantine of twenty-four hours. I wrote a note to the American consul, Mr. Evangelides, a Macedonian by birth, educated in America, who came alongside of our steamer, and with whom we had a most interesting conversation.[4] "I am satisfied," said he, "with regard to Greece. Her people are making the greatest sacrifices to acquire knowledge, and when this is the case, I expect everything. You see our town: those houses on the conical hill are Syra proper, those which cover the shore at its base form another city called Hermopolis. The place was a little village in the time of the Greek revolution; it has now a population of twenty thousand. Of these, three thousand are

pupils in the different schools. In my own school are thirty-one boarders, of whom seventeen pay for their board and instruction; the rest are poor boys. In twenty years it will be hardly possible to find a Greek who cannot read."

Syra, you know, is but a little island on the Greek coast, and the city which bears that name owes its prosperity to its schools, which make it a place of resort not only from Greece, but from all parts of Europe and Asia, where the Greek race is found.

While at Athens, we visited the school in Dr. Hill's house, of which his lady was the founder, and had the principal management. The number of pupils is about three hundred. We were conducted through the different rooms by a Greek lady, educated at the school, who spoke English with great neatness, as well as fluency, and with just enough of a foreign accent to remind us that it was not her native language. The first department, or infant school as it is called, contained, I should think, fifty or sixty children of remarkably intelligent physiognomy. "These little creatures," said the Greek lady, "sometimes neglect their work, but never their lessons." They were taught, as were all the other classes, by assistants, who, with one exception, were educated in the school. Another department was called the ragged school, in which were one hundred and thirty girls distributed in different rooms. They were all children of the very poorest class, who were here taught reading, writing, mental arithmetic, needlework, etc. They were all of Greek families, with the exception of three German children, whom I distinguished from the rest at a glance by their fair complexions and quiet physiognomies.

In another part of the school were the children of persons in better circumstances, who were taught grammar, geography, English, and Ancient Greek. They rose as we entered, and, led by their teacher, a young lady, a native of Greece, sang a little hymn in English. In a yet higher class of young ladies, numbering about twenty, the studies are advanced to drawing, algebra, and other higher branches of education, and the study of Ancient Greek is continued with more critical exactness. I was now in a country where the young ladies

—Read in Greek the wrath of Peleus' son,[5]

pass their graver hours with Plato, and, for light reading, turn the pages of Xenophon. I was shown a set of Greek classics, belonging to a young lady who assisted as a teacher in the school.

At this school, which is doing a vast deal of good, and which is constantly pressed with applications for the admission of pupils which it is obliged to decline or postpone, I heard the same account of the eager thirst of the Greeks for knowledge. "Offer a Greek child," said Dr. Hill, "a toy or a book, and he invariably chooses the book. He prefers the book to anything else you could give him, sweetmeats or coins, no matter what the

value of the coin you offer may be. The Greeks," continued Dr. Hill, "are susceptible, in a high degree, of the influence of example, and with a proper system of education I should hope everything from them. The danger is, however, that in unlearning their superstitions, as they are doing, they may lay aside with them all reverence for religion, and all the restraints which religion imposes. I fear that this is the case with those who are educated at the government schools, and that these have made the Greek character worse instead of better, so far as their influence extends."

Notwithstanding this severe judgment, I cannot think that those whose desire of knowledge makes them submit to privations and hardships in order to acquire it are in a very bad way. They acknowledge and act upon a higher motive than the gratification of their appetites. They are learners in the school of self-denial, which is the basis of all virtue, and the only school in which an elevated character is ever formed.

While at Athens, I was curious to inform myself of the controversy in which Dr. Jonas King, the learned orientalist, has been engaged. He is a schoolmaster to the Greeks in another way, and, I believe, with equal success. You know he resides at Athens in the quality of a missionary. He preaches in Greek to a congregation of about thirty persons. The Greek constitution secures liberty of worship and speech on religious subjects, to persons of "all known religions." The law at the same time directs that no person shall revile the religion of another, and provides certain penalties against those who transgress this rule. Dr. King, in the exercise of the liberty guaranteed by the constitution, freely discussed the question of the adoration of the Virgin. His views were controverted, and he supported them by a pamphlet expressing no opinion of his own, but giving extracts, in the original Greek, from the fathers of the Greek church— Chrysostom, Basil, and others[6]—in which they spoke of the Virgin as not a proper object of adoration. From this moment the controversy became a persecution on the part of his adversaries. He was arraigned on a charge of reviling the Greek Church. He employed able counsel, who undertook his defence on the ground that he had reviled no man's religion, but had merely expressed his own opinion on a religious question, with that freedom which the constitution allows. He was taken to Syra, in order to be tried, but the popular fury against him had been inflamed to such a pitch that it was feared that if he were landed he might be torn in pieces, and he was accordingly brought back to Athens. A principal reason of the popular excitement was the excommunication which had been fulminated against him by the Greek priesthood, denouncing him as a godless blasphemer, with whom all the faithful were forbidden to hold any communication, or to have the most indifferent transaction in life.

At length he was tried at Athens by the Areopagus.[7] He was zealously defended by his counsel, but the court declared him guilty of reviling the

Greek Church, and sentenced him to imprisonment. He was put into a dungeon with common malefactors—a dungeon so crowded, filthy, and damp, that, if arrangements had not afterward been made, allowing him to pass the term of his confinement, which was a short one, in the house of his jailer, his friends believe that he could not have lived to the end of it. A sentence of banishment was also pronounced against him, to which he has paid no heed. "If they come to carry me out of the country," said he, "I shall not resist, but until that is done, I shall remain."

It was during these proceedings that one Sunday a large crowd of Greeks, led by a priest of their Church, assembled in his house and garden to hear one of his discourses. His subject was the duty of religious toleration. At the close the priest asked a question concerning some things advanced in the discussion, to which Dr. King gave a prudent answer. The priest then demanded an explanation of certain positions laid down in another discourse, which Dr. King declined giving at that time, observing that he would agree to appoint almost any other day for the discussion. The multitude immediately joined the priest in demanding that the discussion should go on at that moment, with such fury and noise that his friends thought his life in danger. It happened at the time that the American consul was absent from Athens, and the functions of the office were delegated to Dr. King. An American flag, a day or two previous, had been received by Dr. King, from Washington. In the midst of the tumult, at the very moment when the multitude seemed ready to tear him in pieces, he bethought himself of the flag, and hastily unrolling it, let it stream from one of the windows. As soon as the mob saw it, their clamors were hushed, they began to disperse in the utmost haste, and in five minutes not one of them was left in the house or the garden.

At present the triumph seems to be on the side of Dr. King. The Greeks are in a fair way to learn from him the lesson of religious toleration. He is under an ecclesiastical curse, as nobody can even speak to him without incurring the censure of the Church; yet everybody now speaks to him: he is exiled for his religious opinions, yet he remains at Athens, and preaches every Sunday without any reserve in the expression of his religious views. He has behaved throughout the whole affair with the greatest intrepidity, and, if we may judge from appearances, has brought his adversaries at last to the conclusion that their best policy is to let him alone. I admire his courage, and rejoice in his success.

On the steamer which took me from Athens to Calamaki, I had a conversation with one of those who led the opposition to the Greek administration, while an opposition existed. He spoke without any reserve on the subject of Greek politics. "The sovereign," he said, "has no sympathy with the Greek nation—has no interest in its welfare; he is still a foreigner, and only thinks of his equipages and his amusements.[8] While there

was an opposition in the Greek parliament to the administration, the complaint was that it prevented the enactment of measures for the public welfare: the opposition exists no longer; and yet nothing is done. Greece should have a respectable navy; her natural situation, with so many islands, peninsulas, gulfs, and harbors, should make us a maritime nation; yet we have no navy. We have but one vessel; we send out our young men to obtain a naval education in England, and when they return we have no employment for them. The Greek race throughout Thessaly, Macedonia, and Epirus are eager to break the chains of the Ottoman government, and join themselves to us; if we had a navy to show the Greek flag in their harbors, they would make the attempt, and the Porte would be compelled to submit. Our laws are unfavorable to commerce, yet commerce flourishes without them—a sign of what our trade and our commercial navy would be, if the laws were friendly, or even just to them.

"You see," he continued, pointing to a portly, healthy-looking gentleman in black, "you see there the king's confessor. That man has more to do with public affairs than all the Greek people. It is he who makes up the cabinet and bestows offices. Pay your court to him, and you may have what place in the government you please. It is by the conferring of offices that the parliament is managed. As soon as an able man appears, he is bought over from the people by being made a minister, or appointed to some other respectable post, in which he must give up his independence of opinion. You know how public men are corrupted. In Greece we are all poor, and are therefore the more strongly tempted."

Such are some of the topics of Greek politics in the mouths of the opposition. What may be said on the other side, I had no opportunity to inform myself. I find myself at the end of my sheet, and, as I have little more to say on the subject of this letter, I will close.

MANUSCRIPT: Unrecovered TEXT: *LFE*, pp. 215–230; first published in *EP* for June 1, 1853.

1. The printed text mistakenly has "Imperative." See Letter 831.
2. Clarkson Stanfield; see 542.6.
3. Acts 17:22–23.
4. Christos Evangelides (d. 1881), orphaned during the Greek revolution of 1821–1829, and brought to New York by an American sea captain to be educated at Columbia College, had inspired Bryant's verses "The Greek Boy," published in *The Talisman for MDCCCXXIX*, p. 254, and a portrait by Robert Weir which accompanied Bryant's poem. See *Life*, II, 73; *Poems* (1876), pp. 170–171. See illustration.
5. This quotation has not been placed, but cf. Bryant, *Iliad*, I.1–2: "O Goddess! sing the wrath of Peleus' son, Achilles. . . ."
6. St. John Chrysostom (c347–407), patriarch of Constantinople, 398–404; St. Basil the Great (c330–379), bishop of Caesarea, in Cappadocia.
7. The supreme judicial court of Athens.
8. Otto I (1815–1867), a Bavarian prince chosen in 1832 by a conference of European powers to rule Greece after its independence from Turkey. Highly unpopular, he was deposed by a military coup in 1862.

833. *To* Frances F. Bryant

Rome, May 9th 1853

My dear Frances.

I did not send off the letter I wrote to you from Trieste,[1] thinking soon to be in Rome, where I should have letters from you. We reached Trieste in a rainy evening, and left it on the 27th of April on a rainy morning very early, in a little steamer with a head wind which soon made me sick. We got to Venice at one o'clock in the afternoon, and stopped at the Hotel Danieli on the water east of the Doge's palace. It was a chilly day and the chain of mountains seen to the north of us all the way from Trieste to Venice were covered with snow. The season at Venice was late, a little later perhaps than it is in our own country and every body was complaining of the inclement and stormy weather which they had passed through. We left Mr. Keith behind us at Trieste, where he chose to pass a few days. We had found him an upright and worthy man, of limited faculties, and little information, though he had been educated at some college or other, and full of whims, some of which afforded us no little amusement.

At Venice I began to grow uneasy, for I saw that my companions were in no hurry to leave it. It is the same beautiful place as ever, notwithstanding that there is a railway crossing to it from the mainland, but every thing I saw reminded me of the time when you visited it with me and I was impatient to get to the place to which we had directed our letters to be sent. At Trieste Mr. Leupp wrote to his banker in Paris, desiring him to send all the letters for him and me, which he might have on hand at the time of receiving the note, immediately to Rome. I think I have mentioned in my last that the banker had previous directions to send to Rome all that should have arrived before the 10th of April.

I went again over the Doge's palace, its grand halls, its sumptuous chambers of state and its prisons, [was] rowed to the Lido and the Armenian Convent, walked in its public garden, visited its museums and collections of works of art, threaded some of its narrow streets and found a ring for you in one of the shops in the great square of San Marco. The place, however, seemed to me much less interesting than it had ever seemed before. In walking with Mr. Durand through one of the streets leading north from the square, I saw a hat—a flexible felt hat, on the head of a middle sized man, to which I called Mr. Durand's attention. My eyes happening to fall below the brim of the hat, I saw that under it was the face of Marcus Spring. I went up and spoke to him; he seemed a little puzzled at first to know who I was with my broadbrimmed white hat and long beard of the same color,[2] but ended by being very glad to see me. That evening we all went to his lodgings, and found with him the Revd. James Freeman Clarke[3] and his wife. Here we heard many things about America which were news to us.

I got away from Venice with Leupp and Durand on the 1st of May in the afternoon of a rainy day, and ran down to Padua by railway, where we passed the night, having first looked at one or two of its churches, at its immense old Hall of Justice, in which are the monuments of the ancient historian Livy and the modern traveller Belzoni,[4] and at the circle of statues surrounding the Prato della Valle, a green meadow within the bounds of the city which you may remember.

Next morning we set out with a vetturino, *Tomaso Scimita*, which is Italian for Thomas Schmidt, for the city of Florence to which he was to convey us in three days and a half, giving us a little time to look at Ferrara and Bologna. Scimita is a native of Pisa and was, when a youth, in the service of an old vetturino Vincente Loglio. He proved himself worthy of his bringing up, and performed all that he had engaged to do. We found the country between Padua and Ferrara much flooded with water from the overflow of the rivers and the profuse rains. The fields of grass were yellow with buttercups, but the crops of grain looked sallow, as if they grew in cold marshes. In some places the country was under water for miles, the rows of mulberry trees rising as out of a lake, the water was even with the floors of the peasants' houses and the poor people were passing from place to place in boats.

We had time to look at the sights usually seen in Ferrara, at Bologna we had nearly half a day; and the next morning passed up among the mountains. As we climbed them we came to where the trees were as leafless as in winter, and the earliest flowers just making their appearance,— tufts of primroses in the sheltered places, violets and anemones resembling our own, and the very *hepatica* of our woods in spring, only bluer. Besides these there were daisies and the crocus, and a flower or two which I did not know. By and by we came to where the snow lay in the hollows beside the way. A fortnight before, they told me it had lain on these mountains several feet deep. In one place there had been a land slide which for the eighth of a mile had carried away the road. Several acres of forest had slipped from their place; there were heaps of mingled turf and fresh earth, and great trees leaning in every direction; or overthrown; and above them on the hill side was a tract of bare loose stones and rocks where trees had once stood. We passed the night at Monte Carelli on the declivities of the Appenines, and the next morning, passing by the Pratolino, with its groves of fir and oak we reached the cheerful city of Florence.

We could not go on immediately to Rome, for the diligence does not go daily, but the next day but one, on a rainy morning, we set out in the railway train for Siena which we reached in a little more than three hours. The railway follows the Arno to Empoli, and then turns southward to Siena. We had a wet journey of nearly two days to Rome. Here I found three letters from home; your own 6th and 7th, and the one from Fanny and Julia.[5] I was rejoiced to hear from you again and to hear that you

were all well, and that every thing had been going on so well. I am glad that you decided to have the Corbell house, which properly belongs to the place.[6]

I was in some hopes to get another from you here, but now it is not likely as Mr. Leupp has this day received from his banker two letters, one of the 29th of March and another of the 16th of April, while none has come for me. I do not blame you for saying that you will never consent to my going to Europe again without you. I shall never for my part wish to do so—but as I am here, and as you say that every thing is going on well at the place and the office I think I shall take a corner of Spain in my way home.

Rome looks much as it did when we saw it together. The judas tree and laburnum are in bloom on the Pincian hill, as when we walked there last. But the villas in the neighborhood of Rome, have suffered much, many of them are in ruins, beaten down by cannonballs and deserted. There are many Americans here—Chapman[7] and Page[8] and C. G. Thompson[9] and Mr. Sturges's son and daughter[10] and Professor Tappan and his family[11] &c. &c. Give my love to Fanny & Julia & the babies and thank the two first for their letter. Tell Julia to write with blacker ink. I could not read all her letter. Yours affectionately and ever

W. C. B.

I heard by way of Mr. Leupp's letters that you were all well.

MANUSCRIPT: NYPL–GR.

1. Letter 831.
2. Crossing the desert, Bryant had grown whiskers which had developed by this time into a long "palmer's beard" (see illustrations).
3. James Freeman Clarke (1810–1888, Harvard 1829, Harvard Divinity School 1833), a Unitarian and active Abolitionist, had edited the *Western Messenger* at Louisville, Kentucky, 1833–1840, in which he published early poems by his friend Ralph Waldo Emerson.
4. Giovanni Battista Belzoni (1778–1823), Italian archaeologist.
5. These letters are unrecovered.
6. It is undetermined whether such a property was acquired by the Bryants at that time.
7. John Gadsby Chapman (Letters 526, 713).
8. William Page (1811–1885), a popular figure painter and portraitist, had done a likeness of Bryant for Charles Leupp in 1848, before leaving in 1849 for a long residence in Italy. *DAA*; Page to Bryant, cJanuary 1, 1848, NYPL–GR; information from James T. Callow.
9. Cephas Giovanni Thompson (1809–1888), a portrait and genre painter whose oil portrait of Bryant was shown at the National Academy in 1843. *DAA*; *NAD Exhibition Record*, II, 156. Bryant mistakenly wrote "G. C. Thompson," here and in Letter 834.
10. These were Jonathan Sturges' two oldest children, Frederick (b. 1833), and Virginia Reed Sturges (b. 1830), later Mrs. William Henry Osborn. Mrs. Jonathan Sturges (Mary Pemberton Cady), *Reminiscences of a Long Life* (New York, 1894), pp. 205, 208.

11. Eli Todd Tappan (1824–1888), son of Senator Benjamin Tappan of Ohio (492.2; Letter 521). The younger Tappan, then teaching mathematics at Ohio University, was president of Kenyon College from 1869 to 1875. *Ibid.*, p. 205..

834.   *To* the EVENING POST

Rome, May 17th, 1853.

This is the season when, in Italy, the earth pours forth flowers with the same profusion as she offers her fruits in September. The gardens are one blush of roses, and the stronger-growing kinds of the rose-tree, both white and red, hang themselves on the walls with a surprising luxuriance of growth and bloom. The forest-trees yet cast a thin shade, but in the meadows the grass stands as high as it does with us in the middle of June, and is intermingled with numberless flowering plants. I rode out the other day to the lake of Nemi; the woody banks on each side of the road from Albano were colored with flowers, the apple-trees beside the way along the heights which surround the lake, showed their flower-buds just swelling with the spring, but in the deep basin below they were already fully open, and the white images of the trees were reflected in the tranquil water.

I wish there were no novelties to be observed at Rome more unpleasant than these. Every morning, at an early hour, the people of the city are awakened by military music, and the tramp of bodies of soldiery is heard as they march through the street. You meet them defiling through the public ways at other hours of the day; you see them performing their manoeuvres and exercises in the public gardens; you hear the drum as often as the sound of bells; soldiers are more numerous in public than even priests. Every pains seems to be taken to let the people know that they live under a military government, which can afford to dispense with their good-will. There are some circumstances, however, which tend to show that the government rules in as much fear as it seeks to inspire. Not a single copy of a journal from France or England is delivered from the post-office, till it is carefully examined to see whether it contains any political intelligence which the government chooses to keep from the knowledge of its subjects, or any political reflections of a nature which it disapproves. If these are found in it, the journal is withheld. A German, employed for the purpose, reads the English journals, and whenever he reports in favor of suppressing them they are destroyed. If the people stand in awe of the government, it is evident that the government dreads the people. There is distrust on one side, and hatred on the other—a condition of things which may last for years, but which, through a little imprudence on the part of the government, or a sudden exasperation on the part of the people, may, at almost any time, be exchanged for a state of open and bloody revolt.

In the midst of the evils of this false system of political organization, there are some tokens of prosperity to be seen at Rome. I have no doubt

that the population of the city has considerably increased within the last twenty years. The proof of this is to be found in the rise of rents, and the difficulty which now exists in finding commodious apartments. I am told that rents have nearly doubled, and that the spacious suites of rooms which a few years since stood vacant in the palaces and other large houses, have now their inmates. This is owing, no doubt, in part to the general growth of the population of Italy during the late long interval of rest from war, and in part to the new facilities for travelling, which bring many more strangers to Rome than formerly, as visitors or residents. The tide, also, which in the ecclesiastical world is setting back toward the usages and opinions of the middle ages, no doubt floats many hither, and adds something to this new growth of Rome. Those who foretold that the Eternal City, in the unhealthy air of her Campagna, would at no distant day become unpeopled, must be content to look to a very remote and indefinite futurity for the fulfilment of their prediction.

Meantime the city is somewhat beautified with almost every succeeding year. Statues and columns are erected; the old irregular pavement of the streets, trodden with so much pain by those who had corns on their feet, has been taken up, and its place supplied by a smoother one, composed of small rectangular blocks of stone, like those used in paving the streets of Paris; a noble causey, with parapets and a pavement of hewn stone, has been lately made over the low grounds just without the gate, as the new Appian way; and the public garden on the Monte Pincio has been embellished with rows of busts, in marble, of the illustrious men of Italy, her sages, artists, and authors. Workmen are now occupied in the garden, forming its walks, and planting them with trees, among which I perceive the evergreen magnolia, the bayonet-leaved palmetto, the date-palm, and other trees of the palm kind, which do not find the climate here too rude for their growth.

There is an occupation at Rome which, if I may judge from what I have seen and learned since I came here, meets with a very liberal encouragement from strangers—I mean the copying of old pictures. A great part of this, performed by native artists who make it their profession, is the merest and easiest journey-work. An American, the other day, bought a whole gallery of these copies, so ill-executed, I was told, that scarce anybody here would have allowed them to remain in his sight. These people forget that a good copy of a great picture is no common thing, and that it requires in him who works it, most of the requisites of a great painter. It is frequently said that a good copy is better than a bad original, which is true enough; but it should be remembered that good originals are not so very much more rare than good copies.

You may, perhaps, like some notices of what the American artists are doing in Rome. Crawford is occupied with his equestrian statue of Washington, designed for the city of Richmond. Around the principal figure,

which is not yet fully modelled, will be placed statues of the contemporary great men of Virginia. Two of these, the statues of Jefferson and Patrick Henry, are already modelled, and plaster casts of them have been obtained. They are of colossal size, and are designed with a manly vigor and disdain of minor graces which quite delights me. If the rest of the monument shall be conceived in the same spirit, it will greatly raise Crawford's reputation.[1] He has a small work under the chisel, the Babes in the Wood, which I hear has been ordered by a gentleman of New York. The children are lying hand in hand, and the redbreast has just beg[u]n his pious office of covering them with leaves. The subject seemed to me beautifully treated.

The other American sculptors at Rome—Mozier, Richard S. Greenough, Rogers, and Ives,[2] are all zealously pursuing their art, and occupied with works which show that there is not one of them who is not likely to surpass what he has already done. Mozier has a statue of Silence, which does him much credit; it is a female figure, standing in an attitude of command, with a calm severity of aspect, the forefinger of the left hand pointing to the lips. Greenough is modeling the figure of a shepherd, attacked by an eagle, which promises well.

Page is here, analyzing the manner in which Titian produced his peculiar coloring, and reproducing some of his heads in excellent copies.[3] But he has done what is better than this: he has painted a portrait of Charlotte Cushman, a fine, solid painting, richly colored, with which not only his friends, but everybody who sees it, is charmed.[4] Terry, a universal favorite with his countrymen, is occupied with a picture of "Samuel and his Mother."[5] C. G. Thompson, who arrived here not long since, is looking at the works of the great Italian painters, and now and then making a clever copy of a head or a single figure. Nichols has very successfully transferred the calm glow of Claude's landscapes into some fine copies which he is making.[6] Wotherspoon is luxuriating on the sylvan beauties of [Lake] Nemi.[7] For my part, I can hardly understand what an American landscape-painter, after satisfying a natural curiosity to see the works of the great masters of his art, should do in Italy. He can study nature to quite as much advantage at home—a fresh and new nature, as beautiful as that of Italy, though with a somewhat different aspect of beauty.

I was the other day in the studio of Gibson, the English sculptor.[8] He showed our party a work in basso-relievo, representing Phaeton attempting to guide the chariot of the sun. It equals in fire and spirit anything the imagination could conceive of such a subject. The horses, with distended nostrils, plunge madly forward through space, seeming as if they would leap out of their harness, and the young charioteer holds the reins with an aspect of uncertainty and alarm. In another part of Gibson's studio was placed a statue, on which he had been trying an experiment that had long occupied his thoughts. The ancients, you know, colored or painted their statues, and this is supposed to have been done by persons who made

it their particular profession. Gibson has a statue of Venus, a very pleasing figure, the hair of which he has colored of a very light warm brown, binding it with a fillet of the most delicate blue, stained the eye with a dim azure, with a tint of a crimson vein or two at the corners, laid the faintest possible bloom on the cheeks, touched the lips slightly with scarlet, and suffused the skin, over the whole form, with a carnation just perceptible, through which the blue stains of the marble appear like wandering veins. The drapery of the figure is left in the original color of the marble, except the border, along which runs a double stripe of pale blue, with another of pale crimson next to the edge. The effect is agreeable far beyond what I should have expected. The marble is deprived of all its appearance of hardness, and the statue has the look of a human figure seen through a soft mist; the outlines seem to blend with the atmosphere.[9]

On my way hither, stopping at Florence, I visited the studio of our countryman, [Hiram] Powers. He had several busts lately executed with his usual skill in giving the expression of character and life, and was then occupied with a figure intended as a representative of our new state, California. In her left hand she holds a divining-rod pointing downward to the mines in her soil, and in her right she conceals behind her back a scourge, intended as an emblem of the calamities which follow the eager search for gold. Powers at present models his figures in a peculiar manner. He builds them up with fragments of dry plaster, cemented by the same material in a liquid state. When any part of the figure requires to be made rounder or fuller, he lays on the plaster with a flexible gutta percha trowel; when it is to be reduced in size, he applies a kind of file or rasp, of which he is the inventor, which never becomes clogged, and is pierced with holes, through which the plaster shoots in a shower. In this manner he completes the model in a shorter time than it could be moulded in clay, and avoids the trouble of taking a cast.

While I am speaking of works of sculpture, let me mention the monument of Titian, at Venice, in the church of Santa Maria dei Frari, erected last year,—more than three hundred years after his death. It stands among the monuments of the statesmen and warriors, the admirals and doges of Venice, as lofty and as splendid as any of them, and in a taste less barbaric. Near the base sit two colossal figures—on the left a bald old man, with eyes closed, representing Time Past, holding a tablet, on which are inscribed the words of the Emperor Charles V., uttered in 1506,[10] commanding that Titian be made a knight and count of the empire; on the right a man in the vigor of life, representing Time Present, with a tablet, on which is engraved the command of Ferdinand of Austria,[11] in 1835, directing a monument to be erected to Titian's memory. Titian sits on the summit of the pedestal, unveiling with his right hand the statue of Isis, or Nature, and laying his left on a volume brought him by a winged youth,—intimating that he derives the inspiration of his aid from the two sources of nature

and religion. On each side of him stand two allegorical figures, one of which, the Muse of Painting, looking forward with lifted eyes as if into the distant future, brings him the wreath of immortal fame. On the wall of the monument, and under the arch over the head of Titian, is beautifully sculptured, in basso-relievo, his noblest work, the Assumption of the Virgin; and four other paintings of his are copied in the same manner, on a smaller scale, in different compartments. On the top of the arch, forty feet from the floor, stands the winged Lion of St. Mark, the emblem of that Venice for whose churches and halls his finest paintings were produced. This monument is the work of Luigi and Pietro Zandomeneghi,[12] and strikes me as one of the finest things of its kind in Venice.

MANUSCRIPT: Unrecovered TEXT: *LFE*, pp. 231–242; first published in *EP* for June 9, 1853.

1. This statue, for the design of which Thomas Crawford (519.3, 519.5) had won a competition in 1849, was later erected in Richmond, Virginia.

2. Joseph Mozier (1812–1870), before 1845 a successful New York merchant; Richard Saltonstall Greenough (1819–1904) of Boston, younger brother of the late Horatio Greenough; Randolph Rogers (1825–1892), former New York drygoods clerk who had come to Italy in 1848, with the help of his employers, to study, and who was commissioned in 1853 to design and model the bronze "Columbus" doors which were installed at the east entrance to the Capitol Rotunda in Washington in 1871; Chauncey Bradley Ives (1810–1894), a New York sculptor who lived in Italy after 1844. *DAA*; *Art in the United States Capitol* . . . (Washington, D.C.: Government Printing Office, 1976), pp. 343–345. The following year Mozier sent Bryant a photograph of his statue *Truth*, suggested by Bryant's poem of 1837 "The Battlefield." Mozier to Bryant, July, n.d., 1854, NYPL–GR.

3. Titian, or Tiziano Vecellio (1477–1576), foremost Venetian painter of the sixteenth century.

4. After several years spent perfecting her art in London, Boston-born Charlotte Cushman (1816–1876) had made a triumphant American tour in 1849–1852 which established her as the leading actress of her native country.

5. Luther Terry (1813–1869), a Connecticut portrait and figure painter long resident in Rome, often exhibited at the American Art-Union and the National Academy. *DAA*.

6. Probably Edward W. Nichols (1819–1871) of New York, a frequent exhibitor at the National Academy. *DAA*.

7. William Wallace Wotherspoon (1821–1888), a New York landscape painter who began showing his pictures at the National Academy and the American Art-Union in 1844. *DAA*.

8. John Gibson (537.3).

9. Gibson's *Venus*, with several others of his tinted statues, was shown at the International Exhibition in 1862.

10. This date should probably be 1556. Charles V (1500–1588), emperor of the Holy Roman Empire, 1519–1558, invited Titian to his court at Augsburg in 1548 and 1550, becoming Titian's great admirer and patron. In 1554 Titian painted for Charles V his great Trinity, "La Gloria."

11. Ferdinand (1793–1875), emperor of Austria, 1835–1848.

12. Luigi Zandomeneghi (1778–1850), and his son Pietro (1806–1866), Venetian sculptors.

835. *To* Frances F. Bryant

Marseilles   May 21, 1853

My dear Frances.

Yesterday we reached this place by the Mongibello a Neapolitan steamer from Civita Vecchia, to which we went on the night of the 18th in a diligence from Rome. It was the first steamer which made the passage directly from Civita Vecchia to Marseilles in which we had an opportunity of going; the other steamers made slow and tedious voyages along the coast, and we should not have arrived much sooner by taking any of them. Today, as soon as we get our passports we shall go northward towards Paris.

Our design of visiting Spain is given up. I am anxious to get home, and Mr. Leupp, who has hitherto been quite disposed to protract his stay abroad as long as possible, is to my great satisfaction almost equally so. In passing through Italy, he was desirous to see more of Venice and of Rome, to which, I for my part was indifferent, or rather averse. John Durand also was desirous of seeing something of Italy, and their wishes as was just, I thought, decided me. If we had gone immediately to Spain on arriving at Trieste, we might have seen something of the country, though even then our visit must have been necessarily a hurried one. At present, the season has arrived when to travel in the south of Spain would be uncomfortable on account of the heat, and the progress of the traveller is slow in every part of the country.

We shall go on to Paris, and after getting some clothes, for we are now pretty ragged, we shall take the steamer for America. I have remembered you in most of the places where there was anything to buy which I thought you would like. At Rome I had a daguerreotype likeness of myself taken[1] that you might see what a magnificent white beard I brought with me from the Desert. Perhaps, however I shall bring the beard home with me. Tell Julia that I did not get her letter with the hint about the coral ornaments sold in Naples till long after I left that city behind me.[2] I shall bring her something, however.

The voyage from Civita Vecchia to this place was an uncomfortable one, as most of our many voyages on the Mediterranean have been. The boats are small, for the most part, except the English ones; and are tumbled and rolled about by one of the most uneasy seas in the world. The accommodations in all of them, except one of the French boats, we have found indifferent, and in most instances wretched. I was dreadfully sick night before last, and such a scene of vomiting and sprawling about I never saw as was exhibited on board our vessel. We had more than a hundred passengers, many of them ladies. I think our party were the only Americans, the majority were English flitting homeward, or to Paris for the summer.

I send with this a letter for the Evening Post which contains notes of

what I observed in Rome of most importance.[3] I was not much interested in this visit to the place, probably on account of my impatience to get home. I went through our old street, the Via Pontefici, several times. The Palazzo Correa, looks just as it did, and so does the rest of the street.[4] The villa Borghese, just without the walls where I used to walk so often, and which you must remember visiting with me, is shut up. Its trees were cut down—not all but a considerable proportion of them in the late revolution.

At Paris I hope to find letters from you. In one of your last you speak of the pleasure I must take in travelling. The pleasure is purchased by a great deal of hardship, among which is the sea sickness I suffer in navigating the Mediterranean; and now that the time I originally set for returning is already past, almost all the satisfaction I might derive from the novelties I see is neutralized by a feeling of uselessness which I cannot control. You know how exact I am in returning from my journeys when their termination depends on *me*.

My love to Fanny and Julia and the children. Give my regards to all my friends who may take the trouble to ask about me— In the hope of seeing you soon, and finding you well I am as always

Affectionately yours
W. C. BRYANT

MANUSCRIPT: NYPL–GR.

1. Unrecovered.
2. Letter unrecovered.
3. Letter 834.
4. From about April 2 until April 28, 1835, the Bryants had lodged in the Palazzo Correa, 57 Via Pontefici. See Vol. I, 7.

836.   *To* the EVENING POST

Paris, June 1st, 1853.

I have just returned from a visit to one of the government offices, in which the Fresnel lights, designed for the light-houses on the French coast, are deposited. The invention of Fresnel[1] is one of the most beautiful examples we have of that skill by which the apparently barren phenomena of science are forced into the service of man.

Light, you know, radiates in all directions. Place a lamp in a tower on a sea-coast, and part of its rays are wasted on the clouds above it, part on the earth below, and part stream to the right and left, where they are not wanted. By a most ingenious arrangement of prisms, Fresnel collected these useless rays and sent them forward in a horizontal direction, parallel with the surface of the ocean, where they must meet the eye of the mariner. An intense light, by this concentration of its beams, is obtained from a single lamp. I desired to see an example of the effect produced, and a lamp was placed within one of Fresnel's circles of prisms, while I stood at the

distance of twenty feet or more. It blazed into my eyes like the rising sun, and I could not bear to look at it.

Lieutenant Bartlett, of the United States Navy,[2] is now in Paris, superintending the purchase of two or three of these lights, for which appropriations have fortunately been obtained from Congress. One of them is shortly to be sent out to America, and will, it is expected, be exhibited for a time at the Crystal Palace.[3] I hope it will be so placed that everybody may see it without cost; for I regard it as a matter of great importance that the perfect manner in which the invention fulfils its purpose should be generally known and acknowledged. The want of good lights on our coast is a scandal to our country. France, with a much smaller marine commerce than ours, has erected Fresnel lights at every part of her borders on the Atlantic and the Mediterranean where the seaman needs the least notice of danger. These strong rays, piercing the fogs and storms, give the necessary warning in any state of the weather. England, with a commerce but little larger than our own, has also adopted the Fresnel lights. We, on the other hand, content ourselves with putting up a few lamps, which glimmer feebly when the air is clear, and are of no use in thick and foggy weather— that is to say, when their light is wanted. We might nearly as well let our lighthouses fall to ruin, and imitate the example of Turkey, which leaves its whole coast in entire darkness.

One or two of the Fresnel lights have already been set up in America, but they are of the original early pattern—before Fresnel and his brother had perfected the invention. I saw one of these at the repository of which I am speaking, and the difference between it and those which are at present used in France is very great. In that model, Fresnel employed only prisms with straight sides; he had no apparatus for making any other; they were put together in small pieces; the light was obstructed by the cement used to confine them in their places, and the stray beams of light which escaped through the space between the prisms, were caught upon mirrors and reflected in the desired direction. But in the new Fresnel lights, the mirrors are laid aside as no longer necessary; the prisms have taken a curved shape; they are larger and less numerous, and the sphere of glass which they form, enclosing the lamp, is of a far simpler and more solid construction, and a more perfect transparency.

I was taken afterward to the workshop where these prisms are made, and whence the western coast of Europe is supplied with the apparatus for its light-houses. Here large wheel-shaped masses of glass, fixed upon tables revolving horizontally, were ground with sand to the proper angle, and finally polished. In another part of the building artisans were at work, framing the turrets of metal and glass in which the apparatus of Fresnel is enclosed. These are roofed with copper, and the iron ribs in which the glass is set are covered on the outside with thin copper bars, so that no

part of the iron is in danger of corrosion by being exposed to the external air.

The great advantage of Fresnel's apparatus lies in the strength of the light which it throws in the direction where it is wanted, but it has two other important recommendations—its economy, and the ease with which it is kept in order. With a single lamp it does what in the old method required thirty, and it dispenses altogether with the clumsy contrivance of reflectors, which are constantly becoming tarnished and wearing out. The supply of oil which is needed is, of course, comparatively trifling. I hope, for my part, that no time will be lost in lighting the whole coast of the United States, through all its degrees of latitude, both on the Atlantic and the Pacific, with the apparatus of Fresnel. The outlay at first would be considerable, but it would be soon made up to the treasury in the diminished expense of maintaining the lights. A liberal appropriation for the purpose made at once, would be an act of the highest frugality for the public treasury, to say nothing of the lives it might preserve, and the cargoes it might save from wreck.

I have been told that Captain Forbes, of Boston, not long since took out with him to America two ship-lanterns constructed on Fresnel's plan.[4] They were found to answer their purpose admirably, as I hear, but the Yankees, with their usual dexterity in applying such resources as they have at hand, immediately hit upon a substitute for Fresnel's prisms of cut-glass, which is a great deal cheaper and succeeds almost equally well. They form the glass into prisms, with the necessary curve, by pressure, and in this way construct a lantern but very little inferior in the strength of its light to those made in the French way.

The other day I went to the church of the *Invalides*, to see the tomb of Napoleon, which has been several years erecting, at an immense cost, and is just completed. There is not on earth so magnificent a mausoleum as that which is destined for the remains of the former Emperor of France. On entering the church I found myself in the midst of a throng hastening in the same direction, and saw before me, at the opposite end of the building, a large altar, blazing with gold, under a gilded canopy, which rested on twisted pillars of black and white marble. In front of it, immediately under the windows of the dome, appeared a circular balustrade of white marble, around which the people were pressing. I joined them, and saw that it enclosed a broad, open space, sunk, perhaps, fifteen feet below the church. There, on a pedestal of blue granite, stood an enormous open sarcophagus of polished porphyry, the lid of which lay near it, on a machine, ready to be slid over it as soon as the ceremony of sepulture shall be performed. On the pavement below, around the pedestal, was a wreath of laurel leaves and berries, wrought of various-colored marbles—among which a vivid green marble, from the quarries of the United States, was conspicuous. Surrounding the sarcophagus, and standing against the pil-

lars which support the floor, was a circle of colossal figures in marble, the meaning of which I did not attempt to study. One of them, a winged figure, with a trumpet by his side, was perhaps the angel of the resurrection, who is to summon the great warrior from his grave on the day of account, when he will be unpleasantly confronted by the multitudes who were slain in his wars. In the recesses behind these statues were sculptures in bas-relief, representing some of the most important events of Bonaparte's history.

In that sarcophagus is soon to be placed the handful of dust which is all that remains of one who, for a few years, was the terror of the world. In its material, its form, and its glittering polish, this massive receptacle reminded me of the huge chests of porphyry found in the newly-opened tomb of Apis, at Sakkara, enclosing the bones of the sacred ox of Egypt. It is thus that, in different ages of the world, the same posthumous honors are paid to a quadruped and a conqueror, by two nations, each claiming in its day the palm of civilization. The Egyptians were the nearer right of the two; they honored the representative of a most useful tribe of animals; the French pay their homage to one whose title to it is, that "with infinite manslaughter" [5] he won an empire which he was not able to keep.

I regretted that I could not look at the sculptures in relief below, except at a distance: they will be accessible, it is said, as soon as the remains of Bonaparte are inurned. I inquired of a friend residing in Paris, when this would be done. "There is a controversy," he replied, "about this matter among the Bonapartists. One party insists that the heart of Napoleon shall be deposited by itself in the church of St. Denys, among the monuments of the former sovereigns of France; but Jerome swears that he will not allow his brother's body to be cut up in that manner.[6] The ceremony of removing his remains to the sarcophagus has, therefore, been postponed for a year."

But we had not yet seen the whole of the monument. Passing beside the glittering altar, we descended a flight of steps to the level of the great Court of the *Invalides*. Here, immediately back of the altar, and under it, I saw the entrance to the tomb, a massive doorway, over which are engraved the words of Napoleon expressing his desire to be buried among the French people on the banks of the Seine. On each side of this passage to the sarcophagus stands a colossal figure, in bronze; one of them bearing, on a cushion, a globe and sceptre, the symbols of dominion, and the other a sword and gauntlet, emblematic of the violence by which that dominion was gained, and, for a brief space, upheld. As we were considering these figures, the voices of priests and a choir, chanting at the altar above, resounded up the lofty dome; it was a litany, nominally addressed to the God of Peace. I looked about me, and saw only the symbols of warlike glory, and encouragement to the pursuit of renown in arms. On the walls were the sumptuous monuments of men who had distinguished them-

selves as the instruments of warlike ambition and conquest—Vauban, Marshal Bertrand, and others.[7] This church itself had been converted into the mausoleum of a conqueror; it was the shrine of Napoleon; this altar formed a part of his monument, and this hymn, whatever its words, was chanted in his honor. I had before me one of the forms in which the Power of Destruction is still worshipped. What a groundless fancy, to suppose that the adoration of a Great Spirit of Evil has become extinct with the race of ancient Persians, or exists only among a few savage tribes! I left the place with the throng, passing out to the street through the Hospital of the *Invalides*—for we were not permitted to retrace our steps to the principal entrance. I left it with a strong impression of the yet imperfect civilization of mankind.

An exhibition of the works of living artists is now open in this city. It contains more than twelve hundred paintings, three hundred and twenty works of sculpture, and two hundred and sixty engravings and architectural designs. These are not half the number of works offered by the artists; about twenty-five hundred were rejected by the committee employed to make the selection, and among these were some which at least deserved a place among the best which were accepted. There was no artist on the committee; those who were named as members declined to serve, and the politicians and public men who finally composed it were probably not the best judges in such matters.

I hope so at least, for the collection is far from being as good as I expected to find it, and I should be glad to believe that it would have been better if the task of selection had been intrusted to a better committee. In the department of sculpture, the want of a high standard of art is perhaps most observable. There are plenty of naked Venuses and nymphs, simpering, leering, and sprawling; and these are oddly enough contrasted with several figures of female saints, wearing an air of theatrical and resolute prudery. An Egyptian maiden stooping with a look of compassion and tenderness to take the infant Moses from his ark of rushes, is one of the few female statues not strictly ecclesiastical which is not vulgar. Of the busts there are some good ones, but many of them have a sort of smirk or an affected attitude. There are several attempts to make something of the head of Louis Napoleon in sculpture, but the subject seems an intractable one, and none of them are successful.

There are many historical pictures—some of them very large, and scarce any of the large ones tolerable. The largest is by Matout,[8] representing Ambrose Paré applying, for the first time in the annals of surgery, the ligature to the arteries of a lamb, after an amputation—an immense failure. The subject is coldly and confusedly treated. The best of this class is the *Death of the Virgin*, by Lazerges,[10] a subject which the painter has managed with dignity and feeling, though the dignity, I must say, rather predominates. The death-struggle is just past, the household stand in sor-

row around the couch of the dead, whose countenance wears the tokens of a happy departure, and a little child is advancing, encouraged by its mother, to lay a handful of roses by the Virgin's cheek. You may judge of the strange sort of things to be seen in this gallery, by what I shall tell you of the *Death of Agrippina,* by Duveau.[11] A large, elderly woman, of a livid complexion, is sitting up naked in her bed, and throwing her arms abroad in the air, facing three half-clad ruffians, with complexions of reddish brown, who rush at her with clubs and daggers, while a scowling maid-servant, behind her mistress, is huddling on her garments, which seem to refuse to cover her. I must not omit to mention a picture by Winterhalter, representing Florinda and her Maidens beginning to disrobe her for the bath, which is very beautiful.[12] Of the landscapes, there are none very remarkable; the best are those which are apparently studied from nature; the larger and more elaborate ones seemed to be painted in forgetfulness of nature. There are portraits in the collection, good, bad, and indifferent; the indifferent forming the largest number.

After all, I am making a criticism which must be the universal one in regard to all miscellaneous collections of the kind. The greater number of the works produced by artists in all ages are unsuccessful, or but partially successful, endeavors after excellence. The works which survive to be the admiration of succeeding times are few in any single year, and in the most prolific years form an exception to the mass of works produced.

MANUSCRIPT: Unrecovered TEXT: *LFE,* pp. 243–256; first published in *EP* for June 16, 1853.

1. Augustin Jean Fresnel (1788–1827), French government engineer and physicist who was widely renowned for his researches on polarized light.

2. Washington Allen Bartlett (1815–1894), United States Navy, 1833–1855. *General Register of the United States Navy and Marine Corps . . . (1786 to 1882) . . .* (Washington, 1882), p. 55.

3. The New York Exhibition, or World's Fair, was held in 1853 in a building resembling London's Crystal Palace (1851), at Forty-Second Street and Sixth Avenue, later the location of Bryant Park.

4. Probably Robert Bennet Forbes (1804–1889), a shipowner and sea captain, and long a promoter of coastal life-saving.

5. This quotation is unidentified.

6. Jerome Bonaparte (1784–1860), Napoleon I's youngest brother, who was king of Westphalia, 1807–1813, and was known in France after 1847 as "Prince Jerome."

7. Sébastien le Prestre, Marquis de Vauban (1633–1707), French marshal under Louis XIV, whose heart was buried in the Hôtel des Invalides by the order of Napoleon Bonaparte; Count Henri Gratien Bertrand (1773–1844), French general under Napoleon, whom he accompanied to Elba and St. Helena.

8. Louis Matout (1811–1888), painter of landscapes and historical portraits.

9. Ambroise Paré (c1510–1590), a French army doctor and a pioneer in humane surgery.

10. Jean Raymond Hippolyte Lazerges (1817–1887).

11. Louis Jean Noël Duveau (1818–1867).

12. Franz Xaver Winterhalter (1806–1873), German court and portrait painter. His "Florinda" is now in the Metropolitan Museum of Art, in New York.

837.   *To* Messrs. Woodman & Co.

Havre   June 6, 1853.

Gentlemen.

Will you do Mr. Leupp and myself the favour to write to him at London, where he will be the remainder of the week, what disposition you have made of the clothes which we have ordered and not received and how the account stands with each of us respectively.[1] If you should have a good opportunity to send the clothes intended for us to London, in the course of the week, he will be there and will take charge of them. . . .[2]

MANUSCRIPT: NYPL–GR (draft) ADDRESS: To Messrs. Woodman & Cie [27 Boulevard des Italiens, Paris].

1. Bryant's "Diary, 1852–1853" notes that on May 25 he ordered coat and trousers from Woodman, "who complains that the *Evening Post* does not come."
2. Unsigned.

XVII

Tumults of the Noisy World
1853–1857
(LETTERS 838 TO 973)

STEPPING ASHORE IN NEW YORK on June 22, 1853, Bryant must have appeared a patriarchal specter, wearing the long white beard he had left unshaven for six months, with his face and high bald forehead scorched by the suns and sand-storms of the Near East. He passed unrecognized by the office clerk sent to meet him, and later at Roslyn by a neighbor for whose mystification he donned a Turkish turban and gown and talked in broken English. He himself was a little disturbed, in reading an article by a German writer on New York journal-ists, to see himself described as a "little, dry, lean old man," and in writing Richard Dana he remarked wryly, "I do not like to think of growing old." But his appearance belied the vigor of his fifty-eight years. Toughened by travels which might have overborne many a younger man, he turned at once to the repair and improvement of his house and grounds at Cedarmere, and to the growing political contest over the spread of slavery into the new western terri-tories.

In July, when the Pierce administration's organ, the Washington *Union*, stigmatized the *Evening Post* as the creature of Abolitionism and read it out of the Democratic Party, Bryant scorned the charge as coming from a "party hack," the servant of an extreme pro-slavery faction. But his sharp criticism of President Franklin Pierce, whose candidacy he had supported grudgingly in 1852, was in truth alienating him from the party in power. When, in January 1854, Senator Stephen Douglas of Illinois introduced in Congress the Kansas–Nebraska Bill, which would in effect repeal the Missouri Compromise of 1820 by opening the territories to slavery, Bryant cut his paper loose from its ties to the Democratic Party and led it firmly into the anti-slavery cause. He charged that Pierce, in his "mad and wicked adhesion to the Nebraska perfidy," was acting as the "tail of Senator Douglas's kite"; that the proposed measures would result in "Afri-canizing the heart of the North American continent." We must, he declared, "oppose an impassable barrier to the admission of any more slave states."

The political resurgence of xenophobia and anti-Catholic prejudice, the defeat of which Bryant had celebrated after the New York election of 1845, produced an American, or "Know-Nothing," Party which elected nine state governors and a large minority of congressmen in 1854. Coinciding with the weakening of older party loyalties, this movement appealed, unfortunately, to many northern opponents of slavery. Bryant had been pleased with signs of growing religious tolerance in the Catholic and Moslem countries which he had lately visited, and he was disgusted to find a reversion to prejudice at home, warning his readers not to be "deluded or frightened into a needless crusade against the venerable and harmless hobgoblins, 'Popery' and 'Foreign

Influence.' " By 1855 he was convinced that the movement had lost its force in the North, but he was disturbed by indications that it had "struck deeper root" in the South, where a leading newspaper proposed the right of a political party to "lay its plans in secret and to secure them from disclosures by oath."

In the fall of 1855, convinced that the southern-dominated Congress and administration had "ceased to serve the cause of freedom and justice," Bryant turned his attention to the nascent Republican Party. The following July he made what was for him a rare commitment to political activism, when he gave the principal speech at a party rally in Yonkers, New York, proposing as the Republican slogan, "Three Cheers for Freedom and Frémont." His uncharacteristic action was impelled by a physical assault made two months earlier by South Carolina Congressman Preston Brooks on Senator Charles Sumner of Massachusetts. Conceding the intemperance of a Sumner speech which provoked the attack, Bryant posed the question "Has the freedom of speech in the United States Senate been put in peril?" If so, he declared, the Constitution has been violated, and "violence is the order of the day; the North is to be pushed to the wall by it." Soon after, his name headed the list of sponsors at a Broadway Tabernacle meeting protesting the attack. The *Evening Post*, which had been serializing Bigelow's life of Republican presidential candidate John Charles Frémont, took up the cause of Free Soil settlers in Kansas against pro-slavery "Border Ruffians" from Missouri, endorsing appeals from the Emigrant Aid Society for funds to support their struggle. The *Post* sponsored a prize contest for a Frémont campaign song, and as the 1856 election drew near, Bryant was hopeful of a Republican victory. His disappointment at defeat was tempered by a large plurality of popular votes for Frémont and the American Party candidate Millard Fillmore over those given the winning Democratic candidate, James Buchanan. Frémont carried eleven northern and western states, allowing Bryant to draw the conclusion that "We have at least laid the basis of a formidable and well-organized party, in opposition to the spread of slavery."

Returning in 1853 to a daily preoccupation with politics, Bryant had written Dana, "I am grinding at the mill again, and find it the same dull work as ever." Despite his dependence on the newspaper for a living, he persisted in a hope that he might escape from journalism to a more strictly literary life. He continued to buy land in Illinois; in August 1854, after a visit to Princeton, he had acquired more than one thousand acres of prairie and timber, as well as town lots. But advertising revenues shrank in the 1854 recession, and Cullen went into debt to his brother John. In 1856 he told Dana, "If it had not been that I lost money about two years since I think I should have nearly got myself clear of the drudgery of my newspaper by this time." In poems of the period Bryant's longing for a quieter life is often intimated; it is manifest in the opening lines of "A Rain-Dream" (1854):

> These strifes, these tumults of the noisy world, . . .
> Oppress the heart with sadness. Oh, my friend,
> In what serener mood we look upon
> The gloomiest aspects of the elements
> Among the woods and fields!

Letters of this time show an almost obsessive concern with his gardens and farm and orchards, never so intense as when, after a winter in Manhattan or travel

abroad, he could get home to Roslyn. In January he requests Chinese sugar millet seeds from the Patent Office in Washington; in the midst of the most severe winter in memory he chafes to take cuttings and make grafts of rare varieties in his pear orchard; in September he writes of digging two hundred bushels of potatoes and harvesting more apples and plums than his family can consume. "My ambition," he tells Dana, "is to have a little fruit for all seasons—straw berries in their time, European grapes in a cold vinery, and pears from August to Easter. I am fussing a little with figs and hope yet to eat one of my own raising." He disclaims special skill as a gardener; it is Julia, he says, who "overwhelms me with everblooming roses, verbenas, and a dozen varieties of the clematis." But in more than one letter he discusses the niceties of floriculture, as when he advises Catharine Sedgwick on late-season blossoms and notes one in particular which Thomas Cole had brought him from Sicily a dozen years before: "I never gather it without thinking of him; it is sweet and fragrant, like his memory."

It was probably Bryant's salvation that he could dissociate his work as a poet from that as a publicist. "I am surfeited with politics in my vocation," he replied to John Bryant's urgent suggestion that he attend a Pittsburgh meeting in February 1856 at which a national Republican Party was to be proposed, "and when I go from home I cannot bear to carry them with me." John Bigelow thought that "this separation of his professional from his poetical life must be taken into account in any effort to explain the uniform esteem in which he was always held as a poet by his country people, while occasionally one of the least popular journalists." In the heat of Free Soil struggles Bryant's poems rarely reflected—even obliquely, as in "A Rain-Dream"—his weekday immersion in political contention. With scarcely an exception, those composed between 1849 and 1857 show his sensitivity to his natural surroundings at Roslyn and his deep affection for those who shared them with him: "The May Sun Sheds an Amber Light," "The Planting of the Apple-Tree," "The Voice of Autumn," "The Snow-Shower," "A Rain-Dream," "Robert of Lincoln," "The Twenty-Seventh of March," and "An Invitation to the Country." Yet the variety of activities to which he willingly devoted his evening hours and sometimes his weekends suggest he could not have suffered for long a quiet country retirement.

Biweekly meetings of the Sketch Club during the 1850s found Bryant almost always present when he was in town. From its start as a casual gathering-place for amateur and professional artists and writers twenty-five years before, the club had become the chief incubator for innovations in the city's cultural life. Though still meeting in rotation at its members' homes, it was host to many of New York's civic and professional leaders and notable visitors from abroad. Among those entertained during this period were American artists Frederick Church, Jaspar Cropsey, Felix O. C. Darley, Regis Gignoux, Horatio Greenough, Thomas Hicks, John Kensett, Louis Lang, Emanuel Leutze, William S. Mount, Thomas Rossiter, and Richard Upjohn. British artists included Alfred Derby, Samuel Laurence, and William Guy Wall. Prominent among writers were George Bancroft, Dion Boucicault, Fenimore Cooper, Ralph Waldo Emerson, Fitz-Greene Halleck, Oliver Wendell Holmes, and William Makepeace Thackeray. Publishers William Appleton and Nathaniel Currier came, as did clergymen Henry Bellows and Jonathan Wainwright, New York governors Washington Hunt and Horatio Seymour, ex-President Martin Van Buren, Judge Charles

P. Daly, and United States Attorney William M. Evarts. Businessmen included railroad presidents William B. Ogden and William H. Osborn, and foundryman Gouverneur Kemble.

Bryant portraits, and landscapes inspired by his poems, continued to appear at National Academy exhibitions. Asher Durand painted his friend in 1853, and after the picture had been engraved for popular subscription gave it as a New Year gift to Mrs. Bryant, who returned "a thousand thanks for making something pleasing of a face which so many have caricatured." Charles Loring Elliott's "Bryant" was shown in 1854, Daniel Huntington's in 1855, and Samuel Laurence's in 1857. In 1853 Durand painted a "Monument Mountain," and in 1854 "The Primeval Forest," suggested by "A Forest Hymn." That year his "Green River" appeared in Bryant's *Poems*, and in 1857 he supplied landscape illustrations for another edition. In 1854 Joseph Mozier sent Bryant from Rome a photograph of his statue *Truth*, which had been suggested by "The Battlefield."

Beginning with its first issue in 1855 *The Crayon*—first American magazine of art criticism—stressed Bryant's aesthetic affinity with the landscape artists. In the first of several articles on "The Landscape Element in American Poetry," his imagery was likened to that of such painters as Durand and John Kensett in its "majestic harmony," its "foreground passages . . . painted to your very feet," its "fine sense of harmony of color," and its subordination of parts to a single "great impression." Durand's first "Letter on Landscape Painting" urged art students to "Go forth, under the open sky, and list / To Nature's teachings," and in later essays he quoted other Bryant verses to make his points. Bryant's opinions on art were solicited; in 1854 his comparison of Cole and Durand in *Graham's Magazine* drew much approval.

Bryant's concern with civic affairs was evident in his frequent appearances as occasional speaker or chairman at public meetings, as well as in his editorial writing. Often addressing political or literary topics, he also spoke to such subjects as "The Improvement of Native Fruits," and "Music in the Public Schools." His early advocacy of a great public playground in New York City was never far from his mind. After the state legislature's authorization in 1853 of parks in both Jones's Wood—the site Bryant had first suggested—and the center of Manhattan Island, real estate and other interests had tried to constrict the parkland and dilute what was left with ornate squares and homes for the wealthy. Bryant fought their efforts; "a few speculators and land-jobbers," he declared in 1854, "begrudge the inhabitants of New York one park of seven hundred acres . . . by their persevering, under hand opposition." With further delay, he warned, "We shall soon be walled in on all sides with brick." He demanded no less than "the whole of Central Park, unencumbered and uncurtailed." When in 1856 the city acquired the land, undiminished, Bryant rejoiced in the *Evening Post* that landscaping could now proceed.

Although his verse composition during this period was slender, Bryant supervised the publication of several new collections, at home and abroad. The Appletons brought out editions in New York and London in 1855 and 1857. In 1854 an authorized volume was printed at Dessau, Germany, the first in a series of "Standard American Authors."

As 1856 drew to a close, Bryant might have feared for his country's future,

were it not, he wrote Dana, that "I rarely despair of any thing, . . . for it is not in my temperament to do so." Following the Republican defeat he pointed to the future obligations of his new party. "It is the condition of great achievements," he wrote, "that they are slowly accomplished. We have, in fact, but just entered on the threshold of this war." Leaving the Democratic Party cost Bryant at least one old and valued friend, for ex-President Martin Van Buren, angered by his defection, canceled his subscription to the *Evening Post*. But Bryant would have been solaced, certainly, to read words written in extenuation of his editorial course by Van Buren's longtime associate, former Attorney General Benjamin F. Butler: "I regard [Bryant] as one of the brightest luminaries of the age—not only in the department of letters but in that also of politics." And after a series of editorials in March 1857 in which Bryant attacked the constitutionality of Chief Justice Taney's dictum in the Dred Scott case denying the status of citizenship to free blacks, he could not have avoided satisfaction had he heard the comment of a Free Soil leader, John Curtiss Underwood: "What a glory it would be to our country if it could elect this man to the Presidency—the country not he would be honored & elevated by such an event."

Precarious as Frances Bryant's health had been for more than two years past, her husband became alarmed late in 1856 when her illness was diagnosed as rheumatic fever. When she seemed to have recovered somewhat by the following April, he was advised, following the custom of that time, to give her a change of air and scene. It was supposed that a long sea voyage might prove especially helpful, so they planned a slow passage across the Atlantic on a sailing packet, followed by about six months on the Continent, to be spent largely in Spain, which none of the Bryants had seen. So, with Julia Bryant and her cousin Estelle Ives, they left New York on May 2, 1857, on the *William Tell*, bound for Le Havre.

838. *To* Richard H. Dana

New York   July 5th   1853.

Dear Dana.

I *thought* you would write to me about these days and this morning I was glad to see your well-known hand on the back of a letter addressed to me. When I came to read it, however, there was something in the middle of it which made me wince. I always read over your letters two or three times, but now when I came to that part of your letter which speaks of old age I found myself hurrying over it, without giving myself time to perceive its full meaning, as a sick man bolts an unpleasant draught without taking its full flavor. I do not like to think of growing old, though I try to reconcile myself to it.

I am sorry to hear such bad news about your daughter. My wife had told me of her visit to New York, and of the ineffectual attempt she made to get her to make a little journey to her place on Long Island. I am sure she bears the sufferings of ill-health meekly; and I hope they will be yet mitigated to her. Your son made a most capital answer to Hillard's attack. The first thing I did in the *Evening Post* on my return was to insert the answer with a few words calling attention to it.[1] He will never have occasion to make another reply of that sort to any thing that Hillard may say in public. I would not exchange your son's chance of "success in life," as they call it, for his. There is something taking, after all in courage; if it be not a virtue in itself it is an ornament and grace to the virtues. A certain respect attends the bold and frank man even if he has scarcely another good quality, and a cowardly good man never wholly escapes contempt.

Your letter has one sign of youth in it. You make my absence from America as twelve months, when I was gone but seven months and a week. I went to London, to Paris to Marseilles to Genoa to Leghorn, to Naples, to Malta, to Alexandria and Cairo. From Cairo I went up the Nile in a government steamer as far as the first cataract, visiting the old temples and tombs on my way. From Cairo on my return I made a journey on a camel across the Shuren Desert to Syria. In Syria I saw almost every thing which travellers visit except the ancient town of Hebron. I bathed in the Jordan and in the Dead Sea—passed several days at Jerusalem, visited Nazareth, the Lake of Tiberias, Mount Carmel, Acre, Tyre, Sidon and Beyroot. From Beyroot I crossed Lebanon and Anti-Lebanon to Damascus, returning by way of Baalbec. From Beyroot a steamer took me to Constantinople; I returned to Smyrna and went in a steamer to Athens, crossed the Isthmus of Corinth to the Gulf of Lepanto and took a steamer for the island of Corfu, a beautiful spot where I passed two or three days. From Corfu I went directly by steamer to Trieste, and from Trieste to Venice—then, after a little stay, to look at the pictures and architecture of the Venetian artists I went by land, to Florence and Rome, and from Rome I came to

Marseilles by way of Civita Vecchia and the Mediterranean. I had ten or twelve days in Paris and a day in London from which I ran down to the Isle of Wight and there embarked in the steamer Humboldt for New York. I had a chilly passage of thirteen days and when I got to New York I seemed to find myself in a hot vapor-bath. In my journey across the desert I let my beard grow and found it so convenient to dispense with the trouble of shaving, that I allowed no razor to pass over my face till I got to New York. One of the clerks of our office was sent down to the steamer to look for me and did not know me when he had found me. I went down to my place on Long Island, put on a Turkish turban and gown, and had a long conversation in broken English with a young lady, our next door neighbor, who really thought that I was an Oriental.[2]

I am afraid, however, that I have come back no younger than I went. I am grinding at the mill again, and find it the same dull work as ever. Was it not singular that the same moment that I got your letter, another was put into my hands enclosing an article about the New York journalists from a Leipsic paper, in which I was described as "a little, dry, lean old man."?[3] The pill was sweetened by several compliments, but it had a bitter flavor, after all.

You are at Manchester [Massachusetts], I see. Why will you not come to my place as soon as you return, and prolong your summer for a few days in this climate? I have new walks in my woods, and a seat or two where you may rest in the shade, and two or three little openings that look out from the forest upon the water. Remember me most kindly to my former patient Charlotte[4] and to your sisters if they are with you.

Yrs very truly

W. C. BRYANT.

MANUSCRIPT: NYPL–GR ENDORSED: X Wm C. Bryant, July / 5th / 53, Ans. July 7th / X This in ans to mine of July [3rd?].

1. The earlier antagonism between Richard Henry Dana, Jr., and George Stillman Hillard (see Letter 757) had flared up again at the Massachusetts Constitutional Convention on June 23, when Dana made remarks about the conservatism of Boston businessmen which led Hillard to say in print, "The bread that he and I both eat comes from the business community of Boston, and . . . we should not strike at the hand that feeds us." In reprinting Dana's reply from the *Commonwealth*, Bryant commented, "Mr. George S. Hillard—the same on whom Mr. Webster, shortly after he changed his course on the slavery question, pronounced a public eulogium—made an attack upon Richard H. Dana, jun., the nature of which will be sufficiently understood from the reply which we publish." *EP*, June 29, 1853.

2. Bryant was accustomed thereafter to amuse his grandchildren by donning this costume (see *Life*, II, 74), which is now in the Bryant Homestead at Cummington. See illustrations.

3. Both letters and the newspaper article are unrecovered.

4. Ten years earlier Bryant had arranged effective treatment for Charlotte Dana's chronic eye trouble. See Letters 440, 448, 462.

839.   *To* Richard H. Dana

New York   July 11, 1853

Dear Dana.

I am very sorry that I was not apprized that your daughter was in town when I returned. My wife supposed that she had gone back to Boston long since, or she would have made a point of calling to see her, in one or two journeys she made to town. She came into New York with me on the Monday after I arrived, during the cool days that we had after that terribly hot weather in the midst of which I landed, and if we had thought there was the least chance of her being yet here we should have looked her up. Say to her that my wife is quite quite concerned that she should have appeared so careless about her.

Now as to Mr. Chilton and his scheme of getting a collection of autographs, "with an ultimate view to their publication in fac simile."[1] I have so many applications for my autograph, that I remember none of them except that of a Philadelphian, it was not Chilton, who did not pay his postage, and whose letter I did not answer—and even his name I have forgotten. Sometimes, but not often, they have asked me for autograph copies of some one of my poems. In that case, I send them a few lines of the peom, a stanza perhaps, and excuse myself from giving the rest by alleging want of time. It may be that I have sent Mr. Chilton something in this way, but if I have I have quite forgotten it. If he has any thing of the sort I am quite indifferent about what he does with it—he may publish it or burn it for aught I care. If publishing it will satisfy any body who wants my autograph, and will prevent his writing to me for it, it will do me a service.

I admit that it is not fair in him to obtain a manuscript for such a purpose without communicating his intention, and I have no recollection of any person whatever applying to me for any scraps of verse to be published in that manner. If such a request had ever been made to me, I think I should have remembered it on account of its singularity. Perhaps, however, Mr. Chilton, in confessing an "ultimate view to publication," meant merely that hereafter when we old gentlemen had dropped off he might give the collection to the world as a curiosity. Who he is, I do not know. If the case were my own, I should send him the verses, and let him know that in attempting to get them without informing me that he wanted to put them into a book he had behaved unhandsomely. A grave and gentle rebuke, such as you know how to give, might do him good.

You have, before this time, my answer to your first letter, and if I may judge from the tenor of your second,[2] must have been astonished at getting the answer so promptly. Don't draw my conduct into precedent, as the lawyers say, and expect me always to be so punctual.

Yrs very truly
W. C. BRYANT.

MANUSCRIPT: NYPL–GR DOCKETED: Wm C. Bryant, July / 11th / 53.

1. No such book has been identified.
2. Neither letter from Dana has been recovered.

840. *To* Daniel Coit Gilman[1]

New York   July 15, 1853.

Sir

Be pleased to make my best acknowledgments to the Committee of the Linonian Society of Yale College for the honor they have done me, by inviting me to attend their approaching celebration.[2] It will be impossible for me to have that pleasure, on account of other engagements.

I am, sir,
Yours respectfully
WM. C. BRYANT

MANUSCRIPT: John Hopkins University Library ADDRESS: Daniel C. Gilman Esq.

1. Daniel Coit Gilman (1831–1908, Yale 1852) was later (1856) the founder at Yale University of the Sheffield Scientific School, of which he became professor of physical and political geography. In 1872 he was made president of the University of California, and in 1875 first president of The Johns Hopkins University. Gilman apparently induced Bryant to join the American Oriental Society, and they corresponded on other matters at least until 1870.
2. This invitation is unrecovered.

841. *To* Julia S. Bryant

New York   July 18, 1853. Monday morning.

Dear Julia

I send enclosed a batch of letters for you. Yesterday we went to church and brought Miss Appleby home with us, and in the afternoon took her to Oyster Bay to see Mr. McCoun and his family.[1] It was the most delightful drive I have had this year; a cool atmosphere, and everything fresh with the shower of the night before. The road by which we returned— through a part of Buckram, was richly embowered all the way with trees, which seem to be twice as tall as they ever were before. Mrs. Holland we found ill and languid, Mr. McCoun well and smiling, Miss McCoun cordial, hospitable and *empressée* [gushing?]—I have not time to hunt up an English word. We returned by the crimson light of sunset and the white light of the moon.

Your mother, I fear will have a solitary week of it—so you must write. I send with this letter a parcel. My regards to Miss G.

Yrs. affectionately
W C BRYANT

MANUSCRIPT: NYPL–GR.

1. Miss Appleby is unidentified.

842.   *To* Eliza Robbins[1]

New York, July 19, 1853.

. . . We have had a great time with the opening of the Crystal Palace here, and the banquet the next day; they used to call such things dinners.[2] I went to neither of them. I like more space than you get at such places. I like air and elbow-room, as you find them about the Pyramids, as at Thebes and Baalbec. Do you know they are going to rail in the ruins of Thebes and Denderah and Edfou, and the other old remains in Egypt, and appoint guardians to take care of them? This will take off something from the effect of the ruins, but it will prevent them from being mutilated and disfigured. I meant to have astonished you with a long white beard—the growth of my chin while wandering in the East—and I sometimes asked myself the question whether Miss Robbins would know my face in such a costume. The day I went to Roslyn I put on a turban, a Turkish silk shirt and striped silk gown, which I got at Damascus, and a pair of yellow slippers, and held a fifteen minutes' conversation in broken English with Miss Hopkins, our next-door neighbor, she thinking all the time that I was a Turk. This is egotism, but I think you would have been interested in the people of the East if you had seen what I did. I do not believe in the theory that there is no chance of recovery for nations that have once degenerated. A great change is going on in the East; religious bigotry is wearing out, and by and by religious freedom will be enjoyed in the Turkish dominions to a greater extent than in any other country except the United States. The missionaries have already successfully introduced girls' schools in the north of Syria. Let the example be followed in other parts of the East, and the reign of barbarism will be over. . . .

MANUSCRIPT: Unrecovered TEXT (*partial*). *Life*, II, 76.

1. Unknown to Bryant, Eliza Robbins had died three days earlier at Cambridge, Massachusetts, at the age of sixty-nine. In an obituary in the *EP* on July 20 Bryant called her "one of the most eloquent and witty persons we have known; . . . her conversations were the delight of her friends." He concluded, "We pen these few words in profound sorrow at her loss."
2. The Crystal Palace Exhibition, of which Bryant's friend and associate Theodore Sedgwick III was president, opened on July 14 with a parade reviewed by President Franklin Pierce. *EP*, July 14, 1853.

843.   *To* Frances F. Bryant

New York   Wednesday   July 28, 1853

Dear F.

Julia was here on Monday and expects to go down tomorrow. I was half dead with dispepsia on Monday, but on going up town I called at Rand's and almost before I knew it Mrs. Rand had some blackberries for

me and her husband, and some cracked wheat boiled. The prescription cured me.

Yesterday Mr. Leupp called to ask me to go with him today to Edmonds's place in Westchester to pass the night.[1] As it rains now it is not likely that he will care to go. I am sorry that you have so bad a week for your carpenters. But perhaps they did not come.

Yrs ever

W. C. B.

MANUSCRIPT: NYPL–GR ADDRESS: Mrs. F. F. Bryant / Roslyn / Long Island ENDORSED: Rand / Cracked corn / & / boiled wheat / for / dispepsia.

1. The banker-artist Francis William Edmonds (487.1) had a home, "Crow's Nest," on the Bronx River in what was then southern Westchester County, New York.

844. *To* Frances F. Bryant

New York   August 11, 1853.

Dear F.

The carriage goes to Roslyn in the sloop Sarah Elizabeth. I was at the sloop this morning and was told by Captain Multy that it could be conveyed with perfect safety and convenience. He will take off the wheels. I suppose you will get it on Saturday morning. Captain Multy paid me the rent for one quarter $15—[1]

This morning I had a note from Mrs. Morton saying that she and Mr. Morton proposed to come to see you on Saturday. I think she will come with me in the boat. Georgine I hear, is still at Presqu' Isle.[2]

It is frightfully hot—90 and 99 yesterday in the shade, and quite as hot today.

Yrs truly

W. C. B.

MANUSCRIPT: NYPL–GR ADDRESS: Mrs. F. F. Bryant / Roslyn / Long Island.

1. Peter and James Multee operated the sloop *Sarah Elizabeth* between New York and Roslyn. Goddard, *Roslyn Harbor*, p. 24. One of them rented a cottage on Bryant's property. See Letter 861.
2. The Hudson River home, at Fishkill, of the late William Denning (1768–1849); see 376.1, 505.1. For the Rutledge Mortons and their daughter Georgine, see Letters 406, 412.

845. *To* John Howard Bryant

New York   August 11, 1853.

Dear Brother.

I think you promised my wife that you would come east this summer, partly for the purpose of seeing the Crystal Palace, and I believe some

others of our friends at Princeton were to come with you. In order that we may have the house clear for you when you come, I should be glad to know at what time, or about what time you expect to make the visit. Please to write if you have made up your mind and tell me how many of you there will probably be. I need not say that we shall all be glad to see you and the rest. Give my regards to your wife and sons.

Yours affectionately
W. C. Bryant.

Manuscript: Chicago Historical Society Address: John H. Bryant Esqre.

846.   *To* Frances F. Bryant

Friday   August 12 [1853]

Dear F.

I wrote to you yesterday that Mr. and Mrs. Morton would come out on Saturday and that our carriage would be brought to Roslyn in the sloop Sarah Elizabeth. I write now lest my letter should have miscarried.

We are now almost melted by the heat. This is the third very hot day and I hope tomorrow will be cooler.

There is another disaster on the Providence and Worcester Railroad.— Two trains dashed against each other and fourteen persons were killed—

Yours ever
W. C. B.

Manuscript: NYPL–GR Address: Mrs. F. F. Bryant / Roslyn / Long Island.

847.   *To* Frances F. Bryant

New York Monday August 15, 1853.

Dear F.

Fanny writes from Niagara a letter dated August 9th in which she says.

"My dear Mother. We went to Albany on Tuesday morning, dined there and rested a couple of hours, then went on to Utica for the night; the next day we reached Niagara before tea rather tired but much better. This afternoon we take the boat for Montreal. I have enjoyed myself very much here. We are on the Canada side; my room large and opening upon a piazza and looking directly on the falls. I only wish you were all here— Julia for the dancing which they have every evening in the concert room— you and father for fine fresh air and the views— Willie and Susan for new ideas. Minna is happy. No New Yorkers here— Mrs. Sarah Jenkins[1] the only person I ever heard of—I forget C. P. Cranch.[2] In hopes the chickens are all well—Love to all Yours affectionately—Fanny Bryant Godwin."[3]

I found on board of the steamer this morning Webster, who is to work this week for the Miss Mudges. You know he is a well-digger by pro-

fession, so I talked with him about our well to be dug between Mott's[4] house and Multy's. He says he can come after he has done working for the Mudges and attend to it. He thought it would be cheaper and in many respects better, to line it with brick uncemented than with stone, if the stone had to be dragged to the place. But when I talked further with him I found that he meant brick manufactured expressly for the purpose, in such a shape as to make them form a regular circle when laid. These are to be obtained from West Neck, but he promised to enquire this morning if there are any to be had at Glen Cove. If there are John might go down for them; if there are not it will be cheaper to use stone.

Webster will call on you this week, and tell you when he will come to dig the well. He owes me a trifle, and I think it will be best to employ him. Our men, as I told him, might work with him.

Yrs ever
W. C. B.

P.S. The weather is so cool that I shall expect you this week.

MANUSCRIPT: NYPL–GR ADDRESS: Mrs. F. F. Bryant / Roslyn / Long Island DOCKETED: My letter to my wife / — August 1853 —.

1. Unidentified.
2. Christopher Pearse Cranch (1813–1892), a Unitarian minister who was also a poet and painter, and a friend of Emerson's and of other Transcendentalists.
3. Bryant mistakenly wrote "Fanny Godwin Bryant."
4. Probably James Mott (1788–1868), member of an old Roslyn Quaker family, and a prominent Abolitionist. His wife, Lucretia Coffin Mott (1793–1880), was even more distinguished in the women's rights, as well as the anti-slavery, movements. Godwin, *Roslyn Harbor*, p. 16.

848.   *To* Frances F. Bryant

New York, Monday   September 19, 1853.

Dear F.

All our friends but John and his wife went in the half past eleven train to Springfield. John who has just left me goes in the Stonington boat at five o'clock this afternoon.[1]

Gourlie has just arrived[;] he called on me this morning looking in good health and spirits. Durand came with him and is off on a visit to his father.[2]

Yrs ever
W. C. B.

MANUSCRIPT: NYPL–GR ADDRESS: Mrs. F. F. Bryant / Roslyn / Long Island.

1. It is uncertain how many of Bryant's Illinois family, in addition to his brother John and wife Harriet, visited Roslyn that summer. See Letter 845.
2. John Durand had left Bryant and Leupp at Paris on June 2 for a visit to Italy with John Hamilton Gourlie (653.1). Bryant, "Diary, 1852–1853."

849. *To* Frances F. Bryant

New York   Thursday   Oct. 6   1853.

Dear F.

I have been perfectly well since I came out here. Fanny has had some troubles which I suppose she will tell you of.

This morning Mr. Leupp called with a watch and a note for Julia, which I send you by Mr. Willis. The note I suppose she will answer.

Did you hear that dreadful story of the end of Joanna Miller of East-hampton? She came to New York, took lodgings at a boarding house, some time last winter, and afterwards went under a feigned name to an hotel at the bottom of Broadway where she died. I will tell you the rest when I see you if you have not heard it.[1]

Yrs ever
W. C. B.

MANUSCRIPT: NYPL–GR.

1. No reference has been found to this case in the *EP*.

850. *To* G. S. McIntosh and others.[1]

New York   October 21, 1853.

Gentlemen.

I am sorry that you did not apply to a more expert grammarian, but I will answer your question. I have never doubted that the word "inexpert" relates to the pronoun "I," which would make this to be the construction:—"I, more inexpert, boast not of wiles" &c.

Yours respectfully
W. C. BRYANT

MANUSCRIPT: Iowa State Department of History and Archives
ADDRESS: Messrs. G. S. McIntosh, Justus White, E. C. Brooks, John Cowles.

1. The manuscript of this letter is accompanied by an undated newspaper clipping explaining its origin. Three young men had asked their Presbyterian minister John Cowles, of Olean, New York, for a gloss on the syntax of Moloch's statement to the fallen angels in Milton's *Paradise Lost* (II.51–53):

> "My sentence is for open Warr: Of Wiles,
> More inexpert, I boast not: them let those
> Contrive who need, or when they need, not now."

The learned clergyman decided that "inexpert" modified "wiles"; the boys referred it to "I." So all "agreed to refer [the question] to the great American Poet, William Cullen Bryant, and abide his decision."

851. *To* Henry R. Schoolcraft

New York   October 28, 1853.

My dear sir.

I thank you very much for the honor you have done me in dedicating to me the fourth volume of your work. In taking notice the other day of the North American Review, I took occasion to say what I thought of the ill nature and petulance of its attack upon you.[1] But works of merit, if they have already made, as yours have done, a favorable impression on the public, easily recover from any mischief which such criticisms can inflict. You are right therefore in pursuing your course without much attention to animadversions so manifestly cavilling and captious.

I am glad to learn that you are steadily occupied with your work and I anticipate from your labors, contributions to our stock of knowledge respecting the aboriginal inhabitants of our country, the value of which will be enhanced by every year that passes.

I am, dear sir,
very truly yours
W. C. BRYANT

MANUSCRIPT: HEHL ADDRESS: Prof. H. R. Schoolcraft.

1. In the course of a review of Volumes I–III of Schoolcraft's *Historical and Statistical Information Respecting the History, Condition, and Prospects of the Indian Tribes of the United States* (Philadelphia, 1851–1853), which appeared in the *North American Review*, 77 (July 1853), 245–262, its editor, Francis Bowen (1811–1890, Harvard 1833), called these "bulky and pretentious volumes" incomplete and unsystematic: "Indeed, we are compelled to believe that one of the principal objects in getting up the work was to afford a profitable job to the engravers." These volumes, ironically, were profusely illustrated with engravings from the work of the distinguished painter of Indian life, Seth Eastman (1808–1875, United States Military Academy 1829), twenty-six of whose paintings now adorn the Capitol in Washington! A brief notice of the *North American Review* for October 1853 appeared in the *EP* on October 15, but Bryant's comments on Bowen's attack have not been located. Nor is there a dedication to Bryant in the copy of Schoolcraft's fourth volume examined for the present edition; perhaps Bryant's reference is to an inscribed volume sent him by the author.

852. *To* George Bancroft

New York   November 9th. 1853

My dear sir.

A request has been made to me, to which I have readily yielded, that I should either speak with you or write to you concerning the wish of the Ingraham Testimonial Committee, to make you President of an Association which they are organizing.[1] They desire to place it under the auspices of the highest talent and character in our country. Not being able to command time for seeing you today I write this note.

You will perceive, on looking at the constitution of the Society, that its plan is a most liberal and comprehensive one. Many of the most estimable of that class whom the tyrannies of Europe have driven to seek refuge here are concerned in it. It proposes, among other things, to establish for that class and their friends, a Reading Room in this city, to serve as a common centre of information. Your acceptance of the office would do them a special service, and I hope—nay I am sure—that you will give the proposal at least a friendly consideration.[2]

I am, dear sir,
Yours very truly
WM. C. BRYANT.

MANUSCRIPT: MHS ADDRESS: Hon Geo. Bancroft.

1. In the summer of 1853 Duncan Nathaniel Ingraham (1802–1891), a naval officer in charge of the United States sloop *St. Louis*, had secured the freedom from detention on an Austrian warship at Smyrna, Turkey, of an Hungarian refugee and revolutionary associate of Louis Kossuth's, Martin Koszta, who had lived in the United States and had applied for American citizenship, and brought him to this country. Ingraham's action was supported by Secretary of State William L. Marcy, and widely applauded by Americans. On October 28 the *EP* reported an "Ingraham Testimonial Committee" which planned to organize a "Society of Universal Democracy," the object of which would be to "bring together and make better acquainted all men, whether Americans or foreigners, who desire the triumph of universal democracy." The society would implement its objective by opening a reading room and diffusing full information on parties, platforms, and other political matters, and by affiliating with like-minded organizations elsewhere.

2. It is uncertain whether Bancroft accepted this office.

853. *To* Cyrus Bryant

New York   Nov. 29, 1853.

Dear Brother.

I got the apples all safe, on the 22d, and am much obliged to you and John and Arthur for the trouble you have taken. The fruit, such of it as I have seen and tried is particularly excellent. Thank little Julia[1] in my name for the big pippin.

I would like you to write as soon as you get this and let me know whether I ought to give Kasson's Despatch the notice of which you speak. I paid $2.50 a barrel for the apples delivered at the office; of this $4.20 was for their conveyance on board the steamer Hendrick Hudson.

With regard to Cullen, I think it very uncertain whether the appointment of cadet at West Point can be got for him. If application is to be made to the Secretary of War I think it ought to be made soon, but I cannot flatter myself with having any influence in that quarter. He appoints the supernumeraries, I believe from what states he pleases. Your best way I think would be to get your application backed by Long John and as

many democrats in your part of the country as you can. If you then think that a letter from me to the Secretary would do you any good I would write it to accompany your application. As a general rule my letters have never done any body any good. Sometimes a formidable array of known party men has an effect. It would of all things be important, I think, to be early on the list of candidates.[2]

If in any thing I can help or advise you, I wish you would let me know.

Remember me kindly to your wife and children. Frances has been quite ill this month with an inflammation of the lungs, but is now again entirely well.

Yours affectionately
W. C. BRYANT

MANUSCRIPT: NYPL–BFP ADDRESS: C. Bryant Esqre.

1. Cyrus Bryant's elder daughter, then eight years old.
2. Cyrus's third son, Cullen, was then fourteen. He was graduated from West Point in 1864 and served in the United States Army until his retirement (as a Lieutenant Colonel?) in 1894. "Long John" is unidentified.

854. To Abraham Hart

New York   December 15, 1853.
My dear Sir.

It is now a year and some months—how many I do not recollect—since I have heard from you.[1] May I ask of you the favor to examine and inform me, how many copies of my poems you have printed since my last draft, and how much I am to draw upon you for?

Yours truly
W. C. BRYANT.

MANUSCRIPT: YCAL ADDRESS: A. Hart Esq.

1. See Letter 779.

855. To Ferdinand E. Field[1]

New York   Dec   19, 1853
My dear sir.

I am about to address you on a subject in which if I seem to inter-meddle officiously I hope you will at least ascribe my conduct to its right interest, and regard it as an error of good will.

It has grieved me to learn of a serious misunderstanding between you and your brother Alfred which threatens to become a permanent one. He has just read to me the correspondence between you, and asked my advice. I answered that I would write to you immediately.

The malady which caused your brother to make the proposals out of which the misunderstanding has arisen is a serious one as I have every reason to believe, and such as naturally to occasion much apprehension. During my absence last winter his friends here were in great concern about him. He left his place to which both he and his wife were exceedingly attached and came to pass the winter in town. In the spring he took what is the best course in all such complaints, he hired a house in the interior, beyond the influence of the sea-air, which is pernicious in such complaints. To have abandoned his home on Staten Island with which he had taken such pains and which he had made so pleasant, was the strongest proof that could be given of the necessity to which he was reduced. I saw him in July or August—I think the latter—free from cough in consequence of the change of air, and though the cough has since recurred, he is much stronger than before.

In regard to the correspondence which has taken place between you and him, allow me to observe that according to my experience letters are a fruitful source of misunderstanding. Owing to the inadequacy or imperfect choice of the expressions used—to the accidental introduction of things better left out, or the casual omission of things which should have been expressed, they often stand in need of verbal explanations to clear up the writer's whole meaning and to avoid offense. The several plans proposed by your brother in consequence of his ill-health, namely to come to Birmingham for a short residence, or to make a journey to the southwest of this country, were as he declares made with no idea of putting either of them in execution without your entire concurrence. If I had written the letters I might have accompanied them perhaps with a more explicit reference to your will in the matter—yet they were after all, in the strictest sense, but plans "proposed" to you and to which he desired your answer. When he found that you did not agree to them he yielded and pressed them no more. I understand from him that he has never desired nor ever meant to express a desire to change the business relations which exist between you, nor has any thought of taking any step which could be construed into a violation of the articles of partnership[2] without your consent. He has established such a reputation for probity and frankness during his long residence among us that I cannot help taking his word in this case.

The modification of the articles of partnership which you require, to protect you from the danger of such violations of it as you thought you had reason to apprehend, he is perfectly willing to make if minded it were any thing reasonable, and for my part I am sure you would not expect any other. The danger I suppose to be that he might absent himself without your consent from the business of the firm. He is perfectly willing, I have his authority to say, to stipulate against this by subjecting either party who shall transgress in this way to a penalty in money.

I am the more anxious that the difference between you should be amicably adjusted as I regard it greatly for the interest of you both that the firm's business should continue on its present footing. It is now I understand [uncertain?], and if it is [passed?] for a short time in the manner it has been, it seems likely that it will put both you and him at your ease. It is of more importance to him than to you inasmuch as he has a family, and this should make it—allow me to say so—more a matter of conscience on your part to deal liberally and magnanimously with him.

May I take therefore the privilege of an old friend in addressing one whom it has been a great satisfaction with me to regard as one of the most just and fair minded men I have known, to beg you, in the treatment of this unfortunate controversy to abate something even of what may seem to you strictly your right for the sake of continuing a business connection so important to the prosperity of you both—but particularly for the sake of avoiding the loss of good will between two persons whom I know and wish to esteem.

I have not communicated to your brother the contents of this letter except that part which relates to the modification of the partnership. With regard to that may I ask the favor of a reply—addressed either to him or me. If you should deem my interference impertinent you will not I am sure condemn my motive.

My wife sends her best regards.

Yrs truly
W C B.

MANUSCRIPT: NYPL–GR (draft) ENDORSEMENT: My letter to / Ferdinand E. Field / about his affairs with / his brother Alfred.

1. This letter apparently survives only in a much revised and barely legible draft.
2. In the hardware export business; see 384.1.

856.   To J. K. Furlong[1]

New York. January 9th   1854.

Sir

The first edition of what I now recognize as my poems appeared in the year 1821.[2] It consisted of The Ages, Thanatopsis and half a dozen others.

I am sir
respectfully yours
W. C. BRYANT.

MANUSCRIPT: Pierpont Morgan Library ADDRESS: J. K. Furlong Esq.

1. Unidentified.
2. Throughout his adult life Bryant consistently excluded from his poetic canon the boyish verses printed at his father's instigation in The Embargo (1808), and its

enlarged second edition (1809). He rarely mentioned these, and then only with impatience, even disgust. See *Life*, I, 75.

857.   *To* F. Hall[1]

New York   February 20, 1854.

Sir.

Mr. Bigelow has not yet returned from Hayti, but is expected soon; probably he will return about the first of next month.[2]

I am, sir,

respectfully yours,

W C BRYANT.

MANUSCRIPT: NYPL–Thomas F. Madigan Collection ADDRESS: F. Hall Esq.

1. Unidentified.
2. From November 1853 until March 1854 John Bigelow traveled in Haiti and the Virgin Islands, sending back letters to the *EP* describing social and political conditions there. Bigelow, *Retrospections*, I, 146–153; Nevins, *Evening Post*, p. 231.

858.   *To* Phillips, Sampson & Co.

New York   February 20, 1854

Gentlemen.—

Until I received your letter, I had not heard that Mr. Hart intended to sell the stereotype plates of which you speak.[1] I have not at present the contract at hand, but I consented to it because its terms were such as suited me better than any others, and I am disinclined to change them or give up any power they reserve to me over my own writings.

I am gentlemen

respectfully yours

W. C. BRYANT.

MANUSCRIPT: NYPL–GR (draft).

1. On February 18 the Boston publishers Phillips, Sampson & Co. had written Bryant that they noted that Abraham Hart of Philadelphia was advertising a sale of the stereotype plates of the octavo edition of his poems, and wondered what price Bryant would ask for their copyright. NYPL–GR. See Letter 854.

859.   *To* Fanny Bryant Godwin and Julia S. Bryant

New York   March 22, 1854.

Dear Fanny and Julia.

We got Fanny's note yesterday, at the very time when we expected you both back in the steamer.[1] I am glad to hear so good an account of your health and of the pleasant time you have had. By the time you return the severity of winter, I think will be over. At present we are almost in the midst of it. Eight or ten days of very bland sunshiny weather have been

succeeded by nearly a week of the very worst and most disagreeable we have had all the season—piercing cold winds, blowing off chimney tops and filling the air with hurricanes of dust, and in the midst of all I have the influenza.

The babies are all very well, and I hear them romping and laughing half the time in the other room. Your mother and myself have been out but little—but tomorrow we are invited to a great dinner at [Phalens?]. Tonight we shall, if I am well enough, go to the Academy of Design, which opens this day a small but very respectable exhibition of pictures, to close again on the 25th of April. The Academy has sold its building at a large advance in the cost.[2] We have an English artist here, a portrait painter, named Laurence, of whom a great deal is said and who has furnished a crayon drawing of Bancroft—a remarkably fine head.[3] Elliott has painted me for Dr. Griswold.—[4]

I could think of forty things more to tell you if I had time, but you will have it all when you get home. Tell Dr. and Mrs. [Samuel Henry] Dickson and the young ladies how much your mother and I thank them for the hospitality to you.

Yrs affectionately
W C BRYANT.

MANUSCRIPT: NYPL–GR.

1. Fanny and Parke Godwin, with Julia Bryant, were then visiting Savannah, Georgia, for Fanny's health. See Letter 861.

2. The National Academy then occupied galleries on Broadway, near Amity Street.

3. The English artist Samuel Laurence (1812–1864) worked in New York from 1854 to about 1861. *DAA*. His portrait of Bancroft was shown at the annual exhibition of the National Academy in 1855. Two years later he exhibited a likeness of Bryant there. *NAD Exhibition Record*, I, 286–287.

4. This portrait, by Charles Loring Elliott (1812–1868), commissioned by Rufus Griswold, was among those at the 1854 exhibition to which Bryant refers. *Ibid.*, 149.

860.   *To* Lyman C. Draper[1]

New York   March 25, 1854

Sir,

I am obliged to the Executive Committee of your [Wisconsin] State Historical Society for the honor they have done me. I perceive that among the ways, pointed out in the circular you have sent me,[2] of contributing to the objects of your association, the gift of books by authors is mentioned. I am preparing to get out a new edition of my poems, which I will endeavor to remember to send.

I am sir
respectfully yours
W C BRYANT.

MANUSCRIPT: The State Historical Society of Wisconsin ADDRESS: L. C. Draper Esq. / Madison / Wis.

1. See 388.1.
2. Unrecovered.

861. *To* Leonice M. S. Moulton

[New York, cMarch 1854]

... My wife, who has been indisposed lately with a severe cold which now affects her eyes, has commissioned me to answer your letter.

"I feel a strong wish to oblige her," was her remark, when she read your letter. But the cottage is already disposed of. It is taken by Miss Jerusha Dewey, sister of the Doctor; you may perhaps know her.

I do not know whether you would think of the house in which Wilson used to live. Captain Multy is about to move out of it, and nobody has yet taken it. I suppose you know that I have purchased it.[1] It is I believe a pretty comfortable tenement, and I should be happy to do any thing in my power to make it more so, to such a neighbor as you would be. If you would care to hear any thing more about it I would call upon you at any time tomorrow.

We are now alone at 53 Lexington Avenue. Fanny has been much afflicted with neuralgia this winter and three weeks since went off to Savannah with Godwin, where she has much improved in health. We sent Julia with her. It would be an act of charity in you to call on my wife. ...

MANUSCRIPT: Ridgely Family Collection TEXT (*partial*): Hoyt, "Bryant Correspondence (II)," 203–204.

1. This house may have been on a parcel of land adjoining Bryant's property which he apparently bought from John Tatterson on May 1, 1852. MS note in Bryant's handwriting, NYPL–GR.

862. *To* Leonice M. S. Moulton

[New York] Friday morning [cApril 10, 1854].

My dear Mrs. Moulton.

Yesterday afternoon I heard that Mrs. Dana[1] had been to look at the Willis Cottage and did not like it. One of her objections to it was the water in the cellar.

My wife has not been to Roslyn since she saw you. She has recently heard from her children in Savannah, and as they are expected to return in a few days this may make a difference in her plans and render the time of her going to Roslyn uncertain. I wish for my part I was there now. Mrs. Dana says the place is beautiful.

Yours truly
W. C. Bryant

MANUSCRIPT: NYPL–Bryant-Moulton Letters.

1. Probably the wife of Charles Anderson Dana (1819–1897), then assistant to Horace Greeley on the New York *Tribune*, and after 1868 renowned as the owner–editor of the New York *Sun*. Dana, an early friend of Parke Godwin's, soon established a summer home at Glen Cove, adjoining Roslyn.

863.   To Leonice M. S. Moulton

[New York] April 25, 1854.

. . . Coming in this morning from the country I find your note—I answer your questions in their order

Willis's store is yet open.

Cooking-stoves are to be had at two places in the village.

No stage-vehicle now runs from the Branch to Roslyn. I came in this morning in the stage coach and steamer by way of Flushing. They go twice a day.

Mrs. Bryant will be very happy to have Mrs. Moulton for her guest, of that I am sure. . . .

MANUSCRIPT: Ridgely Family Collection TEXT (*partial*): Hoyt, "Bryant Correspondence (I)," 68.

864.   To Rufus W. Griswold

New York   April 26, 1854.

My dear sir.

I have found at Roslyn a few of my brother's verses pasted in a scrap book. I have copied the accompanying ones, which I hope may answer your purpose.[1]

I am sir
Yours truly
W   C   BRYANT.

MANUSCRIPT: New York University Library ADDRESS: Dr. R. W. Griswold.

1. These particular verses of John Bryant's are unidentified, but they were probably among nine of his poems included by Griswold in the revised edition of his *Poets and Poetry of America* (Philadelphia, 1856), pp. 367–370.

865.   To Prosper M. Wetmore?[1]

New York, April 26, 1854

. . . I have seen the picture of Washington by Sharples. It is a fine picture and most interesting, inasmuch as it represents Washington in the vigor of manhood, some years before Stuart's portrait of him was taken. The countenance expresses thought, resolution, sensibility, and a high degree of physical energy.

I regard the discovery of this picture as an event of great importance.[2]

W. C. BRYANT.

MANUSCRIPT: Unrecovered TEXT: *The Sharples Portraits of Washington* ([New York? 1882?]), p. 8.

1. Though the recipient of this letter is not identified in the printed text, it seems to have been Prosper M. Wetmore (227.1, 523.1), who was for some time Chairman of the Executive Committee of the New-York Historical Society, and to whom Washington Irving wrote a similar letter. *Sharples Portraits of Washington*, p. 6; Vail, *Knickerbocker Birthday*, p. 90.

2. The British artist James Sharples (c1751–1811) came to Philadelphia about 1793, and later settled in New York with his wife and two sons, all artists. Although he died in New York, he had apparently taken with him on a visit to England two portraits of George Washington and one of the president's wife which he had painted soon after coming to this country, and there they came into the hands of a private collector. At Irving's insistence, one portrait of President Washington was brought to New York and exhibited at the New-York Historical Society in April 1854. On April 13 Irving wrote Wetmore, "Mr. Bryant and myself are equally anxious . . . that these portraits . . . shall not again leave the country." But, though all three pictures were later shown here, they remained permanently in England. One of the two George Washington portraits is in the National Portrait Gallery, London. *Sharples Portraits of Washington*, pp. 1–6, *passim*; *DAA*; *The Concise Dictionary of National Biography*, *Part I* ([London] Oxford University Press [1969]), p. 1187.

866.   *To* Fanny Bryant Godwin

[New York] Thursday May 4. [1854]

Dear Fanny.

I have a letter from your mother this morning. She says, "Mrs. Moulton is not willing to part with her sideboard. I wish you or Julia would find one at some of the auction stores."

I write to you because Julia may come out with me. If she stays in town let her see this letter, and if she goes out she might look in at some of the places where such things are sold.

Your piazza—the floor—was to have been painted yesterday if it did not rain—but as it did I presume the painting was postponed. Mrs. Moulton got to Roslyn on Monday and is busy getting together her things. She is to set somebody to clean house for her and go back to town for a servant. "This,["] says your mother ["]makes slow business for me."

Yours affectionately

W. C. B.

P.S. I send the letter—[1]

P.S. I have a letter from John. His son Henry—a fine youth—is dead— The disease was consumption—the death was unexpected.[2]— W. C. B.

MANUSCRIPT: NYPL–GR.

1. Frances Bryant's letter is unrecovered.

2. John Howard Bryant's son Henry died in April 1854, at nineteen years of age.

867. *To* Frances F. Bryant

[New York] Wednesday Morning   May 17th. 1854.

Dear Frances.

Dr. Dewey has written to me to ask that we and Julia will visit them in June. He will be down he says in about a fortnight, when he will talk with us about the visit. Not a word is said in the letter about Jerusha.

I heard yesterday morning that on Monday afternoon, four men, at work at the Clay Banks in Glen Cove were struck with lightening, one of them it was thought was killed.

On my bureau I find a bill from the Home[1] of $3.83 with a handkerchief of Julia's.

John Durand called yesterday to ask if I had any objection to his father's portrait of me being engraved. He wants another sitting.[2]

The children are all well.— Please let John come to the Branch for me on Friday afternoon. I saw Webster yesterday morning. He said there was a Dickinson—a well digger, near Glen Cove whom he would try to get for me.

Ever &c

W. C. B.

MANUSCRIPT: NYPL–GR.

1. Possibly the *Home Journal*, a popular magazine conducted since 1846 by George Pope Morris (194.6) and Nathaniel Parker Willis (309.3, 665.5).

2. At some time late in 1853 Asher Durand completed duplicate portraits of Bryant, taken in alternate sittings. One was done for the Bryant family and the other for the Century Association. In 1854 the artist's son John Durand undertook a subscription for an engraving of the portrait, Bryant's copy of which was sent to the studio of Alfred Jones (1819–1900) in Boston for that purpose. From March to July 1855, the art journal *The Crayon*, conducted by John Durand and William James Stillman (1828–1901), announced weekly that the engraving would soon be ready for subscribers. But it was not published until 1858, after the artist himself had given it finishing touches with the graver. *Catalogue of the Engraved Work of Asher B. Durand* (New York, 1895), pp. [3]–11; Daniel Huntington, *Asher B. Durand: A Memorial Address* (New York, 1887), p. 26; *EP*, November 13, 1878. See Letters 869, 878; Frances Bryant to Asher Durand, January 1, 1855, NYPL–Asher Brown Durand Papers.

868. *To* Richard H. Dana

New York   May 26, 1854.

Dear Dana.

I am just now going into the country to remain till Monday when I set out on a journey to Illinois with my wife.[1] It will not be easy for me to do what you ask in regard to the portrait of Coleridge, but I have put the thing into the hands of an intelligent young man in our office, who has promised that he will attend to it.[2]

I have not read the life of Hartley Coleridge of which you speak, but your recommendation makes me resolve to do so.[3]

As to my poems with illustrations; that is an idea of my bookseller's. There is I suppose, a class of readers—at least of book-buyers, who like things of that kind; but the first thing which my bookseller—it is Appleton—has promised to do, is to get out a neat edition of my poems in two volumes *without* illustrations. The illustrated edition is a subsequent affair, and though I have as great a horror of illustrations as you have, they will I hope hurt nobody. I am not even sure that I will look at them myself.[4]

What you say of the doings of our government I am sorry not to be able to disagree with. It seems to me that never was public wickedness so high-handed in our country as now.[5]

Remember me kindly to Charlotte of whose improved health I am glad to hear. For her throat I am satisfied that the air of the interior is the thing. Did you ever think of it[?] It is becoming a common remedy here.—

Yours ever
W. C. BRYANT

MANUSCRIPT: NYPL–GR DOCKETED: Wm C. Bryant / May 26/54 PUBLISHED (*in part*): *Life*, II, 78.

1. No other reference by Bryant to this trip has been found, but the Bryants apparently left New York for Princeton, Illinois, on May 29, and were home before the first of July. On June 10 Cullen bought from his brother John a parcel of land in or near Princeton. David J. Baxter, "William Cullen Bryant: Illinois Landowner," *Western Illinois Regional Studies*, 1 (Spring 1978), 11. See also Cyrus to Cullen Bryant, July 16, 1854, NYPL–GR.

2. Dana's letter which drew Bryant's responses herein is unrecovered.

3. Probably *Poems by Hartley Coleridge. With a Memoir of His Life by His Brother*, 2 vols. (London, 1851).

4. In 1854 D. Appleton & Co. of New York published an unillustrated edition of Bryant's *Poems* in two small volumes, and a larger illustrated edition, with "Seventy-one Engravings from Drawings by Eminent Artists."

5. The Kansas–Nebraska Bill, then on its way to passage by Congress, and the arrest in Boston of the runaway Anthony Burns under the Fugitive Slave Law two days before this letter was written, turned Bryant and the *EP* against the administration of President Pierce and the Democratic Party. In one editorial after another during the early months of 1854, Bryant had condemned what he called the "Nebraska fraud being perpetrated by Senator [Stephen A.] Douglas," which, he said, was "Africanizing the heart of the North American continent" (*EP*, February 9, 1854). On March 5 he charged, "The President has taken a course by which the greater part of this dishonor is concentrated upon the Democratic Party. Upon him and his administration . . . and upon the Democratic Party who gave the present executive his power of mischief, the people will visit this great political sin of the day." And, leaving for Illinois at the end of May, he concluded, "If it should become the custom of the long-flourishing republic of the United States to erect statues to the authors of the abolition of slavery, the first should be erected to the authors of the fugitive slave bill, and the second to the authors of the Nebraska bill." *EP*, May 29, 1854.

869. *To* Richard H. Dana

New York, July 14, 1854.

Dear Dana,

John Durand, a son of the artist was my fellow traveller in the East. The other day, I told him the substance of what you had written to me concerning his father's portrait of me. He expressed a wish that his father might have the benefit of your criticisms, and yesterday called and took a copy of that part of your letter which relates to the picture and said he should send it to his father in the country.[1]

Professor Channing, I hope, will publish his book. It would, I think, be well received. All his old pupils want it, of course, and all who have heard of him from his old pupils, so that it would be sure of an introduction to the public, and if only fairly introduced it would be pretty sure to make its own way.[2] I do not know that Phillips and Sampson are much in the way of publishing books of this kind. Ticknor & Fields, and Little Brown & Co. are, I think, more so. In our city Appleton would be as good a bookseller as he could have. Putnam was a little crippled for a time, but he is now, I believe cautious, and as a matter of course does not publish very extensively.

I have two editions of my poems in press, one in two volumes, and the other a cheap one, in one volume. This morning I have corrected the last page of the first volume. As to the illustrated edition, it is to be slow in making its appearance, and I give myself no trouble about it. It is, I believe, to have wood engravings.

Remember me most kindly to your daughter and sisters. If you do not come this way in a few months I shall be tempted to come to Boston to have a look at you again. . . .[3]

MANUSCRIPT: NYPL–GR DOCKETED: Wm C. Bryant, July / 14/54.

1. Presumably Dana had seen Asher Durand's portrait of Bryant in Boston, where it had been sent for engraving. See 867.2. Dana's letter is unrecovered.
2. Edward Tyrell Channing's *Lectures Read to the Seniors in Harvard College* was published posthumously in 1856. See 54.1; 749.4.
3. Conclusion and signature missing.

870. *To* Estelle Anna Lewis[1]

[cJuly 20, 1854]

. . . I am fond of both the painting of Cole and Durand. Cole has the bolder hand, and, I think, worked with more freedom. He was earlier a painter than Durand, and to this owed, I have no doubt, much of that vigor and confidence which is apparent in all his works. In this respect, however, Durand is constantly improving, as his later works have the most strength. Cole sought always to infuse into his paintings some great moral

or religious idea. I am not certain that he did not sometimes make this design too obvious. This is never the case with Durand, who seems to love art more for her own sake. They were both close observers of nature—men of great industry and an accurate hand. Durand, in general, imitates nature with truest paint; Cole, with the same power, did not always deem its exercise to the same extent necessary or even ancillary to his design.

Both Cole and Durand hold a place among the first landscape painters of modern times; indeed, I think, among the first of any time. If I were to be asked what other painter in that department I would prefer to Durand, I should say—*no one*. There are no landscapes produced in any part of the world which I should more willingly possess than his. . . .

WILLIAM C. BRYANT

MANUSCRIPT: Unrecovered TEXT (*partial*): E. Anna Lewis, "Art and Artists of America," *Graham's Magazine*, 45 (October 1854), 322.

1. Estelle Anna Blanche Robinson Lewis (1824–1880), a poet and magazine writer, had written Bryant on July 11, 1854 (NYPL–GR),

I am writing, for Graham's Magazine, a series of critical and biographical essays. Durand and Cole will be my next subjects. May I ask you to give me, in the form of a letter, some opinions of the artistic merits of these eminent landscapists?

It has always seemed to me that there was much in common between yourself and these gentlemen, and that anything you might be pleased to say of their genius would have the warmth of kindred sentiment.

871.   *To* John Bigelow

[New York] Friday, July 21. [1854]

I gave the first part of *Blair's* lucubrations as a leader today with some slight changes for the sake of perspecuity.[1] As you take the wheel on Saturday,[2] I have left the work of editing the second article to you as you will perceive.

W. C. B.

MANUSCRIPT: NYPL–GR DOCKETED: W C Bryant.

1. These "lucubrations," written perhaps by Francis Preston Blair (1791–1876, Transylvania 1811), editor and politician and a strong opponent of the Kansas–Nebraska Bill, were apparently two unsigned articles appearing as leading editorials in the *EP*: "The Nullifiers in the Ascendant" (July 21), and "How the Nullifiers Passed the Nebraska Bill" (July 22).

2. The Bryants were about to visit Cummington; see Letter 872.

872.   *To* Frances F. Bryant

New York   Tuesday   July 25, 1854.

Dear Frances.

I have a letter from Ellen[1] in which she says.

"The stage that passes through this place leaves Hinsdale Tuesdays Thursday and Saturdays, after the first trains from Springfield and Albany arrive, and reaches Cummington about noon. If you can leave New York Wednesday morning, by the Harlem railway, you will reach Hinsdale at night and can take the stage the next morning; or if you prefer, you can take the evening boat to Hudson, and then the railroad to Hinsdale by way of Chatham, reach[ing] this place at noon. I shall look for you on Thursday noon, and if I do not see you then, shall certainly expect you on Saturday."

I have written to Ellen to expect us on Thursday week.

Do not forget to send for my shoes, and make Henry attend to the well-cover.

Write to me how Miss Dewey gets on. I enclose a letter for her and one for you.

Yours ever
W. C. B.

MANUSCRIPT: NYPL–GR.

1. Bryant's niece, Ellen Mitchell (738.1), then living in Cummington.

873. *To* William L. Marcy[1]

New York   July 25, 1854

Dear Sir.

I write this, not to ask a favor, but to make a suggestion. Mr. E. Felix Foresti[2] of this city was sometime since appointed American Consul at Genoa, but the Sardinian government refused to recognize him. He has since visited Washington, where he was kindly received by the President who assured him that the administration intended yet to do something for him.

I wish to say that the fulfilment of this intention, while the recollection of Mr. Foresti's rejection by the Sardinian government is yet fresh in men's minds would be creditable to the administration. The world would then see that when our government takes up a worthy man it does not drop him because some European king takes a fancy to object to him. It seems to me that the intention expressed by the President was dictated by a proper regard to national policy and a feeling of what was due to our national dignity.

I have known Mr. Foresti ever since he came to this country, which is about eighteen years. He is a man of more than common merit, highly endowed both by nature and education, and of a solidity of judgment not usual among political exiles. He was bred to the law and held a judicial situation in his native country. He would make a good figure as Charge to one of the South American republics, or in a semi-judicial post or any

situation in which a good knowledge of the general principles of law, or
of the law of nations was required.

I am sure that almost any other government would take the course
which the President has intimated to Mr. Foresti his design to take, and I
am equally certain that it would be generally applauded.[3]

I am, sir,

very respectfully

Your obt servt,

W. C. BRYANT.

MANUSCRIPT: LC ADDRESS: Hon Wm L. Marcy.

1. William Learned Marcy (1786–1858, Brown 1808), a Van Buren Democrat, and
a former governor of New York and United States senator, served as Secretary of War
under President Polk, 1845–1849, and as Secretary of State in the Pierce administration,
1853–1857.

2. Eleutario Felice Foresti (1793–1858), after being exiled from Italy as a member
of the secret revolutionary society, the *Carbonari*, came to the United States in 1836.
He was professor of Italian at Columbia and New York universities from 1839 to 1856,
and apparently took office as United States consul at Genoa in the year of his death.
See 559.3.

3. Marcy replied to this letter on August 2 (NYPL–GR), "The President was informed some time ago that Mr. Foresti was willing to take the office of Consul at Constantinople & his name was sent to the senate for that appt. The nomination is now
pending before that body. I know of no reason why it has not been acted on."

874.   *To* George Bancroft

New York   July 26, 1854.

Dear Bancroft.

Mr. Foresti, whom you know very well, is a little uneasy that a promise
made him is not yet fulfilled. After he had been appointed Consul at
Genoa, and the Sardinian government had refused to recognize him as
such, he went to Washington and was told by the President that he should
have some other office. The grace and effect of such a thing consists in
doing it in season, while the occasion of it is yet remembered. I have written to Mr. Marcy about Mr. Foresti's case, and the good effect of showing
a little spirit &c.

I do not know whether you ever meddle in such matters. If you do,
Mr. Foresti would take it as a great favor, should you be inclined to say to
the President or to any one who has influence with him a word in his behalf.[1] Besides, you would have the pleasure of obliging a man of great
merit. Mr. Foresti would fill with credit any station which requires a
knowledge of the law of nations, or of the principles of general law. He is
well endowed both by nature and education and is of a more solid cast of
mind than most political exiles.

My regards to Mrs. Bancroft and to your sons if they are with you.

Yours very truly
W. C. BRYANT.

MANUSCRIPT: MHS.

1. Since his retirement as ambassador to Great Britain in 1849, George Bancroft had been living in New York and writing successive volumes of his *The History of the United States from the Discovery of the Continent*, of which six volumes had been published by 1854. "Although personally unconcerned with active politics during his fifties," writes his biographer, "Bancroft kept close watch of the fortunes of his [Democratic] party." Russell B. Nye, *George Bancroft: Brahmin Rebel* (New York: Knopf, 1945), p. 203. On August 14 Bancroft replied from Newport (NYPL–BG) that he shared Bryant's good opinion of Foresti, and would help in any way he could.

875. *To* Julia S. Bryant

[Roslyn, *c*July 30, 1854]

Dear Julia

Ellen says that the stage leaves Hinsdale on Mondays Thursdays and Saturdays in the morning for Cummington. If we leave New York on Wednesday we can reach Hinsdale that night, and setting out for Cummington the next morning can reach it on Thursday noon.

You must be ready therefore on Wednesday next to go on with us to Hinsdale. It is possible that your mother will choose to leave New York on Tuesday and pass the night at Barrington; but if she should not and we should leave this place on Wednesday we shall want you to be ready and at the station with every thing prepared to go on with us.

Yours affectionately
W   C   BRYANT

MANUSCRIPT: NYPL–GR.

876. *To* Julia S. Bryant

Roslyn, Monday, July 31, 1854.

Dear Julia.

Your mother does not go to town this morning as she expected, and it is possible may not go to day. If she should not she will not be at Great Barrington tomorrow.

She was attacked yesterday with a diarrhoea, attended with considerable debility. If she is better at noon, she may, however, go to New York to day. If not better, you may not see her this week. There is nothing alarming in the complaint, but it will be imprudent to journey till she is stronger.

At all events I wish you to be ready and at the station, on Wednesday prepared to join us, though it is possible we may not come.

Miss Dewey is getting on famously, and looks better than before she was ill.

Remember me kindly to Mrs. Ives and Estelle and all our friends.

Affectionately

W. C. BRYANT

MANUSCRIPT: NYPL–GR.

877. *To* an Unidentified Correspondent

SARATOGA CONVENTION.

New York, Aug. 5th, 1854.

To the Hon.

Sir.

The enclosed Circular will advise you of the object of the *Peoples'* *Convention*, to assemble at *Saratoga Springs, on the 16th of August*, and of the parties with whom the call originated.[1] It appears to be warmly responded to throughout the State, and there is reason to anticipate an assemblage of Delegates representing all parties and shades of opinion, whose deliberations, if wisely conducted, can hardly fail to have an important bearing upon the political destinies of our country.

We know, Sir, that you are not insensible to the magnitude of the issues, which the repeal of the Missouri Compromise, ending the confidence essential to all honorable union, has forced upon the citizens of the free States; and we believe that you appreciate, as we do, the grave occasion which the passage of the Nebraska Act presents for consultation, conciliation and mutual concession between those who, having long been, politically, opponents, are brought near together by the wanton outrage upon rights and principles which they cherish, not as whigs nor as democrats, but as the common heritage of American citizens.

Thus knowing and believing, we beg leave respectfully and frankly to ask what in your opinion will be the wise and proper course to be pursued by the Convention, to ensure among our citizens (who already heartily agree in their judgment upon the bad faith and the insolent aggression of the slave power, aided by northern allies) such an effective unity of action, as will serve to check its extension, rescue the Federal government from its control, and restore the Free States to their rightful position in the Federal Union.

Touching the manner in which this unity of action is to be effected, there will be differences of opinion, and perhaps no slight practical difficulties, resulting from olden ties and associations, which your wisdom and experience (looking beyond the immediate concerns of the day and of the State to the future conduct of the Federal Government, involving the happiness and the honor of our republic,) may teach us successfully to avoid and overcome.

We trust, therefore, that you will be kind enough, at as early a day as you shall find convenient, to favor us with your views on this grave sub-

ject, simply for our own guidance, if you shall so limit them, or otherwise, as we should prefer, with permission to use them as we may think proper.

We have the honor to be, Sir, with great respect,

Your fellow citizens,

[Signed]   JOHN JAY

HENRY B   DAWSON

WILLIAM C   BRYANT

J   M   BOYD

Committee of Correspondence.[2]

P.S. Since writing above, we have resolved to hold a Mass Meeting in the Park, on TUESDAY, the 8th inst. at 6 o'clock, P.M. when we shall feel ourselves both honored and gratified by your presence.[3]

We trust, under any circumstances, that you will favor us with an early reply to this communication, addressed to JAMES M. BOYD, 95 Maiden Lane, N.Y.

MANUSCRIPT: (printed letter): Illinois State Historical Library.

1. On May 25, 1854, President Pierce signed into law the Kansas–Nebraska Bill, which repealed the Missouri Compromise of 1820 by opening to slavery the western territories north of the 36° 30′ parallel from which it had previously been barred. Furor among anti-slavery northerners in both major political parties hastened the dissolution of party loyalties, as Democrats and Whigs splintered into "fusion" and "anti-Nebraska" and "republican" committees and conventions. In July "Republican" parties were organized in Michigan and Wisconsin.

Between January and May Bryant had repeatedly warned against passage of the Kansas–Nebraska Bill, proposed by Democratic Senator Stephen A. Douglas of Illinois. On February 27, under the caption "The Duty of the People," he remarked that "Not a word, uttered against the contemplated enormity of the Nebraska bill, is superfluous." Now, in August, he joined anti-slavery Whigs and radical Democrats in planning an "Anti-Nebraska" convention at Saratoga Springs, New York, called to organize a new party and choose a fusion platform and nominees for state offices. The circular mentioned in this letter is unrecovered.

2. John Jay (1817–1894), grandson of the statesman and chief justice of the same name (1745–1829), was an anti-slavery leader and social reformer. Henry Barton Dawson (1821–1889), an English-born New York businessman and historian, later edited *The Historical Magazine*, a forerunner of the *American Historical Review*. James M. Boyd was a hardware merchant doing business at 95 Maiden Lane. *Rode's New York City Directory for 1850–1851*, p. 58.

3. At this meeting of several thousand people it was adopted as a "permanent principle that slavery shall be no longer allowed in an existing territory or new state." With Bryant one of those presiding, delegates, including his fellow committee members, were chosen for the Saratoga convention. *EP*, August 9, 1854. On August 15 the *EP* announced its own platform for the meeting: "No More Slave States." But that meeting was adjourned, after much discord, to await the result of the regular Whig convention; when it reconvened on September 26 at Auburn, New York, its delegates endorsed the Whig state ticket. Of this action the *EP* commented the next day that a statewide anti-slavery sentiment would assure a Whig victory on that single issue; thus the Democrats would be supporting "the representatives of great heresies in our national politics, and a system of waste and corruption in the administration of our state affairs."

878.   *To* Richard H. Dana

New York   August 11, 1854.

Dear Dana.

Young Durand was in my office, this morning with a letter from our modest friend, his father. He copied from it, at my desire, the enclosed passage, occasioned by your remarks on his portrait of me.[1]

With regard to that portrait I omitted to say in my last, that the expenses of the engraving had been, I believe, fully provided for by subscription here, before the picture was sent to Boston. It was sent for because the engraver wished to begin his work.

Yours ever
W. C. BRYANT.

MANUSCRIPT: NYPL–GR DOCKETED: Wm C. Bryant / Aug. / 11/54.

1. Neither Asher Durand's letter nor the passage from it has been recovered.

879.   *To* Orville Dewey

New York, August 15, 1854.

. . . I sometimes almost wish my place was sold, more on my wife's account than any other; but I am not sure that she would get well any faster anywhere else than there, where we have a pretty genial climate, and seabathing, which I think does her a great deal of good. The twelve hours' railway travel (to Sheffield) of which you speak affrights me; and then your spring is so long in coming, and your winter pounces upon the fields and woods in such a hurry. I think we must stay in these latitudes, though the bribe you offer us to go north is very tempting. Why cannot that series of papers which is to make the world stare be written without my coming to Sheffield?[1] Try number one, and enjoy their astonishment from your lurking-place. . . . My brother John is here, and I, the printer, am putting in type for him a little volume of his poems.[2] I hope there is nothing vulgar or mechanical in being a printer. Horace Walpole, you know, the most fastidious of men, had a press at Strawberry Hill, and printed there the Odes of Gray. . . .[3]

The world within ten or twenty years past has not been growing any better than I can see, although my excellent neighbor, Joseph Curtis, whose cheerful views of things are a great support to me, sees differently.[4] One reason why the world makes no more progress in goodness is that we all begin life at the same point; we all set out from the pure natural man at our birth. People overlook that fact, it seems to me, when they talk of the progress of the age, and imagine that the son of a good wise man is, as soon as he is born, as virtuous and enlightened as his father. . . .

MANUSCRIPT: Unrecovered TEXT (*partial*): *Life,* II, 77–78.

1. Dewey had written Bryant from his home in Sheffield, Massachusetts, on May

13, 1854, "Will not you and Mrs. Bryant come to see us in June? Do. It is a long time since I have sat on a green bank with you, or anywhere else. I want some of your company, and talk, and wisdom. The first Lowell lecture I wrote was after a talk with you here, three or four years ago. Come, I pray, and give me an impulse for another course. . . . I shall be down in New York on business a fortnight hence, and shall see you, and see if we can't fix upon a time." *Autobiography and Letters of Orville Dewey, D.D.*, ed. Mary E. Dewey (Boston, 1884), pp. 233–234. Dewey's twelve lectures before the Lowell Institute in Boston were published in 1864 under the title, *The Problem of Human Destiny; or, The End of Providence in the World and Man.*

2. *Poems, by John Howard Bryant* (New York: D. Appleton, 1855).

3. Horace Walpole, fourth Earl of Orford (1717–1797), operated a private printing-press at Strawberry Hill, his home in Twickenham, England, where, in 1757, he published the two Pindaric odes which established Thomas Gray (1716–1771) as the leading English poet of his day.

4. Joseph Curtis (1782–1856), an improvident manufacturer and a practical philanthropist among New York's youth and underprivileged poor, was at various times director of the House of Refuge, superintendent of public primary schools, and a founder of the Public School Society. He lived in Hempstead not far from Bryant's Roslyn home. See Edward C. Mack, *Peter Cooper, Citizen of New York* (New York: Duell, Sloan and Pierce [1949]), pp. 132–134; Catharine Maria Sedgwick, *Memoir of Joseph Curtis, A Model Man* (New York, 1858), *passim*; *Life*, I, 336; 942.1.

880.   *To* Frances F. Bryant

[New York] Thursday   Aug   24th   1854

My dear Frances.

I send you two letters and enclose one for Miss Dewey.

Bigelow will it is expected, be in town today; but I cannot come out tomorrow as there will be many things to talk over and arrange,—so at least I think

Yours   ever
W   C   B.

Willis called yesterday to tell me the news.—

MANUSCRIPT: NYPL–GR.

881.   *To* Benson J. Lossing[1]

New York   Aug. 25th, 1854.

My dear sir.

I have just returned from a journey,[2] and find your kind letter.[3] It will not be possible for me to accept the obliging invitation it contains. I never deliver public lectures, and if I did, my time is now so much occupied that I could not write one for your Lyceum.[4]

I am, sir,
very respectfully,
Yours.
W. C. BRYANT

MANUSCRIPT: Cornell University Libraries ADDRESS: B. J. Lossing Esq.

1. Benson John Lossing (1813–1891), a wood engraver and popular historian, was associated from 1846 to 1869 with William Barritt in the engraving business in New York City. In 1850–1852 he published a *Pictorial Field Book of the Revolution*, and in 1866 *The Hudson from the Wilderness to the Sea* (reprinted in facsimile in 1972), profusely illustrated with his own drawings.

2. Perhaps to visit Orville Dewey; see Letter 879.

3. Unrecovered.

4. Lossing, a member of the New-York Historical Society, may have extended this invitation for its lecture series, in which he participated. Vail, *Knickerbocker Birthday*, pp. 135, 345.

882.   *To* John Howard Bryant

New York   September 1st, 1854.

Dear Brother.

I wrote you yesterday; but your letter of the 28th of August having this moment arrived[1] I must give you the trouble of reading this. As to the building of another house on the lot where my brick house stands,[2] it is out of the question at present. I have no money to spare, not a penny. The times are what we call hard in New York and threaten to become harder yet and the engagements into which I have entered will take up all my means and require strict economy besides.[3] So I think both the plans— that of building a kitchen to the old house, and that of building a new house on the same lot must stand over. I cannot even consider them at present.

Yours truly,

W   C   BRYANT.

MANUSCRIPT: WCL ADDRESS: Jnº H. Bryant Esq.

1. Neither letter has been recovered.

2. Built in 1846; see Letter 597.

3. On May 15, 1854, Bryant and Bigelow had bought from their partner, Timothy Howe (503.2), his three-tenths share of the *EP* properties, committing themselves to pay him $6,685 on demand, and a total of $15,000 within five years. At the same time they took into a full one-third partnership Isaac Henderson, who had joined the *EP* in 1839, first as clerk and later as bookkeeper (Nevins, *Evening Post*, pp. 237–238). Though nominally liable for his partners' debt to Howe, it seems likely that Henderson was unable to pay it for the time being. In fact, on November 1, 1854, Cullen gave John Bryant a demand note at seven percent for $1,450, which suggests that John helped him to discharge his first commitment to Howe on the 15th of that month. Note in Bryant's hand, NYPL–GR. See the MS record of semi-annual dividends of the *EP*, 1828–1849, with a record of shareholders and stock transfers, NYPL–GR.

883.   *To* Henry Kirke Brown

[New York] Tuesday   September 12, 1854

Dear Brown

I wrote you a note this morning which by mistake was sent to the

postoffice to let you know that Dr. [Samuel Henry] Dickson and his wife of Charleston are with us at Roslyn.

Will you and Mrs. Brown come and see them and us. Come on Friday or Saturday and stay as long as you can.

Yours truly,
W. C. BRYANT

MANUSCRIPT: Henry Kirke Brown Papers, Yale University Library.

884. *To* Frances F. Bryant

New York   Sept. 26. 1854.

Dear F.

I put two letters into the post office for you this morning.

Mrs. [John] Gibson will not come out this week. She is at Lake Mahopac and is to stay there another week. The Dicksons are at Hastings.

Mrs. Ida Pfeiffer[1] called on me this morning—a little thin woman, with a very dark complexion and pretty good teeth. She wanted to see the public institutions and I gave her letters[2] to Simeon Draper[3] and Joseph Curtis.

Do not look for the key to Miss Dewey's house, for it is in my pocket.

Yrs ever
W. C. B.

MANUSCRIPT: NYPL–GR.

1. Ida Reyer Pfeiffer (1797–1858) was a widely traveled German whose published accounts of her journeys were translated into English and published in numerous British and American editions. Before visiting the Near East in 1852–1853 Bryant had probably read her *Visit to the Holy Land, Egypt and Italy* (London, 1852).

2. Unrecovered.

3. Simeon Draper (1804–1866) was a New York Whig politician and later a supporter of the Seward–Weed faction in the Republican Party. In 1864–1865 he was Collector of Customs for the Port of New York. For Joseph Curtis, see 879.4.

885. *To* Frances F. Bryant

New York   October 11, 1854   Wednesday morning.

Dear Frances.

I have this moment opened a letter from Dr. Dickson, dated October, the day not given but the postmark is the 8th. He found his daughters Sarah and Bell quite sick but the day he wrote they were convalescent. The child's nurse was attacked the same morning and the child had the hooping cough.

The whole city is sad at the terrible disaster which has befallen the steamer Arctic, and, it is supposed, another vessel. Gourlie the first mate, it is possible, may have been saved.[1]

Do not forget—if you have not attended to it, to let Wright[2] have his money.

Yours ever
W. C. B.

P.S. I hear nothing yet from Mr. Felt[3] and Dr. Dewey—

MANUSCRIPT: NYPL–GR.

1. Word had just reached New York that the American steamship *Arctic*, on which Bryant and Leupp had traveled to Liverpool in November 1852, had sunk with great loss of life in the North Atlantic Ocean on September 27, after colliding with another ship in the fog off Cape Race, Newfoundland. Among those presumably lost, besides John Gourlie's brother, the chief officer, were the wife, son, and daughter of the ship's owner, Edward Knight Collins (794.3). See Letter 801; *EP*, October 11, 14, 16, 1854.

2. Probably a Roslyn workman.

3. Probably Rev. Joseph Barlow Felt (1789–1869, Dartmouth 1813), president of the New England Historic Genealogical Society, and best known for his *Ecclesiastical History of New England* (1851, 1862).

886. *To* Julia S. Bryant

New York   Wednesday morning   October 18th 1854.

Dear Julia

Your mother is rather better, though she still complains of her stomach.

Susan is getting on very well with the house. She has lots of women to help her.

We hear nothing of Agnes Maxwell.[1] Godwin is detained here longer than he expected, by some matters of business, so I send this by mail.

Yours affectionately
W   C   BRYANT.

MANUSCRIPT: NYPL–GR.

1. See 812.2.

887. *To* P. P. Wells[1]

New York October 24, 1854.
Office of the Evng. Post.

Dear Sir.

The bearer Mr. Skidmore is a reporter for the Evening Post.[2] I am desirous of obtaining some report of the doings of the coroner's jury called, as I understand in the case of a patient of yours, in which I suppose the Coroner goes beyond the proper functions of his office. Can you do any thing to help him to the notes of the examination as far as it has proceeded? If so you will much oblige me by doing so and also by informing him as to the time and place to which the inquest is adjourned. It is my

object, if the proceedings be of the nature I suppose, to make them the subject of some animadversions.[3]

Yours respectfully
W. C. BRYANT

MANUSCRIPT: UVa.

1. Dr. Wells was a founding member in 1849 of the Hahnemann Academy of Medicine, a development from the New York Homoeopathic Society, of which Bryant was a past president. See 420.6; Leonard Paul Wershub, *One Hundred Years of Medical Progress: A History of the New York Medical College Flower and Fifth Avenue Hospitals* (Springfield, Illinois: Charles C. Thomas [1967]), pp. 16, 43.

2. Skidmore has not been further identified.

3. On October 7 a twelve-year-old Brooklyn child, Agnes Lotimer, had died of convulsions after having been under homoeopathic treatment for two months by Dr. Wells. Though an autopsy performed by two other physicians found no cause for suspicion, the Brooklyn coroner, one Dr. Ball—an allopath—called a jury to inquire whether Wells was guilty of malpractice. Held intermittently for three weeks and reported in detail in the *EP*, the hearings became a lengthy debate between proponents of the opposing systems of medicine. Among homoeopathic physicians appearing for Dr. Wells were Bryant's medical associates John Franklin Gray, A. Gerald Hull, and Benjamin Franklin Joslyn. During the testimony Bryant charged, in an *EP* editorial captioned "An Inquest Extraordinary," that the coroner was legally unjustified in holding an inquest, but was "wielding the functions of his office against his enemies the homoeopathists." Although Dr. Ball tried the patience of his jurors in an attempt to refute Bryant's charge, they declared themselves unqualified to pass judgment on the efficacy of homoeopathic treatment, and found the death due to natural causes. See *EP*, October 31 and November 6, 1854, and *passim*.

888. *To* Susan Fenimore Cooper[1]

New York   November 17, 1854.

Dear Madam.

I thank you very much for the beautiful volume you have caused to be sent me and for the honor you have done me by inscribing the work to me.[2] I should have judged, even before I saw it, that nobody could be better qualified for the task of making an anthology of the finest things said by the poets of a country life, than you who have given a proof of the great love you bear it by describing it more charmingly than any other writer. Your book is of the more value, inasmuch as it is made up of poems not found in the ordinary collections and shows that there are yet in the garden of English poetry flowers as sweet as any that have been already gathered.

I am, madam,
with great regard
Your obt servt.
W. C. BRYANT.

MANUSCRIPT: YCAL ADDRESS: To Miss Susan F. Cooper.

1. See Letter 730.

2. *The Rhyme and Reason of Country Life; or, Selections from Fields Old and New. By the Author of "Rural Hours"* . . . (New York, 1854).

889. *To* Samuel Jones Tilden

New York, November 23, 1854.

My dear sir,

 I have called at your office twice to-day on some business of my own. Will you oblige me by letting me know when you are in your office, that I may come and bore you?

Yours truly,

W. C. BRYANT

MANUSCRIPT: Unrecovered TEXT: *Letters and Literary Memorials of Samuel J. Tilden,* ed. John Bigelow (New York and London: Harper, 1908), I, 105.

890. *To* William J. Stillman[1]

New York December 4th, 1854.

Dear sir.

 I send you the poem I promised the other day.[2] You need not give yourself the trouble to send any thing to me in return. I shall want to see a proof. If you can suggest a name for it you will oblige me.

Yours truly

W C BRYANT.

MANUSCRIPT: HEHL.

 1. Stillman, also writing art criticism for the *EP*, was then engaged in preparing the first issue of *The Crayon.*

 2. In its first number, January 3, 1855, p. 25, *The Crayon* carried this poem, to which Stillman attached the title "A Rain-Dream." MS in HEHL. See *Poems* (1876), pp. 326–330; Stillman, *The Autobiography of a Journalist* (Boston and New York, 1901), pp. 225–226; *DAA.* Bryant and Stillman had become acquainted as fellow-passengers aboard the *Humboldt,* returning from Europe in June 1853. Bryant, "Diary, 1852–1853." For the same number of *The Crayon* which carried "A Rain-Dream," Stillman had written, under the pseudonym "G. M. James," an article, "The Landscape Element in American Poetry. BRYANT" (pp. 3–4).

891. *To* Theodore Sedgwick III

New York Dec. 5, 1854.

My dear sir.

 I am sorry to send your article back it is so clever; but I had already and long since, made up my mind not to do in the Evening Post, what the article will do if published. The discourse is very rightly appreciated almost every where—perhaps, the public judgment is a little severe upon it,

and it is hardly worth while to interfere, especially as any thing like your article appearing in the Evening Post may be misunderstood.[1]

Meantime I am glad you are so far recovered as to be cross and combative.[2] I should have come to see you; I have thought of doing so again and again, but my wife's illness made me anxious and took me to Roslyn when I was not obliged to be here, and then I had some perplexities of business which occupied me when I was not at work for the paper. I have all the directions for getting to Owl's head and back on the same day which my wife, good soul, procured for me, and which I carry about with me in my hat, meaning some day to avail myself of. There is more work for me, somehow, at the office this season than usual, and more care of every sort elsewhere. My regards to Mrs. Sedgwick and the young ladies.

Yours truly

W C BRYANT

MANUSCRIPT: HCL ADDRESS: T. Sedgwick Esqre.

1. Sedgwick's article, and the discourse to which Bryant refers, are unidentified.

2. Having given up his law practice and traveled in Europe for his health in 1850–1852 (see Letter 736), Sedgwick had so far recovered as to serve as president of the Crystal Palace Exhibition in 1853. The nature of his more recent illness is uncertain.

892. *To* J. A. Sessions[1]

New York December 14, 1854.

Sir.

Your letter asking me to deliver a lecture before the Association of which you are the Secretary has just been put into my hands.[2] It is not in my power to accept the invitation you so obligingly communicate, for this reason among others, that I have no time to spare either for writing or delivering public lectures.

Yours respectfully

W. C. BRYANT.

MANUSCRIPT: University of Michigan Library ADDRESS: Mr. J. A. Sessions.

1. Unidentified.

2. Letter unrecovered.

893. *To* an Unidentified Correspondent

New York December 21st 1854.

Sir.

The poem of Thanatopsis first appeared in the North American Review, then a monthly, somewhere about the year 1815; it might be a year or two earlier or later.[1] My father took the manuscript with him to Boston and gave it to the conductors of that periodical.[2] It had not at that time

either the introduction or conclusion, which were added, I think, in 1821. The poem was written several years before its publication.[3]

> I am, sir,
> respectfully yours
> W. C. BRYANT

MANUSCRIPT: Chapin Library of Rare Books, Williams College.

1. *North American Review*, 5 (September 1817), 338–339.
2. See 46.2.
3. See William Cullen Bryant II, "The Genesis of 'Thanatopsis,'" *New England Quarterly*, 21 (June 1948), 163–184.

894.   *To* Fanny Bryant Godwin

> New York   December 23   1854.

Dear Fanny.

I send you the $2— I owe you in change for the [fine?]—

With this I send a note from Julia. Will you find the things of which she speaks and send them down by the bearer—

> Yrs ever
> W   C   B.

MANUSCRIPT: NYPL–GR.

895.   *To* Gulian C. Verplanck

> New York   December 28th   1854.

Dear Sir.

Several of your friends who esteem your personal character, admire your intellectual endowments and place a high value on your public services, unite in a request that you will do them the favor to dine with them at the Rooms of the Century in Eighth Street. Should you accept the invitation, they desire that you will appoint the time according to your own convenience.

> We are sir,
> with the highest
> regard, &c.
> W. C. BRYANT[1]

MANUSCRIPT: NYPL–Berg ADDRESS: To the Hon Gulian C. Verplanck.

1. This invitation to Verplanck, who had served as chairman of the Committee of Management of the Century Association since its establishment in 1847, is in Bryant's handwriting, with his signature followed by those of thirty-one other members. In 1857, upon the incorporation of the Century as a club, Verplanck became its first president. See Robert W. July, *The Essential New Yorker: Gulian Crommelin Verplanck* (Durham, North Carolina: Duke University Press, 1951), pp. 251–252. An accompanying letter of the same date from Charles M. Leupp to Verplanck comments, "The number has been restricted to the capacity of the rooms." NYPL–Berg.

896. *To* Andrew H. Green[1]

New York   Jan. 4, 1855.[2]

Dear sir.

I have no copy of any part of the snow shower of which any mere man could make any thing.[3] The manuscript sent to the printer was not returned to me.

I have perpetrated something since in the way of verse, which has been contributed to "the Crayon," and is now in type.[4] I send you a rough draft of it which I happen to have kept.

Yours truly
W C BRYANT.

MANUSCRIPT: Brown University Library ADDRESS: Andrew H Green Esq. / No. 43 Wall Street DOCKETED: Letter from / Hon William C. Bryant / 1854.

1. Andrew Haswell Green (1820–1903) was a law partner of Samuel Jones Tilden. In 1857 he became treasurer of the Board of Commissioners for Central Park, which was established that year by the state legislature. Henry Hope Reed, *Central Park, A History and Guide* (New York: Potter [1972]), p. 17.
2. Bryant mistakenly wrote "1854."
3. This poem, "The Snow-Shower," was first published in *The Knickerbocker Gallery* (New York, 1855), p. 81. See *Poems* (1876), pp. 323–326.
4. "A Rain-Dream." See 890.2.

897. *To* George P. Morris[1]

New York   Jan. 4, 1855.

My dear sir.

I send you herewith a volume which I have not seen noticed in the Home Journal, though I think it not wholly unworthy of one. Will you look at the last poem, if you should not have time to read any of the rest?[2]

Yours very truly
WM. C. BRYANT.

MANUSCRIPT: HEHL ADDRESS: Gen Geo P. Morris.

1. See 194.6; 867.1.
2. Bryant probably refers to the small one-volume edition of his *Poems*, published by D. Appleton in 1854. The last poem in the volume (pp. 252–254) is entitled "The Conqueror's Grave," written in 1853 and first published in *Putnam's Magazine* for January 1854. See *Poems* (1876), pp. 318–320. This seems to be a unique instance in Bryant's correspondence of his soliciting a notice of his own work; he must not have been aware that a month earlier Morris' periodical, in a brief notice of the volume, had commented, "Such an edition—just the one to read aloud from at the family fireside—will be welcomed by the multitudes of admirers of this world-renowned American poet—the first of his class and of the age." *The Home Journal*, 460 (December 2, 1854), 2.

898.   *To* J. J. Flournoy[1]

New York   January 13th, 1855.

Sir.

I return your verses according to your request, with a remark or two concerning them. Being without the sense of hearing, it could only be by a happy combination of observation and ingenuity that you have acquired so good a knowledge of the laws of metre and rhyme as were necessary to the production of your poem. In the last line of the second stanza however the measure is a little imperfect, besides which, the act attributed to Aurora, namely, *brushing* the dew, does not quite please me. The last line in the third stanza, seems to me not the precise one which you would have chosen were it not for the rhyme. In the last stanza there is also a bad rhyme which I have underscored.

There are one or two other little matters in the poem upon which a verbal[ist?] might perhaps pass an unfavorable judgment, but my vocation is not that of criticism. I do not pretend to pass a judgment on the poetry of others. Besides a poet must make himself; no man was ever made a poet by criticism. A true poet by repeated efforts of composition learns at last to perceive in what his writings are deficient—so far at least as respects their literary execution, and there is very little which he can learn from any body else.

I am sir
respectfully yours
W C BRYANT.

MANUSCRIPT: NYPL–GR (draft) ADDRESS: J. J. Flournoy Esqre ENDORSEMENT: My Letter to / J. J. Flournoy / Jan 1855.

1. John Jacobus Flournoy (1806–1879), of Athens, Georgia, was a miscellaneous prose writer, and author of about fifteen books and discourses.

899.   *To* Mrs. A. E. McDowell[1]

New York   January 13th, 1855.

Madam.

I have been so very busy lately that I have not found time to reply to your letter till now.

Your project is a praiseworthy one and I hope it will succeed. It is not possible for me however to give it any aid in the way you mention. My time is so much occupied that I have little leisure for composition except for my own journal, and when I write at all for other publications it is in fulfilment of some engagement already subsisting. If I held as fluent a pen as some other writers my power of answering such demands would be

much greater, and I should not be obliged to meet them as I now am by constant refusals.

> I am, Madam,
> with great respect
> Your obt Servt.[2]

MANUSCRIPT: Haverford College Library ADDRESS: Mrs. A. E. McDowell.

1. Neither Mrs. McDowell nor her "praiseworthy" project has been identified.
2. Bryant apparently forgot to sign this letter.

900. *To* Frances F. Bryant
[Third Letter][1]   New York   February 8th   1855.—Thursday.
Dear Frances,

I thought I should hear again from you today, but have been disappointed.

We begin to fear that the snow will blockade you in Berkshire. We have quite a deep snow here and the sleighs make the streets merry, though it is very cold yet. It has been fearfully cold—for two days I could not keep my room at Fanny's warm. I went to Mrs. Cronkhite's[2] on Tuesday evening, partly to get warm but did not succeed. Fanny did not go with me. A great many of your acquaintances were there who inquired about you and Julia.

Willie has done coughing, but the business has been taken up by Minna and Annie[3] who cough for half an hour together in chorus.

My own health is perfectly good, except an ugly *crick* as they call it in the neck, which is wearing off. We begin to think it is about time for you to come home. If we suffer so much by the cold here we infer that you must be nearly killed by it. There is a fine snow falling yet, and the wind drifts it somewhat. As soon as the roads are well open we shall expect to see you. Love to J[ulia]. Regards to all. Yrs ever

> W. C. B.

MANUSCRIPT: NYPL–GR.

1. Bryant's note. His two earlier letters are unrecovered.
2. Probably Mrs. J. P. Cronkhite; see 812.3.
3. Bryant's three oldest grandchildren, then five, ten, and seven years old, respectively.

901. *To* Evert A. Duyckinck[1]
                              New York   February 25, 18[55]
My dear sir.

I have not seen the book of which you speak, but if you are willing

to have any thing to do with it, I am confident of its merit. I shall be proud to [see?][2] the poems you mention included in the collection.[3]

I am, sir,

very truly yours

W. C. BRYANT.

MANUSCRIPT: Swarthmore College Library ADDRESS: E. A. Duyckinck Esqre.

1. See 471.2.
2. Word omitted.
3. Probably Evert A. and George L. Duyckinck, *Cyclopaedia of American Literature, Embracing Personal and Critical Notices of Authors . . .* , 2 vols. (New York, 1856). This includes a dozen of Bryant's poems, wholly or in part, on pp. 183–190.

902.   *To* John Howard Bryant

New York, March 5, 1855

Dear Brother

I have a deed from you and another from Olds, both of them I suppose at Princeton, which I shall be obliged if you would look up and send me. At the same time will you give me a list of my lands in Illinois, which I am a little uncertain about in the many changes which have been made.

The *Evening Post* begins to look up, though the money does not yet come in. The advertizing business may run better. I hope to be able to pay your note next year.[1]

[President Franklin] Pierce has done one good thing—the veto of the Collins line bill. I do not think he is pecuniarily dishonest, and probably he now perceives that policy requires him to be on the side of those who are against carelessly squandering the public money.[2]

My regards to your wife and son. I am every day expecting an answer to my letter. My wife sends her love.—

Yours truly

W. C. BRYANT

P. S. My wife says I must tell you that she is better. The rest are all well.

MANUSCRIPT: BCHS ADDRESS: Jn. H. Bryant Esq. TEXT: Keith Huntress and Fred W. Lorch, "Bryant and Illinois: Further Letters of the Poet's Family," *New England Quarterly,* 16 (December 1943), 641–642.

1. See 882.3. There had been a moderate financial depression in 1854.
2. President Pierce had just vetoed a congressional appropriation bill which would have awarded $858,000 to the Edward K. Collins steamship line for carrying mail from New York to Liverpool in twenty round trips during the year. In an *EP* editorial on March 5 Bryant praised his action, pointing out that during the preceding four years the company had been paid $2,629,000 for carrying mail on which the total postage paid amounted to only $734,000.

903. *To* John Howard Bryant

New York   March 10th   1855.

Dear Brother.

I have your letter with the receipt and another paper enclosed.[1] With regard to your coming east this summer, there are several circumstances in favor of it, which I did not mention in my last. In the first place, my wife has taken the house at 53 Lexington Avenue for the summer, and you could go immediately to it on your arrival in New York. She has done it on purpose that she might have a place to receive her friends on their way to Roslyn. After this summer it is probable that Fanny and her family will live in the country, and that the house will be let to somebody else. This would be a great saving of expense in going and coming and a great convenience in visiting New York occasionally. As to the cost of living, the times do not make so much difference at Roslyn as in New York. The main part of what is consumed in my family comes from my farm.

Then again we are all alive and well now, and it is convenient for us to receive you. Another year may make a difference in some of these conditions.

It would be therefore, desirable to us and in some respects pleasanter and more convenient for you to come this summer. What I shall do in repairing my house I cannot say. I have a carpenter on the farm of whose services in this way I might avail myself.

Do as seems to you good in regard to coming this season. If you should not we shall be glad to see you hereafter. My regards to Harriet and your son.

Yrs truly

W   C   Bryant

My wife and daughter desire their love to all. My wife I think gets better daily.

W. C. B.

MANUSCRIPT: NYPL–BFP.

1. Unrecovered.

904. *To* S. N. Holliday[1]

New York   March 15, 1855.

Sir

On receiving your letter[2] dated nearly three months since I laid it by with a view of answering it at my leisure, and unfortunately forgot it, till I found it the other day among some of my papers. This is my apology for not answering it sooner.

I cannot give you any information of the occasion which suggested to

my mind the idea of my poem of Thanatopsis. It was written when I was seventeen or eighteen years old—I have not now at hand the memorandums which would enable me to be precise—and I [believe it was composed in my solitary rambles in the woods. As it was first committed to paper, it began with the half-line—"Yet a few days, and thee"—and ended with the beginning of another line with the words—"And make their bed with thee." The rest of the poem—the introduction and the close—was added some years afterward, in 1821, when I published a little collection of my poems at Cambridge.][3]

respectfully yours
W. C. BRYANT.

MANUSCRIPT: Saint Louis Mercantile Library Association ADDRESS: S. N. Holliday Esq. PUBLISHED (in part): *Poetical Works*, I, 329–330.

1. Unidentified.
2. Unrecovered.
3. The manuscript is incomplete; matter in brackets is supplied from a partial text in *Poetical Works*, I, 329–330.

905.   *To* Charles Gould

[New York] Wednesday   March 28 [1855]

Dear Mr. Gould.

I have the Sketch Club at 53 Lexington Avenue on Friday evening. Will you do me and them the favor to meet them?[1]

Yours truly
W. C. BRYANT.

MANUSCRIPT: HCL.

1. According to the surviving Sketch Club minutes, Gould (Letter 773) did not attend this meeting at Bryant's home on March 30. Information from James T. Callow.

906.   *To* John Howard Bryant

New York, March 29, 1855

Dear Brother

In regard to your coming to the East, we wish you to take your own time. Come as early as you please, we shall be glad to see you and be ready for you. I have lately been passing a week at Roslyn and next week my wife goes down for the summer.

I have hesitated somewhat to accept Mr. Bingham's proposition for this [reason?].[1] When I had the two lots entered I designed one of them for each of my daughters. The lot No. 69 was to be Fanny's as I have made it so by my will. If it is sold the proceeds ought to be secured to her, so that

she could receive the interest. I have therefore concluded to have the place sold for the price you mention and the amount secured to Fanny. The payment of $250 would not be at all desirable, in this point of view. What I wish is that she should have the interest until the money is paid, and then that the principal should either be lent out again or invested for her benefit, in some kind of property the value of which will be certain to increase. So, if Mr. Bingham buys the house and lot let the proceeds be secured to Mrs. Fanny Bryant Godwin of Roslyn, Queens County Long Island—or rather New York, for she is yet in New York—but let me have the papers.[2]

My wife suggests that if you have more hams and smoked beef—particularly the former, than you have occasion for—and if, moreover, the cost of sending them to New York be not too great—of which you are better able to judge than we—that you should put up a box of them and despatch it to me at New York and I will pay you the price they bear at Princeton. But do not take any trouble about the matter unless they can be sent for a reasonable charge.

Frances desires her love to you all and bids me tell you that she is glad you are coming. She will soon write to tell you so. We are all pretty well. My own health has been uncommonly vigorous since I saw you last. My regards to your wife and son.

Yours truly
W. C. Bryant

P. S. We pay 15 cts a pound for hams here. You can therefore calculate whether they can be profitably transported to this place. At my place only two pigs were killed last fall, which makes our supply of hams very small.

W. C. B.

Manuscript: BCHS text: Keith Huntress and Fred W. Lorch, "Bryant and Illinois: Further Letters of the Poet's Family," *New England Quarterly*, 16 (December 1943), 642–643.

1. The printed text has "occasion."
2. On April 7, 1855, Bryant's lot Number 69 in Princeton was sold to Dolan P. Bingham for $2,500. David J. Baxter, "William Cullen Bryant: Illinois Landowner," *Western Illinois Regional Studies*, 1 (Spring 1978), 10.

907. *To* Frances F. Bryant

Wednesday afternoon   April 11, 1855

Dear Frances.

I send you inclosed a letter from Adeline.[1] You will see it is full of matter. I also send a little note to Dennis.[2]

Mr. Evangelides called this morning to inquire whether you were at home; he was desirous to see Mrs. Brown.[3] I shall try to see Mr. [Alfred?]

Field before I come out. If the weather continues as cold as it is now I shall probably not come out till Saturday. If it grows warm I may—I do not care to go to Flushing if it is *very* cold. I have seen nobody yet, nor have I heard any thing of consequence since I came to town.

Yours ever
W. C. B.

MANUSCRIPT: NYPL–GR.

    1. Mrs. Austin Bryant.

    2. Probably a workman on Bryant's Roslyn property.

    3. No other indication has been found that Christos Evangelides (Letter 830; 832.4) visited the United States at this time. Mrs. Brown is unidentified.

908. *To* Richard H. Dana

New York   April 20, 1855.

Dear Dana.

My wife and I were very glad to get your letter. The account you give of the consequences of Charlotte's accident interested us greatly. We had heard nothing before so particular or so much to be depended on. I do not wonder that your own health was in the end affected. As the milder weather comes on, I hope you will both find yourselves the better for it. Considering the nature of the accident it was a mercy that she survived. The effect on her nervous system, I suppose, continues after the other consequences have passed away and will be comparatively slow in leaving her.[1]

If it should appear to you that a softer temperature at this season would be of advantage to either of you, you must remember that we have a place on Long Island where you will both be welcome guests. My wife has not been so well as usual for some months past, but is in a good way, and is gradually coming up to the old mark. She is not now as strong as formerly, but even in that respect she is gaining. She had a nervous attack last autumn, which left her very weak, unable to bear noise, or much talk of any kind, and disagreeably affected by any appearance of haste. She gave up the care of the household for a little while, but it is now again in her hands; though we try to prevent her from encumbering herself with too many matters at once, and to moderate her zeal for keeping every thing in order.

I cannot review Mr. Wallace's book. I am not deep enough in the philosophy of art to do it satisfactorily to myself, and then I write no more reviews, except for very strong and pressing reasons. I have spoken to Godwin, who has something to do with Putnam's Magazine, and he has promised to see if he can find some suitable person to write a review of the book, and I will speak to Stillman of the *Crayon* about it, when I next see him.[2]

Remember me most kindly to your daughter and sisters, and believe me

as ever, truly yours,
W. C. BRYANT.

MANUSCRIPT: NYPL–GR ENDORSED: Wm C. Bryant Ap. 20th / 55 Ans. May 20th

1. The nature of Charlotte Dana's accident is unknown.

2. *Art, Scenery and Philosophy in Europe*, by Horace Binney Wallace (1817–1852, Princeton 1835), published posthumously at Philadelphia in 1855, was reviewed in *The Crayon*, 1 (June 13, 1855), 371–372, probably by William James Stillman (890.1). In 1853 Parke Godwin had become an associate editor of the new *Putnam's Magazine*.

909. *To* Evert A. Duyckinck

Roslyn   May 28, 1855

My dear sir.

I have as you will see made some corrections of the press and one or two corrections of fact in the proofs you have sent me.[1] Perhaps I should have said more of Dr. Bliss, if so, you can supply the deficiency. He was of so generous a temper as often to yield his own just rights in order to meet the expectations of authors for whom he published. I was glad to be able to repay in some degree his kindness to me by obtaining for him an office in the custom house, after he had lost the greater part of his property by unfortunate speculations in real estate.[2] This, I think is the only public office that I was ever able to obtain for any body during a pretty long political life.

Theophilus Parsons was the editor of the Literary Gazette when I first began to write for it,[3] but it passed afterwards into the hands of James G. Carter,[4] who was much interested in the subject of public education and took an active part in the introduction of normal schools into this country. I think the first we had were in Massachusetts. Of Mr. Parsons I can tell you nothing. I never saw him but once and had little communication with him. With the exception of the part he took in conducting the Gazette, I only know that he published not very long since a volume of Essays of a religious character. He is a Swedenborgian, as you doubtless know.

The facts in the notice of John H. Bryant which appears in Griswold's Poets of America were furnished him by me. I could not well add any thing of importance to them without communicating with my brother, which I shall be able to do soon, as I expect him in the second week of June. If that will do, I will get something out of him at that time and send it to you. Meantime my daughter has copied one of his poems, which I enclose with this.[5]

The anecdote related in your note concerning Thanatopsis and the

Inscription is not quite exact. I did not send the poems to be published in the North American Review, nor was the stratagem of ascribing one of them to my father one which I should have practised. They were taken to Boston by my father, without speaking to me on the subject. He had found them among the papers left by me at Cummington while I was in another part of the state. In receiving them from him the conductors of the Review must have misunderstood him in regard to their authorship. I recollect very well that they were surprized when I told them that I wrote both. The beginning of Thanatopsis—that is to say the first sixteen lines, and the conclusion, that is to say the last fifteen were written by me in 1821, when I prepared my little collection of poems for the press. The close of the Inscription was added at the same time.

I am sir
very truly yours
W   C   BRYANT

MANUSCRIPT: NYPL–Evert Augustus Duyckinck Collection ADDRESS: E. Duyckinck, Esq.

1. Proofs of the biographical article on Bryant in the *Cyclopaedia of American Literature*. See 901.2.
2. See Letter 489.
3. See Letter 94.
4. See Letter 124.
5. Manuscript unrecovered.

910.   *To* Catharine M. Sedgwick

New York, July 16th [1855]

... Enclosed I send you a memorandum of yours which was found among some loose papers on our library-table at Roslyn. You must have missed the receipt for beer, at a time when nothing fermented, of a liquid kind I mean, can be bought and sold.[1] We must go back to what we can make in our households. It is to be hereafter with drinks as it would be with tissues if all the cotton and woollen mills were stopped by law, and we were obliged to wear linsey-woolsey and other homespun cloths. The ferment will, I suppose, cause the planting of large apple-orchards again, and we shall hear the creak of the cider-mill with the return of the autumnal frosts; but, in the mean time, bushels of currants must be squeezed, and the beer-tub—shall I call it vat, for dignity's sake?—must take its old place among household furniture. I wish I could tell you how the receipt succeeds. I compounded some beer after it on Saturday, but I must wait till Saturday next before it is fit for drinking. The season is too warm for the happiest cerevisial fermentation. March and October, you know, are the accepted seasons in the old world—but why is October made to correspond to March?

I see you have the *clematis grandiflora* among the names on your

memorandum. If you want a flower which blooms later, more abundantly, and almost as splendidly, put down the *clematis Sieboldii*. It is just now in season. The flowers are remarkably persistent; they open before they are half grown, and you see the petals broadening and lengthening from day to day, growing more flower-like and delicate in texture, and brighter in color, for ten days together, or more—quite unlike most of the tribes which prepare their beauty in secret, and open when they have attained their full perfection, and then in a few hours are withered. There is something unsatisfactory about those flowers which fade so soon after they unfold. I can overlook the fault only in the *marvel of Peru*; the mirabilis, noon-sleep—the Spaniard calls it Don Pedro; it grows wild in Cuba, naturalized, I suppose. The Don is welcome to drop his blooms of one morning, he repairs the waste so liberally, and comes out upon you with such glory and wealth of compensation the morning after. I have a variety of that flower, the perfumed sort, of which I must gather some of the seeds and send you. It was brought by Cole, the painter, from Sicily, and I have had it in my garden ever since; I never gather it without thinking of him; it is sweet and fragrant, like his memory.

The visit which you and your brother made to us is one of the pleasant memories of Roslyn. We often speak of it, and wish, for your sakes, the weather had been finer, and, for our own, that your visit had been longer.[2] I begin to think that railways, after all, are not the great things that some people pretend; they are smoky, noisy, giddy, dull, clumsy means of going from place to place. If we could only drop in upon you some afternoon, and return the same night or early the next morning, that would be something to talk of. My wife is quite as well as when you were here; too much like Martha—cumbered with many things.[3] If I could only untwist the legs of that wretch Care from her neck and pitch him into—our pond, I would celebrate the event, perhaps, in a poem. I wonder if there is any medium between too much care and not enough to keep the mind in wholesome activity. I think that Sindbad, when he shook off the Old Man of the Sea, made thorough work of it, and walked, thereafter, without any burden on his shoulders.

Roslyn is as fresh as May. The season has been showery, but, on the whole, agreeable—indeed, quite so. Every other day a shower, or, if not a shower, a mist going up in the night to water the earth, and disappearing with the sunrise. The children, who are quite well, are revelling among the latest cherries and the earliest gooseberries, both prodigiously fine this season. We have all of us gone through with "Christie Johnstone" and "Peg Woffington," and find that they deserve all you and your brother said of them.[4] The pleasure they gave us is one of the obligations under which your visit laid us. . . .

MANUSCRIPT: Unrecovered TEXT *(partial)*: *Life*, II, 82–83.

1. A New York State anti-liquor law, passed in 1855, was declared unconstitutional soon afterward by the courts.

2. Catharine Sedgwick and her brother Charles had visited the Bryants at Roslyn some time that spring. Charles's letter of appreciation, dated June 11, is in *Life*, II, 81–82.

3. Cf. Luke 10:38–42.

4. Novels by Charles Reade (1814–1884), both published in 1853.

911.   *To* Henry W. Longfellow

New York   July 25, 1855.

My dear sir,

Professor A. Walchner with whom I believe you have had some correspondence, has desired that I should write you a line concerning a work which he wishes to submit to your inspection. If you could aid him in this matter you might render a material service to a worthy and accomplished man, who has a large family dependent on him for bread, and whose success in this country, I am sorry to say has not been equal to his merits.[1]

I am sir
faithfully yours
W. C. BRYANT.

MANUSCRIPT: HSPa ADDRESS: Prof. H. W. Longfellow.

1. Friedrich August Walchner (b. 1799), *Darstellung der geologischen Verhältnisse des Mainzer Tertiärbeckens und seiner Fossilen, Fauna und Flora* [Karlsruhe? 1850?]. No reply to this letter has been recovered. Longfellow was then summering at Newport, Rhode Island, and working under pressure to prepare his long poem "The Song of Hiawatha" for publication in November. But only a little over one-third of Longfellow's letters written during the period 1854–1856 have been recovered. *The Letters of Henry Wadsworth Longfellow*, ed. Andrew Hilen, 4 vols. (Cambridge: The Belknap Press of Harvard University Press, 1966–1972), III, 406, 487–489.

912.   *To* Henry D. Gilpin[1]

New York   July 26, 1855.

Dear sir,

The bearer of this note is Mr. Weyman Law Reporter for the Evening Post. The object of his visit is to obtain an early copy of the decision of Judge Kane in the case of Passmore Williams which is looked for here with a good deal of interest.[2] If in any way you could facilitate his object you would confer a real favor on the conductors of the Evening Post and in particular on

Yours faithfully
W   C   BRYANT

MANUSCRIPT: UVa ADDRESS: Mr. Gilpin / Philadelphia.

1. Henry Dilworth Gilpin (1801–1860, Pennsylvania 1819), a Philadelphia lawyer

who had been a United States attorney in eastern Pennsylvania, and briefly Attorney General in Martin Van Buren's cabinet, had retired from politics in 1841 to become a cultural leader in Philadelphia. Earlier, he had been editor of the *Atlantic Souvenir* when Bryant had contributed poems to that gift annual in 1825–1826. See Letter 118.

2. When a North Carolina slaveholder, Colonel John Hill Wheeler (1806–1882), had passed through Philadelphia on his way to New York to take ship for Nicaragua the previous year, having been appointed United States minister to that country, a female slave he was taking with him had been advised by one Passmore Williamson of her right to freedom in a free state, and assisted to escape. Williamson was later arrested and charged with her abduction. When he was found guilty before federal judge John Kintzing Kane (1795–1858, Yale 1814), the *EP* attacked the decision as "a denial of the constitutional power of Pennsylvania to pass laws excluding slaves from her territory," and warned its readers, "There is a plan to force slavery upon the free states as well as upon the territories, and we must meet and repel it at once." *EP*, July 26, 28, 31, 1855.

913.   *To* Frances F. Bryant

Tuesday evening   July 27   1855.

Dear F.

Yesterday Mr. John Durand called to say that he would like to come out to Roslyn tomorrow. Immediately I despatched a note[1] to Mr. Leupp to ask him to come also. He told me last evening he determined to come as soon as he got my letter, but on going home he found Gideon Lee[2] at his house, which may possibly make it uncertain whether he comes.

Yours ever

W. C. B.

MANUSCRIPT: NYPL–GR.

1. Unrecovered.
2. Charles Leupp's father-in-law and business partner; see 487.1.

914.   *To* Rufus W. Griswold

New York   July 28, 1855.

My dear sir.

My brother is about making a collection of his verses for publication. He has no perfect copy of the poem entitled the Traveller's Return, which I sent to you the other day and of which I afterwards had a proof from you.[1] Can you oblige me by letting me have a proof of it or a copy in some other form.

Yrs truly

W   C   BRYANT

MANUSCRIPT: HCL ADDRESS: Dr. R. W. Griswold.

1. John Howard Bryant's "The Traveller's Return" was printed in a revised edition of Griswold's anthology, *The Poets and Poetry of America*, in 1856, pp. 369–370.

915.   *To* Messrs. Dix & Edwards

August 24, 1855.

Mr. Bryant has at present nothing finished of the sort mentioned in the note of Messrs Dix & Edwards, and is so much occupied with other matters that he could not have any thing ready in season for the October number of the Magazine.[1]

[unsigned]

MANUSCRIPT: HCL.

1. In 1855 the publishers Dix & Edwards acquired from George Palmer Putnam *Putnam's Monthly Magazine,* of which the editor was then Charles Frederick Briggs (1804–1877), assisted by George William Curtis (1824–1892) and Parke Godwin. Frank Luther Mott, *A History of American Magazines* (Cambridge: Harvard University Press, 1957–1968), II, 419, 427. Dix & Edwards' note to Bryant is unrecovered.

916.   *To* Messrs. Childs & Peterson

New York   Aug. 29, 1855.

Gentlemen.

The specimen of Mr. Allibone's Critical Dictionary of Authors[1] which you sent me has given me a high idea of the industry exactness and various reading of the author. I think it promises to be one of the most valuable works of reference which have been produced in the present century. The plan appears to me excellent, though difficult, but the difficulty has been happily overcome by the author's extraordinary research.

Truly yours,
W. C. BRYANT.

MANUSCRIPT: HEHL ADDRESS: To Messrs Childs & Peterson.

1. Samuel Austin Allibone (1816–1889), *A Critical Dictionary of English Literature* (Philadelphia: Childs & Peterson, 1858, 1871).

917.   *To* Frances F. Bryant

[cSeptember 1, 1855.]

Dear Frances.

If you find the *papers* please put them in my little drawer on the right hand—but do not give yourself much trouble about it. The Horticultural meeting at which I speak takes place on the 25th of September[1]—Be at home before that time.[2]

Your brother Egbert [Fairchild] is here in town and says he *must* go back today. He promised to come in again this morning but has not yet called.

Yours ever
W. C. B.

P. S. I wrote you yesterday that I had found your box. On Monday I mailed two letters for Egbert junior.

W. C. B.

MANUSCRIPT: NYPL–GR.

1. At this meeting of the New York Horticultural Society, actually held on September 26, 1855, in the rooms of the Mercantile Library, Bryant spoke on "The Improvement of Native Fruits." This was printed in the *EP* on September 27, and in Bryant's *Orations and Addresses*, pp. 269–282, where it is misdated 1856.
   2. Frances was then visiting relatives in Ogdensburg, New York.

918. *To* Julia S. Bryant

New York   Sept   3d   1855

Dear Julia.

I think it would be well to give Henry the bellows of which you spoke and tell him to blow off the sulphur from the grapes.

But I write this note to ask you to say to Dennis that I wish him not to take any of the heap of barrilla ashes for the wheat land. I want to keep it all for a top dressing.

I will write to you again when I have seen Mr. [Mulin?].

Yrs affectionately
W   C   BRYANT.

MANUSCRIPT: NYPL–GR.

919. *To* Frances F. Bryant

New York   September 3d   1855.   Monday morning.

Dear Frances.

I have just come to town from Roslyn where I left every body well and every thing in good order. I have put Edward Setton[1] into the cottage, finding the place so much run over by people who had no business there, that I thought it better to take the risk of one tenant than of forty. Dennis and Henry understand all about him and will have an eye on him. Henry takes to gardening with a good deal of zeal, and I doubt not that I shall find him immediately quite as serviceable as Kropf.[2] Julia has packed up the pear marmalade for the Fields, and this morning it was ready to be put on board of the boat.[3] Jessie[4] is back at the cottage. Fanny and the children are well. The country is as green as ever, and yesterday after a hot morning came a smart little shower of rain which was followed by so fresh and bright an evening, that we all wished you were with us to walk out and look at it and enjoy the grateful airs from the west.

The new edition of my poems to be published by Appleton is now out, and he has sent me a check for $476.00.[5] I shall now be able to send out a few more copies to my friends.

I hope you will not find the climate too cool for you on the St. Lawrence. Here the temperature is very agreeable, though cool for the season. I hope likewise that you will adhere to your resolutions of being prudent in regard to what you eat and drink. You may not be able to get all the kinds of fruit that we have at Roslyn, but there will be no want of apples I suppose, and stewed apples in the morning are as wholesome I think as any thing that you could take. Make all the haste you can to be well and strong and let me know often how you get on, and how you occupy yourself.

I shall send you the Evening Post daily till I hear from you that you are on the point of returning. Rachel the tragic actress begins her performances this evening.[6] You must contrive to be back before they are ended.

Remember me kindly to your brothers and their families.

Yours ever
W. C. BRYANT.

MANUSCRIPT: NYPL–GR.

1. Not further identified.

2. Evidently an earlier gardener.

3. Presumably this was to be shipped to some members of the Field family in England.

4. Ann Jeannette (Cairns) Willis (1828–1858), Mrs. Richard Storrs Willis. See 791.1. She was the eldest of three daughters of William and Ann Eliza Cairns (795.1).

5. In 1855 D. Appleton reprinted Bryant's 1854 *Poems* in one- and two–volume editions.

6. The celebrated French tragedienne Rachel (1821–1858) performed in New York from September 3 to November 17, 1855. Her last performance on any stage was given in Charleston, South Carolina, the following December, when she caught a cold which resulted in her death from tuberculosis two years later. Odell, *Annals*, VI, 447–450. Though it is uncertain whether he saw Rachel perform in New York, Bryant had enjoyed her performances at Paris in 1845 and 1849. See his "Diary of a European Tour, 1845," October 27, NYPL–GR; and "Diary, 1849," September 8.

920.   *To* Frances F. Bryant

New York   Wednesday morning, Sept. 5, 1855

Dear Frances.

I was truly rejoiced to hear from you this morning,[1] that you had made so pleasant a journey, and reach Ogdensburg[2] in such good health. You may be disappointed that I do not send you the velvet bows for which you write; but I cannot have them without going to the house, and that will take time that I cannot spare. This afternoon I am engaged to go to Pell's place at West Point,[3] from which I return on Friday morning, and the same day go out to Roslyn with Rosetta Morton whom Julia has invited. [George W.?] Morton will either go out that day or the next. So you see you must wait till the beginning of next week.

I send you two letters which have just been put into my hands, along with one from Victoria [Gibson] for Julia. My own health is excellent. I will write again on Friday.

Yrs ever
W. C. B.

MANUSCRIPT: NYPL–GR.

1. Letter unrecovered.
2. Here, and in Letter 923, Bryant mistakenly wrote "Ogdensburgh."
3. Alfred Pell owned property at Buttermilk Falls (later Highland Falls) near West Point, on which he was building a summer home. Bigelow, *Retrospections*, I, 163.

921. *To* Frances F. Bryant

New York September 13th 1855—Thursday.

Dear Frances.

This is my fourth letter. From you I have received two.[1]

On Tuesday afternoon I left the Battery in a steamer for Mr. Spring's place at Perth Amboy.[2] Edward Spring was on board a handsome youth, and the Revd. Mr. Longfellow.[3] Both Mr. L and myself had engaged to meet Mr. Spring at his counting house, he at half past two and I at a quarter to three, but neither of us found him in and went to the steamboat without him. Our passage took two hours, and was quite a pleasant one. I was glad to renew my acquaintance with the shores of the strait between Staten Island and New Jersey, along which you may remember we once passed in our way to Mrs. Griffith's.[4] We landed at the town of Perth Amboy, and crossed the peninsula or cape on which it stands to the other side where it is washed by the mouth of the Raritan. Here the company have their buildings in a pleasant situation, about a mile and a half from the place where I landed. Edward showed me the grounds, which look barren and neglected, and were infested with swarms of mosquitoes. At six o'clock Mr. Spring arrived in the last boat, having been delayed in consequence of forgetting that we were to leave in the three o'clock boat. We took tea in Mr. Spring's house, in which Mrs. Spring's father, Mr. Buffum is lying very ill, and probably near his end.[5] After tea several of the people from the great stone building in which so many families live came in, and sang a hymn at Mr. Buffum's particular request. Mr. Spring then took me over to see the building, which I will not weary you with describing. It gives each family all its rooms on one floor. I saw nothing attractive either in the place or their mode of living. Luckily, my bed-chamber was not infested with mosquitoes as the parlor was, though the doors and windows were protected by netting, and I passed a comfortable night. Mrs. Spring desired a great deal of love to you.

I find that I have not expressed myself so as to give you a very distinct idea of the place. I will try to do that when I see you. If you should think

of visiting it, I would wait till the mosquito season is over, besides that at present while Mr. Buffum is so ill, the visit would hardly be as pleasant as at another time.

It is very hot here at present; yesterday, the day that I came up in the morning from Perth Amboy was hotter still—a melting day. Julia had heard nothing from Estelle [Ives] when I left—I think—or had heard that she could not come at present—at all events she told me that she did not expect her now.

Is it not time for you to come home[?] I am expecting every day that the cool weather will set in—it will be sure to do so before you have time to get back. I hear from Fanny today that the plums are nearly gone and I shall have to betake myself to the baked apples.—

My regards to your brothers and their families.

Yours ever
W   C   BRYANT.

MANUSCRIPT: NYPL–GR.

1. Neither recovered.

2. Marcus Spring (1810–1874; see 583.2), who had earlier been a director of the Fourieristic North American Phalanx in Red Bank, New Jersey, withdrew from that communal colony in 1853 to establish, with others, the Raritan Bay Union at Eagleswood, near Perth Amboy, New Jersey. *The Papers of Frederick Law Olmsted. I. The Formative Years: 1822–1852*, edd. Charles Capen McLaughlin and Charles E. Beveridge (Baltimore: The Johns Hopkins University Press, 1977), p. 385.

3. Edward, then eighteen years old, was the son of Marcus and Rebecca Buffum Spring. Samuel Longfellow (1819–1892, Harvard 1840), youngest brother of Henry Wadsworth Longfellow, had been minister of the Unitarian Society of Brooklyn since 1853.

4. The writer Mary Griffith (326.9).

5. Arnold Buffum (1782–1859), Quaker anti-slavery lecturer, and first president of the New England Anti-Slavery Society, in 1832.

922.   *To* Cyrus Bryant

New York—or rather Roslyn—September 15th, 1855.

Dear Brother.

I have been careless about answering your letter,[1] and have no apology to make for it except that the question you put required some reflection and consideration and it was more convenient to put off the reply than to make it on the spot as I should have done.

If I were you I would have but two colors. I would have the window blinds and the cornice of the same color. If I had the body of the house painted A according to the samples in Downing's book or B. I would paint the cornice and blinds C. D it strikes me is not a bad color and if I adopted that I would have the cornice and window blinds F.[2] I do not for my part think that a house with cornice and window blinds of the same color looks

ill; though perhaps that would be more suitable for a house of wood in which but one material is used. In a brick house it may be well to distinguish the wooden cornices doors, window frames and blinds by another color.

You wrote to me some time since inquiring about a table for a study or library. The one I had in view and concerning which I spoke to you is of this form. It should be about two feet and seven inches in height four feet or four feet and two inches in length and about three feet wide on the top. In the middle is an open space for the knees to  go under the table with one drawer over it on each side and the ends are occupied each with a double pile of drawers from the floor to the top. At one end might be a sliding leaf to be drawn out when you want to enlarge the top of the table, or when more than two persons want to write at it. At the other end might be a leaf to let part way down, behind which large engravings or maps might be kept. I have thus given you the dimensions of the table, and its plan as nearly as I can.

There is another matter on which you have desired information; our ancestry. On the Bryant side I can go back no further than Ichabod Bryant our great grandfather, who came from Raynham to West Bridgwater in 1745 and died in 1759. His wife was Ruth Staples, but who was her father or where she came from I cannot find. Ichabod Bryant lived in Titicut a parish formed out of a part [of] South Bridgwater and a part of Middleborough. I find that there were Stapleses in Titicut.

I find by the History of Scituate—Dean's[3]—that John Bryant, a house carpenter and "an active and useful man," was a freeman of Scituate in 1639. He married Mary Lewis daughter of George Lewis of Barnstable in 1643. Her sons were John, Samuel, Benjamin, Joseph, Jabez, Thomas Daniel and Elisha. The son John, a lieutenant, in the militia, I suppose, had five sons, John 3d, Jonathan, David, Joshua and Samuel. The other son, Benjamin's family went to Chesterfield. Thomas became a squire, and was the father of Peleg Bryant and of the Revd Lemuel Bryant, of Quincy "a man of extraordinary powers and singularities." Whether this John Bryant senior was our ancestor I have not been able to discover.

Our grandmother Silence Howard, wife of Philip Bryant was the daughter of Dr. Abiel Howard, of West Bridgwater, who was the son of Major Jonathan Howard who died in 1739. He was the son of John Howard who came from England and settled first in Duxbury in 1643, and next in West Bridgwater in 1651. He lived in Miles Standish's family when young. He died about 1700.

I give the Snell genealogy. Thomas Snell from England settled in West Bridgwater in 1665, and was probably the largest landholder in the town. He married Martha, daughter of Arthur Harris. His son Josiah married Anna Alden a grand daughter of Hon. John Alden who came

over in the Mayflower in 1620, and by her had Zechariah Snell who was one of the early settlers of North Bridgwater and father of Ebenezer Snell our grandfather.

The Packards run thus. Samuel Packard with a wife and one child came from Windham in England and settled in Hingham in 1638 whence he came to West Bridgwater where he died in 1684. His son Zacheus married Sarah Howard daughter of the first John Howard & was the father of Abiel Packard our great grandfather, who married Sarah Ames, daughter of John Ames.

The Revd James Keith a Scotchman educated at Aberdeen came over in 1662 aged 18 years and was the first minister of Bridgwater. He married Susannah Edson daughter of Deacon Samuel Edson, and his daughter Mary Keith became the wife of Ephraim Howard, a son of the first John Howard. By Ephraim Howard she had a daughter Jane, who married Nehemiah Washburn, and became the mother of Silence Washburn, wife of Dr. Abiel Howard our great grandfather.[4]

If you want any further information as to the family pedigree I will give it so far as it can be collected from Mitchells History of the Families of Bridgwater.[5] I am sorry not to be able to go as far with the Bryants and Stapleses as I can with the others.

I think I have now fully discharged a duty which has long lain as a burden of my conscience. I hope you will make some allowance for one who is very busy and hates to write. Tell me if I have omitted any thing and I will supply it. My best regards to your wife and children.

Yours affectionately
W. C. BRYANT.

Postscript. I find after all that I have not answered your question in regard to the composition of the colors. I have no doubt, for my part, that lampblack and yellow ochre, in being added to the zinc, would give you all the colours you have in Downing. In the three first, there would I think be a little lamp black and ochre; in the last three only yellow ochre. The Ohio paint, mixed in a small proportion, gives a colour that is not disagreeable. I had my bridge and my grape house painted with zinc and yellow ochre, the color of new wood. The best way is first to mingle the paint in small quantities and paint a board or shingle with it, letting it dry, as an experiment. I did this in painting my bridge and grape house.

W. C. B.

MANUSCRIPT: Presbyterian Historical Society ADDRESS: C. Bryant Esq.

1. Unrecovered.

2. A[ndrew] J[ackson] Downing, in *Cottage Residences; or, A Series of Designs for Rural Cottages and Cottage Villas, and Their Gardens and Grounds . . .* , 4th ed. (New York, 1853), p. 16, offers "specimens . . . of six shades of color highly suitable for the exterior of cottages and villas." A, B, and C were gray; D and F were "drab or fawn."

3. Samuel Deane, *History of Scituate from its First Settlement to 1831* (Boston? 1831).

4. Accounts of the Bryant ancestry are given in *Life*, I, 47–51, and in George Tremaine McDowell, "The Youth of Bryant: An Account of the Life and Poetry of William Cullen Bryant from 1794 to 1821," Unpublished Ph.D. diss., Yale University, 1928, pp. 1–5, 244–251.

5. Nahum Mitchell, *History of the Early Settlement of Bridgwater, in Plymouth County, Massachusetts, Including an Extensive Family Register* (Boston, 1841).

923. *To* Frances F. Bryant

[No. 5]

New York   Monday   September 17th   1855.

Dear Frances,

I rejoice to hear so good an account of your health, and considering the favorable effect it has had upon your spirits I am really glad that you made the visit to Ogdensburg. When you think you have gained all the benefit from it that might be reasonably expected we all hope that you will come back with as little delay as possible. I have just come in from Roslyn and have found your third letter here.[1] At Roslyn every thing is going on pretty well. The men are getting in the potatoes—a much larger yield than we have had since the potato disease made its appearance—we shall have nearly 200 bushels. The orchard gives a liberal supply of fine large apples and we have yet more plums than we can dispose of without sending them to the neighbors. Frances the cook is to leave us tomorrow. The reason for not keeping her word, given by her, is that she cannot get on with Mary. I tried hard to make peace, and Mary promised every thing, but the cook was inexorable, declared that she would not live in a place where so many stories were told and insisted on going off before the end of her month and without notice. Do not give yourself any trouble about the matter nor hurry yourself to come home, on that account. Shall I try to find somebody else?

Mr. Tilden came down to Roslyn on Saturday and came in this morning. He is as you know a candidate for the office of Attorney General of the State.[2]

They are talking of a branch railway from Hem[p]stead Branch to Glen Cove with a station at Roslyn back of Mr. Schenck's. The people in Glen Cove are very eager to have it made, and I was told had subscribed or engaged to subscribe $40.000 and Alderman Charlick has promised to get as much more at Roslyn. Whether there is a prospect of doing any thing I cannot yet tell.—[3]

I send this to Ogdensburg, inasmuch as I am not sure of your being at Rochester or Bloomfield. If you have left Ogdensburg I suppose they will send it after you.

Yours ever,

W. C. BRYANT.

MANUSCRIPT: NYPL–GR.

1. Unrecovered.
2. Samuel J. Tilden was defeated in the election for that office in 1855.
3. The Glen Cove Branch of the Long Island Railroad, with a station at Roslyn, was not opened until 1865. Goddard, *Roslyn Harbor*, p. 23.

924.   *To* Frances F. Bryant

Roslyn   Sept 30, 1855

My dear Frances.

Now that I know from your letter to Minna precisely when a letter is likely to reach you I write again. I sent off on Tuesday last a letter from Fanny for you to Ogdensburg and shortly afterwards got one from you informing me that you were at Rochester, though you did not say how long you would be there. We are all as impatient to have you back again as you can be to get home. For my part I find Roslyn a dull gloomy sort of place, which it never seemed to me before. Yet every thing goes on well, and the weather has been uncommonly pleasant. The grapes have ripened well; the golden chasselas was ripe the earliest. We nearly stripped the vines—there were two of them and sent off baskets of the clusters to our neighbors. Mr. Cairns seemed quite surprized and talked immediately about having a cold vinery of his own; but I found in the course of the conversation that he was afraid of two things—thieves and poultry. A vine fence however he thought, after some discussion, would protect the grapes from both. Mr. McCoun brought over a carpenter last Thursday to take the measure of our grape house. Julia was absent at the drawing lesson.

I got off both the speeches last week without any accident, except that in the speech before the Horticultural Society I forgot a few things, was obliged to pause a moment, and finally went on without them, copying Bonaparte's example who when he encountered a fortress which was not easy to take left it behind him and conquered the country beyond. I sent to you copies of the Evening Post containing reports of both of them. The banquet at the Crystal Palace was a splendid affair, but both that place and the exhibition room in the Mercantile Library, I found bad for speaking in; it required immense powers of voice for one to make himself heard.[1]

Last Sunday John Durand came down; this time I am fortunately alone. On Tuesday Fanny goes to town to make arrangements for letting the house, and to get servants. I go into town tomorrow and hope not to return without you. Fanny wants Mrs. Sutphen to leave the house, but Julia and I—Julia went in, on Wednesday, to be present at the Horticultural Exhibition and the Crystal Palace affair—told her that she might stay till you come back, at least.[2] Mr. [Joseph] Curtis now and then becomes possessed with the notion that you have got back, and comes over to offer you the hospitality of his table. A kind old gentleman. Remember me kindly

to Mrs. Tobey and to Mr. F[rederick] A. Tobey and his wife and the rest of the family and tell Mr. Tobey that I wish he would bring down his wife to see how the farms on Long Island look and give us the benefit of his western skill and experience.

Yours ever

W. C. BRYANT.

P.S. Monday mng. Oct 1, 1855. I have just come to town and get your letter.[3] I find also Mr. Thayer[4] at the office who has just left Col. Kinney at Nicaragua.—[5] I do not think of any thing to add—except that Mr. Dewey was at the Crystal Palace and preached here yesterday—and that we all wish to see you back.

Yours ever

W. C. B.

MANUSCRIPT: NYPL–GR.

1. On September 26 Bryant delivered his address on the improvement of native fruits before the New York Horticultural Society at their exhibition in the rooms of the Mercantile Library. See 917.1. On the following evening, at a "Book Publishers Festival" in the Crystal Palace attended by authors, artists, and publishers, he took as his theme the "promise of American authorship, given by the appearance of Cotton Mather," which "has never been redeemed until now," and wondered why no one had written the "Lives of Eminent Booksellers," epitomized, he thought, by the career of his own early publisher, Elam Bliss, "an upright, generous man of a munificent spirit and every moral quality that could dignify his vocation." EP, September 27, 28, 1855.

2. This tenant of Frances Bryant's rented house at 53 Lexington Avenue, Mrs. Sutphen, is otherwise unidentified. See Letter 903.

3. Unrecovered.

4. William Sydney Thayer (1829–1864, Harvard 1850) joined the EP staff about 1852. He was made Washington correspondent in 1856, and apparently served briefly as managing editor in 1859–1860. Nevins, Evening Post, pp. 242, 256, 315.

5. Colonel Henry L. Kinney, a Texan promoter whose exploits Thayer had been covering for the EP, was attempting to set up an independent American colony on a vast tract in Nicaragua to which he had a dubious claim. He was soon pushed aside, however, by the greater filibustering adventures of William Walker (1824–1860), who made himself president and dictator of that central American country in 1856–1857, and was finally court-martialed and executed in Honduras in 1860. Nevins, Ordeal, II, 373–374, 405–508.

925. To A. G. Carll[1]

New York Oct. 25, 1855.

Dear sir.

I have been called upon by John T. Diossy Esq. of Richmond county,[2] who asks me what I know of Mr. Rider, the member of Assembly from Queens County,[3] who is talked of as a candidate for State Senator to be nominated by the Republicans. I could tell him very little of Mr. Rider, but what I had heard of him I could say was favorable. Could you oblige me so far as to say whether he is right on the slavery question, and likely

to hold his views firmly and not allow himself to be tampered with? Your answer might be directed to me if you prefer it; but I would rather that you would write directly to Mr. Diossy at No. 1, Nassau Street in this city, as he is anxious to have the information at the earliest moment.

Yours very truly
W. C. BRYANT.

MANUSCRIPT: Haverford College Library ADDRESS: A. G. Carll Esq.—

1. Unidentified.
2. John T. Diossy was a bookseller, with a residence at 149 West 38th Street. *Trow's New York City Directory*, p. 229.
3. James Rider (1806–1876), of Jamaica, Long Island, a banker, was a member of the New York State Assembly in 1855, and of the State Senate, 1856 and 1857. *New York Times*, May 1, 1876; Franklin B. Hough, *The New-York Civil List from 1777 to 1857* . . . (Albany, 1857), pp. 299, 144. Rider's views on slavery have not been determined.

926. *To* Frances F. Bryant

New York, Nov. 13, 1855

Dear Frances,

On arriving here I found several notes from Mrs. Cyrus Field[1] which I forward, though you will get them too late. I shall look in a moment this evening and make an apology. I have also a letter from Frederick Tobey informing me that he has sent us three barrels of apples and a [pot of butter?]. I have also a letter from Cyrus [Bryant]—all well there.

The Club meets on Friday night at Mr. Leupp's[2] so I shall not come till Saturday.

Yrs ever
W. C. B.

MANUSCRIPT: NYPL–GR.

1. Mary Bryan Stone Field (1817–1891), the wife of Cyrus West Field (1819–1892), a brother of David Dudley Field (492.4), who was a paper merchant until 1852, when he retired from that business to promote the development of an Atlantic cable.
2. This meeting of the Sketch Club was held on November 16 at the home of Charles Leupp on Madison Avenue and Twenty-Fifth Street. Information from James T. Callow.

927. *To* William Makepeace Thackeray[1]

[New York, cNovember 13–14, 1855]

My dear sir

I called at the Clarendon today to ask you to come to a little club of artists and their friends who meet on Friday night at Mr. Leupps in Twenty fifth Street corner of Madison Avenue where I am staying. Mr. Leupp would have called to give you the invitation himself but he is suddenly called out of town. Your friend Mr. Laurence will be there and has prom-

ised me if you are at leisure to call for you.[2] We meet at 8 o'clock and are generally on the ground early.[3]

Yours truly

W C BRYANT

MANUSCRIPT: NYPL–GR (draft) ADDRESS: Mr. Thackeray.

1. In the fall and winter of 1855–1856 the English novelist William Makepeace Thackeray (1811–1863) made a second lecture tour of the United States.

2. Samuel Laurence (see 859.3), who had settled in New York City in 1854, had painted or drawn crayon portraits of many British and American literary men, including his friend Thackeray, as well as Bryant, Bancroft, Longfellow, and Lowell. *DAA; NAD Exhibition Record*, I, 286–287. He was an occasional guest at meetings of the Sketch Club.

3. Neither Laurence nor Thackeray attended the Sketch Club meeting on November 16. Information from James T. Callow. Bryant apparently renewed his invitation some weeks later, for on January 29, 1856, Thackeray wrote him to regret that a lecture engagement in Philadelphia would prevent his accepting an invitation to dine with Bryant that evening. Letter in NYPL–GR.

928.   *To* Cyrus Bryant

New York   November 15, 1855.

Dear Brother.

I got your letter day before yesterday.[1] By good luck I have got two slender tubers of the *dioscorea*, one of which shall be yours. I think you will have to plant it in pots as soon as you get it, to be sure of keeping it through the winter—cutting it in pieces of two inches and a half in length, and laying horizontally under an inch of earth. Send for it as soon as you please.

Yrs truly

W. C. BRYANT.

MANUSCRIPT: BCHS.

1. Unrecovered.

929.   *To* William Gilmore Simms

New York   November 16   1855.

My dear sir.

James H.[1] Hackett Esq. with whose histrionic reputation you are well acquainted, visits Charleston in company with his son, and will hand you this letter.[2] His amiable character and engaging social qualities have gained him a large circle of friends here, and I take the liberty of commending him to that kindness which I have myself experienced at your hands.

I am sir

very truly yours

W C BRYANT.

MANUSCRIPT: NYHS ADDRESS: Wᵐ Gilmore Simms Esqre. / Charleston / South Carolina ENDORSED (by Hackett): Not in the city / whilst I stopped there / Dec 1855—.

1. Bryant mistakenly wrote "A."
2. Bryant had known the veteran stage comedian James Henry Hackett (1800–1871) since he had headed a prize committee in 1830 which chose for Hackett James Kirke Paulding's play *The Lion of the West.* This had given Hackett one of his most popular roles, that of Colonel Nimrod Wildfire. See Vol. I, 260; Odell, *Annals,* III, 502.

930.   *To* Christiana Gibson

New York   Nov. 25, 1855

My dear Miss Gibson

It was very ill-natured of the doctor to keep you another season in Edinburgh when your friends were dying to see you here. Do not let the winds of that lofty capital blow you away before the return of Spring. Is it certain that your physician's prescriptions will be more effectual than the society of your friends in America would be? What is it that the author of the Proverbs says "doeth good like a medicine"?[1] You see that moral influences were recognized, thousands of years since to be as potent over the health as the drugs of the apothecary. I hope you have fallen into the hands of a sensible man, who knows that medicines very often do more harm than good. If you come back mended in health, we shall be glad to have spared you so long.—

[unsigned]

MANUSCRIPT: NYPL–GR (draft).

1. Prov. 17:22; "A merry heart doeth good like a medicine, but a broken spirit drieth the bones."

931.   *To* Thatcher T. Payne[1]

[New York] December 27   1855.

Dear Payne.

I have, I think, no engagement which will interfere with my coming to your house, this evening, though I shall be obliged to traverse a good deal of space between this and eight o'clock. I should be glad to see your family again as well as to meet Dr. Palfrey,[2] and if I do not find myself over fatigued I will come.

Yours truly
W. C. BRYANT.

MANUSCRIPT: UVa.

1. See 126.2.
2. John Gorham Palfrey; see 482.4.

932. *To* Charles Mason[1]

New York, January 13, 1856

My dear sir.

In the distribution of seeds of the Chinese Sugar millet—or sugar cane—I hope to be remembered. If I am not mistaken, there are seeds of this plant at the Patent Office, which are to be sent to persons in different parts of the country, and being myself somewhat of a farmer on Long Island, I shall be obliged if you will send me a parcel.[2] I have also a brother in Illinois who is a nursery gardener by profession, and who has written to me to procure him seeds of the plant. May I ask you, therefore, in your distribution to send a parcel to

Arthur Bryant
Princeton
Bureau County
Illinois,

and another to

W. C. Bryant
New York

and greatly oblige

Your friend
W. C. BRYANT.

MANUSCRIPT: Unrecovered TEXT: "Life and Letters of Judge Charles Mason of Iowa . . . , 1804–1882," ed. Charles Mason Remey (Washington, D.C., 1932), I, Chapter III.8.45. Typescript in Columbia University Libraries ADDRESS: Chas. Mason, Esqre.

1. Mason had substituted briefly for William Leggett as an *EP* editor during Bryant's absence abroad in 1834; see 312.4.
2. From 1853 to 1857 Mason was United States Commissioner of Patents at Washington. No reply to this letter has been recovered.

933. *To* John Howard Bryant

New York   January 28, 1856.

Dear Brother,

I leave it to your judgment to make such an arrangement with regard to the land I wrote you about,[1] as you think best. As you observe I do not mean to be at any expense in fencing it. They may have it for four or five years if they want it—but unless you should see reason to judge otherwise, I think five years would be long enough. It is not very likely that I shall want to sell before that time—and if I do, I must wait.[2]

The letter answering the inquiries made by Mr. Bigelow, came early to hand, and I gave it to him that he might do as he pleases in regard to the land. He informs me that there is a kind of family quarrel about it which may perhaps prevent any thing from being done.

You speak of cold weather in Illinois. We have had cold weather too; this is the thirtieth day of sleighing in this city—a most extraordinary thing for New York, where the snow generally lies but a short time. Not only has there been sleighing but good sleighing, a deep solid bed of snow which has been no where worn out or melted down to the pavement. At this moment it is snowing very fast, and it looks very much as if the January thaw, the inevitable January thaw—would be pretermitted this year. Just now I am staying with my family in town, the Long Island railroad being now and then obstructed by the snow, but I shall get down there as soon as I can to cut scions from the Seekel pear trees, and make arrangements for grafting a few of my grown trees with the Aremberg, the Winter Nelis and the *Paradis d'Automne*—or rather Autumn Paradise. I am concerned that the tree from which you took cuttings is not the muscadine—it wants the musky flavor and perfume. I cannot see that it was ever grafted or budded and think it must be a natural fruit—the Roslyn pear it might be called.

We are getting on finely in politics. The Emigrants' Aid Society at present occupies a good deal of the public attention.[3] Subscriptions are collecting, with the intention of increasing its funds to $200.000 which is all that is wanted, but this fact I believe they do not mean to publish in the newspapers. Whenever they build a hotel they receive half the town lots which become the property of the association. Within four years they estimate that the funds will amount to two millions, which will be enough to people all New Mexico and Western Texas after Kansas shall have been admitted as a free state. Mr. Pierces message on Kansas has done a great deal of good in creating a feeling favorable to the emigration scheme.[4] Pierce and his confederates are sinking deeper and deeper every day.

I am glad to hear so good news of your wife and son. Their visit to the eastern states probably did them both good. Remember me very kindly to both.

Yours truly
W. C. BRYANT.

MANUSCRIPT: NYPL–BFP.

1. Letter unrecovered.

2. No record of Bryant's leasing Illinois land at this time has been found.

3. The New England Emigrant Aid Company was formed in February 1855 to promote organized anti-slavery migration from the northeastern states to Kansas Territory. Its chief promoter was the Massachusetts educator and legislator Eli Thayer (1819–1899), later a United States congressman.

4. In a special message on January 24 President Pierce attacked the emigrant aid groups for acts which, he said, antagonized the people of Missouri, "whose domestic peace was thus the most directly endangered," and he called the Free State movement in Kansas "revolutionary." Nevins, *Ordeal*, II, p. 417.

934. *To* Fanny Bryant Godwin

New York   Jan. 31, 1856. Thursday morning.

Dear Fanny.

Your mother as I understood her last night has concluded not to come out to Roslyn this week. She saw Mrs. Cairns last evening who said that you were desirous that she should remain in New York awhile for the sake of rest and recreation, and the extreme cold that we now have, has I think made her more willing to stay. I shall not come till she does.

We are all well. Julia was out at a party last night at Mr Fields and the night before at Miss Kirklands. We have an invitation to Mrs. R[obert] Sedgwicks on Saturday evening, and to Mrs. Butlers (Susan Sedgwick's)[1] on Tuesday.

I send you ten dollars which I wish you to give to Dennis—He said he wanted some money—and please help me to remember that I have paid it to him so that I may charge it when I come to Roslyn.

Love to the children—

Yrs affectionately
W   C   BRYANT

MANUSCRIPT: NYPL–GR ADDRESS: Mrs. F. B. Godwin.

1. Catharine Sedgwick's niece, Mrs. Charles E. Butler.

935. *To* John Howard Bryant

New York, February 15, 1856.

. . . I cannot go to Pittsburg. I do not like public meetings.[1] I do not like consultations. I am surfeited with politics in my vocation, and when I go from home I cannot bear to carry them with me. If I were not a journalist, perhaps the case would be different. Then we have such a frightful winter, and I am anxious to seize the first moment of milder weather to see to some things at my place at Roslyn. The travel on the railways is often obstructed, and the ferries are choked with ice. That the consultations at Pittsburg will be among honest men is probable enough, but I am not a very firm believer in the honesty of parties. All parties include nearly all sorts of men, and the moment a party becomes strong the rogues are attracted to it, and immediately try to manage it. If they want its help for no other purpose, they want it to get into office, or perhaps simply to become notorious, which satisfies some people's ambition.

As to Kansas, I am not sure that there will not be some blood shed. But, blood or no blood, I am quite certain that it will be a free State. The whole city is alive with the excitement of the Kansas news, and people are subscribing liberally to the Emigrants' Aid Society. The companies of emigrants will be sent forward as soon as the rivers and lakes are opened— in March, if possible—and by the first of May there will be several thou-

sand more free-state settlers in Kansas than there now are. Of course they will go well armed. . . .

MANUSCRIPT: Unrecovered TEXT (*partial*): *Life*, II, 88–89.

1. In an unrecovered letter, John Bryant had apparently urged his brother to attend a meeting at Pittsburgh on February 22–23 of Free Soil and anti-slavery leaders from most of the northern states. John was one of several delegates from Illinois to this convention, at which a national Republican Party was brought into being. Edward Magdol, *Owen Lovejoy: Abolitionist in Congress* (New Brunswick, New Jersey: Rutgers University Press [1967]), pp. 135–140.

936.   *To* Frances F. Bryant

New York   March 3d   1856.

Dear Frances.

The waggon went smoothly enough this morning till we got a little beyond the Williams place. After that, in getting through the deep snow we came to two places where the road was in such a state that we had to get out to prevent it from being overturned. I would not come out if I were you till I heard that the snow in these places had been shovelled out or thawed away.

Mr. Culver has just called, and brought a request from Mrs. Hopkins[1] that you should come up with him tomorrow. I have sent word that I could not let you go [to Great Barrington] till the weather became milder, when I knew it was your intention to come. He gave me an account of Mr. Henderson's[2] illness. He was failing for some time but did not seem to suffer much—he said he was well enough. He went however to see Mrs. Clark, the clairvoyante or spiritual doctress. She described his case, he said exactly, but he would not take her medicines—roots and herbs—regularly. She told him he was in danger of epilepsy. At length, some eight or ten days before his death, he became so ill that he was obliged to keep his room and soon afterwards became deranged. Dr. Parks was employed, and after a few visits gave him up. Mrs. Clark was then employed and somewhat relieved him; his derangement, however, continued. He did not recognize James when he came; Charles was not there. He often refused to take medicines, except when little Jessie gave them to him. A short time before his death he seemed for a very few hours to suffer great agony; afterwards he became easy and soon dropped away without a struggle. The disease Culver thinks was principally about the kidneys, the loins and small of the back were discolored; Culver calls it mortified. Before he was confined to the room he had for a long time appeared differently from usual; he did not seem to care to live. At table, he had no appetite and would sometimes say grace twice over. These are all the particulars I can now remember from Mr Culver's somewhat unconnected account.

Ralph Taylor has quite recovered from his very dangerous illness, in

which he was near dying. He employed both Dr. Collins and Doctress Clark, but he took only the medicines of the female practitioner. Jessie Culver has been quite ill, but is now well again. Charles Hopkins is particularly well. The rest of our friends in Barrington are as well as usual.[3]

John Baltz was here this morning and I paid him his note. He wants to raise money on a mortgage which he has on his place at Newark. I gave him a letter to Charles Taylor.[4] He looks well and says his family are well. He has a farm of ninety acres at Oswego, four miles from Aurora, in Illinois.

I enclose some letters. I would send Henry as soon as possible to see his German. Let me know whether I am to come out next Sunday.

Yours ever
W. C. B.

MANUSCRIPT: NYPL–GR.

1. Frances' sister Mina, Mrs. Charles W. Hopkins (38.5).
2. Allen Henderson, husband of Frances' sister Esther (38.4).
3. James and Charles were Allen Henderson's sons. Ralph Taylor had been Bryant's roommate during his early years in Great Barrington; see 95.3. Others named in the foregoing paragraphs have not been further identified.
4. Charles Taylor was at one time a Great Barrington storekeeper. Baltz is not further identified.

937. *To* Frances F. Bryant

Office of the Evening Post
41 Nassau Street, cor. Liberty.
New York, April 7   1856

Dear Frances.

I sent a telegraphic message to Rochester this morning as soon as I arrived and I get no answer though it is nearly three o'clock. I shall write by mail as soon as I get one.

Fanny has been here. She has engaged the Irishman, but can get no girl. The boy is well.

Ever yours
W. C. B.

MANUSCRIPT: NYPL–GR.

938. *To* Frances F. Bryant

Office of the Evening Post
41 Nassau Street, cor. Liberty.
New York, April 9th   1856. Wednesday morning.

Dear Frances.

I can get no answer to the message I sent on Monday—though I have often sent to the Telegraph Office, and have directed the message to be

repeated. I can only suppose that the message has been sent to the house of Dr Tobey and that it is not understood—they probably do not understand what is to be done in order to reply.

Dennis is reengaged, and will bring you this.

I have just heard from the telegraph office that the second message was sent yesterday afternoon and that perhaps I may get an answer today.

> Yours ever
> W. C. B.

MANUSCRIPT: NYPL–GR.

939.   *To* Frances F. Bryant
> [New York] Wednesday, April 9. [1856] 12 o'clock M.

Dear Frances.

Half an hour ago I received the enclosed telegraphic despatch from which you will see that what we feared has come to pass.

About the same time the letter from Mrs. Hopkins which I also send was brought me.[1]

> Yours ever.
> W. C. B.

MANUSCRIPT: NYPL–GR.

1. The telegram and letter, neither recovered, apparently reported the death of one of Frances Bryant's near relatives in western New York state.

940.   *To* Julia S. Bryant
> New York   Wednesday morning   April 16   1856

Dear Julia

Will you send word to the Miss Hopkins's[1] that Mr. [Joseph] Curtis was buried yesterday afternoon. I was at the funeral. A discourse was preached by Mr. Bellows in his church to a crowded audience. After the services, the people present defiled down the middle aisle to take a last look at their friend, and went out at the side aisles.

Mr. Curtis died of a congestion of the brain on Saturday evening.

> Yours affectionately
> W. C. BRYANT

MANUSCRIPT: NYPL–GR.

1. The Bryants' next-door neighbors at Roslyn.

941.   *To* Frances F. Bryant
> New York   April 22, 1856.

My dear Frances.

I came into town this morning and got your note of Saturday.[1] Julia got yours yesterday. I am glad to learn that you had so pleasant a time in

travelling to Great Barrington and that you find the roads in such a condition that you can easily go from place to place. If you have had such
weather, however, as we have had for the last three days you must be almost under water. Sunday and Monday and this morning it rained co-
piously; the cisterns are full again, and the green grass in some places almost begins to wave in the wind.

My building materials arrived on Saturday. Next week, Tuesday or
Wednesday Mr. Wood begins. Henry remains at Fanny's with a little increase of wages. Fanny has got a new girl with whom she thinks she will
be satisfied, an Irish cook who has lived in Connecticut. Twalmley has
gone home till his lame foot is healed and then he is to call on me. Edward
is hard at work in the garden, which begins to look decently. The peas are
out of the ground, and are growing well.

As for the human beings at Roslyn they are all doing well. Mr. Stevens has had one or two persons to look at his place, but I have not heard
that any body has bought it. Mr. Cairns improves, it is thought slowly.
The children are all well.

I think I shall come on Saturday; it will not do to be absent longer,
if I go to Roslyn on Tuesday as I think I ought. My regards to all our
friends in Great Barrington.

Yours ever
W. C. BRYANT.

MANUSCRIPT: NYPL–GR.

1. Unrecovered.

942. *To* Julia S. Bryant

New York   April 24. 1856   Thursday afternoon.

Dear Julia

I find that the type of the article respecting Mr. Curtis[1] has been distributed, so that it cannot go into the weekly. It was the fault of Mr. Weyman,[2] who thought the news *local*. I have sent Miss Jenny [Hopkins] however, the copy of the daily containing it.

I enclose you the letter of your mother. Keep a look out for the Con-
cord Grape from Parsons.[3]

Yours ever
W C BRYANT.

MANUSCRIPT: NYPL–GR.

1. An *EP* obituary of April 15 remarked of Joseph Curtis (879.4), who had died on
the 12th, "His activity of mind, which was extraordinary, was devoted to the noblest
end—the good of his fellow-creatures. . . . He was one of the few persons we have
known, whom age did not make less hopeful." See Letter 940.
2. See Letter 912.
3. Probably Samuel Bowne Parsons (1819–1906), of Flushing, Long Island, a

nurseryman who later successfully imported Italian honey bees and Valencia oranges into the United States.

943. *To* Edwin D. Morgan and Others[1]

New York   April 28th   1856.

Gentlemen

It may not be in my power to be present at the meeting at which you have done me the honor to request my attendance,[2] but I fully agree with you as to the importance of a combined effort to assert the rights of the great body of American citizens against the encroachments of an oligarchy —a class of proprietors who seek to subject all other interests, even the most sacred and dear to their own.

Even if the question were merely whether we should stand by our old neighbors—our friends and kinsmen, who have lately left us for a new home west of Missouri, the occasion would be a fitting one to call forth all our zeal and unite all our strength. If we desert them in their hour of need, we shall be justly branded as cold-hearted, selfish and cowardly. No nation in the history of the world was ever so faithless to the obligations of humanity as to be indifferent to the fate of the colonies it had planted. With the republics of antiquity it was a matter of course to answer the calls of their colonies with instant sympathy and aid. England would cover herself with infamy, if she were to allow one of her colonies, appealing to her for protection, to be brought by force under the sway of an absolute government. In the present case the call made upon us is for a species of succor which will cost us no sacrifice, the cheap and peaceful aid of our votes. The votes of the great, prosperous, and powerful North are all that is required to deliver the settlements on the Kansas from the combination of fraud and violence formed to wrest from them their rights and compel them to submit to laws which their representatives never enacted. We raise committees, we organize a system of charity when our benevolence is appealed to by the people of a foreign country in distress. Ought we to do less for our own countrymen? Let us organize the entire region of the free states, with such aid as we can obtain from the just and well disposed of the slave states, into a great association for breaking up the conspiracy against the rights of our countrymen and kindred at the West who look to us for help. Every generous feeling allies itself with the sense of justice in favor of the cause in which you are engaged.

I am gentlemen
with great regard
Your obedient Servant
WM. C. BRYANT.

MANUSCRIPT: NYHS ADDRESS: Messrs. E. D Morgan, / Anthony Bleeker, / Wm M. Evarts, / C. C Leigh, / Jno Bigelow. PUBLISHED: *Life*, II, 89–90.

1. Edwin Denison Morgan (1811–1883), a New York banker, and president of the Hudson River Railroad, was Republican governor of New York, 1859–1862, and from 1863 to 1869 a United States senator. The other addressees were John Bigelow; Anthony J. Bleecker (1799–1884), a real estate auctioneer and a founder of the Republican Party; William Maxwell Evarts (1818–1901, Yale 1847), a lawyer and prominent Republican who became Secretary of State under President Rutherford B. Hayes; Charles C. Leigh is identified in *Trow's New York City Directory*, p. 490, as a crockery merchant located at 232 Bleecker and 183 Spring streets.

2. This was a large public meeting held on April 29 in the Broadway Tabernacle, the purpose of which was "to oppose the measures and policy of the present national administration for the extension of slavery over territory embraced within the compact of the 'Missouri Compromise,' and in favor of repairing the mischiefs arising from the violation of good faith in its repeal, and of restoring the action and position of the federal government on the subject of slavery to the principles of Washington and Jefferson." Bryant's letter was one of a number read at this meeting. See *EP*, April 29, 30, 1856.

944. *To* Frances F. Bryant

New York   May 14. 1856   Wednesday mng.

Dear Frances.

I went to the wedding yesterday after writing the leader in yesterdays paper and was in time. The house is three doors from Mr. Willis's and Mr. Sullivan who lives there is a partner of Wilson G. Hunt's. I made a sort of acquaintance with him on board one of the steamers returning from Europe. His wife is a buxom fresh coloured lady from New Jersey, and a particular friend of Miss Brittain's on which account the marriage took place there. There were thirty or forty people present and Dr Hawks performed the marriage ceremony. After the service there was a lunch and punch—as well as champagne. Of the ladies some wore their bonnets and some did not, all were in long sleeves. Dr Gray and all the family were there great and small. Mrs. Cornelius Lawrence was present and pelted me with a storm of invitations to come to her place, and not to be frightened from coming by any "suspicions" or any thing of the sort. Daniel Lord and his wife were there, Regina Morton, a Mr Tuckerman, not whom you know, &c. There were many inquiries about you. Dr. Hull was sorry you could not come. I made all sorts of apologies.[1]

The bride is pretty with a well developed figure, though small, fresh cheeks, plenty of soft brown hair and I think hazel eyes. She did not seem much flustered. Dr Hull looked thin and hollow cheeked. I will tell you the rest when I see you.

Yrs ever

W. C. B.

MANUSCRIPT: NYPL–GR.

1. The principals in this wedding were apparently a Miss Britain, not otherwise identified, and Dr. Amos Gerald Hull, Jr. (1810–1859). See 405.4. The guests who can

be identified are Wilson G. Hunt, a reform candidate for mayor of New York who was defeated by Fernando Wood, a Democrat, in 1854, and was later a promoter of the Atlantic Cable; Rev. Francis Lister Hawks (656.2); the wife of former mayor Cornelius Lawrence (314.1); Daniel Lord (1795–1868), a New York attorney who had represented John Jacob Astor (1763–1848). The Bryants were acquainted with the critic and essayist Henry Theodore Tuckerman (1813–1871), who had written *A Memorial of Horatio Greenough* (New York, 1853); the wedding guest was probably his cousin Frederick Goddard Tuckerman (1821–1873), the poet.

945.   *To* Frances F. Bryant
Office of the Evening Post,
41 Nassau Street, cor. Liberty.
New York, May 21, 1856. Wednesday morning.
Dear Frances.

I was at Mrs Gibson's last evening. They had received Miss Christiana's letter, and seemed pleased to hear that she was to remain with you for a few days. Mrs. Gibson bid me tell you that she thanked you for the care you were taking of her. They were all quite well. *No hoy novedad* [No news today], as the Spaniards say. I called also on Mrs. Robert Sedgwick, who has made a visit to Mrs. Channing her sister—a visit of seven weeks. She found her in a sort of stony apathy of inconsolable grief, and succeeded a little in bringing her to a more cheerful temper.[1]

I must come out on Friday. Next week Bigelow wants to be absent and I must be here every day

Yours ever
W. C. B.

MANUSCRIPT: NYPL–GR.

1. Edward Channing (Letter 947) had died on February 7, 1856.

946.   *To* Frances F. Bryant
[New York] Wednesday evening, June 11, 1856.
Dear Frances.

I send you a little letter from Ellen [Mitchell] enclosed.

Mr. Bigelow did not get home till today. I have written a letter to Mr. Alden telling him that I cannot come to Easton at present.[1] I suppose you have heard that Ogden Butler son of Mr. Charles Butler is dead.[2] His disorder was a consumption; the scrophulous complaint in the hip seemed to be translated to the lungs and its progress was rather rapid. His funeral took place last Sunday. I send this by Mrs. Willis who goes out tomorrow, though I suppose it possible that you may come in today. Next Wednesday evening is the Annual Strawberry Festival of the Century, when those

must be here who can. I have some other news for you but I suppose you will hear it before I come home, and I had rather not write it.

Yours truly
W. C. B.

MANUSCRIPT: NYPL–GR.

1. Joseph Alden (1807–1885), then teaching at Lafayette College in Easton, Pennsylvania, was later the president of Jefferson College, 1857–1862, and principal of the state normal school at Albany, New York, 1867–1882. In 1877 Alden published at New York *Studies in Bryant. A Text-Book*, with an introduction by Bryant. Bryant's letter to Alden is unrecovered.

2. Ogden Butler, son of the lawyer and railroad builder Charles Butler (1802–1897), and nephew of Benjamin Franklin Butler (374.1), died at the age of twenty-seven.

947. *To* Richard H. Dana

New York   June 23, 1856.

Dear Dana,

My English acquaintanceship is not very extensive, and I am more scrupulous about giving a letter of introduction to an Englishman than to one of my own countrymen. Cooper once said to me that he would give nobody a letter to an Englishman. We Americans are quite too apt to address letters of introduction to persons whom we scarcely know, and the English, knowing that we have this infirmity, are perhaps inclined to hold us to stricter rules in this matter than they would hold their own countrymen.

Nevertheless I send you a letter for your son,[1] which may answer for an introduction to the courts of law, and perhaps to other persons of distinction—a letter to Mr. Edwin Field a lawyer of large practice in London, with whom I became acquainted through his brother, an excellent friend of mine, and who gave me while in England some letters that were quite useful to me. Through him I became acquainted with Mr. Crabbe Robinson, the friend of Wordsworth and Coleridge and a man of uncommon conversational powers. I shall never forget a pleasant day passed with Mr. Edwin Field, Robinson, Fripp an artist, and a young Puseyite clergyman whose name I have forgotten at a pleasant village on the Thames.[2]

I am sorry you do not find it convenient to pass the summer at your place on the sea-shore. If it were not for my occasional retreats to the country I do not know what would become of me. If you cannot go to your own place, will not you and your daughter think of coming for a short time to mine[?] We will not insist on either of you knowing any thing of the last new book. I am sure I rarely do—unless it be the book of your friend Channing which I have read—or rather parts of it for I have not finished the volume—with much satisfaction. It is very sensible and just; he was a good thinker, and yet I did not find so much warmth and earnestness of

manner, so much of the power of carrying along the reader in spite of himself as I expected. The biography is exceedingly well done.[3]

For the political state of the country, I acknowledge that it is bad enough, and yet I do not despair of it— I rarely despair of any thing, in fact; for it is not in my temperament to do so. It looks very much, at present, as if the administration at Washington, and the party that supports it were about to meet with a signal overthrow in the elections. If their conduct be wicked, it is a comfort to me that there are so many who condemn it.

I am not much absorbed in farming. The man whom I have on my place goes rather deeper into it than I wish he would. My ambition is to have a little fruit for all seasons—straw berries in their time, European grapes in a cold vinery, and pears from August to Easter. I am fussing a little with figs and hope yet to eat one of my own raising, but I have not succeeded yet. Julia is an anthomaniac, and overwhelms me with everblooming roses, verbenas, and a dozen varieties of the clematis. But gardening is merely my recreation, and does not withdraw me from literary pursuits. If it had not been that I lost money about two years since I think I should have nearly got myself clear of the drudgery of my newspaper by this time. At present, I have no desire to leave the field till I see what is to be the result of the November election.

You have an excellent practice of filling your sheet when you write a letter. My brain is not so "forgetive" as yours I believe, and after writing a while I can think of nothing more to set down. It wants the stimulus of a reply to set it in motion again. So you must be content with three pages in lieu of four, for this time at least. Re . . .[4]

MANUSCRIPTS: NYPL–GR (draft and final) ENDORSED: Wm C. Bryant, June / 23rd / 56.— Ans. 21.

1. Letter 948.
2. See Letter 545.
3. Edward Tyrell Channing, *Lectures Read to the Seniors in Harvard College* (Boston, 1856). Richard H. Dana, Jr., contributed a biographical memoir to this posthumous book.
4. Conclusion and signature missing.

948.   *To* Edwin W. Field

[New York   June 23?   1856]

My dear sir

The bearer of this letter is Richard H. Dana jr. author of a work which has been very extensively read on both sides of the Atlantic, "Two Years before the Mast." He is the son of my friend Richard H. Dana the poet, and is himself one of the most distinguished advocates of Massa-

chusetts. He desires while in England to see something of your courts and of those who are distinguished in the profession of law. He has some hereditary claim to be interested in this subject, as his grandfather was . . .[1]

May I ask you to give him such assistance in his . . .[2]

MANUSCRIPT: NYPL–GR (draft).

1. A portion of the manuscript is missing here. Young Dana's grandfather was Francis Dana (1743–1811, Harvard 1762), chief justice of Massachusetts, 1791–1806.

2. Several versions of this fragmentary sentence conclude the very rough draft.

949. *To* Frances F. Bryant

New York   June 25, 1856. Wednesday—

Dear Frances,

Mr. [Isaac] Henderson tells me that blinds are made here and fitted on for five and sixpence a foot—which is sixpence less than they cost at the Branch. But the maker he says, would probably not send out to Roslyn a workman to fit them on—and something might be deducted for that. I shall inquire.— If I had the measure I might perhaps engage them immediately.

Yours ever
W. C. B.

P. S. I send this by Mr. Moulton to his wife who goes out I suppose to-morrow.

MANUSCRIPT: NYPL–GR.

950. *To* Calvin Durfee[1]

New York   July 4th   1856.

Dear sir.

It is with great reluctance that I ever consent to write verses for particular occasions, on account of the difficulty and in some cases the impossibility of producing any thing with which I am satisfied. Moreover I have arrived at that time of life when it seems to me that I ought to leave such tasks to youthful poets who may be supposed to be more easily moved by casual impulses. My poetic vein also, owing I suppose to disuse, is become more capricious and unmanageable than formerly.

In regard to the hymn which you have done me the honor to ask me to write, I have done as I sometimes do on such occasions; I have considered whether there is any thing to be said which I could say *well*, without taking more trouble than I have now leisure to take. It is not my fault if I have arrived at a negative conclusion. I must rely therefore on your good nature to excuse me. The subject certainly admits of poetic treat-

ment—but you know what merely middling things all such verses are apt to be even when from the pens of clever writers.[2]

I am sir

with much regard yours,

W   C   BRYANT.

MANUSCRIPT: WCL ADDRESS: Calvin Durfee Esqre.

1. Calvin Durfee (1797–1879) was secretary of the Society of Alumni of Williams College.

2. In 1859 Bryant wrote for Durfee an account of his life at Williams College in 1810–1811, which was published in Durfee's *History of Williams College* (Boston, 1860), pp. 106–108. See *Life*, II, 86–88. In 1863 he contributed to the fiftieth anniversary celebration of the class of 1813, in which he had been briefly enrolled, verses entitled "Fifty Years," published after Bryant's death in *Poetical Works*, II, 327–330.

951.   *To* Julia S. Bryant

Roslyn   July 29   1856   Tuesday morning.

Dear Julia.

I am glad that you find a sojourn at Florence so much to your taste, and particularly that you have taken so kindly to early rising, and exercise before breakfast. I have now no doubt that you will come back in better health, and if the old proverb be true wiser than you went "Early to rise," you know, &c. I only wish that Fanny were more contented with the place, but perhaps she is by this time accustomed to wheaten grits for breakfast. There is no doubt in my mind that the diet prescribed by Dr. Munde[1] is the best for her.

We are getting on very well here. I am passing a few days at Roslyn superintending the draining of the marsh about our little sheet of water and looking to the carpenters, who are now pulling down the old wood house while I write. With the kitchen part they have got on quite well, and the problem of getting out of the main building into it from the second story and from the kitchen part into the garret is happily solved.

Since you left us we have had no rain—at least until now while I am writing, when a very penurious shower is falling which does not promise to continue long. The grass in many places has become withered and crisp and every green thing languishes. The sky has been thick with a dull dust colored haze, and the weather for a good part of the time quite hot. I hope the few drops we have this morning betoken that the draught is at an end.

Your mother I take for granted has written you all about the burning of Mr. Robert Stuart's house.[2] The other Stuart was sorely bested with the asthma while here and has taken quite a prejudice against the Roslyn climate. He went away on Saturday morning.

If you are all pleased with your sojourn at Florence and think it is

doing you good—Fanny I hope is converted ere this—suppose you stay a few days longer—a week if it suits you, beyond the fortnight.

Your flowers have been a little neglected I fear during your absence, but they have not suffered much. The grapes are growing as fast as they can and I think will ripen earlier than last year.

Love to Fanny and Ellen if they are with you.

I am dear daughter—
affectionately yours
W. C. BRYANT.

MANUSCRIPT: NYPL–GR ADDRESS: Miss Julia Bryant.

1. A German physician who conducted a water-cure sanitarium in Florence, near Northampton, Massachusetts.

2. Naval Lieutenant Robert Stuart, Jr. (d. 1863), and his bride of 1855, the former Ellen Elizabeth Cairns (1826–1893), occupied a house her mother had built for them on Hempstead Harbor, "Locust Knoll," near Bryant's Cedarmere. Goddard, *Roslyn Harbor*, pp. 33–34; Cairns Family Genealogical Chart, prepared by Helen Marlatt, Bryant Library, Roslyn. The "other Stuart" is unidentified.

952. *To* Julia S. Bryant

Roslyn   August 2d   1856.

Dear Julia.

Your mother got your letter yesterday. We are glad to know that the bathing and air of the place agree with you so well. Stay as long as you think it is doing you good, and you are contented. I wish you had told us about Ellen—whether she submitted to the water treatment.[1] I am in great haste and cannot write you a long letter. We are all well—Dennis has been sick, but your mother and I have cured him. Mr. Kline[2] brought back his Johnny quite ill—we cured him also—we or nature. Your mother has had a languid time with pain in her limbs and is better. The whole world is about us, attracted to Cedarmere by wages—high wages too—hammering, pounding plastering, ditching. I am glad tomorrow is Saturday. Fanny's children also all well—except that some of them have a troublesome influenza. Your mother sends love.

Yours affectionately
W   C   BRYANT.

MANUSCRIPT: NYPL–GR.

1. In the mid-nineteenth century Northampton and its neighboring village Florence were noted for their water cures, numbering among their patients Harriet Beecher Stowe and Major Thomas Jonathan Jackson—later Confederate general "Stonewall" Jackson. *Northampton, Massachusetts* ([Northampton Chamber of Commerce, 1966?]), p. 10.

2. Probably George B. Cline, a Roslyn schoolteacher who became Bryant's estate steward in 1858. See Bigelow, *Bryant*, pp. 265–266.

953. *To* Catharine M. Sedgwick

[Roslyn] August 8, 1856

I did not hear till yesterday of the calamity which has overtaken your family in the loss of your brother. I should rather say has overtaken us all—for it is the common misfortune of all who knew him.[1] Your letter which I did not receive till the 2d of August, just after I had sent off a letter to him gave me reason to fear a fatal termination of his disease; and one from Mr. Dewey which came to my hands at the same moment contained some strong expressions of concern on his account.[2] But the death of those we love and wish to keep with us almost always has the effect of a terrible surprise, even though we are prepared for it by their gradual decline. He seemed the very man who should be spared to the latest term of human life, to show how beautiful and lovely old age might be. One can scarce imagine a spectacle more delightful than the serene evening of such a life as his—the day of existence on this sphere drawn to a midsummer length, ending in a genial sunset—and as the truly good grow better as they grow older, the graces of his character heightened to the last.

But this was not to be and it seems almost a profane intermeddling with such a grief as this at such a time to suggest any thoughts which tend to reconcile the mind to such a dispensation. Yet I may be allowed to say that the very virtues which make his friends grieve are the source of their consolation, when we think that the more we have lost in him, the more he is sure to have gained. If few have lost so much as you, for that very reason few have the occasion of being so largely comforted.

I was very much struck not very long since at the answer of one to whom the prospect of life seemed uncertain, and whom I was endeavoring to console with the hope of a happier state of existence— "It will be no heaven to me["] she answered, ["]if my friends are not there." She was one who if she departed then must leave those who were dearest to her behind. The delights of the next life I am sure are not selfish; they *must* be social. ["]I go to prepare a place for you," said our Saviour to his disciples—[3] The good who depart before us have all this office, it is they who will make a great part of the heaven for which we hope. Every passage of those we love into the next life prepares it for our reception if we are worthy to follow them.

I hope I commit no impertinence in addressing you these words—so little words. My wife bids me write, and I trust to her instincts in a matter in which my own natural reserve might have dictated a silence which if less demonstrative would have been equally full of sympathy. Meantime she desires me to say to you how deeply she takes part in this sorrow.

I am dear [friend?]
very truly yours
W C B.[4]

MANUSCRIPT: NYPL–GR (draft) ADDRESS: Miss C M Sedgwick— PUBLISHED (*in part, with changes*): *Life*, II, 90–91.

1. After a long illness, Charles Sedgwick had died at his home in Lenox, Massachusetts, on August 3, 1856. *Life and Letters of Catharine M. Sedgwick*, ed. Mary E. Dewey (New York, 1871), p. 364.
2. None of these three letters has been recovered.
3. John 14:2–3.
4. A short postscript is illegible.

954. *To* Julia S. Bryant

Roslyn   August 11th, 1856. [Monday][1]

Dear Julia.

Your mother has had frequent headaches of late, in consequence, I think, of her many cares, and I think your being here would be a sensible relief to her. It would allow her to make her escape for a short time from all the noise and clatter we have constantly about us. Moreover, the carpenters will be ready in a few days to begin upon your room, and we want you to decide what changes shall be made. We have thought therefore that it would be well for you to come home, at the end of this week. Please bring Dr. Munde's bill with you and thank him in your mother's name and mine for the attention he has paid to your case.[2]

The workmen employed on our house are getting on very well. In some respects we have been obliged to change the original plan, and in some respects we perceive now that we might have planned better than we have. On the whole, however, we are satisfied—I am for my part very well satisfied with the alterations we have made in the old part of the building and with the new part. It is more convenient than most houses, and in some respects more convenient than any I ever lived in. There are yet huge piles of rubbish lying about it, which are growing larger rather than smaller.

When you return do not come by Great Barrington. Fanny says the route is both circuitous and expensive, and will be perplexing to you on account of being obliged to change cars so often at the intersections of the railways, where the baggage must be changed from one conveyance to another. If you wish to go to Barrington it would be better to go thither immediately from New York.

Your mother sends her love. . . .[3]

MANUSCRIPT: NYPL–GR.

1. The brackets are Bryant's.
2. The nature of Julia's illness is undetermined.
3. Conclusion and signature missing.

955.   *To* Alfred B. Street[1]

[Roslyn, Long Island, August 11, 1856]

... Your invitation is most kind and there is no man in Albany from whom I should be prouder to receive such an offer of hospitality. But I am confined to these latitudes, repairing my house, building a new kitchen, making drains, reclaiming a marsh and making basins for my springs. At this time every moment I can spare from the paper must be given to the superintendence of my workmen at my place in the country. ...

MANUSCRIPT: Unrecovered TEXT (*partial*): American Art Association Catalogue, May 14, 1914, No. 160.

1. Alfred Billings Street (1811–1881), a lawyer and poet, was the director of the New York State Library at Albany. The nature of his invitation is undetermined.

956.   *To* Messrs. Dix & Edwards

New York   Sept. 2   1856

Gentlemen.

If the bundle of papers which I sent yesterday to Mr. Curtis is still with you, please allow Mr. Rakemann, the bearer, who is one of the Committee to adjudge the prize to the author of the best Frémont Song, to look at them.[1]

Yrs truly

W   C   BRYANT.

MANUSCRIPT: HCL ADDRESS: Messrs Dix & Edwards.

1. In May 1856 the *EP* had printed an account by John Bigelow of the life of John Charles Frémont (1813–1890). After the nomination of that soldier–explorer in June as the first Republican candidate for the presidency, Bryant brought the *EP* to his support in what was for him a rare political speech, at a Republican rally in Yonkers, New York, concluding with the slogan, "Freedom and Frémont." During the summer the *EP* offered two prizes of $100 each for the best campaign songs in English and German. The winning English contribution, by the painter–poet Thomas Buchanan Read (1822–1872), appeared in the *EP* on October 6. George William Curtis (1824–1892), then an editor of *Putnam's Monthly Magazine*, was a reformer active in the anti-slavery movement. He had introduced Bryant at the Yonkers meeting as one "known to our country-men as the first of our citizens in every respect," one whose line from "The Battlefield," "Truth crushed to earth shall rise again," expressed a "sentiment worthy to be the watch word of freemen in all time." *EP*, May 19 and 24, July 12, October 6, 1856; Nevins, *Evening Post*, pp. 231, 252. Rakemann is unidentified.

957.   *To* Julia S. Bryant

Great Barrington   Friday afternoon   September 26th   1856

Dear Julia.

I shall leave this place tomorrow for New York, having delivered my speech.[1] Your mother with Major Hopkins and your aunt expects to fol-

low me on Monday—so that you will have them all on Tuesday. I write that you may have every thing ready.

There has been an immense throng here—eight thousand people at the fair, and every thing has passed off well. Mrs. Henderson is very infirm, but apparently slowly improving. Estelle [Ives] cannot come now.

Yours affectionately
W   C   BRYANT

P.S. Willis and his wife expect to come to Roslyn on Tuesday.

MANUSCRIPT: NYPL–GR.

1. Bryant spoke at the annual fair of the Berkshire Agricultural Society, to which he had addressed several odes during his residence in Great Barrington in 1816–1825. See 39.3. His 1856 speech apparently was not preserved.

958.   *To* John Howard Bryant

New York, October 14, 1856

Dear Brother

As soon as I received your last,[1] I caused its contents to be communicated to our Fremont Committee. Its account of the politics of Illinois was confirmed by other letters in their possession. They said they should immediately take measures to send speakers into your state, which I believe has been done.

We expect a favorable report from Pennsylvania to-morrow. The Buchanan men here are desponding, and it seems to be thought that if the State election goes against them, the Presidential election will go against them also. I do not think that certain, however, though it is probable.[2]

There is good hope of New Jersey. If the means can be provided of getting the Fremont voters to the polls, we stand the best chance of the two. They have a practice in New Jersey of providing conveyances for the voters at the expense of the general election fund of the party to which they belong. The Buchanan men will lose no votes for want of money to pay the carriage hire of those who vote.

New York we regard as perfectly safe for Fremont. The Fillmore party—their agents and leaders at least—brag high, but they either know better or are grossly deceived themselves.[3] Both they and the Buchanan party—their active men and journalists at least make common cause against the free-soilers, though I think they will not come to a formal coalition; the mass of each party not being at all prepared for it. Such a measure would ruin them both. They would be glad to come to an understanding, I fully believe, but the people are in the way.

We are keeping up the contest with the best hopes of success. A very large class of persons who never took any interest in elections before are zealous Fremonters now—among these are clergymen and Quakers and indifferents of all sorts. These men will swell the vote for Fremont in the

choice of electors; but will not make much figure at the previous State elections.[4]

The season thus far has been beautiful with us. I have had a tolerably fair supply of apples, both in quantity and quality. My dwarf pear trees have produced pretty well. Our Vicar of Winkfield was loaded. My two Urbaniste trees were quite fruitful, and so was my Bon Chretien fondante and Louise Bonne de Jersey. The Portugal Quince was full of fruit. In all respects the year has been a fruitful one with us on Long Island.

I am sorry to hear so bad an account of your pear trees. If in the dry weather you had wet the mulching with a pailful of water to each tree, and put stones, if you could find them on the mulching, if not sticks, the moisture would have been retained a long time.

Remember me kindly to all. We are all pretty well.

Yrs truly

W   C   BRYANT

MANUSCRIPT: NYPL–BFP ADDRESS: Jno H. Bryant Esqre. PUBLISHED (in part): Life, II, 91–93.

1. Letter unrecovered.

2. In June 1856 the new Republican Party nominated as its first presidential candidate John Charles Frémont; earlier that month the Democrats had chosen as their candidate James Buchanan (1791–1868, Dickinson 1809) of Pennsylvania, a former senator, Secretary of State, and minister to Great Britain.

3. Former President Millard Fillmore (1800–1874) of New York was the presidential candidate of the Native American, or "Know-Nothing," Party, composed chiefly of disgruntled former Whigs with an anti-foreign and anti-Catholic bias.

4. In the national election on November 4, Buchanan received 174 electoral votes; Frémont, 114; and Fillmore, 8. But Buchanan's popular vote fell short of the combined tally of his opponents by more than 375,000; thus he became a minority president. Nevins, Ordeal, II, 510. On the next day the EP commented editorially, "If we have not carried the United States, . . . we have at least laid the basis of a formidable and well-organized party, in opposition to the spread of slavery—that scheme which is the scandal of the country and of the age."

959.   To Frederic Tudor[1]

New York   Oct   23   1856.

Dear sir

Through our common friend Dr. Piper[2] I have received your very kind invitation to visit your place at Nahant.[3] His account of it—to say nothing of the picture he drew of its amiable inmates, had raised in me a strong curiosity to see a spot which you have made beautiful in spite of Nature—if perhaps I should not rather say by a skilful turning of Nature— a curiosity which my wife shares with me. She has desired me when I acknowledge your civility, to return her thanks to you and Mrs. Tudor, and to say for her as I do for myself that only the lateness of the season and some engagements at home prevent us from accepting the invitation at

present. We have never yet seen Nahant and since your hospitable invitation includes another season we hope to have that pleasure hereafter.

> I am sir
> yours very truly
> W C Bryant.

MANUSCRIPT: NYPL–GR (draft) ADDRESS: Frederick Tudor Esq.

1. In 1806 the Boston businessman Frederic Tudor (1783–1864) had pioneered in shipping ice to the West Indies, eventually establishing a highly lucrative worldwide trade. He was a younger brother of William Tudor (1779–1830), a politician, author, and founder and first editor in 1815 of the *North American Review*.

2. Dr. R. N. Piper of West Groton, Massachusetts, was a horticulturalist and amateur artist who later wrote articles on fruit culture for the *EP*. Piper to Bryant, March 3, 1866, and Bryant to Piper, March 9, 1866, NYPL–GR. See also Letter 997.

3. A resort on the Massachusetts seacoast north of Boston.

960. *To* Cyrus Bryant

> New York   October 31, 1856.

Dear Brother.

You ask me to transfer the Evening Post, which is now sent to Mr. Daniel Bryant, to yourself.[1] I have directed it to be stopped from going any more to him; but if you want it I think you can afford to take it. That he does not agree with its political views, is certainly a very good reason why he should not take much interest in reading it, as it is at present conducted, and if Buchanan should be elected, which God forbid, it will probably be less to the taste of Buchanan's friends than it now is. I have many personal friends who will not touch the paper.

> Yours truly
> W C Bryant.

MANUSCRIPT: NYPL–BFP ADDRESS: C. Bryant Esqre.

1. Bryant probably refers to his father's cousin, but it is uncertain where Daniel Bryant was living at this time.

961. *To* Frances F. Bryant

> New York   November 6th, 1856.

Dear Frances.

I called on Mrs. Robinson last evening. Her husband has been ill with a remittent fever of the typhoid type, and is still quite weak, so that he scarcely goes out.[1] Accordingly, neither she nor Mary can come out at present to Roslyn. I saw the young lady, and gave her a particular invitation, but her mother cannot dispense with her company yet. I have ordered the candles and isinglass—so you will send for them. I shall not come home till Saturday evening.

Mr. William Appleton has returned from Europe, after an absence of five months. He has seen he says the design for the new illustrated edition of my poems, which is to be out in July next[2]—I do not suppose he has seen all—they are, he says very fine—he thinks finer than Longfellows. The landscape sketches furnished by Durand are used in them and the American character of the scenery is well preserved. Laurence's head of me is to be the portrait.[3]

Yours ever
W. C. B.

MANUSCRIPT: NYPL–GR.

    1. Edward and Therese Robinson; see 399.2.

    2. In 1838 William Henry Appleton (1814–1899) and his father, Daniel (1785–1849), had founded the firm of D. Appleton and Company, Bryant's principal publishers from 1854.

    3. See 927.2. The edition referred to here was *Poems by William Cullen Bryant. Collected and Arranged by the Author. Illustrated with Seventy-one Engravings. From Drawings by Eminent Artists* (New York and London: D. Appleton and Company, 1856). This was printed in London by R. Clay.

962.   *To* Samuel H. Dickson

New York   Nov. 17   1856

Mr dear sir

Your letter of the 9th. instant with its enclosure came safely to hand.[1] I wish you had waited a day or two longer that you might have informed me of the arrival of the wine and how you found it. The trouble I have taken in the matter is very little, indeed it is not so much as I ought to have taken, for I might have written earlier to Mr. Hammett to inquire what had become of the *lagrima* which I ordered.[2] My excuse for not doing so is that in his first letter to me Mr Hammett spoke doubtfully of its being sent immediately for want of opportunity.

If none of us have written to you for some time past it is not because we have "forgotten" you and yours, as you express it. We often talked of you, and with the deepest sympathy, when one of your family was called from you. We heard of you through the Dewey family, and their account of you all seemed like renewing the pleasant intercourse of former days. Dr Dewey with his wife and Miss Mary passed a few days with us on their return to the north.

My wife would be the happiest creature in the world could she accept your kind invitation for Wednesday evening, but unfortunately she is in the country confined with the inflammatory rheumatism. My own engagements will prevent me from being present.

I am dear friend
very truly yours
W   C   BRYANT

MANUSCRIPT: NYPL–GR.

1. Letter unrecovered.

2. Probably Henry Pinckney Hammett (1822–1891), a South Carolina cotton manu-facturer. It was probably his cotton mill near Augusta which Bryant visited in March 1849, and described in Letter 671. On December 6, Dickson replied (NYPL–GR) that he had received the wine.

963. *To* Parke Godwin

New York Dec 2 1856

Dear sir

Mr Titus[1] has just called to say that the Superintendent of Public In-struction will probably be removed, and to ask if you would like it. The salary he thinks is $2500—the duties may or may not be laborious; neither he nor I know.[2]

Mr. Titus's office is 34 Liberty Street, where he will be day after tomorrow.

Yours truly
W. C. BRYANT

MANUSCRIPT: NYPL–GR ADDRESS: P. Godwin Esq.

1. Probably Jacob Titus; see 766.6.

2. Godwin did not take this position; see Letter 969.

964. *To* Messrs. Childs & Peterson

New York January 15, 1857.

Gentlemen,

The merits of Dr. Kane's recent work are so universally acknowl-edged, that it seems superfluous to praise it.[1] It is a record of one of the most daring, and so far as the interests of science are concerned, one of the most successful enterprises of modern times, and is written in a most in-teresting manner—a manner which gives the reader a high idea of the in-tellectual and moral qualities of the author.

I am, gentlemen,
respectfully yours,
W. C. BRYANT.

MANUSCRIPT: Indiana University Library ADDRESS: Messrs. Childs & Peterson.

1. Elisha Kent Kane (1820–1857, M.D. Pennsylvania 1842), *Arctic Explorations* (Philadelphia, 1856). This was Kane's account of his hazardous experiences, as leader of the second Grinnell Expedition (1853–1855), which contributed to a fuller explora-tion of northern Greenland than had previously been made.

965. *To* Julia S. Bryant

New York January 16, 1857

Dear Julia,

I got your letter of this morning. The letter for Josephine I mailed to Mrs. Josephine M. Stewart, care of David Stewart Esqre. Baltimore, Maryland, which I am sure will reach her.[1] When you write to a lady always address the letter to her by her own name if you know it—and then though you direct it to the care of the wrong person she will be apt to get it. Whether her husband be John or David Stewart I am uncertain, but as they are brothers, if the one gets it who is not the lady's husband, he will be very sure to send it to her.

The Long Island Rail road has been somewhat obstructed by snow, and when your mother went out a fortnight since she was detained several hours. Since that time it has been clear I believe as far as Farmingdale. The ferries have been much obstructed, and the boats delayed by ice, particularly the South Ferry, so that persons who took the cars had to go by way of Fulton Ferry. Yesterday your mother, after putting it off a day or two on account of the cold weather, went down to Roslyn taking with her the woman who lived at Mrs. Miller's, and whom she designs for Fanny. Tomorrow I shall follow, with the intention of remaining till Tuesday.

I am glad that you are so well entertained at Barrington and so studious besides. Tell Mrs. Ives from me that she must keep a tight rein over you and hold you firmly to your studies, so that if you take any thing from the time you should give them on one day you may a little more than make it up the next—the little more being a voluntary penance for the negligence.

There was a gay time at the Century on the evening after you left—and a very stupid one I am told last evening at the Academy of Music, when they danced for the benefit of the poor children—a cold crowded comfortless room—a chilly jam and that was all. Adele Hoyt[2] was married yesterday—I forget to whom, but it was some young man, who is now out of the market.

Give my best regards to Mrs Ives and Ma'amselle, and to Julia[3] and all our friends in Barrington.

Yours affectionately
W. C. BRYANT.

MANUSCRIPT: NYPL–GR.

1. Leonice Josephine Moulton Stewart (1834–1922) was the wife of John Stewart (1826–1901), a Baltimore merchant. She was the daughter of Mr. and Mrs. Joseph White Moulton. Hoyt, "Bryant Correspondence (I)," 69.

2. Probably a daughter of Jesse Hoyt (230.6).

3. Julia Fairchild, Frances Bryant's niece.

966. *To* Julia S. Bryant

New York January 29, 1857.

Dear Julia.

Your mother is very ill with an attack of acute rheumatism. For some time she had suffered a good deal from a sensation of extreme chilliness which was succeeded on Thursday night by fever and severe internal pains. I was at home, at Roslyn, blockaded by the snow. We did not know what to make of it at first—some of the symptoms resembling those of lung fever, but on Sunday night it declared itself as a decided rheumatic complaint. I came in on Monday morning in an open sleigh, saw the doctor the next morning, and on Tuesday took out his prescription. I found her suffering still more than when I left her. She cannot move herself in bed, and cannot be moved without excrutiating pain. It seems to me the most painful of diseases. This morning I left her very little better, though she had slept during the night after two sleepless nights. I regard the sleep as a favorable symptom.

I think therefore you had better return with as little delay as may be. Your mother will come to town as soon as she is well enough, but in the meantime she is much better there than here. I shall go to Roslyn again tomorrow after seeing Dr. Gray. Susan is taking care of your mother, but I doubt not your presence would be a comfort to her; though much company—or rather much prattle, tires her.

The only news I can tell you of Roslyn is that Stuart has returned, that Mr. and Mrs Cairns are in town at a house in Broadway where they can see every thing that passes from the windows, that Roslyn harbor is sheeted with ice from side to side, and the streets for a month past have been merry with sleighs. Fanny gets letters from her two children at Eagleswood[1] who seem quite contented. The two youngest have the prevalent influenza and the mother also has a touch of it. I have engaged Dennis for another year—the other arrangement fell through. Dennis is to live in the Cottage where Edward now is. Mr. Stevens did not care to engage it.

Please give my kind regards to Mrs. and Miss Ives and Julia Fairchild and all our friends at Barrington. I think your mother would have been glad to get letters from you oftener—but I hope the time which you would have given to writing letters has been passed in study.

Yours affectionately

W. C. Bryant.

MANUSCRIPT: NYPL–GR.

1. See 921.2.

967.   *To* Fanny Bryant Godwin

New York   March 31, 1857

Dear Fanny.

I will do what I am able but I think you ought not to allow yourself in too strong hopes of success. Mr. Godwin must first send in his name, as a candidate, and I will speak to such of the Trustees as I happen to know.

Since I began to write this note Dr. [Henry James] Anderson has called. The subject was new to him and he said, that he thought that nobody could fill the Professor ship better than Godwin—but he added "you know the prejudices of these people—the Trustees." He expressed himself highly favorable to the appointment.[1]

Yours ever,

W. C. B.

MANUSCRIPT: NYPL–GR.

1. See Letter 969.

968.   *To* Benjamin F. Butler[1]

New York   April 17th, 1857.

My dear sir.

I have lately got out an edition of my poems carefully revised, the first perfectly accurate one I think which has appeared. Will you do me the favor to accept the accompanying copy. The *subject* of the last poem in the second volume may perhaps interest you if the verses should not.[2]

Yours very truly

WM. C. BRYANT.

MANUSCRIPT: WCL ADDRESS: Hon. B. F. Butler.

1. See 374.1.
2. "The Conqueror's Grave," in the 1855 edition of Bryant's *Poems*. See *Poems* (1876), pp. 318–320.

969.   *To* Alexander W. Bradford[1]

New York   April 23d   1857.

Dear sir.

Among the persons who have made application to the Board of Trustees of Columbia College of which you are a member for the Professorship of History, is Parke Godwin Esqre. I wish to say in his behalf, that he is addicted by a strong inclination to historical studies, that he is remarkably diligent and persevering in literary pursuits, that he is a man of more than ordinary facility and clearness in the communication of knowledge, and that I know of nothing in his character or mode of life which would be

inconsistent with the dignity of the station he aspires to fill, or that would obstruct his usefulness in discharging its duties.[2]

> I am, sir,
> with great respect
> Yours &c
> WM C. BRYANT

MANUSCRIPT: Boston Public Library ADDRESS: To the Hon. A W Bradford.

1. Alexander Warfield Bradford (1815–1867), a lawyer, was New York City surrogate, 1848–1858.
2. Godwin failed of this appointment, which went to Francis Lieber (217.2). See Parke Godwin to Frances Bryant, May 22, 1857, NYPL–GR.

970. To John Howard Bryant

Great Barrington   April 24th   1857

Dear Brother.

I think any way in which it is most for your convenience to arrange the matter of the Bingham notes will suit Fanny.[1] I told her that you would take the whole amount $2,750 and send her your note for it. But if it be more for your convenience to do as you propose in your letter of April 15th,[2] will you take the trouble to write to her yourself on the subject?

I am sorry to hear such bad news of Austin's[3] health but he has naturally a strong constitution, and I hope will get happily over it.

The weather in our neighborhood has not been as severe as with you, but it has been uncommonly cold, and exceedingly inconstant. My early potatoes, however, were planted the last week of March and have been above the ground more than a week. The European violets in my garden have been out for four weeks. Our wheat is very little winter-killed. A few cherry trees have been split by the extreme cold, as was the case last winter—but the splitting of the cherry tree does not seem with us as it does with you, necessarily to occasion the death of the tree, though I have no doubt it makes it short lived. [I][4] perceive that it is only the very free growing varieties of the cherry tree that are subject to split with us—the marvello and the duke kinds do not split in such winters as we have. Some of the duke varieties produce delicious fruit.

I am here with my wife on a visit to see her sisters previous to our sailing for Europe. She wrote a letter to you which went in the mail ten days since, I think. The notes of Bingham I sent some time since. My wife is pretty well recovered from the attack of rheumatism she had last winter and I am in hopes that the sea voyage will give her strength which she yet wants.

Remember me kindly to all.

> Yours affectionately and truly
> W. C. BRYANT

MANUSCRIPT: Mrs. Mildred Bryant Kussmaul, Brockton, Massachusetts ADDRESS: John
    H. Bryant Esq.

    1. See 906.2.
    2. Unrecovered.
    3. Cullen's elder brother had just entered his sixty-fifth year.
    4. Word omitted.

971.   To Richard H. Dana

Great Barrington   April 24th, 1857.

Dear Dana.

    I am here with my wife on a visit to her sisters, before sailing for
Europe, to which I am to take her and Julia very shortly. Her health has
not been so good as usual for the last two years, and last winter she suffered dreadfully with an attack of acute or inflammatory rheumatism. I
am in hopes a sea voyage will give her strength, and therefore we go in a
sailing packet, that there may be a fair trial of its effect. I write this as a
kind of farewell letter, as I cannot take leave of you personally. May I not
hope to hear from you sometimes when abroad? Your letters are among
the very pleasantest I receive here, but in a strange country they will be
more welcome still.

    I am rejoiced to hear that Charlotte has so far recovered. The gradual
improvement which has been going on in her case, seems to make it not
improbable that she may wholly get over the effect of her accident.

    Your attack on the word "commence" quite delighted me. "Com-
mence" is the torment of my life; I can hardly help rebuking roughly any
body who uses it in my hearing. If it be a young person I am pretty sure
to give a short lesson. Trench's book, of which you speak so favorably I
have looked into.[1] I like all his books.

    The lady whom you met at the concert was Miss [Christiana] Gibson
a very good friend of our family. She has a great veneration for eminent
men, and counts it among the lucky accidents of her visit to Boston that
she fell in with you. I shall see her before sailing and will then explain the
matter of your seeming inattention to her. The forgetfulness of names is so
frequent an accident with me that I no longer consider it awkward as you
call it. It is an infirmity of which I am no more ashamed than I am of my
grey hairs.

    I shall let you know, if I do not forget it in the hurry of departing,
how to address your letters to me abroad—but if I do not and you will
send them to the office of the Evening Post with a desire that they may be
forwarded to me I shall get them duly. My best regards to your daughter.

I am, dear sir,
very truly yours
W. C. BRYANT.

MANUSCRIPT: NYPL–GR PUBLISHED (in part): Life, II, 94–95.

    1. Probably Richard Chenevix Trench (1807–1886), The Study of Words (1851).

972. *To* Ellen S. Mitchell

[April 1857][1]

Dear Niece

I write to trouble you with a matter in which I am sure you will take some interest. I would have written directly to your husband if I had not forgotten all but his middle name and surname.

The headstone of my fathers grave is broken and lies on the ground. I wish to have a new headstone or footstone—massive and solid and with a new inscription. What I wish is that your husband should engage some suitable person in Dalton to cut the stone and put it up in a solid and durable manner so that the frosts will not displace it. I should be glad if he would make a bargain with this person to do it within a reasonable time and let me know the terms. I will send the money immediately.[2]

I wish to do this because I am going with my family to Europe this spring—as early as the beginning or middle of next month—and I would be glad to have the matter put in turn before I go.

My wife who has been ill this winter with the inflammatory rheumatism accompanies me as well as Julia. We may be back in six months or may stay longer.

In the hope of hearing soon from your husband I am

affectionately yrs

W C BRYANT.

MANUSCRIPT: NYPL–GR (draft) ENDORSED: My letter to Ellen / S Mitchell—Apl. 1857, / about my Fathers Monument.

1. See Bryant's endorsement on this draft letter.
2. Accompanying this letter is a draft in Bryant's hand of the inscription later placed on Peter Bryant's gravestone in the Bryant Cemetery at Cummington. See 58.3, and the illustration in Volume I.

973. *To* James T. Fields[1]

New York   May 1, 1857.

My dear sir.

I had hoped to have sent you a copy of Thanatopsis before this, but I have been too busy to write it off. You shall have it, if I send it from Europe for which I sail tomorrow.

Yours truly

W. C. BRYANT

MANUSCRIPT: Wellesley College Library ADDRESS: James T. Fields Esqre.

1. This is the earliest recovered letter in a long correspondence between Bryant and James Thomas Fields (1817–1881), who was later (1861–1870) editor of the *Atlantic Monthly*, and whose Boston firm of Ticknor and Fields published Bryant's translations from Homer in 1870–1871.

XVIII

A Sea Change and Spain
1857
(LETTERS 974 TO 1006)

LEAVING NEW YORK in the spring of 1857 Bryant was redeeming a promise made to his wife toward the end of his journey to the East in 1853: "I do not blame you for saying that you will never consent to my going to Europe again without you. I shall never for my part wish to do so." On each long excursion since he and Frances had taken their young daughters abroad in 1834 he had seen places they had hoped to visit together but had failed to do so because of his sudden recall to his newspaper. Now they would fill those gaps in shared experience. After revisiting Paris and Heidelberg, which by now Julia had nearly forgotten, and exploring the Low Countries, familiar only to him, he would guide his family and his niece Estelle Ives across Switzerland and France to the Pyrenees and into Spain.

Although their four-week sea voyage was occasionally rough, Bryant escaped seasickness for the first time, and they all enjoyed shipboard diversions—shuffleboard and whist, guidebooks and novels, conundrums, and desultory conversations. Their fellow-passengers were congenial; Bryant particularly enjoyed long conversations in French with a Catholic priest, Father Cenas, who had seen much of South America and was especially enthusiastic in his appraisal of Chileans, red and white. Reaching Le Havre at the end of May, the Bryants followed this itinerary:

June 1: Rouen; 2–19: Paris (excursion to Versailles); 20–22: Brussels; 23–25: en route Amsterdam via Antwerp, Rotterdam, The Hague; 26–28: Amsterdam (excursion to Zaandam); June 29–July 10: en route Heidelberg via Zwolle, Steenwijk, Leeuwarden, Groningen, Leer, Hamm, Deutz, Cologne, Bonn, Königswinter, Koblenz, Wiesbaden, Frankfurt.

July 11–19: Heidelberg; 20–21: en route Zurich via Freiburg, Basel, Waldshut, Schaffhausen; 22–26: Zurich (excursion to Schmerikon, Weesen, Bad Ragaz, Bad Pfäfers, Wallenstadt); July 27–August 5: en route Geneva via Horgen, Zug, Immensee, Kulm, Weggis, Lucerne, Aarburg, Olten, Bern, Thun, Lauterbrunnen, Grindelwald, Interlaken, Boltigen, Zweisimmen, Saanen, Bulle, Vevey.

August 6–16: Geneva (excursion to Chamonix); 17–22: en route Bagnères-de-Luchon via Lyons, Nîmes, Narbonne, Toulouse; August 23–September 8: Bagnères-de-Luchon.

September 9–16: Bagnères-de-Bigorre (excursion to Luz, Lourdes); 17–24: Pau; 25–26: Bayonne; September 27–October 4: San Sebastián.

October 5–9: en route Burgos via Vergara, Vitoria, Briviesca; 10–13: Burgos; 14–16: en route Madrid via Aranda, Cabanillas; October 17–November 17: Madrid.

November 18–30: en route Málaga via Albacete, Villena, Alicante, Murcia, Cartagena, Almería.

December 1–14: Málaga (excursion to Granada): 15–23: en route Marseilles via Oran, Algiers; 24–31: Marseilles.

Bryant found great changes in Paris, beautified by new boulevards and public buildings being developed by Baron Haussmann under Napoleon III, whose plans for the sumptuous city made life there much dearer, and threatened to leave the poor man "hardly where to lay his head." While the ladies shopped, and their former Heidelberg friend Eva (Hepp) Mercier instructed the girls in French, Bryant saw pictures at the Louvre and at exhibitions, and talked with Senator Charles Sumner of Massachusetts, seeking recovery from bodily injuries suffered the previous year in Congress, and with American Minister John Young Mason, who mistook him for an obscure Virginia versifier and consequently was unaware of his visitor's identity as the caustic critic of his diplomatic qualifications four years earlier. Sumner praised the spas he had lately visited in the Pyrenees, increasing Bryant's desire to spend some time there.

Leaving Paris, the party made short visits to the chief cities of Belgium and the Netherlands, and after crossing northern Holland by steamer, carriage, and canal boat, entered Germany at Emden and went by rail to Cologne and up the Rhine and the Neckar to Heidelberg. Along the way Bryant dutifully escorted his charges into the principal museums and churches, and passed a day in a pauper colony, but most of their time was spent in outdoor sightseeing. At Brussels they saw the zoo and the botanical garden and listened to a band concert; they drove around the Antwerp docks and the Harmonce Gardens; from the Hague they went to the seashore at Scheveningen, where they caught the queen stepping from a bathing-machine for her morning bath, and dined at the fashionable bathhouse restaurant; in Amsterdam they wandered through the Brook Garden and the most absorbing zoo Bryant had ever seen. Crossing the Ems estuary into Hanover, their little steamer ran on a sandbar, causing them to miss the Cologne train at Emden. From Deutz on the Rhine they joined a religious procession crossing the boat bridge to Cologne, visiting the unfinished cathedral and the ancient church of Saint Ursula, where Bryant was impressed by its display of the skulls of eleven thousand virgins behind glass, in a room whose walls consisted of their marrow bones!

At Königswinter they climbed the thousand-foot Drachenfels, Bryant afoot and the ladies on donkeys, for a sweeping view of the river, then took a steamer to Koblenz and went on to Wiesbaden. Here, served by "half a dozen German Naiads, two or three . . . pretty," they drank hot mineral water tasting "a little like chicken broth." They sampled the waters as well at Langenschwalbach and Schlangenbad, and watched gamblers at their hotel, before visiting Frankfurt to see Goethe's birthplace and Danneker's statue of *Ariadne on a Panther*, then continued by rail to Heidelberg. It was hot, so they settled in the Prinz Karl Hotel for a quiet week, searching out such former friends as they could find.

Unexpectedly, at their hotel they met Rev. Robert Waterston and his wife, the former Anna Cabot Lowell Quincy, of Boston, with their daughter Helen. This chance encounter marked the start of an intimacy with the Unitarian minister which would continue until the end of Bryant's life. As they followed the Neckar, or climbed the hills around Heidelberg, Bryant impressed his compan-

ion as possessing a "robust nobleness, with quiet repose," seeming a close and exact observer of nature, in the presence of which "a sense of beauty and harmony . . . quivered through his whole being." Much as he admired Bryant's writings, Waterston thought the man "far more than the best that had proceeded from his pen." The Bryants and the Waterstons would meet again nine months later at Naples, under less happy circumstances.

The Bryants had acquired a Dutch guide, John Bolender, fluent in English and somewhat addicted to drink, who would accompany them as far as Madrid. Passing through the Black Forest to Freiburg, where Bryant admired the cathedral spire and Holbein's *Adoration* in the choir, they spent a night at the old Hotel of the Three Kings overlooking the Rhine in Basel. They followed the river to the great falls at Schaffhausen, then went on to Zurich and sailed up its lake to enter the Alps at Bad Ragaz, where Bryant walked and the ladies rode a wagon to Pfäfers high above. Crossing from Zurich to Lake Zug, they climbed Mount Rigi, Frances in a sedan chair and the rest on horseback— though Bryant noted in his diary, "I walked the greater part of the way leaving the horse to my courier." After a night on the summit at Kulm, they awoke to trumpets calling them to enjoy a "clear, glorious view" of the snow-topped Alps at sunrise. Frances wilted in the heat while walking down toward Weggis on Lake Lucerne, but Cullen found her another chair, and they took a steamer to the city. On the mountain they had met Bryant's Sketch Club friend Beckwith, with whom they now walked the old wooden bridges of Lucerne, with their long-ranging frescoed gables, over the rushing waters of the Reuss, and paid their respects at Thorvaldsen's pathetic memorial to the Swiss Guards of 1792. At Bern they found Professor Hagen, self-exiled from Baden, who walked with them under the cool arcades and across the Aar to the comical bear pits, and took them through the new parliament buildings and an exhibition of industrial arts which reinforced Bryant's respect for Swiss ingenuity and dexterity.

On their way through the Bernese Oberland to Vevey the travelers spent two nights at Grindelwald, and here, below the towering white peak of the Jungfrau, Bryant walked on the glaciers and entered their grottoes of clear blue ice. Then, after a "sultry" night in the valley at Interlaken, where he was impatient with crowds of idle tourists—"we had not crossed the sea to see fine people," he wrote Christiana Gibson; "there are too many of them in New York"—he found a carriage for the trip over the Simmental to Saanen, and down to Vevey for the crossing by steamer to Geneva. Bryant found that city much changed, physically and politically, since his visit in 1849. The old walls had given way to gardens and boulevards and a handsome lakefront, and the city's patrician rulers were yielding control to a popular party; "The emancipated Catholics," Bryant observed, "are building themselves a magnificent church on the west side of the Rhone, and priests, in cocked hats and long black skirts, go hobbling about in the city of Calvin." He found acquaintances in Geneva, and conversed with an English botanist and his wife who collected and pressed rare plants, but he most enjoyed an excursion to Chamonix on the shoulder of Mount Blanc, where he climbed and wandered across the Mère de Glace.

From Geneva the party moved rapidly by rail and diligence through Lyons, Nîmes, Narbonne, and Toulouse to Bagnères-de-Luchon in the Pyrenees, the most attractive summer resort, said Bryant, he had seen in Europe. Here, "sick

of staring at curiosities and wonders," they stayed for a fortnight. Bryant thought his wife's health better than when she had left home, and began to believe their journey an effective restorative. Further relaxing stays, at Bagnères-de-Bigorre, Pau, and Luz, readied the travelers for their journey through Spain, which Bryant foresaw as more strenuous than any yet undertaken. The country, he wrote Charles Leupp, lagged as far behind the rest of western Europe as the tail of a snake from its head. Railroads were only just begun, diligences overcrowded and uncertain, and carriages for hire little better than springless wagons. Travel in Spain, Cullen wrote his brother John, was nearly as taxing as that between Illinois and Oregon, and few Spaniards, even in Madrid, understood English.

Some of Bryant's biographers, unsure of his fluency in Spanish, and ignorant of the details of his three-week journey from San Sebastián to Madrid, have inferred that his way was made easy by letters from Archbishop John Hughes of New York to clerics and religious along his route. In truth, Hughes's one general letter of introduction reached Bryant only after he had been three weeks in Madrid and found other means of acquaintance. The source of the Bryants' introduction to cultivated Spanish society before reaching the capital was, rather, an acquaintance Estelle Ives had made in New York with the son of a Spanish professor whose widow and daughters lived in San Sebastián. These attractive ladies took the Americans in tow during their week in the Basque capital, and, before they left, referred them to a friend in Vitoria, who in turn gave them letters to others in Burgos. As a result, the visitors were attended in each city by courteous hosts, each of whom, Bryant noted, "placed his house at our disposition." The Americans were hospitably received at convents and houses of mercy, joined evening promenades on alamedas and in gardens, and were accompanied to churches and cathedrals. At a fair in Vitoria Bryant enjoyed seeing hundreds of oxen, many "noble animals," and was much amused at the pig market, learning a trick which might have spared him pain as a farm-boy, and might still be useful at Roslyn: that, "with a man or woman at each ear and another pulling him by the tail, a pig can be driven with as much certainty as any other animal." At Burgos he was awed by the magnificent cathedral, but at a bullfight he was sickened by the slaughter of the beasts and horrified to see that the horses being gored by the bulls had been blindfolded. Afterward, he confessed, "we went to the cathedral to compose ourselves."

On their slow progress over rough country roads, in a jolting vehicle drawn by mules which were sometimes helped by oxen, as well as in town visits, the travelers could communicate only in Spanish. Bryant talked with drivers and fellow-travelers and innkeepers, even those who knew little Castilian, and found accommodations, he wrote Leupp, at "all manner of Spanish inns, from the *venta*, where they give you nothing to eat . . . , to the *parador*, where they profess to give you every thing." Reaching Madrid, he was prepared to join an educated circle of Spaniards in their own language.

Though they had found no American representatives at the cities in the north of Spain, at Madrid and thereafter the Bryant party were warmly received by American diplomatic and consular personnel. The minister to Spain, Augustus Dodge, and his wife, attended and entertained them almost daily. Dodge introduced Bryant to the secretary of the university, who helped

him find suitable lodgings and took him to an impressive academic convocation, and to the great national museum, the Prado, which Bryant visited repeatedly, and thought the finest he had ever seen. At the Dodge home he met the former Secretary of Legation, Horatio Perry, and his wife, poet-novelist Carolina Coronado, whose home was one of Madrid's popular salons. Here Bryant went often, sometimes with, and at times without, his family. Mrs. Perry, known familiarly as *La Coronilla* ("Little Crown"), was a romantic in life as well as in art, and seemed greatly taken with the white-bearded American thirty years her senior. Bryant's diary record of their meetings suggests that he was both charmed and amused by his hostess. At their second meeting she received him in her boudoir in an "elegant wrapper," and the next time in a darkened room because she "suffered much" from "bad eyes." He read and translated some of her verses, and to his brief note of comment on them she returned an "impassioned answer." At parting she gave him her picture, which she surrendered "only with tears," and she promised him, "I am going to learn English in order to read your writings." Frances Bryant seems on one occasion to have felt a twinge of jealousy; after an evening with the Perrys Julia wrote in her diary, "Mother pronounced it stupid while Father greatly enjoyed his chat with a poetess."

Bryant found his visits to the Perry home rewarding in other ways; an anonymous letter which found its way into print in New York noted, "A pretty poetess has taken possession of Mr. Bryant, and at her house we meet, informally, almost every evening, the most distinguished men in Spain—authors, ministers, politicians, etc., who seem eager to know and pay reverence to the American poet." Among these men—and women—were the young orator and professor of philosophy Emilio Castelar y Ripoll, later first president of the Spanish republic; Candido Nocedal, influential cabinet minister; novelist and poet Angela Grassi; historian and former prime minister Joaquin Pacheco y Gutiérrez Calderón; critic–dramatist Eugenio Hartzenbusch, director of the National Library; and two editors of Madrid's democratic daily paper, *La Discusion*, Manuel Ortiz de Pinedo and Nicolás María Rivero.

Other diversions added to the visitors' pleasure in Madrid. Mrs. Dodge shopped with the ladies, and took the Bryant party to see Teodora Madrid and Julian Romea in a play by Tirso de Molina, and Bryant rode horseback with her husband in the Queen's park. Buckingham Smith, Secretary of the American Legation and a scholar and translator, introduced Bryant to the National Library, and, through the Brazilian ambassador, found him a guide to replace the Dutchman Bolender, who had proved dishonest as well as intemperate. Bryant met old acquaintances in the former Spanish ambassador to the United States, Angel Calderón de la Barca, and his Scottish wife, a writer, who persuaded Bryant to translate verses of the poet Francisco de Rioja, which he published later as "The Ruins of Italica."

After a month in Madrid the travelers left for Alicante on the coast, traveling with comparative ease as far as Almansa, terminus of the new railway. Here they continued in a rough cart, which they dismissed when they found they might ride the last stretch on a work train loaded with stone. Tired of being jolted over wretched roads, the ladies boarded a steamer at Almería for Cartagena, while Bryant made his way overland in a series of wagons. After some delay Frances and the girls reached Cartagena, where Cullen joined them for

the voyage to Málaga. Here, as in Alicante, they were entertained by the American consul, who also joined them on an excursion to Granada. A letter from a Madrid acquaintance to the governor of the Alhambra secured their admission to areas normally closed to visitors, and, presenting Archbishop Hughes's letter to the archbishop of Granada, Bryant gained entry to the vault of Ferdinand and Isabella in the royal chapel of the cathedral.

On December 12 the party boarded the steamer *Normandie* at Málaga, bound for Marseilles by way of North African ports. They were leaving Spain, Bryant wrote, with regret, "without having had more than a mere glimpse of the country and its people." But traveling had been slow and difficult, and, beyond his concern for his wife's health, which had begun to worsen, he was committed to showing Italy to Julia and Estelle.

Leaving port, the passengers were awakened violently two hours later when their ship rammed and nearly sank a Dutch freighter entering the harbor. Though the *Normandie* was little damaged, the mishap held them two days longer at Málaga. The voyage was otherwise uneventful, except for visits to Oran and Algiers, and a night when the steamer rolled dead in the water off Majorca with engine failure. Bryant was intrigued by the interplay of European with Moorish and Oriental cultures in Algeria, speculating over the political future of the French colony and the likelihood of its becoming Europeanized. Though he would have liked to have visited interior villages and seen something of the valleys among the Atlas mountains, he had taken passage for Marseilles, and the ship was leaving, so his party sailed for the Mediterranean metropolis, which they reached on Christmas Eve. Here Frances and Estelle each caught the prevalent grippe, and while he awaited their recovery Bryant began to catch up on his correspondence with the *Evening Post*. On New Year's Eve, thinking his patients "decidedly better," he engaged steamship passage for Naples.

974.   *To* John Bigelow

Ship William Tell in the
English Channel   May 30, 1857.

My dear sir.

We are now about a hundred miles from Havre and I write this that I may put it into the post-office immediately on my arrival at that place. We have had for the most part not an unpleasant passage, though the captain calls it the most so that he has made in his life at this season of the year, when a quick and agreeable passage to Europe may generally be depended upon. My family have borne it very well.

I left on my table an Epic Poem in a roll of paper, with the name and residence of the author written in pencil on the outside. Will you do me the favor of causing it to be sent to him, if he has not already called for it.

There are two matters on which it would have been well if I had spoken to you before I left New York, that you might if you please make them the subject of animadversion or speculation.

I was informed, not very long before my departure that the Mr. Delano who lived in China,[1] would be glad to give me some information in regard to the present condition of that country, and that he was in possession of some very interesting facts relating to the process of depopulation now going on among the Chinese race both by means of their civil wars and their wars with other nations. I am not aware that this matter has at all attracted the attention of public writers, nor do I know whether the facts are of a nature to justify the idea of a gradual future decline of the Chinese race in numbers—a fate which has been endured by other large families of the human species—but the subject appeared to me worthy of being looked into.

The other matter is the state of our prison establishments on Blackwell's Island. Miss Sedgwick gave me some information in regard to it, and I desired Mr. Hills[2] to make some inquiries the result of which he may possibly have communicated to you. The superintendent Dr. Sanger[3] is said to be a drinking man, and under his management great disorders are allowed to prevail. Although women are confined there, there is no matron at the place—which is saying almost every thing against it. Women are delivered of children more than nine months after their commitment. The punishments are often barbarous and the relaxations of discipline are as bad as the punishments. These abuses I thought worthy of being inquired into and if there was no error in the representations I had heard fully exposed, and made the subject of discussion and remonstrance till a reform was effected.[4]

Havre   June 1st   1857.

We arrived here last evening after a slow and tedious voyage up the Channel. We are all well, and in comfortable quarters. The unanimous

opinion of the ladies, who composed more than three quarters of our passengers is that Captain Funck is the best creature in the world. He takes
as much care for their comfort on shore as he does on board. I find Mr
Vesey the American consul here in daily expectation of being removed.
He is a personal friend of General Dix who has written to him that nothing can save him. The post is a lucrative one and is wanted for somebody
who has done party work.[5]

Will you do me the favor to see that the enclosed letter goes to its
destination?[6]

Yours very truly
W C BRYANT

MANUSCRIPT: NYPL–GR (draft) ADDRESS: Jno Bigelow Esqre. PUBLISHED (in part): Life,
II, 95–96.

1. Warren Delano (1809–1898), maternal grandfather of Franklin Delano Roose-
velt, was a New York merchant who had spent many years in China. His wife, the
former Catherine Robbins Lyman (b. 1824), was the daughter of Dr. Peter Bryant's
old friend Judge Joseph Lyman of Northampton. See 8.1; Vol. I, 62.
2. Probably an EP reporter, though no record has been found of his employment
as such.
3. Not further identified.
4. No comment on this matter has been found in the files of the EP for the month
of June 1857.
5. William Henry Vesey (see 707.4), United States consul at Le Havre since 1853,
continued in that office until 1860, and was appointed to a similar post at Aix-la-
Chapelle in 1861. In 1870 he was transferred to Nice. U. S. Consular Officers, 1789–1939.
6. Letter unidentified.

975.   To the EVENING POST

Paris, June 11, 1857.

There are some things which can only be done in Paris, or at least can
only be done by Frenchmen, and one of these has furnished for the last
fortnight a most attractive spectacle for the people of this place and those
who visit it. The French not only delight in scenic effect, but produce it
with a dexterity, despatch and success which find no parallel elsewhere.

A few weeks ago the interior of the Palais de l'Industrie, the Crystal
Palace of France, built among the trees of the Champs Elysées, was a bare
and empty space, with a floor of dust and gravel, and rafters streaming
with cobwebs. The order for an exhibition of flowers was given, and in
three or four weeks the dusty waste was transformed into a fresh and
beautiful garden. I went to see it the other day—a hot day for the season.
We passed from the entrance to the garden through an alley embowered
with evergreens, young pines and firs, planted for the occasion, filling the
cool air with resinous odors. On each side of the alley were benches, inviting the visitor who might be wearied with his walk, to rest awhile.
Thence we passed into the vast area beyond the columns which support

the galleries, and here the floor was covered with a bright green turf, close-ly shaven, formed into hillocks and gentle slopes, surrounding beds of shrubs and other plants in full bloom, and intersected by winding walks. Here were thickets of rhododendrons of different varieties; here was a group of our own mountain laurel, as beautiful as any seen in our forests; here were showy companies of azaleas of all tinges of color, from bright scarlet to pure white; here were beds of roses and wildernesses of gerani-ums, pampered into innumerable diversities, perfuming the air. All had their roots in the soil; and a friendly soil it seemed, for though the exhi-bition had already lasted a fortnight, there was nothing faded or withered; every blossom and leaf was as fresh as it could have been in its native bed. The tropical flowers themselves seemed not to miss, under this immense canopy of glass, their own genial climate. A young date-palm stood on one of the hillocks, with plants of its own latitudes clustering and blooming around it.

In the midst of the area a little fountain threw up its waters, which formed themselves into what had the appearance of a winding brook. A rustic bridge bestrode the little stream, which, to say the truth, was not quite so transparent as one of our country brooks, for it was the turbid water of the Seine; but it was glassy enough on the surface to make a mirror for some magnificent water-plants whose roots were steeped by it. Two black swans from New Holland, as we crossed the bridge, were stand-ing on the brink of the water, each supported by one broad foot, the other coiled up under the body, and the head tucked under one wing. As we approached, they suddenly pulled out their heads from under their wings, put the uplifted foot to the ground, uttered a clanging cry, and taking to the water sailed off among the groups of calla and iris that fringed the bank.

The exhibition was visited by a crowd of people, and groups of smart-ly-dressed Parisian ladies were hovering about the flowers like butterflies. Among the roses exhibited were some fine new varieties, which it is the fashion of the day to name after eminent military commanders. A large blush-rose bears the name of Lord Raglan, and a larger, with flaming blood-red petals, the name of General Jacqueminot.[1] I believe this is re-garded as a very desirable addition to the stock of roses.

As I was about leaving the place, I observed a gentleman looking at me with a very attentive scrutiny, as if he thought he might have seen me before. A second glance sufficed me to recognize him; it was Mons. Vatte-mare, author of the system of International Exchanges,[2] looking as fresh as any of the flowers in their beds around him. He hurried me off to a place under one of the galleries, where he had a little niche, in which were suspended in rows ears of maize of different varieties, from the State of New York, and on the table lay the two quarto volumes of the Natural History of the same State, which treat of its botany. The ears of Indian

corn, I was not displeased to see, made a much better appearance than the samples from Algeria, which were suspended on a wall immediately opposite. As we were talking about them, two Orientals, with glittering black eyes and jet black beards, wearing the high, shaggy Persian cap—one of them with features so regular and finely formed that they might have served as a pattern for an ideal bust—came up, and addressing Mons. Vattemare in French, asked him for some of the ears of maize to take to their own country. "I will give you them, and a great many other things beside," he answered, delighted to find the opportunity of pushing his system of international exchanges in a new quarter. In the midst of the dialogue which followed, and which was carried on with great spirit and earnestness on the part of Mons. Vattemare, I took my leave.

The same day I went to an exhibition of the works of Paul Delaroche, whose reputation as a painter is as great in the United States as here. Shortly before his death he expressed a desire to paint a picture the subject of which should be of universal interest, in order to give the proceeds to unfortunate artists and workmen in the studios of artists. His friends have thought that the best method of fulfilling a design which the artist himself was only prevented from fulfilling by death, would be to assemble all his pictures in one gallery and give the profits of this exhibition to the charitable fund of the Association of Artists, Painters, Sculptors, &c., of which Delaroche was President. His works have accordingly been brought together from various collections, private and public, in this country, in England and elsewhere. They illustrate, curiously, the gloomy character of his genius. You look about the walls, and you are in the midst of deathbeds, executions, assassinations. The least interesting of these pictures is the death of Queen Elizabeth. The gigantic old woman, sprawling on her couch upon the floor, her harsh features livid with mortal disease, is a horrid object; nor is there any thing in the rest of the picture to make amends for the disagreeable impression produced by this principal figure. The series of portraits of Napoleon forms of itself a tragedy, and a most impressive one. The first of these is "Napoleon crossing the Alps," with which the American public is familiar. As he is making his way through the mountain snows, you see that he is revolving his great plans of conquest. You read in the eye of the young adventurer untameable resolution and absolute confidence in his own fortunes. In the next picture, "Napoleon in his Closet," you have him in the noon of life, his ambitious desires gratified, and the continent of Europe at his feet. His eye is lighted up with a proud satisfaction, as he contemplates the strength and security of the power he has founded by his single arm. In the third painting, "Napoleon at Fountainebleau," you see the great egotist after his fall, older, grosser in person, arrived at the palace from a hasty flight, his boots spattered with mud, his riding coat not laid by; one arm hanging over the back of the chair, as if never to be removed, and his eyes staring into fu-

turity with the fixed, sullen gaze of despair. In all these portraits the artist has shown a power which, it seems to me, should place him in a high rank among painters, even if he had done nothing else.

Manuscript: Unrecovered text: *LT* II, pp. [11]–16; first published in *EP* for June 24, 1857.

1. Lord Fitzroy James Henry Somerset, first Baron Raglan (1788–1855); J. F. Jacqueminot (1787–1865), a French general.

2. The French ventriloquist and impersonator Nicolas Marie Alexandre Vattemare (1786–1864), who first appeared on the New York stage in 1839, had promoted a system of book exchanges between libraries and museums which enjoyed a considerable success between 1841 and 1851, particularly in the United States. At Paris in 1853 Vattemare had shown Bryant a portion of a 10,000-volume "American Library for the City of Paris" which was to be housed in the Bourse. Bryant, "Diary, 1852–1853," June 1, 1853.

976. *To* Julia Sands

Paris   June 17, 1857.

My dear Miss Sands.

My wife who is cumbered with much getting ready for our journey, has assigned to me the duty of replying to your very welcome letter.[1] We shall set out for the Rhine shortly, by way of Belgium, and our little party[2] begin even to talk of taking Holland in their way—the Rhine you know finishes his course in Holland and one cannot be said to have fairly seen the Rhine, till one has seen the country where he enters the sea—just as you cannot judge of a man's character till you know his life from its beginning to its end.

We have had a pleasant journey from Havre to Paris and a pleasant visit to this city, except that the sightseeing and the shopping and the colloquies with dress makers, and milliners, and lace-women, have been rather fatiguing to some of us. Our passage across the Atlantic was not so pleasant as we expected at this season of the year. Our Captain, who has been forty years or more a commander, declared that it was a regular winter passage, and the very worst that he had ever made at this time of the year. He is one of the best creatures in the world, and did every thing he could think of, to make the passage agreeable, and that without any suggestion, on our part or the least ostentation on his. We are in comfortable lodgings in the Hotel des deux Mondes, Rue d'Antin, up only one flight of stairs—all the more convenient but all the damper for that, very near our bankers, and near the Tuilleries and the Louvre, and not far from the Boulevards. We have a large sitting room, elegantly and commodiously furnished and two bed-rooms with hot woollen mattresses, placed on spring mattresses, so high in the middle that you lie constantly in fear of rolling out of bed, and for these rooms and the service of the waiter, chambermaid &c, we pay 24 francs a day. Every thing is dearer at Paris than it was four years ago. The Emperor has been demolishing houses by hundreds, breaking paths through the most thickly peopled parts of the

city—for the extension of the Rue Rivoli, and for the new Boulevards, so that a poor man has hardly where to lay his head. Stately buildings have been erected in their room, for which high rents are demanded, and when rents are high every thing is dear. Meantime the city has been beautified and embellished in other respects at the public expense; the government buildings have been repaired, the Louvre has been magnificently finished, with pedestals and niches, from which a mob of statues look down upon its spacious courts, and into the surrounding streets; old churches have been completed or restored. They who live in so sumptuous a city cannot be allowed to live as cheaply as in a country village. The only thing really cheap at Paris, says Mr. Mason, our minister,[3] is the cab hire; and travellers accordingly indulge in it to a great extent. I went the other day to Mr. Mason's to get my passport viséd for the different countries we expect to see. I went into the office of the Secretary of Legation, to whom I had a letter, not expecting to see any body else, but I had been there but a few moments when Mr. Mason came halting up the steps, and the Secretary introduced me. He mistook me at first for Daniel Bryan of Virginia, who published some bad poetry twenty or thirty years since.[4] His manner was friendly and agreeable, and he talked very pleasantly for a quarter of an hour, and I believe would have talked away the rest of the morning if I had staid. I know he read the comments of my paper on his appointment, but I am not certain that he ever connected my name with them.[5] The paralytic stroke evidently has not damaged his intellect.

I have come to the end of my sheet. My wife and daughter desire their love to you and Miss Hoyt. I think they are both stronger than when they left home. My wife bears the journey as well as I had any reason to expect.

Yrs very truly.
W. C. Bryant

[Write again as
soon as convenient]

[Paris, June 18th[6]: I was near sending off my letter without telling you half the news. I saw Mr. Sumner two days since—the senator—who had just returned from a journey to the Pyrenees, and who was enraptured about the beauty of the scenery, as well as that of the valley of the Loire. An absence of eighteen days—such is the rapidity with which travelling is now performed on the railways—has enabled him to visit the city of Pau, and the neighboring watering-places, to some of which he made his way on horseback over fields of snow, and also to go to chateau after chateau in middle France and on the Loire. He was looking exceedingly well—too fat, rather; in fact, he had lost something of the intellectuality of his expression, which was exchanged for a comfortable, well-fed look. He inquired very eagerly about the state of politics in our country, and seemed highly gratified to learn that everybody was dissatisfied with the decision in the Dred Scott case, and, although the court had declared negroes not

to be citizens, nobody at the North but a few old bigots to judicial infallibility acknowledged the decision to be law. He talked a good deal about his health, which is slowly mending—and but slowly—a certain painful sensibility of the spine being still present, which until lately has hindered him from taking exercise by walking. He referred to several of his speeches like a man who is conscious that his opinions and his affairs are an object of interest to the public, and discussed with me the character of Senator Butler, the news of whose death had just been received.

It is evident that Mr. Sumner must get well more rapidly than he has been doing for the past year to be able to go back to his seat in the Senate as a working member, or even an occasional talking member.][7]

MANUSCRIPT: UVa PUBLISHED (in part): Life, II, 96–97.

1. Dated New York, May 24, 1857; addressed to Frances Bryant. MS William Cullen Bryant II.

2. Consisting of Cullen and Frances, their daughter Julia, and her cousin Estelle Ives.

3. John Young Mason (1799–1859) of Virginia, former congressman, Secretary of the Navy, and Attorney General, served as United States minister to France from 1853 to 1859.

4. Daniel Bryan (1795–1866), of Rockingham County, Virginia, who published three volumes of poems between 1813 and 1826, on such subjects as Daniel Boone and the Marquis de Lafayette.

5. Upon Mason's appointment as minister to France in 1853, Bryant had called him "a man of mild manners, convivial habits, indolent in business, and known, but not in any way distinguished, in public life," and concluded that Mason had "no qualifications" for the position. EP, October 12, 1853.

6. The balance of this letter, unrecovered in manuscript, is supplied from Life, II, 96–97, and is placed within brackets.

7. On May 22, 1856 Senator Charles Sumner of Massachusetts (751.1) had been violently and repeatedly clubbed, as he sat at his desk in the United States Senate, by Congressman Preston Smith Brooks (1819–1857) of South Carolina, following what Brooks considered slurs cast on his uncle, South Carolina Senator Andrew Pickens Butler (1796–1857), during the course of a Sumner speech on the Kansas crisis. Sumner's injuries kept him from the Senate until December 1859. With most northern anti-slavery leaders, Bryant was outraged by this act, which he laid to pro-slavery "poltroons as well as ruffians." And he asked editorially, "Are we to be chastised as they chastise their slaves? Are we too, slaves, slaves for life? . . . Has the freedom of speech in the United States Senate been put in peril?" EP, May 23, 24, 1856.

977.   To the Evening Post

Heidelberg, July 14, 1857.

I have made, with my family, the tour of Belgium and Holland, and coming down from Friesland by one of the Hanoverian railways to the Rhine, am resting for a few days in Heidelberg. We are the more disposed to suspend our somewhat rapid journey here, on account of the heat of the weather, which is very great, one hot day succeeding another, with no interruption from showers, the sky being as intensely dazzling as our own.

While in the northern part of Holland, I made a visit to the pauper colonies of Fredericksoord and Willemsoord, in the province of Overyssel. Here are tracts of sandy soil covered with heath and shrubs, which, from the time when they were first formed from the bottom of the sea, till now, have been abandoned to utter barrenness. The great calamity of Holland is pauperism, and somewhat more than thirty years ago a benevolent society was formed for the purpose of settling the poor, who had become a public charge, upon the waste lands of the kingdom, with a view of reducing them to cultivation. They purchased a tract of land, mostly uncultivated, in the province of Overyssel, where they made a beginning with some of the poor of Amsterdam, who had been thrown upon the public charity. The colony thus established has now increased to a considerable community, yet it has made, I suppose, as much impression upon the vast mass of pauperism in Holland, as the Colonization Society has made upon the mass of slavery in the United States.

We took a carriage at the ancient village of Steenwyck, and proceeded over a road so sandy that we were obliged to travel very slowly, and rendered almost impassable in some places by an attempt to macadamize it. We passed several comfortable looking tenements of the peasantry, with little flower gardens in front of them, and at length the coachman said, "We are in the colony."

I could not see that the habitations of the paupers seemed any less comfortable than those of the district through which we had just passed. They were neat brick buildings, spacious enough to contain, besides the rooms for the family, a stable for the cow, a place for the pig, and a room for the fuel. Near each was a little garden surrounded by a well-pleached hawthorn hedge, and outside of the hedge a ditch; for the Hollander, from mere habit, always surrounds his domain with a ditch, whether there is any occasion for it or not. Back of the gardens were fields of rye and barley and other crops, and beyond, in places, was a forest of shrubs and dwarf trees, looking like the scrub-oak plains on the worst parts of Long Island; and, in places, extensive wastes, the like of which is not seen in our country, covered with dark heath of a purple tinge, and stretching out of sight.

The Director was not at home, and we were accompanied over the village by one of the bookkeepers, who was ready to communicate what he knew, but who spoke French, the only language we understood in common, very imperfectly, and in a low tone of voice. He took us into several of the dwellings. The first we entered was that of a widow from Groningen, who had two or three children able to work at the loom. It was a miracle of neatness. The woman had established in the outer room her summer kitchen, in which were the pig-pen and stable, and had made it as clean as the nicest parlor in our own country. We looked into the winter room—it was as nice as a new sideboard just from the cabinetmaker's. She had a comfortable bed in a little closet, after the Dutch fashion. In a

room above were the beds of the children, in a kind of boxes on each side. Notwithstanding these appearances of comfort, the woman took our courier aside, and complained bitterly of the hardness of her lot. She affirmed that she was half starved, and begged him to intercede with the Director in her behalf. When the matter was afterwards mentioned to the bookkeeper he said that there was no end to the complaints of these people, and that the more they got the more they asked for. We went into another house, in which was a good-looking family of both sexes, well clad, and living in a manner which had every appearance of thrift. The rooms glittered with the display of crockery and polished metal utensils, and were hung with cheap engravings.

We were taken to the manufactory of the village, a room full of looms, where coarse cotton cloth is woven by the children between twelve and eighteen years of age, for the Dutch soldiery in the East Indies. The looms were clashing merrily—the girls, in particular, jerked the shuttles backward and forward with incredible swiftness. "These children," said the bookkeeper, "earn a great deal for their families; in fact, those who come to our colony must either work or starve; if they are obstinately idle, they get nothing to eat."

We were shown the school-house—a building with two spacious rooms, in which the children were taught according to the liberal system of public education established in Holland. The school had been suspended for a while, as the building was undergoing repairs. Religious teachers are provided for the colony—a Protestant, a Catholic, and a Jewish Rabbi. The colonists receive copper and iron tokens for their labor, and this forms the money of the colony. With these they purchase the necessaries for which they have occasion, from the magazines of the colony, where every thing is sold but intoxicating liquors, the sale of which is forbidden.

I could obtain no exact information of the profit or loss of this enterprise. "These people," said the bookkeeper, "cost the society a great deal. They come from the cities unaccustomed to the work we require of them, and often with families of very young children, who are of too tender an age to work. They must be subsisted, and their subsistence is a heavy charge."

There are now about four hundred families in the colony, numbering two thousand six hundred persons. To prevent the excessive growth of the community, and to confine the operations of the institution to their original object, all the young, on reaching the age of twenty, are obliged to leave it, as well as all the young who marry. As the older members drop off, their places are supplied by paupers from the towns. In the mean time thousands of acres have been reclaimed from their primeval wild state, and turned into productive fields.

MANUSCRIPT: Unrecovered TEXT: *LT* II, pp. 17–21; first published in *EP* for August 1, 1857.

978. *To* the Evening Post

Bern, Switzerland, August 1, 1857.

The Swiss are among the most ingenious of the European nations; they possess in a high degree the constructive faculty; you have only to look at their houses to be convinced of this. It seems to me that they are the best carpenters in the world. The Swiss peasantry are lodged, I believe, in more spacious dwellings than any other peasantry in Europe—dwellings as admirably suited to their climate as they are picturesque. Under their overshadowing roofs, which form a shelter from their hot suns in summer, they hang the outer wall with balconies and galleries, which form passages above the deep snows of their winters. The ends of the beams and rafters and the braces are shaped into ornamental projections, so that what would otherwise be the deformity, becomes the grace of the building. The Swiss were long ago the best bridge-builders in Europe, of which the bridge at Schaffhausen, destroyed by the French in the latter part of the last century, constructed entirely of timber, with a span of 365 feet, yet without any support except at the two ends, was a remarkable example. In the long winters of the Alpine regions, the peasants employ themselves in carving, with their penknives, figures and images and objects of various kinds out of wood, with all the patience and nicety of Chinese artisans, and a hundred times the elegance. On the high-roads in the valleys of the Bernese Oberland, the traveller will have the children of the herdsmen trotting beside him, offering him for a single franc the miniature of a Swiss cottage, carved with all the delicacy of frost work.

It is clear that if all this dexterity and patience were directed to the great branches of manufacture, the Swiss must excel. It is so, in fact. I have just come from looking at an exhibition of Swiss industry now open in this beautiful city. An intelligent American gentleman went through it with me, who was as much surprised as myself, both at the variety of the manufactures and their excellence. The spectacle was to me the more interesting because the manufactures of Switzerland prosper without any of those helps which, in the opinion of some, are indispensable—without prohibitory or protective duties, or indeed, high duties of any kind. They prosper, too, in a country surrounded by powerful governments which yet adhere to the protective system, and on which the Swiss have never thought it for their advantage to retaliate.

It must be admitted that the Swiss have some important natural advantages for manufacturing pursuits. Their mountains abound with ores of the useful metals; enormous forests are at hand to supply the furnaces in which these ores are smelted, and the torrents which rush down the mountain sides wield the hammers by which the metals are beaten into plates and bars. A calculating Yankee would be shocked to see the proportion of water-power in this country running to waste. Mills might be built on the Swiss streams to manufacture for the world, without much

disfiguring the grand aspect of Swiss scenery. In going up any of their mountains, you hear the bells of the herds for a vast distance around you. A million of neat cattle are fed in the pastures, with a million and a quarter of sheep and goats, and the woods which supply fuel for the forges and founderies furnish bark for tanning the skins of these animals. In the forest cantons the driver of your carriage will point out, from time to time, in some gorge of the mountains, where the stream comes down through the forest, a large building in which glass is made. The manufacturer in Switzerland has had the advantage from the first, that he has no tax to pay on the crude material which he employs.

I was not, therefore, unprepared to see in the exhibition at Bern a creditable display of objects wrought of iron and other useful metals. Here were fire engines, locomotives for the railways, which the people of the Confederation are industriously building in all parts of their country; engines for the steamers on the lakes, and machines for calico-printing—all of admirable workmanship; here were stoves for kitchen and parlor, of cast or sheet iron, which certainly in finish, if not in other respects, were beyond what we produce in our country; here were busts and statuettes in cast-iron, well designed, of a smoothness of surface equal to porcelain, and great precision of outline. Geneva had sent muskets, rifles and fowling-pieces, beautifully wrought, and there were samples of cutlery from the workshops of Thurgau, A[a]rgau, Bern and Glarus, which might almost bear comparison with the cutlery of Great Britain. The Swiss make their own pins in the mills at Schaffhausen. Of their watches I need say nothing, since in that branch of industry they work with greater nicety and cheapness than the people of any other country, and even furnish a large proportion of the mechanism of what are called English watches. Five cantons of Switzerland employ in watchmaking thirty-six thousand persons.

Beside the iron stoves, there were porcelain ones—white porcelain—of elegant forms, a much pleasanter and more cleanly piece of furniture than the iron ones we have at home. I cannot say much for the samples of table porcelain in the exhibition; they were of the homeliest kind, and had no pretensions to elegance. Of the plainer kinds of glass there was a respectable share, and of elegant plate glass a few samples. Switzerland furnishes the bottles for her own wines and mineral waters. The tanners of the country have by no means an idle time of it, if I might judge from the quantity of the leather, including morocco and patent leather, and the exquisitely tanned skins of the chamois goat, with which the walls of one of the lower rooms were hung.

What most surprised me in the exhibition was the perfection which the silk manufacture had attained. The silk cloths of Zurich, both light and heavy, were of excellent quality, though they wanted the beauty of the French tissues, but the ribbons of Basle and Zurich vie with those of France in texture, lustre, beauty of design and brilliancy of color. Several

ribbon-looms were in the exhibition—light, ingenious machines—in one of which a landscape, and in another a bouquet of flowers of different colors and shapes, were woven. The housewives, I suppose, would expect me to mention the beautiful sewing-silks of Aargau.

There are woollen mills in Zurich and elsewhere, but the quality of the goods produced is not fine; the Swiss sheep, I believe, are rather coarse-woolled. The hair of the goat is wrought into elegant and showy tissues—plaids generally, and of brilliant colors. The cotton cloths are strong and serviceable; the printed cottons are of two kinds—the calicoes and the muslins; the calicoes ugly, and the muslins delicate and beautiful. Fields of flax often meet the eye in Switzerland, and acres of linen at this season are seen bleaching by the streams. There were many good samples of linen in the exhibition.

One of the most remarkable departments of Swiss industry is embroidery, and of this there were many superb samples. In one of these, the maidens of Appenzell had embroidered their Jungfrau on an immense curtain of white muslin. Another from the canton of St. Gallen had flowers in high relief, the petals raised from the muslin and turning back against it, as in a carving. In other samples were fountains and forests; others were of architectural design, intermingled with graceful human figures. There are in Appenzell and St. Gallen six thousand persons who live by this sort of needlework.

Of course there were many samples of carving in wood, but these were excelled by the carvings in ivory—an art which seems to have sprung naturally from the national skill in wood-carving. Among these I noticed a little group of trees, wrought with such delicacy that it seemed as if the foliage must tremble and turn with the wind.

In the north they slay animals for their fur; but the Swiss finds a substitute for fur in the skins of the birds which haunt his lakes. There were numerous samples of muffs, tippets and cuffs formed of this material; some of them of a silvery whiteness, others nearly black, all of them extremely light, smooth and glistening. The names of the birds which had been made to yield this singular contribution to the national fair were annexed to the articles—they were mostly water-fowl of the grebe family, and the kinds related to it. These were the *mergus merganser*, the *anas ferina*, and others which I do not remember.

Among the frolics of Swiss ingenuity I noticed a group of stuffed skins, the wild quadrupeds and native birds of Switzerland, so skilfully adjusted that one could scarcely believe that they were not alive. On the shelves of what seemed a mountain-peak, were owls of different kinds, and other birds, feeding their wide-mouthed young; eagles tearing a pigeon in pieces, foxes lurking behind the crags, a chamois climbing a rock, and another apparently listening on the summit for the approach of his enemies from below. Another was a water-fall pouring over a rock, formed of

some composition in such a manner as to avoid that patched appearance which generally belongs to rock-work, and half draped with wild herbage.

I fear I have tired the readers of this letter, as I have done myself, with this recital; but I hope that I have given them some idea of the variety, the pertinacity and the success of Swiss ingenuity.

The manufactures were exhibited in the barracks near the northern gate of the city, but there was another department of the exhibition, that of the Fine Arts, which was held in the new Palace of the Confederation. The palace, not yet finished, is a sumptuous building, in the Byzantine style, worthy to be the place of assembly for the representatives of a republic like Switzerland. The quarries around Bern yield a light-brown sand-stone, which, when first taken from its bed, is as easily chipped as chalk, and of this the palace is built. It surrounds three sides of a quadrangle, with a massive balcony in the front of the building resting on richly-carved brackets, and on the other side, within the quadrangle, a vaulted ante-room resting on columns, through which is the principal entrance. From the balcony, and the terrace on which the palace stands, you have a view of the green valley of the Aar immediately below you, and beyond the hills which bound the valley rise the snowy summits of the Bernese Oberland.

I found less to interest me in the annual exhibition of Swiss works of art than I had hoped. A Swiss friend, who accompanied me, directed my attention to a large historical picture, by Volmar of Bern,[1] representing the battle of Morgarten, in 1315.[2] It is painted with a good deal of knowledge, but it looked to me as if the artist had conceived and studied each figure separately, and then put them all together in a group as he best might. The light is lurid and like moonshine. There were several historical pictures of a smaller size, by Vogel of Zurich,[3] full of commonplace faces and draperies like leather. The landscapes were better. There were a few exceedingly spirited drawings of Swiss scenery in water colors. Calame of Geneva[4] has an excellent picture in the collection, called "The Torrent." Grisel of Neufchatel, Isen[r]ing of St. Gallen, Jenni of Solothurn, Kaiser of Stans, Koller of Zurich, Meyer of Luzern, and Zimmermann of Geneva, had all clever landscapes in the gallery[5]—representations of Swiss scenery, the contemplation of which ought to make a man a landscape painter if any thing can. But this is a mere "muster-roll of names," and I have no time for more particular remark.

MANUSCRIPT: NYPL–GR (partial draft) TEXT: LT II, pp. 22–29; first published in EP for August 29, 1857.

1. Joseph Simon Volmar (1796–1865).

2. At this mountain on the border of Schwyz and Zug cantons, a small Swiss force defeated the Austrian army on November 15, 1315. This battle signaled the beginning of Swiss independence.

3. George Ludwig Vogel (1788–1879), historical and landscape painter, and engraver.

4. Alexandre Calame (1810–1864).

5. Georges Grisel (1811–1877); Johann Baptist Isenring (1796–1860); Friedrich Jenni (1825–1878); Heinrich Kaiser (1813–1900); probably Johann Rudolf Koller (1828–1905); probably Jost Meyer am Rhyn (1834–1898); Frédéric Zimmermann (1823–1884).

979. *To* Orville Dewey

Bagnères-de-Luchon, August 27 [1857]

. . . We were all delighted the other day to get news from you and yours in the pleasant letters from your quiet home in Sheffield.[1] They came to us in the midst of our journeyings through Switzerland, as we were drifting rapidly about in the currents of travel that rush through that country in the summer, and make it a scene of bustle, almost of tumult. And they brought with them an air of rest and old times, and of good talks on the banks of the Housatonic.

I presented your letter to Mr. Chenevière,[2] who received me very graciously, called on us twice, and gave me a volume of his discourses, which seem to me very good. He was astonished that one for whom he had conceived so high an esteem as his friend "Dewey" should ask if he yet remembered him. I find him a little unhappy at the change which has taken place in Geneva. "Your town," I said to him, "looks prosperous and flourishing." He shook his head; "material prosperity, I grant," he answered. "The radicals are a power, and material prosperity is all they think of. In other respects we are going back. They have shoved aside all the citizens distinguished for character and talent, and put the direction of affairs into the hands of inferior men—*et nous en sommes contre*.[3] Then, party hatred is at times intensely fierce." The truth is that one of those changes has been effected in Geneva which are taking place in all parts of the world where there is any element of freedom in the government. The popular party has extended the right of citizenship, which ten years since was the prerogative of those only who were of the national church, to persons of every communion, a measure which has broken down the Genevese aristocracy. It is very likely the change has been accomplished with some loss as well as gain, and that some pleasant old characteristics of the Genevese social life [have][4] been sacrificed. In pulling up the big weeds in my garden at Roslyn, it has often happened that I was obliged to take up with them some flowers—some useful plant which I would gladly have saved, but could not, its roots were so closely intertwined with the wild ones I must extirpate. But you would hardly recognize Geneva for the same place. Shallows of the lake filled up; rows of stately houses, with broad streets between, built on the level space, thus usurped from the water; massive quays and breakwaters, advancing into the lake, form a spacious port for the skippers; the old fortifications of the town utterly demolished, and converted into public grounds and building lots, and Geneva overflows into the fields. I could hardly believe my eyes. The emancipated Catholics

are building themselves a magnificent church on the west side of the
Rhone, and priests, in cocked hats and long black skirts, go hobbling
about in the city of Calvin.

We saw some of the most remarkable points of Switzerland—Schaffhausen, Interlaken, Grindelwald, the Baths of Pfeffers, Zurich, Luzerne,
Berne, Chamouni[x]. My wife, you will be surprised to hear, went up
Mount Righi, or rather was carried up, and tried to walk down, but gave
out at about two thirds of the descent, and was obliged to call in another
set of bearers, who took her down to Weggis very comfortably in another
chair. Switzerland has sweltered nearly all summer in a torrid heat, but
we had a cool journey from Geneva through Lyons, Nismes, and Toulouse, to this place. Here we are among the Pyrenees—in another Switzerland, with blacker rocks and darker verdure, corn and the vine growing
higher up the mountains, and a livelier race of men and women, who chatter what is left of the ancient language of the Troubadours. From four
o'clock in the morning until ten at night the street before our windows
resounds with the talk of women in strange head-dresses, made of red and
yellow handkerchiefs, and to the cracking of whips by the men, who sometimes startle us with a noise like that of the snapping of timbers in a great
conflagration. Luchon is the most attractive summer residence I have seen
on this side of the Atlantic. Here we have cool airs, extensive promenades
of deep and ample shade, a fresh and flowery turf, rapid streams, cascades,
clear brooks, picturesque mountains, and the greenest valleys winding
away in almost every direction, and all this under the glorious sunshine
of the south of France.

A warm sulphur spring brings many invalids to the place; and the
beauty of the scenery and the agreeableness of the climate attract thousands of others from every country of Europe, among whom, however, are
very few English. I have not been content for my part to stop until I got
here; but here we shall stay, at least till the rage of the dog-star is over.

AUGUST 31st: Luchon is as pleasant as ever, and we have no thought
of quitting it at present, only we begin to long for the sight of some familiar face. We all wish we could have a glimpse of your kind Sheffield
faces. The next thing to a sight of your faces would be a sight of your
letters. Tell Mary[5] I do not understand what she means by sending me
her "respects," nor do I recollect anything in my note addressed to her in
New York[6] which should have provoked it. . . .

MANUSCRIPT: Unrecovered TEXT (partial): Life, II, 99–101.

1. One of these letters was probably that of Dewey to Bryant, June 28, 1857, NYPL–
BG.

2. Jean Jacob Caton Chenevière (1783–1871), a theological writer and professor
of theology with whom Orville Dewey had apparently become acquainted while taking
the water cure at Geneva during his European visit in 1841–1843.

3. "And we are against it."

4. In the printed text, "has."

5. Orville Dewey's daughter, and biographer.
6. Unrecovered.

980. *To* Christiana Gibson

[Bagnères-de-Luchon, September 3, 1857]

My dear Miss Gibson,

My wife insists upon your letter[1] being answered, now that we have at last a few days of repose, and I being the most expeditious workman at getting up a letter the business of writing the answer is put upon me. It is a convenient excuse you perceive for getting rid of a little ink.

I remember that when last abroad you were in raptures with Interlaken. We too were at Interlaken passing through it on our way to Grindelwald and again passing two nights and a day at the place on our return, but we were not tempted to remain. It lies beautifully among its grand mountains and rapid rivers and I even saw fruit trees—I love trees—but there were two objections to the place. It was fiercely hot, and full of company coming and going, a perfect mob of English moving about and meeting you at every step—it was a dressy sort of place too—and we had not crossed the sea to see fine people—there are too many of them in New York.[2] So we bore away from Interlaken to Vevey through the Simmenthal and from Vevey to Geneva, and from Geneva after visiting Chamonix, to this place—making a little stop at Lyons—much embellished and beautified lately, at Nimes full of ancient remains, and at Toulouse— . . .[3]—and finally settled at this place. —Here is the only spot I have for the first time been willing to rest a little. The truth is that my wife and I are fairly sick of staring at curiosities and wonders, and still more tired of tumbling about the world in search of them. So we have fixed ourselves here till the summer heats are over, in what is said to be the finest spot among all the Pyrenees, in spacious and pleasant lodgings in a lively street—too lively sometimes, with a servant woman who toils very anxiously to earn a little daily gratuity, and with meals sent from the neighboring hotel—and all this among the finest promenades I ever saw, in one of the freshest of valleys traversed by roaring rivers, and a noble brotherhood of mountains overlooking it. We have here a street which is always humming with the chatter of a thousand voices and in which you constantly see women in gay colored headdresses walking to and fro, with here and there a Spanish pedlar in his gay colored costume and parties of people on horseback setting out and returning from excursions, the guides cracking their whips with a crackle like a great fire. Among these are well dressed ladies—many have on travelling dresses with broad round hats. Luchon is not uncomfortably warm as we have found all the rest of the continent this summer, except the north part of Holland.

My wife I am glad to be able to say is on the gaining hand. She makes some little expedition every day, and is stronger than when we left home.

I took her up the Righi in a chair, and she saw the sun rise over the Bernese Oberland. She has had several donkey rides, though she does not profess to like them much, and I think I shall get her home so well mended that she will look "amaist as well's the new." Julia and Estelle get on very harmoniously and pleasantly together; they are quite enterprising and plan more excursions than I with all my activity think it best to make.

We were glad to hear through you of the visit which your mother and father are making to Scotland. We hope it will be of service to both of them—indeed it can hardly fail to be—freedom from care and native air will buoy them up again if any thing can. What is medicine to blunt the effects of care[?] What is a surgeons skill worth in setting a dislocated limb every evening if it is to be put out again regularly every morning? The cause must be removed—must cease to act—and [it] is idle to deal with the effect—which is constantly reproduced. Taking medicine to cure the effects of care, without taking medicine to cure the mischief done by care unless you can get rid of the care is like putting arnica on a wound which is torn open as fast as it heals. . . .[4]

MANUSCRIPT: NYPL–GR (draft) PUBLISHED (in part): Life, II, 98–99.

1. Unrecovered.
2. "Interlaken has the appearance of a watering place and is full of idle people." Bryant, "Diary, 1857–1858," August 3, 1857.
3. Three words illegible.
4. The portion of this letter (the second paragraph) printed in Life, II, 98–99, differs so radically from the draft manuscript as to suggest that Godwin may have had access to the final copy, though it seems more likely that he simply exercised his editorial pen, as so often elsewhere.

981. *To* the EVENING POST

Bagnères de Luchon, Hautes Pyrenées,⎱
September 8, 1857.   ⎰

Much as my countrymen travel, there are few of them, I think, who come to the warm springs or baths of Luchon—the Bagnères de Luchon, as they are called here—and few are aware what a charming spot it is, what a delightful summer climate it has, and how picturesque is the surrounding country. It is Switzerland with a more even temperature, a longer summer, a serener sky, and mountains which less capriciously veil themselves in fogs at the moment you wish to get a sight at them. The black rocks with which they are ribbed crumble into a darker and apparently a richer soil, which lends the verdure of their sides a deeper tinge. Here, at Luchon, I see fields of maize and millet half-way up the mountain sides, and patches of buckwheat, now in bloom, whitening almost their very crests.

At Geneva I fell in with an English gentleman, who has been botanizing industriously on the continent for seven years, and had not seen his

native country in all that time. We told him we were going to Bagnères de Bigorre. "Go rather to Bagnères de Luchon," he answered. "You will there be in the heart of the Pyrenees, while at Bigorre you would be only among their lower declivities. Luchon is the finest spot in all the Pyrenees. The accommodations are good; they do not fleece you there as they do here in Switzerland; the English have not got there yet. Besides, you will have about you such a magnificent mountain Flora." We took his advice, and set out for Bagnères de Luchon. But first I must say a word of Geneva.

It was hard to believe it the same place which I saw eight years since.[1] The popular party which now rules Geneva have pulled down the old walls and forts, within which it seems to have been fancied that the city might sustain a siege; these have been converted into public promenades and building lots. Geneva is now an open city, like all our own towns, and is spreading itself into the country. Where Lake Leman begins to contract itself into the Rhone, and the blue waters rush towards their outlet, large spaces on each side, lately covered with water, have been filled up with the rubbish of the forts, and massive quays and breakwaters extending into the lake, have been built to form a secure harbor for the shipping. Long rows of stately buildings, of a cheerful aspect, with broad streets between, have been erected by the water side. Enterprising men have been attracted from other parts of Switzerland and from foreign countries, by the field here opened to their activity, and with them come swarms of strange work-people. Catholic priests, in their big cocked hats and long black gowns clinging to their legs, are now a frequent sight in this city of Calvin; and the Catholics, now at length admitted to full citizenship, are building an elegant church on the west bank of the Rhone. One need not wonder that those who liked the old order of things should lament that the Geneva of to-day is no longer the Geneva of their youth.

In our way to Luchon we stopped for a short time at Lyons, which I found almost as much changed in four years as Geneva in eight. It seems to have caught the rage of demolition and reconstruction from Paris. A broad street, like one of the Boulevards of the metropolis, running from the *Place de Bellecour* to the hills, has been opened through the heart of the city, by beating down the mass of old houses, separated from each other by narrow and gloomy passages, and constructing others of a more cheerful architecture in their place. They call the new street the *Rue Imperiale*, to mark its epoch. In a paved square opened in the middle of this street, I saw a group of workmen engaged in putting up the statues of a fountain, and not far off a crowd of them busy in erecting a bank of elaborate Italian architecture. Near the northern extremity of the street another company were occupied restoring and enlarging the Hotel de Ville.

We passed a day and a half at Nîmes, in the comfortable and spacious Hotel du Luxembourg—Nîmes, at this season, quiet, dull and silent as the vast interior of its own grand Roman amphitheatre. Its principal com-

merce at the moment seemed to consist in disposing of the enormous quantities of fine melons which I saw heaped on the pavement in its streets. Nîmes is a city for a winter residence; the August sun glared upon us so fiercely that we were withered by the heat. I found the turf under the bowers of evergreens, in the garden above its famous fountain, scorched to snuff with the summer fervors. I remembered its freshness and the sweet December sunshine that rested upon it nearly four years since, and almost wished it were December again. Yet, even amidst this quiet, some new buildings were going up at Nîmes: several elegant houses and a church of a remarkably graceful Gothic model, the light and airy shafts and arches carved out of the cream-colored stone, so easily wrought, with which they build in this country. There was some activity of a different kind—they were fitting up the amphitheatre for a bull-fight the next Sunday, but the keeper of the building compassionately assured us that it was a very different thing from a Spanish bull-fight, and that there was no danger in it either to the bull or to the human combatants.

From Nîmes to Toulouse, with the exception of Montpelier, the environs of which seemed pleasant, and where the air of the sea breathed upon us with a refreshing coolness, our journey was through an arid and almost shadeless country. Frontignan, famed for its grapes, as the delicious varieties which bear its name with us testify, was no exception; nor Cette, which sends its white wines to our market; nor dirty Narbonne, where we got a luxurious dinner and passed a night with the fleas. As we approached Toulouse the aspect of the country softened, but there was the same dreary and melancholy lack of verdure, the same absence of groves, shade-trees and grassy turf, for which no appearance of fruitfulness can compensate— and yet the country is abundantly fertile. The city of the Troubadours detained us only long enough to look at its curious old churches, and to drive through some of its handsome promenades, and we took the diligence the next morning for this place, passing over the broad plains of the Garonne and through several very dirty French villages—for the further south you go in France the more dirt you find—till at length we came to where the Garonne comes plunging and roaring from the mountains. It was like the effect of enchantment to pass, as we did, from a dust-colored landscape into a valley of luxuriant verdure, from a flat level to grand mountain scenery, from silent streams to sounding torrents, from a sultry atmosphere to airs cooled by the eternal snows of the glaciers.

The baths of Luchon, supplied by hot sulphur springs which gush from a mountain side, have been frequented for the last two hundred years. For generation after generation has the ingenuity of man been exerted to render the place attractive, to multiply its accommodations, and make the most of its natural beauties. Shady walks into which the noon sun cannot penetrate, with seats of stone, squares planted with pleasant trees—one of these is entirely planted with American trees, the catalpa

and the tulip-tree—paths beside the roaring torrents, paths climbing the mountain sides, paths into the thick forests, terraces from which you look down into the valleys and far away among the mountain peaks—these you have all around you; and then there are excellent carriage roads which take you to picturesque old turrets, and along the windings of beautiful valleys, and beyond these, bridle roads which lead to cascades, to solitary highland lakes and to lofty summits of mountains. There are guides whose occupation it is to accompany travellers to the most remarkable points of this region, and the calling is often hereditary—the father training his sons to it from early boyhood. They are a hardy race of men, healthy by their occupation, obliging and serviceable from habit; they hunt wolves, bears and the wild goat in the mountains, when the season of the baths is over; and there is no place in the Pyrenees to which they will not agree to conduct you. They frequently take travellers to the top of the Maladetta, the highest peak of the Pyrenees, covered with perpetual snow, and only first ascended, about twelve years since, by M. De Franqueville.[2] The other day three of them dragged an Englishman to the top of the *Pic de la Pique,* or *Pic de la Picade,* a slippery-looking pinnacle of rock, not far from the Maladetta, with sides almost perpendicular, which had never before been scaled.

If any of the readers of these letters should visit Luchon, I can cheerfully, without disparagement to any of his brethren, recommend one of these guides, Bertrand Estrujo, who is certainly a favorable specimen of his tribe. Estrujo is a fine, broad-chested figure of a man, with a good-natured face, and civil, obliging manners. He will tell you the legends of the region through which he takes you, and when these are exhausted, will sing you a song in French or Spanish, or in the *patois* of the mountains, as you may choose; or if there is nothing to be said, and you are tired of silence, he will crack his whip with a succession of reports like a rolling fire of pistol shot—a sort of tattoo turned off from the tip of the lash, which is shivered into fibres and left floating in the air like gossamer. Estrujo will give you excellent horses, or if they are not always precisely what you desire, will apologize so ingeniously for their defects, or throw in such skilful commendations of their real merits, that you can hardly help being satisfied.

The main part of Luchon is a shabby village, with dirty-looking houses, and narrow, winding streets, on each side of which is a paved gutter, the channel of a swiftly-flowing little stream, diverted from the torrent of the *One,* in which the women are sometimes seen washing their clothes. But the south end of Luchon, called the *Cours d'Etigny,* in which the visitors to the baths have their lodgings, is a noble street—broad, planted with a fourfold row of elms and lindens, and bordered with large, commodious houses, in nearly all of which apartments are let. To the south, this pleasant street terminates at the stately building erected to contain the baths,

and the pleasure ground surrounding the spring where the waters are dispensed to those who drink them, and just at this season it presents, all day long, one of the gayest spectacles I ever saw.

At an early hour arrive the diligences; the street is immediately in commotion; troops of servant-women in head-dresses of bright-colored handkerchiefs, red and yellow, run after them and crowd around them, offering the newly arrived travellers apartments in the houses of their employers. You hear a sound of small bells; a herdsman is driving his cows to their mountain pasture, or a woman has brought her goat to your door to be milked. Companies of people, men and women, are departing on horseback—each with a guide, who is known by his cap, short jacket and loaded leathern valise strapped in front of his saddle. They are setting out, perhaps, for the beautiful *Vallée du Lys*, where the meadows at this season are as fresh and flowery as our own in June, or to the *Lac d'Oo*, a blue pool, high among the mountains, surrounded by dark pinnacles of rock flecked with fields of snow, from one of which a white cataract plunges, roaring, into the lake. Or, perhaps, they are going to the summit called the *Pic de l'Anticade*, from which you look down into the valleys of Catalonia, or to that called the *Port de Venasque*, whence you look down into those of Aragon and over the mountains of that province. If the company consist of one or three, and these are men, perhaps they are about to ascend the Maladetta. Carriages are drawn up before the doors of the houses; they are waiting to convey the lodgers to the old town of *St. Beat*, in a narrow rocky gorge of the Garonne, or further on, to the *Pont du Roi*, on the frontier of Spain, or to *St. Bertrand de Cominges*, renowned for its ancient Gothic church, or to the *Cascade des Demoiselles*, on the Pique. A sedan chair, with two strong-limbed bearers, passes through the street; it contains a patient whom they are carrying to the baths; two or three people in thick cloaks, and hoods covering their heads and faces, are walking in the other direction; they are bathers returning to their lodgings. People are setting out upon a morning walk; a lady and her children are trotting by on donkeys, with women for donkey drivers; they are going to the Cascade of Montauban, or to that of Jaze, or to the terrace called La Sauniere, from which you look down upon Luchon and its green and shady valley. If they are more adventurous, perhaps they are bent upon climbing to the summit of Superbagneres, the mountain from the base of which flow the sulphurous springs that supply the baths. A group of priests, in their black robes and cocked hats, are passing; the priests throng to Luchon, and love to saunter in its shady alleys, and are often seen in the cavalcades that go out upon excursions among the mountains. There go two Sisters of Mercy, in their flowing hoods of white muslin; they are on a visit to the lodging-houses, to ask donations for the hospital of Luchon. Two ragged, brown, slender men, in their red caps, knee-breeches, stockings without feet, and hempen sandals, are driving their

loaded asses through the street; they are peasants from one of the neighboring Catalonian villages. Spanish pedlars in laced jackets and small clothes of brown velvet, are moving about the streets, taking off their caps to almost all they meet, and offering their wares. Others of them have piled their glistening foulards from Barcelona, their packages of linen and their silk shawls around the foot of one of the great trees in the street, to attract the attention of the passengers.

When the shadow of the mountain begins to fall on the well-kept grounds below the edge of the forest south of the bath-house, which is at about four o'clock in the afternoon, a crowd of visitors in little groups seat themselves in chairs on the terrace in that spot. Walk among them and you will hear spoken the accented dialect of Southern France; you will hear French; you will hear Spanish, but no English. It is not quite exact to say, however, as my English acquaintance at Geneva said, that the English have not got to Luchon yet. At the Lac d'Oo, which we reached at the beginning of a pelting storm of rain and hail, we fell in with a party from Liverpool, of whom five were ladies, who came, soused and dripping, into the cabin among the rocks where we were taking our luncheon. They were "doing up" the Pyrenees, I think, in a fortnight, conscientiously seeing every thing set down for them to see in their guide-books, and as they were provided with water proof cloaks, they defied wind and weather. They whipped through the list of sights in a space of time that seemed to me incredibly short, and then went off to Toulouse in the night. The English who come here do not stay long, but look at what is remarkable and depart.

Our party have not been so faithful to the duty of sightseeing, contenting ourselves with a selection from the usual excursions. One of these we made to the *Pic de l'Anticade*. It is a green mountain summit within the Spanish dominions, grazed by cattle under the care of Catalonian herdsmen. The roar of a hundred waterfalls rose at once to our ears from the valley of the Garonne below, where I counted eleven villages lying east of us—Busost and Bïla, and—a Catalan woman, who had followed us up the summit to beg, gave us their names, but I have forgotten the rest. Below us eagles were wheeling about the crags; and to the south, where the Garonne came down from the mountains, vast and dense forests reached far down the valley. "In these forests," said our guide, "we go to hunt bears in winter. Wolves too, are found there, and where the rocks are steep, the *isard*, our mountain goat." To the west of us rose the mountains of Aragon, and, half seen through the mists, the white summit of the Maladetta. Our guide gave us the etymology of the name in this legend:

"Our Saviour," said he, "was passing over the mountain, when he met a shepherd and his dog. The dog flew at our Saviour and bit him, the shepherd making no effort to prevent it. Since that time a curse has rested on the mountain; it is covered with perpetual snow, and the shepherd and

his dog keep their station there yet. They were seen not long since, but, on being approached, they disappeared. You understand now why the mountain is called the Maladetta or the Accursed."

When the autumnal weather begins to grow chilly at Luchon, the visitors generally, if they do not go home, migrate to Bagnères de Bigorre, as we propose to do to-morrow, though the temperature is still soft and genial here.

MANUSCRIPT: Unrecovered TEXT: *LT* II, pp. 30–40; first published in *EP* for October 3, 1857.

    1. See Letter 699.
    2. Not further identified.

982. *To* the EVENING POST
San Sebastian, Province of Guipuscoa, Spain,⎱
September 28th, 1857.⎰

Since I wrote you last, I have made a short sojourn at Bagnères de Bigorre and another at Pau, to say nothing of a brief stay at Bayonne. Bagnères de Bigorre, a pleasant watering-place, is too much like Bagnères de Luchon, in most that is characteristic, to need a very particular description. Like that place, it lies high, in a cool atmosphere. At the foot of a long hill break out, I think, nearly a dozen warm springs, of different temperatures and different degrees of mineral impregnation, each of which has its building fitted up with baths, and each of which asserts its specific merits in healing certain ailments, so that whatever be your malady, it will go hard but you will find some practitioner of medicine to recommend one or the other. Broad paths, embowered with trees, some of them planted long ago, lead from one spring to the other, along rivulet or hill side. Here you meet the visitors to the place, whether they come for the waters or the air, idly sauntering; here you meet with patients carried in sedan chairs, or resting on the benches. Sometimes it is a well-dressed lady from Paris, or one of the provincial towns of France, in a bonnet of the newest pattern, and sometimes a *bourgeoise*, equally well dressed, with no bonnet at all. Sometimes it is a man in the garb of the laboring class, beside whom sits or walks his plain wife, employed on her knitting; sometimes it is a woman with her distaff, industriously twirling the spindle as she threads the long alleys. Bigorre is a town of lodging houses, and affords ample accommodations for all these classes. The peasants go out to shoot game for them among the mountains; the fruits of the south of France are brought to them from the plain of Tarbes, and peasant girls gather strawberries for them all summer long, going higher and higher up the Pyrenees, from July to October. For their spiritual wants large provision is made; the Catholics have here several churches, among the finest of which is that of the Carmelites, newly built, and close to their new convent, a

good sample of the Romanesque style. I cannot think it improved by the fresco behind the altar, just finished from a design by Horace Vernet, representing Elijah taken up into heaven.[1] Elijah is an Arab, with a peaked beard, and the Bedouin head-dress bound on his forehead by a cord of camel's hair. Elisha is a stout friar in a brown gown, catching at the mantle which falls from his master, and an angel in a blue robe and white wings, hovering above the chariot of fire, holds the reins and guides the horses. The whole conception strikes me as poor and commonplace. The Protestants have also their temple, where a French clergyman, who preaches with great simplicity and earnestness, conducts the worship, with a considerable congregation, mostly of the laboring class.

At Pau, where we were delayed a few days by the indisposition of one of our party, we found only silence and slumber. Of the English who throng it in winter, on account of the softness of its climate at that season, those alone remained who were lying in its cemetery. Those who, about this time, are on their way home from St. Sauveur, or Luz, or Cauterets, or some other of their famous watering-places in the Pyrenees, stop now and then just to look at the castle of Henry the Fourth[2] and the park, and then go on. I saw a "list of visitors" advertised on an English sign, and applied to see it. "No," I was told, "we do not make it out till winter." I was looking for a pair of cork soles for one of our party. "They are not arrived yet," was the answer; "it is too early in the season." In short, Pau was in its summer sleep; and though it was past the middle of September, the sun blazed with a heat like that of August, and the trees in the handsome Park, which overlooks the brawling current of the Gave, yielding to a few months' drought, were fast dropping their yellow leaves. At length the long-wished-for showers fell, and we set out, one fine bright morning, for Bayonne—the whole country steeped and fresh with rain. Our carriage bowled over one of those broad, smooth, well-kept macadamized roads of France, with massive stone bridges, and parapets wherever the ground descends on either side of the way, which impress one strongly with an idea of energy and precision in the workings of the power of government. The rain soon returned—we travelled on in a deluge—and it has been raining ever since. After passing through a fertile country, bordering the Gave of Pau, we climbed into a barren region, which the prickly gorse and the rigid heath made gay with their unprofitable flowers, and then entered among pine forests, scarred with long yellow wounds to make the trees yield them turpentine. These gave place at length to gardens and country seats, and almost before we were aware, our carriage rolled through the gates of a fortified city, and we were in Bayonne.

I was surprised at the green and fresh appearance of the fields around Bayonne, after so long a drought. The neighborhood of the mountains on the one side, and of the sea on the other, perhaps so temper the air as to give the country this verdurous aspect, while so much of the south of

France at this season is of the color of ashes. Bayonne is a half Spanish town; the guests in its hotels are in a considerable proportion Spanish; it maintains an active regular trade with Spain, to say nothing of what is done by the smugglers, who in the passes of the Pyrenees set the agents of the government at defiance; its shops have, many of them, Spanish signs, and it is the point from which diligences set out to all parts of Spain. Bayonne lies on two rivers which here meet on their journey to the ocean, a league from their mouth, and far enough inland to deprive the sea winds of their bleakness in winter. Beyond its walls a public promenade shaded with noble trees surrounds nearly the whole city.

We found quarters at the *Hotel du Commerce*, where we went up to our rooms by dirty staircases, and where half a dozen serving maids, all rather tall, very thin, very sharp-featured, and most of them talkative, attended to the wants of the guests. What with talking and waiting on the guests, the poor creatures, although they applied themselves to both duties with all their might, seemed to have more work on their hands than they were able to perform, and the comfort and convenience of the guests suffered no little in consequence. I had occasion to observe, in passing through the streets, that the women were rather taller, besides being considerably thinner and sharper featured than those I had seen in the more eastern departments.

We took places the other morning in the diligence that travels between Bayonne and San Sebastian, and passing a long alley of trees, and leaving behind the belt of handsome country seats by which Bayonne is environed, we ascended a height from which we saw the Atlantic ocean spread before us. In green and purple it lay, its distant verge blended and lost in the mists of the horizon. I cannot describe the feeling awakened within me as I gazed on that great waste of waters which in one of its inlets steeped the walls of my own garden, and to the murmur of which on a distant shore, those I loved were doubtless at that moment slumbering. From time to time, as we went on, we descended out of sight of the sea, and rose again to see it flinging its white breakers against the land. The peaks of the Pyrenees were all the while in full view, and we were approaching the region where their western buttresses present an eternal barrier against the assaults of the ocean, which to the north of them have hollowed out the Gulf of Gascony.

The scenery to the south of Bayonne presented the same fresh and verdant appearance as that in its immediate neighborhood to the east, but the houses had a Swiss look, with their overhanging eaves, supported by the projecting rafters, and here and there a balcony on the gable ends, which were striped with upright wooden posts, imbedded in the stucco, and painted red. The rest of the exterior was neatly whitewashed, and the windows were hung with shutters, painted red or green. This is the fashion of Basque architecture, for we were now among the Basque race, though

yet several miles from the Spanish frontier. The road was full of peasant men and women, coming and going; the men in flat blue caps, short jackets, and wooden shoes, many of the younger wearing scarlet sashes; and the women for the most part barefoot, their heads bound with gay cotton kerchiefs, and their petticoats tucked up for the convenience of walking in the wet roads. Of both sexes a large proportion had the look of premature old age; yet among the older men I saw many of a rather striking appearance, with their high Roman noses, and gray hair flowing down upon their shoulders. It was the women who had the prerogative of carrying all the burdens, some of them bearing large jars, and the others enormous broad baskets poised on their heads.

Through village after village we went, till we came to where the little river Bidassoa, flowing through a green valley, parts the sovereignties of France and Spain. At Behobie, the frontier village of the empire, a French official in red mustaches looked at our passports and allowed us to go upon the bridge; at the other end of the bridge, a Spanish official, with dense coal-black eyebrows, looked at them also, and signified to us that we were at liberty to set foot upon the soil beyond. We were now in Spain; yet the aspect of the dwellings was exactly the same as in the region we had just left, and the costume of the peasantry unaltered, except that the scarlet sash was more frequently seen, the wooden shoes were exchanged for hempen slippers or sandals, and the women wore their thick, long hair gathered into a single braid, which sometimes descended nearly to their feet.

A short drive brought us to the main street of Irun, the first Spanish town—a steep, well-paved street, between tall houses—tall for so small a place—with balcony above balcony, from which women were looking down upon us and the crowd about us. The clean street and the well-built houses gave us a favorable idea of the country on which we had entered. We stopped at Irun to pay a tax of two pesetas on each foreign passport, and to open our trunks for the inspection of the custom-house officers, who seemed disposed to give us as little trouble as they could. Before we reached the frontier, our conductor had made his preparations for passing free of duty a few goods which he had brought with him. He first stuffed his garments, under his blouse, with a variety of merchandise, among which was a pair of patent leather half-boots with elastic ancles. "Here," said he to the postilion, handing him a heavy piece of worsted goods, "button this under your waistcoat." The man complied without a word, and seemed only a very little the more corpulent for this addition to his bulk. "Madam," said the conductor again, addressing himself to a female passenger, and taking a new lady's cloak from a pasteboard box, "will you do me the favor to let this hang on your arm for the rest of the journey?" The lady consented; the custom-house officers found nothing chargeable with duty, and our trunks being replaced on the diligence, away we rolled towards San Sebastian.

While waiting at Irun, I had time to look at the people about me, for it was a holiday, and the peasantry from the neighboring country were in the streets, mingled with the inhabitants of the town. They had a hardy look; we should call them in America rather short; but their frames were well knit, with broad shoulders, a healthy complexion, and a not unpleasing physiognomy; the women seemed of scarcely less vigorous make than the men. This was the pure Basque race, the posterity of the ancient Cantabrians, who had kept the mountain region to themselves from the earliest period known to history, preserving their old impracticable language, and many of their primitive customs. I could not help looking for something striking, characteristic, and peculiar in a branch of the human family which had so long kept itself distinct from the others, but I did not see it; they seemed cast in the common mould of our species. But as we went on, I saw other indications that we had passed out of one country into another —narrower roads, unprotected by parapets where they led along a hillside; hedges untrimmed, lands less sedulously cultivated; fields lying waste and red with withered fern, and fruit-trees less carefully tended. On the French side of the Bidassoa the apple orchards looked fresh and flourishing; here they were shaggy with moss and nearly bare of leaves, bearing instead, heavy bunches of misletoe, which had fastened on the branches and were now in bloom. A considerable part of the tilth was Indian corn, but neither here nor in any part of the south of France were the harvests of this grain such as an American farmer would be proud of. The stalks were small, and each of them produced but a single short and light ear.

Between Irun and San Sebastian we found ourselves on the verge of what seemed a lake among the mountains. "The port of Passages!" said a fellow-traveller, pointing towards it. I looked and saw where a chasm opened between dark and jagged rocks to the Atlantic ocean—a breach in the mountain wall of the Pyrenees, through which the tides flow and sleep in this quiet basin. The passage through which they enter is overlooked by castles which have nothing to guard. Three vessels only were lying where a whole navy might ride in safety from the storms; they were moored beside a poor-looking little town. "It is a noble port," said my fellow-traveller, "but neglected, as every thing else is in Spain." The river of Renteria runs into it and forms shallows with the deposites it brings down from the highlands.

At Irun we had taken our fourth postilion after leaving Bayonne, a meagre, crooked man, with sharp features, shrivelled cheeks, a hooked nose, and a little projecting knob of an under lip; not to forget a hollow scar on the right temple. He held voluble dialogues with the conductor, in which I distinguished some words identical with the Spanish, but of the rest I could make nothing. "What are they talking?" I asked of my next neighbor. "It is the dialect of Gascony," he answered; "the postilion is from Bayonne." But the postilion's eloquence was not confined to one

language. He was somewhat of a wag, and gave us an imitation of the petulant tones of French declamation, and then, changing to a grave and quiet manner, dealt out a few proverbs and pithy sayings in Castilian. He had, besides, a joke in Basque for almost every young female we passed with a basket on her head. As we were approaching, through a narrow, fertile valley, the peninsula on which San Sebastian is built, a troop of boys greeted us from a little distance with shouts, and the smallest of them all, standing in the middle of the road, and seemingly calculating the course of our vehicle, placed a four-cornered stone exactly in the path of our left wheels, and then leaped aside to see the jolt it would give us. Our fluent Gascon instantly turned his horses a little to the right, and discharged at the offender a crack of his whip, which made him start, and a volley of loud words, which, for aught I know, might have been the purest and most classical Basque ever spoken.

Our vehicle crossed a bridge over a shallow arm of the sea, and entering the peninsula, passed through an avenue of poplars, part of the Alameda [public walk] of San Sebastian, near which stands a wooden amphitheatre erected not long since for bull-fights, and went slowly through the gates of the city, which is surrounded on all sides by strong walls, except on the west, where it stands against the steeps of Mount Orgullo, a conical rock, rising four hundred feet from the sea at its base, crowned with a castle, and bristling with other fortifications. Our baggage had to undergo another inspection, and then we were allowed to take it to the Hotel Lafitte, in the street of San Geronimo, where we climbed up a gloomy staircase to dirty chambers. Our French host apologized for the dirt, which was no fault of his, he said, for he had no wife, and only Spanish domestics; but he would endeavor to make amends for the dirt by the excellence of the dinners; and in this, as his profession was that of cook, I must admit that he kept his word.

MANUSCRIPT: Unrecovered TEXT: *LT* II, pp. 41–51; first published in *EP* for October 22, 1857.

1. Probably the Frenchman Émile Jean Horace Vernet (1789–1863), best known for his paintings of military subjects. See 2 Kings 2:11.
2. Birthplace of Henry IV (1553–1610), king of France, 1589–1610; and, as Henry III, king of Navarre, 1572–1610.

983. *To* the EVENING POST

San Sebastian, Spain, October 5, 1857.

It was a matter of course, that in lodgings so neglected by the housekeeper as those I described in my last, we should find the fleas uncomfortably numerous. The mosquitoes did their part to keep us awake, but a walk the next day on the rocky mount at the foot of which San Sebastian is built, made amends for the annoyances of the night. The west wind

had been blowing with some strength for several days; and the agitated ocean was rolling its mighty breakers on one side of us into the bay of Concha, and on the other up the river Urumea, and in front of us dashing them against the base of the rocks on which we stood. The two sublimest features of nature are the sea and the mountains; and it is not often that in any part of the world you see them in their grandeur side by side. Here, at San Sebastian, you have the Pyrenees looking down upon the Atlantic. To the northwest of the city, the sea flings its spray against the dark rocks of Mount Ulia, to the southwest it beats against the steeps of Mount Frio, crowned with lighthouses, and beyond, in the same direction, a lofty promontory stretches, like a sentinel of that mountain range, far into the great deep. As we looked inland from the height we stood, we had before us an amphitheatre of mountains, with peaked and wavy summits, embosoming the country about San Sebastian; at our feet lay the little city with its little artificial port, made by massive seawalls, and containing its little commercial marine, and beyond the port, where the billows rolled in upon the sands, we saw a row of bathing tents, near which ladies were taking their morning bath, and at some distance were men on horseback, urging their animals into the surf.

From this place, resounding only with the roar of the ocean, we returned to streets as noisy with the voices and occupations of men. I think San Sebastian the noisiest place I was ever in, and that with scarcely any help from the rattling of carriages or the tramp of horses' feet. I seem to be perpetually in the midst of a crowd of children, just let loose from school. The streets resound from early morning to eight o'clock at night with all manner of childish and infantile cries; they are calling to each other in their shrillest accents; they are shouting, crying, singing, blowing penny whistles, clattering castanets. Then you hear artisans of almost every trade, engaged in their work—blacksmiths striking their anvils, tinkers mending brass-kettles, cobblers hammering their lasts; you hear the screech of the file, the grating of the saw, and the click of the stone-cutter's chisel. Parrots are screaming to each other across the streets; and oxen are dragging loaded carts, running on plank wheels without spokes, which creak lamentably as they go. Besides all this, there is a most extraordinary yelping of dogs at San Sebastian. Once in ten minutes a dog is flogged, or somebody treads on his tail or toes, and he makes the whole town ring with his complaints.

"Let me show you San Sebastian," said our host, soon after we had returned from our walk. He took us to a balcony, projecting from one of the windows. "There," said he, "on one side, at three or four rods distance, you see the city wall. In the opposite direction, the street extends a few rods further, to that gate, through which you pass to the port. That is the length of San Sebastian." Our host then conducted us to a balcony on the cross street. "Here," said he, "a few doors to the right, the street ends at

the rock upon which the citadel is built; look to the left, and you see where the same street terminates at the city wall. That is the breadth of San Sebastian. You have now seen the city; it is but a village, and would be nothing without its citadel." I was obliged to agree with Monsieur Lafitte as to the extent of the city; which, however, within the narrow circuit of its walls, is compactly built, and can be made no larger; yet in this space are crowded ten thousand persons. The streets are straight, crossing each other at right angles, and rather narrow; the buildings are four stories in height, including the ground floor; and each story, even in the case of the wealthier class, is occupied by a separate family; and as the windows are open all day, scarcely a baby cries in San Sebastian without being heard all over the city.

In one place I found silence; it was Sunday; and I entered the church of Santa Maria, erected in the beginning of the last century. Without, the church has a festive aspect, like that of a theatre, the front being carved into scrolls and escutcheons, flourishes and garlands, and heads of cherubs projecting from among foliage. Within, the massive pillars, faced on each of their four sides with Corinthian pilasters, spread from the richly ornamented capitals into richly ornamented cornices, and from these sprout into ribbed arches of a broad span; the whole in what would be called a corrupt style of architecture, but which has a certain imposing and magnificent effect, and that is perhaps the best test of architectural merit. The church was crowded with worshippers, of whom four-fifths were women, and of these a considerable proportion were of the more opulent class. All were in black veils, the national costume; not a bonnet was to be seen; all were on their knees, with their faces turned towards the altar. I observed among them many fine countenances, and was struck with the appearance they showed of being profoundly absorbed in the offices of devotion. All were motionless, save the priest at the richly ornamented altar, with his bows and genuflections; all was silence, save the prayer he murmured, and the tinkling of the little bell, which announced some peculiar part of the ceremonies. The thick walls of the building excluded all sounds from the streets, and on the platform before it all games are rigorously forbidden.

I came out of the church, and entering the street which led to my hotel, found myself, at once, in a perfect hubbub of noises. Pianos were jangling in the houses; servant girls were screaming to each other in Basque, and uttering shouts of laughter; the chorus of childish voices was shriller than ever; the very parrots seemed to utter their cries with more energy, as if in honor of the holiday; it appeared to me that of all the inhabitants of the city not one was silent. Close to our hotel, and within sight of its windows, lies the great Plaza of the town, and this was full of people, notwithstanding an occasional thin shower of drizzling rain. Here children of different ages were playing their noisy games; some were skipping their ropes, some dancing in a ring and singing, some dancing by

themselves and snapping their castanets. Apart from these, some young people were dancing the fandango the young men in flat scarlet caps, scarlet sashes, and hempen sandals tied with scarlet galoon. The tumult of merriment grew more riotous about twilight. A flute was played at one of the corners of the streets, and a band of young girls capered up and down to the music, with shouts of laughter. About nine o'clock all was comparatively quiet, and soon after that hour the watchman of the city began to utter his cries; for it would be inconsistent with the genius of the place to leave the night to its natural silence. At every stroke of the hour and of each intermediate half hour, he proclaimed the time of night in a deep, melancholy tone, as if lamenting its departure. *"Las dos dadas"*; *"las dos y media dadas"*; *"las tres dadas,"* &c., &c., were repeated again and again as he paced the street, in a voice which grew less and less distinct, until it was lost in turning some distant corner. This went on till daybreak, when other sounds began to be heard, which gradually swelled into the usual tumult of the day.

We have made some pleasant acquaintances here, the wife and two daughters of a late professor in a literary institution,[1] whose kind and gracious manners make good the claim of courtesy to strangers, which is one of the boasts of the people of San Sebastian. The young ladies took us one beautiful evening to walk on the Alameda, a public ground beyond the city gates, planted with poplars, at the mouth of the Urumea, where the waves of the sea rush, with a loud roar, upon the sands. It was just about sunset, and the green between the city walls and the Alameda was covered with groups of nurses and little children, who had come out both for the sake of the air and the music of a military band, which played occasionally, while a small body of soldiery were going through their exercises. I was struck with the healthy look of these children. Some of the older ones, little bare-headed creatures, looked like dolls, with their abundant jet black hair, white skins, and eyes like beads of black glass. The troops, as twilight came on, took up their march for the city, the band playing as they went, and the nurses placing their young charges on their shoulders, hurried back with them.

We saw several ladies walking unattended in the Alameda. "Is that the custom here?" inquired one of our party. "By all means," was the answer. "Young ladies go out in the evening, unaccompanied, without scruple. We are all known here, and that protects us; we are as safe as in our parlors. Even if we were not known, we have confidence in our people. The city gates are never shut even at night, nor are our doors fastened during the day time, and it is not for fear of theft that they are locked at night. Thefts here are very rare, and nobody thinks it necessary to be on his guard against them."

I was glad to hear so good an account of the morals of the place in one very important respect, and it seemed to be confirmed by what I saw at

our hotel. The doors of our rooms had no fastening, and seemed never to have had any. On speaking of this to our host, he assured us that a lock was quite unnecessary, as nothing was ever stolen. While I am writing this letter, he has surprised me by assuring me that he never even locks his outer door at night.

Of one nuisance, from which I had found no other part of the continent wholly free, I had seen nothing here; there are no beggars. In France you will often see, at the entrance of a village, a post, bearing a large wooden tablet, with an inscription purporting that in those precincts begging is strictly forbidden, and under it a fine, ragged fellow will hold out his hand and whimper for charity. Here the same prohibition exists and is respected. "What do you do with your beggars?" I inquired. "Follow us," said our young friends, "and we will show you." We crossed the Urumea by the bridge of Santa Catalina, and passing through another alley of poplars, entered a large building, erected in 1840, on the site of a former Franciscan convent. "We put our beggars here," said one of our companions; "this is the House of Mercy for the district of San Sebastian." We entered a large court in the centre of the building, with trees and a fountain in the midst, and many of the inmates of the place sitting or moving about—the tasks of the day being finished. At the entrance was a chapel, dimly lighted, from which issued strains uttered by the children of the place, chanting a part of their evening worship. All weaned children abandoned by their parents, and all orphans, are received into this institution; all persons in the district found begging are brought hither, stripped of their rags, scoured, put into clean clothing and set to work.

As we returned, we could not help speaking of the softness of the evening. The young ladies with us, and those who were walking in the Alameda, had on only light summer dresses, with nothing on their heads save the thinnest of black veils, fastened to the hair behind, and falling down on the shoulders. "We have no extremes of heat and cold," they said; "the heat of the summer is not intense, the autumn and spring are delightful, and the winter rather rainy than frosty."

At this season we find the weather remarkably agreeable; the heats of noon are temperate, and the evenings are like the blandest summer evenings in our own climate. During the week which we have passed at San Sebastian, we have not felt the slightest autumnal harshness in the air, even at night. The leaves are falling from the trees, not because the frost has nipped them, but because they are old. "You are going to Vitoria and Burgos," said my banker, the other day. "You are going to a country where the weather is very different from what it is here, where it frequently changes from warm to cold, and where the winters are extremely severe, as they are with you in New York." The people of San Sebastian claim that their city is exempt from epidemic or local fevers, and from intermittent fevers, both of the bilious and typhus type. In summer the people

of Madrid resort to it, for the refreshment of its air and for sea-bathing; and the Plaza is a gay scene with these visitors promenading at nightfall, and afterwards. At present you see bare-headed señoras walking in the Plaza till near ten o'clock, or sitting under the arches which surround it, but they are the ladies of the city.

I went again the next morning, with one of our party, to the House of Mercy, and was shown over it by one of the Sisters of Charity of the order of San Vincente de Pablo, who have the care of it, and who are fifteen in number. She was a plump, healthy-looking person, with an agreeable smile, a full, black eye, in which lurked an arch expression, and thick lips shaded with jetty down. She carried a bunch of keys, and opened one room after another for our inspection. "Here," said she, "is one of the sleeping-rooms of the women." It was a long apartment, on the second floor, with thirty beds ranged in rows on each side; a bed for each person; clean beds, with coarse linen sheets, woollen mattresses and pillows, resting on enormous straw beds underneath; the room was clean and amply ventilated. She showed us in succession the other sleeping-rooms of the females, those of the men, and those of the children, all of them equally clean and comfortable, and in airy rooms. We descended to the ground floor. "Here," said she, "is the workshop of the men." A dozen looms were clashing in the room she showed us, and at each a man was driving the shuttle. In one corner several men were employed in mending clothes; in another sat men mending shoes; before the door a man was winding linen thread upon a reel. In other parts of the building women were employed in spinning, after the manner of this country, twirling the spindle in the fingers; others were knitting, others sewing, others by the side of a huge laver, were washing; others in a kitchen as clean as a Dutch kitchen, were busy over huge caldrons, in which soup was preparing for the inmates. All were employed, but all seemed inclined to make their labor as easy as possible. There was none of that alacrity shown in their exertions which we saw in the pauper colonies of Holland, where a system of proportional compensations is adopted.

We were taken to the school, where the children of the institution are taught. The system of instruction does not go very far, but they are taught to read, write, and compute; and we saw some respectable specimens of penmanship in the square Spanish style. In the school several young girls were employed in embroidering, and some neat samples of their skill in this art were shown us. The medicine room contained, in glass jars and gallipots, neatly labelled and arranged, drugs enough to kill twice the number of the inmates of the House of Mercy; but we were gratified to learn that not much use was made of them. One department of the institution is a Hospital, with ample wards and a large number of beds, most of which, I perceived, were unoccupied. Here the same scrupulous neatness seemed to prevail as in the other rooms, and the same care-

ful attention to ventilation. The Hospital is divided into two departments, the medical and surgical; in the surgical departments for males
there was no patient—beggars do not often break their bones—in that of
the women there were but two or three.

In passing through the various compartments of the institution, we
were taken into the bread-room, where one of the Sisters of Charity was
occupied in dividing the loaves into rations. There was a finer and more
delicate kind of bread for the patients in the Hospital, and a coarser kind,
yet light and sweet, for the healthy inmates. "You do not let your people
suffer from hunger," said I, to the sister who had charge of this room.
"No," she replied, "of hunger they never complain; their great suffering
is from thirst; they get enough to eat, they acknowledge, but they do not
get enough to drink." The history of the Almshouse of San Sebastian is,
in this respect, I suppose, like that of other almshouses, and people qualify
themselves for admission to it by the same practices.

As we took leave of our smiling and cheerful conductress, a venerable
lady presented herself, who held the place of Lady Superior among these
Sisters of Charity, and who was on a visit to the institution. She inquired
from what part of the world we came, and being told from North America,
began to speak of her acquaintances in Mexico. It was not easy to make
her comprehend the distance of New York from Mexico, so we did not
insist much on that point. As we had seen the House of Mercy in San Sebastian, she told us we must see that of Tolosa, which was, if any thing,
still more admirably managed; and if we were going to Madrid, we must
see the one at Madrid. Finally, she went and brought another distinguished
sister, whom she introduced to F.,[2] and after a short colloquy, in which
the recommendation to visit the House of Mercy at Tolosa, and the one
at Madrid, was repeated, they both embraced and kissed my companion,
and took their leave.

For myself, I wished to see a little of the environs of the city, in the
way in which they could be seen to most advantage, and I strayed off on a
pedestrian exercise to the valley of Loyola, a pretty spot on the river
Urumea. An excellent road led me to about two miles from the city, along
which Basque women with huge baskets on their heads were passing; the
younger of them having for the most part fine figures, and some of them
pleasing faces. They kept up a lively dialogue with each other as they
went, and made the valley ring with their laughter. To my greeting of
buenos dias, they replied with the still more idiomatic greeting of *agur*.[3]
The road on which I was passing at length degenerated into a bridle road,
over which, however, I could see that the rude carts of the country had
stumbled, but it still led by country houses, and fields of Indian corn and
apple orchards. Here vineyards once flourished, from the fruit of which
a poor wine called *chacoli* was made, and none of any other kind was allowed to be brought into San Sebastian till the *chacoli* was drunk out. The

repeal of this prohibition, I suppose, led to the abandonment of the grape culture, and now there are no vineyards; yet the vine has taken possession of the soil, and, on each side of the way, twines its unfruitful shoots with the blackberry bushes and hazels, and a sort of green briar, almost as prickly as that of our own country.

MANUSCRIPT: NYPL–GR (draft fragment) TEXT: *LT* II, pp. 52–64; first published in *EP* for October 26, 1857.

1. A Señora Satrustegui and her daughters, whose brother Estelle Ives had met in New York. These attentive ladies gave Bryant letters to acquaintances in Vitoria and Madrid. Bryant, "Diary, 1857–1858," October 4, 1857; 985.1, 994.8.
2. Frances Bryant.
3. "Good-bye."

984. *To* the EVENING POST

Vitoria, Province of Alava, Spain,⎞
October 8th, 1857.⎠

It was an oversight not to mention in my last that the House of Mercy at San Sebastian owed its flourishing condition to private beneficence. Many persons have given it large sums; among others, Don Antonio de Zavaleta,[1] a native of the city, who, having emigrated to Havana and become rich, bequeathed to it in 1837 one hundred and twenty thousand dollars. I asked the Sister of Mercy in the thin white hood and blue petticoat, who conducted us over the place, what was the number of its inmates. "We have in the whole," she replied, "about four hundred persons. In the almshouse there are a hundred and four men, about ninety women, mostly old, and ninety boys or more. The girls, who are not so many as the boys, and the patients in the hospitals, make up the number." There is a department of the hospital of which she said nothing, and which, of course, was not shown us, the *Sala de Maternidad*, or Hall of Maternity, a sort of Lying-in Hospital, a refuge, as it is called in a Spanish pamphlet lying before me, for *mujeres embarazadas*,[2] in which the strictest secrecy is observed as to the name of the person admitted, and the place whence she comes, these being known only to the chaplain. Her only designation is a certain number; so that the news of the morning in this department of the Hospital is that the doctor has been called to Number Three, and that Number Seven is as well as could be expected.

Do not suppose, however, that this is the extent of what the good people of San Sebastian do for the poor. They have their charitable associations here, as well as with us; and sixteen ladies are the agents by whom the contributions thus gathered are distributed among those who, in their opinion, need and deserve relief.

All the English who come to San Sebastian, visit, of course, the graves

of the British officers who fell in the siege of the place, in 1813,[3] and in the bloody civil war twenty-three years later, in which England took part. They lie almost in the shadow of the citadel, on a part of Mount Orgollo, which looks across the sea towards England, among enormous blocks of stone scattered about, as if a sudden convulsion of the earth had broken them from the mother rock. I cannot imagine a grander place of sepulture than these craggy steeps, beside the ever-murmuring ocean. We went up to the top of the citadel, which, by command of the government, is now open to citizens and strangers without distinction, and looked out upon a magnificent panorama of sea and mountain, of which the central part, to the landward, was the valley of Loyola, where it is said the founder of the Society of Jesuits was born,[4] and through which the Urumea flows, fringed with tamarisks.

The time had arrived for us to leave San Sebastian, and on the 5th of October we took leave of our most obliging host, the only fault of whose hotel was the want of a hostess, and set out for Vitoria in a carriage hired for the purpose. It was a wet morning, but of this we had warning the evening before; for a strong wind was bringing up black clouds from the west, and driving the billows of the Cantabrian ocean into the bay of Concha, with such fury that, but for the sea wall which protects the narrow isthmus leading from the city, it seemed as if they would force their way across it and make the place an island. I had been to the Alameda as the sun was about to set, and returned on account of the wind; but I met a throng of persons going out, among whom were bare-headed ladies, with their veils of black *tulle* fastened, on the back of the head, to their abundant tresses, and falling down on the shoulders; but the figure which most drew my attention was a priest, holding his hat before him on his breast. The hats of the priests in the south of France are of liberal dimensions; but here, in the genial atmosphere of Spain, their brims expand to a magnificent size. As the least breath of wind would otherwise blow them off, the wearers roll up the brim on each side, over the crown, as we roll up a map, or as the Spaniards roll up a bit of paper to make a cigar. In this way the reverend clergy of these parts contrive to carry on their heads a cylinder of felt and fur, nearly a yard long. The priest whom I met had found it impossible to keep his head covered in the fury of the wind, but, unwilling to lose his walk on the Alameda, was carrying it before him with an air of meek resolution, quite diverting. Two hours later, a thunder shower broke over the city; and as a thunder shower here does not clear the air, as with us, but is the beginning of rainy weather, the next morning dawned in rain.

I must say to those who travel in Spain, that if they wish to avail themselves of the accommodation of the diligences, in their journey to Madrid from the towns in the north of the kingdom, they should endeavor to do it before the first of October. Until that time there are local dili-

gences—that is to say, there are public coaches passing between San Sebastian and Vitoria, Vitoria and Burgos, and so on, in which you can always secure seats beforehand, and set out at a convenient hour. After the
first of October these are generally withdrawn, and you must either hire a
private carriage, or take your chance for a passage in the diligence from
Bayonne, which may arrive crowded with travellers, and perhaps in the
night. We lingered at San Sebastian late enough to miss the local diligence, and were obliged to hire a vehicle at an exorbitant price.

Our course was up a narrow, winding valley, watered by the Oria, at
that time swollen and turbid with rain, pouring down a torrent almost as
yellow as gamboge. On each side were fields of maize ready for gathering,
among which were a few green turnip patches, and here and there a fresh
grassy meadow, while higher up on the hill-sides was a rougher and less
verdant pasturage, among gorse and heath and withered ferns. Scattered
over these wastes were chestnut trees loaded with fruit, and short, stumpy
oaks, the boughs of which had been cut away for fagots, and now sprouted
with a multitude of twigs. The Spaniards do not seem to care for trees,
except when planted in a public walk near a town. I have scarcely seen
one allowed to shoot upward, and extend its boughs laterally, as nature
would have it; wherever a tree grows in the country, it is made to yield
fuel; they poll the oak and reduce it to an ugly bush; they strip the branches
from the sides of the elm, and make it look almost like a Lombardy poplar.
In this state trees rather deform than embellish a landscape.

About two miles from San Sebastian, a man belonging to the laboring
class, who was walking towards Tolosa under a blue cotton umbrella,
asked permission to stand on the hinder step of our carriage, which was
granted. He was a good specimen of the Basque race; of middle stature,
but vigorous make, and a healthy color in his cheeks. Over a white cotton
shirt he wore a knit blue one of woollen, neatly tied with tasseled cords;
on his left shoulder he carried the brown round jacket of the country,
which clings to the shoulder of the Basque peasant like his cap to his head,
whether he be sitting or standing, riding or walking, or even gesticulating.
The man spoke but little Castilian, but was very much disposed to be
communicative. He gave us the names of the places through which we
passed, and was quite inclined to talk of the abundant crops of the season.
"We have plenty of maize this year," he said, "and a large crop of beans.
The apples have failed, and we shall make scarcely any cider, but then
there are so many chestnuts!" On this subject he was almost enthusiastic,
and seemed to imagine that nearly every question we put to him had
some relation to the chestnut crop. We looked about us, and saw that he
had reason to be as eloquent on this head as his scanty vocabulary would
allow, for the chestnut groves on all the hills were heavy with fruit, which,
whiter than the leaves, spotted and bowed the branches. Millions of bushels will be gathered from these groves; a considerable part will form the

food of the peasantry, and the rest will be sold in the towns, or carried abroad.

The Oria is one of the most considerable manufacturing streams of Spain. We passed several large buildings, which our Basque friend informed us were woollen mills; others we perceived to be forges, in which the abundant ores of these mountains are smelted and wrought into bars. There is also a cotton mill here, owned by the brothers Brunet, of San Sebastian. A little beyond the village of Lasarte we passed a handsome building of this kind; and very near it stood the most showy country house I had seen in Spain. In this region scarce any thing is done in the way of laying out or embellishing grounds; the art of landscape gardening is almost unknown; but here was an example of it which fairly dazzled our eyes. The walls of the house were of brilliant white; the windows were surrounded with a bright blue border, edged with a line of crimson; and it stood amidst grounds washed by the river, elaborately laid out, and carefully tended, traversed by gravel walks, winding among fresh grass-plots, and by plantations of choice shrubs, and through orchards of fruit trees. These grounds were enclosed with hedges, as neatly trimmed as any you see in England. This was doubtless the dwelling of the proprietor. I looked on the other side of the way, and there, close to the road, was a long, shabby building, two stories in height, with many doors, at one of the upper windows of which I saw a thin, brown woman, in a dress of the color of her skin, combing her hair. Behind the building were no gardens, but, instead, the space was occupied by heaps of prickly gorse, which had been cut for the fuel of the kitchens. These were, probably, the habitations of the people who wrought in the mill.

We could not see much of Tolosa, which we reached after a journey of about four hours, on account of the rain, and we had been told at San Sebastian that there was nothing in it worth seeing; but there is an ill-natured rivalry between the two cities. We were set down at the *parador* of Don Antonio Manuel de Sistiaga, a very clean inn, where a chatty young woman waited upon us, and gave us, among other dishes, trout fried in oil, which our party found quite palatable, and a plentiful dessert of peaches, pears, and grapes. Happening to mention the mosquitoes at San Sebastian, I was assured that there were none at Tolosa, nor fleas either, except in houses occupied by careless people. From Tolosa, in the afternoon, we followed the same picturesque, green valley, passing by iron mills, the machinery of which was moved by the current of the Oria, until we reached the little village of Bensain, where a yoke of oxen was fastened before our three mules, and we were dragged up into a wild region, among mountain summits and wastes overgrown with prickly shrubs. Here, after we had dismissed our oxen, we entered Villareal, a poor village lying in a little hollow, where we met the first beggars we had seen in Spain. An old woman rang a little bell at one of our carriage windows, and a little

boy whimpered a long prayer for alms, in Basque. Not far from this place we took on another yoke of oxen, and slowly climbed a lonely mountain road, full of short turns, while the darkness of the night gathered round us, and drove the rain violently against our carriage windows. Not long after we had reached the summit a light appeared, and when we came opposite to it our coachman stopped his mules, alighted, and went into a little building, where we saw at the windows and the open door several men in a military uniform. It was a station of the *Guardia Civil*, a body of armed men by whom the highways are watched; presently our coachman reappeared with a lighted segar in his mouth and a flaming military coat on his back. He was followed by a man in the same uniform, carrying a carbine, who took his station on the hinder step of our carriage, kindled a match, took a good look at our party by its flame, lighted his segar by it, and began smoking away quite at his ease. To our questions he returned civil and copious answers. It was his office, he said, sometimes to accompany carriages on that road, but his presence with us that night was altogether accidental, inasmuch as he happened to be at the station, and wished to go to Vergara. There had been, he added, no robberies thereabouts for some time past—only one, in fact, within the year, and before that none for a long time. I inferred, from the strain of his talk, that he wished to magnify his office; but the rest of our party were confident that it was his regular duty to attend carriages, passing up and down the mountain in the hours of darkness, and protect them from robbers, and that he was with us for that special purpose.

We now rolled down the mountain, with our new guard clinging faithfully to the back step, rattled through Anzuelo, with its great houses and dark streets, and entering Vergara, stopped at the *Parador de las Postas*, as nice a place as an English inn, where we found a good-looking landlady and neat-handed domestics, and rooms as clean and bright as a Dutch parlor, with excellent beds. "Do not look for luxuries, or even for what you call comforts, in the inns on your journey to Madrid," said one of our friends at San Sebastian. "These you will not find, but you will find great cleanliness." We have been thus far agreeably disappointed in seeing the promise of cleanliness so well fulfilled.

When we left Vergara, the next morning, the fogs were hanging about the grand rocks and mountains in which the place is embosomed, and here and there touching with their skirts the Deva, which brawled through it. We went up the stream, through another green valley. At a little distance from the town a healthy-looking young woman, in a white knit basque and blue petticoat, with a gay kerchief tied round her head, and another crossed over her bosom, three strings of red beads round her neck, and a large flat basket strapped over her shoulders, suddenly made her appearance, standing on the step at the back of our carriage. We supposed she was there by some understanding with the coachman; and as

she had a bright, cheerful face, we had no objection, and immediately entered into a dialogue with her. Her name, she said, was Eusebia; she could read a little; she subsisted by sewing; she had been on a visit to Vergara, and was now returning to Vitoria, where she had a brother. As we proceeded, we frequently saw peasant boys watching flocks of long-woolled white and black sheep on the mountain sides; and in one place a man and woman were busy in pulling something from the ground. "They are gathering fern," said Eusebia. The whole region, in fact, at certain heights from the valley, was discolored with ferns, which had turned of a dull red. The girl pointed to some large stacks of the same color, standing by the houses of the peasants. "They spread them," she said, "under the feet of the cattle."

They have grand names in Spain for ugly villages—Mendragon, Archivaleta, Escoriaza, Castanares—through all which we passed, the good-natured Eusebia naming them for us. At length our coachman, who had made himself hoarse and tired the day before, with shouting at his mules and flogging them, and was now beginning to urge them forward by the same methods, perceived by the shadow of the carriage on the road-side that he had a superfluous passenger, and giving her a cruel cut or two with the long lash of his whip, compelled her to get down. We were sorry to lose her, since, though not very fluent in Castilian, she told us many things which we wished to know.

As the fog cleared away, lofty peaks of bare rock, of a whitish hue, were seen rising above the greener summits by which we were surrounded. We took on a pair of oxen, and climbed a ridge of the Cantabrian mountains. People were gathering chestnuts along the way; boys, mounted on the trees, were striking off the fruit with poles, and women below were stripping them from their husks, and carrying them away in bags poised on their heads. We passed an old, walled town, Salinas, below which, in a deep ravine, murmured the Deva; and here salt springs break out of the earth, the waters of which are intercepted on their way to the river, and evaporated to salt, by artificial heat. We saw the smoke rising from the salt-works, three or four hundred feet below us.

It cannot be said that every thing stands still in Spain; they are certainly improving their roads, and that is one important mark of progress. We were travelling on an excellent macadamized road; but on the opposite side of the deep glen of the Deva was another, leading around the curves of the mountain, with a gentler ascent. "That," said our coachman, "is the new road to Vitoria."

"Why do you not travel it?" I asked.

"Because," he replied, "it is longer. It is not so steep, nor so uneven; but it is a league further to Vitoria by that way."

It is not easy to turn the Spanish people from the old track. They like old customs, old prejudices, old roads.

Beyond Salinas we were accosted a second time by beggars. Several children trotted by the side of the carriage, asking alms, and at the summit of the mountain sat a ragged man, with a head of enormous size, attended by a boy, whom he sent forth as his messenger to the passers-by. We were now in a country of pastures—a cold, high region, from which descending gradually, we emerged into fields of tilth, and found ourselves on the plain of Vitoria. Here the Zadorra eats its way through the crumbling soil, till it issues from the plain by a pass among the mountains to the west. We drove through a dreary straight avenue of poplars, between a vast extent of fields ploughed for the next harvest, and passing by the steep streets of old Vitoria, seated on a hill, entered the new town, between goodly rows of houses built within the last five years.

At the *Parador de las Postas*, to which we had been recommended, we could find no rooms; and at the *Parador Viejo* only gloomy ones. We applied at the *Parador Nuevo*, where a dame of stately person, with the air of one who unwillingly confers a favor, showed us more cheerful ones, which we took, notwithstanding the unprepossessing manners of the hostess. We have since found her ungracious demeanor imitated by her handmaids.

I must postpone to another letter what I have to say of Vitoria.

MANUSCRIPT: Unrecovered TEXT: *LT* II, pp. 65–77; first published in *EP* for November 19, 1857.

1. This benefactor of the House of Mercy has not been further identified.
2. "Pregnant women."
3. In a nine-day battle against French forces led by Marshal Nicolas Jean de Dieu Soult (1769–1851), a British army under Arthur Wellesley, first Duke of Wellington (1769–1852), carried San Sebastian, suffering severe losses.
4. St. Ignatius of Loyola (1491–1556).

985.   *To* the EVENING POST

Burgos, Old Castile, October 13, 1857.

On arriving at Vitoria, my first care was to deliver a letter of introduction with which we had been furnished by kind friends at San Sebastian. The gentleman to whom it was addressed was not in, but the lady of the house received me with great courtesy, and said: "This house is yours, and we are entirely at your disposal. If any thing occurs to you in which we can be of the least service, command us freely. *He*," meaning her husband, "is just now walking out, but we shall call to-morrow morning on you and your family." To offer one's house is one of the indispensable forms of Spanish politeness.

After this, we all went to see the public grounds, of which Vitoria is so proud—the Florida and the Alameda. The Florida is a flower-garden, bordering the new part of the city, crowded with the most brilliant flow-

ers, in bloom—roses, dahlias, verbenas of numerous varieties, and plants of still rarer kinds. A few persons were slowly pacing the gravelled walks which led through this gay wilderness. We followed them into a little park of old trees, among which stood, here and there, a colossal statue on its pedestal, and from this a long avenue of trees conducted us to the Alameda.

The Alameda of Vitoria is a park, I should think, of some fifteen acres, irregularly planted with trees, and on account of this very irregularity, prettier than most public grounds of the kind in Spain. A few huge, tall old ashes, scattered about, tower above the elms, poplars, and locust trees by which they are surrounded. Priests with the enormous brims of their hats rolled up on each side; students at the University, preparing for the same vocation, in cocked hats of a military form, and long black cloaks; ladies, in their black silk vests or more substantial mantillas; stooping, elderly gentlemen in the sleekest of beavers, and younger men in soft hats, were walking with a leisurely pace up and down among the trees. We were disagreeably reminded that we were no longer in the soft climate of San Sebastian, for a wild, chilly wind was blowing roughly from the west. Notwithstanding this, we met, on our return through the avenue, a considerable number of bareheaded ladies walking out to the Alameda.

The gentleman to whom my letter was addressed called the next morning—a most courteous person, who renewed the offers of service made by his lady.[1] He would hardly allow us to praise Vitoria. "No sir— no," he replied, when I spoke of its cheerful aspect. "Vitoria has nothing to attract the attention of the stranger; we have no beautiful public buildings; we have no museums; we have no public amusements; our only resource of this sort is a reading-room. You have seen, you say, the Florida and the Alameda; you have then seen all that Vitoria has to show you. It is a poor kind of place; the old part is badly built, with narrow streets; the new part is pretty enough, built after the style of Madrid, but there is little of it yet." He admitted, however, that the city was increasing in population and extent; and really it had a thriving air; the houses were in good repair, the streets were kept carefully clean, and where they descended southward to the plain new buildings were going up. Trains of loaded mules were constantly passing under our windows, shaking their little bells; donkeys with burdens bigger than themselves, were driven along by skinny countrywomen, or black-eyed country maidens, and sometimes the poor animal had to bear a stout peasant, sitting sideways; diligences of enormous size, crowded with passengers and heaped with baggage, jarred the pavement as they thundered over it. At the hours when the streets were least thronged, the street-cleaners made their appearance, in their peculiar costume—a high, shaggy, black cap, and a sort of dark brown tunic, reaching below the knees, and bound round the waist with a leathern girdle.

"We can show you something beside the Florida and Alameda," said

another gentleman, to whose civilities we had been recommended; "we have at Vitoria a picture of the Crucifixion, by a famous painter; and I will take you, if you please, to see it." Under his guidance we clim[b]ed the eminence on which Old Vitoria is built, passing one or two rows of buildings recently erected, with arcades over the sidewalks, and mounting, by occasional flights of steps, till we reached the narrow, quiet streets among which stands the cathedral. Several groups of sauntering ecclesiastical students, though queerly attired themselves, seemed to find something quite as strange in our appearance, for they stared at us with great curiosity. The boys were not content at staring, but shouted to each other to look at us.

The cathedral is an old Gothic building, with nothing remarkable except a peculiarity which deforms its architecture—that is to say, a kind of bridge, thrown across the nave from each column to its opposite neighbor, about half way from the floor to the roof. A boy opened the shutters which darkened the sacristy, and showed us the picture which we had come to see—not a Crucifixion, but a Dead Christ, attributed to Ribera.[2] The head and figure are too merely handsome to suit our conceptions of the Saviour; but they are finely painted. At the feet of the body kneels Mary Magdalen, her hands pressed together with a look of despair; the sister of Lazarus stands by its side in a more subdued sorrow, while Mary, the mother, who supports it, raises her eyes in sadness, but with a look of trust, to heaven. The effect of the picture is injured by the introduction of several cherubs, hovering about, with their pretty baby faces distorted by crying.

I went again to the Alameda the second day after our arrival, a little before sunset. A violent wind was driving over the clouds from the west, and the place was deserted. Instead of the promenaders I had seen the day before, there was a flock of long-woolled sheep, black and white, which were to appear at the fair the next day. They were biting the short grass, and little girls were sweeping together and putting into baskets the leaves which the wind was tearing from the trees. I continued my walk beyond the Alameda into the open country; it was a bare, bleak expanse of stubble-fields, or grounds freshly ploughed, or those in which ploughmen were guiding their oxen and scattering seed. There was not a grove, not a thicket, not a belt of trees, to break the force of the wind that swept over it. Only a few lines of meagre poplars appeared, making three or four great roads, which led across the plain to the city.

"Where do you walk when the weather is bad?" I asked of one of my new acquaintances at Vitoria. "We take to the *arquillos*," he replied; "we walk in the arcades which surround the *Plaza*, or in those under the new buildings which you have seen on the hill. The arcades are a great resource in winter, for we cannot do without our daily walk." The winters at Vi-

toria I was told are often severe. The climate is not warm enough for vineyards or the cultivation of the olive. Sometimes the snow lies for a month on the ground, yet the sleigh is unknown here; the pools are often sheeted with ice, yet nobody skates.

I had not yet exhausted all that Vitoria had to show me, whatever my friends might say. The next morning, on looking out at my window, I saw three women, each with a long switch in her hand, and before them walked three long-legged, flat-sided pigs of the country, which by allowing them to proceed very leisurely, and pick up what they could find worth eating by the way, were driven with uncommon success. This was the commencement of a fair which was to be held that day in Vitoria. Soon, small flocks of sheep and goats, oxen in pairs, pigs in companies of four or five, began to come in from the country, and mules and donkeys loaded with all manner of country products. Booths and stalls were opened about the *Plaza* and the vacant spaces in its neighborhood, and the buying and selling began. The market-place was spread with fruits, the principal of which were huge piles of tomatoes, and mountainous heaps of sweet red pepper, the pods of which were often five or six inches in diameter. I strayed among the stalls, and found the countrywomen providing themselves with gay kerchiefs and coarse prints, and the men buying caps, waistcoats and shoes. They did not seem to me so good-looking as the country people about San Sebastian; they were a wind-dried race, as adust as the fields they tilled; skinny women and shrivelled men. Among the flat Basque caps were many of the black velvet ones of Castile, and instead of hearing only Basque spoken, as at San Sebastian, I often listened to the clearer and softer Castilian. Castilian is, in fact, the language of the city, though in the country Basque is also spoken.

In one place I saw at least five hundred yoke of oxen, for in this country of tilth the ox is the great helper of man. Many of them were noble animals, with short heads, like those on ancient medals and gems, massive necks and deep ample chests; and all were of a soft, light-brown hue. In one corner a group of donkeys stood, absolutely motionless; in another a flock of goats, white and black, some of them with thin, flat, twisted horns, were restlessly moving about. Here were gathered the long-woolled sheep, with their white and glossy or jet black fleeces; there were the merinos, which in this country are carefully guarded from extremes of temperature, and which here, as with us, wear their fine close fleeces plastered with dirt.

I must be forgiven if I took most interest in the pig market. The pigs, of which I think I never saw the equals in length of legs and thinness of figure, and many of which had bristles curling over their backs, like the hair of a spaniel, had been well fed to keep them quiet, and as long as they were allowed to lie together and sleep on the pavement, they made no disturbance. It was amusing to see the buyer and seller standing over

them, earnestly discussing their good and bad points, like horse-dealers at a fair. But as soon as the bargain was struck, the transfer was made, and the new proprietor attempted to drive off his pig, the swinish nature was roused, and an open rebellion was the consequence. I heard a frightful screeching in one part of the street, and looking that way, saw two men and one woman engaged in trying to get one of these animals into the new home assigned to him. The men had each hold of one ear, and the woman was pulling him vigorously by the tail, to induce him to go forward. Towards the close of the day, as the peasants were returning home from the fair, I saw several pigs conducted to their new abodes in this manner, and came to the conclusion that, with a man or woman at each ear and another pulling him by the tail, a pig can be driven with as much certainty as any other animal.

I asked one of my new acquaintances at Vitoria how many of these people could read and write. "Too many of them cannot," he answered, "but we have now a liberal system of public education, and with the next generation the case will be quite different. In all the country neighborhoods schools are established, and men of competent education sent out to teach in them. To these the poorest man may send his children, and in these they are taught to read, write and compute. In the considerable towns we have schools of a higher class, in which the sciences are gratuitously taught. I am told that there is a law, but I have not seen it, obliging all parents to send their children to the elementary or other schools."

I was interested to learn, what he afterwards told me, that although in the rest of the kingdom of Spain the salaries of the teachers were directly paid by the government, yet that in the Basque provinces so much of the democratic element was preserved that the separate communities provided for the compensation of their own teachers.

The time at length arrived for us to leave Vitoria, and we set out one rainy morning in a poor sort of carriage, hired specially for the purpose, for there was no room in the diligences for our party. It was drawn by three strong mules, driven by an intelligent-looking and obliging Castilian, who had enough to do in urging them forward by shouting and cracking his whip over their heads. Each of the animals had its name; the leader was *Capitana*; the right-hand mule next to the wheel was *La Platera*, and the left-hand one *Macho gallardo*. *Macho gallardo* was a large, sleek creature of his kind, who had to hear his name shouted and to feel his back pommelled twice as often as either of his companions. I have observed that in Spain the strongest and sleekest mules get the greatest number of blows; being of a robust constitution, they bear them better and mind them less. Our coachman would shout *Capitanâ! Capitanâ!* laying a particular stress on the last syllable—*La Platera! La Platera!* and next *Machô! Machô!* and then, leaning forward, would deal on the sleek, comfortable-looking *Macho gallardo* a storm of hearty blows with the stock

of his whip. *Macho* shook his long ears and sometimes slightly mended his pace, and sometimes crept on as before, just as the humor took him.

From the brown expanse of stubble and ploughed fields around Vitoria, we rode into a region of sandy hillocks, abandoned to pasturage and ragged with tufts of furze. Descending from this and following out the Zadorra through a pass among the hills, here and there made pleasant by a few trees, we reached at length the plain watered by the Ebro, an inconsiderable stream, a string of glassy pools connected by slender brawling shallows, on the banks of which the stubble-fields were interspersed with a few vineyards, heavy with their black fruit. A little beyond, we entered a wretched town called Miranda de Ebro. The moment our carriage stopped we were surrounded by a swarm of beggars, old and young, male and female, wrapped in yellow-brown rags, and with yellow-brown faces. I must do the Castilian beggar, however, the justice to say that, generally speaking, he does not whine like a French beggar. He first seeks to attract your attention, and then prefers his petition. Here, at Miranda, I was accosted with the epithet *Caballero! Caballero!* [Sir! Sir!] and once or twice I was touched on the elbow, but if I paid no attention, they went no further; the beggars of Miranda are too proud to ask alms of one who will not look at them.

At Miranda de Ebro, all baggage of travellers coming from the Basque provinces into Old Castile undergoes as strict an examination as when they cross the Spanish frontier from France. Besides opening and rummaging our trunks and travelling bags, a custom-house officer crawled into our carriage, and almost turned it inside out, looking into the boxes and pockets, peeping under the seats, and feeling all over the lining. At Miranda, miserable as the place appears, is a tolerable inn, where we got a good breakfast and some excellent pears, and after an interval of two hours, set out quite refreshed. At a little distance from our stopping place we descended into a little valley, so finely varied with gentle and graceful slopes, and overlooked by rocky mountain summits, so jagged, and toothed, and blue, that we involuntarily exclaimed: "How beautiful would all this be, if there were but a little green turf and a few trees!" Close by was the village of Ameyugo, and a little stream with a pretty name, the Oroncillo, flowed through the valley, on the brink of which grew several elms; but the peasants had stripped them of their side branches, and forced them to shoot up in slender columns of small twigs, like cypresses.

We were entertained by the sight of a man, who followed on horseback close to our carriage, as if to shelter himself from the wind, that blew a drizzling rain into his face. He wore the black velvet cap of the Castilian, with its two worsted tassels; an ample cloak made of black sheep's wool, which, having faded into a dull brown, had been refreshed by an enormous patch of the original color; knee breeches, and below them a pair of leathern gaiters, half open at the sides, to show the stockings. His com-

plexion was that of the faded part of his cloak. His feet rested in a pair of heavy stirrups, which were studded along the edge of the sole with brass nails. Once or twice he leaned forward over the pommel of his saddle, and laid himself down on his horse's mane; it was his mode of taking his *siesta*; in short he was asleep, as was evident by the passive manner in which his body swayed from side to side. At length, as we were entering a rocky pass beyond Ameyugo, he sat upright, and entered into conversation with us.

"A poor country," said he—"a poor country. They get little wheat from these rocks; but these are nothing to what you will see a little further on." He was right. A little further on we entered the pass of Pancorvo. I had not seen, in the Alps or the Pyrenees, any passage between mountain walls so wild and savage, and surrounded by rocks piled in such strange and fantastic forms; perpendicular precipices of immense height; loose masses so poised that they seemed ready to topple on our heads; twisted ribs, beetling crags, and sharp needles of rock. I thought of the lines in Shelley's translation of Faust:

> "The giant-snouted crags, ho, ho!
> How they snort and how they blow—"[3]

and almost expected these strange horned masses to move with life, and utter voices as strange as their forms. In this pass, the French boast that in the War of the Peninsula a small body of their soldiers held Wellington at bay, and compelled him to turn aside from the great highway to Biscay. There is nothing said of this in the English guide-books.

From the pass of Pancorvo our mules were flogged and shouted through smooth, bare, wintry-looking valleys, along which a railway route had been surveyed, as a channel of communication between Bayonne and Madrid; the signal posts were still standing. We alighted at Briviesca, pleasantly situated on the Oca, with a decent and spacious inn, full of guests. Some of our party were a little concerned at being told that there was neither milk, butter, nor cheese in the place; but we made a comfortable meal notwithstanding. I had heard much of Castilian gravity, but there was none of it in the inn at Briviesca; it rang with laughter nearly the whole night. I walked over part of Briviesca the next morning, before setting out, and found it a dirty place, badly paved and apparently in decay. I saw a good many brown beggars, but half the rest of the population resembled them in looks and attire. The next day we climbed a dreary height, to what our coachman told us was the highest table-land in Spain: a cold, bleak, bare region of pasturage, rough with pale, hoary furze and greener juniper bushes, and here and there a stubble-field. Descending from this, we descried at a distance the citadel of Burgos on a hill, and near it the towers of the majestic cathedral. We entered the town and obtained lodgings at the Fonda de las Postas, one of the best hotels in Spain, with a civil hostess, clean rooms, and most attentive handmaidens.

MANUSCRIPT: Unrecovered TEXT: *LT* II, pp. 78–90; first published in *EP* for November 24, 1857, where it is dated October 14.

1. Señor Leopoldo Antonio de Olalde, to whom Bryant had been given a letter in San Sebastian; see 983.1. He, in turn, introduced Bryant to Don Luiz Diaz Oyuelos, of Burgos. See 986.2; Bryant, "Diary, 1857–1858," October 7, 10, 1857.

2. José Ribera (*c*1590–*c*1652), a Spanish religious painter. The Bryants' guide to the cathedral was the son of their landlord at San Sebastián, M. LaFitte. Bryant, "Diary, 1857–1858," October 7, 1857.

3. II.49–50.

986. *To* the EVENING POST

Burgos, October 14, 1857.

The first aspect of Burgos, the ancient city of the Cid[1] and the chief city of Old Castile, is imposing. As the traveller looks at the castle on its hill, with its surrounding fortifications; the massive remains of its ancient walls; its vast cathedral, worthy, by its magnificence, to have exhausted the revenues of an empire; its public pleasure-grounds, stretching along the banks of its river, almost out of sight; the colossal effigies of its former kings, standing at the bend of the stream called the Espolon; and its stately gate of Santa Maria, where the statues of the Cid and other men of the heroic age of Spain, frown in their lofty niches, he naturally thinks of Burgos as the former seat of power and dominion. Another look at the city, consisting of a few closely-built streets around its great cathedral, produces the effect of disappointment. Yet the town is much more populous than the guide-books represent it to be; they put down its population at twelve thousand, while the recent enumeration makes it thirty-two thousand.

After we had dined and given a satisfactory answer to our civil hostess, who inquired whether we had dined well, I lost no time in delivering a letter of introduction, with which I had been kindly furnished at Vitoria. I was received with the usual forms of Spanish civility. *Esta casa es suya,* "this house is yours," said my new acquaintance, Don Luis,[2] a phrase which, I am told, must be addressed to you on such occasions, or you cannot consider yourself as a welcome visitor.

We all went next to the Alameda; but it was yet too early for the company with which it is thronged in fine weather. Straight rows of poplars, elms, and locust trees extend northward along the banks of the Arlanza, for a great distance, and between them are beds of flowers. In these long avenues it is easy for one to walk himself tired, without often passing over the same ground.

The next morning, Don Luis, the gentleman to whom I had an introduction, called with a friend of his, Don Pedro, to take us to the cathedral. I shall not weary those who may read this letter, with a formal description of the building, of which there are so many accounts and so

many engravings. No engraving, however, nor any drawing that I have seen—and I have seen several by clever English artists in water-colors—gives any idea of the magnificence and grandeur of its interior. The immense round pillars that support the dome in the centre of the building, rise to a height that fatigues the eye. Your sight follows them up, climbing from one noble statue to another, placed on pedestals that sprout from their sides as if they were a natural growth, until it reaches the broad vault where, amid crowds of statues and the graceful tracery of the galleries, the light of heaven streams in and floods the nave below. It is one of the merits of the cathedral of Burgos, that numerous and sumptuous as are the accessories, they detract nothing from the effect of its grandeur, and that the most profuse richness of detail harmonizes genially with the highest majesty of plan. The sculptures in relief, with which the walls are incrusted; the statues, the canopies, the tracery, even the tombs, seem as necessary parts of the great whole, as forests and precipices are of the mountains of Switzerland.

As I stood under the great dome and looked at its majestic supports, I was strongly reminded of the mosques at Constantinople, built in the time of the munificent Saracen dynasties. It was impossible not to recognize a decided resemblance between them and this building, so different from the cathedrals of the North. The cathedral of Burgos was evidently designed by a mind impregnated with Saracenic ideas of architecture; its towers, wrought with a lightness and delicacy which makes them look as if woven from rods of flexible stone, are of the northern Gothic; but its dome in the centre, with the enormous round pillars on which it is uplifted, is Oriental. It is wonderful how perfect is the preservation of the purely architectural parts of this cathedral. The sculptures have been, in some instances, defaced in the wars by which Spain has suffered so much; the carvings about the altar have been in some part destroyed, and inadequately restored; but time has respected the stones of the building, and from the pedestals of the columns up to their capitals, they look almost as fresh from the chisel as they must have looked four centuries ago.

We were taken, as a matter of course, to the chapel called *del Santisimo Cristo*, in which is a figure of Christ on the Cross, of the size of life, with his head bowed in the final agony. It is a clever but somewhat frightful representation of the last sufferings of the Saviour, but the devout of Burgos hold that it exceeds the ordinary perfection of art, and attribute to it the power of working miracles. In a book lying before me, I am informed that, according to the "generally received opinion," it is the work of Nicodemus.[3] "It is of leather," said Don Luis, "and so much like the living body, that the flesh yields to your touch, and when you withdraw your finger, recovers its place."

We had passed through most of the chapels, including that magnificent one of the Condestable, in which lie the bones of the founders—one

of the Velasco family and his wife—under a broad marble slab, supporting their own colossal statues, exquisitely carved in marble, with coronets on their heads, and ample robes of state, rich with lace and embroidery, flowing to their feet. As we were about leaving the cathedral by the principal entrance, Don Luis took me into the chapel of Santa Tecla, to the north of the great portal. "This," said he, "is the latest built of all the chapels, and it is easy to see that it is not of the same age with any of the others." I looked about me and felt as if I had suddenly fallen from a world of beauty into a region of utter ugliness. The chapel in all its parts is rough with endless projections and elaborate carvings, without meaning or grace, and blazes with gilding; the general effect is tawdry and ignoble. How any architect with the example of the cathedral before him, and the beautiful chapels which open from it, could have designed any thing in so wretched a style, I cannot imagine.

We dined that day at the ordinary, or *mesa redonda*, which was served at two o'clock, the fashionable hour at Burgos. With the exception of one or two, who sat at the head of the table, the men wore their hats while eating. The Spaniards consider the eating-room in a hotel as much a public place as the great square, and consequently use much the same freedom in it. I saw the guests at the table turn their heads and spit on the floor. They shovelled down the chick peas and cabbage with the blades of their knives, which they used with great dexterity. They were polite, however; not one of them would allow himself to be helped to any dish until after all the ladies; at the dessert they offered the ladies the peaches they had peeled, and they rose and bowed when the ladies left the room. On going out, we were again met by the hostess, who hoped that we had dined well; and being assured that we had, expressed her pleasure at the information.

The talk at the table was principally of the bull-fight, which was to take place that day at Burgos. I took a turn after dinner with Don Luis and Don Pedro on the new public walk, the *Paseo de la Tinta*, extending along the Arlanza for the space of a league, and found it almost deserted; only here and there a solitary stroller, and a few children with their nurses. From time to time the air was rent with the shouts of a multitude, at no great distance. "It is the clamor of the spectators of the bull-fight," said Don Pedro; "the public walks are forsaken for the *plaza de toros*. I do not know whether your sight is as good as mine; but do you see that crowd of people on the hill?" I looked in the direction to which he pointed, and beheld an eminence, nearly half a mile from the broad circular amphitheatre of rough boards erected for the bull-fight, thronged with people. "There," said Don Pedro, "is a proof of the interest which is taken in these spectacles. Those people cannot pay for admission to the amphitheatre, and therefore content themselves with what little they can see of it from that distance. All Burgos is either in the amphitheatre or on the hill."

Not quite all Burgos, however, was at the bull-fight. As we walked on, we met a few priests, and next a throng of young men, nearly a hundred in number, walking two by two, dressed in long black gowns, and black caps, the brims of which, made to turn up close around the crown, were cut into points like a coronet. They looked hard at me as they passed, seeing something, I suppose, exotic in my appearance. "They are young men designed for the church," said my Spanish friends; "the priests are rarely present at the bull-fights."

I had made an engagement to go the next morning to *Las Huelgas*, a Cistertian convent close to the city, and to the secularized Carthusian convent, about a league off. At nine o'clock a clumsy carriage, built like a small omnibus, was at the door of our hotel, drawn by five mules, gay with tags and tassels of crimson and white, and guided by two coachmen—one who sat on the box, held the reins and cracked the whip, and another, sitting beside him, whose business it was to leap down and run with the animals, turn them where it became necessary, and flog them into a gallop. We proceeded to the house of Don Luis, where we took in Don Pedro and the matron of the family, with her niece, a young married lady, who seemed to me to realize in her person the ideal of Spanish beauty—regular features, lips and chin as finely moulded as those of an antique statue, large dark eyes, redundant dark locks, a face of the most perfect oval, plump, white hands, and a stately form, rounded to a certain Junonian fulness.

As soon as we had left the paved streets and crossed the Arlanza, our second coachman—a lithe, light young fellow—began whipping the mules over the macadamized road, laying heavy thwacks on the sturdiest of them, till he had got them into a rapid gallop, himself running by their side like the wind. He then sprang upon the box, and we rattled on till a loaded wagon, drawn by ten mules, came in our way, when he was off his seat in an instant to guide the beasts and prevent a collision. The moment the pace of his mules flagged a little, he was by their side plying his whip, and once or twice the principal coachman leaped from the box to help him.

At length we turned off from the great highway, and struck out into a wretched, uneven road, like all the crossroads in Spain, even under the walls of the cities, and were jolted along for some distance beside an enclosure with high walls, over which fruit-trees were peering. "It is the orchard and garden of the convent," said one of our Spanish friends. We next drove through a lofty gateway, and entered a broad, paved court, in the middle of which stood a large building with windows secured by iron grates, and a church beside it. On three sides of the court were dwelling-houses and offices. "There," said our Spanish friends, "live the chaplains of the convent and the other persons employed in its service."

We went immediately to the room of the portress, where we held a

short dialogue with two or three slatternly-looking young servant-girls. It was too early yet to see the Lady Abbess; it was not quite ten o'clock. We had but ten minutes to wait, however, and at the end of that time we were informed that we were at liberty to go up to the convent grate. We ascended a cold, narrow staircase, to a little room, in which was an iron grate in the wall, and close to the grate were a little table and five chairs, in which the ladies of our party seated themselves. A sliding shutter behind the grate was withdrawn, and through the opening we saw a thin old lady, of a lively aspect, come almost bounding into the room on the opposite side. She was in the garb of her order—an ample white woollen robe, with very wide sleeves, and a white cap with a black peak, to the summit of which was fastened a black veil, falling over the shoulders. She kissed the elder of the Spanish ladies through the grate, with all the fervor of an old acquaintance, shook hands with the younger, bowed graciously to the rest, and began to talk in the most animated manner. "And these friends of ours," she asked, "where are they from?" "From America." "Ah, I have a nephew in America, at Cordova, in Peru, and he likes the place much; perhaps they know him." We had a little difficulty in making clear to her mind the distance between New York and Cordova, in Peru; but she went on to give the history of her nephew, his wanderings and his settlement at last in Peru. "And you are going whither?" she asked again. "To Valencia, to Alicante, to Seville, probably, and Granada, and, finally, to Rome." "Ah, to Rome! You will have much to see in Rome. But I have a nephew in Seville, and I will give you a letter of recommendation to him, and he will show you every thing you may desire to see in the place."

The interview lasted about half an hour, after which the Abbess again kissed the Spanish matron, shook hands with the eldest lady of our party, and wishing us a good journey, and commending us to the care of God, departed with as light and quick a step as she came.

Entering the church of the convent, we heard a sound of silvery voices; they proceeded from a large and lofty side-chapel, separated from the church by a massive iron grate, reaching from the floor to the ceiling, behind which we beheld the nuns moving in procession, and chanting as they walked. Several of them seemed quite young, and looked pretty in their singular attire. "Those whom you see in white hoods," said one of the ladies who accompanied us, "are novices; they wear the costume and submit to the rules of the order for a year, at the end of which they either take the veil, or, if they please, return to the world. If, at the end of the year, they find that they have a vocation to a religious life, they are received into the order, and go out of the convent no more." "These nuns," she afterwards added, "are Bernardines, and the rule is not an austere one. They are all of noble families; their convent is richly endowed; each of them has her own waiting-maid, and they live in comfort."

As we were listening to the chant of the nuns, we were accosted by a

youth in a black gown, with a white scarf over his shoulder, who pointed
to a little square window in the wall, and signified that the Lady Abbess
desired to speak with us. We went immediately to the window. "I thought
you might like to look into this chapel," said the Abbess; "it is the famous
Chapel of St. Ferdinand, who took upon himself the order of knighthood
here; and here are buried all the infantas of Spain." We could perceive
that the place was full of monuments, of which, however, we could take
but a very imperfect view. "Farewell again," said the Abbess, "I shall not
fail to send the letter for my nephew." At this time, several persons in the
priestly garb began chanting a litany near to where we stood, with deep,
mellow voices that filled the lofty walls and seemed to make them shiver.
"These nuns have good music among their other comforts," we said to
each other, but we had no time to hear more of it; so we returned to our
carriage, and were dragged by the galloping mules towards the *Cartuja*.[4]

MANUSCRIPT: Unrecovered TEXT: *LT* II, pp. 91–101; first published in *EP* for December 2, 1857.

1. Rodrigo Diaz de Vivar, El Cid Campeador (*c*1030–1099), Spanish soldier and
hero whose exploits are the subject of much later literature.
2. Don Luis Diaz Oyuelos; see 985.1.
3. The Pharisee who helped to bury Jesus. John 3:1–21; 19:39–42.
4. Carthusian monastery.

987.   *To* Charles M. Leupp

Madrid   October [26][1] 1857

Dear Leupp.

I am at length where you and I have often talked of going[2] and have
found it no great exploit to get here. If it had not been for my family for
which it was impossible for me to find places in the diligences, crowded
at this season with passengers I should [have] found travelling in Spain
by no means inconvenient—so far at least as we have gone. I have been
obliged to hire a special conveyance from San Sebastian to this place—
making stops of some length of course at Vitoria and Burgos. If I had
been by myself I should have ventured upon the route by Valladolid and
Segovia,—a considerable circuit, and the roads, they say, are not good. The
journey from Burgos to this place was tedious enough; it took four days,
but it made us acquainted with the country, and we all feel that we know
the more of Spain for it. It has given us experience of all manner of Spanish inns, from the *venta*, where they give you nothing to eat and which is
a sort of khan, to the *parador*, where they profess to give you every thing.
The young ladies with me complain of being nearly eaten up by fleas on
the road, but I can assure you, that you and I found a hundred fleas in
Palestine to one that I find in Spain. We are well repaid for all the inconveniences of the journey, and all of us acknowledge it, by what we see

in Madrid. We stopped at the Hotel called Peninsulares, the best in the city—and a tolerable one; but we have now rooms in what they call a *casa de huespedes* [boardinghouse] at No. 7 Calle de Alcalá, where we are much better accommodated and much better served.

We have met with a great deal of civility in Spain—in their way they have shown us every attention—it is not their habit to give dinners but they have accompanied us about every where and have helped us to understand as much of their country as one could see in the short time we have been here. Spain is a backward country, following the rest of Europe at some distance— Spain is like the tail of a snake a good way from the head but dragged along after it nevertheless. She is making railroads which will be done in a few years. From Madrid to Valencia one will be opened in a few months—from Madrid to [Bayonne?] in a few years, and then the barriers which have kept foreigners out will be broken down and a flood [of tourists?] be let in. . . .

MANUSCRIPT: NYPL–GR (draft).

1. The day of the month has been supplied from Bryant's "Diary, 1857–1858," of the same date.
2. See, for instance, Letter 835.

988. *To* Messrs. John Munroe & Co.

Madrid   October 27th   1857.

Gentlemen

I have this morning drawn the last thousand francs on the letter of credit furnished me by you last June. I directed the cashier of the firm to which I belong at New York to lodge with your banking house at New York on the first of August $500 and the same sum on the 1st of every month afterwards so that by this time I presume you have received notice of $1500— being deposited in this way since I left Paris. I thought that I was to return the letter of credit when it was exhausted but Messrs H. O. Shea and Co. insisted on retaining it, saying it remained with them.

What I now wish, and the purpose for which I write this, is to ask that another letter of credit may be sent me for such amount as you may think proper. —Will you also do us the favor, after sending on to Madrid with the letter of credit, such . . .

MANUSCRIPT: NYPL–GR (incomplete draft).

989. *To* the EVENING POST

Madrid, November 1st, 1857.

In our way to the *Cartuja* we soon turned aside into a road still more wretchedly uneven than the one which had led us to *Las Huelgas*. After half an hour of severe jolting it took us through a massive gateway, by

which the possessions of the convent were once entered; but the rest of the enclosure has entirely disappeared. Half a mile from this, we stopped at an imposing Gothic edifice on a hill. This was the convent, and we turned to look at the extensive view it commanded—the view of a broad, smooth vale, stretching league beyond league—of the brown color of the soil, without trees and without houses, except a village to the right, and the city of Burgos to the left. "You should see it in early summer," said Don Pedro, "when it is luxuriant with vegetation." A ragged fellow conducted us into the building, where we passed through long, beautiful, silent cloisters, from the roof of which, in places, the fresco flowers and stars were falling in small flakes, till we reached the chapel, and here a priest, who was already occupied with a French artist and his lady, took charge of us. From the chapel and the other rooms, all the fine pictures have been carried away, and we were shown in their stead what were not worth looking at—some wretched things by a monastic brother. But what most attract and repay the attention of the visitor, are the monuments of the father and mother of Isabella the Catholic,[1] and of her youthful brother, quaintly and delicately carved in alabaster, with a singular combination of grace and grotesqueness—the grace always predominating—in which twining stems, foliage and flowers, figures of quadrupeds and birds, of men and women, and, among these, warriors, patriarchs an[d] evangelists, all exquisitely and airily wrought, are clustered together in marvellous and endless complication.

One of the cells of the Carthusian monks was shown us—a little chamber, with a plank bed on which he slept, covered only with his brown cloak. Opening from it was the little garden, with its separate wall, which he tilled alone; and on another side, the little oratory, where he knelt and prayed. "Here," said Don Pedro, pointing to a little opening from the cell to the cloister, "is the window through which the friar received his meals, to be eaten in solitude." As we were about to go out, I said to Don Pedro, "Is it the custom to give a fee here?" "No"; he replied, with some quickness, "not by any means." I could not help suspecting, however, that there was something in the rules of Spanish politeness which dictated this answer, for at that moment we passed into the *Campo Santo*, or burial-ground of the convent—a spacious area enclosed by the building, spotted with little hillocks, where the monks in utter silence dug their own graves, and Don Pedro said, "You see that part of the ground has been dug up and sown with grain. The ecclesiastics who take care of the building do this to piece out a scanty livelihood, for the government only allows them a *peseta*, the fifth part of a dollar, a day." The graves had no monuments, but close to the newest of them, where the earth had still a broken appearance, stood an iron cross, with the lower end driven into the ground. As we stepped from the burial-ground into the cloisters, and the priest locked the door after us, I put a trifle into his hand, which he received with an air that showed he expected it.

That afternoon, at the special urgency of Don Pedro—for I wished to postpone the spectacle till I should arrive at Madrid—I went with one of our party to a bull fight. "This is the last day," said our Spanish friend; "to-morrow the amphitheatre will be removed, every plank of it, and we shall have no more combats for a year." We found the place, which they told us was capable of containing six thousand persons, already full of people impatiently drumming with their feet, to hint that it was high time for the sport to begin. Nine-tenths or more of them were of the laboring class, and their bright-colored costumes, particularly those of the women, gave the crowd a gay appearance. Many children of various ages were among them, and some of these, showily dressed and attended by nurses, were evidently of opulent families. We took our places in the uppermost circle, under a narrow sort of roof which sheltered us from the sun; below us was range after range of seats open to the sky, descending to the central circle, the arena, in which the combats were to take place.

An alguazil [a constable], in black, first rode round the arena, pro-claiming the regulations of the day. He was followed by a procession of the performers, in their gay dresses; the *picadores*, glittering with gold and silver lace, on horseback, with their broad-brimmed hats and long lances; the *chulos* on foot, with their red cloaks; the *banderilleros*, with their barbed shafts, wrapped in strips of white paper; the *matadores*, with their swords; and lastly, three mules, gayly caparisoned, with strings of little bells on their necks, who were to drag out the slain bulls. Loud shouts rose from the crowd, and then a door was opened, and an enormous bull, jet black, with massive chest and glaring eyes, bounded into the arena. He ran first at the *chulos*, who shook their cloaks at him, but his rage appeared soon to subside. A *picador* put his lance against the animal's forehead, but he shook it off and turned away. The *chulos* again came capering about him and trying to provoke him, but he pursued them only a few steps. Then rose the cry of, *Ah, que es manso! que es manso! codarde! codarde!** Finally, the people began to call for the dogs. *Los perros! los perros!* rose from a thousand throats. Three large dogs were brought, which, barking loudly, flew at the bull with great fury. He took them one after another on his horns, and threw them up in the air; one of them he caught in his fall, and tossed him again. The dogs tore his ears into strings, but they were soon either disabled or cowed, and only attacked him warily, while he kept them off by presenting to them first one horn and then the other. Then the dogs were withdrawn and the *chulos* tried him again, but he would not chase them far; the *picadores* poked at him with their lances, but he declined to gore their horses. The crowd shouted vigorously, "Away with him! away with him!" and at length the door by

[Bryant's note]
    * "Ah, how tame he is! how tame he is! a coward! a coward!"

which the bull had entered was set wide open, that he might make his retreat. But the bull would not go; he was not minded either to fight or quit the field. "Kill him! kill him!" exclaimed a thousand throats—and the signal was given, in obedience to which one of the *matadores*—the *primera espada* [chief bullfighter], as the Spaniards call him, just as the Italians say *prima donna*—made his appearance with a red cloak on his arm, and a long, glittering, straight sword in his right hand. He shook the cloak at the bull, who made a rush at it, while the *matador* at the same moment attempted to pierce the animal to the heart through the chine. Three times he sought to make the fatal pass; at the third he was successful, burying the blade up to the hilt. A torrent of blood flowed from the creature's mouth, he staggered and fell; a sound of little bells was heard; the three mules, harnessed abreast, came in, and dragged out the lifeless carcase.

Another bull, of smaller size, but of more savage temper, was then let into the arena. He ran fiercely at the *chulos*, chasing them into the places of shelter built for them beside the barrier, and the crowd shouted, *"Es muy bravo, ese! muy bravo!"** A *picador* touched with his lance the forehead of the animal, who instantly rushed towards him, raised with his horns the horse he rode, and laid him on the ground, ripping open his bowels. I then perceived, with a sort of horror, that the horse had been blindfolded, in order that he might not get out of the way of the bull. The *chulos* came up with their red cloaks, and diverted the attention of the bull from his victim, while the *picador*, who had fallen under his horse, was assisted to rise. Four other horses were brought forth blindfolded in this manner, and their lives put between the *picador* and the fury of the bull, and each was killed in its turn, amidst the shouts and applauses of the crowd.

One of the *banderilleros* now came forward, provoked the bull to rush at him, by shaking his cloak before his eyes, and leaping aside, planted one of his barbed shafts with its paper streamers, in each of the animal's shoulders. Others followed his example, till the bleeding shoulders of the bull were garnished with five or six *banderillas* on each side. The creature, however, was evidently becoming tired, and the signal was given to finish him; a *matador* came forward and planted a sword in his heart, but he made a violent effort to keep his legs, and even while falling, seemed disposed to rush at the *chulos*.

I had now seen enough, and left the place amidst the thunders of applause which the creature's fall drew from the crowd. I heard that afterwards three more bulls and six horses were killed, and that an addition had been made to the usual entertainments of the *plaza*, with which the

[Bryant's note]
  * He is very fierce, that fellow, very fierce!

people were not well pleased. A class of combatants appeared, called *pega-dores* ["paper-hangers"], who literally took the bull by the horns, allowing him to toss them in the air, and one of them was much hurt by his fall. "It is a Portuguese innovation," said my friend Don Pedro, rather innocently, as it seemed to me, "and it is a horrible sight for us Spaniards. We do not like to see a man tossed like a dog."[2]

I hoped in this letter to give some account of my journey from Burgos to Madrid, which was not uninteresting, though neither exactly pleasant nor comfortable; but my letter is already too long. I am pained to hear such bad news from the United States—such accounts of embarrassments and failures, of sudden poverty falling on the opulent, and thousands left destitute of employment, and perhaps of bread.[3] This is one of the epidemic visitations against which, I fear, no human prudence can provide, so far, at least, as to prevent their recurrence at longer or shorter intervals, any more than it can prevent the scarlet fever or the cholera. A money market always in perfect health and soundness would imply infallible wisdom in those who conduct its operations. I hope to hear news of a better state of things before I write again.

MANUSCRIPT: Unrecovered TEXT: *LT* II, pp. 102–108; first published in *EP* for December 2, 1857.

1. Isabella I (1451–1504), queen of Castile and León.
2. The Bryants' guide at Las Huelgas and the Cartuja was Don Pedro de Carranza, a friend of Don Luis Diaz Oyuelos. Since both Frances and Julia Bryant were indisposed on the afternoon of October 12, Bryant and Estelle Ives went with Don Pedro to the bullfight. After this "spectacle," which Bryant had wished to postpone until he reached Madrid, and in which his sympathies seem to have lain more with the blindfolded horses than with the slaughtered bulls, Bryant recorded, "We went to the cathedral to compose ourselves." "Diary, 1857–1858," October 12, 1857.
3. The sudden financial panic of 1857 was severe in the industrial North and the Middle West; it had relatively little effect on the agricultural South. Nevins, *Ordeal*, III, 176–197, *passim*.

990. *To* the EVENING POST

Madrid, November 5, 1857.

While at Burgos, I was taken to the Audiencia, as the principal court is called, in which justice is administered. In one room were three judges in black caps and lace ruffles about the wrist, but with no other distinguishing costume, and before them a clerk and another officer of the court were sitting, while an advocate, perched in a kind of tribune by the wall, was reading a manuscript argument in a monotonous tone. There were no auditors except those of our party, and this I did not wonder at, for I cannot imagine any thing less likely to awaken curiosity or fix attention. In another hall were three judges, and a person—the *escribano*, I believe, or

clerk—was hurrying through a law paper, which he read with a slovenly articulation, that showed it to be some matter of form. Of course, there was nothing here to detain us long.

The next morning, the 14th of October, at an unreasonably early hour—if the truth must be told, it was two o'clock, for we had been assured that we could not otherwise arrive at Aranda that night, and there was no endurable stopping-place till we got to Aranda—we left our quarters at the *Fonda de las Postas* with some regret. The attentive and cheerful handmaidens who commonly waited upon us, Catalina and Juanita, had got a little breakfast ready for us. I asked Catalina, a stout, round-faced girl, with a pair of what are sometimes called butter-teeth, and who spoke Spanish with some peculiarities of pronunciation, whether she was a Castilian. "No," she replied, "I am from the north of Spain. The girls in this house are all Basques; the mistress, though she is a Castilian, will have no other. The Castilian girls are dirty." I supposed there was some truth in what she said; my subsequent experience confirmed it.

It was a starlight morning when we left Burgos; the mules ceased to trot when we had proceeded a little beyond the city gate, and our two drivers got down from the box and walked beside them in silence. We had the same equipage which had previously conveyed us to *Las Huelgas*, but both coachmen and mules seemed to have lost all their spirit, and were transformed to the merest plodders. After we had proceeded thus for about an hour, the moon rose, and showed us the same broad extent of bare plains which we had seen about Burgos. I had fallen into a doze, when our two *cocheros*, having again mounted the box, awoke me by singing. They sang together a long Castilian ballad, of which I could make but little; it was chanted to a monotonous, melancholy air, with harsh and somewhat nasal voices, reminding me somewhat of the sort of singing I had heard from the Arabs in Egypt and Palestine. As we were slowly climbing a hill, two men came from the road-side, and looked sharply and scrutinizingly into the window on the back of our carriage, bringing their swarthy faces close to the glass. The coachmen sang for about an hour, and then the principal one began to crack his whip, which the beasts who drew us well understood to mean nothing, and, accordingly paid no attention to it.

When the sun rose, we found ourselves in the valley of Lerma, where the soil looks fertile, and where the Arlanza winds among soft slopes, which would be beautiful if the country had any verdure. All that it has, belongs to a few vineyards on sunny declivities. The Duke of Lerma makes a conspicuous figure in history,[1] and the name suggests ideas of magnificence, so that when we drew near to the wretched, decayed old town which bears it, we were not a little disappointed. It had a ruined look, and was dreary, though the pleasantest golden sunshine lay upon it. Its church, formerly a collegiate church, has not been damaged by time, only a thun-

derbolt fell upon its tower a few months since and forced its three bells out of their places. Beyond Lerma, the country became again the brown, dismal region which we had seen further back, without trees, grass, springs or streams, the stubble-fields and tracts fresh from the plough only diversified by wastes, ragged with furze, the pale foliage of which could not be called green.

We stopped at a village called Quintanilla, at an inn, consisting of stables as the ground floor, and dwelling rooms above, like most Spanish inns; it was built of bricks dried in the sun, and its upper floor was a foot higher on one side than on the other. Near at hand was the place from which the building materials were taken, a deep pit in the ground. A tall, grim, slatternly woman, with a prodigiously sharp voice, gave us a sort of breakfast over-seasoned with garlic, but made tolerable by good bread and plenty of grapes. A dessert in Spain is as much a part of the breakfast as of the dinner, and plates of fruit always conclude the early meal.

When we resumed our journey, we needed not to be told that we were in a great high road between city and city, for it actually swarmed with huge, high-loaded wagons, drawn each by ten or a dozen mules in pairs, heavy-wheeled carts of a like description, trains of loaded mules with their sturdy guides, and peasant men and women, trudging on foot or jogging along on donkeys. Among these were a comfortably dressed man and woman, carrying a child between them, and keeping their donkeys on a gentle trot, whom we passed regularly every day of our journey, and who must have got to Madrid nearly as soon as we. At Gumiel, which we passed in the afternoon, it was a delight to the eyes to see half the country overspread with vineyards, though sallow with the season, and though the plants were low, without stalk or prop, and almost trailed on the ground. Here we fell in with large parties of laboring people, of both sexes, travelling on foot, some astonishingly ragged and dirty, and others in clothes tolerably whole and clean. It was remarkable how the raggedest and dirtiest herded together. They had all a merry look, and were evidently amused at something exotic in our appearance, for they pointed us out to each other, laughing and chatting in what was doubtless very good Castilian. "These are the people that gather the grapes; it is the time of the vintage," said one of our coachmen. The vintage, in fact, is a joyous time in all countries, and I no longer wondered that these ragged people wore such bright faces.

A little before nightfall we reached Aranda, and stopping at a wretched inn, found the dirty streets of that wretched place full of vintagers. I walked out among these blinking Castilians, in their knee-breeches and velvet caps, some of them wrapped in great brown cloaks, lounging and gossiping about. The old pavement of the town had been trodden deep into the earth, and was covered with dust; a large, long building of much pretension, with turrets, probably once a palace, stood

unroofed, and moss was gathering on the broken eaves. Beyond it murmured the Duero, flowing under a stately bridge, with a little plantation of locust trees on the opposite bank; but just before I reached the Duero, I was surrounded by an atmosphere which decided me to proceed no further. On my left, close to the road, was a little enclosure of about half an acre, surrounded by a low, broken stone-wall, which, to judge by its appearance, was a place of universal resort for the people of Aranda. If they could quote Shakespeare, it seemed to me that there was not one of them who might not say with reference to that spot,

"Oh, my offence is rank; it smells to heaven."[2]

I returned to our inn, and was almost as much astonished at what I saw in the street which passed under its back windows. The servant women of the house had their faces literally plastered with dirt. They managed, however, to put clean sheets on our beds, and to give us a quarter of roast lamb and some bread for supper. We inquired of our coachman whether there was not a better inn in the place, but he replied that they were all alike, which we afterwards discovered was false, for the diligence companies have established a parador in the place, where travellers are very passably lodged.

We had an uncomfortable time that night with the fleas, which, I suppose, swarmed up from the stables below; and we were not sorry to leave our beds and our dirty inn with early light. We got down stairs by stepping over the bodies of about a dozen muleteers, who, wrapped in their blankets, lay snoring on the floor of an antechamber, and proceeded on our way through a country of vineyards, to which the laborers were going at an early hour. From some of them the fruit had already been gathered, and goats were let in, attended by a keeper, to browse on the foliage. In others, they were collecting the clusters into enormous baskets, which were to be carried to the wine-press on the backs of mules and asses; the animals stood by, waiting to be loaded. We stopped at one large vineyard, asked for some grapes, which were given us with full hands, and the people seemed surprised when we offered to pay for them.

At Boceguillas, where we made our midday halt, we found a decent inn, and were waited on by two or three comely and cleanly-looking young women, with whom our two drivers seemed on very friendly terms. A few hours' drive afterwards brought us to what we were glad to see, a grove of scattered evergreen oaks, rising, with their dark green dense tops, out of the ash-colored waste. Fatigued as our eyes were with looking on barren earth and brown rocks, I can hardly describe the delight with which we gazed on those noble trees, close to some of which we passed. This grove, which covers several hundred acres, had doubtless been spared for the sake of its fruit; for it is this oak that produces the *bellota*, the sweet acorn,

gathered and eaten raw by the people; in Madrid it is sold at almost every corner of the streets.

We had a range of mountains before us, and were rising at every step into a chillier atmosphere, when our vehicle stopped for the night in the neighborhood of a little village, at a large, dismal building, called *Venta de Juanilla*, or Jenny's Tavern. A well-dressed man, with a boy by his side, was standing at the entrance, and as we alighted, hurried into the house, and began to call for rooms. Jenny was not at home, but there were two half-wild servants in the house, one of whom was remarkable for her breadth of chest, resounding voice, and bright, round eyes; and these girls, after some rummaging for keys, got rooms, both for the gentleman's party and our own. We could get nothing to eat, however, till Jenny herself, a short, dark-browed woman, came home from the village and opened her pantry. Our apartment consisted of a sort of sitting-room, with a bare tile floor, and was scantily lighted by four panes of glass, set in the wooden shutters. Into this sitting-room opened two dark rooms, called alcoves, in each of which were two beds. This arrangement of sitting and sleeping-rooms is very common in Spain, south of the Basque provinces.

The party who had preceded us in getting rooms, consisted of a gentleman and his wife, who were fashionably attired, with two children and two maidservants. They were travelling in a cart, covered with an awning of white calico, and drawn by two mules. They had resorted to this method of travelling, because it was not possible, at this time of the year, to obtain seats for so many in the diligence from Bayonne, and probably, also, because it was less expensive than such a conveyance as our own. These carts are a sort of moving couch, I was told; the bottom is covered with mattress upon mattress, and the passengers travel quite luxuriantly, though, of course, very slowly.

The covered cart, with its passengers, set out before us the next morning; and at five we came from our gloomy rooms, and continued the ascent of the mountain range which divides Old from New Castile. Smooth russet-colored pastures sloped on each side to the road, where trickled a little brook, which, in the course of thousands of years, had worn that narrow pass. At the summit, about sunrise, in a keen, cold atmosphere, we came to the village of Somosierra, seated among rocks and mountain hollows, looking almost like a little nook in the mountains of Switzerland, with rivulets from the higher summits running through the fields, and keeping them green. Hard by the village was a forest of oaks, and there were thickets growing luxuriantly by the road side.

We ran down the mountain, passing our friends in the covered cart, and leaving all this verdure behind us. Our mid-day rest we took at Buitrago, a small, decayed place, with an old fortress, once doubtless a place of strength, and two churches, each of which bore on its tower a large stork's

nest. Our stopping-place was a *venta* of the primitive sort. A young girl showed us a room, and when we asked for something to eat, she answered, "We can give you nothing here, but if you want any bread or fruit, there is a *plaza* beyond the nearest church, where you can buy it." We had no alternative but to follow her suggestion; we got some bread, grapes and pomegranates, and made a frugal repast in our carriage; the two coachmen in the mean time had found their way to the kitchen fire, and had managed to get up for themselves a banquet of stewed meat and Windsor beans.

While the mules were resting and feeding, we walked about the place. A little without the town I met with a winding row of granite pillars, a quarter of a mile in length or more, some of which had been thrown down and lay on the ground, and of some only the pedestals remained. At length I discovered that they had formerly borne stone crosses—one or two supported them yet—and that the series ended at the portal of the principal church of Buitrago. Here, then, in former years, the good Catholics must have paid their devotions, stopping and praying at the foot of each cross, in turn; until, at length, in some of the wars of Spain, sacrilegious hands threw them down, to be raised no more.

Crossing this row of pillars was a road never marked with the trace of wheels, which led towards the Lozoya, flowing in a rocky glen. We were surprised at the beauty of the scene which lay before us, and sat down on rocks black with moss to gaze at it. In front of us ran the little river, in which, further up the current, women were washing linen and spreading it on the bank. Immediately opposite to where we sat, rose a hill-side, from which stood forth here and there narrow perpendicular precipices, as tall as the churches of the town, in a natural park of large evergreen oaks, and willows beginning to turn yellow with the season. A little to the right the river spread into a still, glassy pool, and then ran off noisily, over sparkling shallows, through a gorge of rocks. Beside us was a hill pasture, on which was a flock of black and white sheep, with their keeper, which seemed literally to hang on the steep where they fed. As we were walking about, one of the party called our attention to a powerful, aromatic odor. Looking about us, we discovered that almost every plant on which we were treading had the odor of wild thyme or lavender. They were of the dullest possible green, with rigid stems, scantily nourished by that arid soil, but they breathed up a fragrance at every step.

On the way back to our carriage we had a less pleasant sight; we saw what becomes at last of the donkeys of Buitrago. Just out of the streets of the close-built little town one of these poor animals lay kicking his last, and not far from it, in a little hollow, were many skeletons of others, some of them bleached white by the weather, and others clean picked, but still red. Two dogs were among them; the foul feeders slunk away when they saw us. We crossed the road to Madrid; and going into the fields on the

side opposite to the town, overlooked the country around it. All was silent; all seemed at first lifeless, and without human habitations; but at length we descried, afar off, two or three men ploughing with oxen, a woman on a donkey, passing along one of the bridle roads—the cross-roads are all of that description—a little village almost out of sight, and near by, in the bottom of the broad valley, what had been once a convent, and the possessor, probably, of much of the land we overlooked. The monastic orders, with the exception of a few sisterhoods of nuns, no longer exist in Spain; the gowns and cowls, brown, white and gray, have wholly disappeared; and the country in which the friars were, less than a century since, the most numerous, is now the last place in which to look for them.

Resuming our journey, we passed through a valley of meagre pasturage, where a brook came glistening down the rocky mountains, and crossed our road. Here had halted a little caravan of loaded wagons and carts, from which the mules had been taken to rest and be fed; and here a group of strapping muleteers lay basking in the sun. As we went up the road, by which we were to pass out of the valley, I saw some of the strangest looking rocks I ever beheld—rocks without angles or sharp corners, yet lying close upon each other by the road side, and looking like enormous puddings or sacks of meal in a heap. To these succeeded pyramids of rock, overlooking a narrow pass, cracked and split in every direction, so that the whole mountain might be pried into fragments by a lever. It seemed as if a mighty blow had been dealt upon the huge mass of stone, shivering it into splinters down to its very base, and yet not displacing a single part. Our road led us from the pass into a plain, where we stopped for the night at a place called Cabanillas. A freckled, light-haired landlady, of extraordinary activity, who performed the parts of chambermaid, waiter and directress of the kitchen, gave us a friendly welcome, a passable dinner, with a plentiful dessert of fruit, and tolerable beds, in two deep alcoves of a large chamber, the floor of which was covered with matting. The genteel family who were travelling in a cart arrived half an hour or so after us, and had the second choice of rooms. It amazed us, after what we had seen of the deliberate manner in which things are done in Spain, to see our landlady flying from room to room, and waiting very satisfactorily on all her guests at once.

The next day was Saturday, and as it was important that I should arrive seasonably in Madrid, in order to see my banker, we took a start, which our principal coachman, on whose advice we acted, called *tempranito*, a little early or so—that is to say, at two o'clock. One of our mules was out of order, and had been left behind; another was that morning hired in his place, to drag us up a long ascent, and a man was taken on the box to lead the animal back. It was wonderful what a difference the hiring of this mule made in the speed with which we travelled. Our *cocheras* seemed determined to get the worth of their money out of him in the

shortest possible time. The whip was plied unmercifully; a storm of thwacks fell not only on the hired beast but upon his fellows in the harness, and we went up the hill in a whirlwind. After an hour or more of flogging and galloping, we came to where the road began to descend, the hired mule was taken out, and we proceeded at the same plodding pace as the day before. In due time the stars faded, the sky brightened, and we found ourselves again in a bare champaign country, destitute of trees and grass, with mountains in sight as bare as the plain.

Our morning halt was at Alcobendas, at a large inn of the primitive sort, chilly, dreary and dirty, with ample accommodations for mules and scanty accommodations for travellers. While the mules were resting we walked about the town, which, compared with some places seen on our journey, had an air of neatness. The dust had been swept from the sides of the streets into the middle, and looking into the open doors as we passed, we saw that the stone floors of the shops, the entrances of dwellings and the courts had undergone a like process. It was encouraging to meet with this proof that the toleration of dirt was not universal. Before one of the doors swung Mambrino's helmet—a barber's basin of glittering brass, with the owner's own name and the addition *"profesor de cirurjia y coma-dron"*—"professor of surgery and midwife." "These men," said a Spanish gentleman of whom I afterwards asked an explanation, "are licensed to bleed, and therefore assume the title of professors of surgery. In the villages, if you wish to be in good company, you must cultivate the acquaintance of the barber and the curate."

From Alcobendas, a weary road, without any habitations in sight, led us to the poor-looking town of Fuencarreal; and beyond Fuencarreal an expanse equally dreary and deserted lay before us. Yet the road was planted on each side with rows of young trees, among which were conspicuous two American species—the locust and the three-thorned acacia; and here and there, by the road side, were nurseries, from which these and the poplar were supplied to the highways. Roads apparently never mended, and meant only for horsemen and beasts of burden, winded away in various directions from the great macadamized thoroughfare on which we were travelling. At length Madrid, with its spires and towers, appeared, lying in what seemed a little hollow of the ash-colored landscape. Through an avenue of very young trees, we reached a stately gate, where a sleek, well-dressed custom-house officer asked us if we had brought with us any thing subject to duty, and being answered that we had not, said that he would not order our baggage to be taken down, but would send a clerk to our hotel to inspect it.

We were then allowed to enter Madrid, and were struck with its lively, cheerful aspect, and its thronged streets. We applied for lodgings at the *Casa de Cordero*, to which we had been recommended. The hostess, who is commonly called *La Biscayina*, offered us two sitting-rooms with

alcoves, inconveniently small for our party, and up three lofty flights of stairs, but showily furnished, for thirty-two dollars a day, including board at the common table. From this place we drove to the *Calle de Alcalá*, where, in the *Fonda Peninsulares*, kept in a building which was once a convent, and which even now had not a single woman in it except those who were guests, we obtained rooms at a somewhat more reasonable rate. The hotels of Madrid have the reputation, which I believe they deserve, of being the dearest in Europe, and the worst to be found in any of the large capitals. As soon as our baggage was brought up to our rooms, a respectable looking man from the custom-house at the city gates made his appearance, and after eyeing first our party, and then our trunks, declined the task of inspection, and wishing us a good morning, left us to settle ourselves in our new abode.

MANUSCRIPT: NYPL–GR (draft) TEXT: *LT* II, pp. 109–123; first published in *EP* for December 29, 1857.

1. Francisco Gómez de Sandoval y Rojas, Duke of Lerma (1553–1625), statesman and cardinal, who effectively controlled the Spanish government as premier from the accession of Philip III in 1598 until 1618, and who greatly enlarged his personal wealth during that period.
2. *Hamlet*, III.iii.36.

991. *To* Caroline M. S. Kirkland[1]

Madrid   November 5th   1857.

My dear Mrs. Kirkland.

I want very much to get a letter from you, and know of no better method than to plague you with one of my own. We are now where my wife and I some years since used often to talk of coming but where of late years we had almost given up the idea of coming: in Spain—a curious old place, with many picturesque and interesting peculiarities, and many others which make travelling inconvenient and disagreeable for people who are delicate in health and easily disgusted. This capital of the kingdom is rather a showy place, with streets of a cheerful aspect and full of all manner of sights and noises; with noble promenades and a Museum of pictures of which I am not sure that it may truly be said that it is the best in Europe—since it is perhaps as rich as any other in the works of the Italian and Flemish schools, and has besides what they have not a very complete collection of the productions of the Spanish school. We are comfortably established—they say the word comfort is not applicable to Madrid, but I must differ from them in this instance—in lodgings where we have the sun nearly all the day and from which we overlook the sauntering multitude which continually throngs the Puerto del Sol. The Queen generally does us the honor to drive once a day under our windows, attended by a guard of cavalry with drawn swords—Toledo blades, I am told.[2]

We have experienced much kindness in the way that people show kindness here. It is not the habit of the country to ask people to dinner; but we have been taken about to see every thing we desire to see, and have had abundant opportunity for practice in the Spanish language, as in Spain scarce any body can speak any thing else.

We are at last in old Spain the oldest country I believe in Europe. All the rest have suffered renovation and repair—all the rest have been changed some what, but Spain I think remains more as Spain was than almost any other country—with the exception that she has lost her ancient splendor. . . .

MANUSCRIPT: NYPL–GR (incomplete draft).

1. See 517.2.
2. Sword blades crafted in Toledo, Spain, have long been esteemed for their strength and elasticity.

992. *To* John Bigelow

Madrid   November 14th   1857.

My dear sir.

I thank you for the letter I had from you some time since giving me an account of the state of things in America[1]—that is to say, of the money market—for that is the great concern of the day, which takes precedence, even of politics. Even in these remote regions where the failure of the New York merchants and the breaking of the New York banks and the fall of our railroad shares has scarce any effect on individual interests, a great deal of curiosity is manifested as to the progress of the reaction, and the state of the American money market at the latest dates, is as regularly chronicled as that of the rebellion in India.[2]

Your letter intimated that it would perhaps be well for me to be in the neighbourhood of Paris about this time, in order to avoid the inconveniences which might result from a collapse of English and French credit. It has not seemed to me that any step of the sort was necessary at present. The commercial disasters of America doubtless are felt severely in their effects in Europe, but the Bank of England is able to stand pretty violent shocks, and as to the Credit Mobilier,[3] though it has got to explode at some time or other, the crash may be postponed for two or three years yet. Those rich old countries do not feel the reaction of speculation so soon as we. In a deep sea it takes a longer time for a storm to stir the waters to the bottom than in a shallow one.

We have had a comfortable time in Madrid though we had—at least the ladies had rather a hard time in getting here. The history of our journey is contained in the letters for the E. P. which I send with this. Our residence here has already extended to four weeks, and in a day or two we think of setting out for the south of Spain, going by railway to Albacete

and thence to the sea shore. I think we shall try for a part of the journey the method of travelling in a covered cart.

Since we arrived here a new ministry has been appointed with Martinez de la Rosa, the poet, orator and politician, who has almost reached the age of Nestor, at its head.[4] The present administration guided by Narvaez and Nocedal[5] was shipwrecked in an attempt to destroy the liberty of the press. Martinez de la Rosa is a constitutional *Moderado*, or liberal, conservative, who professes to respect the freedom of the press, though he holds in a good degree to the policy of repression, and thinks the *Progresistas* a set of premature and injudicious reformers. Since he has been in power his ministry has been the object of constant attacks from the liberal and the ultra liberal journals. The discussions of the press have certainly been conducted with the utmost freedom so far as the composition of the ministry, its acts hitherto, and its future policy are concerned. They are able too and often so sensible rational and enlightened, that I have been both surprized and delighted—though there was perhaps no occasion for surprize, for good sense is the same in all countries.

I write this letter principally with a view to answer what you say concerning Judge Kent. I do not see any objection to the arrangement of which you speak—indeed, it may prove to be a wise and judicious one.[6] It is important to give the paper a character of permanence in order to prevent its pecuniary value from being the sport of accident, if for no other reason. If the number of its supports be increased it may lose some of these without danger of being much diminished in value. Not that I think the Evening Post to stand in any present need of reinforcement. The opinion of Judge Kent respecting it is as wise and just a one as he ever gave in court; I can find fault with it in but two respects—its orthography which is often slovenly, and the occasional admission of bad poetry. I should like to know, however, what American newspaper is faultless in these respects. With regard to good sense, justice, impartiality, the bold defence of the weak against the strong, and the exposure of incompetence and rascality in public office I do not know of any paper like it.

My wife desires her best regards to you and Mrs. Bigelow, and bids me say that she has followed your advice and Mr. Henderson's in coming to Madrid. I am not sure, however, that she is any the better for it. She has been much inconvenienced with indigestion ever since she has been here. The climate of Madrid is very peculiar and disagrees with many constitutions. Remember me also very kindly to Mrs. Bigelow and the gentlemen of the office. Julia also desires her kind remembrances to you and Mrs. Bigelow. I am, dear sir,

very truly yours
W   C   Bryant.

P. S. I have been somewhat straitened for money in consequence of the smallness of the sum deposited to my credit with J. Munroe & Co. in

New York. In ordinary times it would not have affected me, but the house at Paris is not willing to issue letters of credit, except when funds are deposited with it to the extent of the credit allowed. It was for this cause that I desired Mr. Henderson in my last, to put a thousand dollars on the 1st of next month with Munroe & Co.—W. C. B.

MANUSCRIPT: NYPL–GR PUBLISHED (in part): Life, II, 101–102.

1. Letter unrecovered.
2. The Indian Mutiny, or Sepoy Rebellion, of 1857–1858, a brief but bloody revolt against British rule in India.
3. A trading bank organized in France under Napoleon III which had encouraged speculation by its excessive profits, and which had lately suffered embezzlement of its funds.
4. Francisco Martínez de la Rosa (1787–1862), a dramatic poet.
5. Ramón María Narváez (1800–1868), who was often Spanish premier after 1844; Cándido Nocedal (1821–1885), a writer, orator, and politician who was several times associated with Narváez ministries. Bryant had met Nocedal on November 4 at Horatio Perry's home. "Diary, 1857–1858"; 993.1.
6. At some time in 1857 Judge William Kent of New York (see 540.10) offered to buy into the EP and to share its editorship, calling it the "best American daily," but his proposal was discouraged by Isaac Henderson, the EP's business partner. Nevins, Evening Post, p. 340.

993.   *To* the EVENING POST

Madrid, November 15, 1857.

I ought not to quit Madrid without saying something of the great capital of the Spanish monarchy, the COURT, as they call the city; and yet, I have seen too little to speak of it as I could wish. The outside of Madrid, however, I have seen, and that is as much as the majority of travellers at the present day see of any thing. Yet there are many native Spaniards who tell you that seeing Madrid is not seeing Spain. "Madrid," said a very intelligent person of this class to me, "is not a Spanish city; it is French—it is inhabited by *afrancesados*, people who take pains to acquire French tastes, and who follow French fashions and modes of living. Those who form the court speak French, and when they use the language of the country, disfigure it with Gallicisms. People here read French books and fill their minds with French ideas; our authors of novels give us poor imitations of Eugene Sue; our writers for the stage translate French dramas. From France our absolutists import their theories of despotism, and our liberals the follies of socialism. If you want to see Spain, you must seek it in the provinces, where the national character is not yet lost; you will find Spain in Andalusia, in Estremadura, in the Asturias, in Galicia, in Biscay, in Aragon; but do not look for it in Madrid."

Yet it is not fair to deny to Madrid certain characteristic peculiarities, even when considered in this point of view. If it be French, it is so after a

manner of its own, and the prevailing Gallicism is modified by the national temperament, by old institutions and traditions, and by the climate.

One of the first places we were taken to see on our arrival in Madrid was the Prado. Here, beyond the pavements and yet within the gates of the capital, is a spacious pleasure-ground, formed into long alleys, by rows of trees, extending north and south, almost out of sight. In the midst, between the colossal figures of white marble which form the fountain of Cybele on the north, to those of the fountain of Neptune in the other direction, is an area of ten or twelve acres, beaten as hard and smooth as a threshing-floor, by the feet of those who daily frequent it. Into this, two noble streets, the finest in Madrid, widening as they approach it, the *Calle de Alcalá* and the *Calle de Atocha*, pour every afternoon in fine weather, at this season, a dense throng of the well-dressed people of the capital, to walk up and down, till the twilight warns them home. They move with a leisurely pace from the lions of Cybele to the sea-monsters of Neptune, and then turning, measure the ground over again and again, till the proper number of hours is consumed. The men are unexceptionably dressed, with nicely brushed hats, glittering boots and fresh gloves; the favorite color of their kids is yellow; the ladies are mostly in black, with the black veil of the country resting on their shoulders; they wear the broadest possible hoops, and skirts that trail in the dust, and they move with a certain easy dignity which is thought to be peculiar to the nation. On these occasions, a dress of a light color is a singularity, and a bonnet attracts observation. Close to the walk is the promenade for carriages, which pass slowly over the ground, up one side and down the other, till those who sit in them are tired. Here are to be seen the showy liveries of the grandees and opulent hidalgos of Spain, and of the foreign ambassadors. It seemed to me that the place was thronged on the day that I first saw it, but this the Spanish gentleman who conducted us thither absolutely denied. "There is nobody here," said he, "nobody at all. The weather is chilly and the sky threatening; you should come in fine weather." The threat of the sky was fulfilled before we could get home, and we reached the door of our hotel in a torrent of rain.

The public walk is one of the social institutions of the Spanish towns; it is a universal polite assembly, to which you come without the formality of an invitation, and from which nobody is excluded; all are welcome under the same hospitable roof, the sky. Here acquaintances are almost sure to meet; here new acquaintances are formed; here the events of the day are discussed—its news, politics and scandal; here the latest fashions are exhibited; here flirtations are carried on, and matches, I suppose, made. The Spaniards everywhere pass a great deal of their time in the streets, and seem to have no idea of coming together to eat and drink. When you have a letter of introduction to a Spaniard, he does not invite you to dinner; but when he tells you that his house is yours, he means to

give you free access to it at all proper hours. I can testify that the Spaniards are hospitable in the sense of giving you their society, and making your stay in their country pleasant, though it is not their habit to feast you. They place you on the common footing of Spanish society, except that, regarding you as a stranger, they study your convenience the more.

Here at Madrid they live upon very unceremonious terms with each other, dropping in at each other's houses in the evening, and calling each other by their christian names, without the prefix of Don or Doña. They get perhaps, if any thing, a cup of tea or chocolate, and a *bi[z]cocho*. I was several times at the house of a literary lady of Madrid,[1] and saw there some of the most eminent men of Spain, statesmen, jurists, ecclesiastics, authors, leaders of the liberal party and chiefs of the absolutists, who came and went, with almost as little ceremony as if they met on the Prado. The *tertúlia* [assembly] is something more than this; there is more dress, illumination, numbers; but the refreshments are almost as frugally dispensed. The stranger in Spain does not find himself excluded from native society, as he does in Italy, but is at once introduced to it, on the same footing with the natives.

I find one objection, however, to the social arrangements of Madrid: that they make the evenings frightfully long. People begin to call on each other after nine o'clock, and when the theatres close, between eleven and twelve, the number of calls increases, and these visitors remain till some time among the short hours beyond midnight. The example of turning day into night is set by the Court. The Queen does not dine till ten o'clock in the evening, and cannot sleep till three in the morning. When I first came to Madrid, I used almost every day, a little after sunset, to hear the clattering of horses' feet on the pavement, and the cry of *la reina, la reina!* and looking out of my window, saw three showy carriages pass, preceded by a small body of cavalry with drawn swords, and followed by another. It was the Queen, taking her early drive. This was the beginning of the day with her, and she was taking the morning air at six o'clock in the afternoon on her way to church. As the days grew shorter, the carriages passed after the lamps were lighted.

Not far from the Prado, and just without the city walls, is the amphitheatre for bull-fights, the favorite amusement of the Spanish people. Here, from May to November, they are held every Monday afternoon, and sometimes on Sundays. One fine Sunday afternoon, just as twilight was setting in, I heard a loud clang of military music, and the tramp of many feet, and looking out of my window on the *Calle de Alcalá*, saw a large body of soldiery coming along the middle of the street, and behind and on each side of them a vast crowd, gentry and laborers together, amounting to thousands. They were just returning from the last bull-fight of the season, which had been postponed from one week to another, on account of the rainy weather. It had been thronged, as usual, with spectators. I inquired

why there were no bull-fights in the winter. "The bulls are less enterprising," was the answer, "and disappoint the people." One of those who are
in the habit of frequenting these spectacles, said to me: "These animals
are, in fact, wild beasts; they are in a savage state when brought from the
extensive pastures in the south of Spain, where they have scarcely seen the
face of man, and have never learned to be afraid of him or of any thing
else. The cold tames them, and makes them inactive." It is wonderful what
delight even people who seem of soft and gentle natures take in this horrid
sport.

The winter amusement of the people of Madrid is the stage. There
are nine theatres in this capital: one of them, the *Teatro del Principe*, in
which the plays of Calderon and Lope de Vega were performed when the
Spanish drama was in its glory, and another, the *Teatro Real*, one of the
finest in all Europe, set apart for the Italian opera. The present condition
of the stage is not made a matter of pride by the Spanish critics. The plays
represented are generally taken at second-hand from the French, though,
it is true, freely altered. One theatre, the *Zarzuela*, performs only Spanish
vaudevilles, which also, for the most part, are of French derivation. A considerable part of the scenic entertainments of Madrid consists in the national dances—the dances of Andalucia, Valencia, Galicia, and other provinces, each performed in the costume of the province from which it is
derived. Yet there is no want of talent here among the comic actors. The
best of them, at least the most famous, are to be seen at the theatre called
El Circo, and of these, the person most talked of now is a lady, Theodora
Madrid,[2] of whom it is said that, eminent as she is already, she is making
every day some progress in her art. Romea,[3] of the other sex, who acquired
a high reputation long ago, preserves it still. There are other performers,
by whom these are ably supported, and who need only to be seen to convince one that humor is a special ingredient in the intellectual character
of the Spanish people. There is no appearance of elaborateness or effort
in their comic acting; nor do they seek to produce effect by excessive exaggeration. It is not claimed, I believe, that Spain has now any eminent
tragedians.

But what shall the idler of Madrid do with his mornings? Seven
streets, if I have counted them rightly, converge at the *Puerta del Sol*,
which tradition says was once the eastern gate of the city, but is now a
large open square in the midst of Madrid. Here, from my window, I see
at every hour of the day a crowd of loungers, who stand and talk with each
other in couples or in groups. Sometimes my eye rests on one who is standing for a long time by himself; perhaps he is waiting for an acquaintance;
perhaps this is his way of passing time, and he is satisfied with simply being
in a crowd, till the hour arrives in which he is to go elsewhere. It is one
characteristic of the people of Madrid that they do not generally seem
overburdened with affairs. Where time is so cheap, where people are so

little occupied with business of their own, it is the most natural thing in the world that they should inquire into that of other people; and this may account for a part of the scandal which is current in Madrid respecting people of note of both sexes, and much of which, I suppose, cannot be true.

While the men gossip at the *Puerta del Sol*, the women see each other in the churches. I am afraid that religion in Spain is beginning to be considered as principally an affair of the women. Just now, however, there is something like a revival of religion in Madrid. The other day, as we were walking on the *Calle de Atocha*, we saw numbers of women, dressed in black, the invariable costume when they pay their devotions, going into a large church: it was, I think, the church of San Isidro. We were about to enter also, but I was stopped, while the ladies of my party were admitted by a man who told me that this was a special occasion, on which men were not allowed to be present. It was then near four o'clock in the afternoon; the windows of the church, as I afterwards learned, were darkened, and it was full of female worshippers, kneeling with their faces turned towards an illuminated figure of Christ. That afternoon the Archbishop of Cuba, who is on a visit to Spain, was to preach. A series of discourses delivered by him to the men, which I am told were attended by crowded audiences, had closed a few days before, and he was now in the midst of his sermons to the women. A lady who attended these daily, said to me: "He preaches with great plainness and simplicity, and his words take hold of the heart. It is not by any of the tricks of oratory that he produces an effect; he awakens emotions of contrition by earnest addresses to the conscience. He is bringing the community, a part of it at least, a sense of its errors and its duties, and in this way is doing much good. The Queen has lately appointed him her confessor, though he would gladly have declined the office."

The task of confessing the Queen, I am afraid, the good man will find a little troublesome. She is very devout, as her daily visits to the churches testify, and the rumor goes that she is very dissolute. It is easier to preach twice a day, and occasionally two hours at a time, as the Archbishop of Cuba is doing, than to manage a royal penitent of this sort.

Since Spain has the electric telegraph, and is beginning to build railways, it would be strange if she had no public lectures. She possesses one public lecturer of great eminence. The other evening I was at the house of an acquaintance in Madrid, when a gentleman, eminent as an advocate and as a writer for the journals, came in from attending an evening lecture of Galiano.[4] Galiano is a politician of that school, in Spain, who desire to keep things as they are, if, in fact, they would not rather put them back to where they were at the end of the last century. The gentleman of whom I speak was expressing himself in the most enthusiastic terms of Galiano's elocution—"You should hear what he says," said the lady of the house turning to me; "he is praising a political adversary." She then inquired of her

friend, what was the subject of the discourse. "It was the social and political condition of England." "And how did he speak?" "*Divinamente! divinamente!* the audience were carried away with the charm of his oratory. Seventy years old is Galiano, seventy years or more, and yet he has lost nothing of the beauty of his voice, or of his power over the attention and feelings of his hearers. Such melodious and magnificent tones and cadences, such glorious periods, such skill in lifting up an audience and letting it down, belong to no other man than Galiano." "And how," I ventured to ask, "would his discourse read if written down?" "You could not read it at all," was the answer. "The style has neither grace nor life; it is neither Spanish nor any thing else; the thoughts are utterly trite and commonplace; it would tire you to death. And yet, into this dead mass Galiano breathes a living soul, by his magical elocution." I have had no opportunity of judging for myself whether the severity of this criticism is deserved.

The great collection of works of art, which goes by the name of the Royal Museum of Painting and Sculpture, and is contained in a large building, rising above the trees of the Prado, is one of the first things which attract the attention of a stranger. You will not, of course, expect me to describe a collection which contains two thousand paintings, hundreds of them standing in the highest rank of merit, and which comprises pictures of every school that existed when the art was in its greatest perfection. At the very first sight of it, I could hardly help assenting to the judgment of those who call it the finest gallery of paintings in the world. The multitude of pictures by the greatest masters the world has produced, amazed me at first, and then bewildered me. I was intoxicated by the spectacle, as men sometimes are by sudden good fortune; I wanted to enjoy all this wealth of art at once, and roamed from hall to hall, throwing my eyes on one great masterpiece after another, without the power of fixing my attention on any. It was not till after two or three visits, that I could soberly and steadily address myself to the contemplation of the nobler works in the collection.

It is the boast of the Museum at Madrid, that not only are all the great schools of art largely represented on its walls, but it possesses a most ample collection of the works of the Spanish masters, who, in their day, maintained an honorable rivalry with their brethren of Italy, and whose full merit cannot be known to those who have never visited Spain. The place is made glorious with the works of the gentle and genial Murillo,[5] whose best productions, spiritual without being highly intellectual, and therefore not reaching the highest dignity, like those of Raphael,[6] have yet a beauty of coloring which Raphael never attained. There are sixty-four paintings by Velasquez,[7] fifty-eight by Ribera,[8] eighteen by Juanes,[9] fourteen by Zubarran,[10] and eighty by Alonzo Cano.[11] I was astonished, after this, to find the walls of one long room almost covered with the works

of Rubens,[12] sixty-two in number, some of them in his noblest style, and others in his more vulgar and sprawling manner. In another quarter, I was lost among the Titians, for Titian,[13] dwelt and painted year after year at the Court of Spain. Paul Veronese[14] is here in a magnificence almost equal to that in which he appears at Venice. Here, too, are some very fine Guidos[15] among the sixteen paintings which bear his name. There are ten pictures by Raphael, in his different styles, and among them is the one called *El pasmo de Sicilia*, which is deemed the pride of the Museum. It represents the Saviour sinking under the weight of his Cross, while near him, several women, agitated with pity, are starting forward involuntarily to his relief. The painter has chosen the moment at which Christ uttered the words: "Daughters of Jerusalem, weep not for me," &c.[16] The action and expression of the picture are marvellously fine, but the coloring is most extraordinary; a hot, red glare lies on the figures, like the light from a furnace; the picture must have been repaired by some injudicious hand. Vandyck[17] has twenty-two pictures in the Museum, some of them very noble ones, and of Teniers[18] there were more than I had patience to count, large and small; some of them were his attempts in the heroic style, and ludicrous enough. Several of the finest landscapes of Claude Loraine[19] are in this Museum.

A small part of one of the halls is occupied with Spanish pictures of the present day, which seem as if placed there on purpose to heighten, by the effect of contrast, the spectator's admiration for the works of the past ages. They look like bad French pictures, painted in the time of David,[20] though among them are two or three respectable portraits. I wonder how, with such examples before them as the Museum contains, any artist could suffer himself to paint in this manner. Of landscapes by Spanish painters, I do not recollect one in all the Museum, though the landscape parts of some of Murillo's pictures, seem to me to have all the grace and freedom of his figures. There is a Spanish landscape painter, however, Villamil,[21] whose works I have heard commended; but an American gentleman told me the other day, that they were not such as he would care to bring home with him. There is no wonder that there should be so little landscape painting, where there is so little country life, as in Spain.

I have not yet said all that I have to say of Madrid, but the letter is already so long, that I shall reserve the remainder for another.

MANUSCRIPT: Unrecovered TEXT: *LT* II, pp. 124–136; first published in *EP* for January 2, 1858.

1. This was the lyric poet and novelist Carolina Coronado (1823–1911), wife of Horatio J. Perry, former secretary of the American legation in Madrid. Bryant formed a lasting friendship with his charming hostess, who gave him a volume of her verses, some of which he later rendered into English, and her autographed carte de visite (see illustration). In 1869 his translation of her prose romance, *Jarilla*, was published in

seven weekly installments in the immensely popular *New York Ledger*. See Stanley T. Williams, *The Spanish Background of American Literature* (New Haven: Yale University Press, 1955), II, 134–137; *Poems* (1876), pp. 339–340, 497–500.

2. Teodora Herbella Lamadrid (1821–1896), long a leading lady on the Madrid stage, visited the United States in 1870.

3. Julián Romea Yanguas (1813–1868). On October 24 the Bryant party went with Ambassador and Mrs. Dodge (994.10; Letter 995) to see a play by Tirso de Molina (1584?–1648), *Marta la Piadosa* ("Pious Martha"), with Lamadrid as Marta and Romea as her lover. Bryant, "Diary, 1857–1858."

4. Antonio Alcalá Galiano (1789–1865).

5. Bartolomé Estéban Murillo (1617?–1682).

6. Raffaello Sanzio (1483–1520).

7. Diego Rodríguez de Silva y Velázquez (1599–1660).

8. José Ribera (*c*1590–1652), nicknamed "Lo Spagnoletto."

9. Vicente Juan Macys (*c*1523–1579), known as Juan de Juanes.

10. Francisco de Zurbarán (1598–1664).

11. Alonso Cano (1601–1667).

12. Peter Paul Rubens (1577–1640).

13. Tiziano Vecellio (*c*1490–1576), known as Titian.

14. Paolo Veronese (1528–1588).

15. Guido Reni (1575–1642).

16. Luke 23:28.

17. Anthony Van Dyck (1599–1641).

18. David Teniers (1582–1649).

19. See 755.2.

20. Jacques-Louis David (1748–1825).

21. Possibly Havana-born Bernardo Villamil Marrachi, whose dates are obscure.

994. *To* the EVENING POST

Madrid, November 17, 1857.

My last letter concluded with a word or two on the present state of the fine arts in Spain. On painting and sculpture there waits a handmaid art, engraving, which invariably flourishes where they flourish; in Spain it has scarcely an existence. The glorious works in the Museum are engraved by Frenchmen. In passing along the streets, I have sometimes been stopped by the sight of an engraving of a Murillo or a Velasquez, exposed in the windows, and read under it, "published by Goupil, in Paris and New York." Yet Spain has, at this moment, an eminent engraver, Martinez,[1] whose engraving of one of Murillo's most beautiful things, "The Dream," I saw in the house of Mr. Calderon de la Barca, late ambassador from Spain to the United States.[2] By him I was kindly taken to the studio of the artist, a modest, laborious young man, who in almost any other country would have a career of improvement, fame, and fortune open before him. He was engaged in engraving Murillo's counterpart to "The Dream," which may be called "The Fulfillment," and had almost finished his task; but when it should be completed, he would lack money to go to Paris and get it printed, and in Madrid the means of taking good impressions of steel and copper plates are wholly wanting. The Queen of Spain

had seen and admired his engraving of "The Dream," and had commanded him to engrave "The Fulfillment;" the artist obeyed, but the Queen had forgotten both the artist and the task she set him. On the wall of his studio hung a proof impression of the portrait of a good-humored looking little girl. "It is the portrait of the Queen in her childhood," said the artist, "and was engraved at her express desire." That, I thought, might be re-membered; but even that the Queen had forgotten.

There are some very fine private galleries of paintings in Madrid, to none of which have I asked admittance; for I have not had time to see even the Museum as I could wish. Among these the most remarkable is, perhaps, that of the elder Medraza, a painter,[3] who in the course of a long life has got together, I am told, a princely gallery of paintings, the estrays of art, single works of great merit once owned by decayed families and others, which by some accident had dropped out of large collections. I have heard its value estimated at a quarter of a million of dollars, and am told that it contains many works of the very highest merit. The veteran artist now wishes to dispose of it, with a view of providing for his children, but he declines all offers for any of the pictures separately. If there be any institution in America—as I suppose, in fact, there is not—which desires to possess a collection of paintings rivalling the National Gallery of Great Britain, the Vernon pictures included, here is an opportunity.

Yet, if old arts have passed away, old usages remain—picturesque usages of the times when Spagnoletto and Alonzo Cano held the brush in their living hands. In our country when we make a Doctor of Laws or of Divinity, the ceremony is very simple—a few Latin words are mumbled, and a parchment scroll is handed, or sent by mail, to the candidate, and the thing is done; but in Spain the occasion is not allowed to pass so light-ly. I was taken the other day, by a Spanish friend, to the University, to see the degree of Doctor of Philosophy conferred. The ceremony took place in a large, lofty hall, hung with crimson, on the entablatures of which were portraits of the eminent authors and men of science whom Spain has produced. At the further end of the hall was a raised platform, on which were seated the officers of the University, at a sort of desk, and in front of them, on benches on each side, the doctors of the different sciences, in their peculiar costume. All wore ample black gowns, but they were distinguished from each other by their caps and the broad capes on their shoulders, both of which were of lustrous silks. The capes and caps of the doctors of theology were white, those of the doctors of philosophy blue, the men of the law flamed in red, the men of medicine glistened in yellow, the doctors of pharmacy glowed in purple. On each side of the presiding officer stood a macer, in black gown and cap, bearing his massive club of office, and on the front edge of the platform, looking down upon the audience, stood two janitors, dressed in the same manner, but with black plumes nodding in their caps. After a strain of music, a young man,

sitting on a front bench on the right side of the platform, and dressed in the costume of a doctor of philosophy, turned his face to the presiding officer, and began to speak. "It is Emilio Castelar," said my Spanish friend; "he is one of the professors of philosophy, *gran democrata, y muy elocuente* —he is not more than twenty-four years old, and yet he is a great advocate."[4] I observed the young man more narrowly; he had a round youthful face, jet black mustaches, and a bald forehead; he gesticulated with Spanish vivacity, in yellow kid gloves. I was not near enough to hear very well what he said, but his discourse, delivered in earnest, impressive tones, seemed to take a strong hold of the audience, for they leaned forward with deep attention, and at the pauses I could hear the murmur of "*Muy bien! muy bien dicho!*" ["Very good! very well said!"]

When he had concluded, a strong built man, who had been sitting on the same seat, arrayed in a black gown with a blue silk cape, but without a cap, arose amidst a flourish of music, and was conducted by the steward, who was dressed like the janitors, except that he wore white plumes in his cap, to a sort of rostrum projecting from the wall, into which he ascended and read a printed discourse prepared for the occasion. This was the candidate for the degree to be conferred. When his discourse was finished, he was led up to the officers of the University, before whom he knelt, and placing his right hand on the leaves of a large, open folio, took the oath of his doctorate. A jewel was then put into his hands, and the steward and janitors brought from another room his doctor's cap, with a sword and a pair of gauntlets, reposing on a blue silk cushion, which were presented to him as emblems of the duty now devolving upon him as the sworn soldier of the truth. Amidst a burst of triumphant music, the presiding officer then threw his arms around his new associate; the other officers embraced him in their turn; he was then conducted through the rows of seats on the platform, to be hugged successively by all the doctors, red, white, blue, yellow, and purple. At the close of these embracings, the steward suddenly struck the floor smartly with the end of his massive truncheon, the music ceased, a few words were uttered by the presiding officer, and the session was dissolved. It seemed to me that in the interval which had passed since I entered that hall, I had been favored with a glimpse of the middle ages.

This was shortly before the feast of All Saints, in which the people of Madrid repair to the sepulchres of their kindred and friends, to deck them with flowers. The day before, all the autumnal roses are cropped, the dahlias, marigolds and china-asters broken from their stems, the beds of verbena and heliotrope rifled, and massive wreaths of the dry flowers of *gnaphalium*, or everlasting, made up, with little inscriptions expressive of affection and sorrow, formed by the same flower dyed black. On the morning of the first of November, a rainy morning, cabs and carriages, the tops of which were gay with baskets of flowers, were passing each other

in the street, on their way to the cemeteries. In the afternoon, the clouds opening to let down a gleam of sunshine, I went out to two of these burial grounds, lying just without the walls, to the north of Madrid. They are large enclosures, laid out in formal walks, planted with shrubs and flowers, and surrounded with a wall from fifteen to eighteen feet high, and as thick as the wall of a fort, with a broad portico in front, extending its entire length. This wall is the place of sepulture; it is pierced with five rows of cells or niches, one above the other, into which the coffins are shoved end-wise, and the openings are then closed with tablets, inscribed with epitaphs. All along the portico, before these repositories of the dead, rows of large waxen tapers were burning, and the tablets were wreathed with every flower of the season. Servants were employed to watch the tapers, who trimmed them occasionally, and as they flared in the wind, gathered the wax that dropped from them, frugally made it into balls, and laid it by. People were sauntering from tomb to tomb, and a bell from a little chapel in the wall was giving out a hard, sharp, monotonous toll. A few persons passed into the chapel, and paid their devotions.

The affectionate remembrance of the dead is beautiful in any shape which it takes. And yet I could not help saying to myself, as I looked at all this: What a different sight will be here, when Time, as at length he must, shall cause this sepulchral wall to crumble in pieces! What rows of grinning skeletons will then be turned out to the air! The sleep of the dead in the bosom of earth is safer from such ghastly profanation.

Near these cemeteries I visited, in company with a Spanish friend, the reservoir which is to receive the waters of the Lozoya, the brawling stream at which, as I have related in a previous letter, we saw the women rinsing their clothes near Boceguillas. The Lozoya is to be brought into the city by an aqueduct about twelve Spanish leagues in length, or forty miles, at an expense of four or five millions of dollars. "They will do the work well," said an American gentleman to whom I was speaking on this subject, "for the Spaniards are good masons, and build for many years." Huge iron pipes lay scattered about, in which the hitherto free stream of the Lozoya is to be imprisoned. We climbed a few feet to the top of the reservoir, and then descended into it. We found it to consist of two spacious and lofty chambers, separated from each other by a thick wall; the floor is of water-lime, and the long rows of massive brick pillars that support the roof are plastered with water-lime also. The work is carried on steadily, and in about two years' time, I am told, for they do not hurry these things in Spain, the Lozoya will run in veins through the streets of Madrid. In several of the principal streets they are now engaged in making passages for it. The pavements are not taken up as is done with us; but a shaft is sunk at some convenient point, and from this the engineers and laborers work like moles under ground, mining the streets lengthwise in the two opposite directions. When the work is completed, Madrid will

have an aqueduct rivalling that of our Croton, though I doubt whether the Lozoya will bring in half the water.

As we traversed these great subterranean chambers, the echoes of which rang to the sound of our steps, I had no longer a doubt for what purpose the similar constructions which I had seen in the East were designed—such for example as the Chamber of the Thousand Pillars—I think that is the name—at Constantinople, the spacious vaults under the tower of Ramleh in Palestine, and others beneath ruined castles and mosques in the Holy Land. They were, I doubt not, cisterns, in which the water falling from the clouds in those thirsty regions, was collected for seasons of drought. The vaults under the mosque of Omar, at Jerusalem, were probably constructed as reservoirs of water.

In speaking of the public entertainments of Madrid, I ought, perhaps, to have included what I have no doubt will, in due time, take the place of the bull-fights—that is to say, the newspapers. I have not been able to buy a newspaper in the streets since I came here, yet the taste for newspaper reading is rapidly increasing; the time is at hand when they will be deemed as much a necessary of life as the matches now sold at every corner for the loungers to light their cigars. A few years since, there were but four or five of them in Madrid, and now there are twenty-four. I have looked them over with much interest; they discuss political questions with ability and decorum; some of the most eminent men in the country write for them. Escosura,[5] now a political exile, used, I am told, while a minister, to write, at stated periods, his newspaper article, and take his *onza*, or fee of sixteen dollars. It appears to me also that these discussions just now are managed with perfect freedom. In fact, the fall of the late ministry is generally attributed to the law of the press, the *ley de imprenta*, as it is called, for which, although it was never regularly enacted, Narvaez and Nocedal had the address to procure from the Cortes an ordinance giving it the force of a law until their next meeting, when it was to be discussed and finally enacted or rejected. This ordinance imposed upon the press in Spain the odious shackles it wears in France, and was intended as an engine of the most perfect despotism. The discontent occasioned by it was so great, and manifested itself so strongly, that the Queen, who does not like trouble, and who dreaded a revolution, got rid of her ministers in some haste; and the bold and once popular Narvaez, and the active, able, and, as his enemies say, the utterly unprincipled Nocedal, have fallen, probably never to rise again. The *ley de imprenta* will always be remembered to their shame.

I hear that there are very few of the daily newspapers of Madrid the expenses of which are fully paid out of their income. It follows that they are supported in part by the contributions of the different parties for whom they speak. Meantime, they keep up the controversy respecting measures and principles with as much spirit and perseverance as the journals of our

own country, without the vulgarity which is sometimes so offensive in our party contests. In some of the Spanish journals questions of political economy are very ably argued; the *Discusion*, for example, maintains the cause of free trade, and exposes the errors of the protectionists with skill and effect.[6]

The new Ministry, appointed since I came to Madrid, of which Martinez de la Rosa, an old constitutional conservative, always consistent, is one of the principal members, and in which Mon,[7] a politician of liberal ideas in regard to commerce, holds the place of Minister of Finance, will, it is thought, be favorable to freedom of trade, and do something to relax the rigor of the system under which the useful arts in Spain languish, and smuggling flourishes. The law of the press will probably be rejected under this administration. The appointments which it has made of Governors of the different provinces have already given great offence to the absolutists. The new ministry have released many persons arrested and thrown into prison, by the order of Narvaez and his colleagues, for no other reason than that they were men whom the absolutists disliked and dreaded.

If newsboys are to be found anywhere in a city you would expect to meet them at the railway stations. Madrid has one station—the commencement of a railway intended to connect the capital with the Mediterranean, and already extending a hundred and sixty miles towards the coast; but at that place nobody ever cries the newspapers, though the trains leave it several times in the day. I was shown over the place a few days since by the gentlemanly superintendent;[8] it was a scene of more activity than I had witnessed since I came to Spain. The station extends over a square of nearly forty acres; hundreds of workmen were engaged in levelling it, and hundreds of others in constructing its workshops and other buildings, while close at hand a private company was putting up a large iron foundry. The trains run to Almanza, a Murcian town, from which one branch will proceed to the port of Alicante, and another to that of Valencia. The branch to Alicante—from twelve to fourteen Spanish leagues in length—is all but finished, and will be opened in the course of the winter; that to Valencia will require more time, on account of intervening rocky hills.

When the entire track shall be completed to Alicante, Madrid will have, for the first time, an easy, quick and cheap communication with a seaport. The little town of Alicante, now the seat of a petty commerce, will start into new life and growth. I suppose that envy of the prospects of Alicante will hasten the completion of the branch to the city of Valencia, and that when the effect upon the prosperity of these two places becomes visible, an emulation will be awakened which will cause railways to be made from Madrid to other cities and other marts of the sea. There is a company already engaged in the project of a railway from Madrid to Bayonne, but its progress is very sluggish. One of the clerks employed in the office of the engineer at Vitoria, told me that if it should be finished in

ten years it was all that could be reasonably expected. A railway from Madrid to Lisbon is also one of the projects of the day.

Whether these projects ever go into effect or not, the opening of a passage by steam to the sea coast will bring the whole eastern and southern coast of Spain into immediate communication with Madrid. All that is produced in those rich districts, all that is woven or wrought in the looms and workshops of Catalonia and Valencia; the fruits of the gardens of Murcia and Andalucia; and the harvests of all their fields, which are now conveyed to the capital by slow, laborious and expensive journeys, on the backs of mules or in carts, or in the rude country wagons called *galeras*, will be brought up from the provinces in a few hours and at little cost. Not only will Madrid be thus brought near to all the ports of the Mediterranean, but by means of the railways proceeding from the French ports, she will become the neighbor of all the northern capitals of Europe. The current of foreign travel which sweeps over the continent, and is only turned away from Spain by the obstacles of bad roads and insufficient and uncertain means of conveyance, will rush in at the opening made for it. From Marseilles, a brief voyage in a steamer to Alicante or Valencia, and eight hours afterwards on the rails, will take one to the seat of the Spanish monarchy.

What effect this will have on the material interests of Madrid, it is easy to see; what agency it may have in hastening changes of another kind, now going on in Spain, is fair matter of conjecture. The world is always in a state of change; but at the present time causes are at work as actively in Spain as elsewhere, which thrust change upon the heels of change more suddenly than ever before. Here is a sea-beach which the tide is rising to overwhelm, and Spain is only a bank lying a little higher than the rest, but equally sure to be submerged.

It is impossible, in the first place, that the monastic institutions, which had flourished for so many centuries in Spain, and struck their roots so wide and deep, and overshadowed so much of its territory, should be wrenched from its soil without great consequences, affecting the character and condition of its people, which even now have but just begun to make themselves felt. The temporary restoration of these orders under Ferdinand the Seventh,[9] was attended with circumstances which engendered bitter resentments, and their present suppression is doubtless final and perpetual. It is impossible, in the second place, that a system of universal education should be adopted in a country without introducing new ideas. The ordinance which obliges parents to send their children to the public schools, is not, I believe, much regarded; but, in the mean time, the number of readers is rapidly multiplying. Again, it is impossible that the liberty of printing should be allowed in any moderate degree, without exploding many old notions and opinions, and adopting others in their place. It is remarkable that, even while the odious *ley de imprenta* has been in force,

it is a law of which even those who framed it have never dared to take the full advantage; and there is every reason to believe that, to a certain extent, the liberty of the press will continue to be enjoyed in Spain. Finally, it is impossible that a free intercourse should exist between nations, as is certain to be the case between Spain and the rest of the world to a much greater degree than ever before, without their borrowing something from each other in ideas and habits. The people of different countries are becoming less and less unlike each other every day, under influences which we cannot disarm of their power if we would.

The administration of public affairs in Spain will probably vacillate from conservative to liberal and from liberal to conservative; the *Moderados* will be in power to-day and the *Progresistas* to-morrow; but these are mere petty agitations of the surface; and underlying them all, and far more powerful than they, and ever steadily at work, are the great causes of change which I have already enumerated. For good or for evil, the operation of these causes must go on. To a hopeful temperament, however, there is nothing discouraging in this. All change, we know, is not for the better; but if Spain should lose some of her old virtues, let us hope that she will acquire some new ones in their place; if her people should learn some new vices, let us hope that they will get rid of some old ones. There will still remain, I suppose, certain distinctive elements of character, in that mingling and proportion of intellectual faculties and moral dispositions which the various families of mankind receive from nature, and which cause them to differ from each other as remarkably as individuals.

I am now on the point of leaving Madrid, and I shall leave it with a certain sadness, as a place in which I have found much to entertain and interest me, and in which I have been treated with much kindness both by Spaniards and my own countrymen. Of the people of the country I ought to carry away a most favorable impression, if such an impression could be produced by unwearied endeavors, with apparently no motive but simple benevolence, to make our stay agreeable. The American minister, Mr. Dodge,[10] is very attentive to the convenience of his countrymen, and a great favorite with such of them as come to Madrid. He is on excellent terms also with the people of the country, and has done, what I think few of his predecessors have taken the trouble to do—acquired their language. He has sent his resignation to Mr. Buchanan, that there may be no hesitation in giving the embassy to any other person; but should the resignation be accepted, it is not likely that the post will be so well filled as it now is.

MANUSCRIPT (*partial*): HCL TEXT: *LT* II, pp. 137–151; first published in *EP* for January 13, 1858.

1. Domingo Martínez Aparici (1822–1898), who had studied in Paris in 1848, and won medals at Madrid in 1856 and 1858, became one of Spain's most distinguished engravers.

2. Bryant had been acquainted in New York with Ángel Calderón de la Barca (1790–1861), whose wife, Frances Erskine Inglis Calderón de la Barca (1804–1882), had published *Life in Mexico During a Two Years Residence in That Country* (Boston and London, 1843), a lively and perceptive travel book, with a preface by William Hinkling Prescott. *Life*, II, 102; Stanley T. Williams, *The Spanish Background of American Literature* (New Haven: Yale University Press, 1955), I, 90; II, 134.

3. Not further identified.

4. Emilio Castelar y Ripoll (1832–1899), in 1873–1874 president of the first Spanish republic; "a great democrat, and very eloquent." Soon afterward Bryant met Castelar at the Perry home. See 993.1; Bryant, "Diary, 1857–1858," November 16, 1857.

5. Patricio de la Escosura y Morrogh (1807–1878).

6. Bryant's presence in Madrid was remarked on in an article appearing on November 4 in *La Discusión*, in which he was called "one of the greatest poets in the world today, and without doubt the first among Anglo-American poets." Two weeks later, at the Perrys', he met the principal editors of this democratic daily, Nicolás María Rivero (1814?–1878), and Manuel Ortiz de Pinedo (1831–1901). Bryant, "Diary, 1857–1858," November 17, 1857.

7. Alejandro Mon (1801–1882).

8. This was Don P. Manuel de Olalde, son of Bryant's obliging guide at Vitoria. See 985.1; Bryant, "Diary, 1857–1858," October 22, 1857.

9. Ferdinand VII (1784–1833), king of Spain, 1808–1833.

10. Augustus Caesar Dodge (1812–1883), American minister to Spain, 1855–1859. See Letter 995.

995. *To* Augustus C. Dodge[1]

Alicante Nov 23 1857

My dear sir

We arrived at this place on Friday afternoon—safely—but the ladies much bruised by performing a part of the journey in a cart—from Almanza to Novelda. At Novelda by good luck we found a locomotive with trucks for carrying stone, and mounting one of them rode to Alicante.

The next morning I got from the Post Office the draft sent me by Munroe & Co. of Paris and enclosed it to H. O'Shea & Co. with directions to pass 4000 reals to your credit which I take it has been done.[2]

The American Consul and his family have been very civil to us on account of your letter of introduction[3]—we have also found here some San Sebastian acquaintances. Your friend Senor Don Juan Trabado &c. de Lánda has been very attentive to us—the silver cups were put into his hands on Saturday—and he will write to you.[4]

We shall soon leave this place for the south but we shall carry with us a pleasant recollection of your kindness and that of Mrs. Dodge to whom please give my best regards.[5] The ladies also desire to be most kindly remembered.

I am dear sir
very truly yours
W   C   BRYANT

MANUSCRIPT: NYPL–GR (draft) ADDRESS: To Genl. A. C. Dodge.

    1. See 994.10.

    2. Arriving at Madrid on October 17, Bryant had found himself short of money, and had borrowed two hundred dollars from Dodge. See Letter 992; Bryant, "Diary, 1857–1858," November 12, 1857.

    3. See 998.1.

    4. See Bryant, "Diary, 1857–1858," November 21, 22, 1857.

    5. Ambassador and Mrs. Dodge had been extremely hospitable to the Bryant party throughout their month's visit in Madrid, helping them find lodgings, entertaining them at dinner and the theater, helping them with shopping, and offering evening entertainment at the ambassadorial home a number of times. *Ibid.*, October 20–November 15, 1857, *passim.*

996.   *To* Messrs. John Munroe & Co.

Alicante   Nov. 23   1857.

Gentlemen

    I have found your letter of the 10th of November at this place with the draft of 7600 reals from Pedro Gil & Co of Paris, on H. O'Shea & Co of Madrid for which I thank you.[1] There could be no proceeding more liberal or better fitted to call forth my best acknowledgments.

    I had directed in addition to the $500 which were to have been deposited on the 1st of November the sum of $1.000 to be deposited with your house in New York on the 1st of December in order that there might be no scruple about supplying me with necessary funds. Since your house has stopped which I very much regret—a regret shared I believe by most Americans in Europe and which I hope will prove but a temporary suspension—I suppose the business which you have managed with so much satisfaction to my countrymen abroad may pass into other hands. If so I hope to be informed of it as early as may be.[2]

    Meantime it is not my intention to return to Paris at present, as you suppose—and I do not know how the mistake arose. I want to see the south of Spain before I leave the peninsula and will therefore thank you to send my letters and papers and those of Miss Ives to Malaga until further advised. . . .

MANUSCRIPT: NYPL–GR (draft) ADDRESS: To Messrs. John Munroe & Co.

    1. Letter unrecovered.

    2. Shortly before leaving Madrid Bryant had learned that his bankers had failed in the severe financial panic of the summer and fall of 1857, which had quickly spread from the United States to Great Britain and France. Bryant, "Diary, 1857–1858," November 16, 1857; Letter 992; Nevins, *Ordeal*, III, 190–191.

997.   *To* the EVENING POST

Carthagena, Old Spain, November 28, 1857.

    We left Madrid on a chilly, rainy morning, the 18th of November, after having waited several days for settled weather, that we might visit

Toledo, to which a friend was to accompany us. The fair day for which we were looking had not arrived, and we reluctantly gave up the idea of an excursion to that ancient city, which has preserved so long the works of her Moorish architects, and tokens of the Moorish dominion among the later works of her Gothic builders, and where they yet forge the famous Toledo blade, not quite equal, perhaps, to the cutlery of Sheffield. How many other old cities of Spain we shall have been obliged to leave behind on our journey! Bilbao, Salamanca, Zaragoza, and a dozen more, all of which we should have visited, had we leisure, and the roads and the weather allowed us. We shall leave Spain, also, without a look at those who range the woods of Estremadura; without seeing any thing of Galicia or the Asturias, and other provinces, which, inhabited by races distinct from each other in character, costume and speech, make up what was once the powerful and dreaded monarchy of Spain. To see Spain well, requires time, and we feel that we are about to leave it without having had more than a mere glimpse of the country and its people.

The wind, as we passed through the walks of the Prado, was tearing off and strewing over the hard-beaten soil the sallow leaves from the elms and other trees, some of which, however, whose foliage had not yet grown old, were still in full leaf, and attested, by the freshness of their verdure, the mildness of the autumnal climate in this capital. To our surprise, for punctuality in the arrangements for travelling is not a common virtue in Spain, the train set out at precisely the appointed hour. It took us along the banks of the Manzanares, beside a canal begun by Ferdinand the Seventh, to connect Madrid with the sea, and after a considerable waste of money abandoned. To the left of our track appeared a church, seated on a high rocky hill, rising out of the plain. "It is the hermitage of Pintovas," said a fellow-passenger. "These churches which you see in solitary places are called hermitages. Until lately, some person devoted to a recluse life had his cell in them, and subsisted on the alms which he got from the faithful. The government has seized upon them, or most of them, professing to regard them as useless for the purpose of public worship, and the hermits, like the monks, have been driven back into the world they had left."

Some forty miles from Madrid we crossed the Tagus, swollen with rain, and carrying to the ocean the soil of Castile in a torrent of yellow mud. Immediately we found ourselves in Aranjuez, among shady walks and trim gardens, rows and thickets of elms, acacias and planes, plantations of fruit trees flourishing in a rich soil, and abundant springs breaking out at the foot of the declivities, and keeping up a perpetual verdure. Here the royal family of Spain have a country palace, and hither it is their custom to come in spring, when the flowers and the nightingales make their appearance, which is much earlier in Aranjuez than at Madrid; but they leave the place as soon as the summer sets in, on account of the in-

termittent fevers which prevail here. The grounds are not laid out with any taste, nor could the place be thought remarkably pretty in our country; yet to our eyes, accustomed so long to the brown fields of Castile, it seemed a paradise. But now the walks were slippery with mud, and we were not tempted to stop. We issued from the valley of Aranjuez, and proceeded to Villasequilla, where we had thought to take the road leading up to the rocks on which Toledo is built; but even this place we were obliged to leave behind, on account of the continued bad weather, and passing by a few solitary cottages, scattered at distant intervals along the railway, and inhabited by persons in the service of the proprietors, at the doors of which we saw the comfortable-looking families of the inmates, the train soon whirled us into the province of La Mancha.

In all its provinces which I have seen, Spain needs a reformer like Dr. Piper in our country[1]—some enthusiastic friend of trees, to show the people the folly of stripping a country of its woods; but in no part of the kingdom is he so much needed as in La Mancha. If the Castiles are deplorably naked, La Mancha is so in a greater degree, if that be possible. Until you begin to approach the Murcian frontier, La Mancha has scarcely a bush; it has no running streams, and scarce a blade of grass makes itself seen; the only green it has at this season is the springing wheat, which the rains have just quickened, and fields of which lie scattered among the tracts of fallow ground. It is a time of rejoicing in Spain when the rains fall soon after the wheat is sown, for that is the promise of a plenteous harvest. When the plant is once put in a due course of growth by timely moisture, it defies the drought of the succeeding season. The last harvest was uncommonly large, and the people are now looking confidently for another year of abundance. I may mention here that in almost all the districts of Spain which produce wheat, it is the practice to let the soil recover its fertility by rest. The surface of the ground is stirred with a little light plough of the rudest make; the seed is then scattered and covered; the harvest is reaped in due time, a harvest of full, round, heavy grains, yielding the whitest of flour, and then the ground is left untilled in stubble, till it will bear stirring again. No growth of juicy clover, or of the sweet grasses we cultivate for cattle, succeeds that of wheat.

But to return to the subject of trees; they say at Madrid: "Aranjuez is overshadowed with trees, and the place is unhealthy in summer; trees grow along the Manzanares under the walls of our city, and on the banks of that river you have the tertian ague." The answer to this is, that the unhealthiness of Aranjuez is caused by its stagnant waters, and that there is no proof that trees make the air in the valley of the Manzanares unwholesome, any more than the pebbles of its stream. It has never been found that the health of a district, subject to fever and ague, has been improved by stripping it of its trees, and letting in the sun, to bake the soil and evaporate the moisture to its unwholesome dregs. It is objected again,

in the grain-producing districts of Spain, that trees form a harbor for the birds, which devour their wheat. For these childish reasons, whole provinces, once independent kingdoms, have denied themselves the refreshment of shade and verdure, have hewn down the forests which covered the springs of their rivers and kept them perennial, and withheld the soil from being washed away by the rains, and have let in the winds to sweep over the country unchecked, and winnow its clods to powder.

Ford, in his "Handbook for Travellers,"[2] says that the rivers of the country are constantly diminishing. I do not know what evidence he has to support this assertion; he certainly produces none; but it may be safely taken for granted, that they have now less depth of water in summer than when their sources were shaded by woods, under which a bed of leaves absorbed the rains, and parted with them gradually to the soil, protecting them from a too rapid exhalation. The beds of many of the rivers of Spain are dry for the greater part of the year, and only form a channel for torrents in the rainy reason. To renew the groves, which have been improvidently hewn away, would be a difficult task, on account of the present aridity of the soil and air, which are unfavorable to the growth and health of trees; but with the increase of their number, it is natural to expect that the work of rearing them would become easier. It will require, however, I suppose, centuries to wean the people of the prejudice of which I speak, and then almost as long a time to repair the mischief which is its fruit.

La Mancha has a look of cheerlessness and poverty, and the intervals between town and town are longer and more dreary than in the Castiles. I hear that the winds in summer, sweeping over this level region without an obstacle, drift the dust of the ways and fields in almost perpetual clouds through the air; but when we passed through it, the earth was yet moist with rain, which here and there stood in broad plashes. The towns which lay in our course, such as Campo de Creptino and others, are mostly, as it appeared to me, built of small unhewn stones, plastered on the outside with red mud, the soil of the country. The inhabitants are a slender and rather small race of men. I saw companies of them employed on the railways near the stations; they seemed to work with a will, and had a healthy look. All over the country, wind-mills, as in the time of the author of Don Quixote,[3] were flinging their long arms about, and in one or two places they stood in a little host on the hill-side. Let me say for La Mancha, however, that just before we passed out of it, between Campo de Creptino and Villarobledo, our eyes were refreshed by the sight of a forest of evergreen oaks, small and thinly scattered, but extending over a considerable tract of country.

Soon after this we glided into twilight and darkness, and at half-past seven reached Albacete, where we left the train and stopped for the night at a passable inn. We were now in Murcia, the land of fruits, and they gave us for dessert what you do not often find in Europe, some sweet and

well-flavored melons. As we were dining, we were beset with people offering to sell us daggers and poniards, which are skilfully wrought in this country, and often prettily ornamented. The fellows were neatly dressed and smoothly shaved, and all wore new black velvet caps. They addressed themselves to the ladies of our party, whom they seemed to consider most in need of their weapons, and it cost a good deal of trouble to convince them that we were *gente de paz* [friends], who had come to the country without the slightest intention of stabbing anybody in it. As fast as we got rid of one of these men, another would make his appearance, until they had all received the same answer, and left us to finish our meal in quiet.

We had no time to look at Albacete, for we left it in the fog and darkness at half-past five the next morning, when the train came along from Madrid. When the fog cleared away at sunrise, we were passing through a forest of evergreen oaks. The trees which had attained any size had been polled so often that their tops were but little broader than their trunks, and when I looked at them, I could think only of so many barbers' blocks in green wigs. We reached Almanza, where the travel on the railway terminates for the present, about eight o'clock in the morning. We breakfasted at a comfortless inn, where a fresh-colored, stately hostess, of ample proportions, paid us little attention, and were waited upon by two remarkably skinny and shrivelled little women.

Our first care was now to procure the means of conveyance to Alicante. We might have proceeded in the diligence to Valencia, which we afterwards found to our cost would have been the most convenient mode, but as we were going to the south of Spain, and the nearest route lay through Alicante, we determined to make the best of our way directly to the place. There was no diligence or any other regular means of communication between Alman[z]a and Alicante. The common conveyance of the country is a *tartana*, which is a sort of cart, a two-wheeled vehicle without springs, but provided with cushioned seats, an arched top, and glasses in front. I found all the *tartanas* already in use, and the owner of the best in town did not expect it back till night, so that we were obliged to take up with the original of the *tartana*, a simple cart of rude construction, with cushioned seats on each side like those of an omnibus, an awning, a covering of painted cloth, and a floor of strong matting. They call this a *carrito*, to distinguish it from the *carro*, which has no seats within, and carries charcoal and cabbages to market. I hired a vehicle of this kind to take us to Alicante, a distance of about sixty miles, in eighteen hours of travel; an allowance of time which seemed to me discouragingly liberal. For my comfort, some gentlemen, who were breakfasting at the inn, assured me that the road was "transitable," as they called it.

In getting ready for our journey, our luggage was fastened to the back of the *carrito* in such a manner as to keep that part disproportionately heavy, and always inclining most inconveniently to the ground. We looked

at the vehicle, and looked at the streets of Almanza, which lay deep in mud, and concluded to walk till we got out of town, picking our way as we best might, by keeping close to the houses. As we went, we met numbers of people with loaded donkeys coming to market, and heavy carts and wagons, staggering through the miry streets, their drivers filling the air with shouts, while at every corner, and at almost every door, stood the idle inhabitants, staring at us or nodding and smiling to each other, and pointing to the *Franceses*, as they call all foreigners in this country. We reached at length the city gate, and passing out upon the broad highway into the open country, turned to admire the site of Almanza, lying in a fertile valley, among craggy mountains. Close beside it rose, immediately out of the plain, a lofty red rock, uplifting a massive castle of the same color, which looked as if the cliffs had formed themselves into walls and battlements.

We now got into our *carrito*, the motion of which was unpleasant enough. The road was said to be macadamized, but this was a figure of speech; no pains had been taken to keep the middle higher than the sides, hollows were formed where the water had softened the ground into mud, the heavy carts and *galeras* had almost everywhere furrowed it with deep ruts; and wherever the mire seemed too deep for a loaded vehicle to struggle through, a heap of coarse broken stone had been thrown in a sort of desperation, which added to the roughness of the way. We were tossed backwards and forwards, and pitched from side to side as we stumbled on. Our driver was a good-natured, careless, swarthy Murcian, José Pinero by name, as lithe as a snake, dressed in black velvet jacket and pantaloons, with a bright parti-colored handkerchief wrapped round his head, and over that a black velvet cap. With a beard and the Oriental costume, he might have passed for an Arab of the purest caste. He spoke a sort of clipped Spanish, with a Murcian lisp, and sat on a little board in front of our cart, doubled up, much as he doubled his whip. We had stipulated for two good horses, but those which were furnished us did not quite answer that description. They were very thin, and looked old and worn out; they were harnessed one before the other, and the leader, who had not been accustomed to draw except with another by his side, had an inconvenient habit of always crowding to the right, so that our Murcian was at his wit's end to keep him in the road.

Beyond Almanza the country had some color; there were bright green fields of wheat and trefoil, and tracts of tilth between, of a chocolate brown, and low brushwood on the hills, of a dark green hue, looking like the stubble of what might once have been forests. Six leagues from Almanza, where pinnacles of bare rock enclose smooth and fertile valleys, we reached, as the night was setting in, Villena, a Murcian town, and stopped at the *Posada de Alicante*, a wretched inn, kept in what was formerly part of a convent, where horses were stabled in the cloisters below, and wide stone stair-cases led to the rooms occupied by the family and their guests above.

As we entered, we heard the tinkling of a guitar and the clatter of castanets, and saw in a vaulted recess, on the ground floor, half a dozen people
sitting on benches, one of whom, a young man, was playing, while before
him a young fellow and a little girl were dancing. We got a great, dreary,
chilly room, with one large window looking out upon the old court of the
convent, and two deep alcoves containing enormous wide beds of straw,
resting on huge bedsteads of beam and plank, the work of some coarse
carpenter; perhaps they were the same on which the bulky friars, the former inmates of the place, had slept. A strapping Murcian woman, loud-
voiced and impudent, and always talking, laid the sheets for us, assisted by
a younger maiden, little, pretty, and quiet. For our evening meal we got
a tolerable soup, but it was with great difficulty that we prevented it from
being flavored with garlic. The elder waiting woman tossed her head, and
expressed her scorn very freely when we gave repeated orders to dispense
with the favorite condiment of her country; but we got the soup without
garlic, notwithstanding. The greatest difficulty we had was in obtaining a
sufficient supply of water for our morning ablutions. A single large washbowl, half filled with water, was placed on a stand in the corner of the
great room, and this was expected to serve for us all. We called for more
water, and a jar was brought in, from which the washbowl was filled to
the brim. We explained that each one of us wanted a separate quantity of
pure water, but the stout waiting-woman had no idea of conforming to our
outlandish notions, and declined doing any thing more for us. It was only
after an appeal to the landlady, that a queer Murcian pitcher, looking
like a sort of sky-rocket, with two handles, five spouts, and a foot so small
that it could hardly stand by itself, was brought in, and for greater security
made to lean against the wall in the corner of the room.

MANUSCRIPT: NYPL–GR (draft) TEXT: LT II, pp. 152–163; first published in EP for
February 10, 1858.

1. Dr. R. N. Piper (959.2).

2. Richard Ford (1796–1858), English author and critic, *Handbook for Travellers
in Spain* (1845).

3. Miguel de Cervantes Saavedra (1547–1616), author of the novel *Don Quixote de
la Mancha* (1605–1615), whose romantic hero tilted with windmills.

998.   *To* the EVENING POST

Cartagena, November 29, 1857.

At an early hour the next morning the muleteers were reloading their
beasts among the arches of the cloisters, where they had been fed, and at
half-past five o'clock we set out among them. We had made our way to the
inn with perfect ease the night before, and one of our party had remarked
upon this to the driver. "You will find Villena a bad place to get out of,"
was his answer, and so it proved, for I do not remember ever to have been

conveyed, in the night, through streets so crooked, narrow and miry. A man had been engaged to keep beside the horses, and guide them at the sudden turns of the streets, but even this precaution did not seem enough. There was not a lamp in the streets, and only a dim starlight in the sky; but luckily, an end of candle was found in the carriage, which, being lighted, helped to show the way. Several times the horses stopped, and required a great deal of encouragement from the driver before they would attempt to draw us out of the sloughs into which we had plunged. Once they turned suddenly about, jerking round the *carrito* in a very narrow passage, with an evident design to return to their stable. At length, after a series of marvellous escapes from being overturned or dashed against the walls of the houses, we reached the Queen's highway in safety, and extinguished our light.

With a passable road, and a better carriage, this day's journey would have been delightful. When the sun rose we found ourselves in a picturesque country, bordering a little stream, the Segura, I believe, and here lay the town of Sax on the side of a hill, which towered above it—a high rock, full of yawning holes and caverns, and crowned with an old abandoned castle. We did not enter, but left it a little way off on our right, basking in the sunshine of a pleasant morning. It rang with the incessant cackling of hens, the cries of children, and the shrill voices of women. Craggy mountain summits all around us kept watch over smooth valleys, and along the *huerta* [irrigated land] which bordered the stream, the peasants were cutting and carrying home the fresh stalks of the maize, which had been sown for fodder. Beside the road were green fields of the Windsor bean and trefoil—the trefoil which is so tender, juicy and brittle in its winter growth, that, as I remember, in Egypt it is often eaten as a salad.

The road, however, seemed to grow worse as the country became more worth looking at; the mire was deeper, and the way marked with deeper furrows by the wheels of the heavy *galeras*. The day before we had discovered that our driver had an unlucky knack of locking the wheels of his cart with those of the other vehicles he met, and once or twice had caused our baggage to scrape in a most perilous manner against their muddy wheels. He was now to show us that his accomplishments went further than this. I had taken a long walk of two or three hours that morning, for it was an easy feat to keep pace with our horses in walking; and now, in approaching the town of Elda, the ladies of our party had become so fatigued with the incessant jolting they had endured, that they dismounted, and picked their way on foot by the side of the road. Our *carrito* had entered the town of Elda, the driver walking beside his horses, when, as it turned a corner, the right wheel striking against the check stone and rising over it, overturned the vehicle with all the baggage, bringing the wheel-horse to the ground. When we came up with our driver, he was looking ruefully at what he had done, and apparently meditating what he should do next.

He soon had plenty of advisers and assistants; and leaving our courier with him to see to our baggage, we withdrew from the crowd that were gathering about us and staring at us most unmercifully, and followed a by-street leading round a corner of the town to where the main road again issued into the fields. Here, while waiting for our *carrito*, we had a good opportunity to observe the situation of Elda. It lies in a rich plain, among mountains; a few date palms, the first we had seen in Spain, rising above the houses and all the other trees, give the place a tropical aspect. We had been made sensible all the morning that we had entered within the bounds of a more genial climate than that of Madrid. The air was like that of early June with us, and there was never a softer or pleasanter sunshine than that which shone about us.

In about twenty minutes José rejoined us with his cart, and we all got in again. By that good fortune which strangely attends some careless people, neither the vehicle, nor the horses, nor the harness, nor our luggage, had sustained the slightest damage. We were now in the *huerta* of Elda; on each side of the road were rows of olive trees, the finest and most luxuriant of their kind, loaded with fruit which was dropping to the ground, with occasional plantations of sprawling fig and branching walnut-trees, under all which the ground was green with the winter crops; but the road between was little better than a canal of mud, and so painfully did our horses flounder through it, that we all soon dismounted a second time, and walked. "You will find the road better a league or so ahead," said a man, who, accompanied by laborers, was trying to make it passable in some of its worst parts.

We walked on more than two miles further, when having left the too fat soil of Elda behind, the road became a little better, and José again received the ladies into his *carrito*. We now began to speculate as to what we should do when we should arrive at our next stopping-place, the *Venta de los Cuatro Caminos*, which is Spanish for the Four Corners' Tavern— whether we should get another cart for our luggage, or whether we should hire donkeys, on which the ladies might make part at least, of our remaining journey to Alicante, a distance of three or four leagues; I could not learn exactly which, for the computation of distances is remarkably inexact in Spain. Just then the plain in which stands the *Venta de los Cuatro Caminos* opened upon us, a broad fertile tract, swelling into pleasant undulations between desolate mountain ridges; and showing at one view three or four considerable villages, the largest of which was Novelda, and beside more than one of which rose lofty groups of palm trees. Our vehicle had already crossed a railway, the unfinished part of that which is to unite Alicante to Madrid, when our courier, who had been walking all the way from Elda, came running after us with the good news that a train of open trucks was to go that afternoon to Alicante, and that if we pleased we might have a passage in it. He had seen the engine smoking at a little dis-

tance, and the fancy had taken him to inquire if that did not offer an easier means of conveyance to Alicante than the one we had. We immediately paid off and dismissed our Murcian driver, who seemed nearly as glad to be spared the rest of the journey, as we were to get out of his cart. But here we were met with a new difficulty; the tickets we had bought for Alicante specified that the passengers should take with them no baggage. On representing our case, however, to the principal persons in charge of the train, they most kindly allowed us to take our trunks and travelling bags along with us, and treated us with the greatest courtesy. After waiting some time for the principal engineer to arrive, and for a shower to pass over, which darkened the sky and smoked on the hills in the quarter to which we were about to proceed, we set out, shielded by our umbrellas from a thin rain beating in our faces. About half the distance between the station of Novelda and Alicante, we stopped to load the trucks with broken stone, a dirty white alabaster, destined to be used in building, after which we went on. The Mediterranean soon glimmered in sight; then appeared a bald rock with a fort on its summit, and the other drab-colored heights by which Alicante is sheltered; and in a few minutes we were at the terminus of the railway. Four Valencians took charge of our baggage, which had required but two porters to carry it in Madrid. When told that so many were not necessary, they answered: "We are not Gallegos; we are not beasts of burden." We followed them through a short avenue of elms, just without the city, beside a plantation of young palm trees, profusely hung with their large clusters of fruit, to the *Fonda del Vapor*, where we found pleasant rooms, and sat down to an excellent dinner, closed by a plentiful dessert of fruit, grapes of the finest quality in enormous clusters, and dates just ripened and fresh from the trees that bore them.

Alicante had not much to interest us, except the kindness of the American Consul, Mr. Leach,[1] and his family, and that of the other persons to whom we had letters, and who did every thing in their power to make our stay agreeable, while we waited for a steamer bound for the southern parts of Spain. It is a decayed town of great antiquity; its people carry on a little commerce in wine, raisins, and a few other productions of the fertile region around it; a small number of vessels lie in its port, and now and then one of them is freighted with wine for the United States. The streets are for the most part unpaved, and I could not succeed in finding a pleasant walk in the environs of the city. "We are too poor to pave our streets," said one of the residents to me; yet the hope is cherished that Alicante will become the seat of a great commerce, after the railway to Madrid shall have been opened. Already they are beginning to build a little, in expectation of that event; but this is done sluggishly. It will require some powerful, immediate impulse to break the dead sleep which for centuries has settled on that ancient seat of trade.

I said that Alicante had not much to interest us; let me recall the ex-

pression. I saw at Alicante what interested me more than almost any thing else which I met with in Spain, the monument of a man most remarkable for active and disinterested beneficence, Don Trino Gonzalez de Quijano, who was the civil Governor of the province of Alicante from the 22d of August, 1852, to the 16th of September in the same year,[2] while the cholera was carrying off its thousands, and filling the province with consternation. In early life Quijano had been a soldier, and was always a zealous constitutionalist. Those with whom he acted had entrusted him successively with the administrative power in several of the provinces of the kingdom, and he had made himself so popular in the Canary Islands, to which he had been sent by the government, that they elected him their representative to the Cortes. Immediately upon his arrival at Alicante, he entered actively upon the work of mercy, superintending in person every measure adopted for the relief of the sick and their families, attending at their bedsides, administering the medicines prescribed by the physicians, providing for the necessitous out of his private fortune, and when that was exhausted, dispensing the contributions of those who were incited to generosity by his generous example. As the circle of the pestilence extended, he passed from one town to another, sometimes in the night and sometimes in the midst of tempests, carrying, wherever he went, succor and consolation, and assuaging the general alarm by his own serene presence of mind. When his friends expressed their fears lest his humane labors might cost him his life, "It is very likely they may," he answered, "but my duty is plain, and if I can check the spread of the cholera by laying down my life, I shall lay it down cheerfully." He was attacked at length by the distemper, but not till he had the satisfaction of seeing its violence greatly abated. "Do not call in the physicians," he said, "it will create a panic and make new victims; let it not be known, if you can help it, that I died of the cholera."

Quijano died, to the great grief of those whom he had succored, and for whom he had literally laid down his life. Three years he lay in his grave, and as soon as the physicians pronounced that it could be done without danger to the public health, his coffin was taken up and opened. The features were found to be little altered; it seemed that even corruption had respected and spared the form in which once dwelt so noble a soul. The people of the province, in silence and wonder, came in crowds about the lifeless corpse and kissed its hand; mothers led up their children to look at all that was left of the good man, to whom they owed their own lives and those of their husbands. The corner-stone of a monument was laid, to which the towns composing the province of Alicante contributed. It stands a little without the northern gate of the city, a four-sided tapering shaft, inscribed with the names of the grateful towns which he succored—Alicante, Alcoy, Montforte, Elche, and others—resting on a pedestal which

bears a medallion head of Quijano and inscriptions in his honor. May it stand as long as the world.

I love and honor Spain for having produced such a man as Quijano. A pamphlet is before me, consisting of the addresses made and poems recited on laying the corner-stone of the monument under which he was again committed to the earth—florid prose and such verse as is easily produced in the harmonious language of Castile. I only wish that in some part of it a plain recital had been given of his numerous acts of beneficence, that I might have made this brief account more particular, and, of course, more interesting.

MANUSCRIPT: NYPL–GR (draft) TEXT: *LT* II, pp. 164–172; first published in *EP* for February 20, 1858.

1. William Leach Giro, born in Málaga of American parents, was United States consul at Alicante from 1853 to 1896. *U. S. Consular Officers, 1789–1939.*
2. Not further identified.

999. *To* the EVENING POST

Malaga, December 2nd, 1857.

I had become quite tired of waiting at Alicante for a steamer bound for the southern ports of Spain; yet the roads were so bad that none of our party but myself would venture to perform any part of the journey by land. I therefore determined to proceed by myself to the city of Murcia, taking Elche in my way, and thence to Carthagena, on the coast, where the others were to join me. At three o'clock in the morning of the 25th of November I was waked and conducted through the miry and silent streets to the office of the diligence. Here I was told that, on account of the badness of the roads, the passengers were not to be sent forward as usual in a *coche*, but in a *galera*, which means a sort of market-wagon without springs, running on a large pair of wheels behind, and a small, low pair next to the horses. In taking my passage, I had paid for a seat in the *berlina*, or *coupé*, as the French call it, and as the *galera* has no *berlina*, I was told that I was entitled to receive twelve reals back. I took the change, and soon found myself packed in the wagon with eight other passengers, who did not seem in the best humor; possibly on account of the change in the mode of conveyance—nor did they quite recover their spirits during the whole journey. They consoled themselves with rolling up small quantities of finely-chopped tobacco in little bits of paper, to make *cigarritos*, and quietly smoking them out. For this purpose every true Spaniard carries with him a little unbound volume of half the size of a pocket almanac, composed of thin leaves of blank paper, one of which he tears off every time he has occasion to make a *cigarrito*, and drawing a quantity of chopped tobacco from a small bag, folds it with quick and dexterous fingers into a compact

cylinder, and lighting a lucifer match with a smart explosion, raises a smoke in as little time as is needed to read these lines. There is one respect in which Spanish industry takes the lead of the world—the making of lucifer matches for smokers. A slender wick of two inches in length is dipped in wax of snowy whiteness, and tipped with a little black knob of explosive matter, looking like the delicate anther of some large flower. Struck against the gritty side of the little box which contains it, the Spanish match starts into a flame which requires more than a slight puff of wind to blow it out, and which lasts long enough for a very deliberate smoker to light any but the most refractory cigar.

Our *galera* was dragged out of town in the glare of two torches, by eight mules, going at a pretty smart trot; but when the light of morning became so strong that the snap of a lucifer match was no longer followed by an illumination of the inside of our wagon, we saw that we were travelling in what could not be called a highway but by a gross misapplication of terms. It was from three to five rods in width, and worn considerably lower than the fields through which it passed, so that the rain-water flowed readily into it, and found no passage out, making it a long, narrow quagmire. Yet we were in the midst of a pleasant *huerta*, for here were groves of olive trees, full of fruit, and rows of the dark green lentisk, from which the fleshy pods had been gathered, and lines of mulberry trees, already bare, and sallow pomegranate bushes, and fig trees beginning to drop their foliage. Above these towered here and there a giant palm, and, finally, at a distance, appeared a great wood of palm trees, which seemed to fill half the horizon, like those which in Egypt overshadow the mounds that mark the site of Memphis, or those through which the traveller passes on his way from Cairo to Heliopolis. We were approaching Elche, the inhabitants of which have tended their groves of palm, refreshing the trees with rills of water guided to their roots in the dry season, and gathering their annual harvest of dates in the month of November, ever since the time of the Moors. I seemed to have been at once taken from Europe, and set down in the East. The work people whom I saw beginning their tasks in the fields, or going to them along the road, reminded me of the Orientals. The Majo cap which they wore, without being a turban, imitates its form in such a manner, that at a little distance it might be easily taken for one; and their gay-colored sashes worn around the waist, their wide white drawers reaching just below the knee, and their hempen sandals, the next thing to slippers, heightened the resemblance. In our journey from Alman[z]a to Alicante we had often, as we approached the sea-coast, met with cartmen and wagoners dressed in this half Oriental garb; but now we were on the spot where it was the household costume, and where the needles were plied by which it was shaped.

Passing by a large plantation of young palms, just beginning to rise from the ground, with trenches from one to another along the rows, lead-

ing the water to their roots, we entered the great wood. There were palms on both sides of the way, standing as near to each other as they could well grow; some of them tall, the growth of centuries, others short, though equal in breadth of stem and reared within the last fifty years. They hung out in the morning sunshine their clusters of dates, light green, yellow, or darkening into full ripeness; clusters large enough to fill a half bushel basket, while their rigid leaves rustled with a dry hissing sound in a light wind.

Our vehicle staggered on in the miry streets, between low stone walls, and amidst a crowd of men and women going forth to the labors of the day, entered the streets of Elche, embowered in this forest. I saw that all the houses had flat roofs—another resemblance to the towns in the East. I looked around me for similar resemblance in the people by whom the place is inhabited, and fancied that I found them. The people have dark complexions, bright, dark eyes, narrow faces, and for the most part high features and peaked chins, and slight and slender figures; such, at least, was the sum of observations made in the slight opportunity afforded me. I did not see the wide white drawers so frequently in the streets as I had seen them in the fields. The knee-breeches and ample brown cloak of Castile were a more common sight.

Our mules were stopped at an inn, where they were to be changed, and where the passengers were told that they could have a cup of chocolate. It was now about half past seven in the morning. In a little room on the ground floor, near the stables, two or three persons sitting at a table were satisfying their early appetite with toasted bread or bi[z]cochos, a sort of sponge cake, which they first dipped in a little cup of very thick chocolate. I followed their example. All over the kingdom the Spaniard breaks his morning fast on chocolate; it is the universal household beverage; the manufactories of chocolate—chocolate mills I might call them—are more numerous than the windmills. Those who take coffee drink it at the *cafés*, as an occasional refreshment, just as they take an ice cream; and the use of tea, though on the increase, is by no means common. The only narcotic in which the Spaniards indulge to any extent is tobacco, in favor of which I have nothing to say; yet it should be remembered, in extenuation, that they are tempted to this habit by the want of something else to do; that they husband their *cigarritos* by smoking with great deliberation, making a little tobacco go a great way, and that they dilute its narcotic fumes with those of the paper in which it is folded. With regard to the use of wine, I can confirm all that has been said of Spanish sobriety and moderation, and must add that I find the number of those who never drink it larger than I had supposed.

In walking about the streets of Elche, I found myself quite as much a curiosity to the people of the place as they were to me, and as they were several hundred to one, the advantage in this encounter of eyes was clear-

ly on their side. So I beat a retreat, and got back to the inn, from which, at a little past eight, we again set out, and splashed out of Elche as we had entered it, among palms standing thick on each side, and overshadowing the muddy way with their scaly trunks, their plumy foliage, and their heavy clusters of fruit hanging down below the leaves, as if to tempt the gatherer. The road now became worse than ever, and, at the request of the conductor, we all got out and walked for a considerable distance. Here were hedges of the aloe plant beside the way, and thickets of that gigantic kind of cactus called the prickly pear were in sight, allowed to grow, I suppose, for the sake of their fruit. We were still in the region of palms, some groups of which were so lofty that it seemed to me easy to prove, by counting the circles in their bark, made by each annual growth of leaves, that they had been planted by the Moors. The village of La Granja, close by a range of bare, brown precipices, had a noble group, and was surrounded by young plantations of palms, which at some future day will screen it from the sight of the traveller till he enters it. At La Granja we passed an extensive orange grove, lying in the mild sunshine, with abundance of golden fruit spotting the dark green foliage, and guarded by a high and thick hedge. We drove through a gap in that range of precipices to Callosa, and here were other orange groves; and now we came at length in sight of Orihuela, where on each side of the way were rows of young palms just springing from the ground, which will one day supply the markets of Madrid.

At this place the diligence stopped to bait, and I had the honor of a seat at the same table with the conductor. A mess of some undistinguishable materials, chopped up with an abundance of garlic, was placed before him, while I contented myself with eggs and bread, a bit of cheese and a dessert of fruit; and we both had the company of the landlady, a very stout and rosy woman, who sat by us and chatted and gossipped incessantly. She was curious to know of what country I was. "A Frenchman, certainly." "No." "Not French; then you must be English." "I am not English." "From Germany, then?" "Not a German, but an American." She looked at me narrowly, as if with a purpose to satisfy herself in what respect an American differed from a European. "And how do you like our country?" I could not but praise what I had seen of it that day. "And you understand all we say?" I would not admit my ignorance of the local dialect, and yet, I confess, I was obliged to pay the strictest attention to be always tolerably certain of what she was saying. In the south of Spain the Castilian loses its clear, open pronunciation, and all its majesty. Among other peculiarities, the natives, who like to do every thing in the easiest way, neglect to pronounce the letter *s* in many words, and decline giving themselves the trouble of articulating the letter *d* between two vowels. Thus, you will hear *este* pronounced *ete*; *dado* in their mouths becomes *dao*; nay, *casa*

is sometimes contracted to *caa*. It is just as if in English we were to say *chet* instead of chest, *louer* instead of louder, and *hou* instead of house.

Before setting out again, I walked about the town, which presented little worthy of notice; Orihuela being curious only in one sense, that is to say, in the disposition which the people in the streets manifest to scrutinize the appearance of those who seem to be foreigners. Beyond Orihuela the road was rough with stones, rammed into the clayey soil, making a kind of rude pavement, over which we were jolted without mercy; but we were compensated for this inconvenience by the pleasant sights which our journey showed us. Along the fertile *huerta*, through which we were travelling, lay here and there extensive olive groves, composed of as fine trees of their kind as I ever saw, stretching away to the right and left, sometimes as far as the ranges of desolate rock that overlook the country. They were loaded with fruit, which was dropping to the ground; and now that the olive harvest was come, the soil under the trees had been carefully levelled, and the peasants were shaking the boughs, picking up the olives, and carrying them away in panniers. Although so late in November, the sun was shining with a genial light, like that of our blandest October days. An hour or two before his setting, I saw where the proprietors had come out to superintend the tasks of the laborers, or to entertain their families and friends with the spectacle of the olive harvest. Amidst groups of the peasantry, vigorously shaking the boughs and filling the panniers, chairs were placed, where, under the shelter of some broad tree, sat ladies, while children sported and shouted around them, or gave their help to the workpeople. At a later hour, as the air grew chilly, we saw several of these parties returning to their houses.

MANUSCRIPT: Unrecovered TEXT: *LT* II, pp. 173–181; first published in *EP* for February 2, 1858.

1000. *To* the EVENING POST

Malaga, December 2d, 1857.

It was nightfall when our conveyance reached Murcia. "Where will you stop?" asked the conductor; "at the Fonda Francesa, I suppose." He was right; and a boy was called to carry my travelling bag and show me the place. I was led through crooked and narrow ways, where in many places the water lay in plashes, to the dreary inn, the best in Murcia, situated in a gloomy street, where a French waiter, who had not been long enough in the country to speak Spanish, showed me a room, and seemed glad to meet with a guest who understood his own language. I had a letter for a gentleman in the Murcian capital, furnished me by a Spanish acquaintance in Madrid, and leaving my luggage at the inn, I made my guide conduct me to his house in the *Calle de Contrasta*. Unfortunately, the gentleman was not in, and I went back to the inn to write up my journal.

The mosquitos interrupted and shortened the sleep of that November night, and at an early hour I was walking about the city and peeping into the churches. The streets of Murcia are narrow and irregular, and some of them have only a narrow strip of pavement on the sides for foot passengers, like those of Damascus. The houses that overlook them are often painted yellow or pink. Of the churches, I found only the cathedral worthy of much attention. It has a tower built after some modification of classic architecture, so lofty and massive that it deserves to be noble and beautiful, but it has neither beauty nor majesty; and the foundation having settled on one side, it leans awkwardly away from the main building. An old Gothic portal forms the northern entrance of the Cathedral, and if the building had been finished according to the original plan, it would have been an excellent sample of the severer Gothic; but as one century went by after another, the later builders, proceeding from east to west, ran into the Roman style, and spoiled the work. One of the chapels at the east end is finished in a very singular and striking manner; the walls are wrought into a net-work of interwoven rods and twigs, here receding to leave niches, and there growing into canopies, pedestals, and other architectural appendages—freakish, but exceedingly ingenious and graceful. The principal front of the Cathedral is in that over-ornamented style into which the Spanish architects, two hundred years ago or thereabout, corrupted the classic orders. It is stocked with an army of statues—the martyrs, saints and confessors of the church—all in violent action, all with fluttering drapery, gesticulating, brandishing crosiers and scrolls, or wielding ponderous volumes. If one could suppose them living, they might seem a host of madmen at the windows and balconies of an insane asylum, ready to fling themselves at the heads of the spectators below; and yet, with all this, there is a certain florid magnificence about this part of the Cathedral which detains the attention.

As I was looking at this array of the church militant, I found myself the object of very close observation from the people in the great square, and to avoid it, entered the Cathedral. In returning to my inn I was stared at, I think, more remorselessly than I had been anywhere else in Europe, except perhaps in North Holland. People would pass me in the street at a quick pace, and then turn to get a good look. Yet the number of odd costumes in the city of Murcia appeared to me greater than I had seen in any other part of Spain. Not to speak of the hats of all shapes—the sugar loaf, the cylindrical beaver, the priests' enormous brim, the cocked hat of the Civil Guard, and the wide-awake, black or brown—not to mention caps of every form, from the velvet one of the *Majo* [young man-about-town] to the broad-topped cap of the Basque, and of every color of the rainbow—here were knee-breeches by the side of pantaloons; here were short, wide, white drawers; worn by men in crimson sashes and white shirts, unjacketed; here were legs cased in embroidered leathern gaiters,

and other legs covered with white or blue woollen hose, reaching from the knee to the ankle, and showing the bare chocolate-colored foot above the sandal; here were some who, over their short, white drawers, wore another garment looped at the sides, and jauntily left half open; and here were men who, in the chill of the morning, wore shawls with broad stripes of brilliant scarlet or crimson, alternating with black and white—a Moorish inheritance—the very *bornous* of the Arabs, which is to be found at this moment in the French shops, where it is exposed as the last ladies' fashion, just from Algiers. Yet, with all this diversity of garb, the slightest new peculiarity attracts attention. You see mustachios on every third man at least, but let one come among them whose beard is not of some well-known familiar cut, and the whole town is electrified with wonder.

I did not wait to see the gentleman to whom I had a letter of introduction, though, if I had, I should have seen Murcia to much better advantage, for the Spaniard is the most obliging of men when you have such an occasion for his attentions; but fearing that the steamer from Alicante might reach Cartagena before me, I determined to proceed. There was a *galera* going out to Cartagena at eleven o'clock that morning; there was a diligence which would set out at nine in the evening. I chose the humbler mode of conveyance, because I preferred to travel in the daytime, though the favorite practice in Spain, I know not why, is to begin a journey in the public conveyances at night.

In a covered wagon, without springs, drawn by three horses, twelve other passengers were packed with me, and we left Murcia by a very passable road which led us through a rich plain, planted with mulberry, fig, pomegranate, lentisk, orange and lemon trees, a few palms towering above them all. My fellow-passengers were mostly mechanics, laboring men and tradespeople, good-humored, obliging, and disposed to make the best of every thing. One of them was a decided wag, and entertained the rest with his jokes. Two wore the wide white drawers of the country, which, as they sat, showed their bare brown knees; they had on crimson sashes, white knit leggings and hempen sandals. The younger of these was as handsome a youth, I think, as I ever saw—his features would have been a study for the sculptor; in Rome he might make his fortune by sitting as a model to the artists.

We rose gradually out of the plain, till, on looking back, the Cathedral of Murcia appeared of a mountainous size beside the city dwellings, and its lofty tower seemed higher than ever. Beyond the city, to the north, stood the solitary rock of Monte Agudo, crowned with its old Moorish castle, under the shadow of which I had passed the day before in approaching Murcia. Still continuing to ascend, we threaded a pass between arid hills, spotted all over with green tufts of a little palmetto, somewhat smaller than the dwarf palmetto of South Carolina and Florida, and then descended into a plain as bare and dreary as those of Castile, bounded by

desolate mountains. The country, sinking gradually towards the ocean side, began to clothe itself with olive groves; we passed through them; entered an avenue of elms, in a fertile *huerta*, and Cartagena was before us, overlooked by half a dozen mountain fortresses, which command her spacious harbor on three sides. We drove through a long street between dingy houses, almost blue with decay, and were set down at the entrance of a large stable. I procured a guide to the Hotel of the Four Nations, *Fonda de las Cuatro Naciones*, kept by a Frenchman, in a narrow, dark lane, leading out of the main street, and here I got a lofty room lighted by one great window, where, for half the year at least, the sun never entered. I remembered my experience at Murcia, and asked for a mosquito net to my bed, but none was to be had, and that night the mosquitos came humming about me.

The hotel, while I was its guest, was more than what its name imported—it was an hotel of six nations. At the *mesa redonda*, or ordinary, were assembled, besides myself, an Italian and his wife, three or four Spaniards, a chattering and sometimes smutty Frenchman, two Germans, one silent and the other excessively loquacious, and two English commercial travellers, one modest and quiet and the other noisy and impertinent. It is generally agreed, I believe, that where there is an innate propensity to loud and conceited talking, the profession of commercial travellers develops it to its fullest extent. Two tiresome days and three tiresome nights I passed at Cartagena, wondering when the steamer from the north would arrive. I employed myself in writing this letter, and for recreation walked about the city and its neighborhood. It was not till the afternoon of the day following my arrival that I discovered what a remarkably fine promenade surrounds the city, along the ramparts, erected when Cartagena was a place of much greater consequence than now.

It commanded a noble view of sea, mountain and valley. To the north of the city, a marsh, in which the mosquitos that tormented me the night before were bred, and in which pools of water were lying, formed an ugly spot; but beyond it, the ground rose gradually into a rich champagne country. As I looked seaward, I thought of the time when the prows of the Carthaginians first broke these blue waters; I thought how they must have admired this noble bay, which they afterwards made the seat of a great commerce, and what a wonder they must themselves have been to the barbarian natives. The palms which I saw at a distance were perhaps the posterity of those which the Carthaginian colonists introduced from Africa. I thought again of the time when the conquering galleys of the Romans sailed in between these rocky promontories, and compelled the colony to submit, and of that still later period when the Moors, coming over from Africa, seized upon it and made it one of their strongholds and their favorite haven, until at length it fell into the hands of the Christians, and gradually declined from its ancient importance.

Cartagena is built on the sides of four rocky hills, enclosed within the circuit of its walls. I climbed to a ruined castle on the top of one of them, where I found part of a Roman wall of hewn stone, wholly undecayed, in which is fixed a tablet bearing a Roman inscription, with letters as sharp and distinct as if freshly cut. Other portions of the castle are said by the antiquaries to be the work of Phoenician hands. Against the Roman wall, spacious vaults, built by the Moors, with the form of arch peculiar to them, still remain; and thus the ruin is a monument of three great dominions, which have successively flourished and passed away.

Cartagena is a dull, dreary town, but it has its spacious amphitheatre for bull-fights. In its markets I found the fruits of the country excellent, abundant, and cheap; its large clusters of grapes still fresh, and its pomegranates of the finest flavor and the amplest size. I was complimented, as I walked the streets, with the special notice of the inhabitants—sometimes rather amusingly manifested. A boy who had seen me approaching at some distance, got together his companions to look at me, and as I passed them, said in a voice which was not intended for my ear—*parece loco*—"he seems to be a crazy man."

You may imagine that I was well pleased, when, on the third morning, the *mozo* [porter] came to my room to announce that a steamer had arrived from the north, the *Tharsis*, which is French or Spanish, or both, for Tarshish, the Land of Gold. A short time afterwards appeared our courier with the news that my family were on board the Tharsis, and expecting me. I was not slow to leave my gloomy lodgings, but I had first to get the leave of the police to go on board the steamer as a passenger. The police officer, as he was about to countersign my passport, expressed his surprise at my surname, which he said was the same with that of a brigadier-general commanding at Cartagena, and he wrote out the name to show that it was composed of precisely the same letters. At last I was permitted to go on board the steamer, which, about sunset, stood out of the bay, and early the next morning dropped anchor in the roadstead of Almeria.

Almeria has left a distinct image in my memory. I see yet its range of bare, white mountain ridges, looking as if calcined by an intense fire, herbless, treeless, reflecting the sun with a glare painful to the eye, and smoking with furnaces in which the lead ore drawn from their bowels is smelted. I see yet its white houses and fortresses at the foot of this range, and eastward of these, towards the sea, its cultivated plain, a sort of *huerta* overtopped by a few palms. The wind blew fresh all day, while our cargo was discharged and lumps of lead were brought to us in boat-loads from the shore. Our steamer rolled incessantly from side to side, which made the loading slow and laborious, and several of our Spanish passengers were so sickened by this motion that they left us. Among them was one who came on board at Alicante, taking passage for Malaga, and who now resolved to perform the rest of the journey by land. This peculiar liability to sea-

sickness, I hear, is a general infirmity of the Spaniards, and from what has come under my observation, I should judge that the remark is true. In a mixed company of passengers, the natives of Spain seemed to suffer most.

We left Almeria a little before sunset, and keeping under the shelter of the shore, with a west wind, we got on pretty smoothly; but when we turned a cape and took a westerly course, the wind came sweeping down the Straits of Gibraltar, and tumbled against us billows that, for aught I know, were formed in the Atlantic. Our steamer was a propeller, and easily affected by the motion of the sea. It was a great relief to find ourselves, towards morning, in smoother water; and when the sun rose upon us, it was the genial and golden sun of Malaga.

MANUSCRIPT: Unrecovered TEXT: *LT* II, pp. 182–191; first published in *EP* for February 3, 1858.

1001. *To* the EVENING POST

Oran, Algeria, December 17, 1857.

It was a beautiful morning on which we landed from the steamer *Tharsis*, at Malaga. The red hills which rise back of the city, and the great Cathedral and the close huddled roofs around it, were lying in a golden sunshine, and the waters of the harbor were swept by airs as mild as those of our June. Nothing could be more bland or more grateful than the welcome which the climate of Malaga gave us—a promise of soft and serene weather, which was kept up to the time of our departure.

They have a way of making strangers who land at Malaga pay an exorbitant tax on their luggage; a fixed rate is exacted for every separate package, great or small, taken from the steamer to the wharf; another for its conveyance to the custom-house, and a certain tribute on every thing brought into the custom-house; and a separate charge on every object conveyed from the custom-house to the hotel. I heard of an American gentleman who, in this way, by some ingenious construction of the regulations in force, was made to pay twenty dollars; and then the rogue who had practised this imposition, told him that if he would do him the honor of employing him when he should leave the port, he would put his baggage on board of any steamer for a fifth part of the money.

In the *Fonda de la Alameda*, one of the best hotels in Spain, we took rooms looking upon the principal public walk of the city—a broad space, planted with rows of trees, mostly elms, which had not yet, on the first of December, parted with their leaves. The sun shone pleasantly into our windows for nearly the whole day, and we felt no need of artificial warmth. The fine weather tempted us out to look at the town, which resembles others in the south of Spain in the narrowness and crookedness of its streets; the same labyrinth of ways, no doubt, which was trodden by the inhabitants ages since, when they wore turbans. It is proverbially said in

Malaga, that a priest cannot turn round in them without knocking off his hat. Many of them have a short stone pillar placed at each end in the middle of the passage, to prevent carriages from attempting to enter. The little dark shops on each side are scarcely larger than the narrow and shallow recesses in which the traders of Cairo and other towns in the East sit squatted among their merchandise; but the dwelling-houses, when the open street doors allowed us a peep at the courts within, had a pleasanter aspect. Here was an open square paved with black and white pebbles, in a sort of mosaic, representing foliage and flowers, and surrounded by a gallery resting on light stone columns with round arches. In the midst, generally, flowed a little fountain, and the place was made cheerful by orange trees and other ornamental evergreens, or by pots of flowers. Our walk took us by two or three fruit markets, in which lay piles of oranges on mats, with lemons scarcely turned yellow, and baskets of pomegranates and medlars, but no grapes. "At this season you must not look for fresh grapes in Malaga," said one to whom I expressed my surprise; "however abundant they may be in Cartagena or Alicante. The wines we send abroad bear so high a price at the present time, that all our grapes go to the wine-press, and after the vintage there is not one to be seen."

One of the earliest walks I took in Malaga conducted me to the Protestant burial-ground, in which lie several of our countrymen. The first grant of a piece of land for this purpose was made by the Spanish government to the late Mr. Mark, the British consul,[1] who obtained it after long and persevering solicitation. Before this, the bodies of those who died at Malaga without professing the faith of the Latin Church, were buried on the sea-beach at low water mark. The funeral procession bore the bier to where the last receding wave left bare the bottom of the deep: a hasty grave was scooped in the wet sands, and the coffin laid in a spot over which the waters would immediately return, and over which no monument could be erected. The soil of Spain, it was held, should not be profaned by the carcasses of heretics, and they were therefore given to the ocean. It was with a good deal of difficulty that Mr. Mark effected a purchase which assured him and his Protestant brethren, that when they died they should not have a more contemptuous burial than was allowed to asses and dogs. He now sleeps in the spot which he vindicated for his own last rest and theirs, and a stately monument is erected to the worthy man's memory.

It is said that after this cemetery was opened, and the bodies of Protestants allowed a last resting-place in Spanish earth, the funerals could not for some time take place without hootings and cries of derision from the populace, and that fears were sometimes entertained lest the funeral services should be riotously interrupted. At present there is nothing of all this, and the Protestant is as welcome to the hospitality of a quiet grave as his Catholic brother.

The burial-place lies on the side of a mount, rising from the sea to

the citadel of Malaga, formerly a stronghold of the Moors, and surrendered by them to the conquering arms of Isabella the Catholic. The rains which fall on this declivity, ragged with scattered groups of the prickly pear, flow naturally into a ravine, which passes by the cemetery, and here they are gathered into a reservoir, from which, in the dry season, they are distributed to the plants growing among the graves. We entered the enclosure by a massive portal, just erected, before which scowled two lions in freestone, and behind which stood a porter's lodge, and went up to the monuments through two rows of geraniums, of the most luxuriant growth and spotted with flowers. "You should see them in January," said the friend who accompanied me, "when they are in a flush of bloom." The walks within were bordered with beautiful tropical plants, which, in this genial atmosphere, seemed not to miss their native climate. The tree called *flores de pascua,* or paschal flower, held forth its clusters of yellow blossoms, around which broad circles of its leaves had parted with their natural green color and took that of blood; the pepper tree, as it is called, drooped its sheaves of delicate, fresh green leaves over the graves, shivering in the slightest breath of wind; nor were rows of cypresses wanting. Among the monuments were those of several of my countrymen; two of them from New York, Lieutenant Coddington and young Mr. Clerke, a son of Judge Clerke.[2] Several graves had the space over them formed into the shape of a coffin, in a kind of shell-work imbedded in cement. At the foot of the declivity occupied by the burial-place, the ocean glimmered and flung his billows against the shore with an angry noise, as if he chafed at being deprived of the dues paid him for so many years—the corpses of the heretics, which used to be buried in the sands of his bed with the bones of sharks and sea-lions.

The original burial-ground has been greatly enlarged by the present Mr. Mark, the son and successor in office of him by whom it was first projected. To him are owing the various embellishments of which I have spoken, and others which I have not mentioned. At present, Americans are allowed a place in it by courtesy and sufferance, and it seems to me that it would be well if our government would, by a small appropriation, secure to its citizens, in perpetuity, the right of sepulture within its limits; which, I am told, might be done.

It was some days after this, that I went with the American Consul, Mr. J. Somers Smith,[3] from whom and whose family we received many kindnesses during our stay in Malaga, to visit the city cemetery. A pleasant winding road conducted us to it from the city gates, between rows of olive trees, and little orange and lemon groves. I was surprised at the splendor of the monuments, as compared with those of the cemeteries of Madrid. The lords of commerce, in Malaga, sleep in far more sumptuous sepulchres than the Castilian nobility. Over the space enclosed by the thick walls of

the cemetery are scattered tombs in the form of chapels, urns or massive pedestals, marble statues on columns of costly workmanship, and elaborate sculptures in relief. The walks, at the time I was there, were bordered with roses and other choice plants, in bloom, carefully tended.

As we stood in the centre of the grounds, admiring the prospect it showed us, the beautiful undulations of the surrounding country—its airy eminences and sunny nooks, and the great ocean to the south—the American Consul remarked that this would be a most desirable region for country residences, if the neighborhood were but safe. "We live within the city walls," he continued, "for the sake of security. If we have country seats, they are always in danger of the visits of robbers."

This is, in fact, the cause which prevents those who enrich themselves by the growing commerce of Malaga, and who build for their families these stately sepulchres among roses and geraniums, from covering the heights around the city with beautiful country seats. The mildness of the winter climate allows the cultivation of almost any tropical plant to which one may take a fancy; indeed, the winter is the season of bloom and verdure. They might embower their dwellings with the palm and the orange, and twenty other beautiful trees, which require a climate where the frost never falls, and the vapors of the air never curdle into snow.

"It was but a little while since," said a resident of Malaga to me, "that we were really afraid to go into the country, except to travel on the great roads which are watched by the civil guard. At that time there was a bandit who, with a few accomplices, haunted the region back of the city, and used to waylay and carry off such persons as he thought likely to bring a large ransom. A poor devil was, of course, not worth the catching, but a rich man or a rich man's son was a prize which was sure to reward his trouble. He would send word to the family of his captive, that on an appointed day he must have a certain sum of money, or a forefinger of their friend would be sent them; or perhaps a harsher message came, that his head would be laid at their door. At last he was shot—it was three or four weeks ago—and his body was brought into town; I saw it; it was that of a man of middle size, but of great apparent hardihood and vigor. The wounds by which he died were given in such a manner, that he must have been shot while asleep. He had been a smuggler in his day; had been detected and imprisoned, and on getting his liberty, betook himself to the profession of a robber. Since his death I have ventured into the country on a party of pleasure."

Some further particulars of this man's warfare upon society, I heard before I left Malaga. Not long before he was killed, he captured a boy just without the city gates, and caused his father to be informed that if within a certain time eleven thousand dollars were not deposited at a place named in the message, the boy's ears would be sent him. The money

was deposited, and the boy restored to his family. He related that he was well cared for, and kindly treated; that he was taken blindfold from one place to another, among the solitary recesses of the mountains, and that only when they reached one of their lurking places, the robbers removed the bandage from his eyes. The name of the bandit whose story I have related—I believe I have it right—was Manuel Diaz; the family name Diaz is very common in Spain, and figures in the history of the wars with the Moors. When I heard these accounts of the Andalusian bandit, I could not help thinking of what I had heard and seen in the East, nearly five years ago—of the dreaded robber of Lebanon, who infested the neighborhood of Beyrout, and was brought into the city a prisoner, while I was there; and of the fear which the inhabitants of Smyrna had of the outlaws in its environs, who held the city in a state of siege on the land side, so that no man of substance could venture to occupy his country place in one of the villages pleasantly seated on the declivities of the mountains.[4]

At Malaga they make with great cleverness little images of baked earth, representing the different costumes seen in the south of Spain. The artist who at present enjoys the greatest reputation is José Cubero,[5] though I believe he has his rivals. In his collection you see the *majo* and the *maja*, the Andalusian dandy and his mate; gipsey men and women; peasants of both sexes, on foot or on donkeys; young people dancing in holiday dresses, hidalgos on horseback wrapped in their ample cloaks; priests in their enormous hats; bandits of the mountains; soldiers; members of the civil guard, with their carbines, and I know not how many more. After the figures have been subjected to a strong heat, they come out of the oven with a clean, sharp outline and of a soft cream color; a workman then takes them, and with a pencil paints the hair, tints the eyes and face, stains the gaiters, tracing them with embroidery, and gives every part of the dress its proper hue. The spirit with which these little figures and groups are designed, and the skill and ingenuity with which they are executed, show a capacity for the plastic art which only needs due encouragement to raise it to something more noble.

MANUSCRIPT: Unrecovered TEXT: *LT* II, pp. 192–200; first published in *EP* for February 20, 1858.

1. Not further identified.
2. Jonathan I. Coddington was a New York lawyer with an office at 17 Wall Street. Thomas W. Clerke was a justice of the New York Supreme Court, with chambers in New City Hall. *Trow's New York City Directory*, pp. 166, 163.
3. John Somers Smith of New York was the United States consul at Málaga from 1850 to 1854, and from 1855 to 1861. He had previously served in a similar office at Cadiz. *U. S. Consular Officers, 1789–1939*.
4. See Letter 829.
5. Not further identified.

1002. *To* the EVENING POST

Oran, Algeria, December 17, 1857.

While at Malaga we went to pass a few days among the remains of Moorish splendor in the city of Grenada. A diligence goes out from Malaga on its way to that place at nine o'clock every night, in which we took places, accompanied by two persons of the family of the American consul, to whom we were indebted for much of the pleasure and interest of the journey. I have already said that the Spaniards like to begin their journeys in the night. A diligence was not long since established which set out for Grenada in the morning, but this departure from old usages met with little favor, and was soon given up.

I shall long remember the journey of that night. It was a soft mild evening, and the moon flooded the whole region with brightness. Our vehicle climbed the mountains north of Malaga, steep beyond steep, while the lights of the city and its harbor were seen for a long time gleaming up from the edge of the ocean far below us. Half way up we passed the Queen's Fountain, *Fuente de la Reyna,* where Isabella the Catholic is said, in one of her triumphant passages through the south of Spain, to have stopped and quenched her thirst. It pours out its waters into a marble basin, murmuring now in the silence of night as it murmured four hundred years ago. Along the road grew a row of evergreen oaks, flinging their dark shadows into the path; below us lay ravines and gulfs, which deepened into indistinguishable darkness; around us stood bold headlands in the white moonlight; a solitary region, tilled but not inhabited; a vast tract covered with vines; vineyard beyond vineyard farther than the sight can reach, where a fierce sunshine beating upon the red soil exalts the juices of the fruit, and whence the vaults of a thousand wine merchants have been filled for century after century.

The village of Colmenar came in sight. "Here," said one of our companions, "live the smugglers of the coast, and here the robbers I told you of have their confederates, and are sometimes harbored." The diligence now descended into a valley, the moonlight faded in thickening clouds, and a little before sunrise we stopped at the town of Loja for our morning cup of chocolate. Loja is known as the birthplace of Narvaez, the late prime minister of Spain, who has acquired an infamous notoriety as author of the law against the liberty of the press. In leaving the place, a turn in the road gave us an opportunity of observing its beautiful situation, on the side of a hill covered with olive groves and other fruit trees, and sloping down to rich meadows, through which wound a stream, the Genil of Grenada, bordered with an ample fringe of unpruned forest trees, nearly all in leaf, though it was now the fourth of December. We had so long been accustomed to seeing forest trees lopped and trimmed, that we gazed with delight on these unmutilated groves, sending forth their boughs in

their native freedom, and wondered at their beauty. Out of this valley we passed into a dreary region of pasturage, where shepherds were tending their flocks of long-woolled sheep, mostly black, and then we descended upon the Vega of Grenada, a vast and rich plain studded with villages. At Santa Fé, where we stopped to change our horses, several miles south of Grenada, a mob of boys came about us, some of them quite comfortably clad, who clamored for alms, and several of whom, keeping pace with our vehicle, ran beside it for more than half the way to Grenada.

At length Grenada lay before our eyes, on a hill-side, with her ancient towers rising over her roofs and her woods, and towering far above all gleamed the snowy summits of the Sierra Nevada, in which her rivers have their source. We drove into the city through a wretched suburb, and were instantly surrounded by a mob of young beggars, who trotted and shouted beside the diligence, while the people gazed and grinned at us from the doors and windows. Every city in Spain has its particular custom-house, and our baggage had, of course, to undergo an inspection, after which we had it sent to the *Fonda de Minerva*, on the Darro, a tolerable hotel, but miserably sunless and chilly at this season of the year. After having dined in an uncomfortably airy saloon, we went out into the pleasant evening sunshine and walked upon the Alameda, planted with majestic elms that overhang a broad space with their long spreading branches, and form one of the finest public walks in all Spain. The extent and beauty of its public walks is one of the most remarkable characteristics of Grenada. They surround the hill on which stands the Alhambra, and intersect its thick woods; they accompany the Genil a considerable way on its course; they follow the stream of the Darro; they border the town at its different extremities and issues.

I am not about to describe Grenada. After what Irving has written of it,[1] I should as soon think of attempting a poem on the wrath of Achilles in competition with Homer. Let me say of it, however, that its site is as beautiful and striking as its antiquities. There is but one Alhambra; there is but one Grenada. Could it have been the taste of the Moorish sovereigns; could it have been their sense of the beauty of nature, which led them to fix their residence in a spot presenting such glorious combinations of mountain and valley, forest and stream; a spot where you hear on all sides the sound of falling waters and the murmur of rivers; where the hill-sides and water-courses clothe themselves with dense woods; where majestic mountains stand in sight, capped with snow; while at their foot, stretching away from the town, lies one of the fairest and most fertile valleys that the sun ever shone upon? However this may be, the place was the fitting seat of a great and splendid dominion.

If in any respect the Alhambra did not correspond with the idea I had previously formed of it, it was in the minuteness of its ornamentation. I did not expect that the figures into which the surface of its walls is

wrought, and which yet, in most places, preserve the sharp outline of a stereotype plate, would prove to be no larger than some engravings in which they are represented. Yet this very minuteness, I must admit, harmonizes perfectly with the general character of the architecture, which is that of the utmost lightness and delicacy possible in buildings of stone. The architecture of the Alhambra is that of the harem; it is the architecture of a race who delighted in voluptuous ease, who wrapped themselves in soft apparel, and lolled upon divans. The Alhambra was the summer palace of the Moorish monarchs—a place of luxurious retreat from the relaxing heats of the season—a place of shade and running waters, courting the entrance of the winds under its arches and between its slender pillars, yet spreading a screen against the sunshine. To this end the stones of the quarry were shaped into a bower, with columns as light as the stems of the orange trees planted in its courts, and walls incrusted with scroll-work and foliage as delicate as the leaves of the myrtle growing by its fountains. Yet, the most remarkable parts of the Alhambra are those lofty rooms with circular vaults from which hang innumerable little points like icicles, with rounded recesses between them. These are as strangely beautiful as a dream, and translate into a visible reality the poetic idea of a sparry cavern formed by genii in the chambers of the rock.

I was glad to see workmen employed in restoring the defaced parts of this palace. The work goes on sluggishly, it is true, but it is a comfort to perceive that the ingenuity of man renews faster than time destroys. I was still more pleased to learn that the clumsy additions with which the Spanish monarchs disfigured the beautiful work of the Moors are to be taken down. On the original flat roofs they built another story, on the sides of which they ostentatiously displayed the arms of Castile, by way of publishing their own bad taste, and this superstructure they covered with a pointed roof of heavy tiles.

"All that," said the keeper of the place, when I expressed my disgust at its deformity, "is to come down; every thing that you see above the Moorish cornice; and the building is to be left as it was at first."

Besides miserably spoiling the general effect, these roofs load the columns below with too great a weight. An earthquake which happened two or three years since made them reel under their burden; it moved several of them from their upright position, and rendered it necessary to prop others with a framework of wooden posts and braces. When the barbarian additions made by the Spaniards shall be removed, it will be easy, I suppose, to restore the columns to their upright state, and the wooden supports will become unnecessary. At some future time we may hope that the visitor will see this palace, if not in its original splendor, yet cleared at least of what now prevents him from perceiving much of its original beauty and grace.

I was told that visitors are no longer allowed admission to the garden

under the walls of the citadel, called the Garden of the Moorish Kings; but a letter to the Governor of the Alhambra, with which I had been furnished at Madrid, opened it to our party. Here an enormous vine, said to be of the time of the Moors, twists its half-decayed trunk around a stone pillar. It looks old enough, certainly, to have yielded its clusters to Arab hands, and perhaps will yet yield them to their descendants, when, in the next century, the Arab race, imbued with the civilization of Western Europe, and becoming fond of travel and curious in matters of antiquity, shall visit hospitable Spain to contemplate the vestiges of power and splendor left in that land by their fathers. Two lofty cypresses, planted by the Moors on this part of the hill of the Alhambra, yet stand in their full vigor and freshness—a sight scarcely less interesting than the Alhambra itself. These trees have survived wars and sieges, droughts and earthquakes, and flourish in perpetual greenness, while generations, and dynasties, and empires have passed away, and while even the massive fortresses built by those who planted them are beginning to crumble. Thus they may outlast not only empires, but the monuments of empires.

A general letter of introduction from Archbishop Hughes, of New York,[2] obtained for us access to the relics of Ferdinand and Isabella, in the Royal Chapel of the Cathedral, and to the vaults below, in which their remains are laid. The mausoleum of these sovereigns before the altar is one of the most superb things of its kind in the world; their colossal effigies lie crowned and sceptred in their robes of state, and on the sides of their marble couch is sculptured the story of their conquests. I was amused by an odd fancy of one of our companions: "Do you perceive," said he, "that the head of Ferdinand makes scarcely any impression on his pillow, while the head of Isabella sinks deep into hers? The artist no doubt intended to signify that the Queen's head was much better furnished than that of her consort."

An ecclesiastic sent to accompany us, by the Archbishop of Grenada, called to an attendant, who brought a light, and removing a carpet on the floor between the mausoleum and the altar, pulled up a trap-door, below which, leading down to a vault, was a flight of steps. We descended, and here we were introduced to the coffins of Ferdinand and Isabella, immediately under the monument which we had just been admiring. They are large, shapeless leaden boxes, in which the bodies of the royal pair were enclosed at their death, and deposited near to the spot where the priests chant their litanies and offer the sacrifice. The contrast between the outside of this sepulchre and what we now saw, was striking; above, in the beautiful chapel, every thing was pompous and splendid, but here lay the dead within a bare dungeon of hewn stone, in dust, darkness and silence. When we again ascended to the chapel, the ecclesiastic caused the crown and sceptre of Isabella, and the sword of Ferdinand, to be brought forth and shown us, along with one or two other relics, among which was a

dalmatico, or ecclesiastical mantle, heavily embroidered with thread of gold by the pious hands of Isabella, to be worn by the priests in the ceremonies of the church. The crown, I must say, appeared to me to be rather a rude bauble of its kind, but it had been worn by a great sovereign.

We could not help regretting, every moment of our stay at Grenada, that we had not visited it earlier in the season; for now the air, after the first day, was keen and sharp, and the braziers brought into our room were quite insufficient to remove the perpetual comfortless feeling of chilliness. Still more fortunate should we have been if we could have visited Grenada in the spring. That is the time to see Grenada, and not to see it merely, but to enjoy it with the other senses—to inhale the fragrance of its blossomed orange trees, and of other flowers just opened; to hear the music of the nightingales, with which its woods are populous; to listen at open windows to the murmur of its mountains and streams, and to feel the soft winds that blow over its luxuriant Vega, and all this in the midst of scenes associated with a thousand romantic memories.

As a town, Grenada forms a perfect contrast with the beauty that surrounds it; it is ugly; the houses for the most part mean, and the streets narrow, winding, and gloomy, in some places without a pavement, and generally, owing to certain habits of the people, nasty. There is a group of beggars for every sunny corner, at this season, and I suppose for every shady one in summer. The people of the place are said to have the general character of the Andalusians; that is to say, to be fond of pleasure, mirth, and holidays, and averse to labor; improvident, lively, eloquent, given to exaggeration, and acutely sensible to external impressions. Every afternoon during our stay, a swarm of well-dressed people gathered upon the public walk on the other side of the Darro, before our windows, where we saw them slowly pacing the ground, and then turning to pace it over again. A few seated themselves occasionally on the stone benches, in spite of the keen air, which they bore bravely. I had a letter to a gentleman, a native of Grenada, an intelligent man, who, under one of the previous administrations, had held a judicial post in Valencia.[3] At his first visit, I spoke of calling to pay my respects to him at his house. "Why give yourself that trouble?" he asked; "I will come to see you every evening." And come he did, with the most exact punctuality, and informed me of many things which I desired to know, and manifested much more curiosity in regard to the institutions and condition of our country than is usual among Spaniards.

In looking across from the Alhambra to the Albaicin, which is the old Moorish part of the town, we saw the hill-side above the houses hollowed into caverns. "There live the gipseys," said our guide; "they burrow in the earth like rabbits, and live swinishly enough together; but in some respects they set a good example; the women are faithful to their marriage vow, and the gipsey race is kept unmingled." A practised eye easily dis-

cerns the gipsey, not merely by the darker complexion and by the silken hair of the women, but by the peculiar cast of countenance, which is more than I have been able to do. "There," said our guide one day, pointing to a man who stood by himself in the street, "there is the captain of the gipseys." For my part, I could not have distinguished him from the common race of Andalusians. He was a small, thin man, of sallow complexion, wearing the *majo* dress—a colored handkerchief tied round his head, and over that a black cap; a short, black jacket, an embroidered waistcoat, a bright crimson sash wrapped tightly round his waist, black knee-breeches, and embroidered leathern gaiters.

The women of Grenada appeared to me uncommonly handsome, and this beauty I often saw in persons of the humblest condition, employed in the rudest labors. The mixture of races has had a favorable effect in raising the standard of female beauty—casting the features in a more symmetrical mould, and giving them a more prepossessing expression. I had frequent occasion to make this remark since I left the province of New Castile. The physiognomy changes, as you pass to the softer climate of the country lying on the sea-coast, where the blending of the different branches of the Caucasian stock has been most miscellaneous and most complete.

On the eighth of December, at ten o'clock in the evening, we took passage in the diligence from Grenada to Malaga, and passing through the extensive olive groves of Loja, in the early dawn of the next morning, we came, about sunrise, to where the road winds with a steep ascent up among bare, bleak mountains. I got out to walk, and was joined by a passenger from another compartment of the diligence. He was a Castilian, who had lived thirty years in Grenada, engaged in trade, and, as I inferred, successfully. "Grenada," he said, "is declining, but it is the fault of the inhabitants. These Andalusians like only to be amused, and there is no contempt like the contempt they have for money. All that they earn they must get rid of; a workman who has a dollar in his pocket will do nothing till it is fooled away. It is therefore that the Grenadans are poor, and their city in decay."

"But what will you say of Malaga?" I asked. "Malaga, you must admit, is thriving."

"It is the Castilians," he replied, "who have made it the prosperous city it is. It was a poor place enough till the Castilian merchants saw the advantages of its situation and settled there." And then he went on to enumerate the eminent Castilian merchants who had built up, as he said, the prosperity of Malaga, until the diligence, overtaking us on a piece of level road, put an end to his eulogy of Castilian enterprise, by an intimation that it was time to take his seat within.

At Colmenar, where we stopped to breakfast, the beggars came about us in such numbers that we could with difficulty get in and out of the carriage, and were obliged to poke them out of our way. Here a passenger

joined us, who spoke of the distemper which of late years destroys the grape. This year, he said, the fruit had suffered more from the mildew than in any previous season; and if no remedy was found, the culture of the vine must be abandoned. I looked round on the almost boundless mountain side, planted with low vines almost trailing on the earth, and thought what a change would occur in the pursuits of the people when these should be uprooted. "That vineyard," pursued he, pointing to a field by the wayside, "is mine; in good years it has yielded twelve hundred arrobas of wine; last year I had but a hundred. It is true, I am in part compensated by the higher price; for the same quantity of must, that formerly brought me three reals, now brings me twenty-four. You see, however, that on the whole, I lose seriously."

We were now descending the mountains towards Malaga, and began to be sensible of its more genial climate. A bright sunshine lay on the red hills, and though the wind blew with great strength, there was in it no harshness or chilliness. We reached Malaga, submitted to an examination of the shirts, night-gowns and slippers we carried with us, and were allowed to take them to an hotel.

Our visit to Malaga was ended. Cadiz and Seville, and the rock of Gibraltar, we had not seen, as we had hoped to do, including a possible excursion to Cordova; but travelling in Spain, even by passing in steamers from port to port on the coast, is slow, and we found that if we proceeded further, it would take more time than we could spare from our intended visit to Italy. A steamer from Rouen, bound to Marseilles by way of Oran and Algiers, made its appearance at Malaga. After some comparison of the advantages of coming this way instead of proceeding to Marseilles by any of the lines which touch at Alicante, Valencia, and Barcelona, we decided in favor of the African route, and took passage in the steamer *Normandie*, which brought us hither.

MANUSCRIPT: Unrecovered TEXT: *LT* II, pp. 201–214; first published in *EP* for February 18, 1858.

1. Washington Irving, *A Chronicle of the Conquest of Granada* (1829); *The Alhambra* (1832).

2. Archbishop John Joseph Hughes of New York; see 213.16. The letter to which Bryant refers is unrecovered. It reached Bryant at Madrid, enclosed in a letter from Isaac Henderson, on November 5. Bryant, "Diary, 1857–1858," November 5, 1857.

3. This was Don Juan de Dios Rodríguez de Escalera, a lawyer, to whom Bryant had been given a letter of introduction by General Serravia y Nuñez in Madrid. *Ibid.*, December 5, 1857.

1003. *To* the EVENING POST

Algiers, December 20, 1857.

It was a beautiful evening when we went on board of the steamer Normandie, anchored in the port of Malaga; the sea as smooth as a mirror,

and the sky in the west flushed with an amber light, which gave its own tinge to every object lying below it. It was not without regret that we found ourselves about to leave the agreeable climate of Malaga, without the hope of finding any thing like it in the countries to which we were going. "This is our winter weather," the residents of the place would say to us, when we spoke of the serenity and genial softness of the season. In fact, winter in Malaga has nothing of that dreary dampness or of those keen winds which make so many days unpleasant in other parts of the south of Europe. From the bleak north wind it is shielded by mountains; and it welcomes rather than dreads the sirocco or south wind. In Africa the hot and dry breath of the sirocco parches the soil and withers its vegetation; in passing over to Italy it loads itself with all the vapors of the Mediterranean; it drenches Naples with rain and involves Leghorn in clouds; but on Malaga it blows genially, bringing in gentle showers. There is just enough of sea between the Spanish coast and Africa to take off its fatal dryness, and to make it a temperate sea wind, instead of the burning wind of the desert. "In fact, we have hardly cold enough in winter," said a gentleman who had lived at Malaga for several years, "to brace us for the heats of summer; and one of the maladies of the country, occasioned by this softness of the climate, is an enlargement of the blood-vessels of the skin—the appearance of varicose veins on the limbs, which often make it necessary to wear an elastic bandage or stocking." I have no doubt, for my part, that the winter climate in Malaga is one of the most equable in every respect, and most friendly to the health of invalids, in the world.

It was five o'clock in the afternoon when we went on board of the steamer Normandie, which had the reputation of being an excellent seaboat, commanded by an obliging and experienced captain; but it was not till a little past nine that we raised anchor and ploughed our way out of the port. At eleven o'clock the sky was bright with stars, and the ocean sleeping in a perfect calm, and I had betaken myself to my berth for the night, when a shock was felt which jarred the vessel from stem to stern, followed by a hurried trampling of feet on the deck above me, a stormy rattling of ropes, and loud shouts. Of course everybody was immediately on deck, and it was found that by some gross stupidity, on one side or the other, we had struck a steamer coming into port, amidships, opening a breach in her side which let in the sea, and caused her to settle fearfully in the water. The first inquiry was, whether we were going down; the next, what had become of the steamer we had struck. The Normandie had sustained no serious injury, and boats were instantly lowered to go to the help of the other steamer; but after the search of an hour or two they returned, not having been able to find her. A violent east wind arose soon after midnight, which tumbled us about most uncomfortably; and the Normandie was kept passing backwards and forwards near the spot where the collision took place, until day broke, when we stood for the port. As

we entered, there lay the vessel we had struck, aground, with her prow in the air and her stern in the water. Immediately after the accident, her commander caused the pumps to be worked by the engine, in order to keep her afloat, and made all speed for the port, where he ran her ashore. Lighters were now at work taking out her cargo. She proved to be a Dutch steamer, bound from Marseilles to Rotterdam.

This accident obliged us to remain two days longer at Malaga, which we only regretted as it was so much to be deducted from our contemplated visit to Italy; but these days were to be passed in a finer climate than Italy can boast. On the evening of the 15th of December we were again summoned on board, but we did not go out of the harbor till the next morning. While we were waiting our departure, I happened to stand near a slatternly woman, who had established herself with a brood of children on a part of the deck among carpets and shawls somewhat after the Oriental fashion. She asked me in Spanish if I was going to Oran. "I am." "Are you a Christian?" The question surprised me a little, but I answered, "Certainly; what are you?" "I am an Israelite." "Born in Oran?" I inquired. "No, I was born in Tangier." "And do the Jews in Tangier and Oran speak Spanish?" "Certainly; they all speak Spanish."

What she said of Tangier and Oran is true of the Jews of all the coast of Northern Africa. When the Hebrew race were so cruelly expelled from Spain,[1] they carried with them, wherever they went in considerable numbers, the language of that country, as spoken and written in their day, and they preserve it yet as their household speech. The Jews of Morocco read the Hebrew scriptures in old Spanish; and I remember to have seen a copy of a folio edition of this translation, printed in Amsterdam for their use. The Jews in Cairo speak Spanish; in the Jews' quarter at Smyrna you will hear the children prattling Spanish; the Jews in Constantinople speak the same language, and an intelligent Greek once told me that Spanish is the language of the Jews of Thessalonica, in Macedonia—so widely did the exile and dispersion of the Spanish Jews diffuse the language of Castile.

As we stood out from Malaga to the southeast, the mountainous coast of Spain, which we were leaving, seemed to rise higher the farther we receded from it. The bare, steep ridges, cloven with hollows deepening from the summit downward, seemed to bathe their feet in the sea, and lost not their dark red hue in the distance. At their base along the shore was seen here and there a town or village, but the buildings on their sides were few, and, I was told, were only those containing the wine presses, to which the grapes are brought in the time of the vintage. We could now understand how, in that extensive region of ravines and precipices, far from the habitations of men, robbers could lurk and elude pursuit.

Next morning we found ourselves gliding along on a smooth sea, opposite to the African coast; a coast of dark mountain ranges, projecting in capes; the shores of Algeria stretching along our right, and behind us. To

the west, rose dimly the heights of Fez. We were now in waters still haunted by pirates. It is generally imagined, I believe, that, since the conquest of Algiers, the inhabitants of the Barbary coast have ceased to plunder the commerce which passes through the Straits of Gibraltar; but this is a mistake. All along that part of the Mediterranean, where the coast recedes between Ceuta on the west and the Habibas Islands to the east, they levy their old tribute on the vessels of Christendom, though in a somewhat different manner. They have their lurking-places among the tall reeds of the shore; and when they descry a vessel becalmed, they put forth in their boats, armed to the teeth, and climbing on board, take what they find worth carrying away. They are a little careful of shedding blood, except in cases of resistance; and carry off no prisoners, contenting themselves with simple pillage. Some attempts, I was told at Malaga, have been made to pursue and punish them, but without success. Their boats were not to be found; it is supposed they had contrived to hide them in the sand, and the sea-robbers who navigated them were safe in their mountains and deserts.

I asked the commander of the Normandie if these robberies were frequent.

"Most certainly," he replied. "In calm weather these waters are unsafe for merchant vessels. It was only about eight months ago that a Bavarian prince, who was in his yacht, amusing himself in this part of the Mediterranean, was robbed by them. You must have seen the account in the newspapers. He did not yield with a good grace, and there was a little encounter, in which he was wounded by a ball in the arm."

We approached the Habibas Islands—dark rocks, rising out of the water, between us and the shore—we passed them, and steered south for the bay of Oran. As we drew near the coast, we were struck with the contrast it presented to the bare, herbless region we left the day before. Its rocky steeps were tinged and brightened with patches and stripes of verdure. About twelve o'clock we reached a landing in the bay at the distance of some five miles from the town of Oran, called by the Spaniards Marsal-quivir—but the French write it, probably with more attention to its Arabic etymology, Merz el-Kebir. Here, on a precipice that rises over the landing, stands a fortress; and at its foot, a French settlement extends for some distance along the road to Oran. A mingled crowd of Franks and Orientals stood on the wharves, and among the latter I observed two or three whose flowing garments of white and blue illustrated, very strikingly, the superior grace and dignity of the Oriental costume.

The moment we dropped anchor, our steamer was surrounded with boats manned by Arabs and Spaniards, who came to take us to land. A dozen Arabs sprang instantly on board, barelegged and barefooted, with smooth-shaven heads and little close red caps, leaping like so many African monkeys over the boxes and barrels on deck, accosting the passengers one

after another in a sort of Arab-French, and seizing on the baggage of those who were about to go on shore. We made choice of a Spanish boatman, as one with whom it was most easy to communicate—a man of enormous breadth of back and shoulders, who took us in his boat to the shore. With him was one of his countrymen, a lively chattering fellow, who was a candidate for the job of taking us in his carriage to the town. I inquired of him how long he had been in Oran. "Eight years," he answered; "I emigrated in the time of the great drought." I had heard of this drought in Alicante; in a considerable part of that province and the adjacent region, there was no rain, they told me, for nine years. "The country," they said, "became almost a desert; the vegetation was utterly dried up; the inhabitants abandoned it; thousands of them went to Oran, on the African coast; and if you were now to go to Oran you might fancy yourself in a province of Spain." Here then, we were at Oran, and found this description true— the common people speaking a less provincial and more intelligible Spanish than those in the country we had just left. I inquired what was the number of Spanish emigrants in the department of Oran. "There are twenty-eight thousand of them," I was answered, "mostly settled on the coast; the number of French is at most fourteen thousand."

We had with us, on landing, a few things which we brought on shore with the design of passing a night or two at Oran; these were carried into the Custom-house, where they were rigorously searched by a stupid fellow in uniform, who would scarcely be satisfied without unfolding every pocket-handkerchief, and turning every stocking inside-out. At length, it fully appearing that we were no smugglers, we were allowed to proceed. The road leading to Oran from the landing is a broad, hard, winding, parapeted highway, cut in the living rock which skirts the sea. One of the first cares of the French government has been to make macadamized roads along the coast, and from village to village, in a region where there had been no roads since the time of the Romans. We passed through the French neighborhood, where women were screeching at their children in the shrillest French, and military veterans in white mustaches were sitting before the doors. Half a mile beyond, we left, on our right, in a little recess of the mountains, the populous village of St. André, entirely peopled by Spanish emigrants. "That village," said our loquacious driver, "is only six years old." I was struck with the verdurous appearance of the shore along which we were passing. The crags that overhung the road sprouted with many different shrubs and herbs of the freshest green; here were beds of blue violets, patches of young grass, white tufts of the sweet alyssum in the clefts of the rocks, and the face of the perpendicular precipices was often draped with pendant strings of a prostrate plant, having thick fleshy leaves, like the air-plant; a sight refreshing to eyes wearied with the glimmer of the sea.

We turned a projecting rock, and found ourselves at Oran, a city of

forty thousand inhabitants, partly lying on the strand and rising up from the water through a ravine to the sides of the hills where stand its forts, old and new. Two lofty minarets overlook its dwellings, with the humbler towers of its two or three churches, and two broad, white, macadamized roads lead from the lower to the upper town. I shall long remember the sights that met our eyes on entering Oran; Arabs in their loose attire of dirty white, sitting in the sun, or walking by loaded donkeys; Zouaves strolling about in their Oriental garb of red and white turbans; soldiers in the ordinary French uniform, marching in companies; Jews in black caps or turbans, and black tunics, talking with Franks, and probably driving bargains; Spaniards in their ample cloaks, with one corner drawn over the mouth, to keep out their great dread, the *pulmonia*, masons and carpenters at work on buildings by the way-side; Franciscan monks in brown gowns; Dominican monks in white; Catholic priests in broad-brimmed Quaker hats, with long beards—for though they must be clean-shaved in Europe, they have permission to wear their beards in Algeria; French ladies in bonnets; French servant women in caps; Arab women toddling about, wrapped in white woollen from head to foot, with but one eye uncovered; other Arab women in calico gowns and coarse crimson shawls on their heads, drawn over the lower part of the face; horsemen reining spirited steeds of Barbary—sometimes a French officer, sometimes a brown Arab, the better rider of the two, and proud of his horsemanship; camels with their drivers resting at an angle of the way; little drays drawn by a single horse or mule, briskly trotting along with an Arab driver; files of mules dragging loaded wagons, and tinkling their little bells, and rattling Droshkas rapidly driven past all these, on their way to the landing or some neighboring villages. Through this miscellaneous crowd we made our way up the hill, and alighted at the *Hotel de France*, where we found rooms looking upon a great public square, in which figures like those we had just seen were constantly passing to and fro, as in a phantasmagoria.

This letter is already so long, that it will not be possible for me to include in it all I have to say of my visit to Algeria; I therefore stop here for the present. Several of my letters from America congratulate me on having wandered beyond the limits of the commercial panic, which has so convulsed our own country. This may be true of Algeria, in which I now write, but it was not quite true of Spain. I had occasion, while at Malaga, to negotiate a draft on my banker at Paris; and being told that there would be no difficulty in doing it, I deferred taking any step in the matter till my return from Grenada. But the panic made its appearance in Malaga during my absence, like the sudden breaking-out of an epidemic. News of the great failures in Hamburg had been received, and several houses which were powerful and prosperous on Monday evening were bankrupt on Tuesday morning. Money seemed to have disappeared in the course of a night; to hear people talk, one would have supposed that

there were not five hundred dollars in all Malaga. So I reduced my draft to half the sum I thought of at first, and even this amount would not have been obtained but for the special good offices of the Consul. I am happy to learn that in America, the cloud is passing over, and that, one by one, the broken links of commercial intercourse are rejoined.

MANUSCRIPT: Unrecovered TEXT: *LT* II, pp. 215–225; first published in *EP* for February 26, 1858.

1. In 1492.

1004. *To* the EVENING POST

Steamer Normandie, Off Majorca.⎫
Malaga, December 22d, 1857.⎭

The city of Oran was held for three centuries by Spain. In 1791 a terrible earthquake shook down a part of the town, and soon afterwards the Spaniards, thinking it not worth while to defend the remainder against the Algerines, who harassed them with continual hostilities, finally abandoned it. I was not surprised, therefore, to find in parts of the town a strong resemblance to those I had lately visited in Spain. Before our hotel, on the other side of the square, was a street of shops, and through this we walked. At its entrance sat half a dozen native vendors of small wares, with their legs tucked under them, on little platforms, in the open air. Of the shops, some were mere niches in the walls, where sat the Oriental traders among their goods; others occupied by the Franks were but little larger, and reminded me of the shops of Grenada and Malaga.

Taking another direction, we entered a street leading to the lower part of the city, and passed through a Moorish portal, rough with arabesque ornaments, into the court of the principal mosque of Oran. Here we found several workmen occupied in making repairs, for the French government charges itself with the support of the Mohammedan worship in Algeria, as it does with that of the Christian and the Jewish worship in France. It repairs and rebuilds the mosques, gives salaries to the Imaums, and makes the Muezzins its dependants and stipendiaries. "You may enter freely," said the workmen, "but if you step on the mats you must first take off your shoes." We entered, and found ourselves in a forest of square and round pillars, supporting Moorish arches and the domes above them, the square pillars standing in a circle under the central dome. The arches were quaintly and superlatively Moorish, the two ends of the horse-shoe approaching very near each other, but in other respects the architecture was exceedingly plain; the capitals were of the rudest workmanship, and the whole interior as white as simple whitewash could make it. "This is a very copy of the great Cathedral of Cordova, which was formerly a mosque," said one who attended us; "in all but the ornamentation and

the dimensions, the two buildings are precisely alike." We walked about on the stucco floor, among the numerous pillars, taking care not to pollute with our shoes the mats with which nearly half the floor was covered. In the eastern part of the building were two worshippers on their knees, with beads in their hands, one of whom took no notice of us, but continued to murmur his orisons and to strike his forehead against the floor, but the other fixed a steady gaze upon us till we withdrew.

From one of the city gates several parallel foot-paths over the green led to an Arab village, which we visited, passing by the Civil Hospital on the right, a modern structure in the Moorish style, and an old fortress on the left, now used as a prison. On each side of the way the grass was long enough to wave in a gentle wind. The village is a collection of low flat-roofed houses, whitewashed, with a broad street running north and south through the middle, and narrow lanes diverging to the right and left among the houses. As we were approaching it, an Arab overtook us, a thin-bearded little man, with a face slightly tattooed in two or three places, and wearing a blue outer garment. He greeted us with *bon jour*, and added, *"vous bromenie?"* I shook my head as not comprehending his question, and he, after repeating it two or three times, substituted the word *basear*. I then perceived that he was explaining the French word *promener* by the Spanish *pasear*, for the Arabs of these parts confound the *p* with the *b*. "Certainly," said I, "we are walking out." "Will you walk to my house?" he asked. I declined, but he immediately repeated the question to one of the ladies, who, not aware of my refusal, accepted the invitation, and on we went under his guidance, until we entered an enclosure surrounded by a wall freshly whitewashed, in one corner of which stood his house, of the same bright color with the wall. Within it, and facing the open door, was a glittering display of small dishes and plates of blue and white porcelain on several rows of shelves; a pallid woman, apparently ill, lay on a mat at one end of the room, and at the other there sat on the floor, with a bright-eyed little girl beside her, a young woman of rather pleasing aspect, extremely fat, with well-formed lips and chin, and large black eyes, wearing a gay-colored handkerchief tied round her head, and another tied under her chin, and a loose blue muslin robe, from under the skirt of which appeared one of her naked feet. On each cheek was a little blue mark, and her jetty eyebrows were joined by a streak of black paint. In her little plump hands, tattooed and stained with henna, she held a bellows, with which she was coaxing a flame in a little furnace filled with charcoal, on which stood a small dish of potatoes. Our host, whose name, as he afterwards told me, was Gannah, found a bench for the ladies and a chair for me, seating himself on the floor; and at a word from him, the little girl took the potatoes from the fire, and put in their place an open tin coffee-pot, full of powdered coffee and water, and the plump round hands of the fat lady again plied the bellows to raise a flame. "You must drink

coffee with me," said Gannah. We sought to decline his hospitality, but Gannah was resolute, and a contest arose, to which I was fortunately enabled to put an end by pointing to the clouds, apparently big with rain, and making the approach of a shower a reason for our hasty departure. While we were excusing ourselves from the importunities of our host, a negro woman in a loose white dress, with bare arms and uncovered legs, as fleshless and almost as slender as the crooked black staff on which she leaned, a bracelet of beads on her bony wrists, a long string of brown beads hanging from each ear, and another round her neck, presented herself at the door, looking in with an aspect of curiosity and a good-natured smile; but a word from Gannah sent her away. Two lively-looking little girls entered and squatted down by the fat lady, but Gannah growled at them till they took their leave also. The young woman, in the mean time, had reached out her plump hands, and taking hold of the dresses of the ladies, one after another, examined them attentively, making some brief remark to Gannah at the close of each inspection. As I rose to take my leave, I put my right hand into my waistcoat pocket, and immediately her open palm was held out to me; I placed a piece of money into it, over which the plump fingers closed eagerly. "It is not well," said Gannah; "it is not well;" but I could perceive he was not displeased.

We returned to the hotel, and amused ourselves with watching the motley crowd constantly moving in the large square under our windows. Among those who contributed most to our entertainment was a group of native youths, from fifteen years old upwards, dressed in the scantiest attire, a red cap and a white woollen shirt, some of them belonging to the pure negro race, and the rest of different degrees of Arab intermixture, who chattered, laughed, shouted, sang, capered, chased each other about the square, and teased each other in a hundred different ways, as long as the sunshine, which had now returned, lasted, and through the brilliant twilight that followed.

The next morning I wandered into a village lying east of the city gates, and inhabited principally by emigrants from Spain, but the signs over the shop windows were all in the French language, which seemed to imply that the gift of reading and writing was possessed in a much greater degree by the French population than by the Spanish. I followed the highway onwards to a gentle eminence, where stood half a dozen windmills, greeting those whom I met in Spanish, and receiving an answer in the same language. From the summit I had a view of the broad plain extending southward to the mountains, a fertile region, where great tracts of springing wheat were separated by intervals of luxuriant grass, which a few cattle were eagerly cropping. A cross-road brought me to the Arab village which I had visited the day before. As I entered it, two youths passed me dressed in the Oriental garb; they were talking to each other in Spanish. Here and there stood a gray-bearded Arab, motionless, in his

white head-gear and white underdress, with a dark-colored outer garment reaching nearly to the feet—thin, spare men, to whom their costume gave a certain air of majesty. Children were playing about, laughing, shouting, and crying, just as children laugh, shout, and cry in the most civilized countries. Women, looking like bolsters placed on end and endowed with locomotion, were stealing along the streets from house to house.

Returning to town from the village, I was surprised by the salutation of *bon jour* from somebody at my elbow, and turning, saw my Arab acquaintance of the day before. "I was going to your hotel to see you," said Gannah. "Come then," I answered, and we proceeded to the hotel together. As soon as he was fairly seated, he drew from under his cloak a fowl, freshly killed, with the feathers on, and placed it on the table. "What have you there, my friend?" I asked. "I have brought you a fowl," answered Gannah, "you will buy it to eat." I explained to him that this would be extremely inconvenient; that we were supplied with every thing at the hotel, and on board of our steamer; that we could not cook his fowl if we had it; and that he would do well to dispose of it in the market. To each branch of my explanation, Gannah returned a resolute "No"; and sat waiting the time when I should enter into a negotiation for the fowl. I lost patience, and leaving the room, sent our courier to get rid of him. Our landlady afterwards told me that this man was very fond of making the acquaintance of strangers arriving at Oran, and was sometimes rather troublesome with his attentions.

In walking that morning about the town, we came to a minaret, and asked to see the mosque. A tall Alsatian soldier presented himself with a bunch of keys, and we discovered that the mosque had been converted into quarters for the troops. He, however, took us to the top of the minaret, commanding a view of the city and its neighborhood. The hills around us were covered with the strongholds of war, rising one over another. I pointed to an old castle, which had a ruinous look. "It is strong enough within," said he; "it is the prison for the natives." Another old fortress near us, he added, was the prison for the colonists. "There," he said, "is the new fort built by the French; yonder is a fortification erected by the Spaniards when they possessed Oran; on that hill-side is the storehouse for munitions; those white tents further up are occupied by the soldiery." I looked down into the streets where people were coming and going, and it seemed to me that at least every fifth man was a soldier. It is thus that the colony is held; the government requires soldiers to keep the colonists submissive, and the colonists require soldiers to overawe and restrain the natives. It is a military colony, subsisting by force and fear; and while my eyes rested on the spectacle before me, I could not help thinking how slow would be the growth of a settlement in our own country, which held its existence on such calamitous conditions.

The Alsatian told me, that in the Arab village which we had visited

the day before, only the poorer part of the native population lived; the more opulent have their dwellings within the gates of the town, and some of them, he added, are as rich as noblemen in France. I directed his attention to several dark mouths of caverns, and doors fitted into the rock, on the hill-side rising to the west of the town. "These," said he, "are underground habitations, where Spaniards live. Last year we had so much rain that the earth and stones over some of these caverns were loosened by the water, and came down upon the poor creatures, crushing them to death."

Another pleasant drive under the rocks, with the dashing sea on one side and the flowery cliffs on the other, brought us back to the fort and landing of Merz-el-Kébir, and at four o'clock in the afternoon we stood out of the bay of Oran, on our way to Algiers. We had a beautiful evening, with the African coast always in sight, and the morning found us gliding over a smooth sea, with the shore on our right rising into dark mountains. It was past noon when we turned to approach the land, and began to distinguish the white houses among the deep green of the shrubs and other vegetation which made the rocky declivities beautiful. "These are the country seats," said a passenger whom we took up at Oran, "not only of the French colonists, but of the rich Jews and of the Moors engaged in commerce. Some of the richest of the Mussulman inhabitants, however, went away when the French came in; went to Tunis, to Morocco, and to Alexandria, and other places where the Mussulmans are the masters."

Now came in sight the city of Algiers, rising from the water up the hill-side, a vast cone of flat-roofed houses, as white as snow, so compact as to look like a gigantic beehive, with not a streak, or patch, or shade of any other color between them; not a red roof nor a shrub to break the uniform whiteness. We passed the pleasant-looking village of St. Eugene, and coming before the town saw where the bay swept deeper inland to the southeast, bordered with a bright green shore and scattered country seats. On expressing my surprise at the number of these, a passenger answered that there was no occasion for surprise, for the police system was as perfect here as in France, and a country residence as safe.

An Arab boatman took us to the land with our baggage, at which the custom-house officers declined to look. We could not obtain rooms at the *Hotel de l'Orient*, where we meant to stop, but obtained them at the *Hotel de la Regence*, a house to which I cannot conscientiously advise others to go. Yet it is well situated on the Place Royale, a broad esplanade, built, it is said, over the cells in which the Christian slaves were formerly confined, and at all hours of the day thronged with men of the various races of the East and West, making it look like a perpetual masquerade. Before the door of our hotel a copious fountain threw up its waters with a perpetual dashing; four rows of orange-trees, protected by a massive iron chain, glittered with golden fruit, and I never looked out that I did not see Arabs or native Jews sitting on the stone benches under them.

The lower part of Algiers, near the water, is a mere French town; it has its broad streets for carriages, its shops with plate-glass doors, its cafés, its restaurants, its theatre, its library, its museum, its statues in the squares, its barracks, its guard-houses, its arcades on each side of the way, like those of the Rue Rivoli in Paris. All that was characteristic, or that recalled the memory of the Moslem dominion, has been demolished. The palace of the Deys, which looked upon the Place Royale, has been pulled down; the ancient cemetery which contained the mausoleum of the six Deys, all elected and murdered within twenty-four hours, has been ploughed up and levelled, to form a square for military exercises. I was soon satisfied with the view of this part of Algiers, and struck into the streets that ascend the hill, of which the town is principally composed. Here I found myself in an Oriental city at once, and soon met with nobody but Orientals. I walked in a sort of twilight, in narrow winding lanes, into which the sun never shone, where the wind never blew, and where the projecting walls of the houses often met overhead. No windows look from the dwellings into those shadowy lanes; nobody was standing at the quaint Moorish doors. Arab men, in their dresses of dull white, were creeping about; I did not hear their voices. I met little companies of native women, swaddled in white, from the crown of their head to where the pantaloons were gathered about the bare ankles, above the slippered feet; they passed me in silence; only the younger looked at me; I could see that they were younger by a glance; for age plants its marks as distinctly about the eyes as on any other part of the face. In a spot where the streets opened a little, I passed a row of Mussulmans sitting on the pavement, with their backs against the wall; they turned their great Oriental eyes upon me, and if I heard their voices at all, it was only a low, indistinct murmur. I could almost fancy myself in a city of the dead, walking among the spectres that haunted it. My own footsteps sounded disagreeably loud in this stillness, and it was a relief to hear the click of a donkey's small hoofs against the pavement, and the voice of his driver urging him along passages where no carriage can pass, and not even a hand-cart was ever trundled. It was a relief, also, to come, as I sometimes did, to a little row of shops where the Moorish traders sat among their goods. Occasionally I saw where houses had been thrown down by the earthquake which happened two years since, and where others had been shaken from their upright position and made to lean against each other. It was clear to me that if the shock had been a little more violent, those narrow streets would have offered the inhabitants no means of escape, and that they would have been hopelessly entombed in their dwellings.

It was some time before I could find my way out of this maze of twilight lanes into the broad streets along the shore, full of light and of activity, and when I did so, it was like a return from the abodes of death to the upper world.

The melancholy impression which this ramble in the streets of Algiers left upon me was not without good reason. "They are dying very fast on the hills, poor creatures," said a resident of Algiers to me the next morning; "their bodies are going to fill their cemeteries. Within two years past, we have had the cholera here, which swept them off by thousands; now they are perishing by famine, and the fevers of the country and other disorders occasioned by unwholesome nourishment. While Algiers was under the rule of the Deys, a native could subsist on a few sous a day, and this was a liberal allowance; now all the necessaries of life are dear, and they are starving; the trade with France has brought in French prices. While the prickly pear was in season, they lived upon that, the cheapest fruit of the country; what they live on now, I am sure I do not know. The French government has lately taken some measures for their relief."

That day closed as the most beautiful days of Italy close, with a glorious amber light at sunset, tinging the whole atmosphere, and streaming in everywhere at the windows, even those which looked north and east. We had dates that day for our dessert at the *Hotel de la Regence*, dates from the palms of the neighborhood, but they were not so fine as the dates of Elche, which we found at Alicante.

MANUSCRIPT: Unrecovered TEXT: *LT* II, pp. 226–238; first published in *EP* for March 5, 1858.

1005.   *To* George B. Cline[1]

Marseilles   Dec   28, 1857

Mr. Cline

I did not write my last letter[2] with so much reflection as I ought. You have not had the advantage from my place this year that you were entitled to expect. I wish therefore that you would take of the wheat which was harvested last summer as you want it enough to make four barrels of flour or thereabouts—which may perhaps last you till the next harvest—and also of the Indian corn enough for a barrel or two if you like it—and of the potatoes what you may want—and if there be any left over let Mrs. Godwin have them rather than sell them.

My wife desires me to say to Mrs. Cline, that she knows that her house is a large one and that it is a good deal of trouble to take care of it. She therefore does not wish her and your mother to do any thing more than to see that no mischief happens to it. She does not wish Mrs. Cline and your mother to spend their time in brushing away cobwebs, and wiping up every particle of dust or rubbing out of every speck of mould—with a general care which provides that nothing valuable shall take hurt we shall be satisfied. As for the old [gaiters?] of mine, they were good for nothing—except to be flung out of the window. My wife is very anxious lest Mrs. Cline and your mother should give themsel[ves] too much trou-

ble. Mrs. Godwin writes that every thing about it looks in the nicest order —and we are afraid that your wife gives too much of her time and care to it— Remember that we are reasonable people and would wish you to do no more than you would expect of us.

Should your mother go west this fall Mrs. Bryant desires that you would get her a good warm cloak or dress and a warm bonnet at my expense for the journey and give them to her from Mrs. Bryant. . . .[3]

[P. S.] We are sorry about the trouble with the [potash?] &c. &c.

MANUSCRIPT: NYPL–GR (draft) ENDORSED: My Letter to Mr. G. B. Cline.

1. George B. Cline (1823–1898) and his wife, Isabella C. Cline (1824–1908), occupied Cedarmere during the Bryants' travels abroad in 1857–1858. Thereafter, until Bryant's death, Cline was his estate superintendent and confidential steward, and later one of the executors of his will. Bigelow, *Bryant*, pp. 265–266, 347. See 952.2.

2. Unrecovered. Bryant's "Diary, 1857–1858" records that he had written Cline most recently on December 2, 1857.

3. John Bigelow seems to have had access to the final copies of this letter and a number of other, unrecovered letters from Bryant to Cline. See Bigelow, *Bryant*, pp. 266–273, *passim*.

1006.   *To* the EVENING POST

Marseilles, December 29, 1857.

The day after our arrival in Algiers was like one of the balmiest days of spring. We all went to see the great Mosque near the *Place Royale*. Before it, a portico of massive Saracenic columns encloses a court in which flows an abundant fountain for the ablutions of the worshippers. Within, the appearance is striking; the massive horseshoe arches, which are crossed by broad horizontal flutings, descend to low, heavy pillars, which have the effect of a grove of vast trunks, spreading upwards into lofty canopies. I cast my eyes beyond them, and there, looking no larger than insects beside these great columns, were half a dozen natives at their morning devotions. A strange-looking man, with an air of abstraction, was wandering about. "He is crazy," said a gentleman who had kindly conducted us to the mosque; "and being crazy, is regarded as a saint and called a marabout." Some of the columns of the mosque had been broken and a part of the wall damaged by the late earthquake, and workmen employed by the government were busy in repairing it.

On our return from this building, we peeped into the hall of an Arab tribunal, where the muftis and cadis still dispense justice. It was a room of very moderate dimensions, on the lower floor, and at that time open to the street, but the magistrates were not in session, though their cushions were ready to receive them. At a little distance from this is the New Mosque, remarkable only for being built in the form of a church, under the direction of a Christian slave, and for the fate of the architect, whose head was

struck off, by order of the Dey, for his audacity in making a temple of the faithful resemble the temples of the infidel.

We followed the main street northward till we issued from the city by the northern gate, the *Bab-el-Wad*, or River Gate; for here a ravine, called by the Arabs the river, descends to the sea, and overlooking it rise the northern walls and battlements of Algiers. From these battlements, they tell you, the Deys caused prisoners of state to be thrown alive, and their bodies being caught on the ends of iron spikes below, they were left to perish by slow tortures. Those who had the means bribed the executioner to strangle them before throwing them down. From the gate, a broad Macadamized road led us up to a public garden, laid out by the French, within which a winding walk, where a species of oxalis, new to me, made a beautiful deep green border, spotted with showy crimson flowers, separated beds filled with the fairest plants of the tropics. Among these was the India-rubber tree; and by the wayside were rows of young palms, of which those that were already ten or twelve years old had stems scarcely a foot in height, for the date-palm is of slow growth, and when it once germinates begins a life of many centuries.

In a nook of the garden stood a group of paper-mulberry trees, the leaves of which were withered and rolled up, as if scorched by fire or seared by frost. I inquired what might be the cause of this phenomenon. "It is the sirocco," answered the gentleman who was with us; "a sirocco which blew here three weeks since. No one, who has not felt the sirocco, can form any idea of its effects; it withers up vegetation in a few hours; it dries up the springs; it bakes the soil, and makes it open in long and deep clefts. Men and animals suffer as much as the plants and trees." The leaves of the paper-mulberry, which is a native of a moister climate, were, it seems, scorched beyond remedy by this wind of the desert, while the leaves of the native trees had recovered their freshness.

About this time the muezzin was proclaiming the noontide hour of prayer from the minaret of a mosque further up the hill, and towards this we proceeded, leaving the garden. We came first to a Moslem cemetery, and here we were in a sacred neighborhood; for here was not only a mosque, but two marabouts, or little Moslem chapels, each containing the remains of some holy man of the religion of Islam; and low arched passages led from one enclosure of the cemetery to another, and from mosque to marabout, and in these passages fountains were gushing for the ablutions of the faithful. Women in white, their faces covered with white veils, showing only the eyes, hovered about the graves, which looked quaintly, with their little borders of thin stone, set edgewise in the ground, and the Arabic inscriptions on the stones at the head. Wherever I turned my eyes, veiled women, dressed in white, were softly coming up the streets from below, or down the paths that led from the top of the hill. Women are the same tender, affectionate, religious creatures in Algiers as in more civilized

countries; they cherish as warmly the memory of the dead, and their hearts open as readily to the feeling of an intimate relation with an omnipresent and benevolent Power.

We entered the mosque, which contained nothing remarkable, and the marabouts, which did. In each of them was the sarcophagus of a saint, and one of them was furnished with two or three, covered with a silken cloth of a dark yellow color, heavy with gold embroidery, and hanging down like a pall. About them women were kneeling, most of them apparently absorbed in their silent devotions, occasionally kissing the drapery of the tomb, but not a word was uttered. The young girls gazed at us with their black, almond-shaped eyes, and one or two of the elder ones looked at us, I thought, as if they wondered what business we had there. The women in Mohammedan countries are excluded from the mosques, but there are other holy places open to them, and they throng to the burial-places and the marabouts. We saw only one or two men, who came in and soon went out again. In one of the marabouts, a man in a large turban, walking with a fantastic gait, approached the tomb of the saint, smiling a silly smile, pressed the embroidered cloth to his lips, and went out with the same smile on his face, touching me gently with his hand as he passed. "Poor fellow," said the gentleman who was with us, "he has lost his wits: his wife died, and he became crazy in consequence."

As we descended the hill, we passed several little companies of women, and some who sat by the wayside and asked alms. One of these was a little thin woman in a clean white dress, whose eyes, which were all of her face that could be seen, gave token of the middle age of life. She silently held out a small hand, with nails sharpened to a point like the nib of a pen, and the ends of the slender fingers were reddened with henna. I see that delicate, thin hand now as I write, and as I always see it when I recollect our walk of that day, and my heart smites me when I think that I put nothing into it.

We afterwards went up to the Casbah, a former residence of the Deys, serving both as a fortress and a palace, but now turned into barracks for the troops. A great deal that was characteristic in this building has been altered or defaced, but the court of the harem, with its slender columns carved in Italy, and the tiles brought from Holland, with which its walls were inlaid, are there yet, though the rooms are occupied by the French officers and their families. There also were the openings in the parapets of the roof, through which the ladies of the seraglio looked upon the town below, themselves unseen. I wondered that the whole was not preserved as nearly as possible in its original state, if not as a curiosity, yet at least as a memento of the conquest of a city which had so long defied all Christendom and compelled it to pay tribute.

The view of the surrounding country from the height of the Casbah is very striking—its fertile valleys in their winter verdure; the dark range

of the Atlas to the southeast, and beyond the Atlas, the snowy range of the Djudjura. A scarcely less interesting sight was before us in the housetops of the natives, where were sometimes seen the women in their light gauze dresses, without their veils, occupied in their domestic tasks. "These housetops," remarked our companion, "were fatal to some of the French, when they first occupied Algiers, and had not learned the necessity of caution. They were naturally curious to get a peep at the Moorish women, and carrying their investigations too far, were shot through the head, without its being ever known from what hand the ball came."

In going down from the Casbah through the dreary maze of dim lanes, that made me think of the passages in an ant-hill, we came to an Arab school, the door of which was open to the street. In the midst of a crowd of boys, seated without any particular order on the floor, sat the long-bearded and turbaned master, in a white Arab dress, with his back against the wall, and a stick in his hand, like that with which the New England farmers drive their oxen, long enough to reach the most distant corner of the room. The boys were all shouting their lessons together, and woe to the wight who was silent.

Just before we entered upon the broader streets of the city, we stopped at a building, once a Moorish dwelling of the first order, in which a French school for young ladies was now kept. A polite young woman showed us over the rooms. Here at the entrance was the spacious ante-room, where the guests of the Moorish owner were lodged, and beyond which no person of the male sex was allowed to penetrate; here was the inner court, with its columns sculptured in Italy, and its fountain in the midst; here were walls gay with Dutch tiles; here was the staircase leading to the secret apartments, and here on the third floor, was the marabout, or little chapel, in which the family offered their prayers. It is now dedicated to the Virgin, a little image of whom, crowned with a chaplet of artificial roses, in miniature, stood on a pedestal. I inquired the number of pupils in this school. "There are one hundred and twenty-nine of them," said the young lady. "Any natives?" "Many; the daughters of Israelites, who here receive a European education."

At an early hour on the following day, we went to visit the markets of Algiers. We followed a street cut through the graves of an old cemetery, where the cells of the dead in the ground could be distinguished in the bank on either side. A large building, too spacious for so slender a commerce, for the present at least, serves as an oil market. Here goat-skins, filled with oil, and shining and slippery with the fluid they contained, lay in heaps on the ground, and around stood groups of people from the interior. "They are Kabyles, the ancient Berbers," said our companion; "they inhabit the Atlas and the Djudjura mountains; observe them closely, and you will perceive in what respects they differ from the Arabs." I took a good look at them, and before I left Algiers, I thought I could generally

distinguish a Kabyle from an Arab. They have a clearer complexion, and features moulded, if not with more regularity, certainly with more delicacy. They are like the Basques, a primitive race, inhabiting like them the mountains which their fathers inhabited in the time of the Roman empire. They seemed to me an intelligent-looking race; and if put into the European costume, they would attract no particular notice in our country, by any peculiarity of physiognomy or color, though immemorially an African branch of the human family.

We entered next the great country market, heaped with all those vegetables which are the summer growth of our own gardens. Here, too, were piles of oranges from Blidah, the finest of their kind, already sweet, while the oranges of Malaga are almost as sour as lemons. Here were men sitting by huge panniers of olives; they were Kabyles, the sides of whose mountains are shaded by olive groves. In an adjoining enclosure, donkeys were tied, and camels were resting on the ground. After eight o'clock this market is closed, the Arab cultivators get upon their donkeys and depart for the villages of the plain; the Kabyles mount their camels, and are on their way to the mountains.

In returning to our hotel, we passed several negro women sitting by the way, with baskets of bread or of fruit for sale, and met others carrying burdens on their heads or in their arms. "These persons," said our friend, "were slaves some years since, and the French conquest set them free. Their conduct since shows what good creatures they are; their former owners have fallen into extreme poverty, and these women support them by their industry." Of course, those who were slaves before the French conquest, which took place in 1830, could not be very young now, yet I was astonished to see how some of them had been dried to skeletons by time and the climate; they seemed the very personification of famine.

This morning, the 20th of December, we received a summons to return to our steamer, which was about to leave the port. We should have thought ourselves fortunate if at this agreeable season—for such we found it on the African coast—we could have found a little time to make excursions into the surrounding country; to visit Blidah, pleasantly embowered in its orange groves; the picturesque village of Ste. Amalie, famous for its Roman ruins; the no less remarkable region of Koleah, celebrated for its magnificent mosque, erected close to the tomb of a benevolent Arab, venerated as a saint; or to penetrate into one or two of the fresh valleys of the Atlas; but we had taken our passage for Marseilles, and otherwise so arranged the plan of our tour that we had no time to spare for Africa. At noon we went on board, and our steamer left the bay. As we receded from the shore, the site of Algiers looked more imposing than ever, with its lofty cone of white houses rising from the edge of the sea, and crowned with the great fortess of the Casbah, and on each side its declivities of vivid green, spotted with country houses.

Those parts of the colony of Algeria which came under my observation, gave me an impression of activity and prosperity. The French seem to take great pride in this offshoot of their power, and apply to the rule of their new provinces all the energy and precision of their peculiar political and social organization. The possession of Algeria, a larger territory than France, though part of it extends over deserts, gratifies their love of dominion, and justifies the claim of their government to be entitled an empire. Yet, the growth of the European settlements is really slow. In the three different provinces of Algeria, the European population, in the year 1852, amounted to 124,000; in 1856 it was 160,000. An increase of thirty-six thousand in four years certainly does not imply that emigrants are very powerfully attracted to that quarter. There may be various reasons for this: they may prefer a country with freer institutions than Algeria offers them; they may prefer a colony maintained at less expense; or they may doubt the healthiness of its climate. I do not refer to the plague, which has several times desolated Algiers, or to the cholera, which two years since made frightful ravages among the native population, but to permanent local causes of disease. Oran, since it came into possession of the French, has several times been visited by fatal epidemics; the year 1850 is memorable for the havoc they made. Yet they will tell you at Oran that the place is healthy and the air pure; and that the only cause of disease is the filthy manner in which the Spanish population live. In the province of Algiers there are numerous places chosen as the site of colonies which are proverbially unhealthy. At Foudouk, twenty-four miles from the capital, the population has been swept off and renewed several times. Of La Chiffa the same thing is said. Bouffarik, on the rich plain of Mitidja, has been called a cemetery, so surely did the colonists who went thither go to their graves. Various other stations of the European population have a reputation which is little better than that of Bouffarik. Yet there are answers ready, when this objection is brought against Algeria as a place of settlement for the superfluous population of Europe. There have been marshes, it is said, which made a pestiferous atmosphere; but the marshes have been drained and the causes of insalubrity carefully removed. No doubt something has been done in this way, but the fact remains, that the country is subject to fevers, and that these are of a peculiarly obstinate character. One who had resided several years in the city of Algiers, said to me: "You would be much interested by an excursion into the country, but you would have to be on your guard against our fevers, even in the winter."

Earthquakes also are frequent and terrible in Algeria, overturning the towns and burying the inhabitants under their walls. Several times has Algiers been shaken by earthquakes into a mass of ruins; the last earthquake, two years since, destroyed several houses and made others unsafe. The whole plain of Mitidja, so late as 1825, was desolated by an earth-

quake, which laid waste several villages, and extending to Blidah, one of
the pleasantest towns in the province, threw down all the dwellings.

Of the hundred and sixty thousand emigrants from Europe, not quite
two-thirds are French. The Spaniards amount to nearly forty-two thousand, and they come from the south-eastern coast of Spain, and from the
Balearic Islands. The hot island of Malta, which sends such numbers to
every part of the East, has furnished seven thousand to Algeria. There is
about the same number of Germans and Swiss, and of Italians there are
nine thousand. The number of Protestants in all this population is a little
less than five thousand; but they have brought with them their worship
and their religious teachers. The rest of the European emigration is Catholic, and the Gallican Church has its bishops in each of the three provinces
of Algeria.

The time must shortly arrive when Algiers will be altogether a French
city, and all the ports on the coast will be inhabited by families of European origin or descent. At present, Algiers is supposed to contain in its
walls and suburbs a hundred thousand persons, chiefly of the original
Moslem population, but of these the number is rapidly diminishing. They
have but few arts or occupations which they can successfully pursue in
competition with the artisans and workmen from Europe; and while this
is the case it will be their fate to waste away from year to year. As they
drop off, their places will be supplied by emigrants from Europe. A vast
mass of Moslem population will remain in the interior, which for a long
time to come will be but slowly affected by the influences of European
civilization.

In the mean time, it may be instructive to hear what the French themselves say of the colony of Algeria. They complain that the great proportion of those who migrate thither from France, do not go to cultivate the
soil, but to make their fortune by some speculation—by the commerce in
wines and liquors, by opening hotels, cafés, and restaurants, by purchasing
lands to be sold at a higher price, and a thousand other ways which involve
no necessity of labor. The proportion of the town to the country population shows this complaint to be well founded. The rural population of
Algeria derived from Europe is but sixty thousand, and of these not quite
fifty thousand are engaged in agriculture. The colony is still too much a
military and commercial colony to increase rapidly.

It was a delightful afternoon when we left Algiers, but before we lost
sight of it, a black cloud gathered above its hills, and, apparently, broke
over it in a deluge of rain. The rain reached us also, a little after sunset,
and then a strong head wind sprung up, roughening the hitherto sleeping
sea, and making the night most uncomfortable. At every high wave, the
rudder of the Normandie had a trick of thumping the timbers on each
side, with a succession of quick and violent blows, which shook the vessel
fearfully, and made sleep impossible. We labored on in this manner until

the second night after our departure, when, as we were passing between Majorca and the neighboring island of Minorca, an accident happened to an air-pump of the steam engine, which obliged us to stop in the middle of our course. For fourteen hours we lay idly rolling on the water, with the mountainous coast of Majorca beside us. The air-pump was at length mended, and we proceeded, gaining next day a view of the snowy summits of the Pyrenees, which sent towards us a keen, sharp wind from the northwest. On the fourth morning we arrived at Marseilles, which gave but a chilly welcome to those who had just left a region glowing with sunshine, and fanned by airs that make the winter only a longer spring. Marseilles is a stately and prosperous city, nobly situated on a harbor, which I wonder not that the Greeks should have chosen as the seat of their commerce with Gaul; but its damp and frosty winds, and its sunless streets, make it just now a gloomy and dreary abode. The *grippe* is a prevalent malady here, and we are only waiting for one of our party to recover a little from an attack of it, to flit to a warmer coast.

MANUSCRIPT: Unrecovered TEXT: *LT* II, pp. 239–252; first published in *EP* for March 6, 1858.

Abbreviations and Short Titles

Bigelow, *Bryant*. Bigelow, John. *William Cullen Bryant*. ("American Men of Letters") Boston and New York: Houghton Mifflin, 1897.

Bigelow, *Retrospections*. Bigelow, John. *Retrospections of an Active Life*. . . . 5 vols. New York: The Baker & Taylor Co., 1909–1913.

Bryant, "Diary, 1849." Manuscript "Diary of a Visit to Europe in 1849. June–Oct." by William Cullen Bryant in Goddard–Roslyn Collection, New York Public Library.

Bryant, "Diary, 1852–1853." Manuscript "Diary of a Voyage to Europe and Asia, 1852–1853" in 3 vols. by William Cullen Bryant in Goddard–Roslyn Collection, New York Public Library.

Bryant, "Diary, 1857–1858." Manuscript "W. C. Bryant's Diary of Travel Abroad, May 1857–June 1858" in 2 vols. in Goddard–Roslyn Collection, New York Public Library.

Bryant, *Orations and Addresses*. *Orations and Addresses by William Cullen Bryant*. New York: Putnam's, 1873.

Cooper, *Letters & Journals*. *The Letters and Journals of James Fenimore Cooper*. Ed. James Franklin Beard. 6 vols. Cambridge: The Belknap Press of Harvard University Press [1960]–1968.

Cowdrey, *AAFA & AAU*. Cowdrey, Mary Bartlett. *American Academy of Fine Arts and American Art-Union*. 2 vols. New York: The New-York Historical Society, 1953.

DAA. Groce, George C., and Wallace, David H. *The New-York Historical Society's Dictionary of Artists in America, 1564–1860*. New Haven and London: Yale University Press [1957].

EP. New York *Evening Post*.

Goddard, *Roslyn Harbor*. Goddard, Conrad Godwin. *The Early History of Roslyn Harbor, Long Island*. Printed by the Author [1972].

Hoyt, "Bryant Correspondence." Hoyt, William D. Jr., "Some Unpublished Bryant Correspondence (I)," *New York History*, 21 (January 1940), 63–70; "Some Unpublished Bryant Correspondence (II)," *New York History*, 21 (April 1940), 193–204.

LFE. *Letters from the East*. By William Cullen Bryant. New York: Putnam's, 1869.

Life. Godwin, Parke. *A Biography of William Cullen Bryant, With Extracts from His Private Correspondence*. 2 vols. New York: D. Appleton, 1883.

LT I. *Letters of a Traveller; or, Notes of Things Seen in Europe and America*. By William Cullen Bryant. New York: Putnam's, 1850.

LT II. *Letters of a Traveller. Second Series*. By William Cullen Bryant. New York: D. Appleton, 1859.

NAD Exhibition Record. *National Academy of Design Exhibition Record, 1826–1860*. 2 vols. New York: The New-York Historical Society, 1943.

Nevins, *Evening Post*. Nevins, Allan. *The Evening Post: A Century of Journalism*. New York: Boni & Liveright [1922].

Nevins, *Ordeal*. Nevins, Allan. *Ordeal of the Union*. 8 vols. New York: Scribner's [1947–1971].

Odell, *Annals*. Odell, George C. D. *Annals of the New York Stage*. V–VI. New York: Columbia University Press, 1931.

Poems (1876). *Poems by William Cullen Bryant*. Collected and Arranged by the Author. Illustrated by One Hundred Engravings from Drawings by Birket Foster, Harry Fenn, Alfred Fredericks, and Others. New York: D. Appleton [1876].

Poetical Works. *The Poetical Works of William Cullen Bryant*. Ed. Parke Godwin. 2 vols. New York: D. Appleton, 1883.

Rode's New York City Directory for 1849–1850, 1850–1851, 1851–1852. New York: Charles R. Rode, 1849, 1850, 1851.

Trow's New York City Directory Trow's New York City Directory for the Year Ending May 1, 1856. Comp. H. Wilson. New York: Trow [1855].

U. S. Consular Officers, 1789–1939. List of U. S. Consular Officers, 1789–1939. Washington, D.C.: National Archives Microfilm Publications, 1964.

Vail, *Knickerbocker Birthday.* Vail, R. W. G. *Knickerbocker Birthday: A Sesqui-Centennial History of the New-York Historical Society, 1804–1954.* New York: The New-York Historical Society, 1954.

Index of Recipients
Volume III

References are to Letter numbers.

Index

The numbers refer to pages.
An asterisk marks a page containing principal biographical data.